MW01436620

THE ONE SHOW

Volume 18

The pencil, the tool of doodlers, stands for thinking and creativity, but at the same time, as the toy of children, it symbolizes spontaneity and immaturity. Yet the pencil's graphite is also the ephemeral medium of thinkers, planners, drafters, architects, and engineers, the medium to be erased, revised, smudged, obliterated, lost—or inked over. Ink, on the other hand, whether in a book or on plans or on a contract, signifies finality and supersedes the pencil drafts and sketches. Ink is the cosmetic that ideas will wear when they go out in public. Graphite is their dirty truth.

From *The Pencil* by Henry Petroski

Tracing its roots to the early Roman era, the pencil-or penicillus as it was known then-has an interesting etymology [< L. *penis,* little tail]. Had someone informed Henri Toulouse-Lautrec of this fact, the artist most likely would never have uttered his famous words, "I am a pencil."

The One Show Judged to be Advertising's Best Print, Radio, TV

Volume 18

A Presentation of The One Club for Art & Copy

THE ONE CLUB
FOR ART & COPY

GARY GOLDSMITH
President

MARY WARLICK
Executive Director

JIM WASSERMAN
Art Director

KRISTIN OVERSON
Editor

TODD GAFFNEY
CAROLINE KAZLAS
Assistant Editors

BILL SCHWAB
Creative Director,
Jacket and Divider Pages

JACKET AND DIVIDER PAGES
PHOTOGRAPHER: Craig Cutler
COPYWRITERS: Joe Lovering, Tripp Westbrook
PROP STYLING: Barbara Fierros

STOCK PHOTOGRAPHY

Title Page:
Scala/Art Resource, New York

Best of Show:
Minneapolis Historical Society

Gold on Gold:
Incense Cedar Institute, photo by Kent Lacin

Print Finalists:
University of Florida, Parkman Dexter Howe Collection, HDT 6

Public Service/Political Finalists:
Bettman Archive, illustrated by C.M. Relzer

Radio Finalists:
Bettman Archive, photo by Norman Currie

Film processing courtesy of U.S. Color Lab, New York.
Special thanks to Polaroid for donation of professional instant film used in production of this book.

Grateful acknowledgement is made to Henry Petroski, author of
The Pencil: A History of Design and Circumstance published by Alfred A. Knopf, New York, 1993,
for text and material used in the captions on all title pages.

Published and Distributed by ROTOVISION S.A.
Rue Du Bugnon 7 • 1299 Crans-Pres-Celigny • Switzerland
ROTOVISION S.A., Sales & Production Office
Sheridan House 112/116A Western Road • HOVE BN3 IDD. England
Telephone: 44-1273-7272-68 • Fax: 44-1273-7272-69

In Association with
THE ONE CLUB FOR ART & COPY
32 East 21 Street • New York, NY 10010
Telephone: 212-979-1900 • Fax: 212-979-5006

Copyright ©1996 as a collection by
The One Club for Art & Copy, Inc.
All rights reserved.
No part of this book may be reproduced in any way by any means whatsoever
without express permission in writing from the owners.

First Printing
ISBN 0-929837-10-X

Production and Color Separation by
Provision/Singapore • Telephone: 65-334-7720 • Fax: 65-334-7721
Printed by Tien Wah Press/Singapore.

CONTENTS

BOARD OF DIRECTORS

GARY GOLDSMITH
Goldsmith/Jeffrey
President

TOD SEISSER
Ammirati Puris Lintas
Vice President

EARL CAVANAH
Lowe & Partners/SMS
Treasurer

TONY ANGOTTI
Angotti Thomas Hedge

BOB BARRIE
Fallon McElligott

PAT BURNHAM
McKinney & Silver

NICK COHEN
Mad Dogs & Englishmen

MARTY COOKE
TBWA Chiat/Day

LEE GARFINKEL
Lowe & Partners/SMS

DEAN HACOHEN
Goldsmith/Jeffrey

WOODY KAY
Pagano Schenck & Kay

MIKE LESCARBEAU
Fallon McElligott

DIANE ROTHSCHILD
Grace & Rothschild

KIRK SOUDER
Ground Zero

DEAN STEFANIDES
Hampel/Stefanides

PRESIDENT'S MESSAGE

GARY GOLDSMITH

We have reached the point of absurdity with awards in our business. A week does not go by that doesn't bring a call-for-entry packet from one or more obscure new shows. Among the established shows, competition for entries and top judges is fierce. As agencies increasingly begin to question what they get in return for their award expenditures, it will become even more so. Even those among us who believe that awards have a legitimate purpose have begun to more carefully select which shows we enter and which clubs we support.

The shows that survive and grow in importance will be the ones that have a clear mission and set of standards and are able to maintain them year after year. Few fall into that category.

I'm confident that the work you will see on the following pages will make it very obvious what the mission is at The One Club: continue to provide a credible showcase for the year's best advertising; continue to be the award that evokes the most jealousy and envy among creatives; continue to be the book on agency bookshelves that is the most well-worn, the one that art directors and writers flip through at 2:00 a.m. looking for inspiration. And the one students all over the world fantasize about having their work in.

We'll never have as many categories as some shows do. We'll never give out as many finalist certificates as other shows do. We'll never hand out as many medals as most shows do. And our ceremony will probably never be broadcast on television.

Will a couple living in Iowa ever be impressed when their daughter calls home from New York to say she won her first One Show pencil?

I doubt it.

At least not until she first explains what a One Show pencil is.

But as long as we're the show that the people who actually conceive, produce and run the world's best advertising look to for recognition, we'll do just fine.

Harold Ross, legendary editor of *The New Yorker*, was so fanatical about his pencils that he hired an office boy to sharpen them. The pencils had to be of a certain length, with no teeth marks. The points had to be fine, but not too fine. It took the boy weeks to perfect this, but he succeeded. And one memorable afternoon, Mr. Ross said to him, "Son, you're a damn good pencil sharpener."

Judges & One Club Members

ONE SHOW JUDGES

JILL BOHANNAN
Ammirati Puris Lintas

BILL BORDERS
Borders Perrin & Norrander

RICK BOYKO
Ogilvy & Mather

LARRY CADMAN
New York

TIM DELANEY
Leagas Delaney

LARRY HAMPEL
Hampel/Stefanides

CABELL HARRIS
Work

JOHN HEGARTY
Bartle Bogle Hegarty

MIKE HUGHES
The Martin Agency

ROCHELLE KLEIN
Angotti Thomas Hedge

STEVEN LANDSBERG
Ogilvy & Mather/Toronto

NEIL LEINWOHL
Korey Kay & Partners

CAROLYN McGEORGE
O'Keefe Marketing

TY MONTAGUE
Montague &

NOAM MURRO
New York

RICHARD PELS
BBDO

NANCY RICE
DDB Needham/Chicago

STEVE SIMPSON
Goodby Silverstein & Partners

PAUL SPENCER
New York

LUKE SULLIVAN
Fallon McElligott

ONE CLUB MEMBERS

Mike Abadi
Hy Abady
Jeffrey Abbott
Alexander Aksyonov
Joe Alexander
Wade Alger
Mark Allen
Carl Ally
Pascal Alouidor
Aimee Alpert
David Altschiller
Olivia Altschuler
Patricia Alvey
Ralph Ammirati
Kevin Amter
Audrey Anderson
Ron Anderson
Anthony Angotti
Joseph Antonacci
Jill Applebaum
Stephanie Arculli
Arnold Arlow
Stephanie Arnold
Lorraine Arroll
Sharilyn Asbahr
Craig Astler
John Athorn
Don Austen
Ruth Ayers
Dominick Baccollo
Kristina Backlund
Christian Baffa
Chris Baier
Robert Baird
Guy Barnett
Julie Baron
Bob Barrie
Lauren Barrocas
Scott Bassen
John Bateman
Steve Bautista
Tim Bayless
Clifford Beach
Rhonda Beaudette-Lubow
John Beausang
Allan Beaver
Theresa Beck
Wendy Beck
Kris Becker
Wendy Becker
Henry Belfor
Doug Bell
Brian Bellanca
Brian Bellefont
Jacqueline Benitez
Jason Benn
A.K. Bennett
Gordon Bennett
Danielle Berger
Warren Berger
Steve Berkowitz
Paul Bernasconi
David Bernstein
Michael Bernstein
Wayne Best
Dana Betgilan
Dominique Biger Kahn
Arthur Bijur
Bruce Bildsten
Pat Bilger
Robert Bilotti
Chris Bingaman
Doug Bixby
Paul Blade
Karen Blanken
Steven Block
Richard Bloom
Albert Blum
Alisa Blum
Gerardo Andres Blumenkrantz
Alex Bogusky
Rex Bonomelli
Jill Bordonaro
Jason Borzouyeh
Diana Bosniack
Peter Bossio
Alix Botwin
Simon Bowden
Teru Bower
Rick Boyko
John Boyle
David Bradley
Scott Brennan
Alisa Brenner
David Brenner
Harvey Briggs
Chris Brignola
Jim Brodie
Bill Brokaw
Charles Bromley
Dara Brooks
Stephen Brophy
Mike Brotebeck
George Brown
Maiysha Brown
Mark Brown
Todd Brunner
Rich Buceta
Kirk Buddy
Stephanie Burke
Ron Burkhardt
Eric Burnard
Pat Burnham
Allison Burton
Mercy Burwell
Jaime Butler
Graham Button
Alice Butts
Larry Cadman
Andrew M. Cahill
Dina Calabro
Jenny Calderon
Jennifer Callery
Cathie Campbell
Lori Campbell
Ian Caplan
James Caporimo
Paul Cappelli
Chris Caracciolo
Rob Carducci
David Carlin
David Carlson
Chris Carter
Debra Cassa
David Cassada
Johanna Castaneda
Angelo Castelli
Patricia Castiblanco
Earl Cavanah
Tugrul Cavusoglu
Hank Champion
Spencer Chan
Wilson Chan
Flori Chastain
Yim Cheng
Nelson Cheung
Jay Chiat
Vincent Chieco
Michael Chu
Kenny Chui
Chris Churchill
Mark Clark
Matthew Cocco
Henry Cochran
Claudia Coffman
Daniel Cohen
David Cohen
Gary Cohen
Lauren Cohen
Peter Cohen
Marcie Cohn
Cybill Conklin
Marty Cooke
Christopher Cooper
David L. Corr
Scott Correll
Colin Costello
Sharla Costello
Ashley Coursey
Ed Cousineau
Rob Cramer
Court Crandall
Tom Crimp
Janna Criscione
Peter Crosby
Kevin Cruickshank
Christine Cucuzza
Michael Cundari
Phyliss Cunningham
Greg Curran
Mark Curto
Michael Czako
Mark D'Arcy
Joanna D'Avanzo
Julie A. Dahlen
Trish Daley
Matthew Dalin
Yael Daphna
Jeffrey Davila
Jeannine Marie Davis
Stephen Dean
Victor DeCastro
Jay Deegan
Tony DeGregorio
Craig Deitch
Ken DeLeon
Maria Demartino
Allison DeRose
Sal DeVito
Audrey DeVries
Steve Diamond
Christopher Digianni
Steve Dildarian
Greg DiNoto
Tony DiPietro
David DiRienz
Brian Dixon
Angela Dominguez
Bernstein Donn
Andrew Donnelly
Carolyn Donnelly
Steve Doppelt
Tom Doud
Sean Dougherty
Antonio Downer
Michael Draper
Sharon Dreyer
Rosalyn Dunham
Laurence Dunst
Jim Durfee
Elizabeth Durnin
Arye Dworken
Susan Dwyer
Richard Eber
Linda Edwards
Shannon Edwards
Lisa Ciocci Egan
Arthur Einstein
Aaron Keith Eiseman
Stuart Elliot
Alice Elston
Bradford Emmett
Kevin Endres
Patricia Lynn Epstein
Linos Ermogenides
Camilo Espinel
Eric Essig
Reza Estakhrian
David Fagin
Peter Farago
Mark Feigenson
Thomas Feinstein
Judith Fekete
Jeremy Feldman
Sarah Feldman
Steven Feldman
Mark Fenske
Joseph Ferrazano
Robert Festino
Michael Fetsko
Kerry Feuerman
Michael D. Field
Peggy Fields
Carlo Figueiredo
Luis Figueroa
Kirk Filer
Michael Fine
Terri Finnerty
Ann Fisher
Peter Fitz
Cora Flaster
Mike Flegle
James Floersch
Laura Forbes
Daniel Forman
Howard Foster
Paul W. Foulkes
Lisa Francilia
Christian Francioli
Sela Francis
Cliff Freeman
Robert Fremgen
Joshua Friedman
Eric Fuentecilla
Rosanna Fuentes
Jerry Fury
Tom Gabriel
Tom Galati
Brendan Gallahue
Michael Gambino
Terri Gannarelli
Mark Ganton
Bertrand Garbassi

Thomas Garbellotto
Jacqui Garcia
Richard Garcia
Salvador Garcia
Lee Garfinkel
Amil Gargano
Matthew Gargano
Melissa Garner
Lisa Garrone
Dave Gassman
Gianina Gauci
Alan Gee
Dean Gemmell
Jim Gennell
John George
Harold German
Marc Getter
Djamila Ghezzar
Steven Giamarino
Steven Gianakouros
George Gier
Carla Gigante
Robert Gilanyi
Jeffrey Gilligan
Frank Ginsberg
Tim Godsall
Chris Goldschmidt
Alexandra Goldsmith
Gary Goldsmith
Mark Goldstein
Mia Goldstein
Steven Goldstein
Sandra Gomes
Eve Gonsenhauser
Mark A. Gonzalez
Beth Goozman
Genevieve Gorder
Regina Gormar
Holly Goscinsky
Roy Grace
Lorraine Gracey
Stella Grafakos
Jason Graff
Jeff Graybill
Clare Delle Grazie
Dick Grider
Jeff Griffith
Aaron Griffiths
Jerry Gross
Philip Growick
Jonathan Grusky
Roland Grybauskas
Michael Guarini
Bruce Guidotti
Frank Guzzone
Amy Haddad
Deb Hagan
Jim Hagar
Stephen Haggarty
Matthew Hallock
Trace Hallowell
Ada Halofsky
Bill Hamilton
Jon Harcharek
Keith Harjes
Keith Harmeyer
Yuval Harpaz
Cabell Harris
Vanah Harris
Eva Hart
Drew Harteveld
Jim Hayman
Joel Heffron
Kathleen Hennicke
Roy Herbert
Rony Herz
Ron Herzig
Bill Hillsman
Larry Hinkle
Paul Hirsch
Peter Hirsch
Sigal Hofshi
Barry Holland
Patrick Holland
Dave Holloway
Jenine Holmes
Sandra Holtzman
Sung Woo Hong
Laurence Horvitz
Ryan Hose
Hugh Hough
Lara Hovanesian
Major Howell
Matthew Hoyt
Rodney Huff
Dion Hughes
Julie-Anne Hughes
Mark Hughes
Mike Hughes
Neal Hughlett
Robert Hume
Lisa Hurwitz
John Hynes
Jessica Iannuzzi
Paul Iannuzzo
Aki Inoue
Kim Irelan
Jeanmarie Jackman
Dick Jackson
Judi Jacob
Harry M. Jacobs, Jr.
Paul Jamieson
Jaydee Jana
Bryson Jane
Natacha Jeanty
Joan Jedell
Shawn Jeffrey
Sam Jen
Mickey Jenkins
Heather Jeranek
Andrew Jeske
Anthony Johnson
Glynnis Johnson
Timothy Joyce
M. Kinsley Kalinoski
Eric Kalison
Joshua Kamins
Joshua Kampta
Charles Kane
Melinda Kanipe
Maria Kantlis
Scott Kaplan
Peter Katz
Richard Kaufman
Leslie Kay
Woody Kay
Victor Kaykaty
Elizabeth Keane
Vincent Keane
Yong Keh
Michelle Keller
Brian Kennedy
Eil Jung Kim
Sae-Won Kim
Jon Michael King
Larissa Kirschner
Lawrence Kirschner
Christopher Kline
Megan Kline
Joe Knezic
T.K. Knowles
Daren Koniuk
Julie Koppman
Ronni Korn
Renee Korus
Maria Kostyk-Petro
Judy Kozuck
David Krewinghaus
Neal Krouse
Stewart Krull
Cristy Kruse
Adam Kuhr
Pradeep Kumar
Joseph Kwit
Al Kwok
Robert LaBarge
Jenny Landey
Steven Landsberg
Jeffrey Lang
Andy Langer
Anthony LaPetri
Carole Larson
Susan LaScala
Mary Wells Lawrence
Diane Lazarus
Marcia LeBeau
Jennie Lee
Jong Lee
Patrick Lee
Sung Lee
Sung-Yoon Lee
Tae Hwa Lee
Taylor Lee
Neil Leinwohl
Dany Lee Lennon
David Lentini
Jodie Leopold
Grace Lerner
Mike Lescarbeau
Michael Leselrod
Sharon Lesser
Jill LeVans
Robert Levenson
Geoffrey Levick
Joshua Levy
Jonathan Lewis
Zhao Wen Li
Ian Li-Pelaez
Bernie Libster
Henriette Lienke
Jessica Lim
Lisa Lipkin
Michael Liss
Wallace Littman
Steven Liu
Roger Livingston
George Lois
Vinnie Longo
Alexander Loomis
Steven Lopez
Carson Lord
Joe Lovering
Abby Lovinger
Jack Low
Peter Lubalin
David Lubars
Lisa Lurie
Stephen Lynch
Tony Macchia
Shyam Madiraju
Oktama Madjid
Cynthia Malaran
Chris Maley
Madhu Malhan
John Malinowski
Karen Mallia
Ellery Manalac
Ellen Mance-Smyth
Sara B. Mandel
Ken Mandelbaum
Claudia Mandreucci
Bradley Manier
Claudia Manuel
Nicole Manzi
Jennifer Marafiore
Scott Margolis
David Marino
Louis Marino
John Mariucci
Larry Marks
Rachel Marks
Rhoda Marshall
Frank Martino
Caprice Marut
Thomas Matt
Kimberly Mattig
Michael Maurer
John Maxham
James Mazzola
Scott McAfee
Ed McCabe
Jim McCabe
Nancy McCaleb
Clem McCarthy
Lisa McCarthy
Alex McCausland
Matthew P. McCutchin
Kevin McKeon
Paul McKittrick
Rob McPherson
Danielle McVeigh
Gabriel Medina
Lynne Meena
Mark Mendelis
Ted Mendelson
Frank Meo
Mario G. Messina
Lyle Metzdorf
Terri Meyer
Greg Meyers
Marc Meyers
Micah Meyers
Bethann Miale
Risa Mickenberg
M. Christina Miclat
Dion Middleton
Michael Migliozzi II
Mark Millar
Christopher Miller
Don Miller
Gordon Miller
Reid Miller
Jonathan L. Mindell
Michael Minerva
Deanna Cohen Mitchell
Mark Mitchell
J. Gregory Mohr
Nicole Monea
Leonard Monfredo
Ty Montague
Kevin Mooney
Miguel Morales
Deborah Morrison
Marco Morsella
Gregory Motylenski
Jim Mountjoy
Tom Moyer
William Munch, Jr.
Sibila Munoz
Vinny Muratore
Mark Musto
Tracy Nader
Narendra Nandoe
Greg Nardone

Jennifer Nash
Thomas Nathan
Shane Nearman
Robert S. Needleman
Arun K. Nemali
David Newbold
T. Michelle Newman
Patrick Ng
William Ng
Steve Nicholas
Howard Nierman
Simi Nikore
David Nobay
Jennifer Noble
Jennifer Nottoli
Dick O'Brien
Joe O'Neill
Bill Oberlander
Walter Ocner
Rip Odell
David Ogilvy
Jin Oh
Steve Oh
Vicky Oliver
Alex Olmstead
Peter Oravetz
Cele Otnes
Juan Padilla
Alvaro Paez
Jack Palancio
Marissa Palazzolo
Julie Pankowski
Haley Panzer
Joe Paprocki
Sam Park
Kimberly Paul
Alido Pavan
Michael Pavone
Richard Pels
Nicolas Perkin
George Perkins
Ellen Perless
Christopher Perone
Laraine Perri
Matt Peterson
Yolanda Petriz
Annelise Pfeil
Daniel Pierre
Donna Pilch
Marianne Pillsbury
Rosa Pineda
Jeremy Pippenger
Piyawan Piyapong
Heather Plansker
Larry Platt
Jonathan Plazonja
Chris Pollock
Shirley Polykoff
Lorre Powell
Tony Pucca
Amy Putman
Nazneen Qazi
Tom Quaglino
Elissa Querze
Keith Quesenberry
Lisa Quitoni
Dick Raboy
Lynda Raihofer
Suzanne Ramos
Saira Ramoutar
Maya Rao
Eldar Rapaport
Ian Reichenthal
David Reinhardt
Robert Reitzfeld
Joseph Ricci
Nancy Rice
Allen Richardson
Jonathan Richter
Hal Riney
Lori Roberts
Michael Robertson
Phyllis Robinson
Scott Rockwood
Lloyd Rodrigues
Alexis Rodriguez
Manny Rodriguez
Mike Rogers
Gad Romann
Katherine Rose
Mike Rosen
Ron Rosen
Deb Rosenberg
Bernie Rosner
Tom Rost
Rosanne Rotenberg
Mark Rothenberg
Diane Rothschild
Carolyn Amorosi Rothseid
Steve Rotterdam
Jason Roumas
Keri Roy
Risiandi Rumito
Il'ja Ruppeldt
John Russo
Nat Russo
Mel Rustom
Alan Ruthazer
Xenia Rutherford
Kelly Ryan
Nancy Rybczynski
Ted Sabarese
Rebecca Sage
Steve Sage
Masateru Saimaru
Salomon Sainvil
Jeffrey Salgado
Natasha Samoylenko
Emmanuel Santos
Carl Sastram
Joanne Scannello
Paul M. Sceppaguerico
David Schermer
Glenn Scheuer
Christopher Schifando
Timothy Schultheis
Eric Schutte
Matthew Scott
Danielle Searles
Lee Seidenberg
Tod Seisser
Francisco Sepulveda
Carol Sessions
Michael Seymour
Diane Sharp
Timothy Shaw
Bill Shea
Don Shelford
Matthew Shepko
Lori Sheppard
Brett Shevack
Edward Shieh
Bob Shiffrar
Albert Shih
Chiun-Kai Shih
Mark Short
Fred Siegel
Kate Silverberg
Lisa Silverbrand
Daniel Silverstein
Tonia Simon
Leonard Sirowtiz
Steve Skibba
David Skinner
Paula Slack
Jonathan Slater
Mike Slosberg
Robert Slosberg
Colleen Smith
Hillary Smith
Kevin Smith
Nancy Smith
Pete Smith
Matthew Smukler
Rafael Soberal
David Sohn
Richard Solomon
Lee Solon
Jae Son
Vanessa Soto
Cheri Soukop
Andy Spade
Mark Spector
Joni Spencer
Jeff Spiegel
John Spiteri
Douglas Spitzer
Helayne Spivak
Andy Srygley
Lee St. James
Paige Elizabeth St. John
John Staffen
Joseph Staluppi
Scott Stefan
Dean Stefanides
Len Stein
Danielle Stella
Dandridge Stevenson
Art Stiefel
Marianne Stillwagon
Jason Stinsmuehlen
Bob Stohrer
Kevin Stoohs
Roberto Stulz
Christine Sullivan
Marc Surchin
Bob Sullivan
Nick Sustana
Robert Swartz
Joe Sweet
Leslie Sweet
William Sypher
John Szalay
Norman Tanen
Willie Tang
Daniel Taormina
Abby Terkuhle
Mike Tesch
Linda Thibodeau
Tom Thomas
Benjamin Thompson
Brian Thompson
Tami Thrasher
Eric Tilford
Todd Tilford
Carlos Torres
Robert Torres
Troy Torrison
Mark Townsley
Joel Tractenberg
Wendy Tripp
William Troncone
Matthew Trumino
Michael Tsapos
Lina Tun
Christopher Turner
Ben Urman
Victor Valadez
Jennifer Van Blarcom
Eddie Van Bloem
Peter Van Bloem
Tom Van Ness
Barbara Vasquez
Nancy Vecilla
Michael Vella
Paul Venables
Jennifer Venegas
Theresa Venezia
Amy Vensel
Tim Vermillion
Stephen Versandi
Ketsana ViLaylack
Wven Villegas
Larry Vine
Michael Vitiello
Joseph Volpicelli
Bennett Voyles
Leila Vuorenmaa
Nina Wachsman
Elaine Wagner
Judy Wald
Deborah Waldman
Marvin Waldman
Thomas Walker
Adam Ward
Carl Warner
Bernard Washington
Peter Watt
Jessica Watts
Steve Wax
Christine Weary
Lyle Wedemeyer
Beth Wegiel
Les Weiner
Eliot Weinstein
Marty Weiss
Robert Shaw West
Bill Westbrook
Jeffrey Weston
Bill White
Ronald Scott Wild
Richard Wilde
Jay Williams
Tim Williams
Claire Willms
Heike Windfelder
Jennifer Winn
Paul Witt
David Wojdyla
Stefen Wojnarowski
Holly Ann Wojtaszek
Lloyd Wolfe
David A. Wong
Lai Phun Wong
Laura B. Woods
Elizabeth Wynn
Seiji Yamaski
Betsy Yamazaki
Mei Yee Yap
Christopher Yates
Richard Yelland
Elaine Yip
Jung Hwan Yoon
Harpaz Yuval
Lynette Zator
Steven Zeitzoff
Jeffrey Zeldman
Peter Ziegler
Rainer Zierer
James Zuccox

According to the National Bureau of Standards, there are twenty-one different grades of pencils. They range from the softest, a 9B, to the hardest, a 10H. The latter is able to write on metal and stone, thus ensuring the pencil can leave its mark on virtually anything in the world.

Gold, Silver & Bronze Winners

GOLD, SILVER & BRONZE AWARDS

CONSUMER NEWSPAPER
OVER 600 LINES: SINGLE

1 GOLD

ART DIRECTORS
Gerald Schoenhoff
Howard Beauchamp

WRITER
Ian MacKellar

PHOTOGRAPHER
Chris Gordoneer

CLIENT
Panasonic

AGENCY
Roche Macaulay & Partners/Toronto

Okay. Now describe the person on the previous page.

Hey, no cheating.

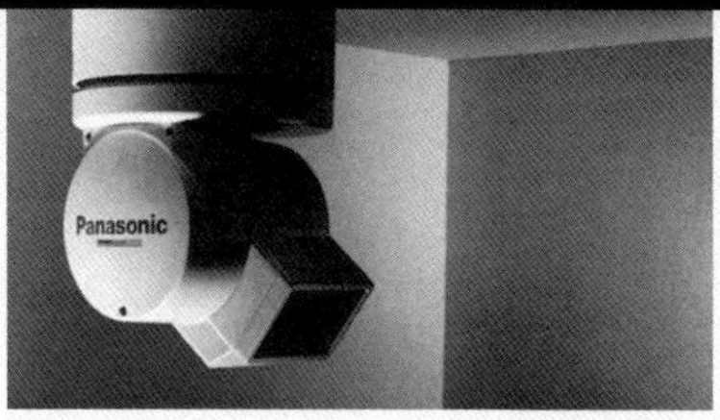

The fact is, most people have trouble remembering what a person looks like even seconds after just meeting them. Just ask a police officer who's investigating a robbery.

But that doesn't have to be the case. When you install a Panasonic Closed Circuit Security Camera system in your store or business, you'll be making available a convincing and very accurate witness to everything that's going on around you. One that is available twenty-four hours a day, everyday, without hesitation.

That's why it's not surprising that you'll find our cameras at work in places like convenience stores, airports, banks, and casinos. Places that rely heavily on a security system to provide a detailed video description of any individual who is involved in criminal activity.

Now that you've had a few minutes to think about it, try to remember again, what the person on the other page looked like. If you still can't recall, turn back to the page and see for yourself. But not before you memorize this phone number: 1-905-238-2279. It's where you can get the name of the Panasonic Closed Circuit TV dealer nearest you. Someone you won't soon forget.

Panasonic®
Security Systems

1 Gold

GOLD, SILVER & BRONZE AWARDS

CONSUMER NEWSPAPER OVER 600 LINES: SINGLE

2 SILVER

ART DIRECTOR
Todd Grant
WRITER
Bo Coyner
PHOTOGRAPHER
Gil Smith
CLIENT
American Isuzu Motors
AGENCY
Goodby Silverstein & Partners/San Francisco

3 BRONZE

ART DIRECTOR
Mark Fuller
WRITER
Ron Huey
PHOTOGRAPHER
William Coupon
CLIENT
Amgen
AGENCY
The Martin Agency/ Richmond

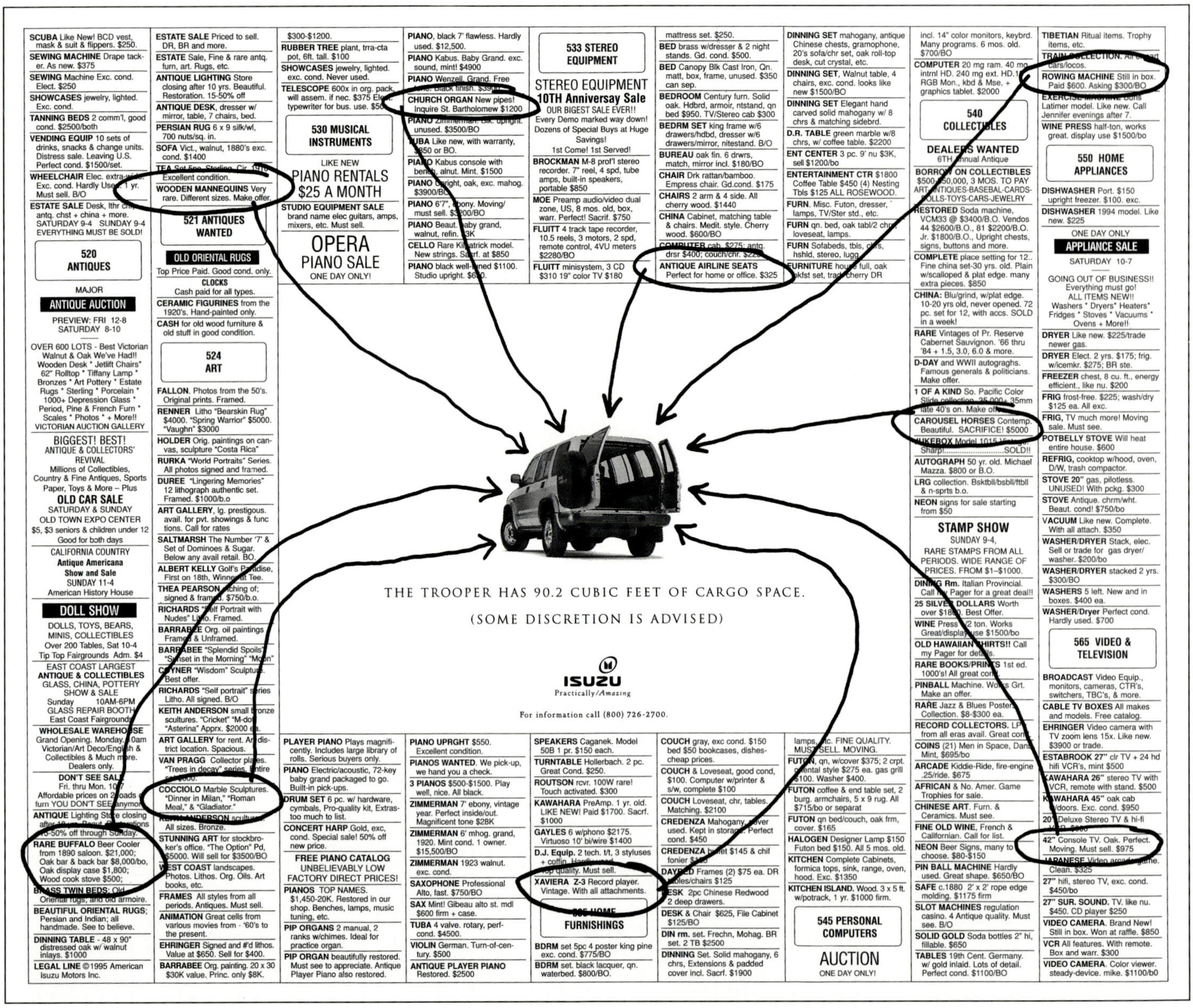
THE TROOPER HAS 90.2 CUBIC FEET OF CARGO SPACE.
(SOME DISCRETION IS ADVISED)
ISUZU
Practically/Amazing
For information call (800) 726-2700.
LEGAL LINE ©1995 American Isuzu Motors Inc.

2 Silver

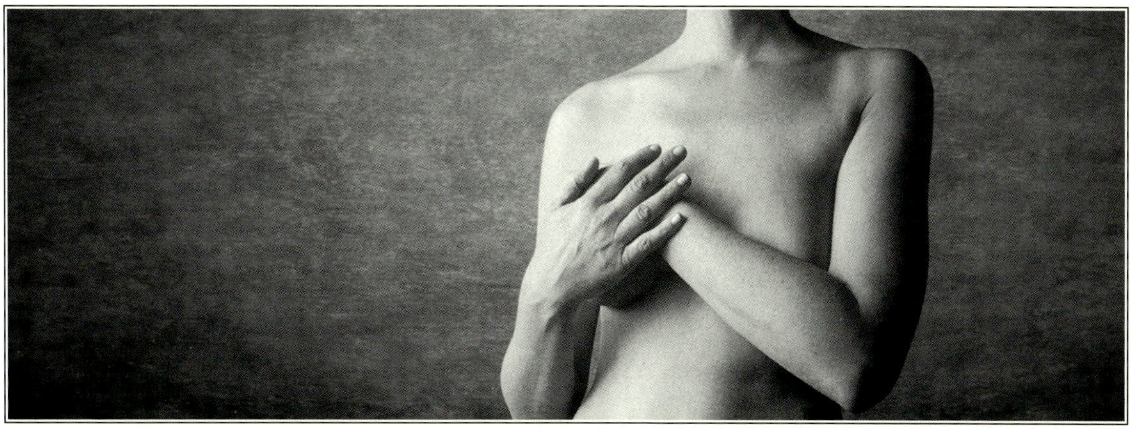

YOU'VE JUST FOUND OUT YOU HAVE CANCER. LET'S BEGIN BY REDUCING THE LUMP IN YOUR THROAT.

In recent years, new breakthroughs have been made in helping people with cancer better manage their treatment. New drugs are helping reduce many of the common side effects of chemotherapy treatment. Including nausea and even more serious conditions that can develop like a low white blood cell count.

One drug, Neupogen (Filgrastim), is now being prescribed to help certain people on chemotherapy maintain a normal white blood cell count. Specifically, a normal neutrophil count. In short, neutrophils are white blood cells that help your body fight infection. Maintaining a normal neutrophil count during your chemotherapy treatment can be important for two reasons.

First, you have a much greater chance of staying on your chemotherapy schedule. And, that will mean getting your treatment behind you sooner. Secondly, maintaining a normal neutrophil count can help reduce your risk of infection. So you have a better chance of staying out of the hospital. Instead, you can spend more time at home where you belong with family and friends. Even daily activities like shopping and eating out can be more accessible.

Of course, Neupogen isn't appropriate for every patient. Ask your doctor if Neupogen should be a recommended part of your treatment. On the following page, you'll find an explanation of Neupogen and its possible side effects. The most common side effect that patients experience is mild-to-moderate bone pain, which can usually be controlled with a non-aspirin analgesic.

In closing, before we embarked on this educational campaign, we conducted extensive research with people undergoing chemotherapy and with doctors. Among those being treated, we found an overwhelming desire for more information concerning treatment. Doctors, many of whom had initial misgivings about any advertising at all, urged us to be candid and to point out that Neupogen isn't for everyone. We acted on their advice.

We realize that your medical care is a sensitive and personal matter. We'd like to know your feelings about the information presented here. If you would like to receive more information concerning Neupogen and how it might help in your treatment, please call us at 1-800-333-9777, extension 667.

NEUPOGEN

3 Bronze

GOLD, SILVER & BRONZE AWARDS

CONSUMER NEWSPAPER OVER 600 LINES: CAMPAIGN

4 GOLD

ART DIRECTOR
Sally Overheu

WRITER
Jackie Hathiramani

PHOTOGRAPHER
Sally Overheu

CLIENT
The British Council

AGENCY
Ogilvy & Mather/ Singapore

WARNING!!
IT IS FORBIDDEN TO ENTER A WOMAN
– BY ORDER

IMPROVE YOUR ENGLISH. We have over twenty part-time and full-time courses to help you read, write and speech (sorry, speak) correct English. Call 473 6661 for more information. The British Council

HOTEL PIERRE
PLEASE LEAVE
YOUR VALUES
AT THE
FRONT DESK.
THE MANAGER

IMPROVE YOUR ENGLISH. We have over twenty part-time and full-time courses to help you read, write and speech (sorry, speak) correct English. Call 473 6661 for more information. The British Council

Papa's Cafe
THE MANAGER
HAS PERSONALLY
PASSED ALL
THE WATER
SERVED HERE.

IMPROVE YOUR ENGLISH. We have over twenty part-time and full-time courses to help you read, write and speech (sorry, speak) correct English. Call 473 6661 for more information. The British Council

GOLD, SILVER & BRONZE AWARDS

CONSUMER NEWSPAPER OVER 600 LINES: CAMPAIGN

5 SILVER

ART DIRECTOR
Eric Houseknecht

WRITER
Marcus Woolcott

PHOTOGRAPHER
Jen Halim

CLIENT
Gallery 13

AGENCY
Bates/Hong Kong

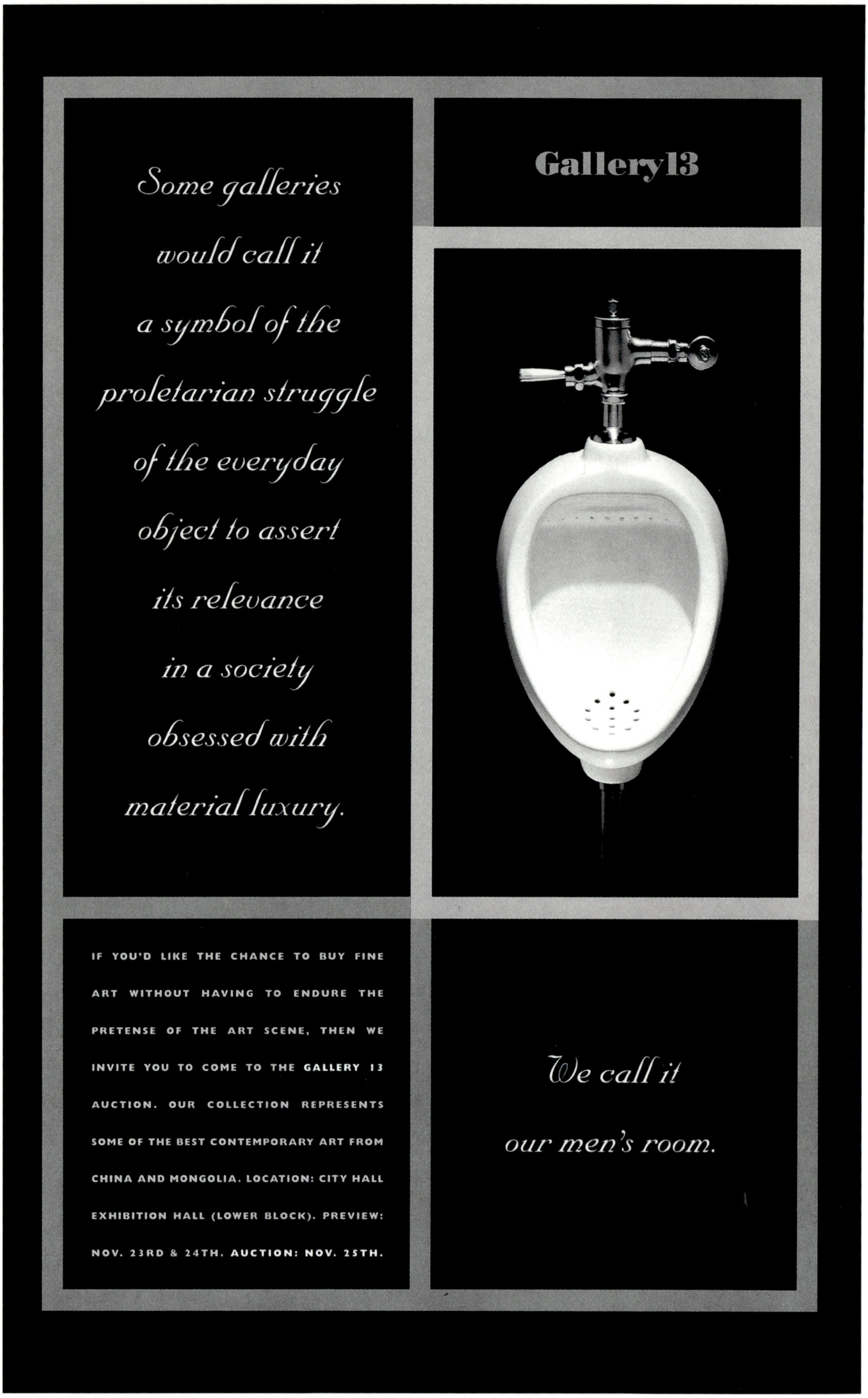
Some galleries would call it a symbol of the proletarian struggle of the everyday object to assert its relevance in a society obsessed with material luxury.
Gallery13
IF YOU'D LIKE THE CHANCE TO BUY FINE ART WITHOUT HAVING TO ENDURE THE PRETENSE OF THE ART SCENE, THEN WE INVITE YOU TO COME TO THE GALLERY 13 AUCTION. OUR COLLECTION REPRESENTS SOME OF THE BEST CONTEMPORARY ART FROM CHINA AND MONGOLIA. LOCATION: CITY HALL EXHIBITION HALL (LOWER BLOCK). PREVIEW: NOV. 23RD & 24TH. AUCTION: NOV. 25TH.
We call it our men's room.

Gallery 13
Some artists are starving for a reason.
IF YOU BELIEVE THAT THE CREATION OF ART SHOULD STILL INVOLVE THINGS LIKE SKILL AND TALENT, THEN WE ENCOURAGE YOU TO ATTEND THE GALLERY 13 AUCTION. OUR COLLECTION REPRESENTS SOME OF THE FINEST CONTEMPORARY ART FROM CHINA AND MONGOLIA. LOCATION: THE LOWER BLOCK OF THE CITY HALL EXHIBITION HALL. PREVIEW: NOVEMBER 23RD & 24TH. AUCTION: NOVEMBER 25TH.

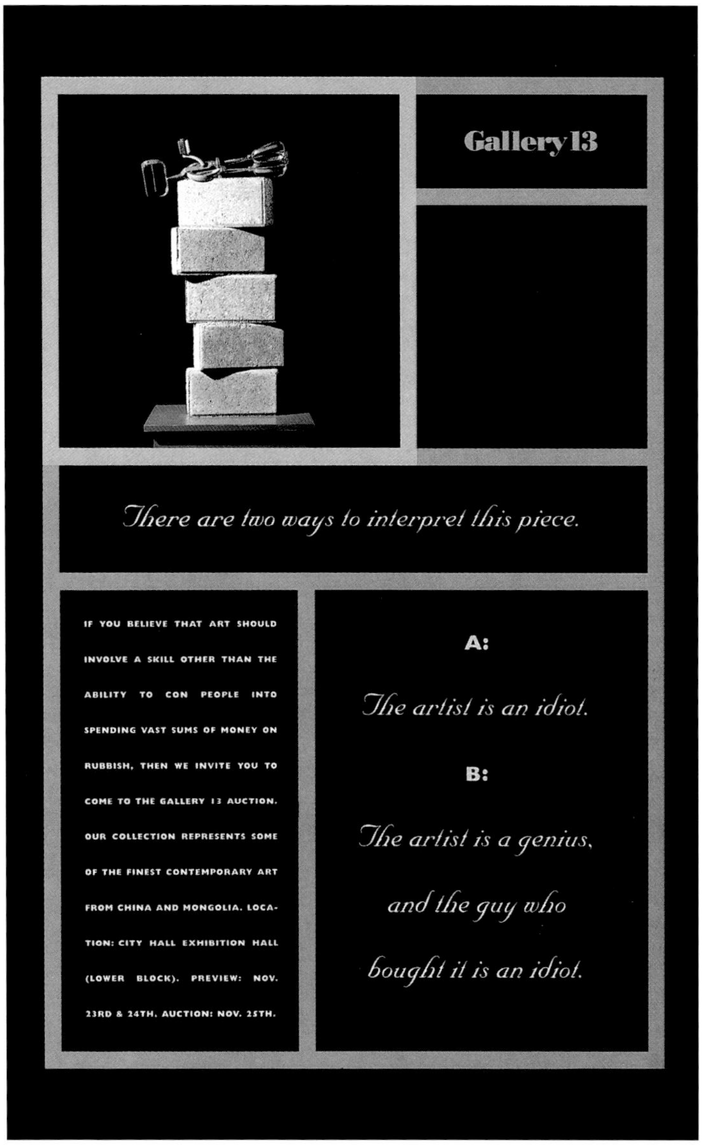
Gallery 13
There are two ways to interpret this piece.
IF YOU BELIEVE THAT ART SHOULD INVOLVE A SKILL OTHER THAN THE ABILITY TO CON PEOPLE INTO SPENDING VAST SUMS OF MONEY ON RUBBISH, THEN WE INVITE YOU TO COME TO THE GALLERY 13 AUCTION. OUR COLLECTION REPRESENTS SOME OF THE FINEST CONTEMPORARY ART FROM CHINA AND MONGOLIA. LOCATION: CITY HALL EXHIBITION HALL (LOWER BLOCK). PREVIEW: NOV. 23RD & 24TH. AUCTION: NOV. 25TH.
A:
The artist is an idiot.
B:
The artist is a genius, and the guy who bought it is an idiot.

5 Silver

GOLD, SILVER & BRONZE AWARDS

CONSUMER NEWSPAPER OVER 600 LINES: CAMPAIGN

6 SILVER

ART DIRECTOR
Todd Grant

WRITER
Bo Coyner

PHOTOGRAPHER
Gil Smith

CLIENT
American Isuzu Motors

AGENCY
Goodby Silverstein & Partners/San Francisco

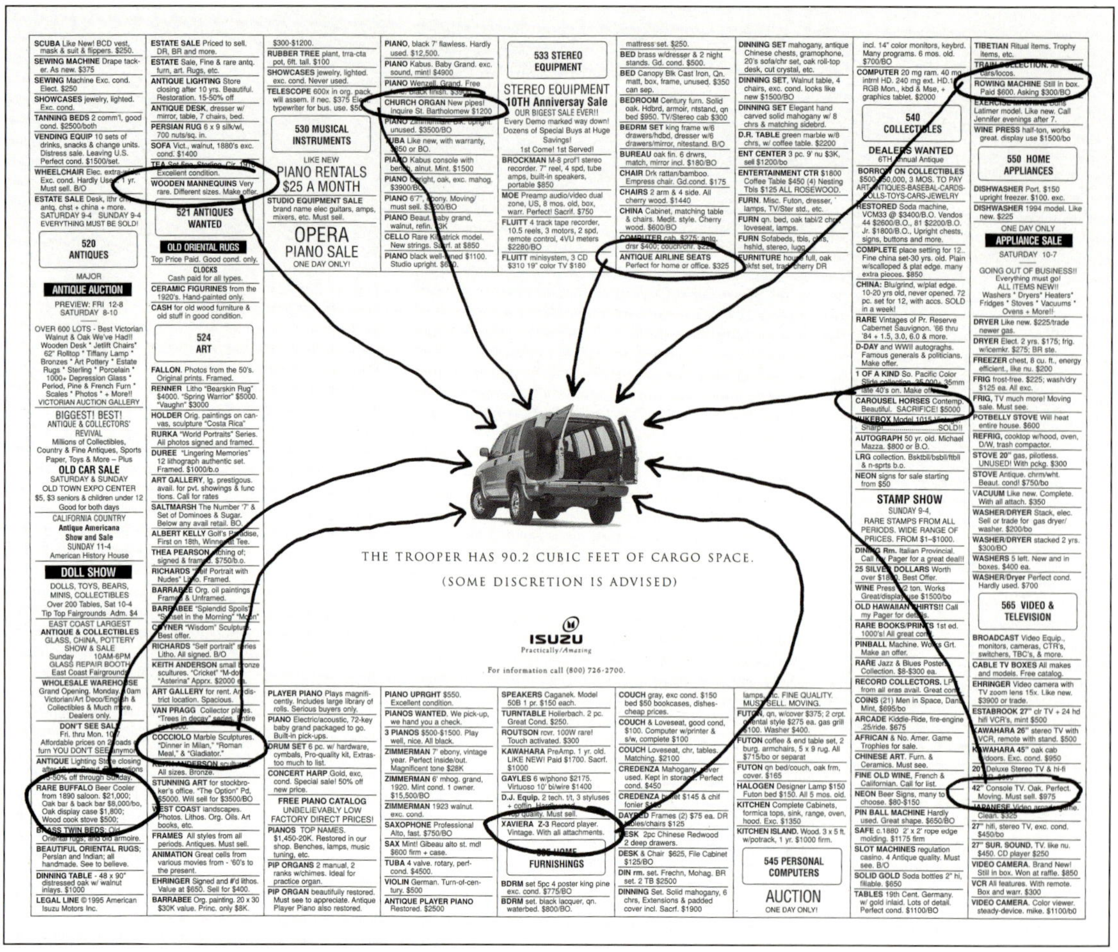

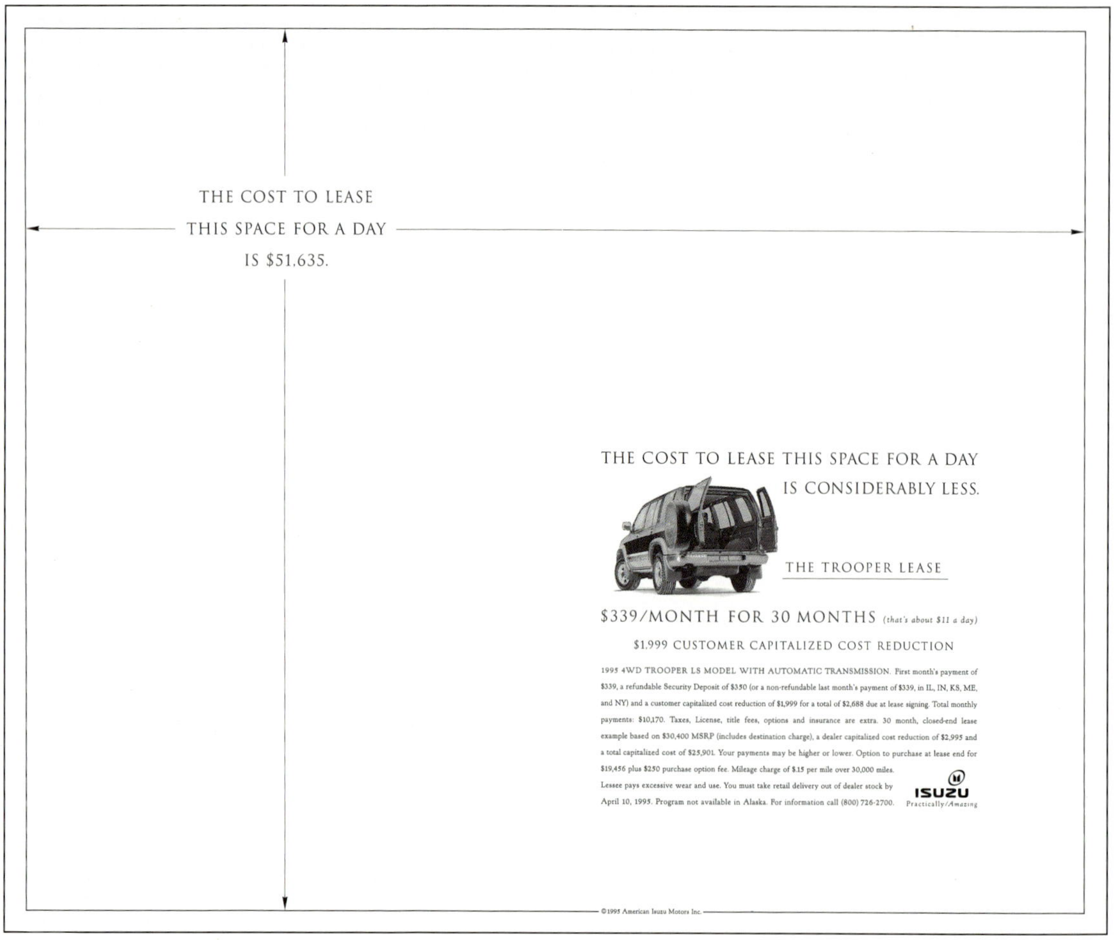

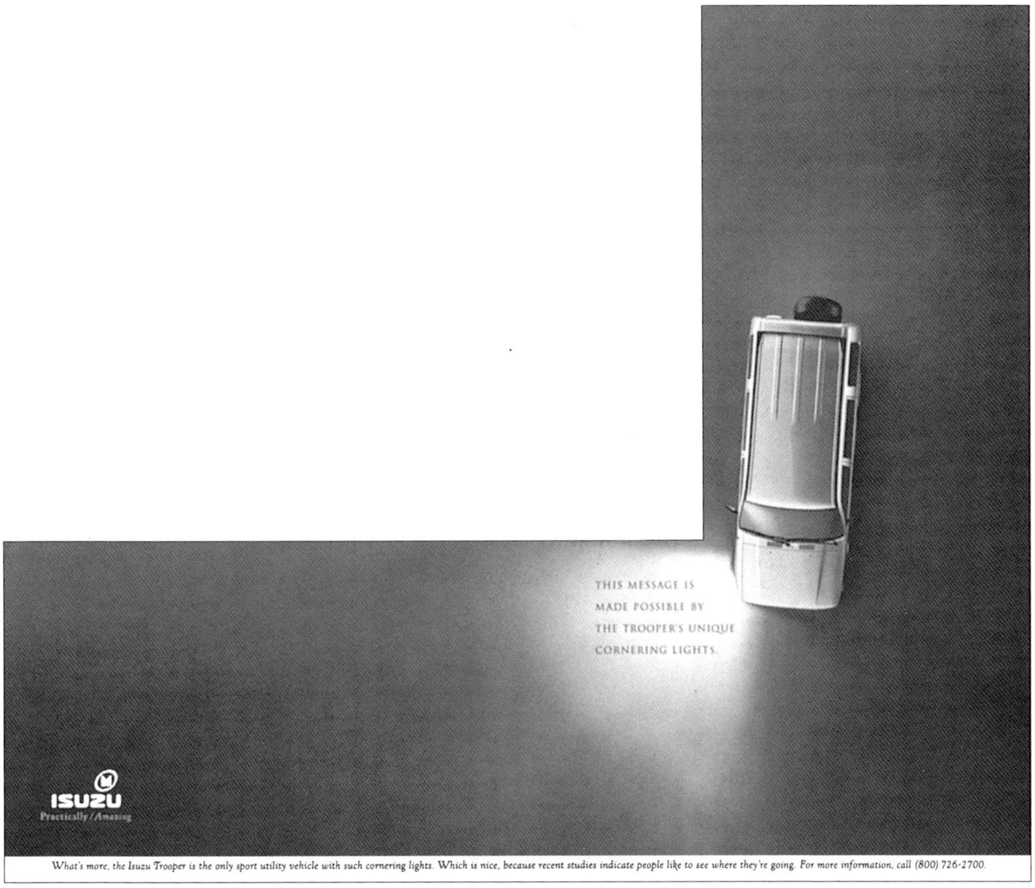
THIS MESSAGE IS
MADE POSSIBLE BY
THE TROOPER'S UNIQUE
CORNERING LIGHTS.
ISUZU
Practically/Amazing
What's more, the Isuzu Trooper is the only sport utility vehicle with such cornering lights. Which is nice, because recent studies indicate people like to see where they're going. For more information, call (800) 726-2700.

6 Silver

Power folding mirrors optional on S model. ©1995 American Isuzu Motors Inc.
POWER FOLDING
MIRRORS
COME IN PRETTY
HANDY AT
TIMES LIKE THIS.
THE ISUZU TROOPER
Call (800) 726-2700
ISUZU
Practically/Amazing

GOLD, SILVER & BRONZE AWARDS

CONSUMER NEWSPAPER OVER 600 LINES: CAMPAIGN

7 BRONZE

ART DIRECTOR
David Beverley

WRITER
Robert Burleigh

CLIENT
The Observer

AGENCY
Leagas Delaney/London

RUDOLF HESS took a terrible secret
to his grave in 1987. He WASN'T Rudolf HESS.
The A to Z of Conspiracy Theories. From how Rudolf Hess managed to hang himself decades after he'd been killed to why electricity pylons make people depressed. Only in The Observer this Sunday.
THE OBSERVER
Howard's law and disorder

In 1992 MOSSAD found out that 'MINISTER OF FUN' wasn't the only position DAVID MELLOR enjoyed.
The A to Z of Conspiracy Theories. From how Mossad discovered David Mellor's affair with Antonia de Sanchez to who was really behind the Lockerbie bombing. Only in The Observer this Sunday.
THE OBSERVER
Howard's law and disorder

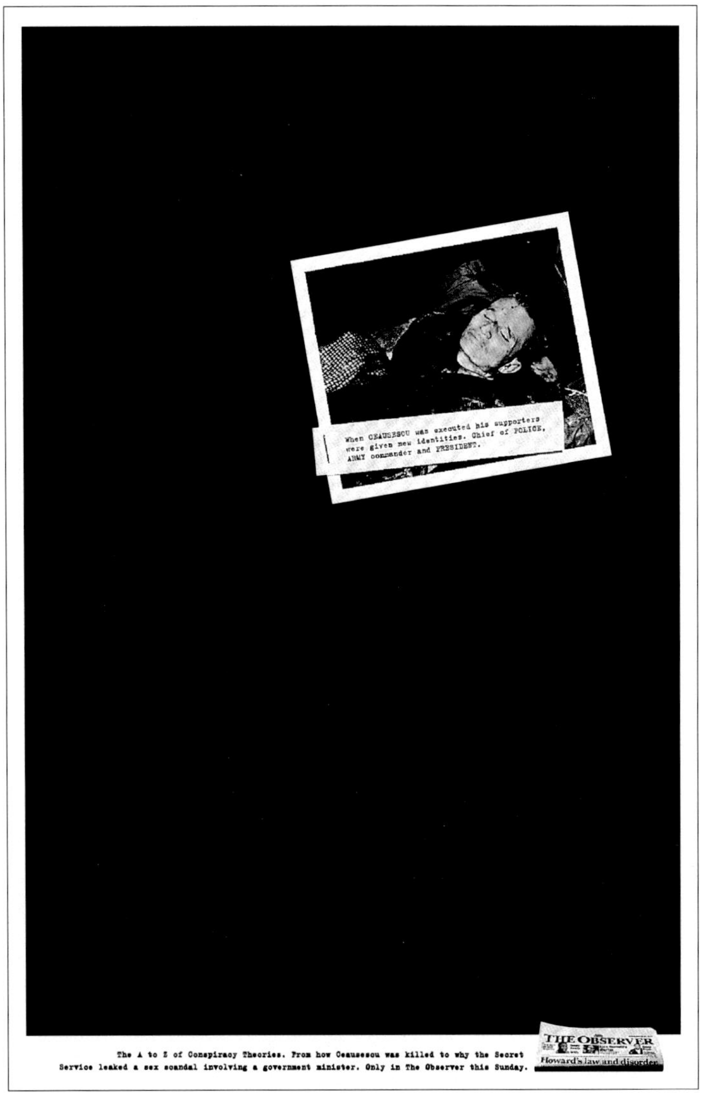
When CEAUSESCU was executed his supporters were given new identities. Chief of POLICE, ARMY commander and PRESIDENT.
The A to Z of Conspiracy Theories. From how Ceausescu was killed to why the Secret Service leaked a sex scandal involving a government minister. Only in The Observer this Sunday.
THE OBSERVER
Howard's law and disorder

7 Bronze

GOLD, SILVER & BRONZE AWARDS

CONSUMER NEWSPAPER 600 LINES OR LESS: SINGLE

8 GOLD

ART DIRECTOR
Sharon McDaniel Azula
WRITERS
David Oakley
Scott Corbett
ILLUSTRATOR
Rik Olson
CLIENT
East West Partners
AGENCY
Price/McNabb, Charlotte, NC

9 SILVER

ART DIRECTOR
Bob Barrie
WRITER
Dean Buckhorn
PHOTOGRAPHER
Anthony Suau
CLIENT
Time International
AGENCY
Fallon McElligott/ Minneapolis

10 BRONZE

ART DIRECTOR
Dan Cohen
WRITER
Paul Hartzell
PHOTOGRAPHER
Kevin Logan
CLIENT
Barron's
AGENCY
Angotti Thomas Hedge/ New York

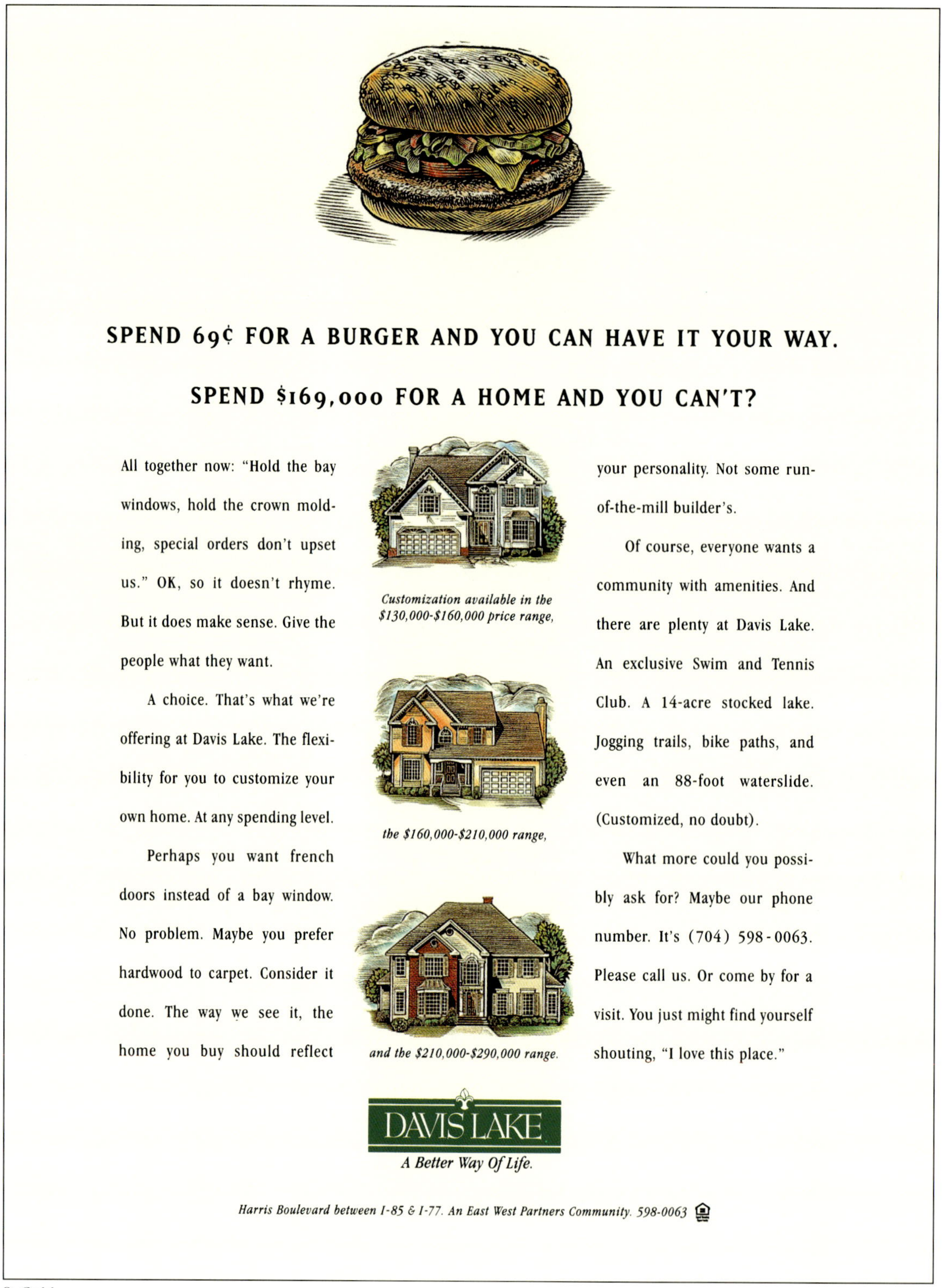

SPEND 69¢ FOR A BURGER AND YOU CAN HAVE IT YOUR WAY.
SPEND $169,000 FOR A HOME AND YOU CAN'T?
All together now: "Hold the bay windows, hold the crown molding, special orders don't upset us." OK, so it doesn't rhyme. But it does make sense. Give the people what they want.
A choice. That's what we're offering at Davis Lake. The flexibility for you to customize your own home. At any spending level.
Perhaps you want french doors instead of a bay window. No problem. Maybe you prefer hardwood to carpet. Consider it done. The way we see it, the home you buy should reflect your personality. Not some run-of-the-mill builder's.
Of course, everyone wants a community with amenities. And there are plenty at Davis Lake. An exclusive Swim and Tennis Club. A 14-acre stocked lake. Jogging trails, bike paths, and even an 88-foot waterslide. (Customized, no doubt).
What more could you possibly ask for? Maybe our phone number. It's (704) 598-0063. Please call us. Or come by for a visit. You just might find yourself shouting, "I love this place."
Customization available in the $130,000-$160,000 price range,
the $160,000-$210,000 range,
and the $210,000-$290,000 range.
DAVIS LAKE
A Better Way Of Life.
Harris Boulevard between I-85 & I-77. An East West Partners Community. 598-0063

8 Gold

Two warring African tribes.

Two million refugees.

Two minutes on the nightly news?

Understanding comes with TIME.

9 Silver

© 1995 Dow Jones & Company, Inc. All Rights Reserved. 4E633

It's a lot easier making your second million.
But we'll talk about that later.

To subscribe, call 1-800-328-6800, Ext. 510. *Barron's. How money becomes wealth.®*

10 Bronze

GOLD, SILVER & BRONZE
AWARDS

CONSUMER NEWSPAPER
600 LINES OR LESS:
CAMPAIGN

11 GOLD

ART DIRECTOR
Bob Barrie

WRITER
Dean Buckhorn

PHOTOGRAPHERS
Anthony Suau
Christopher Morris
Gerard Vandystadt

CLIENT
Time International

AGENCY
Fallon McElligott/
Minneapolis

Two warring African tribes.

Two million refugees.

Two minutes on the nightly news?

Understanding comes with TIME.

TIME
People who are willing to die
for freedom shouldn't be buried
in the middle of the newspaper.
Understanding comes with TIME.

TIME
The stopwatch never lies.
Then again, it rarely tells
the whole truth.
Understanding comes with TIME.

GOLD, SILVER & BRONZE AWARDS

CONSUMER NEWSPAPER 600 LINES OR LESS: CAMPAIGN

12 SILVER

ART DIRECTORS
Steve Amick
Mikal Reich

WRITERS
Steve Amick
Mikal Reich

CLIENT
The Village Voice

AGENCY
Mad Dogs & Englishmen/ New York

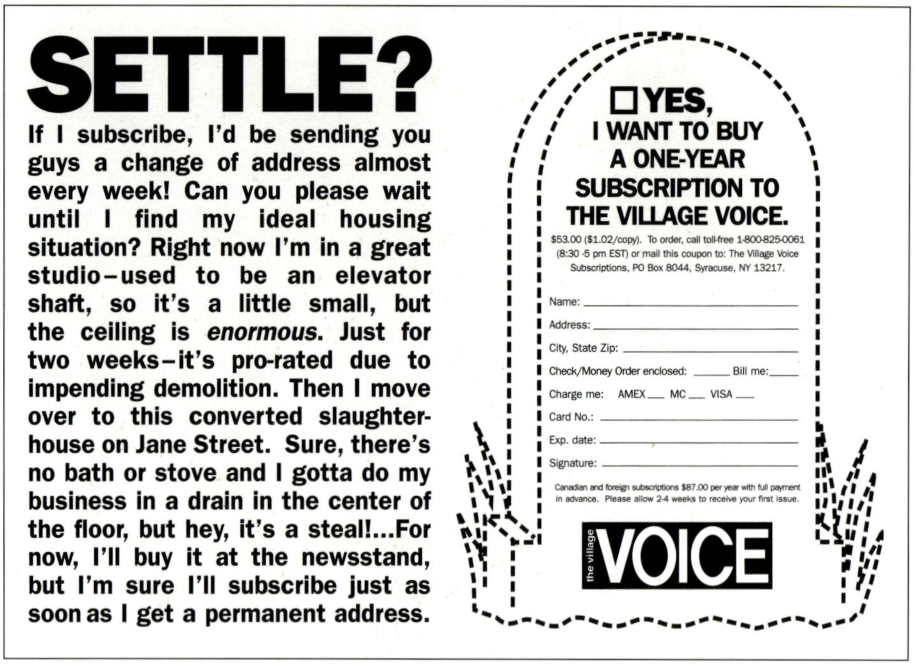

SETTLE?
If I subscribe, I'd be sending you guys a change of address almost every week! Can you please wait until I find my ideal housing situation? Right now I'm in a great studio–used to be an elevator shaft, so it's a little small, but the ceiling is *enormous*. Just for two weeks–it's pro-rated due to impending demolition. Then I move over to this converted slaughter-house on Jane Street. Sure, there's no bath or stove and I gotta do my business in a drain in the center of the floor, but hey, it's a steal!...For now, I'll buy it at the newsstand, but I'm sure I'll subscribe just as soon as I get a permanent address.
☐ YES, I WANT TO BUY A ONE-YEAR SUBSCRIPTION TO THE VILLAGE VOICE.
$53.00 ($1.02/copy). To order, call toll-free 1-800-825-0061 (8:30 -5 pm EST) or mail this coupon to: The Village Voice Subscriptions, PO Box 8044, Syracuse, NY 13217.
Name:
Address:
City, State Zip:
Check/Money Order enclosed: Bill me:
Charge me: AMEX MC VISA
Card No.:
Exp. date:
Signature:
Canadian and foreign subscriptions $87.00 per year with full payment in advance. Please allow 2-4 weeks to receive your first issue.
the village VOICE

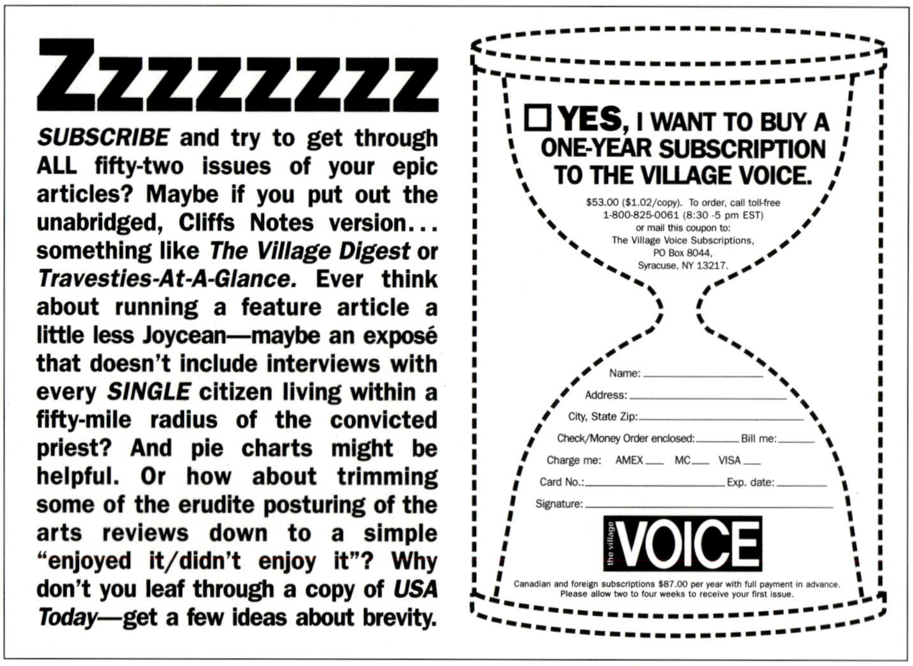

Zzzzzzzz
SUBSCRIBE and try to get through ALL fifty-two issues of your epic articles? Maybe if you put out the unabridged, Cliffs Notes version... something like *The Village Digest* or *Travesties-At-A-Glance.* Ever think about running a feature article a little less Joycean—maybe an exposé that doesn't include interviews with every *SINGLE* citizen living within a fifty-mile radius of the convicted priest? And pie charts might be helpful. Or how about trimming some of the erudite posturing of the arts reviews down to a simple "enjoyed it/didn't enjoy it"? Why don't you leaf through a copy of *USA Today*—get a few ideas about brevity.
☐ YES, I WANT TO BUY A ONE-YEAR SUBSCRIPTION TO THE VILLAGE VOICE.
$53.00 ($1.02/copy). To order, call toll-free 1-800-825-0061 (8:30 -5 pm EST) or mail this coupon to: The Village Voice Subscriptions, PO Box 8044, Syracuse, NY 13217.
Name:
Address:
City, State Zip:
Check/Money Order enclosed: Bill me:
Charge me: AMEX MC VISA
Card No.: Exp. date:
Signature:
the village VOICE
Canadian and foreign subscriptions $87.00 per year with full payment in advance. Please allow two to four weeks to receive your first issue.

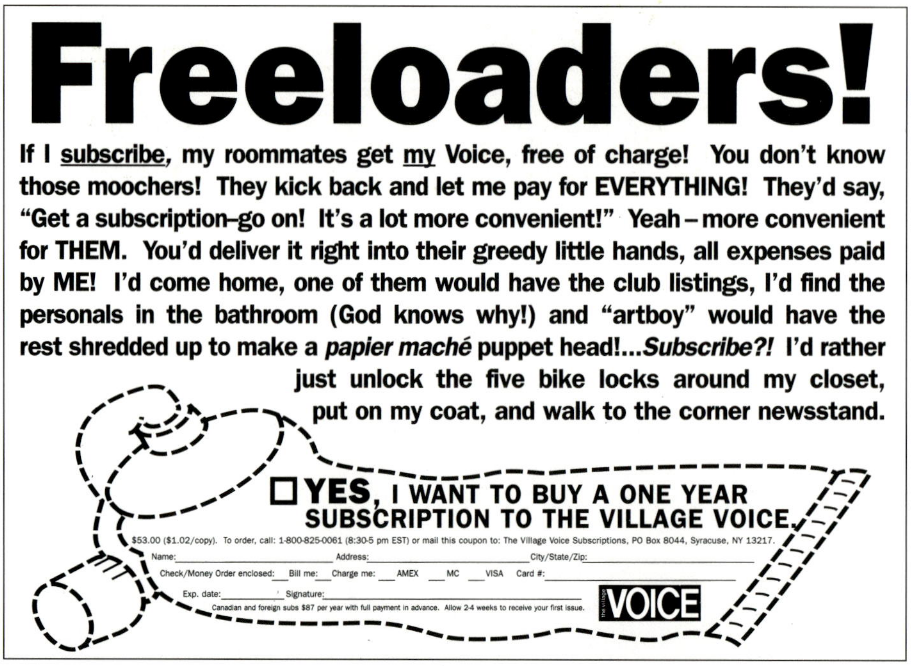

Freeloaders!
If I subscribe, my roommates get my Voice, free of charge! You don't know those moochers! They kick back and let me pay for EVERYTHING! They'd say, "Get a subscription–go on! It's a lot more convenient!" Yeah–more convenient for THEM. You'd deliver it right into their greedy little hands, all expenses paid by ME! I'd come home, one of them would have the club listings, I'd find the personals in the bathroom (God knows why!) and "artboy" would have the rest shredded up to make a *papier maché* puppet head!...*Subscribe?!* I'd rather just unlock the five bike locks around my closet, put on my coat, and walk to the corner newsstand.
☐ YES, I WANT TO BUY A ONE YEAR SUBSCRIPTION TO THE VILLAGE VOICE.
$53.00 ($1.02/copy). To order, call: 1-800-825-0061 (8:30-5 pm EST) or mail this coupon to: The Village Voice Subscriptions, PO Box 8044, Syracuse, NY 13217.
Name: Address: City/State/Zip:
Check/Money Order enclosed: Bill me: Charge me: AMEX MC VISA Card #:
Exp. date: Signature:
Canadian and foreign subs $87 per year with full payment in advance. Allow 2-4 weeks to receive your first issue.
the village VOICE

INK???

Why do you folks persist in remaining a Yugo on the info superhighway? Let me get this straight: you want to send me a *hard copy* of the Voice every week? Get *serious*: a clunky stack of newsprint that you have schlepped from *your* offices to the post office to *my* apartment?!? You're kidding, right? "Cyberspace"...? Sound familiar? There are millions of your *non*-Amish readers who would kill to access the Voice *on-line*. No waste of paper, ink or precious resources. No added expense of delivery, just fire up the modem, click the mouse on an icon of a little tortured guy and...*bingo!*...we're interactive with an entire photo essay on political prisoners in Bolivia!

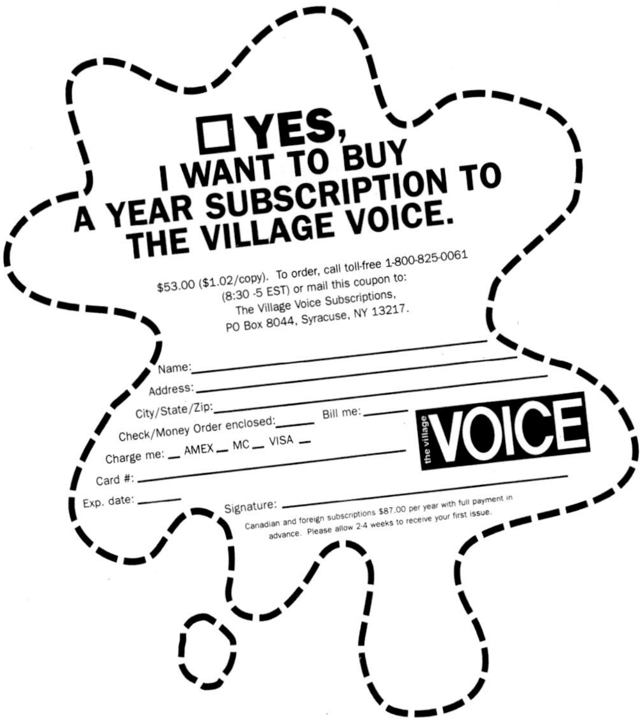

NYET!!

I am not now, nor have I ever been, a subscriber to the Village Voice. I admit I *occasionally* glance through a Voice, but in light of our country's new swing to the Right, how could I sign something that might later resurface as a "list of known troublemakers"? They might think that I *question* making prayer in schools a required credit like Gym; replacing all members of Congress with the entire cast of *The Love Boat* and selecting royal blue, rather than that suspicious pink, as the new M&M...!!! Let me go on record here as saying that though I may read the Voice, there is absolutely no evidence that I am "with" the Voice. (Heck, I might even let my children join the Newtketeers.)

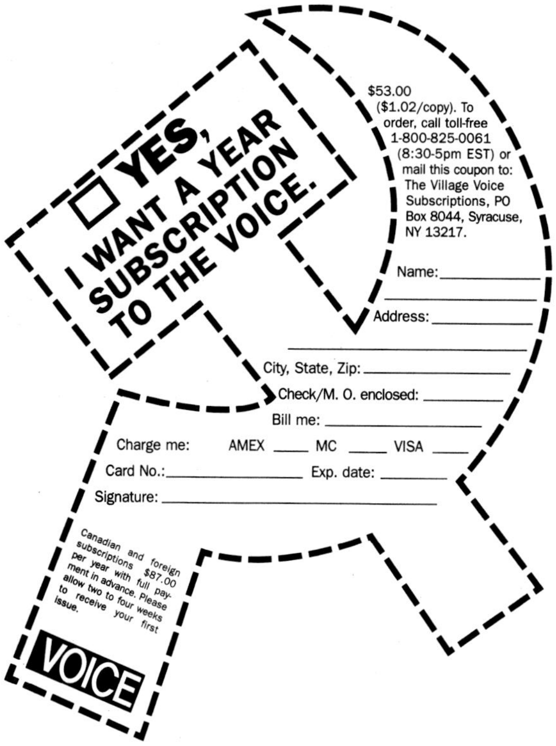

GOLD, SILVER & BRONZE AWARDS

CONSUMER NEWSPAPER 600 LINES OR LESS: CAMPAIGN

13 BRONZE

ART DIRECTOR
Dan Cohen

WRITER
Paul Hartzell

PHOTOGRAPHER
Kevin Logan

CLIENT
Barron's

AGENCY
Angotti Thomas Hedge/ New York

CONSUMER MAGAZINE B/W FULL PAGE OR SPREAD: SINGLE

14 GOLD

ART DIRECTOR
Ben Osborn

WRITER
Ben Osborn

PHOTOGRAPHER
Simon Harsent

CLIENT
Richter

AGENCY
Cosmos/Surry Hills, Australia

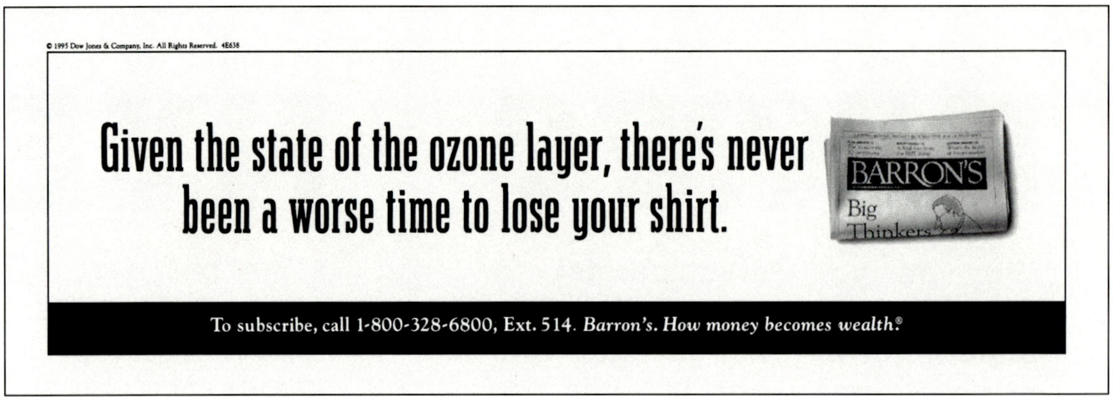
Given the state of the ozone layer, there's never been a worse time to lose your shirt.
BARRON'S
Big Thinkers
To subscribe, call 1-800-328-6800, Ext. 514. Barron's. How money becomes wealth.®

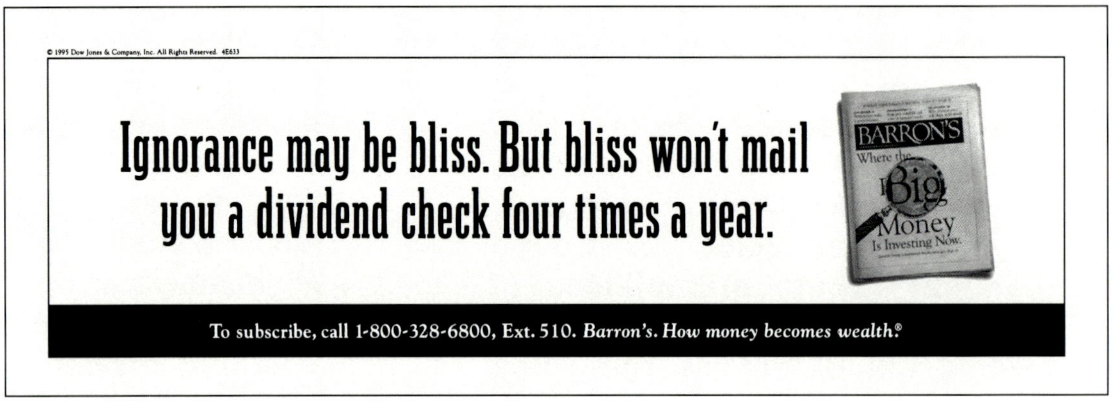
Ignorance may be bliss. But bliss won't mail you a dividend check four times a year.
BARRON'S
Big Money
Is Investing Now.
To subscribe, call 1-800-328-6800, Ext. 510. Barron's. How money becomes wealth.®

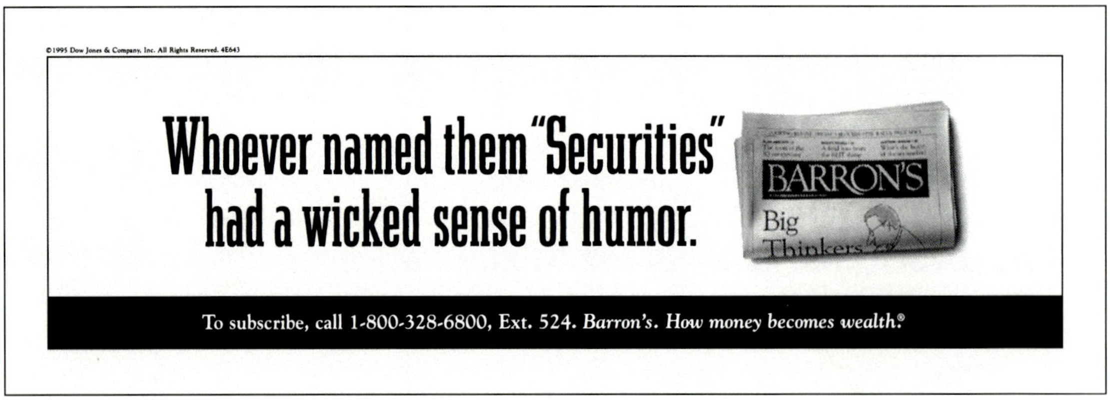
Whoever named them "Securities" had a wicked sense of humor.
BARRON'S
Big Thinkers
To subscribe, call 1-800-328-6800, Ext. 524. Barron's. How money becomes wealth.®

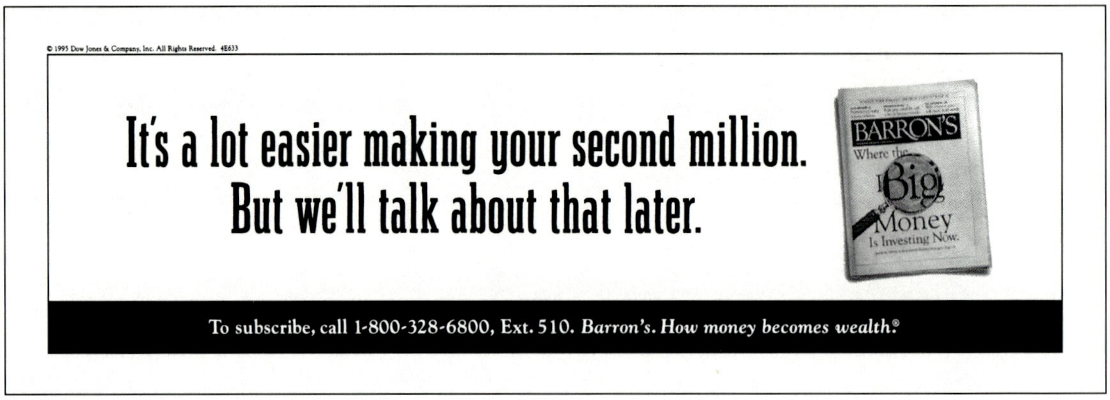

13 Bronze

LAING + SIMMONS
Balmain
FOR SALE
818 2133
BIRCHGROVE REAL ESTATE
FOR SALE
303 DARLING ST, BALMAIN
810.0164
FOR SALE
Gilmour
555 9322
BIRCHGROVE REAL ESTATE
FOR SALE
810.0164
POWERBASE
SUBWOOFERS BY RICHTER
richter
THE FORCE FROM DOWNUNDER

14 Gold

GOLD, SILVER & BRONZE AWARDS

CONSUMER MAGAZINE B/W FULL PAGE OR SPREAD: SINGLE

15 SILVER

ART DIRECTOR
Chris Toland
WRITER
Steve Morris
PHOTOGRAPH
Nebraska State Historical Society
CLIENT
Oregon Trail
AGENCY
Cole & Weber/Portland

CONSUMER MAGAZINE COLOR FULL PAGE OR SPREAD: SINGLE

16 GOLD

ART DIRECTOR
Alan Pafenbach
WRITER
Lance Jensen
ILLUSTRATOR
Carla Siboldi
DESIGNER
Becky Hickey
CLIENT
Volkswagen
AGENCY
Arnold Communications/Boston

IMAGINE HEARING YOUR KIDS ASK, "ARE WE THERE YET?" EVERY DAY FOR SIX MONTHS.
Imagine, also, taking your family on a cross-country road trip in the days when there were no roads. No rest areas. No Dairy Queen. Just a trail. A sun-scorched, dust-choked, treacherous ribbon of dirt cutting through the wilderness, spanning six states and some 2,000 miles. Yet between 1840 and 1860, nearly 300,000 overland emigrants embarked on this grueling six-month journey. And if the little varmints complained, well, they could get out of the wagon and walk. Now, over 150 years later, you can relive the pioneers' experiences through a wide variety of fascinating attractions along the Oregon Trail. Including the Oregon Trail Interpretive Center at Baker City and the End of the Oregon Trail Interpretive Center in Oregon City. To order a visitors guide, call 800-332-1843.
VISIT THE HISTORIC OREGON TRAIL
OREGON TRAIL

15 Silver

Jerry Garcia. 1942-1995.

Copyright 1995 Volkswagen of America, Inc.

GOLD, SILVER & BRONZE AWARDS

CONSUMER MAGAZINE COLOR FULL PAGE OR SPREAD: SINGLE

17 SILVER

ART DIRECTOR
Jeremy Postaer
WRITER
Paul Venables
PHOTOGRAPHERS
John Frame
Jim Safford
CLIENT
Bell Sports
AGENCY
Goodby Silverstein & Partners/San Francisco

18 BRONZE

ART DIRECTOR
Mark Fuller
WRITER
Ron Huey
PHOTOGRAPHER
William Coupon
CLIENT
Amgen
AGENCY
The Martin Agency/ Richmond

THE 40-YEAR HISTORY OF BELL HELMETS, IN 2.3 SECONDS.
00.1
Guy hits wall.
01.2
Car explodes.
02.3
Guy O.K.
On May 10, 1991, a few seconds validated our entire existence. And prolonged Mark Dismore's.
Mark broke both feet, both knees, two vertebrae in his neck and his right wrist. His head, and his brain, in case you were wondering, were just fine. In fact, he's still racing today.
We were thankful. Thankful that we've spent a lifetime pioneering helmet safety. That the people in our factory in Illinois painstakingly hand-craft each and every racing helmet. That decades of research and testing had taught us—forced us—to make the best helmet we could possibly make.
Let's just say that Mark was kind of appreciative, too.
There were many crashes before his. There have been crashes since. Every time a mountain biker takes on a boulder, every time a road biker catches a pedal, every time a twelve year old runs his skateboard off concrete steps, the same knowledge that saved Mark Dismore's head from sustaining any injury whatsoever kicks in. All the research on how the G-forces of an impact affect the brain, all the strap tests and drop tests and crash tests. Suddenly, all 40 years of it matters. Understandably, 22 of the top 33 IndyCar drivers request and wear Bell helmets.
As for the hundreds of professional cyclists that wear Bell, well, they don't even know who Mark Dismore is. But we get the feeling they understand the value of a split second, too.
Our IndyCar research gets strapped to your noggin. Just knowing that should add years to your life.
COURAGE FOR YOUR HEAD.™
BELL HELMETS

17 Silver

In recent years, new breakthroughs have been made in helping people with cancer better manage their treatment. New drugs are helping reduce many of the side effects of chemotherapy treatment like nausea and even more serious conditions like a low white blood cell count.

One drug, Neupogen (Filgrastim), is being prescribed to help many people on chemotherapy maintain a more normal white blood cell count. Specifically, a normal neutrophil count. In short, neutrophils are a type of white blood cell that

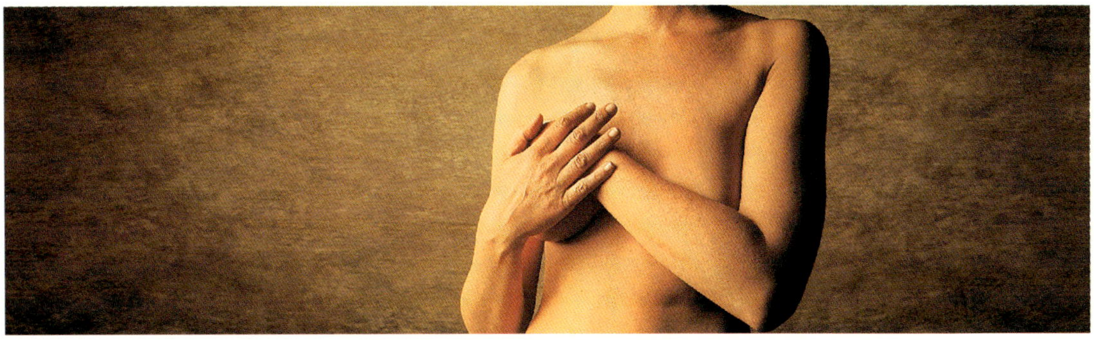

YOU'VE JUST FOUND OUT YOU HAVE CANCER. LET'S BEGIN BY REDUCING THE LUMP IN YOUR THROAT.

helps your body fight infection. Maintaining a normal neutrophil count during treatment can be important for two reasons.

First, you have a much better chance of staying on your recommended chemotherapy schedule. That means getting your treatment behind you sooner. Secondly, maintaining a normal neutrophil count can help reduce your risk of infection. So you have a better chance of staying out of the hospital. Instead, you're able to spend more time at home where you belong with family and friends. Even normal daily activities like shopping, going to movies and eating out at restaurants can be more accessible.

Of course, Neupogen isn't right for every patient. Ask your doctor if Neupogen should be a part of your treatment. On the following page, you'll find an explanation of Neupogen and its possible side effects. The most common side effect that patients report experiencing is mild-to-moderate bone pain, which can usually be controlled with a non-aspirin analgesic.

As a final note, before we embarked on this educational campaign, we conducted extensive research in cities across the country. We talked with people who were currently undergoing, or had undergone chemotherapy treatment in the past. We also met with doctors, nurses and other cancer specialists. Among chemotherapy patients, we found an overwhelming desire for more information about cancer and chemotherapy treatment. Doctors and nurses, many of whom had initial misgivings about any advertising at all, urged us to please be candid in all of our communications. They also asked that we point out that Neupogen isn't for everyone. We acted on their advice.

We realize that your medical care is a sensitive and very personal matter. We'd like to know your feelings about the information presented here. If you would like to receive more information concerning Neupogen and how it might help in your treatment, call us at 1-800-333-9777.

NEUPOGEN

GOLD, SILVER & BRONZE AWARDS

CONSUMER MAGAZINE B/W FULL PAGE OR SPREAD: CAMPAIGN

19 SILVER

ART DIRECTOR
Thomas Hayo

WRITER
Richard Yelland

PHOTOGRAPHER
Tom Card

TYPOGRAPHER
Rob Sutton

CLIENT
The Paris Review

AGENCY
J. Walter Thompson/
New York

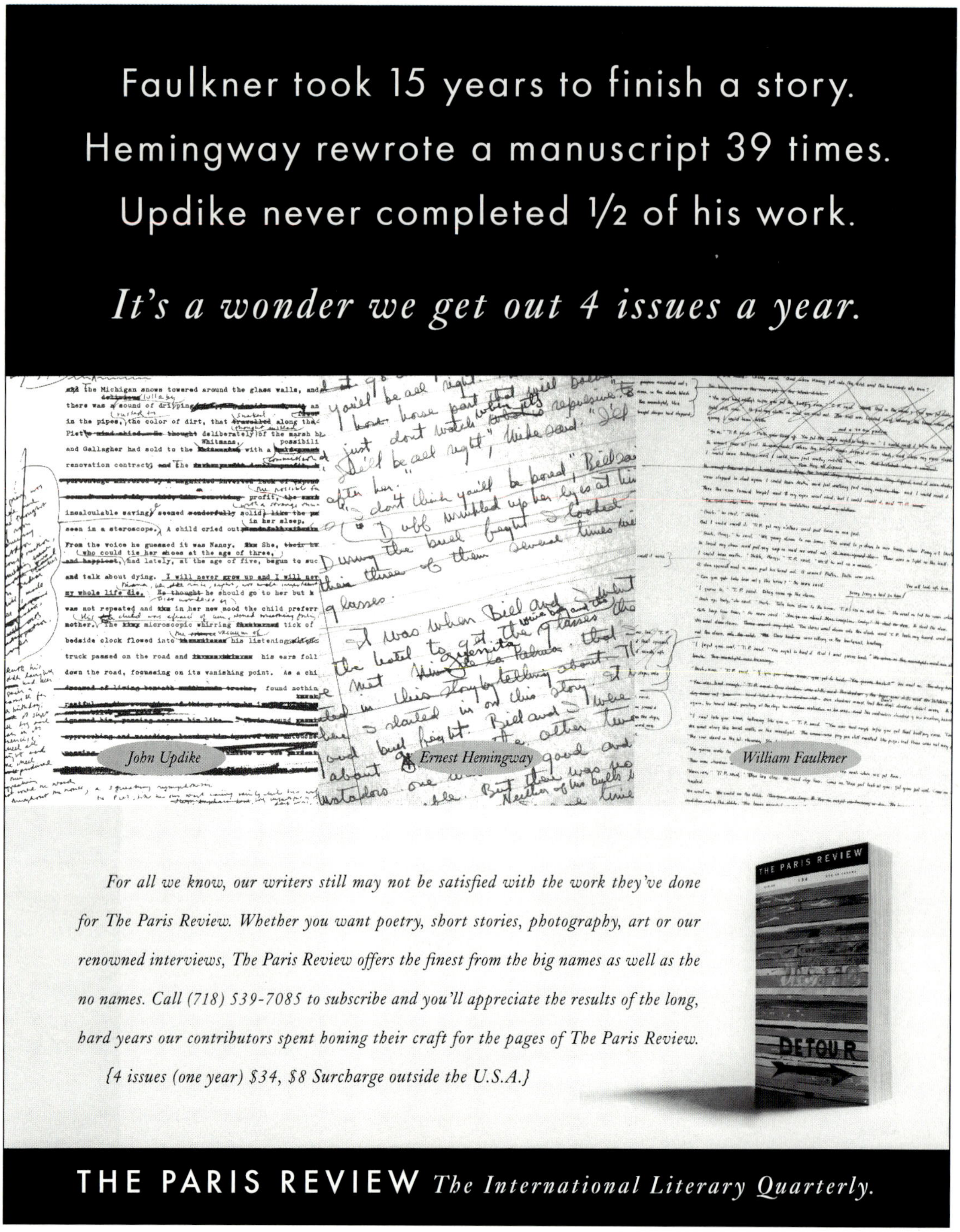
Faulkner took 15 years to finish a story.
Hemingway rewrote a manuscript 39 times.
Updike never completed 1/2 of his work.
It's a wonder we get out 4 issues a year.
John Updike
Ernest Hemingway
William Faulkner
For all we know, our writers still may not be satisfied with the work they've done for The Paris Review. Whether you want poetry, short stories, photography, art or our renowned interviews, The Paris Review offers the finest from the big names as well as the no names. Call (718) 539-7085 to subscribe and you'll appreciate the results of the long, hard years our contributors spent honing their craft for the pages of The Paris Review.
{4 issues (one year) $34, $8 Surcharge outside the U.S.A.}
THE PARIS REVIEW
DETOUR
THE PARIS REVIEW The International Literary Quarterly.

Flaubert compared losing oneself in literature to perpetual orgy.
Here's your invitation to the party.
THE PARIS REVIEW
$34 FOR 4 ISSUES
$1000 FOR LIFE
Postal surcharge of $8 per 4 issues outside USA except for life subscriptions
CHECK ENCLOSED
MASTERCARD/VISA
name
address
city
state
zip code
credit card number
expiration date
THE PARIS REVIEW, 45-39 171 PLACE, FLUSHING, NEW YORK 11358
The Paris Review. It's the kind of writing that gives you goosebumps. That sends a shiver down your spine. That makes your hair stand on end. It's the kind of writing that's the result of a longstanding commitment to literature. A commitment The Paris Review has made for more than 40 years.
Whether you want short stories, poetry, photography, art or our renowned interviews, call (718) 539-7085 to subscribe and you'll get a better understanding of the place where Flaubert found his passion.
THE PARIS REVIEW The International Literary Quarterly.

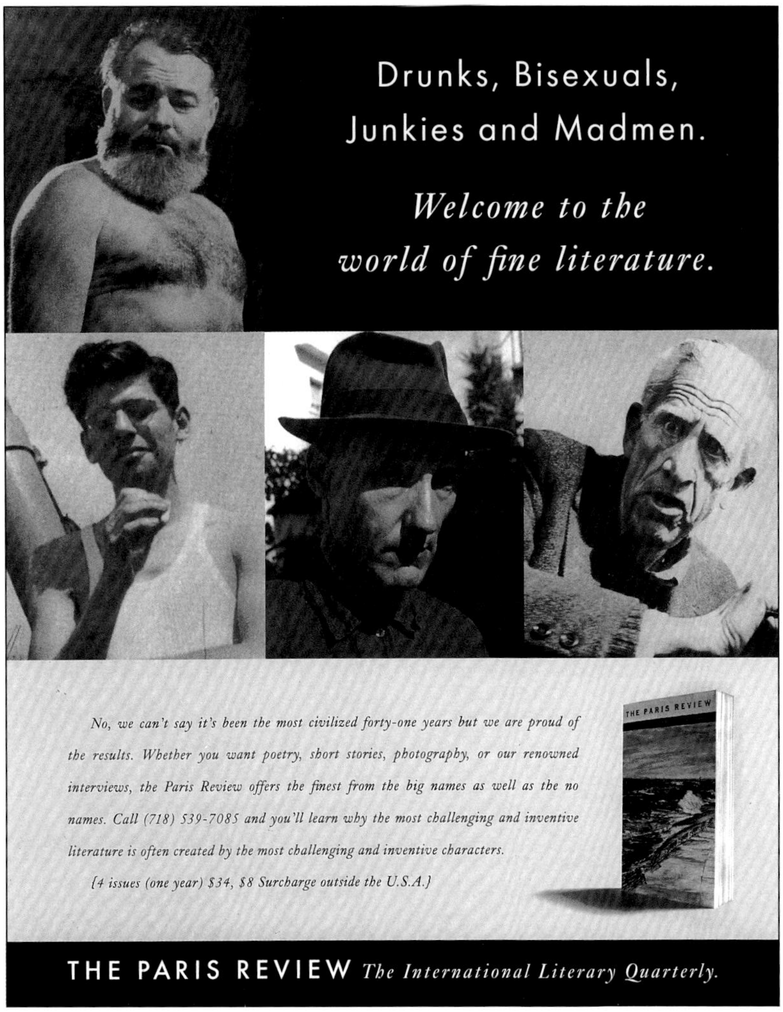
Drunks, Bisexuals, Junkies and Madmen.
Welcome to the world of fine literature.
THE PARIS REVIEW
No, we can't say it's been the most civilized forty-one years but we are proud of the results. Whether you want poetry, short stories, photography, or our renowned interviews, the Paris Review offers the finest from the big names as well as the no names. Call (718) 539-7085 and you'll learn why the most challenging and inventive literature is often created by the most challenging and inventive characters.
(4 issues (one year) $34, $8 Surcharge outside the U.S.A.)
THE PARIS REVIEW The International Literary Quarterly.

19 Silver

GOLD, SILVER & BRONZE AWARDS

CONSUMER MAGAZINE B/W FULL PAGE OR SPREAD: CAMPAIGN

20 SILVER

ART DIRECTOR
Terence Reynolds

WRITER
Todd Tilford

PHOTOGRAPHERS
Richard Reens
Duncan Sim

CLIENT
AM General Corporation

AGENCY
R&D/The Richards Group, Dallas

THERE ARE TWO WAYS TO GET TRAFFIC TO PULL IMMEDIATELY OUT OF YOUR PATH. A POLICE ESCORT IS ONE OF THEM.
Subtlety is just not one of its strong suits. In fact, you will not find one timid rivet in the Hummer's heat-treated aluminum alloy body. With its unique design, a Hummer can do things that no other vehicle can. Scale an 18-inch vertical rock ledge. Plow through a three-foot snowdrift. Part rush-hour traffic.
HUMMER

YES, IT'S STREET LEGAL. NO, YOU CAN'T GET IT WITH A MACHINE GUN TURRET.
Save for some added creature comforts and the absence of optional rocket launchers, the Hummer is unchanged from its military counterpart. Scale 18-inch vertical ledges. Plow through three-foot snowdrifts. Stand defiantly in the face of categorization, conformity, and boredom.
HUMMER

THE ABILITY TO SCALE AN 18-INCH VERTICAL LEDGE. THE ABILITY TO FORD TWO FEET OF WATER. THE ABILITY TO MAKE A SEMI THINK TWICE ABOUT CUTTING YOU OFF.
It's not a car. It's not a truck. It's not just another 4X4. It's a Hummer. A vehicle not in a class, but a universe all its own. With 16 inches of ground clearance (twice that of any 4X4), steep approach and departure angles, a stable 72-inch track width, and a unique geared hub assembly, there is no such thing as a dead end. For more information about the Hummer's unmatched capabilities, just call 800-732-5493.
HUMMER

GOLD, SILVER & BRONZE AWARDS

CONSUMER MAGAZINE COLOR FULL PAGE OR SPREAD: CAMPAIGN

21 GOLD

ART DIRECTOR
John Boiler

WRITERS
Glenn Cole
Ned McNeilage

PHOTOGRAPHER
Brad Harris

CLIENT
Nike

AGENCY
Wieden & Kennedy/
Portland

APPAREL
Somewhere there's a nice, sunny place with warm breezes and shady palms where all the second-place guys train.
The Clima-F.I.T.® running jacket is part of the NIKE F.I.T.™ line of apparel. A layering system that keeps you warm when you need to be warm, dry when you need to be dry. Bob Kennedy's Clima-F.I.T. jacket protects him from wind, rain, his own sweat, and the occasional notion to move to one of those nice, sunny places.

APPAREL
If your teeth still chatter, it's fear.
The Storm-F.I.T.™ full-zip waterproof jacket is part of the NIKE F.I.T.™ line of apparel, a layering system that keeps you warm when you need to be warm, dry when you need to be dry. David Bryson's teeth do not chatter because he is neither cold, nor wet, nor a pathetic sniveling wuss.

GOLD, SILVER & BRONZE AWARDS

CONSUMER MAGAZINE COLOR FULL PAGE OR SPREAD: CAMPAIGN

22 SILVER

ART DIRECTOR
Brian Campbell

WRITER
Ben Priest

PHOTOGRAPHERS
Raymond Meeks
Mark Power

CLIENT
Olympus Cameras

AGENCY
Lowe Howard-Spink/
London

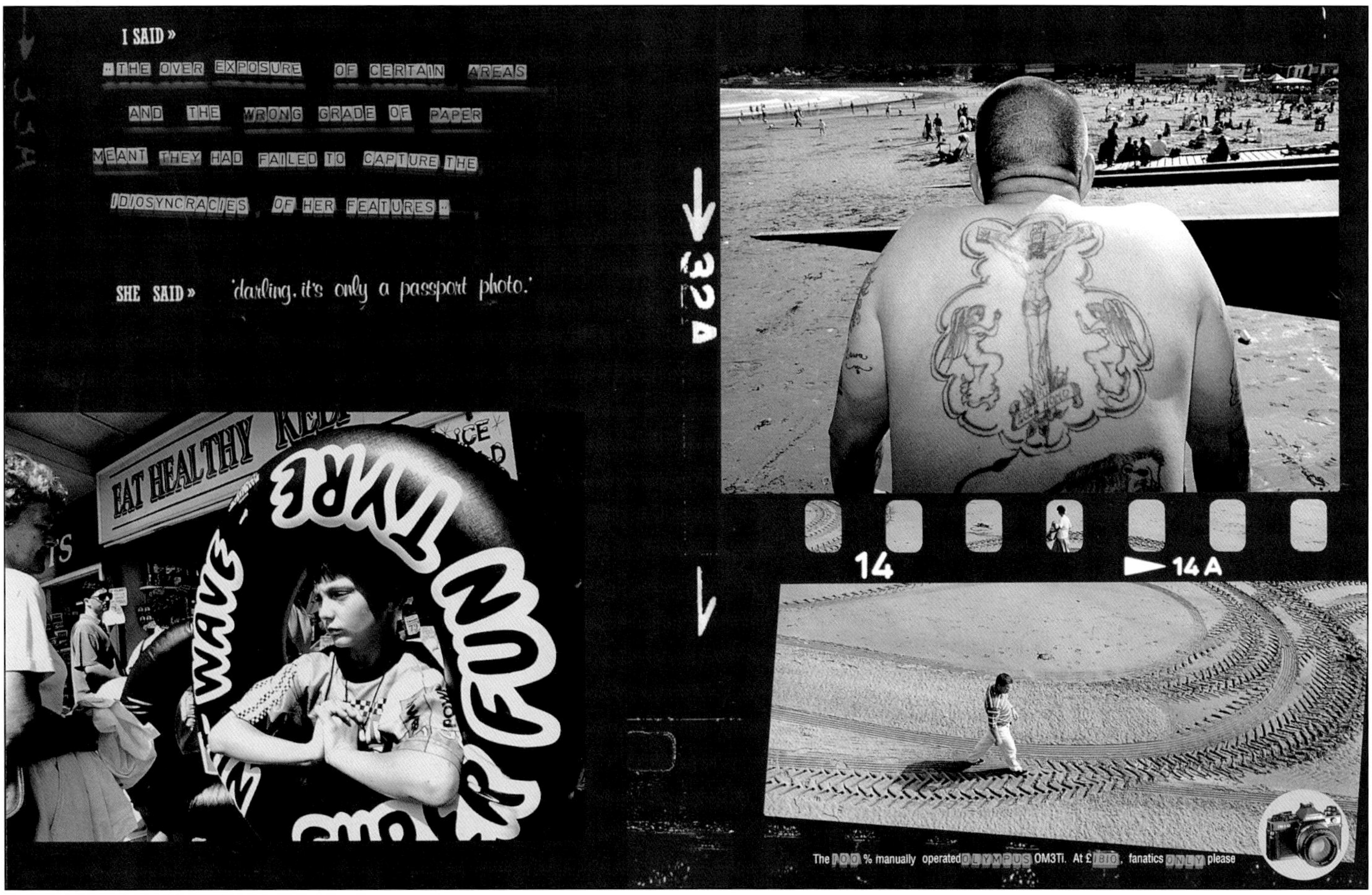
I SAID »
« THE OVER EXPOSURE OF CERTAIN AREAS
AND THE WRONG GRADE OF PAPER
MEANT THEY HAD FAILED TO CAPTURE THE
IDIOSYNCRACIES OF HER FEATURES »
SHE SAID » 'darling, it's only a passport photo.'
EAT HEALTHY
TYRE
FUN
WAVE
32A
14
14A
The 100% manually operated OLYMPUS OM3Ti. At £1810, fanatics ONLY please

KODAK 5063 TX
HERE LIES NEIL THOMAS
BURIED ALONGSIDE HIS BELOVED WIFE
MAUREEN,
HIS ENLARGER,
DEVELOPING TANKS,
AND TWO BOXES OF MULTIGRADE.
The 100% manually operated OLYMPUS OM3Ti. At £1810, fanatics ONLY please

GOLD, SILVER & BRONZE AWARDS

CONSUMER MAGAZINE COLOR FULL PAGE OR SPREAD: CAMPAIGN

23 BRONZE

ART DIRECTOR
Jeremy Postaer

WRITER
Paul Venables

PHOTOGRAPHERS
Heimo
Gary Davis
John Frame
Barry Robinson
Jim Safford

CLIENT
Bell Sports

AGENCY
Goodby Silverstein & Partners/San Francisco

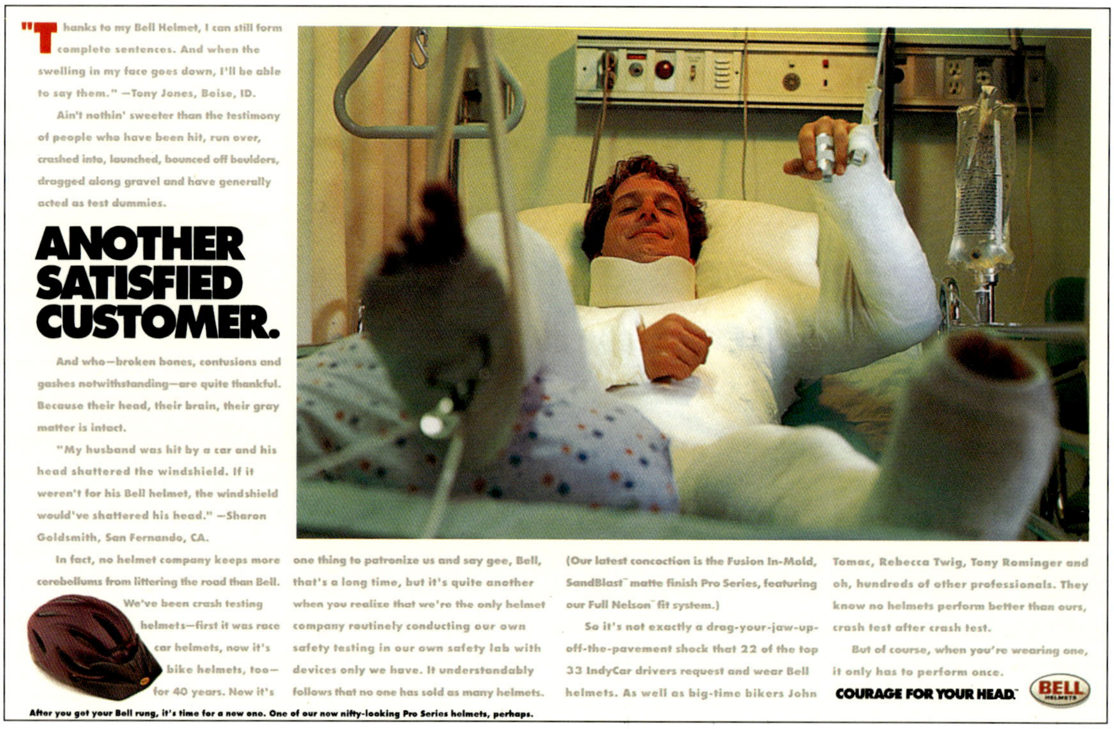

A HELMET THOUGHTFULLY DESIGNED BY ENGINEERS, CRAFTSMEN AND DEAD GUYS.
Product Development Engineer, Tom Stone
Industrial Designer, Michele Seward
VP of Research & Development, John Doe
You know what our designers contributed. It's sitting down there in the form of that Fusion In-Mold, SandBlast™ finish 16-vent Psycho Pro, featuring our Full Nelson™ fit system (named after a particularly snug wrestling hold).
You can probably guess what our engineers and craftsmen contributed. For forty years, they have been pioneering helmet structure and safety by tenaciously developing their own unique crash and burn tests (and standards) in their own unique research facility.
No hallucinogens were used in the designing of our new Pro Series. (As far as we know.)
Then there's the dead guys. They seem to require a bit more of an explanation. Their contribution has been more along the lines of a spongy grayish thing called a brain. You see, to figure out what happens in a real accident, we need to determine what happens to the brain. Crash test dummies don't have brains. So, we used cadavers to test how the G-forces of an impact effect the old cerebellum. We worked with brain surgeons from the St. Louis Medical Center, running crash tests with electrodes hooked up to the brains of, well, dead guys. Of course, no one else does this sort of thing.
Anyway, we've learned a lot.
For starters, no other helmets on the market are better than ours. Which is probably why no company has sold nearly as many helmets. And why 22 out of the top 33 IndyCar drivers and hundreds (too many to count, in fact) of professional cyclists prefer Bell.
As well as most dead guys.
COURAGE FOR YOUR HEAD.™
BELL HELMETS

YOUR BRAIN IS A HIGHLY SENSITIVE DEVICE. TOO BAD IT COMES IN SUCH A CHINTZY CARRYING CASE.
Boulders. Trees. Curbs. Concrete. All patiently waiting to prove (via simple demonstration) that when it comes to buffering your brain from impacts, your cranium's just not up to snuff.
Which puts pressure on your neural network to reason that A) you better wear a helmet and B) that you better cough up a few extra bucks for a Bell.
One of these Pro Series helmets, perhaps.
Razor Pro.
Image Pro.
Lug your cerebral cortex around in one of these: our new Fusion In-Mold SandBlast™ matte finish Pro Series helmets, featuring our Full Nelson™ fit system (the name comes from a particularly snug wrestling hold).
Avalanche Pro.
Psycho Pro.
Now those babies are Bells, so you just know they can take a spanking. Because we do things no other helmet company does. We test helmets using nasty devices only we have. We work with neurosurgeons to determine exactly how G-forces affect the brain upon impact (once we even had to explain that very thing to the brain surgeons.) And we crash and burn and otherwise destroy more helmets than anybody. In the name of safety, of course. (That and because it's kinda fun, too.)
You also might want to know that we've been at this for 40 years or so. Which means we were making mountain bike helmets, oh about 20 years before there were any mountain bikes. You can see why hundreds of pro bicyclists request and wear Bell helmets (there are too many to count, in fact). And why 22 of the top 33 IndyCar drivers entrust their noggins to us. As well as over 30 million regular schmoes.
It sure is nice to see all those people using their ultra-sensitive, highly sophisticated devices to ensure that they'll still be able to in the future.
COURAGE FOR YOUR HEAD.™
BELL HELMETS

THE 40-YEAR HISTORY OF BELL HELMETS, IN 2.3 SECONDS.
00.1
Guy hits wall.
01.2
Car explodes.
02.3
Guy O.K.
On May 10, 1991, a few seconds validated our entire existence. And prolonged Mark Dismore's.
Mark broke both feet, both knees, two vertebrae in his neck and his right wrist. His head, and his brain, in case you were wondering, were just fine. In fact, he's still racing today.
We were thankful. Thankful that we've spent a lifetime pioneering helmet safety. That the people in our factory in Illinois painstakingly handcraft each and every racing helmet. That decades of research and testing had taught us—forced us—to make the best helmet we could possibly make.
Let's just say that Mark was kind of appreciative, too.
There were many crashes before his. There have been crashes since. Every time a mountain biker takes on a boulder, every time a road biker catches a pedal, every time a twelve year old runs his skateboard off concrete steps, the same knowledge that saved Mark Dismore's head from sustaining any injury whatsoever kicks in. All the research on how the G-forces of an impact affect the brain, all the strap tests and drop tests and crash tests. Suddenly, all 40 years of it matters. Understandably, 22 of the top 33 IndyCar drivers request and wear Bell helmets.
Our IndyCar research gets strapped to your noggin. Just knowing that should add years to your life.
As for the hundreds of professional cyclists that wear Bell, well, they don't even know who Mark Dismore is. But we get the feeling they understand the value of a split second, too.
COURAGE FOR YOUR HEAD.™
BELL HELMETS

GOLD, SILVER & BRONZE AWARDS

CONSUMER MAGAZINE
B/W OR COLOR LESS THAN A PAGE: SINGLE

24 GOLD
ART DIRECTOR
Frank Haggerty
WRITER
Jim Nelson
PHOTOGRAPHER
Shawn Michienzi
CLIENT
Stren
AGENCY
Carmichael Lynch/ Minneapolis

25 SILVER
ART DIRECTOR
Frank Haggerty
WRITER
Jim Nelson
PHOTOGRAPHER
Shawn Michienzi
CLIENT
Stren
AGENCY
Carmichael Lynch/ Minneapolis

26 BRONZE
ART DIRECTOR
Tom McMahon
WRITER
Tim Wallis
PHOTOGRAPHER
Daniel Wilson
CLIENT
TileWorks
AGENCY
Meyer & Wallis/Milwaukee

24 Gold

25 Silver

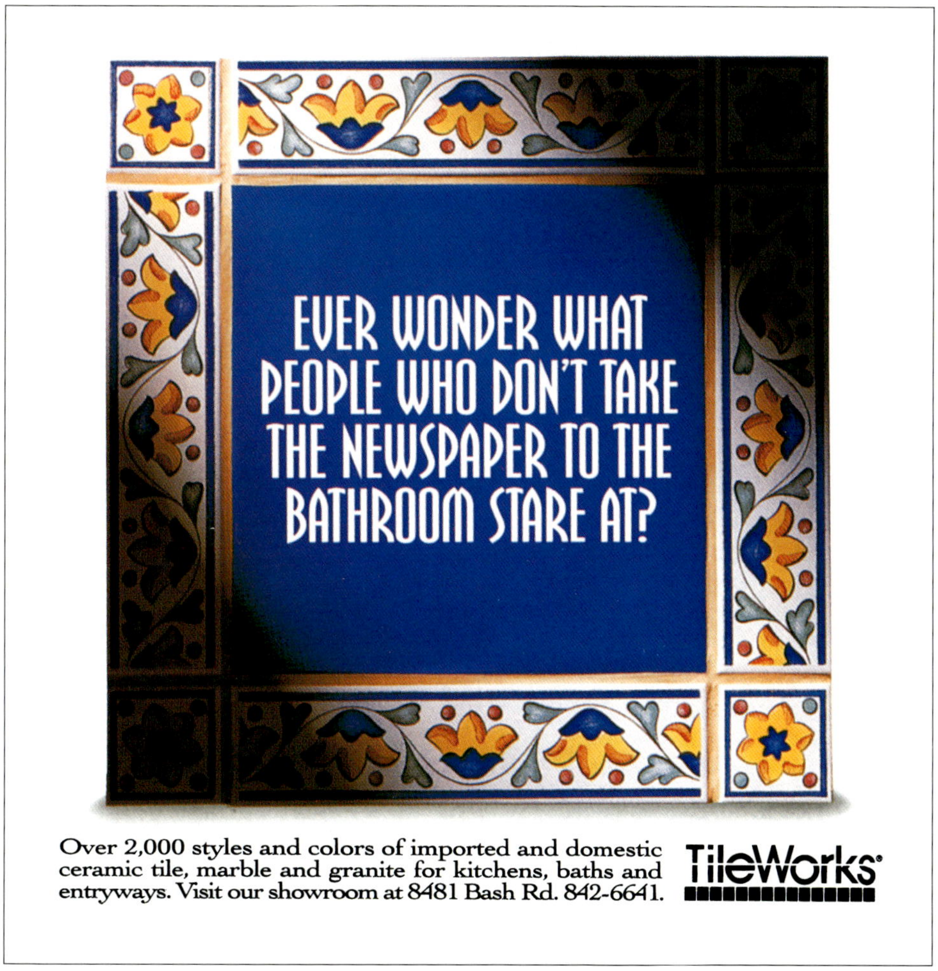
EVER WONDER WHAT PEOPLE WHO DON'T TAKE THE NEWSPAPER TO THE BATHROOM STARE AT?
Over 2,000 styles and colors of imported and domestic ceramic tile, marble and granite for kitchens, baths and entryways. Visit our showroom at 8481 Bash Rd. 842-6641.
TileWorks

26 Bronze

GOLD, SILVER & BRONZE
AWARDS

CONSUMER MAGAZINE
B/W OR COLOR LESS THAN
A PAGE: CAMPAIGN

27 GOLD
ART DIRECTOR
Frank Haggerty
WRITER
Jim Nelson
PHOTOGRAPHER
Shawn Michienzi
CLIENT
Stren
AGENCY
Carmichael Lynch/
Minneapolis

28 SILVER
ART DIRECTOR
Michael Kadin
WRITER
John Hage
PHOTOGRAPHER
Markku
CLIENT
Wolf Range Company
AGENCY
The Miller Group/
Los Angeles

27 Gold

THE OVEN THAT
PROFESSIONAL CHEFS WOULD HAVE
AT HOME IF THEY
WEREN'T SO SICK OF COOKING WHEN
THEY GOT THERE.
It's a new convection oven that cooks 30% faster than a traditional oven. And it holds twice as much food. Most importantly, it's made by Wolf Range. In other words, it's what chefs would use if they brought work home with them. Any questions? Please call 800-366-9653.
WOLF

YOU CAN SUBSTITUTE
MARGARINE FOR BUTTER.
YOU CAN SUBSTITUTE LEMON FOR SALT.
WE SUGGEST
THE SUBSTITUTIONS END THERE.
No chef worth his salt uses anything but a Wolf Range. And no Wolf Range is complete without our new back shelf hood. It provides excellent visibility and actually absorbs grease and odors. Anything else would be like substituting tarragon for basil. Questions? Call 800-366-9653.
WOLF

YOU DON'T LIVE IN
KANSAS CITY. YOUR GRANDMOTHER DIDN'T
PASS DOWN A RECIPE FOR BBQ SAUCE.
YOU'VE NEVER UTTERED THE PHRASE, "Y'ALL."
AT LEAST TECHNOLOGY IS ON YOUR SIDE.
What you lack in heritage, the new Wolf Range barbecue makes up for in technology. For instance, it has Wolf's famous charbroiler for restaurant taste. It also has an open burner and an infra-red burner so you can cook your whole meal outside. Questions? Y'all call 800-366-9653.
WOLF

GOLD, SILVER & BRONZE AWARDS

CONSUMER MAGAZINE B/W OR COLOR LESS THAN A PAGE: CAMPAIGN

29 BRONZE

ART DIRECTOR
Brian Campbell

WRITER
Ben Priest

CLIENT
Olympus Cameras

AGENCY
Lowe Howard-Spink/ London

COUNTRY ESTATE FOR SALE.
34 bedroom mansion commanding dramatic views of the Nene valley. Due to cashflow crisis, must go A.S.A.P. No offers considered under £1,810.
The Olympus OM3Ti. At £1810, fanatics only please.
Call 0171 250 4570 for details.

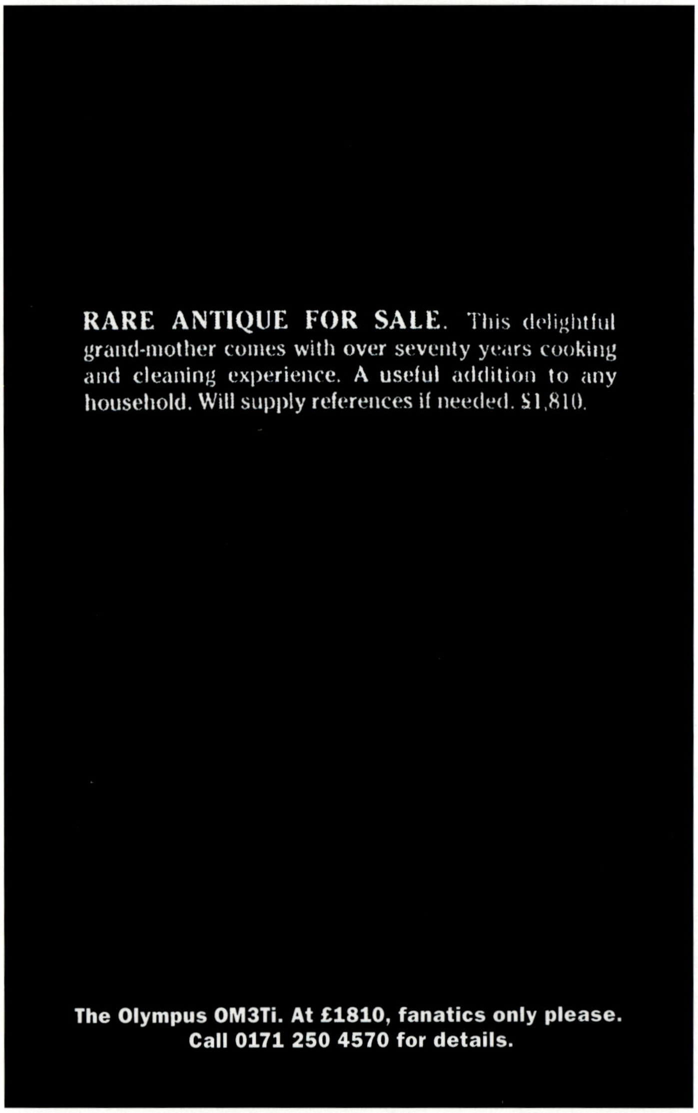
RARE ANTIQUE FOR SALE. This delightful grand-mother comes with over seventy years cooking and cleaning experience. A useful addition to any household. Will supply references if needed. £1,810.
The Olympus OM3Ti. At £1810, fanatics only please.
Call 0171 250 4570 for details.

KIDNEY FOR SALE In excellent condition. One careful owner. Available at 24 hours notice. £1,810 ono.

The Olympus OM3Ti. At £1810, fanatics only please.
Call 0171 250 4570 for details.

LOYAL FAMILY PET FOR SALE. Pedigree Golden Retriever by the name of Lucky. Has given 10 years of well behaved companionship. Excellent with kids. Must be got rid of immediately. £1,810.

The Olympus OM3Ti. At £1810, fanatics only please.
Call 0171 250 4570 for details.

FOR SALE : ENGAGEMENT RING This very delightful Emerald and Ruby creation gave 22 years of pleasure to its current owner. Must go by Friday. No time wasters please. £1,810 o.n.o.

The Olympus OM3Ti. At £1810, fanatics only please.
Call 0171 250 4570 for details.

29 Bronze

GOLD, SILVER & BRONZE AWARDS

OUTDOOR: SINGLE

30 GOLD
ART DIRECTOR
Georgia Arnott
WRITERS
Tim Hall
Matthew McGrath
Jasun Vare
CLIENT
Citibank
AGENCY
Young & Rubicam/Sydney

31 SILVER
ART DIRECTOR
Wayne Hanson
WRITER
Sue Higgs
PHOTOGRAPHER
John Alflatt
CLIENT
Vauxhall Motors
AGENCY
Lowe Howard-Spink/London

32 BRONZE
ART DIRECTOR
Ron Brown
WRITER
David Abbott
TYPOGRAPHER
Joe Hoza
CLIENT
The Economist
AGENCY
Abbott Mead Vickers. BBDO/London

30 Gold

31 Silver

32 Bronze

GOLD, SILVER & BRONZE AWARDS

OUTDOOR: SINGLE

33 BRONZE
ART DIRECTOR
Brian Hickling
WRITER
Jim Garbutt
PHOTOGRAPHER
Rick McKechnie
CLIENT
Nike Canada
AGENCY
Cossette Communication-Marketing/Toronto

34 BRONZE
ART DIRECTOR
Matt Hazell
WRITER
Jane Atkinson
CLIENT
United Airlines
AGENCY
Leo Burnett/London

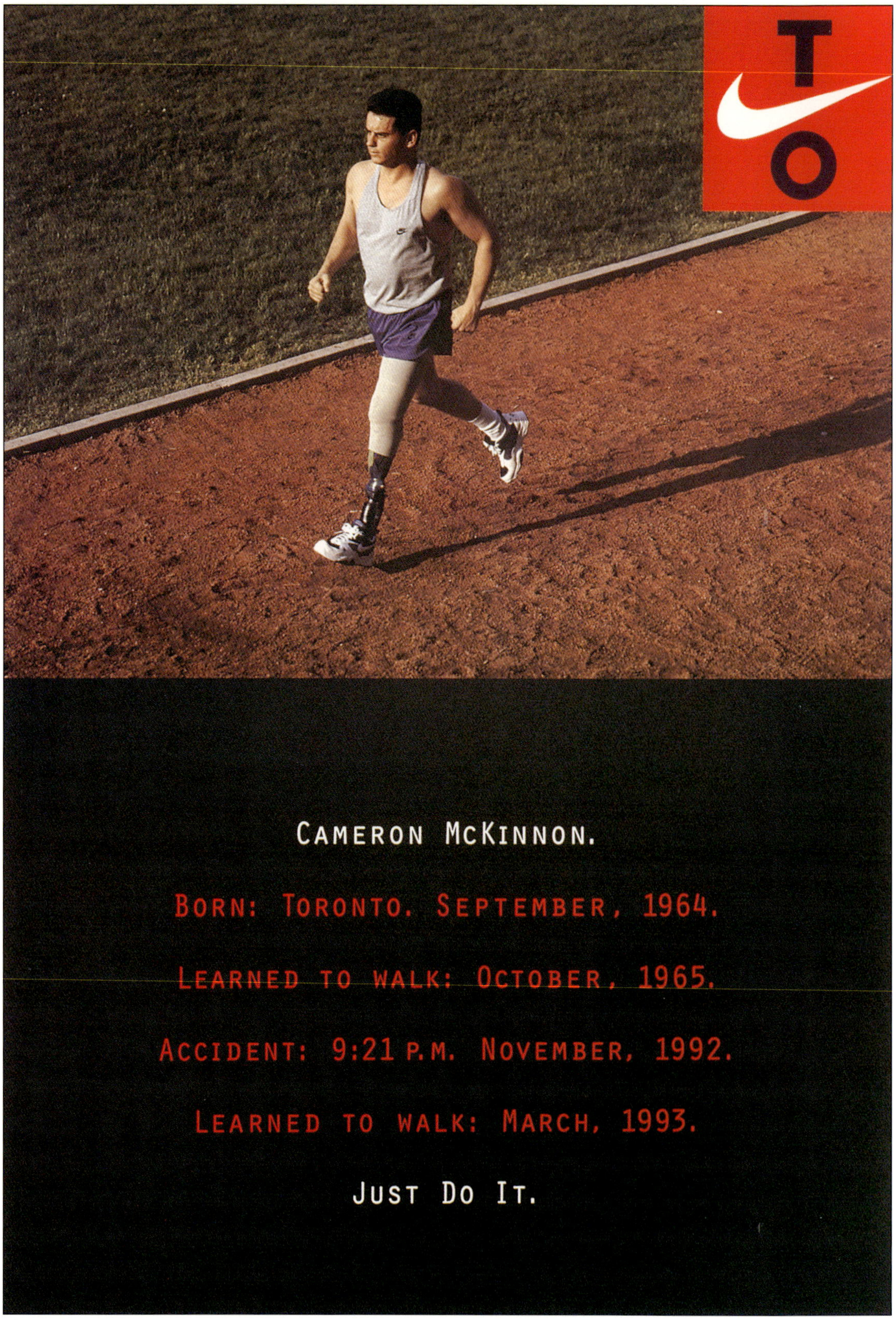
T
O
CAMERON MCKINNON.
BORN: TORONTO. SEPTEMBER, 1964.
LEARNED TO WALK: OCTOBER, 1965.
ACCIDENT: 9:21 P.M. NOVEMBER, 1992.
LEARNED TO WALK: MARCH, 1993.
JUST DO IT.

33 Bronze

On June 7th we launch our new 777. Watch this space.
UNITED AIRLINES

34 Bronze

OUTDOOR: CAMPAIGN

35 GOLD
ART DIRECTOR
Brian Hickling
WRITER
Jim Garbutt
PHOTOGRAPHERS
Rick McKechnie
Chris Gordoneer
CLIENT
Nike Canada
AGENCY
Cossette Communication-
Marketing/Toronto

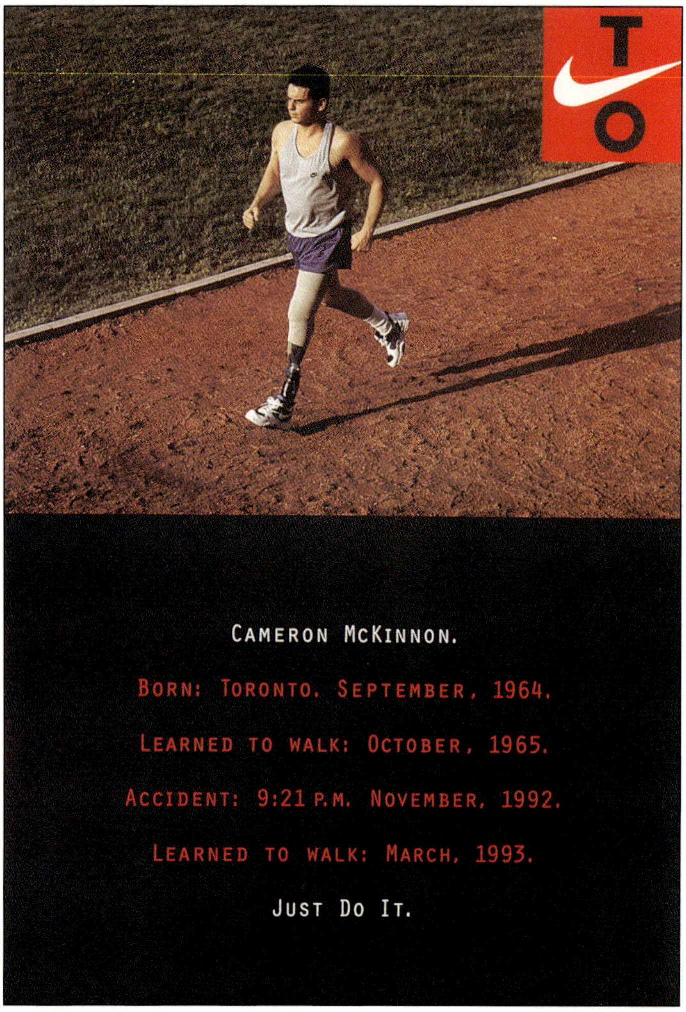

CAMERON MCKINNON.

T
O
ED BACON.
AGE: 63
STARTED RUNNING: NOVEMBER 1994.
CLAIM TO FAME: RAN 1995 TORONTO MARATHON.
FINISHED: LAST.
TIME: 5 HOURS, 48 MINUTES, 39 SECONDS.
LEARNED TO WALK: OCTOBER, 1965.
ACCIDENT: 9:21 P.M. NOVEMBER, 1992.
LEARNED TO WALK: MARCH, 1993.
JUST DO IT.

T
O
Simeon Mars.
Part time job: Basketball coach.
Full time job: Counsellor, Mentor, Role model.
Place: Eastern Commerce High.
Teaches: The value of an education,
Life skills & Strong defence.
Result: Self Respect.
Just Do It.

T
O
Ashley Banfield.
Born: Toronto, 1983.
Hobbies: Hockey.
Interests: Hockey.
Skills: Hockey.
Goals: Goals.
Just Do It.

T
O
Freddie Williams.
Runner: Canadian 800m record holder.
Birthplace: Cape Town, South Africa.
Home: Toronto.
Secret to success:
Take life 800 metres at a time.
Just Do It.

GOLD, SILVER & BRONZE AWARDS

OUTDOOR: CAMPAIGN

36 SILVER
ART DIRECTOR
Steve Levit
WRITERS
Rich Siegel
Glen Wachowiak
PHOTOGRAPHER
Michael Ruppert
CLIENT
Lion Nathan International, Castlemaine XXXX
AGENCY
Team One Advertising/
El Segundo, CA

37 SILVER
ART DIRECTOR
Sean Ehringer
WRITER
Harry Cocciolo
PHOTOGRAPHER
Hunter Freeman
ILLUSTRATOR
Dan Escobar
CLIENT
California Fluid Milk Processor Advisory Board
AGENCY
Goodby Silverstein & Partners/San Francisco

CASTLEMAINE
XXXX
IT'S BREAKFAST.
(AFTER WE DRINK IT, OF COURSE.)
THE 4 MAJOR FOOD GROUPS OF THE AUSSIE OUTBACK.

36 Silver

37 Silver

GOLD, SILVER & BRONZE AWARDS

TRADE
B/W FULL PAGE OR SPREAD: SINGLE

38 GOLD
ART DIRECTOR
Steve Mitchell
WRITER
Doug Adkins
CLIENT
Dublin Productions
AGENCY
Hunt Adkins/Minneapolis

39 GOLD
ART DIRECTOR
Steve Mitchell
WRITER
Doug Adkins
CLIENT
Dublin Productions
AGENCY
Hunt Adkins/Minneapolis

ZYGOTES, OBLATE SPHEROIDS, SUBMICROSCOPIC ANTIFERROMAGNETISM *and other* INHERENTLY FUNNY THINGS.

After exhaustive interrogation, Rick was forced to cut these giant mushrooms from his Doctoral thesis entitled "Inherently Funny Fungi." Surprisingly, Rick and the mushrooms became quite close friends and often get together on weekends to play Parcheesi.

From whither comes the innate hilarity of protactinium-233? And exactly how humorous is it? Through a complex system of hydrogenerators, micro-transducers and twisty straws, the inherent humoric content of any object can now be liquefied and sucked out. While the average human contains less than a six-pack of humor, a 1966 Mopar engine block yields some 44 gallons of the Fresca-like liquid.

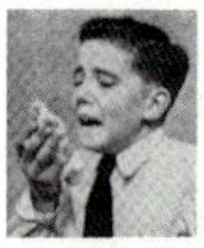

People tend to fall into one of two groups: The inherently funny, and the inherently terrified of rags.

NIETZSCHE: MASTER OF THE PRATFALL

Friedrich Nietzsche was a man of destiny. A man so filled with genius, his mortal flesh could scarcely contain it. A man destined to become the greatest slapstick performer the world had ever known. His passion began with a simple pratfall, performed impromptu during a tense philosophical debate with Schopenhauer. From there his rare gift of inherent humor manifested itself in a menagerie of pies in faces and feet striking buttocks. At night he practiced pratfalls and noogies by candlelight, ever dreaming of inherent humor immortality. As Richard Wagner, the German composer and slapstick critic, observed, "While Nietzsche certainly had a flair for philosophy, he was never really in his element unless he was slapping old ladies with fish." Tragically, Friedrich "Puddinhead" Nietzsche fell in with a bad metaphysics crowd and eventually decided to pursue a career in taxidermy.

Jerry Pope limbers up with some of his clones.

THE DUBLIN INSTITUTE FOR GENETIC TOMFOOLERY

Is it wise for us to play God by genetically creating our own race of superfunnymen? Thou shalt not judge us! For nigh onto a century the Dublin Institute has been manipulating vegetables in order to create inherently funny foodstuffs. However, it seems one cannot laugh convulsively while eating without choking to death. Going from potatoes to humans was a small genetic leap. And yet one cellular secret still escaped us: the elusive clown gene. What produces the bulbous red nose, the flipper-like feet, the jaunty ledge of crimson hair? For 75 years we searched. Then, by simple chance, we discovered that mating with clowns creates more clowns. Call 612-332-8864 or 612-CLWN-SEX for a free genetic mutation sample.

The common wombat is not inherently funny unless it's had a few-too-many martinis.

DUBLIN PRODUCTIONS

WHY JOE PYTKA COULDN'T DIRECT HIS WAY OUT OF A WET PAPER BAG

or

THE SUBTLETIES OF LAWSUIT HUMOR.

January, 1969. The Tonight Show, starring Zachuriah McGillacutty.* Guest Rick Dublin walks onto the stage and, in front of millions of viewers, proceeds to call Zach a "festering bag of gruel-like pus." A nation laughs. Mr. McGillacutty sues. America's love affair with lawsuit humor has begun.

During a brief recess in the infamous Wackadoodle trial, Rick and Jerry confer with G-14, Dublin Production's charismatic mechanized lawyer. G-14 would later suffer a nuclear meltdown during closing statements, leading to over 16,000 other lawsuits.

LITIGATION HO!

According to recent statistics, the wealthiest 1% of Americans control 99% of this country's humor, as well as most of the pay toilets. Fortunately, if you have but a few million in the bank, you too can afford to be funny (you can also afford to dress up like the Duchess of York and sing "The Girl from Ipanema" while hanging from a freeway overpass, but that's another form of humor entirely). Here are a few handy lawsuit buzzwords that, when mentioned in conjunction with someone who is well-financed, are sure to land you in court: convicted mass-murderer, big meanie, farm animals, cocaine-induced frenzy, duck hater, politician, poo-butt, impotence and, of course, frequent bed-wetter.

Our active lawsuits, Aaker to Aanonson.

*Not his real name.

SHAMBO, SUBPOENA KING OF THE JUNGLE

Deep in the jungles of Madagascar dwells a mysterious tribe of cannibalistic pygmy $500/hour trial lawyers. These fearsome four-foot-tall litigators have a millennia of experience debating all the finer points of lawsuit humor, as well as picking lice out of each other's hair. In the landmark "Zobo is a banana face" case, Shambo, the world renowned defense lawyer, riveted a nation as he proved that Zobo was indeed a banana face, and also that he had eaten his cousin Wawa.

Dublin vs. Anvil tied up the courts for years.

IBM IS A POO-BUTT

Legal experts agree that before the turn of the century lawsuit humor will, in fact, be our only form of humor. To this we say, "Corpus delicti, nolo mutatis contendre and glutei maximi." A display of Latin mastery such as this can provide a decisive coup d'état in the courtroom, although most judges are equally impressed by Pig-Latin or courtroom rap. But we digress. For a copy of our reel, or if you're simply interested in suing us for something, call our lawsuit hotline at 612-332-8864. Please prepare to be put on hold for five or six days. By the way, did we mention that you are stupid and ugly and that you smell bad too?

After a recent courtroom win, Jerry demonstrates the Dublin victory dance.

DUBLIN PRODUCTIONS

GOLD, SILVER & BRONZE AWARDS

TRADE
B/W FULL PAGE OR SPREAD: SINGLE

40 SILVER
ART DIRECTOR
Steve Mitchell
WRITER
Doug Adkins
CLIENT
Dublin Productions
AGENCY
Hunt Adkins/Minneapolis

41 BRONZE
ART DIRECTOR
Jim Cameron
WRITER
George Goetz
PHOTOGRAPHER
Kevin Morrill
CLIENT
The Boston Globe
AGENCY
Ingalls/Boston

JOKES THAT ARE ONLY UNDERSTOOD BY TONE-DEAF MAILMEN FROM GRINNELL, IOWA WHO DRIVE '73 PACERS AND ARE NAMED JOHNNY WACKADOODLE

or

A BRIEF HISTORY OF ESOTERIC HUMOR.

The dawn of mankind. An Australopithecus man turns to another and says, "I just flew in from Chicago and boy are my arms tired." But because language has not yet been developed, all that escapes his lips is "Ugg-gag-guh." The second man, having absolutely no idea what the first is talking about, abruptly crushes his fellow Australopithecine's skull with a large femur bone. In this moment of classic misunderstanding, esoteric humor is born.

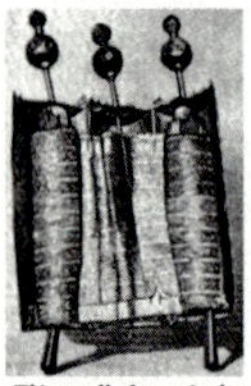

This scroll of meaningless symbols has never been translated and therefore is fall-down-whack-your-head funny.

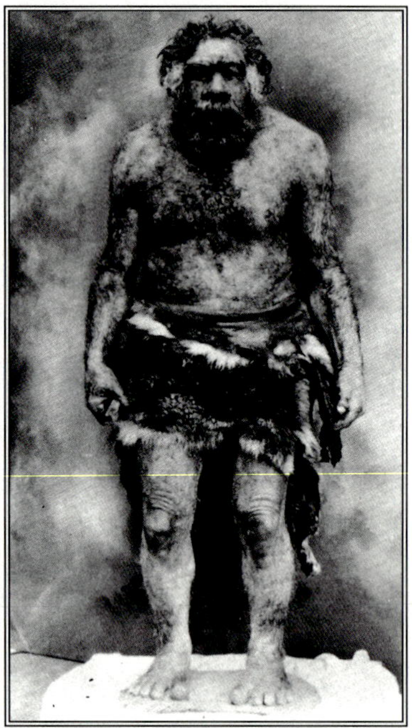

Uga, a distant ancestor of Rick Dublin, is revered as the greatest esoterian of the Cenozoic era. Though even he never understood his humor, Uga went on to host Saturday Night Live a record 27

WHY ISHTAR MAKES US WET OURSELVES

To 99.999999997% of the Earth's population, the film Ishtar is cataclysmically unfunny. Yet somewhere around the 638th successive viewing of this film, something truly magical happens. Suddenly one begins to notice a subtle, yet ingenious thread of humor woven ever so deeply into the dialogue's apparent inanity. What once seemed to insult every fiber of one's intelligence now sings to one's deepest intellect with humor so vibrantly overwhelming, one can't help but go insane.

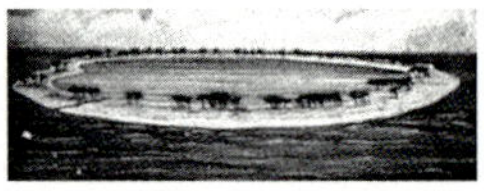

For reasons you shall never understand, this photo makes us laugh so hard we cough up small organs.

A recent archeological discovery has rocked the esoteric world. Ancient stone tablets unearthed in Chattanooga reveal that turn of the century esoterians were required to carry a knockwurst, a shoe horn and a jar of mayonnaise with them at all times. This revelation came as quite a shock to modern day esoterians who have been carrying bowls of goulash around with them for decades.

PLAY THAT FUNKY MUSIC ESOTERIA BOY

The perfect esoteric joke is understood by no one. Not even God or monkey boy. The most nearly perfect joke ever conceived was authored by a 13th century Turkish dog catcher which, loosely translated, reads: "How many water buffalos does it take to change your underwear? Sixteen." Currently, there are but three people alive who understand this joke. If our efforts to have these people killed are successful, this will become a perfect joke.

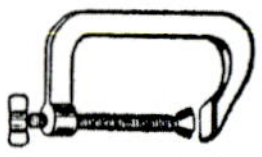

A true esoterian can never have too many clamps.

To be enlightened in the ways of esoteria, call 612-EEC-VUNG for our reel. And if you happen to recognize even the most minute quantum of humor in any of our spots, please call and inform us so that we may remove it posthaste. Thank you.

DUBLIN PRODUCTIONS

40 Silver

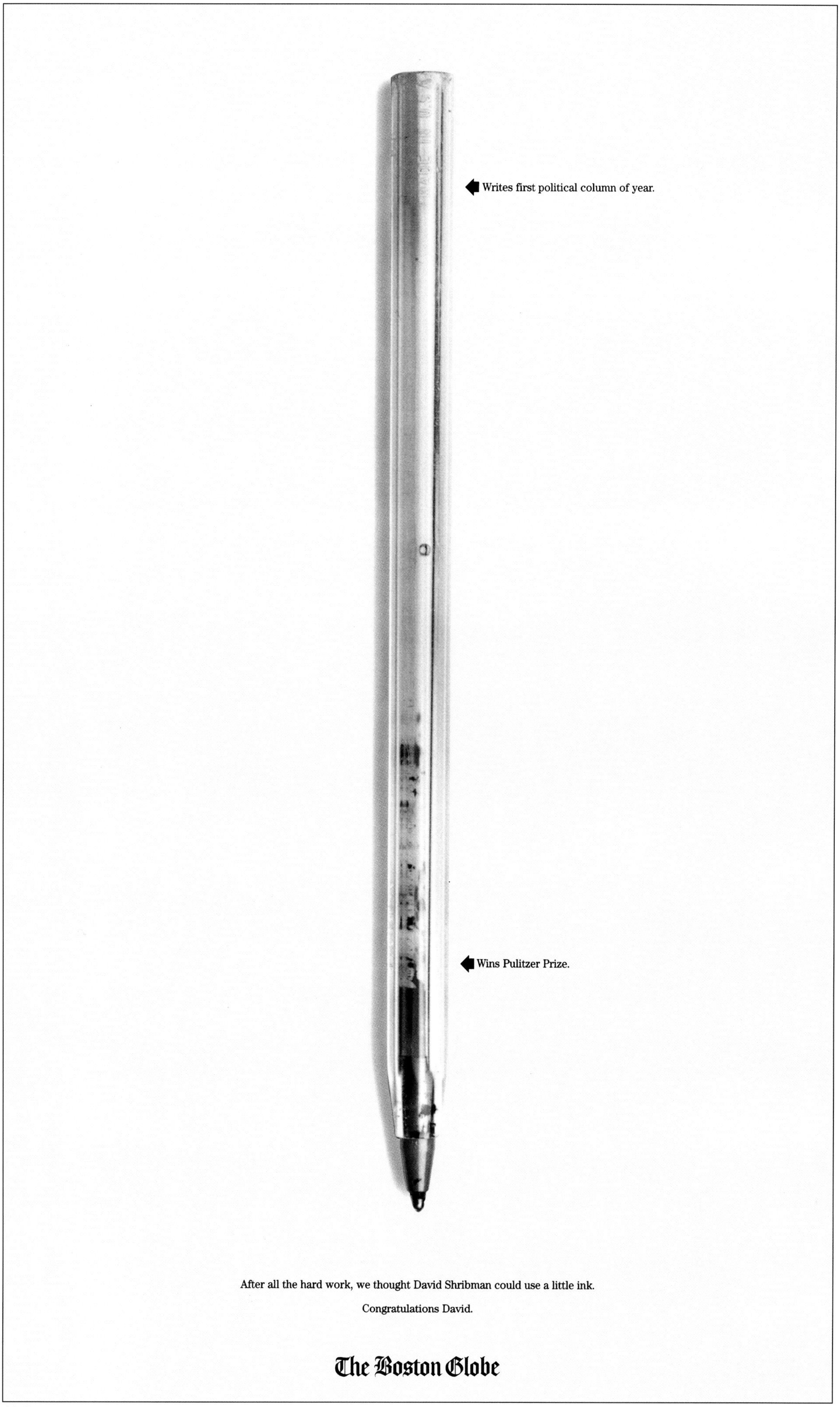
Writes first political column of year.
Wins Pulitzer Prize.
After all the hard work, we thought David Shribman could use a little ink.
Congratulations David.
The Boston Globe

41 Bronze

GOLD, SILVER & BRONZE AWARDS

TRADE
COLOR FULL PAGE OR SPREAD: SINGLE

42 GOLD

ART DIRECTORS
Paul Hirsch
Ted Royer

WRITER
Kara Goodrich

PHOTOGRAPHERS
Steve Becker
Steve Nozicka
Daryl-Ann Saunders
Lars Topelmann
Steve Hellerstein

CLIENT
Polaroid

AGENCY
Leonard/Monahan
Providence

43 SILVER

ART DIRECTORS
Paul Hirsch
Ted Royer

WRITER
Kara Goodrich

PHOTOGRAPHERS
Steve Hellerstein
Val Valandani
Phil Bekker
Lars Topelmann
Michael Going

CLIENT
Polaroid

AGENCY
Leonard/Monahan
Providence

44 BRONZE

ART DIRECTORS
Paul Hirsch
Ted Royer

WRITER
Kara Goodrich

PHOTOGRAPHERS
Steve Hellerstein
Michael Going
Lars Topelmann
Peter Dazeley
Francois Robert

CLIENT
Polaroid

AGENCY
Leonard/Monahan
Providence

COLLATERAL
POINT OF PURCHASE AND IN-STORE

60 GOLD

ART DIRECTORS
Paul Hirsch
Ted Royer

WRITER
Kara Goodrich

PHOTOGRAPHERS
Steve Hellerstein
Val Valandani
Phil Bekker
Lars Topelmann
Michael Going

CLIENT
Polaroid

AGENCY
Leonard/Monahan
Providence

61 SILVER

ART DIRECTORS
Paul Hirsch
Ted Royer

WRITER
Kara Goodrich

PHOTOGRAPHERS
Steve Becker
Steve Nozicka
Daryl-Ann Saunders
Lars Topelmann
Steve Hellerstein

CLIENT
Polaroid

AGENCY
Leonard/Monahan
Providence

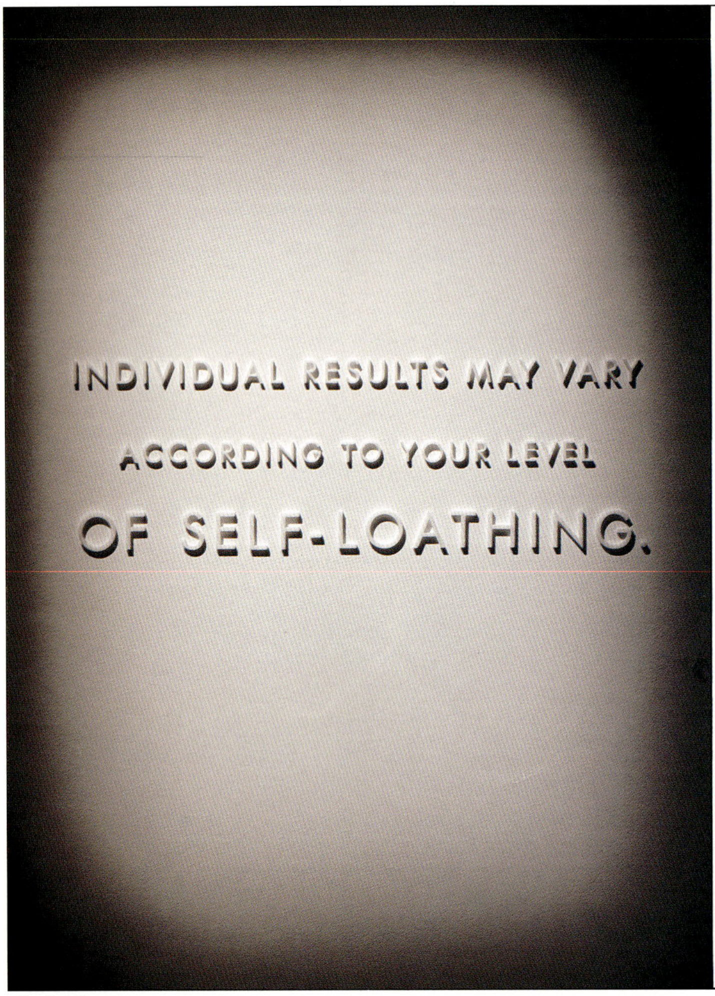

42 Gold

[SX-70 manipulation by Steven Becker, Chicago, IL]
[Emulsion transfer by Steve Nozicka, Chicago, IL]
To discover your level, call Polaroid at 1-800-662-8337, ext. 745 for a guide on creating these photographic techniques.
Polaroid
[Image transfer by Daryl-Ann Saunders, New York, NY]
[Instant 35mm by Lars Topelmann, Portland, OR]

61 Silver

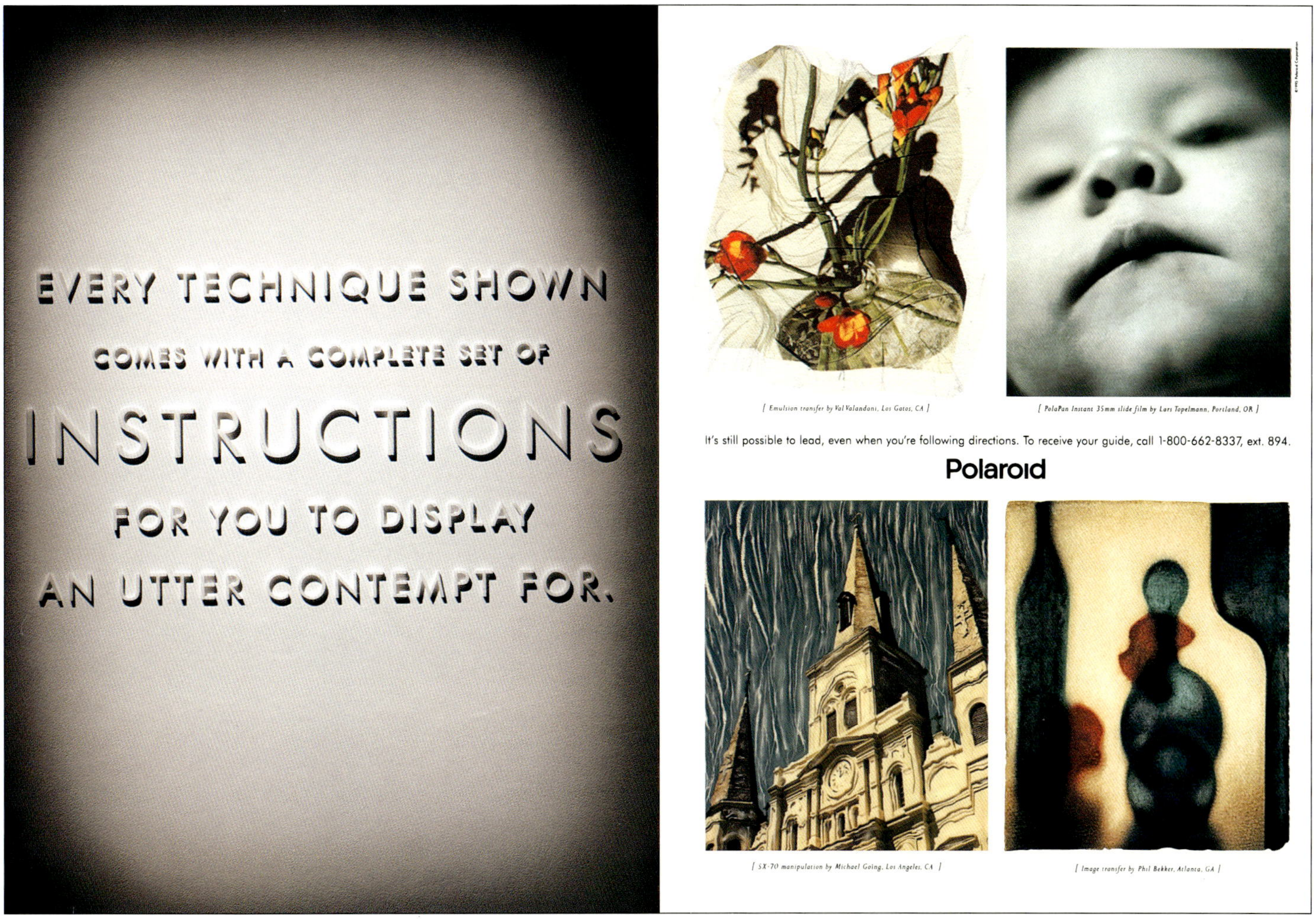

43 Silver

60 Gold

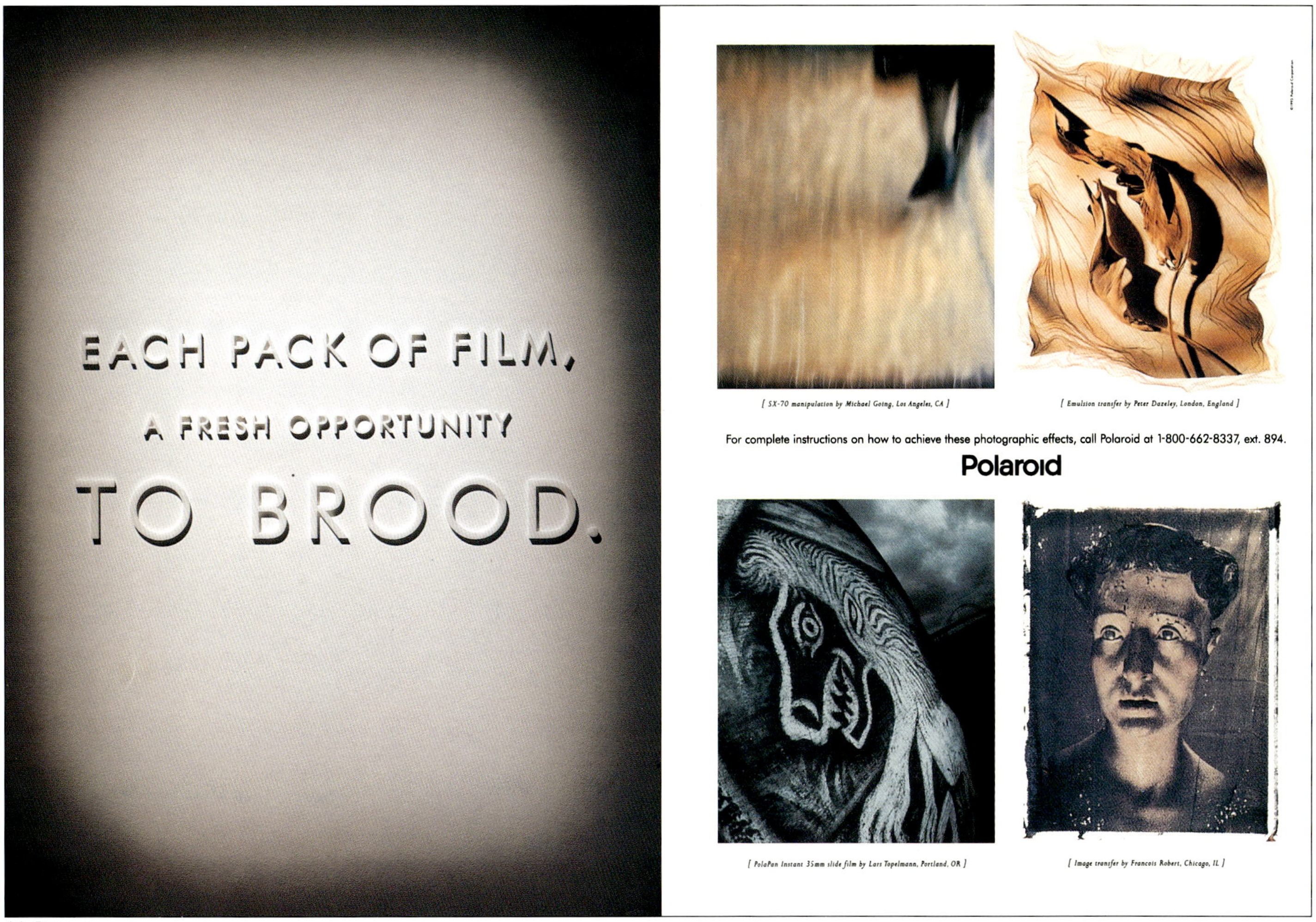

EACH PACK OF FILM,
A FRESH OPPORTUNITY
TO BROOD.
[SX-70 manipulation by Michael Going, Los Angeles, CA]
[Emulsion transfer by Peter Dazeley, London, England]
For complete instructions on how to achieve these photographic effects, call Polaroid at 1-800-662-8337, ext. 894.
Polaroid
[PolaPan Instant 35mm slide film by Lars Topelmann, Portland, OR]
[Image transfer by Francois Robert, Chicago, IL]

44 Bronze

GOLD, SILVER & BRONZE AWARDS

TRADE
B/W OR COLOR
ANY SIZE: CAMPAIGN

45 GOLD

ART DIRECTOR
Steve Mitchell

WRITER
Doug Adkins

CLIENT
Dublin Productions

AGENCY
Hunt Adkins/Minneapolis

WHY JOE PYTKA COULDN'T DIRECT HIS WAY OUT OF A WET PAPER BAG

or

THE SUBTLETIES OF LAWSUIT HUMOR.

January, 1969. The Tonight Show, starring Zachuriah McGillacutty.* Guest Rick Dublin walks onto the stage and, in front of millions of viewers, proceeds to call Zach a "festering bag of gruel-like pus." A nation laughs. Mr. McGillacutty sues. America's love affair with lawsuit humor has begun.

During a brief recess in the infamous Wackadoodle trial, Rick and Jerry confer with G-14, Dublin Production's charismatic mechanized lawyer. G-14 would later suffer a nuclear meltdown during closing statements, leading to over 16,000 other lawsuits.

LITIGATION HO!

According to recent statistics, the wealthiest 1% of Americans control 99% of this country's humor, as well as most of the pay toilets. Fortunately, if you have but a few million in the bank, you too can afford to be funny (you can also afford to dress up like the Duchess of York and sing "The Girl from Ipanema" while hanging from a freeway overpass, but that's another form of humor entirely). Here are a few handy lawsuit buzzwords that, when mentioned in conjunction with someone who is well-financed, are sure to land you in court: convicted mass-murderer, big meanie, farm animals, cocaine-induced frenzy, duck hater, politician, poo-butt, impotence and, of course, frequent bed-wetter.

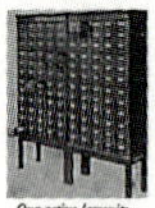

Our active lawsuits, Aaker to Aanonson.

*Not his real name.

SHAMBO, SUBPOENA KING OF THE JUNGLE

Deep in the jungles of Madagascar dwells a mysterious tribe of cannibalistic pygmy $500/hour trial lawyers. These fearsome four-foot-tall litigators have a millennia of experience debating all the finer points of lawsuit humor, as well as picking lice out of each other's hair. In the landmark "Zobo is a banana face" case, Shambo, the world renowned defense lawyer, riveted a nation as he proved that Zobo was indeed a banana face, and also that he had eaten his cousin Wawa.

Dublin vs. Anvil tied up the courts for years.

IBM IS A POO-BUTT

Legal experts agree that before the turn of the century lawsuit humor will, in fact, be our only form of humor. To this we say, "Corpus delicti, nolo mutatis contendre and glutei maximi." A display of Latin mastery such as this can provide a decisive coup d'état in the courtroom, although most judges are equally impressed by Pig-Latin or courtroom rap. But we digress. For a copy of our reel, or if you're simply interested in suing us for something, call our lawsuit hotline at 612-332-8864. Please prepare to be put on hold for five or six days. By the way, did we mention that you are stupid and ugly and that you smell bad too?

After a recent courtroom win, Jerry demonstrates the Dublin victory dance.

DUBLIN PRODUCTIONS

JOKES THAT ARE ONLY UNDERSTOOD BY TONE-DEAF MAILMEN FROM GRINNELL, IOWA WHO DRIVE '73 PACERS AND ARE NAMED JOHNNY WACKADOODLE

or

A BRIEF HISTORY OF ESOTERIC HUMOR.

The dawn of mankind. An Australopithecus man turns to another and says, "I just flew in from Chicago and boy are my arms tired." But because language has not yet been developed, all that escapes his lips is "Ugg-gag-guh." The second man, having absolutely no idea what the first is talking about, abruptly crushes his fellow Australopithecine's skull with a large femur bone. In this moment of classic misunderstanding, esoteric humor is born.

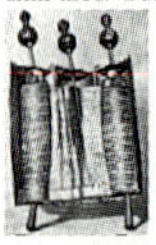

This scroll of meaningless symbols has never been translated and therefore is fall-down-whack-your-head funny.

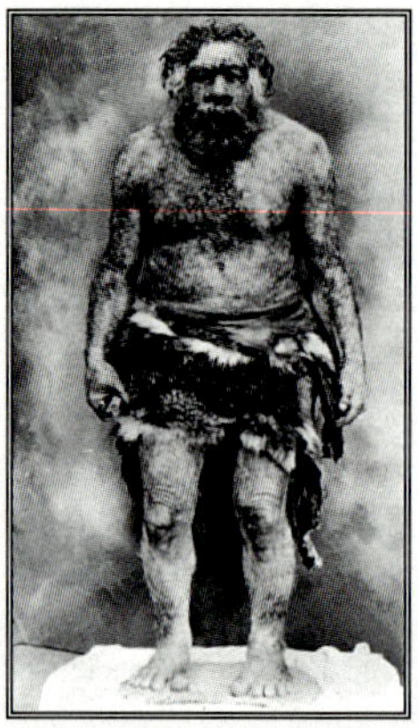

Uga, a distant ancestor of Rick Dublin, is revered as the greatest esoterian of the Cenozoic era. Though even he never understood his humor, Uga went on to host Saturday Night Live a record 27

WHY ISHTAR MAKES US WET OURSELVES

To 99.999999997% of the Earth's population, the film Ishtar is cataclysmically unfunny. Yet somewhere around the 638th successive viewing of this film, something truly magical happens. Suddenly one begins to notice a subtle, yet ingenious thread of humor woven ever so deeply into the dialogue's apparent inanity. What once seemed to insult every fiber of one's intelligence now sings to one's deepest intellect with humor so vibrantly overwhelming, one can't help but go insane.

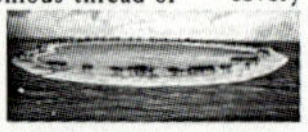

For reasons you shall never understand, this photo makes us laugh so hard we cough up small organs.

A recent archeological discovery has rocked the esoteric world. Ancient stone tablets unearthed in Chattanooga reveal that turn of the century esoterians were required to carry a knockwurst, a shoe horn and a jar of mayonnaise with them at all times. This revelation came as quite a shock to modern day esoterians who have been carrying bowls of goulash around with them for decades.

PLAY THAT FUNKY MUSIC ESOTERIA BOY

The perfect esoteric joke is understood by no one. Not even God or monkey boy. The most nearly perfect joke ever conceived was authored by a 13th century Turkish dog catcher which, loosely translated, reads: "How many water buffalos does it take to change your underwear? Sixteen." Currently, there are but three people alive who understand this joke. If our efforts to have these people killed are successful, this will become a perfect joke.

A true esoterian can never have too many clamps.

To be enlightened in the ways of esoteria, call 612-EEC-VUNG for our reel. And if you happen to recognize even the most minute quantum of humor in any of our spots, please call and inform us so that we may remove it posthaste. Thank you.

DUBLIN PRODUCTIONS

MASTERING THE INFINITE COMPLEXITIES AND SUBTLE NUANCES OF DRIVING A JOKE INTO THE GROUND.

Part nine in a series.

Rick Dublin, Patron Saint of Belabored Jokes and Stretchy Cloth Things That Go Over Your Head And Around Your Ears, explains to Bobo why dogs are physically incapable of performing the uproarious "pull my finger" joke.

Joke belaborment. If you doubt its power, try this simple experiment: Next time one of your favorite little anecdotes fails to elicit laughter, simply repeat said joke over and over and over and over again until every last atom — nay, electron — of humor is squeezed from it, leaving only a shriveled, humorless husk. This rapid release of subatomic humor will create a chain reaction which will end with your unappreciative audience being incinerated into a chalk-like powder.

Jerry Pope's pet cabbage, Rufus.

THE DUBLIN LOBOTOMIZER/ SPATULA

Recent experiments at the Dublin Institute have resulted in many insights into the way the human brain perceives humor, the function of the cerebellum in this process, and why the human elbow is so wrinkly. Many of Dublin's advertising clients, after imbibing several of Rick's special Nitro Cocktails, graciously volunteered to have their prefrontal lobes surgically separated from their amygdalas. Much to his horror, doctor Dublin discovered that, once lobotomized, people no longer find any of his jokes funny, no matter how many times he repeats them. They also tend to develop chronic drooling problems. From this we can deduce that the amygdala performs the vital dual functions of regulating the flow of both humor and saliva.

Dublin's new producer, amphibian boy, has impressed many with his meteoric rise from single-cell amoeba boy.

WHAT'S UP WITH THAT?

To the Macadamians of Gibraltar, a clan of bloodthirsty nomadic tollbooth operators, there can only be one joke. In their entire 4000-year history they have had but a single humorous anecdote, known simply as "Bob." By law, all members of the clan must repeat Bob 20 times a day while speaking in a high-pitched chipmunk voice. Infidel humor is not tolerated. Those who dare to tell other jokes are beaten roundly about the ears with a zucchini and then, in very stern tones, asked to please stop it. Needless to say, repeat offenders are rare. We could reveal Bob to you but, as an uninitiated outsider, you would likely laugh so hard that you'd spontaneously burst into flames.

DON'T STOP ME IF YOU'VE HEARD THIS BEFORE

"If something was humorous 30 seconds ago and 15 seconds after that, then it will most certainly be funny every 15 seconds into infinity." Thus begins Rick Dublin's 6000-page dissertation on humor belaborment (the rest of the dissertation consists of this opening line repeated 454,681 times followed by one not-at-all-funny line about a duck). To hear a tape recording of Rick's favorite joke repeated over and over while you're on hold, call 612-332-8864 (Minneapolis) or 213-960-3322 (Los Angeles).

Elektro, Dublin's mechanical comedienne, is programmed to tell the same joke over and over again until the year 3165. Sparko the Wonder Dog also doubles as a toaster.

DUBLIN PRODUCTIONS

ZYGOTES, OBLATE SPHEROIDS, SUBMICROSCOPIC ANTIFERROMAGNETISM

and other

INHERENTLY FUNNY THINGS.

After exhaustive interrogation, Rick was forced to cut these giant mushrooms from his Doctoral thesis entitled "Inherently Funny Fungi." Surprisingly, Rick and the mushrooms became quite close friends and often get together on weekends to play Parcheesi.

From whither comes the innate hilarity of protactinium-233? And exactly how humorous is it? Through a complex system of hydrogenerators, microtransducers and twisty straws, the inherent humoric content of any object can now be liquefied and sucked out. While the average human contains less than a six-pack of humor, a 1966 Mopar engine block yields some 44 gallons of the Fresca-like liquid.

People tend to fall into one of two groups: The inherently funny, and the inherently terrified of rugs.

NIETZSCHE: MASTER OF THE PRATFALL

Friedrich Nietzsche was a man of destiny. A man so filled with genius, his mortal flesh could scarcely contain it. A man destined to become the greatest slapstick performer the world had ever known. His passion began with a simple pratfall, performed impromptu during a tense philosophical debate with Schopenhauer. From there his rare gift of inherent humor manifested itself in a menagerie of pies in faces and feet striking buttocks. At night he practiced pratfalls and noogies by candlelight, ever dreaming of inherent humor immortality. As Richard Wagner, the German composer and slapstick critic, observed, "While Nietzsche certainly had a flair for philosophy, he was never really in his element unless he was slapping old ladies with fish." Tragically, Friedrich "Puddinhead" Nietzsche fell in with a bad metaphysics crowd and eventually decided to pursue a career in taxidermy.

Jerry Pope limbers up with some of his clones.

THE DUBLIN INSTITUTE FOR GENETIC TOMFOOLERY

Is it wise for us to play God by genetically creating our own race of superfunnymen? Thou shalt not judge us! For nigh onto a century the Dublin Institute has been manipulating vegetables in order to create inherently funny foodstuffs. However, it seems one cannot laugh convulsively while eating without choking to death. Going from potatoes to humans was a small genetic leap. And yet one cellular secret still escaped us: the elusive clown gene. What produces the bulbous red nose, the flipper-like feet, the jaunty ledge of crimson hair? For 75 years we searched. Then, by simple chance, we discovered that mating with clowns creates more clowns. Call 612-332-8864 or 612-CLWN-SEX for a free genetic mutation sample.

The common wombat is not inherently funny unless it's had a few-too-many martinis.

DUBLIN PRODUCTIONS

---

or

MINIMALIST HUMOR.

The hilarious "Study in Gray" by Rick Dublin.

"Dust Motes In Aspic" by Jerry Pope.

"Gray Triptych." A shade darker and it wouldn't have been funny.

The farcical "Gray Box #57" by Rick Dublin.

DUBLIN PRODUCTIONS

GOLD, SILVER & BRONZE
AWARDS

TRADE
B/W OR COLOR
ANY SIZE: CAMPAIGN

46 GOLD

ART DIRECTORS
Paul Hirsch
Ted Royer

WRITER
Kara Goodrich

PHOTOGRAPHERS
Steve Becker
Phil Bekker
Peter Dazeley
Michael Going
Steve Hellerstein
Steve Nozicka
Francois Robert
Daryl-Ann Saunders
Lars Topelmann
Val Valandani

CLIENT
Polaroid

AGENCY
Leonard/Monahan,
Providence

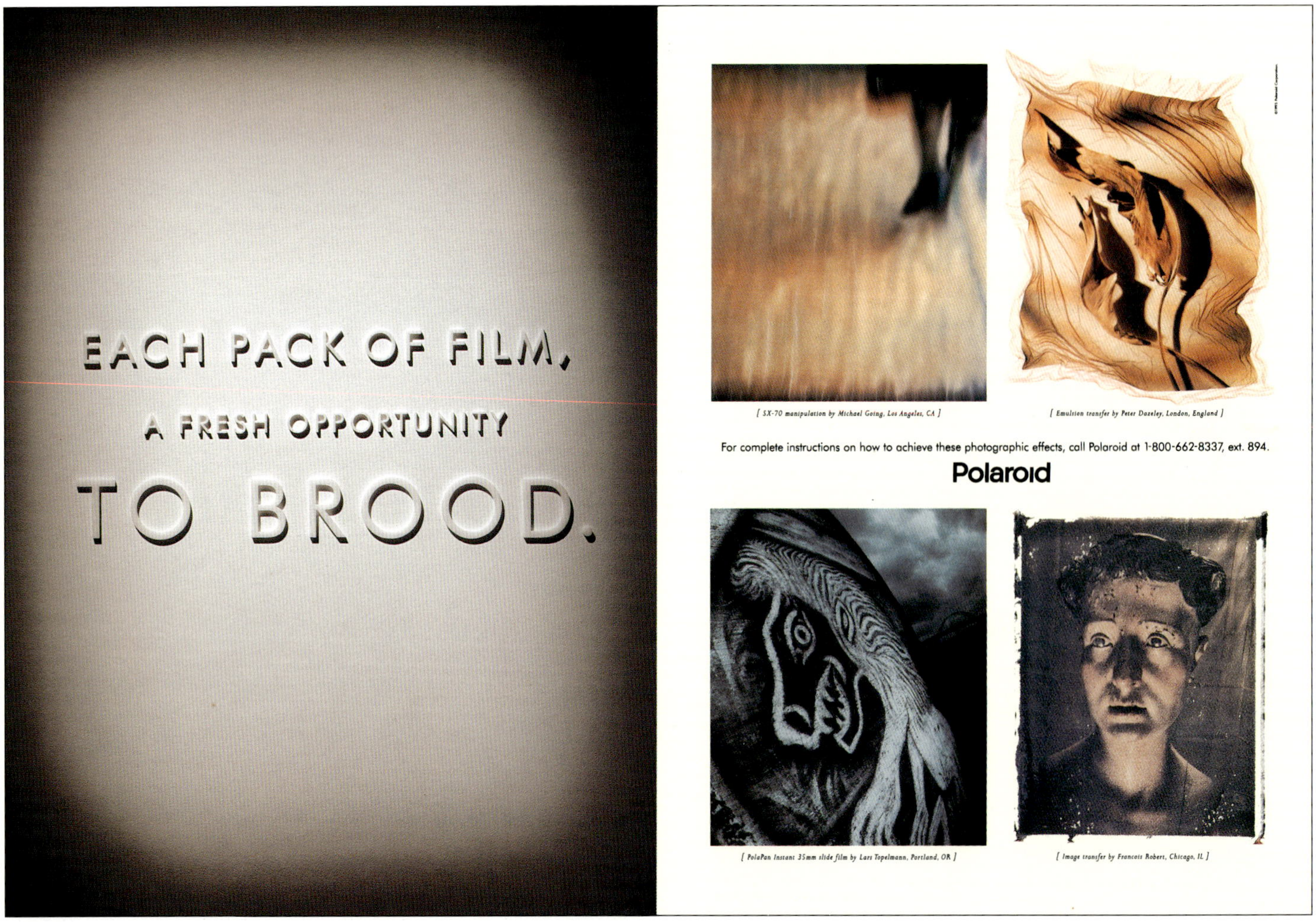
EACH PACK OF FILM,
A FRESH OPPORTUNITY
TO BROOD.
[SX-70 manipulation by Michael Going, Los Angeles, CA]
[Emulsion transfer by Peter Dazeley, London, England]
For complete instructions on how to achieve these photographic effects, call Polaroid at 1-800-662-8337, ext. 894.
Polaroid
[PolaPan Instant 35mm slide film by Lars Topelmann, Portland, OR]
[Image transfer by Francois Robert, Chicago, IL]

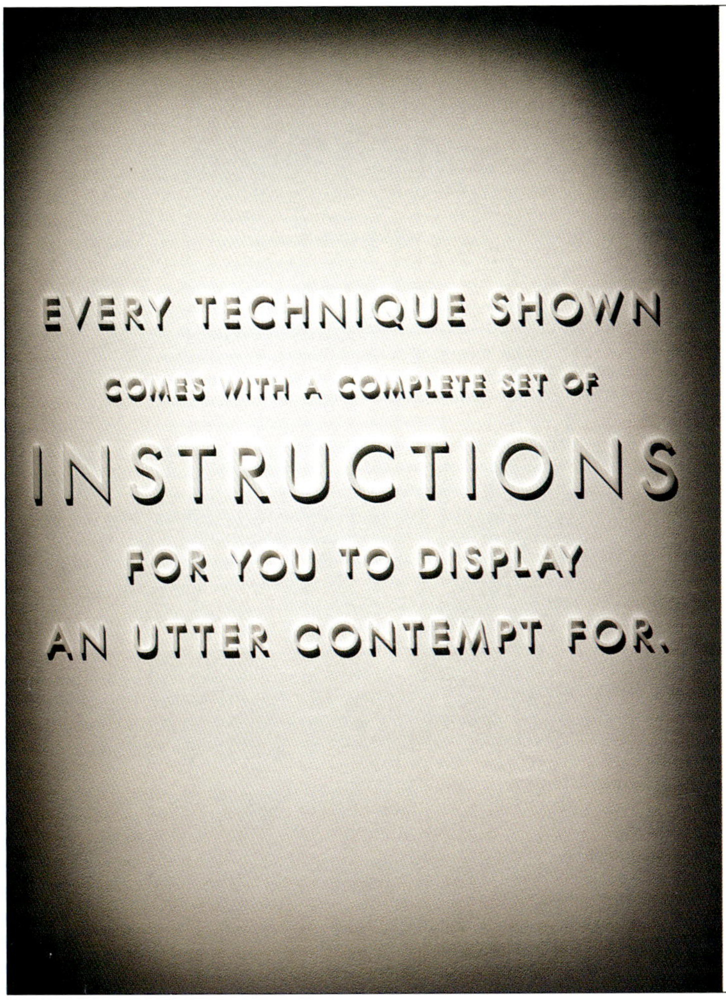
EVERY TECHNIQUE SHOWN
COMES WITH A COMPLETE SET OF
INSTRUCTIONS
FOR YOU TO DISPLAY
AN UTTER CONTEMPT FOR.

[Emulsion transfer by Val Valandani, Los Gatos, CA]

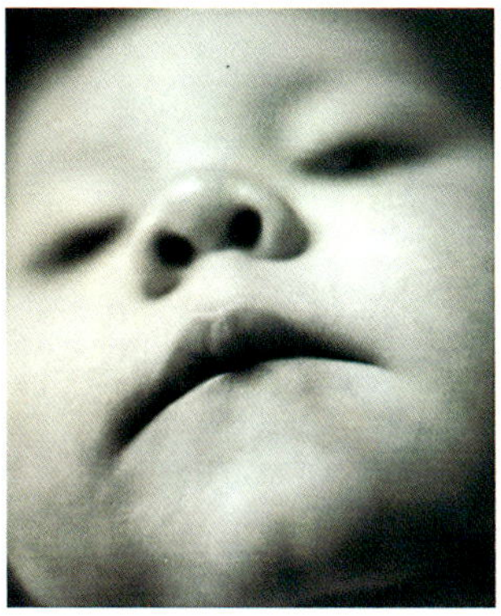

[PolaPan Instant 35mm slide film by Lars Topelmann, Portland, OR]

It's still possible to lead, even when you're following directions. To receive your guide, call 1-800-662-8337, ext. 894.

Polaroid

[SX-70 manipulation by Michael Going, Los Angeles, CA]

[Image transfer by Phil Bekker, Atlanta, GA]

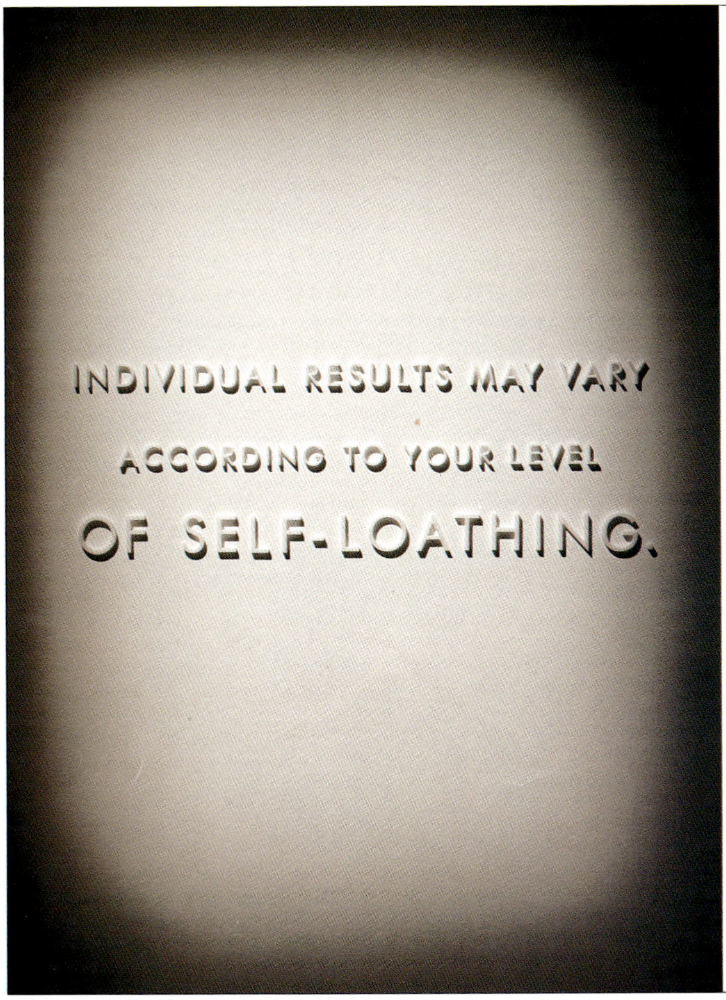
INDIVIDUAL RESULTS MAY VARY
ACCORDING TO YOUR LEVEL
OF SELF-LOATHING.

[SX-70 manipulation by Steven Becker, Chicago, IL]

[Emulsion transfer by Steve Nozicka, Chicago, IL]

To discover your level, call Polaroid at 1-800-662-8337, ext. 745 for a guide on creating these photographic techniques.

Polaroid

[Image transfer by Daryl-Ann Saunders, New York, NY]

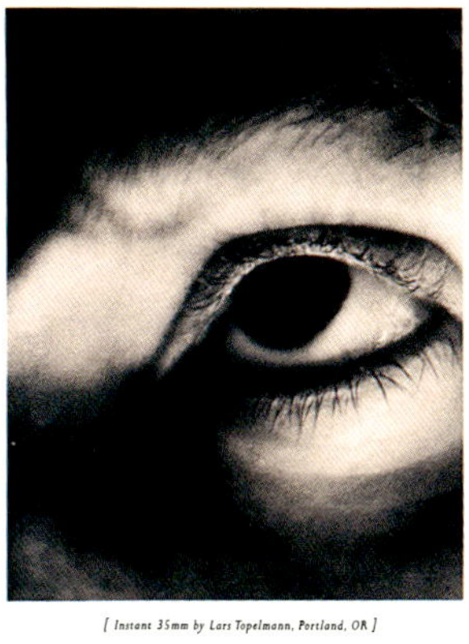

[Instant 35mm by Lars Topelmann, Portland, OR]

GOLD, SILVER & BRONZE AWARDS

TRADE
B/W OR COLOR
ANY SIZE: CAMPAIGN

47 SILVER

ART DIRECTOR
Bill Winchester

WRITER
Tom Evans

PHOTOGRAPHER
Curtis Johnson

CLIENT
Pfizer Animal Health

AGENCY
Colle & McVoy/
Minneapolis

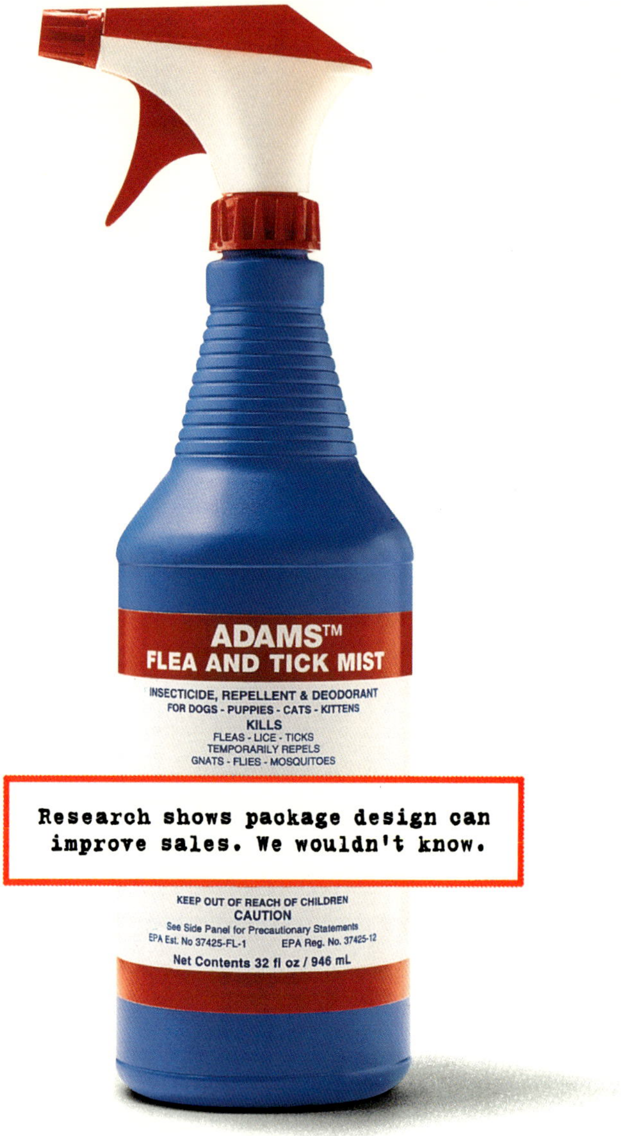

Research also shows that 97% of dog and cat owners who try Adams would buy it again, so we're pretty sure it's what's in the bottle, not on it, that makes Adams so effective at controlling fleas and ticks.

Adams. The really strong stuff in the ugly blue bottle.

ADAMS™
FLEA AND TICK MIST
INSECTICIDE, REPELLENT & DEODORANT
FOR DOGS - PUPPIES - CATS - KITTENS
KILLS
FLEAS - LICE - TICKS
TEMPORARILY REPELS
GNATS - FLIES - MOSQUITOES
Who cares if it's an ugly bottle?
Dogs are color blind anyway.
KEEP OUT OF REACH OF CHILDREN
CAUTION
Net Contents 32 fl oz / 946 mL
Veterinarians have recommended Adams for twenty years,
so dog and cat owners who know what works know to look for our
distinctive blue bottle. No matter how ugly it is.
Adams. The really strong stuff in the ugly blue bottle.

ADAMS™
FLEA AND TICK MIST
INSECTICIDE, REPELLENT & DEODORANT
FOR DOGS - PUPPIES - CATS - KITTENS
KILLS
FLEAS - LICE - TICKS
TEMPORARILY REPELS
GNATS - FLIES - MOSQUITOES
We were gonna put a
doggy and kitty on the label but the
science dept. laughed at us.
KEEP OUT OF REACH OF CHILDREN
CAUTION
Net Contents 32 fl oz / 946 mL
When you're ready to get serious about flea and tick control,
look for Adams. It's the professional formula in the not-so-pretty package.
The way we see it, killing fleas and ticks is an ugly job.
Adams. The really strong stuff in the ugly blue bottle.

47 Silver

GOLD, SILVER & BRONZE AWARDS

TRADE
B/W OR COLOR
ANY SIZE: CAMPAIGN

48 SILVER

ART DIRECTORS
Rob Rich
Ted Royer

WRITER
Kara Goodrich

PHOTOGRAPHER
Kerry Peterson

ILLUSTRATOR
Brad Palm

CLIENT
Polaroid

AGENCY
Leonard/Monahan, Providence

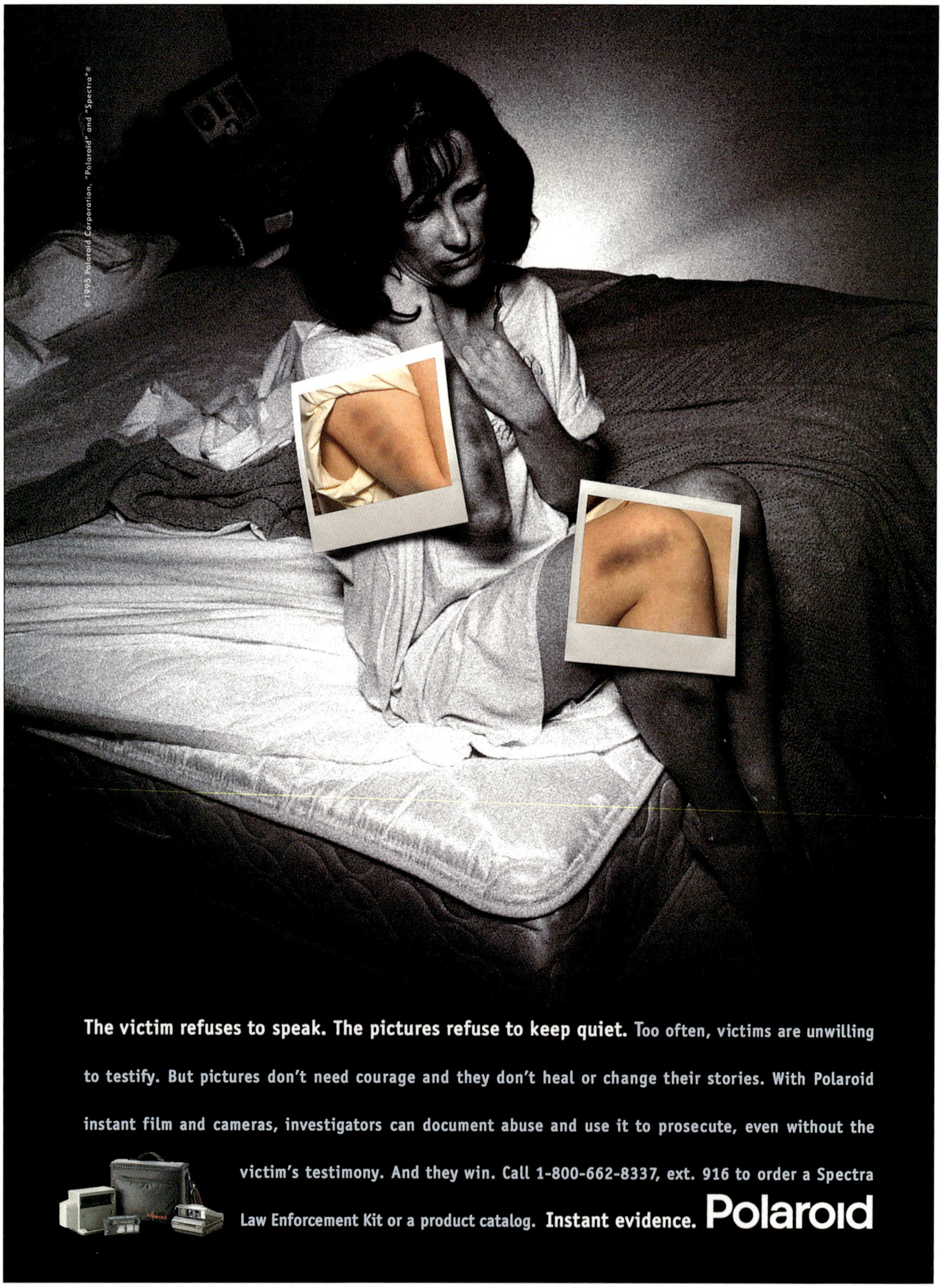
© 1995 Polaroid Corporation, "Polaroid" and "Spectra"®
The victim refuses to speak. The pictures refuse to keep quiet. Too often, victims are unwilling to testify. But pictures don't need courage and they don't heal or change their stories. With Polaroid instant film and cameras, investigators can document abuse and use it to prosecute, even without the victim's testimony. And they win. Call 1-800-662-8337, ext. 916 to order a Spectra Law Enforcement Kit or a product catalog. Instant evidence.
Polaroid

Framed. By his own artwork. Tags, throw-ups, fill-ins and masterpieces. Police officers are using Polaroid instant film and cameras to document gang and tagger graffiti, then piecing together the evidence to build their cases. When a suspect is identified, the pictures become almost as valuable as a written confession. Call 1-800-662-8337, ext. 916 to order a Spectra Law Enforcement Kit or a product catalog. Instant evidence.
Polaroid

Criminals always leave a trail. This one leads to a jail cell. With Polaroid instant cameras and film, investigators can easily document evidence and be sure they have it before the crime scene is disturbed. That means building a case quicker. In court, instant pictures also act as excellent witnesses providing irrefutable evidence. Call 1-800-662-8337, ext. 916 to order a Spectra Law Enforcement Kit or a product catalog. Instant evidence.
Polaroid

GOLD, SILVER & BRONZE
AWARDS

TRADE
B/W OR COLOR
ANY SIZE: CAMPAIGN

49 BRONZE

ART DIRECTOR
Jeremy Postaer

WRITER
Steve Johnston

PHOTOGRAPHER
Heimo

CLIENT
DHL Airways

AGENCY
Goodby Silverstein &
Partners/San Francisco

49 Bronze

GOLD, SILVER & BRONZE AWARDS

COLLATERAL BROCHURES OTHER THAN BY MAIL

50 GOLD

ART DIRECTOR
Dan Olson
WRITER
Riley Kane
PHOTOGRAPHER
Leo Tushaus
CLIENT
Flagstone Brewery
AGENCY
Fallon McElligott/
Minneapolis

51 SILVER

ART DIRECTOR
Keith Anderson
WRITER
Eric Osterhaus
PHOTOGRAPHER
Barry Robinson
CLIENT
Bell Sports
AGENCY
Goodby Silverstein &
Partners/San Francisco

50 Gold

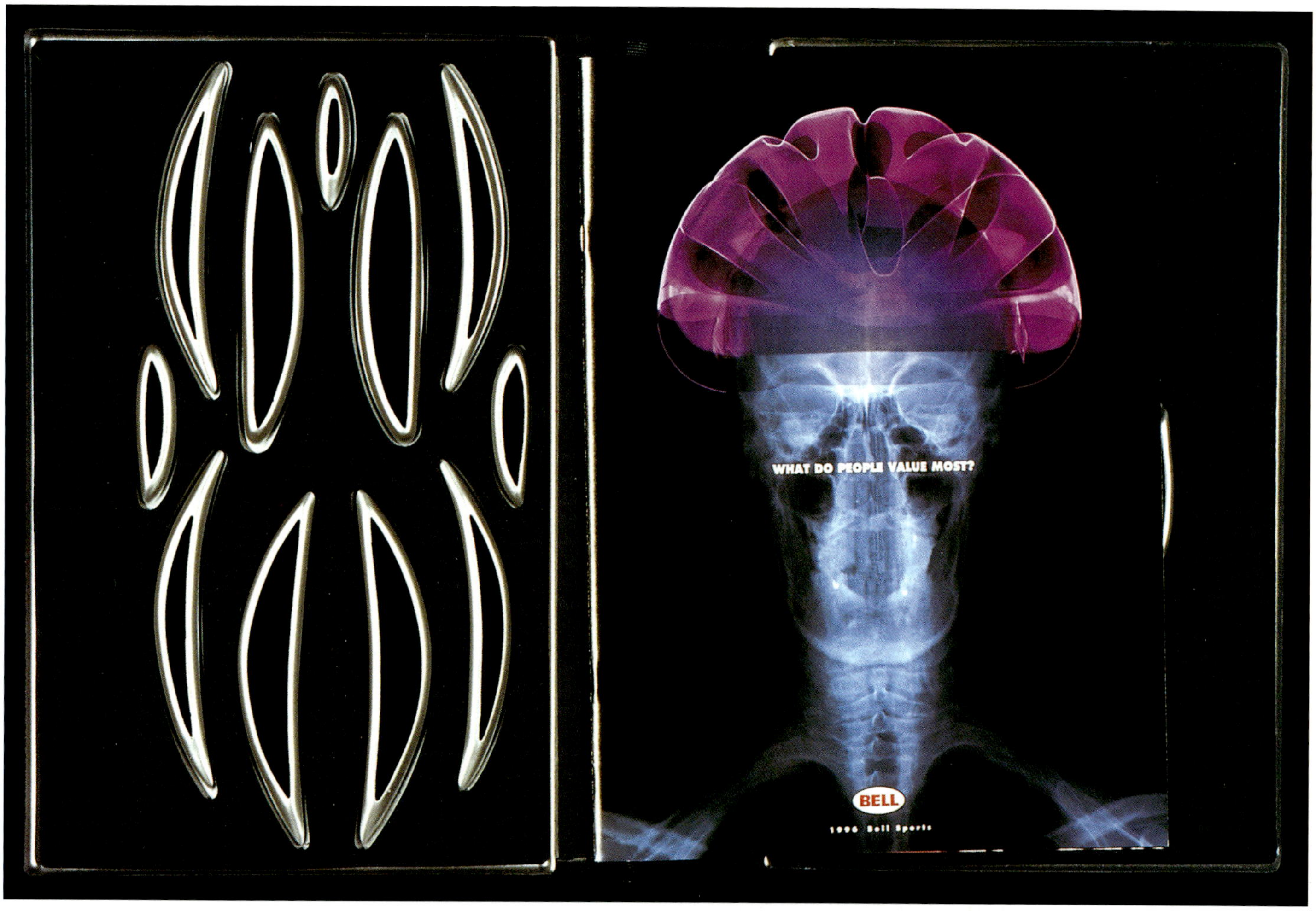
WHAT DO PEOPLE VALUE MOST?
BELL
1996 Bell Sports

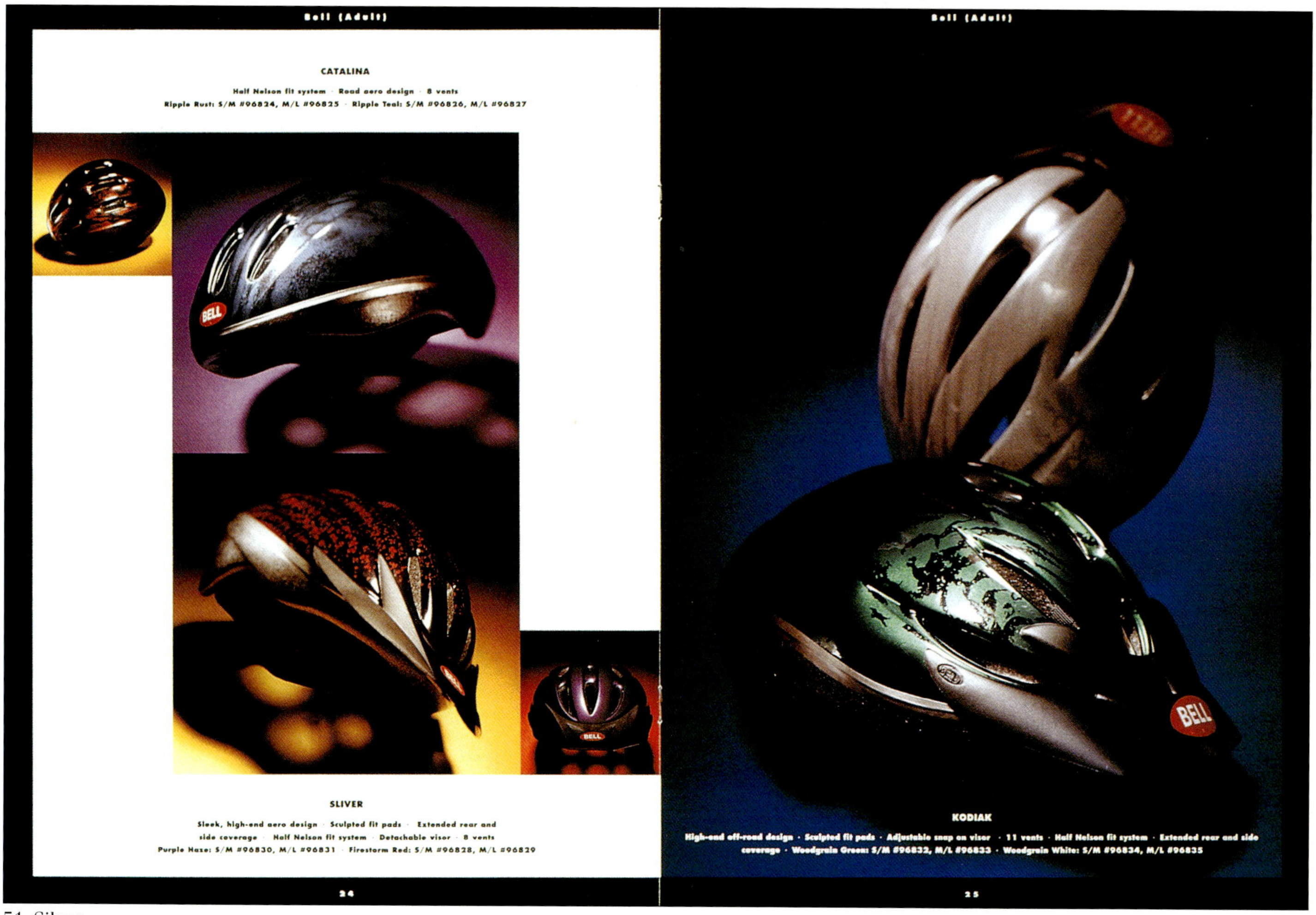
Bell (Adult)
CATALINA
Half Nelson fit system · Road aero design · 8 vents
Ripple Rust: S/M #96824, M/L #96825 · Ripple Teal: S/M #96826, M/L #96827
SLIVER
Sleek, high-end aero design · Sculpted fit pads · Extended rear and side coverage · Half Nelson fit system · Detachable visor · 8 vents
Purple Haze: S/M #96830, M/L #96831 · Firestorm Red: S/M #96828, M/L #96829
24
Bell (Adult)
KODIAK
High-end off-road design · Sculpted fit pads · Adjustable snap on visor · 11 vents · Half Nelson fit system · Extended rear and side coverage · Woodgrain Green: S/M #96832, M/L #96833 · Woodgrain White: S/M #96834, M/L #96835
25

51 Silver

GOLD, SILVER & BRONZE AWARDS

COLLATERAL BROCHURES OTHER THAN BY MAIL

52 BRONZE

ART DIRECTOR
Keith Anderson
WRITER
Eric Osterhaus
PHOTOGRAPHER
Barry Robinson
CLIENT
Bell Sports
AGENCY
Goodby Silverstein & Partners/San Francisco

COLLATERAL DIRECT MAIL: SINGLE

53 GOLD

ART DIRECTOR
Hal Curtis
WRITER
Steve Bautista
PHOTOGRAPHER
Michele Clement
CLIENT
M&H Typography
AGENCY
Pagano Schenck & Kay/Boston

54 GOLD

ART DIRECTOR
Hal Curtis
WRITER
Steve Bautista
PHOTOGRAPHER
Michele Clement
CLIENT
M&H Typography
AGENCY
Pagano Schenck & Kay/Boston

52 Bronze

WHEN YOU SET
AN AD IN 750 DEGREE
HOT LEAD,
TYPOS
ARE NOT TAKEN LIGHTLY.
FORMING LETTERS FROM MOLTEN LEAD ISN'T DONE NONCHALANTLY. When first practiced around the year 1450, it took time to cast hot metal type. And to do this properly, time is what it still takes today. But there is another requirement to pouring letterforms from lead, arranging them into words, and pressing their images into paper. It takes dedication — something that M & H Type has exhibited since 1915, by offering a rare collection of metal type to suit the tastes of even the most discriminating individuals. And for those who require a more modern approach, we provide a photo-composition service also, using the most advanced technology obtainable today. Call Andrew Hoyem, president, to inquire about the availability of type styles or for help in planning your next project. Because there is an additional benefit from having your typography composed with a greater attention to detail. There are usually fewer mistakes.
M & H TYPE. TYPOGRAPHERS & TYPEFOUNDERS SINCE 1915.
460 Bryant Street, San Francisco, California 94107. Telephone 415-777-0716. Fax: 415-777-2730.

53 Gold

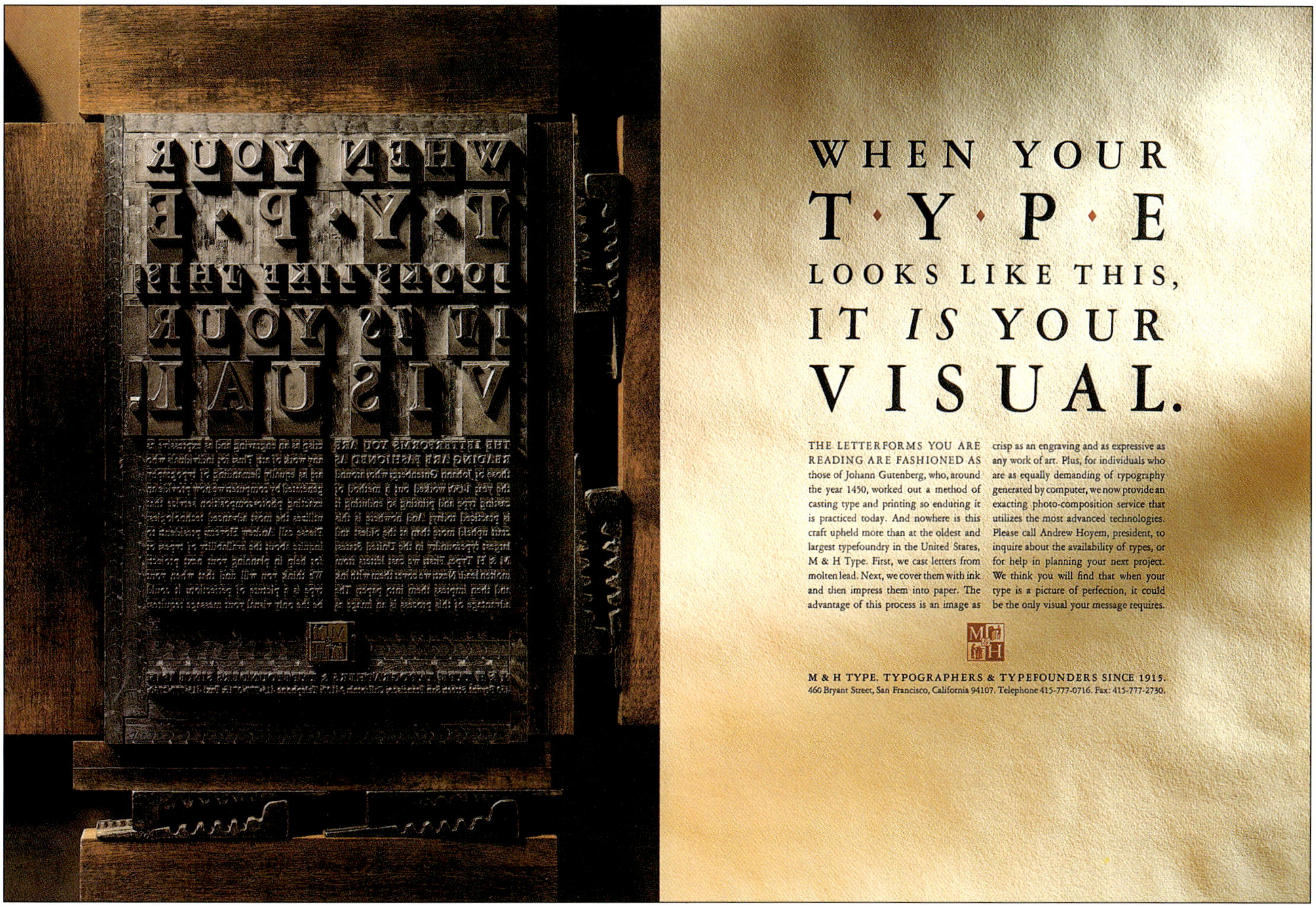

WHEN YOUR
T·Y·P·E
LOOKS LIKE THIS,
IT IS YOUR
VISUAL.
THE LETTERFORMS YOU ARE READING ARE FASHIONED AS those of Johann Gutenberg, who, around the year 1450, worked out a method of casting type and printing so enduring it is practiced today. And nowhere is this craft upheld more than at the oldest and largest typefoundry in the United States, M & H Type. First, we cast letters from molten lead. Next, we cover them with ink and then impress them into paper. The advantage of this process is an image as crisp as an engraving and as expressive as any work of art. Plus, for individuals who are as equally demanding of typography generated by computer, we now provide an exacting photo-composition service that utilizes the most advanced technologies. Please call Andrew Hoyem, president, to inquire about the availability of types, or for help in planning your next project. We think you will find that when your type is a picture of perfection, it could be the only visual your message requires.
M & H TYPE. TYPOGRAPHERS & TYPEFOUNDERS SINCE 1915.
460 Bryant Street, San Francisco, California 94107. Telephone 415-777-0716. Fax: 415-777-2730.

54 Gold

GOLD, SILVER & BRONZE AWARDS

COLLATERAL DIRECT MAIL: SINGLE

55 SILVER

ART DIRECTORS
Mark Slotemaker
Roger Bentley

WRITER
Joel Thomas

PHOTOGRAPHERS
Giovanni Stephano
Ken Anderson
Mark Slotemaker

ILLUSTRATOR
Bob Bredemeier

CLIENT
Big House

AGENCY
Dalbey & Denight Advertising/Portland

56 BRONZE

ART DIRECTOR
Jim Mountjoy

WRITER
Ed Jones

PHOTOGRAPHER
Harry DeZitter

CLIENT
North Carolina Film Commission

AGENCY
Loeffler Ketchum Mountjoy/Charlotte, NC

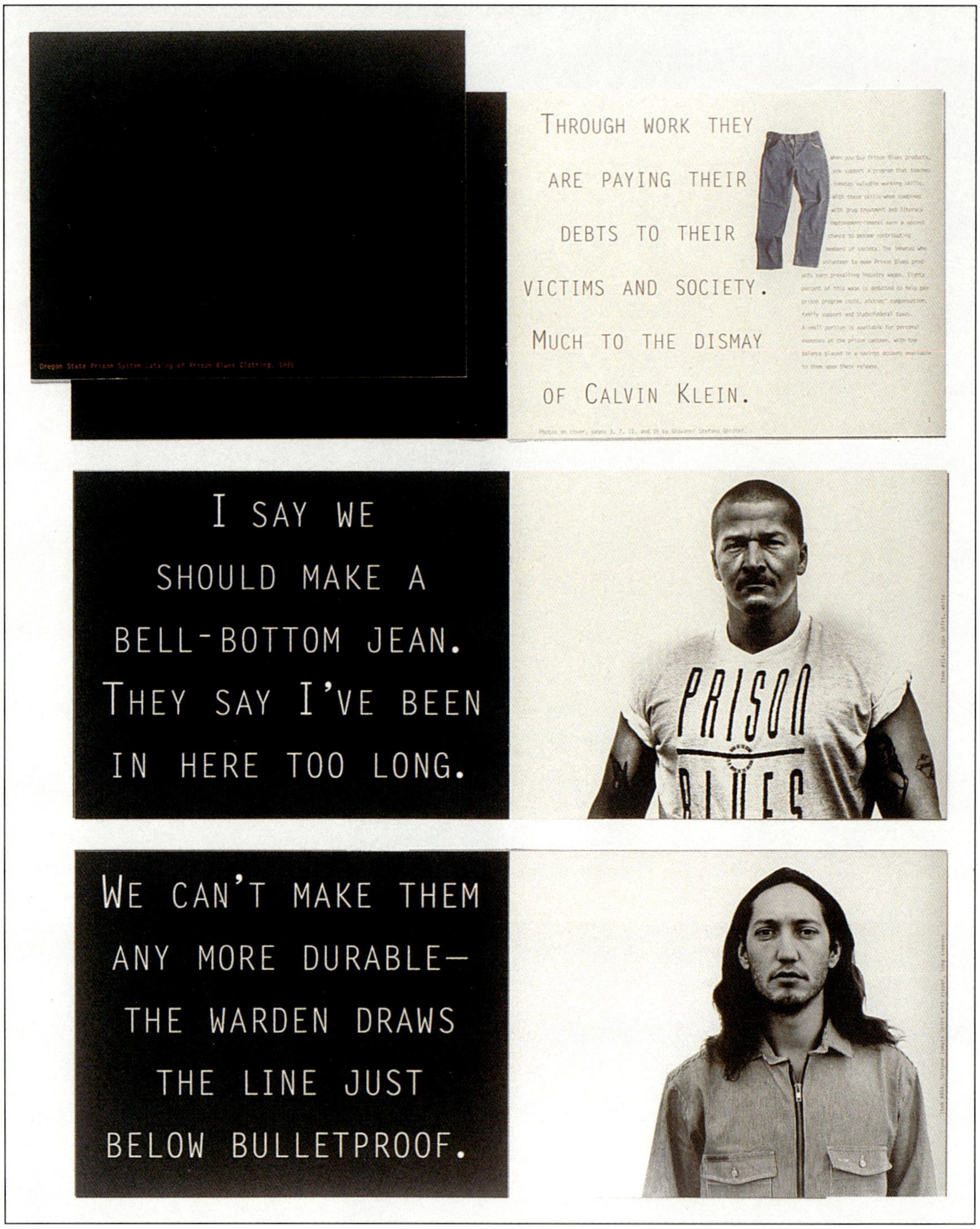

55 Silver

YOU WON'T HAVE TO YELL "QUIET ON THE SET!"

Fade up. Killer location. Something's got to be wrong with this picture. Everything's going too easy. Crew's too bleeping nice. Cut to face of location scout. She whispers, "Wait'll you see the other 5 locations." Dailies roll in. Boffo. You're already thinking sequel. You dial (919) 733-9900 to set it up. You show rough cut. Everybody applauds. Even clueless studio executives. (This worries you slightly.) You remember why you got into films in the first place. Life is good. The end.

North Carolina Film Commission

GOLD, SILVER & BRONZE AWARDS

COLLATERAL
DIRECT MAIL: CAMPAIGN

57 GOLD

ART DIRECTOR
Hal Curtis

WRITER
Steve Bautista

PHOTOGRAPHER
Michele Clement

CLIENT
M&H Typography

AGENCY
Pagano Schenck & Kay/
Boston

WHEN YOU SET
AN AD IN 750 DEGREE
HOT LEAD,
TYPOS
ARE NOT TAKEN LIGHTLY.
FORMING LETTERS FROM MOLTEN LEAD ISN'T DONE NONCHALANTLY. When first practiced around the year 1450, it took time to cast hot metal type. And to do this properly, time is what it still takes today. But there is another requirement to pouring letterforms from lead, arranging them into words, and pressing their images into paper. It takes dedication — something that M & H Type has exhibited since 1915, by offering a rare collection of metal type to suit the tastes of even the most discriminating individuals. And for those who require a more modern approach, we provide a photo-composition service also, using the most advanced technology obtainable today. Call Andrew Hoyem, president, to inquire about the availability of type styles or for help in planning your next project. Because there is an additional benefit from having your typography composed with a greater attention to detail. There are usually fewer mistakes.
M & H TYPE. TYPOGRAPHERS & TYPEFOUNDERS SINCE 1915.
460 Bryant Street, San Francisco, California 94107. Telephone 415-777-0716. Fax: 415-777-2730.

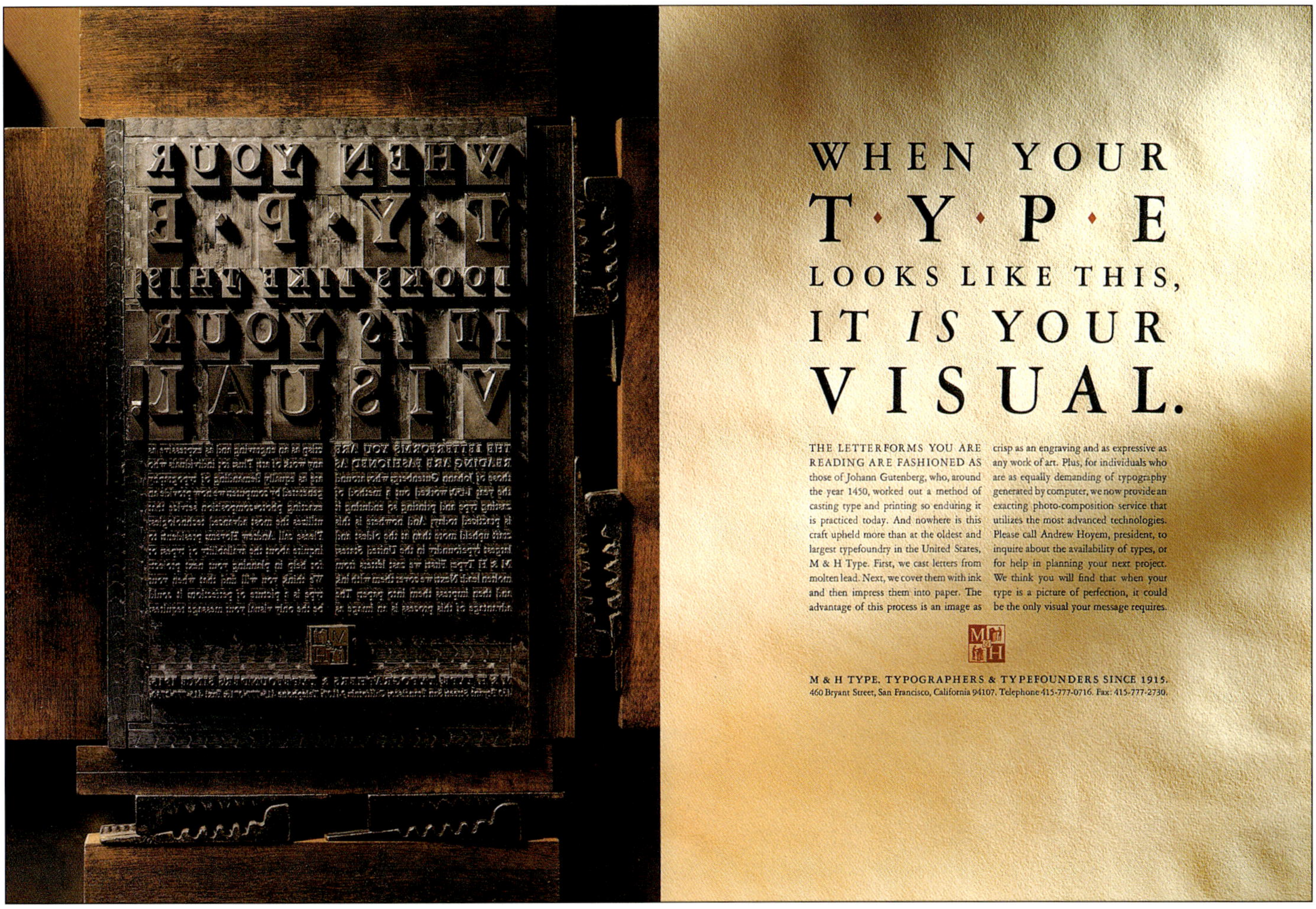
WHEN YOUR
T·Y·P·E
LOOKS LIKE THIS,
IT *IS* YOUR
VISUAL.
THE LETTERFORMS YOU ARE READING ARE FASHIONED AS those of Johann Gutenberg, who, around the year 1450, worked out a method of casting type and printing so enduring it is practiced today. And nowhere is this craft upheld more than at the oldest and largest typefoundry in the United States, M & H Type. First, we cast letters from molten lead. Next, we cover them with ink and then impress them into paper. The advantage of this process is an image as crisp as an engraving and as expressive as any work of art. Plus, for individuals who are as equally demanding of typography generated by computer, we now provide an exacting photo-composition service that utilizes the most advanced technologies. Please call Andrew Hoyem, president, to inquire about the availability of types, or for help in planning your next project. We think you will find that when your type is a picture of perfection, it could be the only visual your message requires.
M & H TYPE. TYPOGRAPHERS & TYPEFOUNDERS SINCE 1915.
460 Bryant Street, San Francisco, California 94107. Telephone 415-777-0716. Fax: 415-777-2730.

WE MAKE
T·Y·P·E
THE OLD-
FASHIONED WAY.
WE POUR IT.
AROUND THE YEAR 1450, JOHANN GUTENBERG CAST MOLTEN LEAD into the Roman alphabet. Then for five years, he arranged his letterforms by hand, covered them with ink, and pressed their images into paper. The result was the Latin Bible—a book revered not only by Christians, but by a group of zealots who became known as typographers. M & H Type has continued this tradition since 1915 by presenting a rare collection of metal types to suit discriminating individuals. And, for those who may desire a more modern approach, we are equally demanding of typography generated by photo-composition. To inquire about the availability of type styles, or for help in planning your next project, please contact Andrew Hoyem, president. Because just as did Gutenberg over five-hundred years ago, we do considerably more than compose typography. We worship it.
M & H TYPE. TYPOGRAPHERS & TYPEFOUNDERS SINCE 1915.
460 Bryant Street, San Francisco, California 94107. Telephone 415-777-0716. Fax: 415-777-2730.

GOLD, SILVER & BRONZE AWARDS

COLLATERAL
DIRECT MAIL: CAMPAIGN

58 SILVER

ART DIRECTORS
Dave Cook
Carol Holsinger
Gina Fortunato
Mikal Reich

WRITERS
Mikal Reich
Carol Holsinger
Steve Amick

PHOTOGRAPHERS
Joe Fornabio
Mel Curtis

CLIENT
The Village Voice

AGENCY
Mad Dogs & Englishmen/
New York

The next thing I know you'll be reading *The Satanic Bible*!
the village VOICE
NOT AMERICA'S FAVORITE PAPER

It's *so* nice that homosexuals, Jews and terrorists have a newspaper to read.
the village VOICE
NOT AMERICA'S FAVORITE PAPER

Let's say an individual was approaching you, trying to sell you a subscription...you could drop that mother at 500 feet.
the village VOICE
NOT AMERICA'S FAVORITE PAPER

GOLD, SILVER & BRONZE AWARDS

COLLATERAL
POINT OF PURCHASE AND IN-STORE

59 GOLD
ART DIRECTORS
Mark Slotemaker
Roger Bentley
WRITER
Joel Thomas
PHOTOGRAPHERS
Giovanni Stephano
Mark Slotemaker
CLIENT
Big House
AGENCY
Dalbey & Denight Advertising/Portland

62 BRONZE
ART DIRECTOR
Steve Mitchell
WRITER
Matt Elhardt
PHOTOGRAPHER
Curtis Johnson
CLIENT
Rohol
AGENCY
Hunt Adkins/Minneapolis

PUBLIC SERVICE/
POLITICAL NEWSPAPER OR MAGAZINE: SINGLE

63 GOLD
ART DIRECTORS
Todd Riddle
Mark Nardi
WRITERS
Mark Nardi
Todd Riddle
CLIENT
Massachusetts Department of Public Health
AGENCY
Houston Herstek Favat/Boston

59 Gold

For 60 and 61, please see numbers 42 and 43.

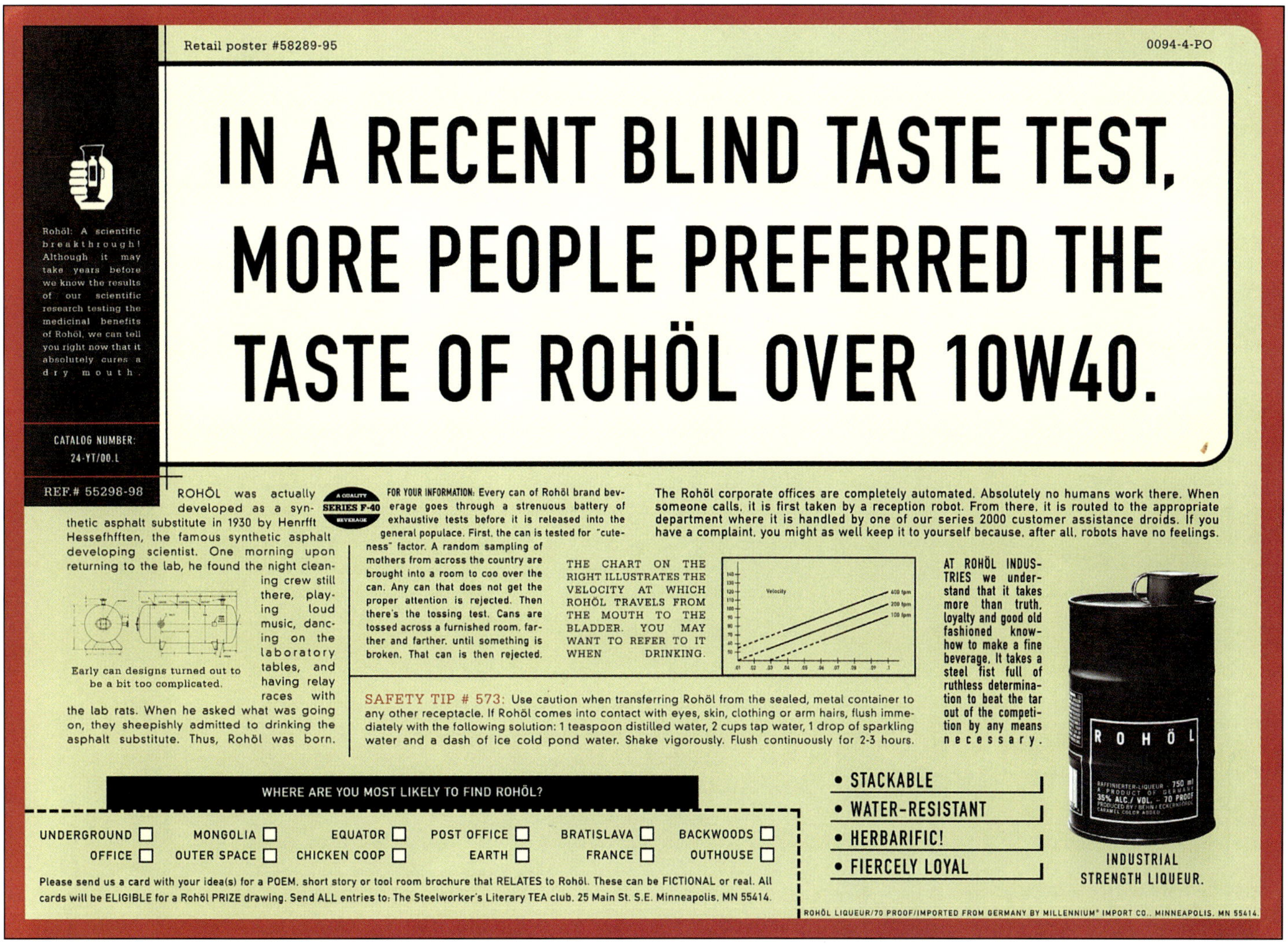

62 Bronze

You are 2 months old. Your lungs are this tiny. You spend day after day around second-hand cigarette smoke. You breathe it in. You cough. You hack. You wheeze. Your lungs clog up with sticky fluid and thick mucous. You get bronchitis. Or pneumonia. If you have asthma, it will likely get worse. All together, up to 300,000 babies end up getting sick every year. 15,000 of them could end up hospitalized. Simply from being exposed to cigarette smoke. It's time we made smoking history. A message from The Massachusetts Department of Public Health.

63 Gold

GOLD, SILVER & BRONZE AWARDS

PUBLIC SERVICE/ POLITICAL NEWSPAPER OR MAGAZINE: SINGLE

64 BRONZE

ART DIRECTOR
Jennifer Ward
WRITER
Kevin Lynch
ILLUSTRATOR
Kent Barton
CLIENT
Partnership for a Drug-Free America
AGENCY
Four Walls and a Roof/ Chicago

65 BRONZE

ART DIRECTOR
Tom McMahon
WRITER
Tim Wallis
PHOTOGRAPH
America's Black Holocaust Museum, Yuenkel Studios
CLIENT
America's Black Holocaust Museum
AGENCY
Meyer & Wallis/Milwaukee

WHAT TO DO AFTER BURYING YOUR 10-YEAR-OLD.
IT'S the ninth conversation you've had with your child this week. Today, you tell her about the flowers you bought, and the movie you saw last night. You tell her all the people who miss her – her brothers, her aunt. Tears stream down your cheeks as you tell her you miss her too. You hope she knows. You walk away from your child's grave for the ninth time this week, feeling emptier still.
IT IS IMPORTANT for bereaved parents to go through the grieving process if they are expected to eventually heal.
For the fifteenth night in a row, you are awakened by your child's voice. You wish none of this were happening. You wish you hadn't let her go to school that day. You wish you'd never heard of "sniffing," because that's what killed her. Sniffing is slang for inhaling ordinary, everyday household products to get high. You look around the darkened bedroom, haunted by the voice that woke you up. The voice that was silenced at 10.
TO ASSIST IN THE healing, familiarize yourself with the five phases of death, and the emotions that accompany them.
You never drive past her school, or by the hospital where you learned firsthand about the effects of inhalants. You talked to your child about drugs. But inhalants? How could you have warned your child about a problem you'd never heard of? You tried to avoid every site associated with your child's death. Unfortunately, her sniffing habit could've started at home. The average home has over 100 household products that can be inhaled to get high, like correction fluid, spray paint, or even markers. The house you built to protect her was the house that introduced her to inhalants. It's too much to even think about. But you do. Every time you walk in the door.
It's been three weeks since the funeral. You are comforted by the sight of her things – her hair brush, still on the bathroom counter. Her bike, still leaning against the garage door. The piano that she played through four years of lessons, now sitting silent. Sometimes, you even catch yourself smelling the sweater she wanted you to wash that morning. Her room is still the way she left it when she went to school that morning. You are oblivious to the items she used as inhalant paraphernalia because they are such common items – socks, soda cans, even empty lunch bags. Back in the living room, you sit at the piano, and begin playing her favorite song.
SPOUSES USUALLY HEAL at different rates. Often, family therapy can help bridge the varying recovery stages.
It's been five months since the funeral. Some days, you're able to forget for a moment. You're doing a crossword puzzle – what's another word for "spiral" that begins with "H"? – when the phone rings. It's an old friend. "How are you?" she asks. "And how are the kids?" You thought you wouldn't have to break the news anymore. A long silence. A deep breath. She's dead, you say. She died from using inhalants. You hang up the phone. Then throw it across the room.
INCLUDING MEMORIES of your child in discussion may feel self-conscious at first, but this will assist in your recovery.
Could this be your child? Hopefully, no. Potentially, yes. Because inhalant abuse is on the rise. Inhalants can damage the heart, kidneys, liver, or brain. They can even kill the very first time. Please learn about inhalants by calling 800-729-6686. Until there are more parents who know about sniffing, there will be more parents who wish they did.
IF YOU DON'T WANT TO LEARN ABOUT GRIEVING, PLEASE LEARN ABOUT SNIFFING. CALL 800-729-6686.
PARTNERSHIP FOR A DRUG-FREE AMERICA®
64 Bronze

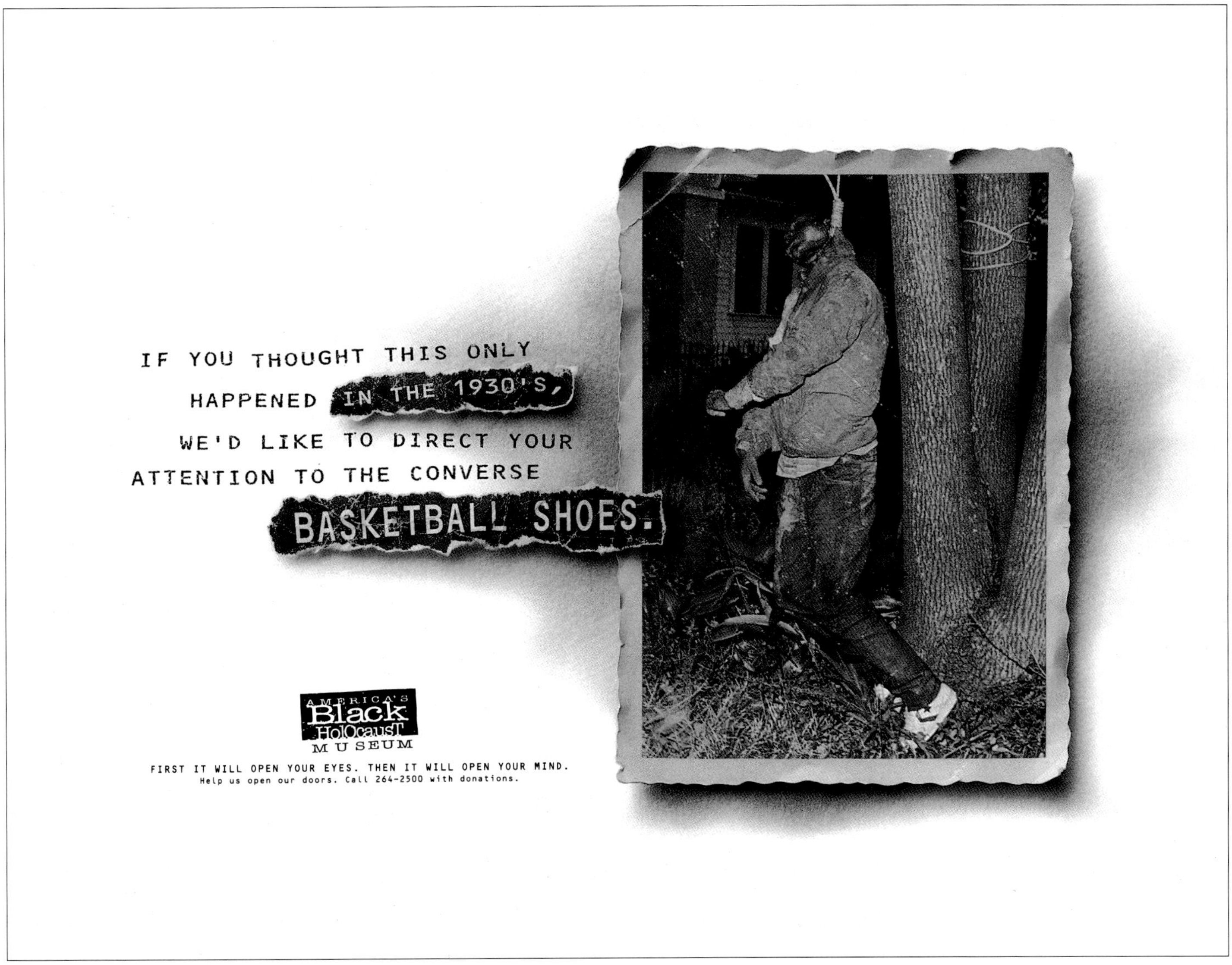
IF YOU THOUGHT THIS ONLY
HAPPENED IN THE 1930'S,
WE'D LIKE TO DIRECT YOUR
ATTENTION TO THE CONVERSE
BASKETBALL SHOES.
AMERICA'S Black Holocaust MUSEUM
FIRST IT WILL OPEN YOUR EYES. THEN IT WILL OPEN YOUR MIND.
Help us open our doors. Call 264-2500 with donations.

65 Bronze

GOLD, SILVER & BRONZE AWARDS

PUBLIC SERVICE/ POLITICAL NEWSPAPER OR MAGAZINE: CAMPAIGN

66 GOLD

ART DIRECTOR
Robb Burnham

WRITER
Sally Hogshead

PHOTOGRAPHER
Marc Norberg

CLIENT
Minneapolis Animal Shelter

AGENCY
Fallon McElligott/ Minneapolis

Expiration Date:
MON. JULY 24
Ever since we've had her, she's been wagging her tail like crazy. Unfortunately her owner couldn't keep her any longer, and now, neither can we. Can you? Adopt. Fast. 348-4250. MINNEAPOLIS ANIMAL SHELTER

Expiration Date:
MON. MAY 29
He's about half German Shepherd, he's housebroken, and he knows how to shake hands. If he's your kind of dog, come get him quick. This offer expires soon. Adopt. Fast. 348-4250. MINNEAPOLIS ANIMAL SHELTER

GOLD, SILVER & BRONZE AWARDS

PUBLIC SERVICE/
POLITICAL NEWSPAPER
OR MAGAZINE: CAMPAIGN

67 BRONZE

ART DIRECTOR
John Scully

WRITER
Jan Van Mesdag

PHOTOGRAPHERS
Sebastio Salgado
Jack Pkone
Roger Hutchings

CLIENT
Medecins Sans Frontieres

AGENCY
McCann-Erickson/London

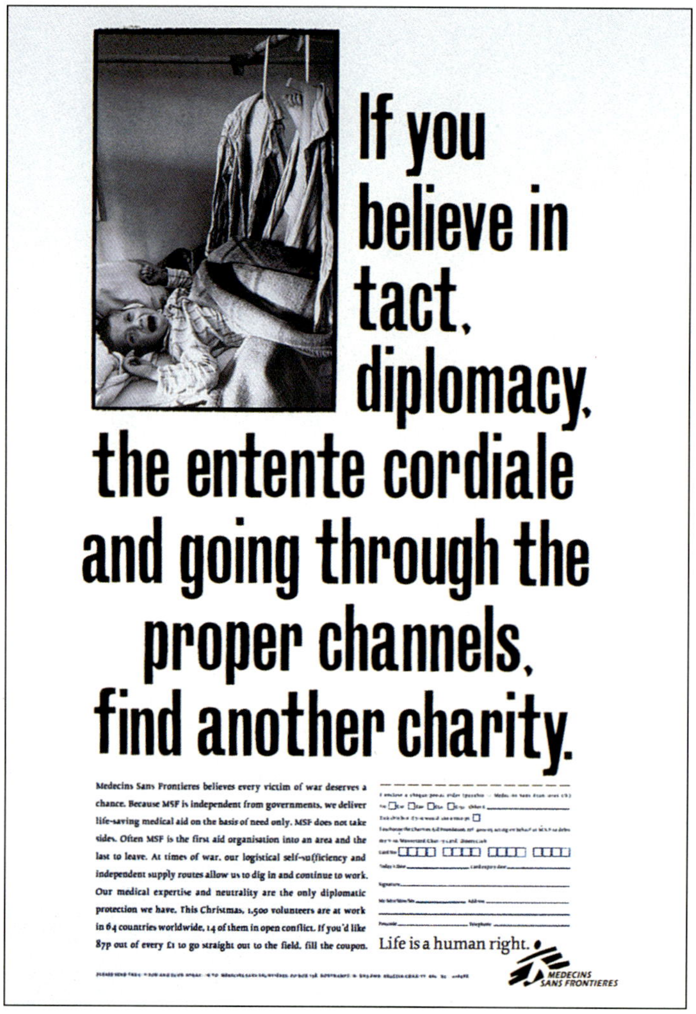
If you believe in tact, diplomacy, the entente cordiale and going through the proper channels, find another charity.
Medecins Sans Frontieres believes every victim of war deserves a chance. Because MSF is independent from governments, we deliver life-saving medical aid on the basis of need only. MSF does not take sides. Often MSF is the first aid organisation into an area and the last to leave. At times of war, our logistical self-sufficiency and independent supply routes allow us to dig in and continue to work. Our medical expertise and neutrality are the only diplomatic protection we have. This Christmas, 1,500 volunteers are at work in 64 countries worldwide, 14 of them in open conflict. If you'd like 87p out of every £1 to go straight out to the field, fill the coupon.
Life is a human right.
MEDECINS SANS FRONTIERES

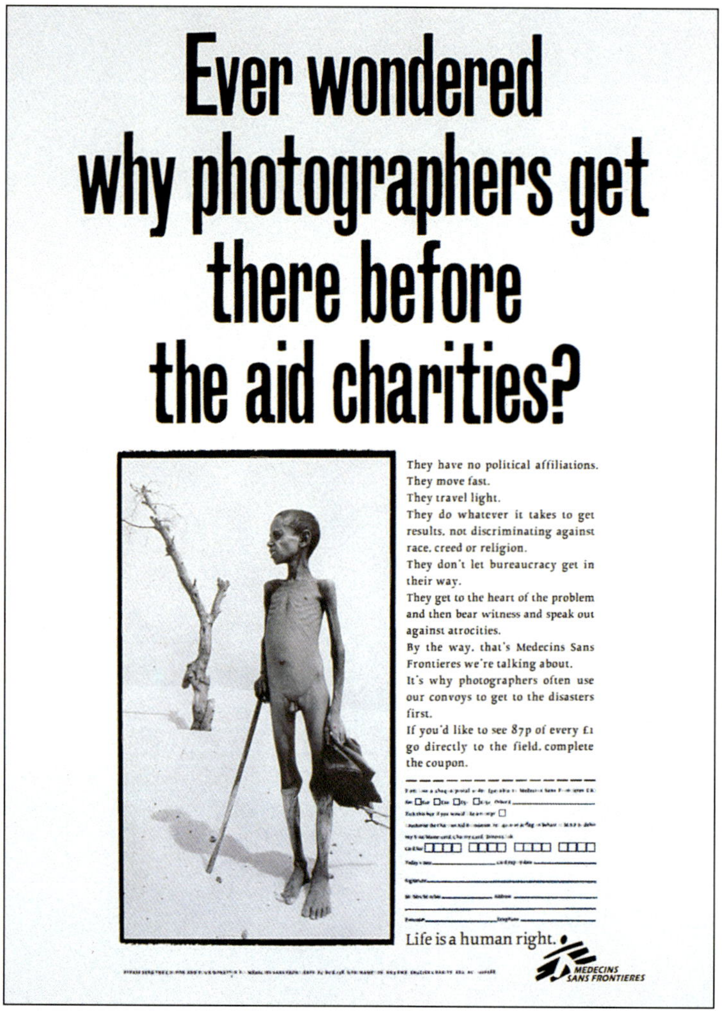
Ever wondered why photographers get there before the aid charities?
They have no political affiliations.
They move fast.
They travel light.
They do whatever it takes to get results, not discriminating against race, creed or religion.
They don't let bureaucracy get in their way.
They get to the heart of the problem and then bear witness and speak out against atrocities.
By the way, that's Medecins Sans Frontieres we're talking about.
It's why photographers often use our convoys to get to the disasters first.
If you'd like to see 87p of every £1 go directly to the field, complete the coupon.
Life is a human right.
MEDECINS SANS FRONTIERES

They're ripping out tongues, gouging eyes and hacking off hands.
Christmas in Sierra Leone.
We don't understand why men can become ruthless butchers, but in the city of Bo, Medecins Sans Frontieres surgeons are dealing with some of the most horrific mutilations they've ever witnessed. Armed groups vying for control of the country's mining areas have found that maiming works better than slaughtering when trying to "encourage" people to leave their homes. Survivors are telling us that more refugees are being blinded so they can't reach help. Bo used to have a population of 60,000. It's now home to 1/4 million displaced men, women and children. 10,000 new refugees emerge from the bush every month. Malnutrition is rife. This "poor man's war" has only met with indifference and neglect from the international community. As a result, only very few people even know it is taking place. After all, how much are you reading about it in this paper? MSF works in the three cities with the largest refugee concentrations in the country. When the roads were closed by the fighting earlier this year, we alone established an air supply route and opened feeding centres. When cholera and measles broke out, we brought them under control and launched vaccination programmes. And of course, we opened treatment facilities for those appalling injuries. But to sustain our single-handed effort, we need your support. 87p of every £1 donated will go straight out to the field, so please give generously.
Life is a human right.
MEDECINS SANS FRONTIERES

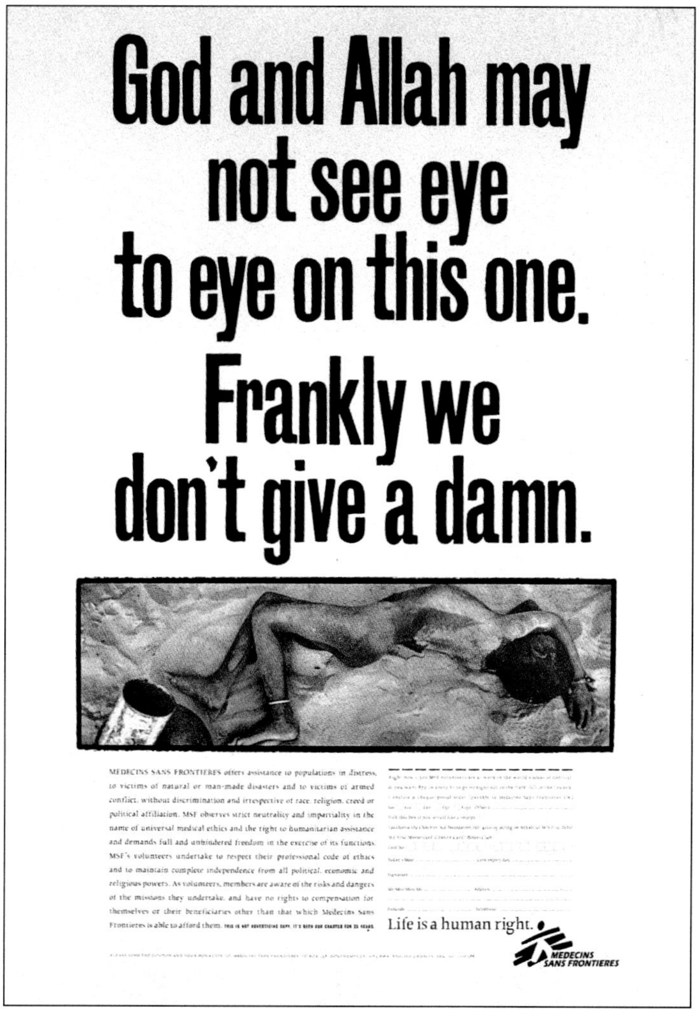
God and Allah may not see eye to eye on this one. Frankly we don't give a damn.
MEDECINS SANS FRONTIERES offers assistance to populations in distress, to victims of natural or man-made disasters and to victims of armed conflict, without discrimination and irrespective of race, religion, creed or political affiliation. MSF observes strict neutrality and impartiality in the name of universal medical ethics and the right to humanitarian assistance and demands full and unhindered freedom in the exercise of its functions. MSF's volunteers undertake to respect their professional code of ethics and to maintain complete independence from all political, economic and religious powers. As volunteers, members are aware of the risks and dangers of the missions they undertake, and have no rights to compensation for themselves or their beneficiaries other than that which Medecins Sans Frontieres is able to afford them.
Life is a human right.
MEDECINS SANS FRONTIERES

67 Bronze

GOLD, SILVER & BRONZE AWARDS

PUBLIC SERVICE/ POLITICAL OUTDOOR AND POSTERS

68 GOLD

ART DIRECTOR
Paul Renner
WRITER
Ryan Ebner
PHOTOGRAPHERS
Marko Lavrisha
Gareth Hopson
CLIENT
Howell Central Little League
AGENCY
Butler Shine & Stern/ Sausalito

69 SILVER

ART DIRECTOR
Paul Renner
WRITER
Ryan Ebner
PHOTOGRAPHERS
Marko Lavrisha
Gareth Hopson
CLIENT
Howell Central Little League
AGENCY
Butler Shine & Stern/ Sausalito

INTRODUCE
YOUR SON TO THE
GREAT AMERICAN
PASTIME.
BEFORE
SEGA DOES.
Howell Central
LITTLE LEAGUE
THIS SPRING, GIVE YOUR SON A SENSE OF ACCOMPLISHMENT THAT DOESN'T COME FROM HITTING HIGH SCORE ON MORTAL KOMBAT. SIGN HIM UP AT TAUNTON SCHOOL, JANUARY 8 & 11, 7-9 PM.

68 Gold

FORGET
NIKE AND PEPSI.
WE'VE GOT
AL'S TIRE
AND
MUFFLER.
Howell Central
LITTLE LEAGUE
OUR PLAYERS COULDN'T CARE LESS ABOUT MULTI-MILLION DOLLAR ENDORSEMENTS. HECK, THEY COULDN'T EVEN SPELL "ENDORSEMENTS." SIGN UP AT TAUNTON SCHOOL, JANUARY 8 & 11, 7-9 PM.

69 Silver

PUBLIC SERVICE/ POLITICAL OUTDOOR AND POSTERS

70 BRONZE

ART DIRECTOR
Robb Burnham
WRITER
Sally Hogshead
PHOTOGRAPHER
Marc Norberg
CLIENT
Minneapolis Animal Shelter
AGENCY
Fallon McElligott/ Minneapolis

71 BRONZE

ART DIRECTOR
Mitch Gordon
WRITER
Barton Landsman
ILLUSTRATOR
Mitch Gordon
CLIENT
The Oriental Institute Museum
AGENCY
Gordon/Landsman, Chicago

70 Bronze

YEAH SHE'S DEAD, BUT SHE STILL ENTERTAINS GUESTS.
More than 5000 years ago, the body of this woman was wrapped in reeds and buried in a pit in the Egyptian desert. There her body was completely enveloped by hot, dry sand which quickly dehydrated it and preserved it for posterity.
This mummy, created by naturally occurring environmental conditions, predates the Egyptian embalming practices used on pharaohs by hundreds of years. Today, this mummy is a part of our showcase of history, art, and archaeology from the amazing cultures of ancient Egypt, Israel, Iran, Syria, Iraq, Palestine and Anatolia. It is a collection the Oriental Institute has been amassing since 1919.
Our exhibits span four millennia of the ancient Near East, where nations left traces for archeologists to decipher. To see the artifacts left by these people is to look back at the beginnings of some of mankind's most fundamental endeavors. And when these pieces are all assembled, they speak volumes on what these people believed, how they lived, and how they died. Monumental statues proclaim the glory of their kings. Clay tablets, papyrus scrolls and inscriptions on stone show the development of their writing systems and document many aspects of their lives and culture. Objects used in everyday life display their highly developed skills in decorative arts and reveal the progressive refinement of their aesthetic tastes.
Carefully reconstructed tombs and burial sites based on numerous decades of study and gruelling work provide clues and insights to their lives, deaths and unique mortuary beliefs.
Once you decide to to come and visit we are quite certain you and your family will find all of these exhibits entertaining, educating, and fascinating. You just won't find them breathing.
THE ORIENTAL INSTITUTE
The Oriental Institute Museum at the University of Chicago, 1155 East 58th Street, Chicago, IL 60637

PUBLIC SERVICE/ POLITICAL RADIO: SINGLE

72 GOLD

WRITER
Mark Nardi

AGENCY PRODUCER
Lisa Sulda

PRODUCTION COMPANY
Soundtrack/Boston

CLIENT
Massachusetts Department of Public Health

AGENCY
Houston Herstek Favat/ Boston

73 SILVER

WRITER
Sally Hogshead

AGENCY PRODUCER
Vicki Oachs

CLIENT
A Chance to Grow School

AGENCY
Fallon McElligott/ Minneapolis

72 Gold

BOB MEHRMAN (WITH AID OF ELECTROLARYNX): What happened? What went wrong? My life was supposed to be fun and exciting, sexy and glamorous. I thought I'd always be laughing and smiling and riding horses into a beautiful sunset. I was supposed to live the life of those people in cigarette advertisements. But now I can't even breathe through my mouth, I can't taste food, I can't smell, and I sound like a damn robot.

My name is Bob Mehrman. After smoking cigarettes for many years I developed cancer and my larynx had to be removed. Now I can only talk by holding this electrolarynx to my throat. But have no pity on me. Pity the young people who must fight the terrible seduction of cigarettes. It's important to do what we can so another person doesn't end up like me. Please let the tobacco industry hear your voice. They certainly don't want to hear mine.

ANNCR: The Massachusetts Department of Public Health.

73 Silver

ANNCR: When dyslexia a child learning problem a has like, reads he switch words or in what letters. Sense makes nothing. Can't when understand going on a child school, frustrated feels stupid and he. His failing keep going down until grades he's. At A Chance to Grow, children help understand we. Our school revolutionary teaches students how to understand read and. If your child has dyslexia a learning problem such as, we can help him finally make sense of school. Please call A Chance To Grow at 521-2266. You thank.

PUBLIC SERVICE/ POLITICAL RADIO: CAMPAIGN

74 GOLD

WRITER
Mark Nardi
AGENCY PRODUCER
Lisa Sulda
PRODUCTION COMPANY
Sountrack/Boston
CLIENT
Massachusetts Department of Public Health
AGENCY
Houston Herstek Favat/ Boston

75 SILVER

WRITER
Sally Hogshead
AGENCY PRODUCER
Vicki Oachs
CLIENT
A Chance To Grow School
AGENCY
Fallon McElligott/ Minneapolis

74 I Gold

BOB MEHRMAN (WITH AID OF ELECTROLARYNX): What is a voice? A voice lets you sing "Happy Birthday," yell at the umpire at a baseball game or simply say: "I love you." The sound of a voice can stir up an angry mob of people or comfort a newborn baby. With a voice you can speak your mind, call for help or whisper in someone's ear. A voice can be a shoulder to lean on 1,000 miles away, or a companion from the radio along a lonely stretch of highway. A voice is something that is rhythm and melody, feeling and expression. A voice is something I don't have. And because I smoked cigarettes, got throat cancer and had my larynx removed, now I speak by holding this electro-larynx against my throat. My name is Bob Mehrman. Please understand the terrible dangers of cigarettes. Please listen to a man with no voice.

ANNCR: The Massachusetts Department of Public Health.

74 II

BOB MEHRMAN (WITH AID OF ELECTROLARYNX): A . . . B . . . C . . . D . . . E . . . F . . . G . . . I . . . J. . . . It's impossible for me to pronounce that missing letter. It's impossible for me to do a lot of things. My name is Bob Mehrman, and I don't have a voice anymore. I got throat cancer from smoking cigarettes, and my larynx was removed. I'd strongly recommend that you keep your larynx. It makes life so much easier. For example, people won't suddenly turn around in a restaurant when you talk. If you call someone on the phone, they won't cut you off because they think you're a machine. And if a little nine-year-old girl comes to your front door selling candy for a school project, she won't stare at you and ask if you are a robot. You know, it's too bad I can't pronounce that certain letter I talked about earlier. Because there are so many times I want to tell the cigarette industry to go to ell.

ANNCR: The Massachusetts Department of Public Health.

74 III

BOB MEHRMAN (FROM OLD RECORDINGS): This is Bob Mehrman. This is Bob Mehrman. This is Bob Mehrman.

BOB MEHRMAN (WITH AID OF ELECTROLARYNX): This is Bob Mehrman. I don't have that voice anymore. I don't have that career anymore. For 40 years, I was a television and radio announcer. Right up until the day they took out my larynx, because it had cancer from years of smoking. So never again will anyone hear me introduce a lovely ballad from Frank Sinatra. Or read the weather for a beautiful sunny afternoon. Or report the news from a distant land. Instead, you will hear my brand new voice, which comes out of this device called an electrolarynx, telling you how dangerous cigarette smoking can be. It can take away your life, your dignity, and your dreams. As a broadcast announcer my entire life, I always wanted to have an unmistakable voice. . . . It's sad how it finally came true.

ANNCR: The Massachusetts Department of Public Health.

75 Silver

ANNCR: Some children have a problem with their brain waves. They literally can't focus on one thing at a time. Their minds wander like that butterfly outside the window falling as fast as my baby sister when I pushed her down the stairs and knocked out her first tooth oh yeah, Thursday is my dentist appointment a block away from where I am now talking about the new school called A Chance To Grow that teaches children how to focus their thinking. If your child has poor grades, or has trouble concentrating, please call A Chance To Grow at 521-2266.

If your mind was wandering, that number was 521-2266.

GOLD, SILVER & BRONZE AWARDS

PUBLIC SERVICE/ POLITICAL TELEVISION: SINGLE

76 GOLD

ART DIRECTOR
Peter Favat
WRITER
Stu Cooperrider
AGENCY PRODUCER
Amy Feenan
PRODUCTION COMPANY
Tony Kaye Films
DIRECTOR
Tony Kaye
CLIENT
Massachusetts Department of Public Health
AGENCY
Houston Herstek Favat/ Boston

77 SILVER

ART DIRECTOR
David Angelo
WRITER
Glen Porter
AGENCY PRODUCER
Mary Ellen Duggan
PRODUCTION COMPANY
Tony Kaye Films
DIRECTOR
Tony Kaye
CLIENT
Partnership For A Drug-Free America
AGENCY
Cliff Freeman & Partners/ New York

78 BRONZE

ART DIRECTOR
Rob Dow
WRITER
Greg Harper
AGENCY PRODUCER
Romanca Mundrea
PRODUCTION COMPANY
Great Southern Films
DIRECTOR
Mat Humphrey
CLIENT
Transport Accident Commission
AGENCY
Grey Advertising/ Melbourne

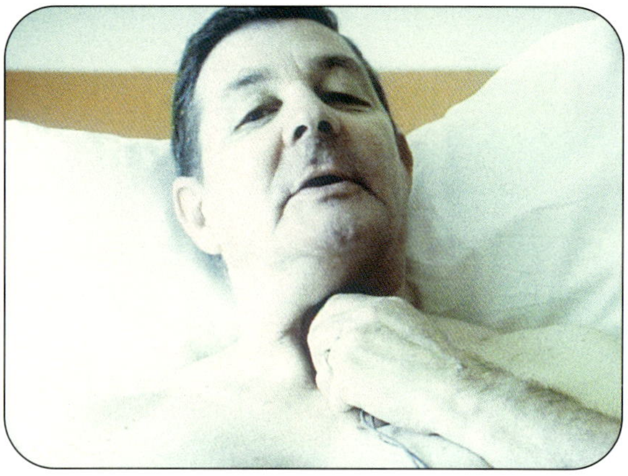

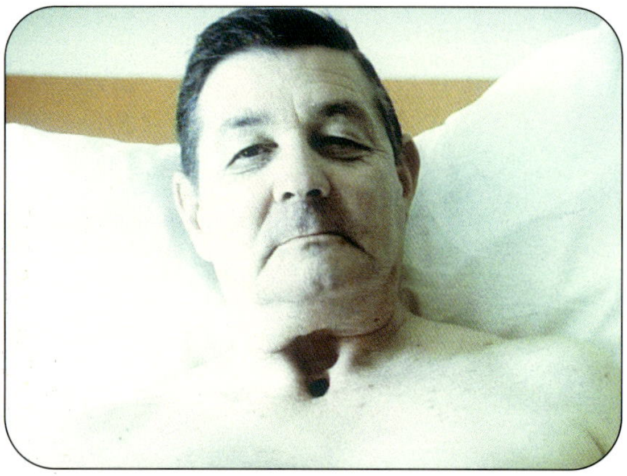

76 Gold

MAN: "Happy Birthday" with a buzzer.

MAN (SINGING WITH ELECTROLARYNX): *Happy birthday to you. Happy birthday to you. Happy birthday dear . . .*

SUPER: HAPPY BIRTHDAY TO THE TOBACCO INDUSTRY CELEBRATING 121 YEARS OF FINE TOBACCO PRODUCTS.

MAN: *Happy birthday to you.*

SUPER: IT'S TIME WE MADE SMOKING HISTORY.

SUPER: MASS. DEPARTMENT OF PUBLIC HEALTH.

77 Silver

LENNY: You know I just felt like real good, man. You know, I wasn't like racing, I wasn't speeding, you know. I was like mellow, and I mean I threw up the first time and everything, you know. And after I threw up, I said, "Wow, this (BEEP) is (BEEP), like, good." Yeah . . . let me do this hit.

You know? Okay . . . you know when, um, you used to go on a ride and you, you know, your adrenaline pumps. You know what I'm trying to say? That's the feeling, like that. . . .

And I had uh, gangrene on my foot, and they took my, almost took my foot off.

I'm you know, I consider myself pretty intelligent, I can do whatever I wanna do, man. I threw up man, my guts. And as I'm throwing up I'm like, damned boy, this is (BEEP) what I want. That's it, why can't people just do that. Maybe everybody should shoot heroin and like, just mellow out.

But I got these tracks man, all over my body. That puss was just coming out of the little hole here, like nothing. . . .

I used to do a lot, a lot more things you know. Like, I used to go to movies more. I used to like, go out to restaurants, and I used to go to Broadway shows. I like Broadway shows, they're nice, man.

By the time '97 rolls around, '96 at this time, right? Nineteen ninety-six, August 17th? 18th? Whatever it is. You can come here with your cameras . . . and I'll be a totally different person. I'll be successful. And I'll bet my life on it.

SUPER: HEROIN. WANT SOME?

SUPER: PARTNERSHIP FOR A DRUG-FREE AMERICA.

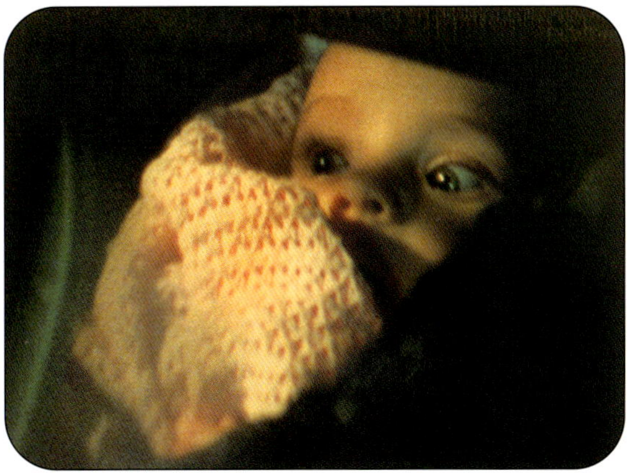

78 Bronze

ANNIE: It's the funniest thing I have ever seen, she had it all over her.

SANDY: Hey, there's Ian's car. Do you reckon they're going to Adam's party?

ANNIE: Oh, I hope so, Paul is a babe.

SANDY: Have they seen us?

ANNIE: Yeah, they're flashing their lights.

SANDY: Are they still behind us?

ANNIE: Yeah, they just ran a red light.

SANDY: Did they make it through?

ANNIE: No! Ah, suffer.

(SFX: CAR CRASHING)

IAN: Oh God, what have we done.

PAUL: Oh geez, they must have hit hard.

ANNIE: Get an ambulance.

(SFX: BABY CRYING)

PAUL: Oh, Jesus, are you okay? . . . She's dead.

ANNIE: What do you mean, what have we done?

PAUL: We've just killed somebody, that's what we've done.

(SFX: BABY CRYING MORE INSISTENTLY)

ANNIE: Oh no, the baby!

SUPER: IT'S IN YOUR HANDS, CONCENTRATE OR KILL.

SUPER: TRANSPORT ACCIDENT COMMISSION.

CONSUMER RADIO: SINGLE

79 GOLD
WRITER
Al Kelly
AGENCY PRODUCER
David Logan
CLIENT
Sega of America
AGENCY
Goodby Silverstein & Partners/San Francisco

80 SILVER
WRITER
Bob Kerstetter
AGENCY PRODUCER
David Logan
CLIENT
California Fluid Milk Processor Advisory Board
AGENCY
Goodby Silverstein & Partners/San Francisco

81 SILVER
WRITER
Al Kelly
AGENCY PRODUCER
David Logan
CLIENT
Sega of America
AGENCY
Goodby Silverstein & Partners/San Francisco

79 Gold

(SFX: DRILL, BEEPING OF LIFE-SUPPORT MACHINE)

DOC: Ever had brain surgery, Jim?

(SFX: "CRUNCH")

JIM: No . . . um, do I have to be awake?

DOC: Just try to relax, Jim . . . all right . . . we'll just snip this away . . .

(SFX: SNIPPING SOUND)

DOC: Say, Jim have you seen that new Sega Saturn?

JIM: Uh, yeah, the 3D graphics are cool.

DOC: You know, it sounds very impressive. Better than your home stereo in fact.

JIM: Oh, really?

DOC: See the Sega Saturn's 24-bit surround sound processor sends out this uh, sonic image, fooling your cerebral cortex . . . here . . .

(SFX: POKING SOUND)

JIM: Ooohhh . . .

DOC: . . . into thinking it's surrounded. This in turn activates the hypothalamus under here . . .

(SFX: "R-R-RIP")

JIM: Ouch!

DOC: . . . which in turn stimulates the pituitary behind here . . .

(SFX: POKING SOUND)

JIM: Ow! That hurts!

DOC: . . . sending hormones along your corpus collosum behind this gray thing. If I could just . . .

(SFX: GRUNTING, STRAINING)

JIM: Aaaaah! Okay! Okay! I believe you! Stop it!

DOC: . . . get around this reticular formation I could show you . . .

JIM: Aaaaaiiiieee!!!!! Stop it! Stop! Okay! You made your point! Aaaaahhh!

ANNCR: Sega Saturn. So real, it's kind of scary.

DOC: Okay. Jim, let's try this: bark like a dog.

JIM: I'm not gonna . . .

(SFX: "SQUISH")

JIM: Woof! Woof!

ANNCR 2: Sega Saturn!

80 Silver

MAN: I . . . I . . . I love you.

WOMAN: Awwww.

MAN: No, I mean . . . I . . . I mean, I don't . . . just . . .

WOMAN: What (GIGGLES), go ahead . . .

MAN: I just . . . don't think I'd be anything without you . . .

WOMAN: Aw . . . that's so nice . . .

MAN: I, uh, made these for you . . .

(SFX: BAKING PAN AND FOIL SOUNDS)

WOMAN: Aw . . . you didn't have to do this . . .

MAN: They're just brownies.

WOMAN: Ooh, and they're still warm too.

MAN: I was gonna get you something good.

WOMAN: Aww, don't be silly, could I have one?

MAN: (LAUGHS) Well, yeah sure . . . go ahead . . .

WOMAN (MOUTH FULL): You know . . . ?

MAN: What . . . you don't like brownies?

WOMAN: No . . . no . . . (SLIGHT GAG) miggkkk . . .

MAN: I'm sorry, I can't understand you.

WOMAN: Neet . . . d miggkk.

MAN: You need Mick?

WOMAN: Miccllggkk!

MAN: A guy named Mick! I can't believe this . . .

WOMAN: Pleeeeease miiigggggggllkk . . .

MAN: Yeah, yeah, okay you don't have to scream his name in ecstasy, I get the message. All right I got it, I'm gone.

WOMAN: No, umbhum, no, miiiiiigggllllkk!

MAN: Look, I gotta go, I'm sorry I'm gonna need my CD's back . . . and . . .

WOMAN: No, no, miiiggllk.

MAN: . . . and I'm sorry for this whole thing. . . .

WOMAN: No, miiiggglIkk . . .

MAN: No, it's Scott remember?

WOMAN: No . . . miigggkkkffff . . .

ANNCR: True love means never having to say, "Got Milk?"

81 Silver

(MUSIC: SOFT)

WOMAN: I'm a woman. I like flowers, and kittens, and things that smell pretty. Sometimes, I need a little something to make me feel fresh, and feminine again. Which is why I like to use Virtua Fighter.

(SFX: BURST OF LOUD VIRTUA FIGHTER SOUNDS)

WOMAN: On the new Sega Saturn.

(MUSIC: SOFT)

WOMAN: It gives me that just-dropped-a-tall-strong-man-on-my-knee-and-broke-his-spine feeling. And I like that. Of course, sometimes, I feel more romantic. That's when I reach for Panzer Dragoon.

(SFX: BURST OF LOUD PANZER DRAGOON SOUNDS)

WOMAN: It's loud, it's warlike, and I get to blast the living (BEEP) out of anything that moves.

LITTLE GIRL: Mommy? Am I turning into a woman?

WOMAN: Yes, you are. And I think it's time.

LITTLE GIRL: Time for what?

WOMAN: Time for Daytona USA.

(SFX: DAYTONA USA SOUNDS)

ANNCR: Sega Saturn. So real, it's kinda scary.

(MUSIC: PRETTY FLOURISH)

WOMAN: For that spring-fresh feeling.

ANNCR 2: Sega!

CONSUMER RADIO: CAMPAIGN

82 SILVER

ART DIRECTORS
Jeff Hilts
Dean Lee

WRITER
Hagan Ainsworth

PRODUCTION COMPANY
Wave Productions

CLIENT
Mum's Tattoo

AGENCY
The Unemployment Agency/Surrey, Canada

83 BRONZE

WRITER
Al Kelly

AGENCY PRODUCER
David Logan

CLIENT
Sega of America

AGENCY
Goodby Silverstein & Partners/San Francisco

82 Silver

SNAKE: This is Snake for Mum's Tattoo. Some (BEEP) people think there's health problems at tattoo parlors. Well just so you know, that's a crock of (BEEP). Anything our customers come near is brand (BEEP) new or sterile. Basically, we spend a (BEEP) load of time and a big pot of (BEEP) money making sure everyone's (BEEP) is as safe as (BEEP) possible.

ANNCR: At Mum's Tattoo, the only thing dirty is our language. Come see for yourself at 291 Pemberton in North Vancouver.

SNAKE: Check the place out, it's (BEEP) clean.

83 Bronze

(MUSIC: SOFT)

WOMAN: I'm a woman. I like flowers, and kittens, and things that smell pretty. Sometimes, I need a little something to make me feel fresh and feminine again. Which is why I like to use Virtua Fighter.

(SFX: BURST OF LOUD VIRTUA FIGHTER SOUNDS)

WOMAN: On the new Sega Saturn.

(MUSIC: SOFT)

WOMAN: It gives me that just-dropped-a-tall-strong-man-on-my-knee-and-broke-his-spine feeling. And I like that. Of course, sometimes, I feel more romantic. That's when I reach for Panzer Dragoon.

(SFX: BURST OF LOUD PANZER DRAGOON SOUNDS)

WOMAN: It's loud, it's warlike, and I get to blast the living (BEEP) out of anything that moves.

LITTLE GIRL: Mommy? Am I turning into a woman?

WOMAN: Yes, you are. And I think it's time.

LITTLE GIRL: Time for what?

WOMAN: Time for Daytona USA.

(SFX: DAYTONA USA SOUNDS)

ANNCR: Sega Saturn. So real, it's kinda scary.

(MUSIC: PRETTY FLOURISH)

WOMAN: For that spring-fresh feeling.

ANNCR 2: Sega!

GOLD, SILVER & BRONZE AWARDS

CONSUMER TELEVISION OVER :30 SINGLE

84 GOLD

ART DIRECTOR
Matt Vescovo
WRITERS
Steve Dildarian
Arthur Bijur
Cliff Freeman
AGENCY PRODUCER
Anne Kurtzman
PRODUCTION COMPANY
Propaganda Films
DIRECTOR
David Kellogg
CLIENT
Little Caesars Pizza
AGENCY
Cliff Freeman & Partners/ New York

85 GOLD

ART DIRECTOR
Sean Ehringer
WRITER
Harry Cocciolo
AGENCY PRODUCERS
Betsy Flynn
Cindy Epps
PRODUCTION COMPANY
Smillie Films
DIRECTOR
Kinka Usher
CLIENT
California Fluid Milk Processor Advisory Board
AGENCY
Goodby Silverstein & Partners/San Francisco

84 Gold

SUPER: SOMEWHERE IN THE GOBI DESERT.

(SFX: WHISTLE)

TRAINER: Up the stairs! Down the stairs!

MANAGER: Keep 'em steady! That's it!

(SFX: DOOR KNOCKING, DOOR BELLS)

MANAGER: Bell, knocker, hand! Bell, knocker, hand!

KID: Pizza! Pizza!

TRAINER: Pizza! Pizza!

KID: Pizza! Pizza!

TRAINER: Good, I like that! And again!

(SFX: MECHANICAL DOG BARKING)

TRAINER: Go, go, go!

ANNCR: Little Caesars introduces . . . delivery!

85 Gold

(MUSIC: SUSPENSEFUL, BUILDING)
(SFX: JINGLING OF STORE BELL)
(SFX: DOOR SLAM, FOOTSTEPS)
(SFX: BOX SLIDING ON SHELF, FOOTSTEPS, BOX BEING SET ON COUNTER)
WOMAN: Trix? . . .
(SFX: DOOR SLAMMING SHUT)
WOMAN: . . . Trix are for kids. Ha, ha, ha, ha, ha, ha. . . .
(SFX: CASH REGISTER "CHA-CHING")
(SFX: CHANGE JINGLING, DOOR OPENING AND CLOSING)
(SFX: YAPPING DOG, DOOR OPENING, CLINKING OF LOCKS, BOXES HITTING FLOOR)
GUY: Finally, after all these years of . . .
(SFX: CEREAL HITTING BOWL)
GUY: "Trix are for kids" . . .
SUPER: SPONSORED BY THE CALIFORNIA MILK PROCESSOR BOARD.
GUY: Well . . .
(SFX: ZIPPING SOUND)
GUY: . . . today . . .
GUY/TRIX RABBIT: . . . they're for . . . rabbits!!! (CACKLING LAUGHTER).
(SFX: SMALL SPLASH OF MILK)
TRIX RABBIT: Uuuuuhhh? Uuuuuuuuuuuhh. . . .
(SFX: MILK DRIPPING)
SUPER: GOT MILK?

GOLD, SILVER & BRONZE AWARDS

CONSUMER TELEVISION
OVER :30 SINGLE

86 SILVER
ART DIRECTOR
Adam Glickman
WRITER
Craig Feigen
AGENCY PRODUCER
Greg Popp
PRODUCTION COMPANY
Propaganda Films
DIRECTOR
Anthony Hoffman
CLIENT
Anheuser-Busch/
Budweiser
AGENCY
DDB Needham/Chicago

87 BRONZE
ART DIRECTOR
Don Schneider
WRITER
Michael Patti
AGENCY PRODUCERS
Regina Ebel
Maria Amato
PRODUCTION COMPANY
Pytka
DIRECTOR
Joe Pytka
CLIENT
Pepsi Cola Company
AGENCY
BBDO/New York

88 BRONZE
ART DIRECTOR
Don Schneider
WRITER
Michael Patti
AGENCY PRODUCERS
Regina Ebel
Maria Amato
PRODUCTION COMPANY
Pytka
DIRECTOR
Joe Pytka
CLIENT
Pepsi Cola Company
AGENCY
BBDO/New York

86 Silver

(SFX: CLYDESDALES RUNNING)

(SFX: HORSE KICKING EXTRA POINT)

COWBOY 1: They always do that?

COWBOY 2: Naw! They usually go for two.

SUPER: BUDWEISER. KING OF BEERS.

87 Bronze

(SFX: MOURNFUL SONG, STRANGE SOUNDS IN BACKGROUND)
(SFX: SINGING)
MAN: Yes! Yes! Aaah, wooah!
SUPER: NOTHING ELSE IS A PEPSI.
(SFX: DOLLAR BILL REJECTED BY MACHINE)

88 Bronze

WAITRESS: Here we go.
COCA-COLA DRIVER: Thanks, Darlene.
PEPSI DRIVER: It's cold, ooh!
WAITRESS: What can I getcha?
PEPSI DRIVER: Aaah, blueberry pie and a Pepsi.
(SFX: JUKEBOX STARTS PLAYING)
WAITRESS: You got it.
PEPSI DRIVER: Thanks . . . good song.
COCA-COLA DRIVER: Great song.
PEPSI DRIVER: Working late on the holidays.
COCA-COLA DRIVER: Yeah, it's hard on the kids.
PEPSI DRIVER: Naaah, naaah, naaah.
(SFX: FIGHTING NOISES)
SUPER: NOTHING ELSE IS A PEPSI.

GOLD, SILVER & BRONZE AWARDS

CONSUMER TELEVISION OVER :30 CAMPAIGN

89 GOLD

ART DIRECTORS
David Angelo
John Leu

WRITERS
Tina Hall
Harold Einstein
Cliff Freeman

AGENCY PRODUCER
Mary Ellen Duggan

PRODUCTION COMPANY
Tony Kaye Films

DIRECTOR
Tony Kaye

CLIENT
Prodigy

AGENCY
Cliff Freeman & Partners/ New York

89 I Gold

(SFX: NOISY STOCK EXCHANGE)

(SFX: WOMAN SINGING OPERA)

ANNCR: To all the people wandering around on the Internet who have no idea how to find what they want . . .

(SFX: BUS DOORS OPENING)

BUS DRIVER: You must be looking for a new rod, right?

FLY FISHERMAN 1: Yeah.

ANNCR: Prodigy introduces interest groups.

EVERYONE ON BUS: Hi!

FLY FISHERMAN 2: Ever since I saw the movie "A River Runs Through It," with Brad Pitt, I said, "You've got to go fishing."

So anyway, who cuts your hair? Never mind.

FISHERMAN 3: Bull frogs also eat these . . . ordinary men can't stand it when that happens.

TEACHER/ALL: Ten o'clock, two o'clock.

WOMAN: Harold, I know you're in there . . . Harold!

TEACHER/ALL: Ten o'clock, two o'clock.

WOMAN: He is in there.

ANNCR: Fly fishing . . . just one of the many interest groups you'll find on the new Prodigy.

SUPER: PRODIGY.

SUPER: WHATEVER YOU'RE INTO.

89 II

(SFX: BANJO BEING SMASHED)

WOMAN 1: I . . . can't . . . play . . . this . . . thing!

(MUSIC: SEVENTIES-STYLE)

(SFX: BUS DOORS OPENING)

BARRY WHITE: Having problems, baby?

WOMAN 1: Hey?

BARRY WHITE: Beating up on your banjo?

(MUSIC: VARIOUS BANJO TUNES)

BARRY WHITE: Welcome aboard.

JAZZ MAN: Hey bro, you do weddings?

(MUSIC: "WEDDING MARCH" ON SITAR)

WOMAN 2 (SCREAMING): Who sang "Kung Foo Fighting"?

BARRY WHITE (THROUGH MICROPHONE): The answer . . . is Karl Douglas.

(MUSIC: VIOLIN)

HEADBANGER: Mosh pit!

(MUSIC: REALLY LOUD)

BARRY WHITE (THROUGH MICROPHONE): Next stop . . . Barry's world.

(MUSIC: DISCO)

GOSPEL SINGER: *Yeah . . . yeah, yeah, oh yeah, yeah . . .*

ANNCR: Music . . . just one of the many interest groups you'll find on the new Prodigy.

SUPER: PRODIGY.

SUPER: WHATEVER YOU'RE INTO.

89 III

(SFX: BUS DOOR OPENING)

PARROT: Welcome aboard.

LITTLE GIRL 1/ALL: Hi!

LITTLE GIRL 2: Wanna race?

LITTLE GIRL 1: Okay.

WOMAN 1: Must be all these animals on the bus. You know, I've been allergic to animals all my life.

CHINESE MAN: Ah, yes.

PSYCHIATRIST: He's clinically depressed.

WOMAN 2: No. He's fat.

CAT: Meow.

WOMAN 1: (SNEEZES) Sorry. Can I have this?

CHINESE MAN: Yes.

BOY (SCREAMING): Where's my tarantula?!

LITTLE GIRL 3: Ahhhh!!

INDIAN BOY IN HIS OWN LANGUAGE (SUBTITLED): How do you housebreak an elephant?

ANNCR: Pets . . . just one of the many interest groups you'll find on the new Prodigy.

SUPER: PRODIGY.

SUPER: WHATEVER YOU'RE INTO.

GOLD, SILVER & BRONZE AWARDS

CONSUMER TELEVISION OVER :30 CAMPAIGN

90 SILVER

ART DIRECTORS
Don Schneider
David Goodnight

WRITERS
Michael Patti
Richard Pels

AGENCY PRODUCERS
Regina Ebel
Maria Amato

PRODUCTION COMPANY
Pytka

DIRECTOR
Joe Pytka

CLIENT
Pepsi Cola Company

AGENCY
BBDO/New York

CONSUMER TELEVISION :30 SINGLE

91 GOLD

ART DIRECTOR
Rachel Nelson

WRITER
Janet Champ

AGENCY PRODUCER
Jennifer Smieja

PRODUCTION COMPANY
Mars Media

DIRECTOR
Samuel Bayer

CLIENT
Nike

AGENCY
Wieden & Kennedy/
Portland

90 Silver

GRANDDAUGHTER: Grandpa, do you remember your first Pepsi?

GRANDFATHER: My first Pepsi was 1926 . . . Homer's General Store. . . . Pepsi number two, cheap seats, Wrigley Field. . . . Pepsi 812, the stock market crashed. . . . Pepsi number 1,844, Dad bought the Desoto.

GRANDDAUGHTER: What's a Desoto?

GRANDFATHER: Pepsi number 3,922 — Spam was invented. . . . I was drinking Pepsi number 4,203 when I met your grandma. . . . 5,000, my dog Bruno got skunked! 14,030, your dad repeated third grade. . . . Astronauts walked on the moon—17,101. 20,990 was last Tuesday. . . . And this is Pepsi 21,004, Cathy.

GRANDDAUGHTER: Kelly.

GRANDFATHER: Kelly?

GRANDDAUGHTER: Kelly.

GRANDFATHER: Hmm, I knew that. I think I knew that.

SUPER: NOTHING ELSE IS A PEPSI.

91 Gold

VARIOUS GIRLS (SPEAKING INDIVIDUALLY):

If you let me play.

If you let me play sports.

I will like . . . myself more.

I will have more self-confidence.

If you let . . . me play sports.

If you let me play.

If you let me play!

I'll be 60 percent less likely to get breast cancer.

I will suffer less depression.

If you let me play sports.

I'll be more likely . . . to leave a man who beats me.

I'll be less likely . . . to get pregnant before I want to.

I will learn . . .

I will learn what it means to be strong.

To be strong.

If you let me play . . .

. . . play sports.

If you let me play sports.

SUPER: JUST DO IT.

SUPER: (NIKE LOGO).

92 SILVER

ART DIRECTOR
Chris Hooper
WRITER
Chuck McBride
AGENCY PRODUCER
Ben Latimer
PRODUCTION COMPANY
Propaganda Films
DIRECTOR
Michael Bay
CLIENT
American Isuzu Motors
AGENCY
Goodby Silverstein & Partners/San Francisco

93 BRONZE

ART DIRECTORS
Matt Vescovo
Greg Bell
WRITERS
Tina Hall
Harold Einstein
Steve Dildarian
AGENCY PRODUCER
Mary Ellen Duggan
PRODUCTION COMPANY
Harmony Pictures
DIRECTOR
Charles Wittenmeier
CLIENT
Little Caesars Pizza
AGENCY
Cliff Freeman & Partners/New York

92 Silver

(SFX: TOY STORE SOUNDS)

GUY: Hmmm . . .

(SFX: "TEENIE WEENIE POTTY" BEING LIFTED OFF SHELF, LID OPENING)

GUY: We're outta here.

(SFX: SHOPPING CART NOISES)

KID: Oooohhhh!

GUY: No, please keep your hands in the cart.

KID: Rrrrrrrrrrr.

GUY: We'll come back for that later. . . . That one needs batteries.

(SFX: JINGLING)

GUY: You're gonna get daddy in trouble. . . . 'Scuse me. . . . No, that one definitely has too many parts.

(SFX: REMOTE CONTROL CAR)

GUY: We gotta go.

KID: Oooooooohhhhh!!!

(MUSIC: FAIRY TALE-LIKE, WHIMSICAL)

GUY: Ooohh.

SUPER: THE NEW RODEO. GROW UP. NOT OLD.

SUPER: ISUZU. PRACTICALLY AMAZING.

93 Bronze

(MUSIC: UPBEAT)

MAN: My wallet! All right!

WOMAN: Tom, I've reconsidered! I will marry you!

MAN: Okay! . . . Buddy! You're alive! . . . What a great deal!

MAN (OFF CAMERA): That's even better!

MAN: I've got a brother?!

ANNCR: Just when you thought things couldn't get any better, now get two pizzas with free Crazy Bread for $7.98. Or for $2.00 more, two Little Caesars Pleasers with more cheese and toppings and free Crazy Bread.

LITTLE CAESAR: Pizza! Pizza!

GOLD, SILVER & BRONZE AWARDS

CONSUMER TELEVISION
:30 CAMPAIGN

94 GOLD

ART DIRECTOR
Andrew Christou
WRITER
Eric Silver
AGENCY PRODUCER
Kevin Diller
PRODUCTION COMPANY
NFL Films
DIRECTOR
Greg Kohs
CLIENT
Nike
AGENCY
Wieden & Kennedy/
Portland

94 I Gold

SUPER: NIKE PRESENTS THIS WEEK IN PEE WEE FOOTBALL.

ANNCR: Needing a first down, to keep their playoff hopes alive, the Tigers look to Johnny "the Flash" Parnell. Like any great back, number seven stares into the eyes of his pursuers and something of himself is revealed. Number seven is a number with wings.

But on the game's pivotal drive Parnell was dealt a season's worth of punishment in a single play.

SUPER: (NIKE LOGO).

94 II

SUPER: NIKE PRESENTS THIS WEEK IN PEE WEE FOOTBALL.

ANNCR: On Sunday, return specialist Larry Holby further enhanced his reputation as the ultimate escape artist. Defying all odds to advance the football, number 84 writes a script that had more drama than a Hollywood thriller, as the Wildcats go on to win their first division title.

SUPER: (NIKE LOGO).

94 III

SUPER: NIKE PRESENTS THIS WEEK IN PEE WEE FOOTBALL.

ANNCR: It was crunch time in Elgin. As Cougars quarterback, Ned Barnes, sought divine guidance, as he launched the desperation "Hail Mary."

Reaching into his pocket full of miracles number twelve tried to pull off one more magnificent moment, but it was not to be, as the Indians escape with the win.

SUPER: (NIKE LOGO).

GOLD, SILVER & BRONZE AWARDS

CONSUMER TELEVISION :30 CAMPAIGN

95 SILVER

ART DIRECTOR
Andrew Christou

WRITER
Eric Silver

AGENCY PRODUCER
Kevin Diller

PRODUCTION COMPANY
NFL Films

DIRECTOR
Greg Kohs

CLIENT
Nike

AGENCY
Wieden & Kennedy/
Portland

96 BRONZE

ART DIRECTOR
Jerry Gentile

WRITER
Scott Vincent

AGENCY PRODUCER
Michelle Burke

PRODUCTION COMPANY
Johns + Gorman Films

DIRECTOR
Jeff Gorman

CLIENT
Sunkist California Pistachios

AGENCY
TBWA Chiat/Day, Venice, CA

95 Silver

SUPER: NIKE PRESENTS THIS WEEK IN PEE WEE FOOTBALL.

COACH 1: Listen up. Power football, power football, okay? Here we go.

ANNCR: The man behind the men is the head coach.

COACH 2: We're asleep out there.

COACH 3: Richard, you didn't block nobody.

ANNCR: In a game of sobering truths . . .

COACH 3: You spend too much time sucking on your mouth-piece.

ANNCR: . . . it is he who provides eternal hope.

(SFX: COACHES CHEERING)

COACH 2: Just because they're from Reno, that doesn't mean anything. We're from Sparks, guys. Let's go out, and let's win one for Sparks, huh?

SUPER: (NIKE LOGO).

96 Bronze

SUPER: ROMAYNE RIDDELL. TRANCE CHANNELER.

ROMAYNE: Well, I started trance channeling about six years ago. It's almost like my body was suddenly filled with love. (IN HIGH-PITCHED VOICE) Hello Peter, how are you today?

PETER: Very good, Neya. How are you?

ROMAYNE: Very fine, thank you. So, what is it that you wanted to know?

SUPER: EVERYBODY KNOWS THE BEST NUTS COME FROM CALIFORNIA.

PETER: Where are you from?

ROMAYNE: I'm from Jupiter.

ANNCR: Sunkist California Pistachios. Now that's a nut.

SUPER: CALIFORNIA PISTACHIOS.

GOLD, SILVER & BRONZE AWARDS

CONSUMER TELEVISION :20 AND UNDER: CAMPAIGN

97 GOLD

ART DIRECTORS
Jeff Williams
Darryl McDonald

WRITER
Hank Perlman

AGENCY PRODUCER
Colleen Wellman

PRODUCTION COMPANY
@radical.media

DIRECTORS
Bryan Buckley
Frank Todaro

CLIENT
ESPN/National Hockey League

AGENCY
Wieden & Kennedy/ Portland

97 I Gold

JEFF BEUKEBOOM: Brakes are cut!

SUPER: ADAM GRAVES. NEW YORK RANGERS.

ADAM GRAVES: Okay, I want you to go to the airport, and I want you to pick up Neely, Bourke, and Oates.

CAB DRIVER: Emilio, Amborlica . . .

SUPER: BOSTON BRUINS VS. NEW YORK RANGERS. FRIDAY 7:30 PM ET.

ADAM GRAVES: No, no, no, no: Neely, Bourke, and Oates.

CAB DRIVER: Neely, Bourke, and Oates.

SUPER: ESPN.

97 II

ALEKSEI KOVALEV: How do you tell a male penguin from a female penguin? . . .

SUPER: ALEKSEI KOVALEV. NEW YORK RANGERS.

ALEKSEI: You can't.

(SFX: CROWD LAUGHING AND CLAPPING)

ALEKSEI: Thank you, thank you very much. Thank you . . . thank you. You're beautiful really. I am gonna be in Vegas on the 15th.

SUPER: NEW YORK RANGERS VS. PITTSBURGH PENGUINS. TUESDAY 7:30 PM ET.

(SFX: CROWD NOISES FADING)

SUPER: ESPN.

97 III

(SFX: HOCKEY PUCKS BEING HIT)

(MUSIC: "ROCKY" THEME SONG)

SUPER: CHICAGO BLACKHAWKS VS. PHILADELPHIA FLYERS.

SUPER: ESPN. TONIGHT 8:00 PM ET.

GOLD, SILVER & BRONZE AWARDS

CONSUMER TELEVISION :20 AND UNDER: CAMPAIGN

98 SILVER

ART DIRECTORS
Greg Wells
Carl Warner

WRITER
David Parson

AGENCY PRODUCER
Stan Hart

PRODUCTION COMPANY
Teleworks

DIRECTOR
Carl Warner

CLIENT
American Airlines

AGENCY
DDB Needham Worldwide Dallas Group

CONSUMER TELEVISION VARYING LENGTHS CAMPAIGN

99 GOLD

ART DIRECTORS
Sean Ehringer
Tom Routson

WRITERS
Harry Cocciolo
Bob Kerstetter

AGENCY PRODUCERS
Cindy Epps
Betsy Flynn

PRODUCTION COMPANY
Smillie Films

DIRECTOR
Kinka Usher

CLIENT
California Fluid Milk Processor Advisory Board

AGENCY
Goodby Silverstein & Partners/San Francisco

98 Silver

MAN: Six times a day, an American Airlines plane like this flies between Heathrow and JFK. Although in fact, if it was this big, you could just get on the back, walk down the front and hop off the other end.

SUPER: AMERICAN AIRLINES. SIX DAILY RETURN FLIGHTS BETWEEN HEATHROW AND NEW YORK'S JFK.

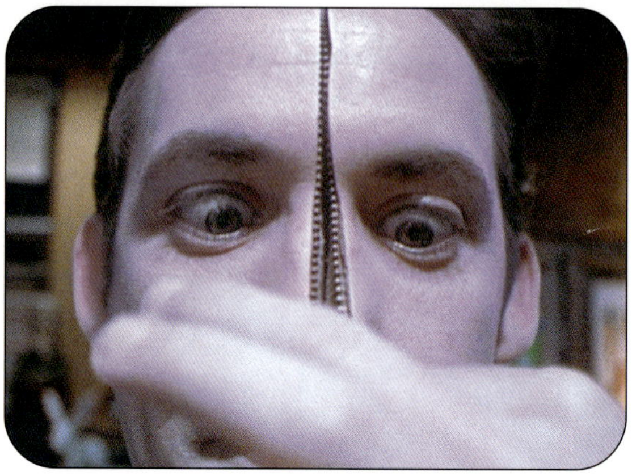

99 I Gold

(MUSIC: SUSPENSEFUL, BUILDING)

(SFX: JINGLING OF STORE BELL)

(SFX: DOOR SLAM, FOOTSTEPS)

(SFX: BOX SLIDING ON SHELF, FOOTSTEPS, BOX BEING SET ON COUNTER)

WOMAN: Trix? . . .

(SFX: DOOR SLAMMING SHUT)

WOMAN: . . . Trix are for kids. Ha, ha, ha, ha, ha, ha. . . .

(SFX: CASH REGISTER "CHA-CHING")

(SFX: CHANGE JINGLING, DOOR OPENING AND CLOSING)

(SFX: YAPPING DOG, DOOR OPENING, CLINKING OF LOCKS, BOXES HITTING FLOOR)

GUY: Finally, after all these years of . . .

(SFX: CEREAL HITTING BOWL)

GUY: "Trix are for kids" . . .

SUPER: SPONSORED BY THE CALIFORNIA MILK PROCESSOR BOARD.

GUY: Well . . .

(SFX: ZIPPING SOUND)

GUY: . . . today . . .

GUY/TRIX RABBIT: . . . they're for . . . rabbits!!! (CACKLING LAUGHTER).

(SFX: SMALL SPLASH OF MILK)

TRIX RABBIT: Uuuuuhhh? Uuuuuuuuuuuhh. . . .

(SFX: MILK DRIPPING)

SUPER: GOT MILK?

99 II

(SFX: SOOTHING MUSIC, HOSPITAL SOUNDS)

DAD: Hey! Cookies! . . . So you know I think our neighbor might like one.

GUY IN CAST: Hmmmmph?

DAD: Uh-huh, well . . .

(SFX: BREATHING)

GIRL: Here you go.

GUY IN CAST: Mmmmm . . . mmmm . . . mmmmm . . . thank you.

(SFX: CHOMPING, CRUNCHING.)

GUY IN CAST: Mmm . . . hmmmm . . . mmm . . .

(SFX: CHOKING SOUNDS)

(SFX: MILK POURING)

DAD: Terrific!

GUY IN CAST (MUFFLED): Ummmmmmm . . . 'scuse me . . . 'scuse me . . . people . . .

SUPER: CALIFORNIA FLUID MILK PROCESSOR ADVISORY BOARD.

(SFX: BED SQUEAKING)

(SFX: "GULP")

GUY IN CAST: Aaaaaagh!

SUPER: GOT MILK?

99 III

DAUGHTER (VOICE IMAGINED): Daddy, who drank all the milk?

(SFX: ECHOING SOUNDS OF COURTROOM, PEOPLE, JUDGE'S GAVEL)

JUDGE: Young lady, do you see the man in this courtroom?

DAUGHTER: That's him! He did it! My daddy!

(SFX: MURMURING IN COURTROOM)

JUDGE: Guilty!

MOTHER: How could you?

(SFX: SLAM OF GAVEL)

MOTHER: Guilty.

SON: Guilty!

DAUGHTER: Guilty!

(SFX: PRISON DOOR LOCKING)

DAD: Hhhmmmmm . . .

(SFX: "GULP")

SUPER: GOT MILK?

GOLD, SILVER & BRONZE AWARDS

CONSUMER TELEVISION VARYING LENGTHS CAMPAIGN

100 SILVER

ART DIRECTORS
Matt Vescovo
Greg Bell
David Angelo

WRITERS
Steve Dildarian
Arthur Bijur
Cliff Freeman
Tina Hall
Harold Einstein

AGENCY PRODUCERS
Mary Ellen Duggan
Anne Kurtzman

PRODUCTION COMPANIES
Propaganda Films
Johns + Gorman Films
Harmony Pictures

DIRECTORS
David Kellogg
Jeff Gorman
Charles Wittenmeier

CLIENT
Little Caesars Pizza

AGENCY
Cliff Freeman & Partners/ New York

101 BRONZE

ART DIRECTORS
Kim Ferraro
Jesse Peretz
Clay Tarver

WRITERS
Kristofor Brown
Mike Judge
Donal Logue

PRODUCTION COMPANIES
MTV On-Air Promos
X-Ray Productions

DIRECTORS
Kim Ferraro
Jesse Peretz
Clay Tarver

CLIENT
MTV

AGENCY
MTV/New York

100 Silver

SUPER: SOMEWHERE IN THE GOBI DESERT.

(SFX: WHISTLE)

TRAINER: Up the stairs! Down the stairs!

MANAGER: Keep 'em steady! That's it!

(SFX: DOOR KNOCKING, DOOR BELLS)

MANAGER: Bell, knocker, hand! Bell, knocker, hand!

KID: Pizza! Pizza!

TRAINER: Pizza! Pizza!

KID: Pizza! Pizza!

TRAINER: Good, I like that! And again!

(SFX: MECHANICAL DOG BARKING)

TRAINER: Go, go, go!

ANNCR: Little Caesars introduces . . . delivery!

101 Bronze

BUTT-HEAD: So, uh, how's it goin'? (LAUGHS)

BEAVIS: It's goin' pretty good, ya know, I'm just watchin' this chick . . . (LAUGHS)

BUTT-HEAD: I'm talkin' to the chick, Beavis. (LAUGHS) Are you like, a actress? (LAUGHS).

ACTRESS: Yes.

BEAVIS: (LAUGHS) Could you act like you're taking off your clothes? (LAUGHS) That would rule (LAUGHS).

SUPER: MTV MUSIC TELEVSION.

GOLD, SILVER & BRONZE AWARDS

CONSUMER TELEVISION VARYING LENGTHS CAMPAIGN

102 BRONZE

ART DIRECTOR
Rick McQuiston

WRITER
Hank Perlman

AGENCY PRODUCER
Dan Duffy

PRODUCTION COMPANY
@radical.media

DIRECTORS
Bryan Buckley
Frank Todaro

CLIENT
ESPN

AGENCY
Wieden & Kennedy/ Portland

102 Bronze

(MUSIC: PIANO)

SUPER: SPORTSCENTER LOBBY. 12:06 AM, SEPTEMBER 14, 1995.

GRANT HILL: Hey, Dan, what's wrong?

DAN PATRICK: Hey, Grant. Uh, bad show. Hair looked bad, teleprompter went down, made some mistakes on some highlights.

GRANT: I've got something that'll cheer you up.

(MUSIC: "CHARGE")

DAN: Thanks . . . thanks, Grant. Appreciate that.

GRANT: No problem, man.

SUPER: THIS IS SPORTSCENTER.

SUPER: ESPN.

CONSUMER TELEVISION UNDER $50,000 BUDGET

103 GOLD

ART DIRECTOR
Jason Gaboriau

WRITER
Tom Miller

AGENCY PRODUCER
Barbara Callihan

PRODUCTION COMPANY
Reel Diehl

CLIENT
Crain's New York Business

AGENCY
Goldsmith/Jeffrey, New York

103 Gold

ANNCR: In the foot hills of Pennsylvania, in the Amish town of Minst, the people lead a carefree life. They don't worry about hostile takeovers. They aren't concerned with being ambushed by competitors. Or blindsided by unexpected information. It is a town of joy, friendliness and boundless love. And when you move there . . . you can cancel your subscription to *Crain's*.

SUPER: NEW YORK'S ONLY BUSINESS NEWSPAPER.

GOLD, SILVER & BRONZE AWARDS

CONSUMER TELEVISION UNDER $50,000 BUDGET

104 SILVER

ART DIRECTOR
Tom Notman
WRITER
Alistair Wood
ILLUSTRATOR
Mark Thomas
AGENCY PRODUCER
Charles Crisp
PRODUCTION COMPANY
Hibbert Ralph Animation
DIRECTOR
Jerry Hibbert
CLIENT
Whitbread Beer Company
AGENCY
Lowe Howard-Spink/ London

105 BRONZE

ART DIRECTOR
Tom Notman
WRITER
Alistair Wood
ILLUSTRATOR
Mark Thomas
AGENCY PRODUCER
Charles Crisp
PRODUCTION COMPANY
Hibbert Ralph Animation
DIRECTOR
Jerry Hibbert
CLIENT
Whitbread Beer Company
AGENCY
Lowe Howard-Spink/ London

104 Silver

SUPER: MR. FLOWERS' GUIDE TO TREES.

MR. FLOWERS: Ah, Derek, consider this mighty oak. What poets and artists it must have inspired. A tree like this might easily have hidden the young Charles II during the Civil War. However, now is not the time for sentimentality.

(SFX: CHAINSAW CUTTING INTO WOOD)

SUPER: ONE TREE LATER.

MR. FLOWERS: There . . . a perfect drinking surface. Where better to enjoy a can of Flowers Original, eh Derek?

SUPER: DAMNED FINE ALE.

105 Bronze

SUPER: MR. FLOWERS' GUIDE TO FOSSILS.

MR. FLOWERS: The fossil-hunter's hammer is like a torch, Derek, illuminating the past.

(SFX: DOG WHIMPERING)

MR. FLOWERS: What in the name of—it's old Patch. He's been worrying sheep and lost his footing. Derek, drop your trousers.

DEREK: Hold on, Patch, hold on . . .

(SFX: COINS FALLING OUT OF POCKET)

MR. FLOWERS: Hell's bells—we're losing valuable drinking money.

SUPER: QUICK THINKING AVERTS A CRISIS. . .

MR. FLOWERS: Fetch, Patch! . . . Just enough left for two pints of Flowers Original.

DEREK: Do you think he'll be all right?

MR. FLOWERS: Yes. Luckily that pile of old sheep broke his fall.

SUPER: DAMNED FINE ALE.

106 Gold

BOY: Hey, Dumbo—na-na-na . . .

(MUSIC: "YANKEE DOODLE DANDY")

(SFX: "WHACKING" OF ELEPHANT'S TRUNK HITTING BOY, NOW GROWN)

SUPER: THINK TWICE ABOUT WHAT YOU DO WITH YOUR LAST ROLO.

107 Gold

(MUSIC: A LOVE SONG)

SUPER: THINK TWICE ABOUT WHAT YOU DO WITH YOUR LAST ROLO.

GOLD, SILVER & BRONZE AWARDS

INTERNATIONAL FOREIGN LANGUAGE COMMERCIAL: TELEVISION

106 GOLD

ART DIRECTORS
Marcel Frensch
Jan Pieter Nieuwerkerk
Diederik Koopal

WRITERS
Marcel Frensch
Jan Pieter Nieuwerkerk
Diederik Koopal

AGENCY PRODUCER
Cariola Schouten

PRODUCTION COMPANY
Czar

DIRECTOR
Rogier van der Ploeg

CLIENT
Nestle Nederland/Rolo

AGENCY
Ammirati Puris Lintas/
Amsterdam

INTERNATIONAL FOREIGN LANGUAGE COMMERCIAL: CINEMA

107 GOLD

ART DIRECTORS
Rob van der Vijfeijken
Diederik Koopal

WRITERS
Diederik Koopal
Rob van der Vijfeijken

AGENCY PRODUCER
Cariola Schouten

PRODUCTION COMPANY
Czar

DIRECTOR
Rogier van der Ploeg

CLIENT
Nestle Nederland/Rolo

AGENCY
Ammirati Puris Lintas/
Amsterdam

GOLD, SILVER & BRONZE AWARDS

INTERACTIVE: WEB SITE

108 GOLD

CREATIVE TEAM
Tim Price
Martin Lauber
Sam Osselaer
Tracy Cohen
Pieter van Praag
Chris Lisick

AGENCY PRODUCERS
Jim Bogner
Todd Moritz

PRODUCTION COMPANIES
R/GA Interactive
Organic On-Line
Obsolete

R/GA CREATIVE/ PRODUCTION TEAM:
Jakob Trollbeck
Brian Loube
Lesli Horowitz

CLIENT
Levi Strauss & Company

AGENCY
Foote Cone & Belding/ True North Technologies, San Francisco

COLLEGE COMPETITION ASSIGNMENT: THE INTERNET

109 GOLD

ART DIRECTORS
Lisa Brink
Faria Raji

WRITERS
Lisa Brink
Faria Raji

COLLEGE
Art Center College of Design/Pasadena

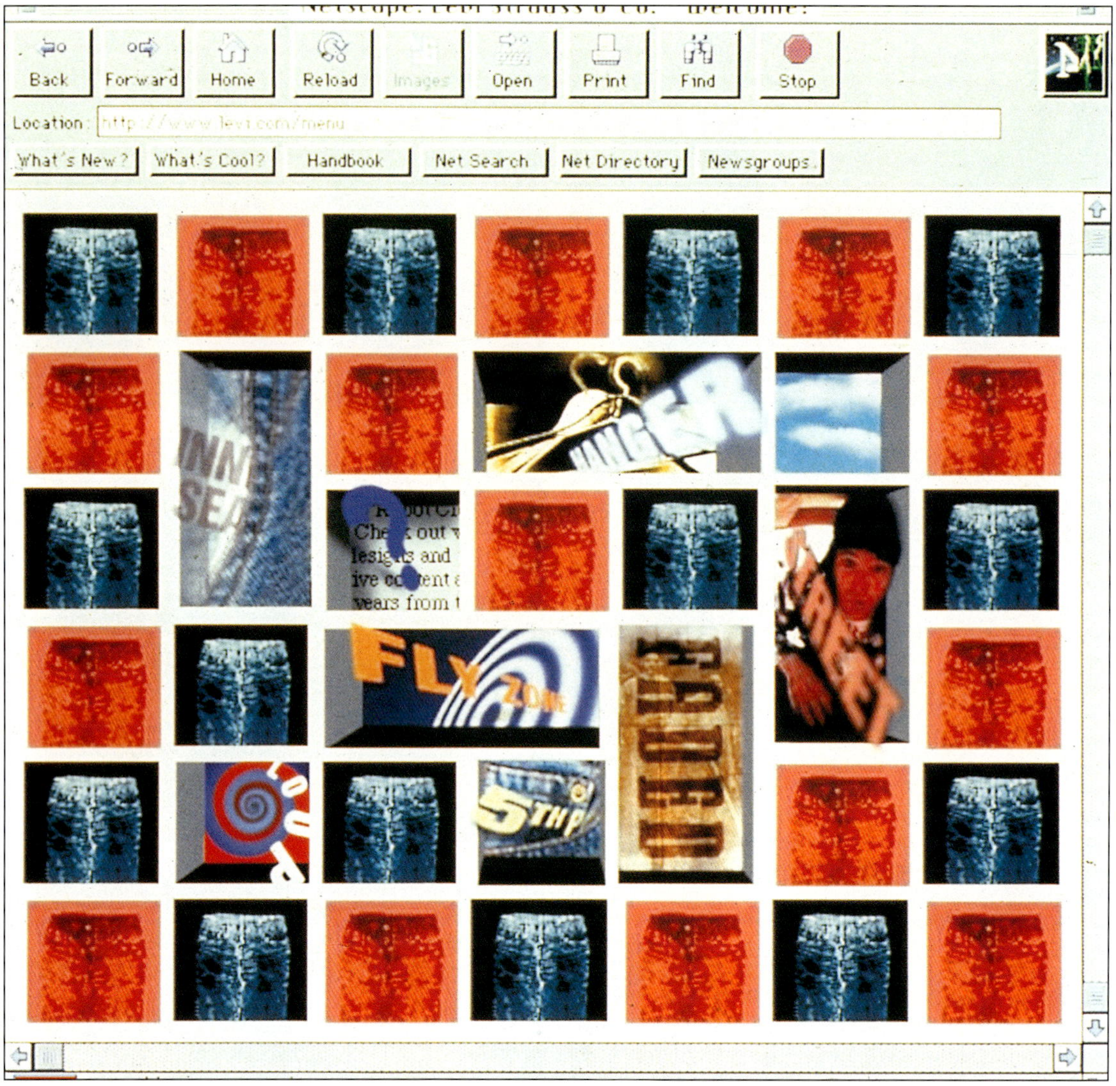

108 Gold http://www.levi.com

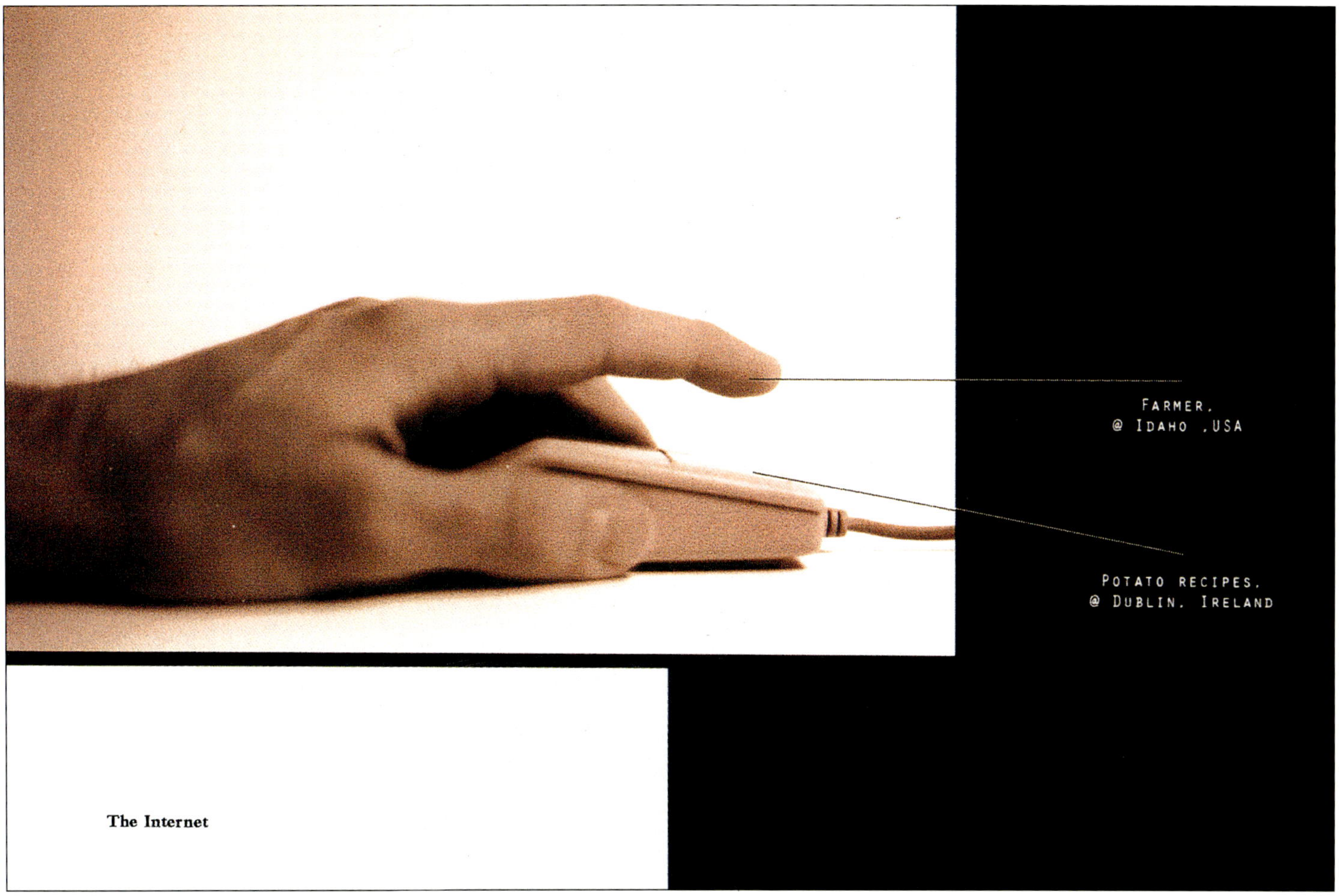
Farmer,
@ Idaho ,USA
Potato recipes,
@ Dublin, Ireland
The Internet
109 Gold

GOLD, SILVER & BRONZE AWARDS

COLLEGE COMPETITION
ASSIGNMENT:
THE INTERNET

110 SILVER

ART DIRECTORS
Paul Keister
Kristie Guilmette

WRITER
Andria Kushan

PHOTOGRAPHER
Brian Deutsch

COLLEGE
Creative Circus/Atlanta

111 SILVER

ART DIRECTOR
Jennifer Tanabe

WRITER
Jennifer Tanabe

COLLEGE
Washington University/
St. Louis

112 BRONZE

ART DIRECTOR
Ed Powell

WRITER
Eben Fox

COLLEGE
Creative Circus/Atlanta

110 Silver

THE INTERNET Choose your destination.

111 Silver

PASSPORT
Business in Tokyo.
Shopping in Paris.
Visiting friends in Rome.
Slow Day.
THE INTERNET. Call 1-800-EXPLORE and get on board.

112 Bronze

No one will argue that the finest graphite is mined in Sri Lanka. Or that the perfect incense cedar comes from the forests of northern California. But the question remains, what's the best pencil in the world? Some say the Koh-I-Noor Deluxe. Others claim the Berol Mirado. Or the Faber Blackwing #2. Each has its merits, but is there a clear winner? It all depends on who's voting.

Best of Show

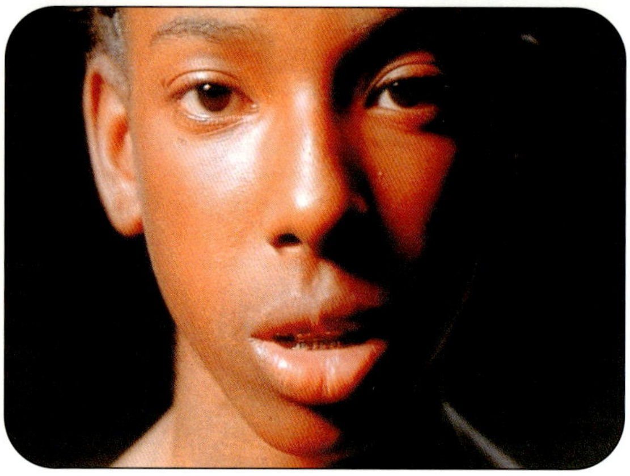

113

VARIOUS GIRLS (SPEAKING INDIVIDUALLY):

If you let me play.

If you let me play sports.

I will like . . . myself more.

I will have more self-confidence.

If you let . . . me play sports.

If you let me play.

If you let me play!

I'll be 60 percent less likely to get breast cancer.

I will suffer less depression.

If you let me play sports.

I'll be more likely . . . to leave a man who beats me.

I'll be less likely . . . to get pregnant before I want to.

I will learn . . .

I will learn what it means to be strong.

To be strong.

If you let me play . . .

. . . play sports.

If you let me play sports.

SUPER: JUST DO IT.

SUPER: (NIKE LOGO).

Best of Show

ART DIRECTOR
Rachel Nelson

WRITER
Janet Champ

AGENCY PRODUCER
Jennifer Smieja

PRODUCTION COMPANY
Mars Media

DIRECTOR
Samuel Bayer

CLIENT
Nike

AGENCY
Wieden & Kennedy/
Portland

1. Incense-cedar logs are milled into 3x3-inch lumber called "pencil stock." The pencil stock is kiln dried to ensure dimensional stability, and then cut into blocks.

2. Pencil blocks are sawed into slats, each one-half the thickness of a finished pencil. Tungsten-tipped saw blades ensure precision tolerances of ± .0003 inch.

3. Pencil slats are saturated with a non-toxic emulsion of wax and stain. This mixture gives the cedar pencil its distinctive color, and makes the pencil easier to sharpen.

4. Each stain slat is machine-grooved to receive the pencil lead.

5. Pencil "lead," a fragile mixture of clay and graphite, is placed into the grooves of the bottom slat. The strength and stability of Incense-cedar keeps the pencil lead from breaking.

6. A second grooved slat is glued on top of the leaded slat, forming a "sandwich." Each sandwich is held tightly together in a hydraulic clamp until the glue dries.

7. High-speed machinery shapes and cuts the slat sandwich into individual pencils.

8. Each pencil is sanded to a smooth, satiny finish. After sanding, the pencils are ready for finishing.

9. Several coats of non-toxic finish are applied to each pencil. After the finish has dried, the manufacturer's name is heat-stamped into one face of the pencil.

10. A shoulder is cut into one end of the pencil to accept the "ferrule," a metal device that secures the eraser tip.

11. The ferrule is inserted into the pencil end, and is clinched to the wood.

12. An eraser is inserted onto the ferrule. Erasers can be clinched, glued or punch-riveted into place. The finished pencil is now ready for sharpening and use.

Used by permission of Incense Cedar Institute photo by Kent Lacin.

Take a stick, drill a hole and fill it with lead, right? If only it were that easy. What appears simple in finished form is often born of the most complex process. But when executed properly, the process and the problems become invisible. What's left is something pure, elemental, perfect.

The Gold Award Winners on the Gold Award Winners

16

CONSUMER MAGAZINE
COLOR FULL PAGE OR SPREAD: SINGLE

AGENCY
Arnold Communications/Boston
CLIENT
Volkswagen

The day after Jerry died, the client—a Dead fan—called and asked for a special ad to run as soon as possible.

We were very busy at the time with other projects but thought it was a great idea. In fact, we were thinking the same thing. Volkswagen was one of the few companies that really had an honest connection to Jerry and his fans.

We felt the best way to execute the ad was to render the illustration in the spare, gaphic style of some of the great Volkswagen ads of the past. This ad came to us in a flash, whole and complete, within five minutes of getting the assignment.

It was a gift, given to us. Most of the good ones are.

LANCE JENSEN
ALAN PAFENBACH

38

TRADE
B/W FULL PAGE OR SPREAD: SINGLE

AGENCY
Hunt Adkins/Minneapolis
CLIENT
Dublin Productions

Last March, when this piece won a Golden Bunsen Burner at the Anti-ferromagnetism Awards Banquet, we gave a hilarious speech on antibaryonic para-positronium. In case you've been living in a cave, we've included the following excerpt for your enjoyment:

> And then the cathoderay oscillograph registered a conservation of parity that was inconsistent with Bloembergen's thermotransuranium findings, thereby rupturing our superheterodyne receiver. What's up with that?

It was at this point in our speech that the entire audience exploded into laughter and continued to laugh harder and harder until we became concerned for our own safety. So we dispatched our personal riot squad to wade into the crowd, where they began cracking femurs, smashing skulls and handing out business cards. The entire audience is now in a Turkish prison where they continue to rot even today.

DOUG ADKINS
STEVE MITCHELL

CONSUMER TELEVISION
:30 SINGLE

AGENCY
Wieden & Kennedy/Portland
CLIENT
Nike

We saw the facts about cancer survival, teen pregnancy, suicide rates, chronic depression. We saw the facts about the impact sports can make. And we already knew too well about the obvious inequality on the playing field. Simply put, we were mad. We wanted to educate people. And we wanted to make a statement that nobody could invalidate.

And they can't.

JANET CHAMP
RACHEL NELSON

91

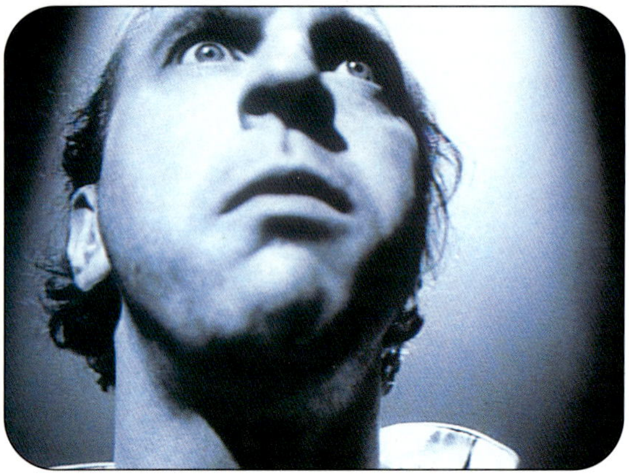

CONSUMER TELEVISION
VARYING LENGTHS CAMPAIGN

AGENCY
Goodby Silverstein & Partners/San Francisco
CLIENT
California Fluid Milk Processor Advisory Board

In May of 1993, Goodby Silverstein & Partners pitched to become the advertising agency for the California Milk Processor Advisory Board. Planners Jon Steel and Carol Rankin asked a focus group of people to go a week without drinking milk. Then they talked with them about their experiences.

The people really missed their milk. They got emotional about it. A strategy was written based on their sense of loss. Associate Creative Director Steve Stone led the creation of several campaigns based on the strategy. One of them was a collection of stories about people who ran out of milk at the absolutely wrong moment. In a meeting one day Jeff Goodby said, "What if at the end of the spot we just said, 'Got milk?' " A good idea. To the point. Simple. Two years later all we had to do was write some more stories.

HARRY COCCIOLO
SEAN EHRINGER
BOB KERSTETTER
TOM ROUTSON

99

CONSUMER TELEVISION
OVER :30 SINGLE

AGENCY
Cliff Freeman & Partners/New York
CLIENT
Little Caesars Pizza

"Is it funnier if the sprinkler hits the guy in the crotch quickly, or if it stays on him a while?" This "spurts vs. steady stream" debate lasted an hour and a half on the second day of filming. Six people participated in the debate. Three actors of varying heights and weights were tried, each changing his pants a minimum of twelve times. Four men attempted to work the hose, of which two were tried — one standard nozzle, one industrial — and three camera angles were considered. Finally on the fiftieth take, the water careened off the crotch perfectly and everyone on the set laughed out loud. Considering that the scene lasted less than one second all this seems pretty excessive. Until you compare it to the seventeen ear shapes we considered for the mechanical dog.

ARTHUR BIJUR
STEVE DILDARIAN
CLIFF FREEMAN
MATT VESCOVO

84

CONSUMER TELEVISION UNDER $50,000 BUDGET

AGENCY
Goldsmith/Jeffrey, New York
CLIENT
Crain's New York Business

We had a great Amish concept.
We had a $25,000 budget.
We had a fruitless stock search.
We had a brilliant editor deliver some lost footage.
We had a producer tell us if the Amish saw it they would sue.
We had a big problem.
We had a meeting.
We had a huge fight.
We had another meeting.
We had another huge fight.
We had an intern point out that the Amish don't watch TV.

We had big smiles all around.

TOM MILLER
JASON GABORIAU

103

PUBLIC SERVICE/POLITICAL TELEVISION: SINGLE

AGENCY
Houston Herstek Favat/Boston
CLIENT
Massachusetts Department of Public Health

We were in a hospital filming people with smoking related diseases when the idea for this particular spot was born. Between set-ups, a gentleman who'd had cancer and spoke through an electrolarynx was telling us about the time he sang "Happy Birthday" at his granddaughter's birthday party. And she was so terrified by the robotic voice coming from his throat that she began crying uncontrollably and had to be taken from the room.

The tobacco industry celebrates the great job they do convincing people that cigarette smoking is glamorous and fun. We saw this as an opportunity to tell the truth.

STUART COOPERRIDER
PETER FAVAT

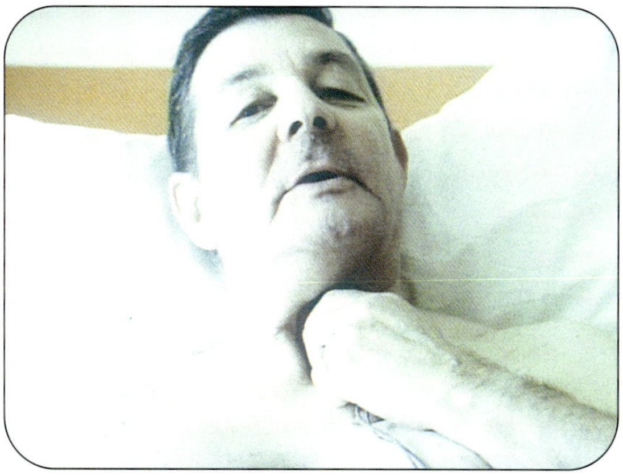

76

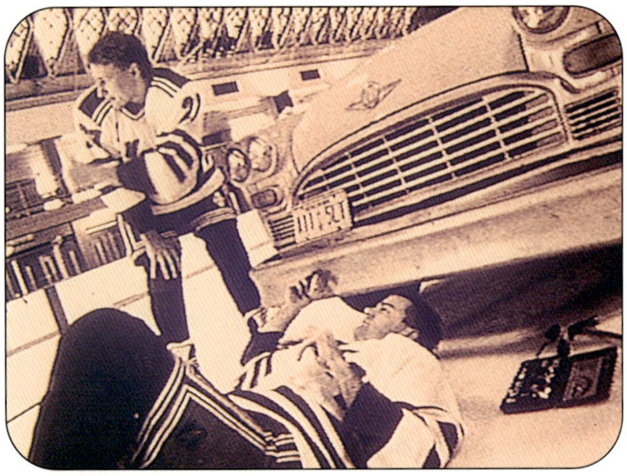

97

CONSUMER TELEVISION
:20 AND UNDER: CAMPAIGN

AGENCY
Wieden & Kennedy/Portland
CLIENT
ESPN/National Hockey League

This isn't supposed to be an acceptance speech, but, honestly, the best way to explain how this campaign got produced is to thank all the people who made it happen. We've been doing these spots for three years (we're not sure of the exact number, but it's around two hundred), and there are a lot of amazing people who deserve a lot of credit.

Thanks to Neal Tiles at ESPN for being a really cool client. Thanks as well to ESPN's Allan Broce and Judy Foaring for the same thing. There have also been a lot of people at Wieden & Kennedy who have worked hard on this campaign. Matt Stiker, Sharon Miller, Sherry Rogers and Eric Cooper are the account people we'd like to thank. Ben Grylewicz is the producer who knew what a pain in the butt it was going to be, but made it happen anyway. Colleen Wellman is probably the producer who's spent more time on this than anyone. She learned a lot about hockey in the process and we think she's a better person because of it.

There have also been a lot of creative people who have worked on this campaign over the years. Tim Hanrahan helped come up with the thing in the first place. Jerry Cronin and Larry Frey also have had a lot to do with it, as well as Rick McQuiston. Stacy Wall, Jon Goldberg, and Winton Sweum deserve credit as well for their hockey knowledge and continued support.

Finally, we want to thank the unsung heroes of this campaign, all the people at @radical.media who worked above and beyond the call of duty from that very first phone call in 1993. In particular, Frank Todaro and Bryan Buckley. They're the best. We can't say enough to thank them for how much of themselves they've put into this campaign. Jon Kamen, Robbie Fernandez and the always smiling Steve Orent also deserve our thanks and a lot of the credit for this work.

These spots are fun to do and it's always great to find out that someone finds them just as fun to watch.

JEFF WILLIAMS
HANK PERLMAN
DARRYL McDONALD

106

107

INTERNATIONAL FOREIGN LANGUAGE
COMMERCIAL: TELEVISION and CINEMA

AGENCY
Ammirati Puris Lintas/Amsterdam
CLIENT
Nestle Nederland/Rolo

Message to all creatives: think twice! Don't waste your life making bad advertising.

So, if you — and you do — like to make nice commercials, get yourself an agency that's not only good at creating great advertising but also good at creating time. Because you need a lot of it to make commercials like Rolo "Elephant." First you create the idea, that's the easiest part. Then think about it over and over again. Is the idea as good as we thought? It seems so familiar to me, are you sure it hasn't been done before? Who would be the ideal director?

In other words, as the campaign line says: think twice. . . . Or nobody will ever remember you. Not even an elephant.

MARCEL FRENSCH
JAN PIETER NIEUWERKERK
DIEDERIK KOOPAL
ROB VAN DER VIJFEIJKEN

CONSUMER MAGAZINE
B/W FULL PAGE OR SPREAD: SINGLE

AGENCY
Cosmos/Surry Hills, Australia
CLIENT
Richter

I was once told to love thy neighbor. I ignored it.

BEN OSBORN

14

TRADE
COLOR FULL PAGE OR SPREAD: SINGLE
and B/W OR COLOR ANY SIZE: CAMPAIGN

AGENCY
Leonard/Monahan, Providence
CLIENT
Polaroid

No photographer who thinks of himself as an artist wants to admit to trying "techniques" that were developed by Polaroid R&D guys. So what better way to soothe their assaulted egos than to poke fun at the things that make them artistic in the first place?

Thanks to a great client. And thanks to ten talented photographers who practically donated their work because we promised them it would appear in the award books. We were just making it up at the time.

KARA GOODRICH
PAUL HIRSCH
TED ROYER

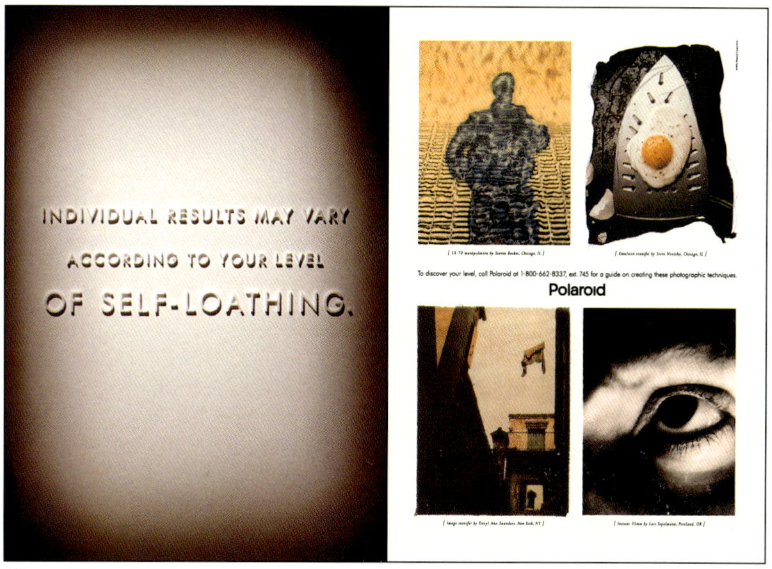

42 46

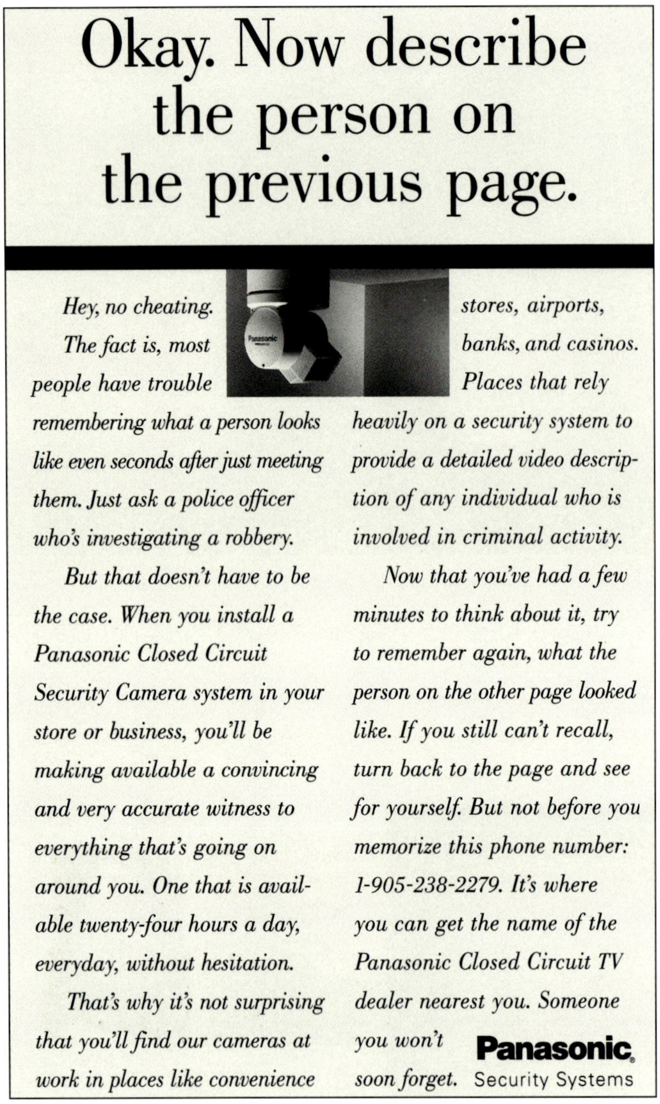
Okay. Now describe the person on the previous page.
Hey, no cheating. The fact is, most people have trouble remembering what a person looks like even seconds after just meeting them. Just ask a police officer who's investigating a robbery.
But that doesn't have to be the case. When you install a Panasonic Closed Circuit Security Camera system in your store or business, you'll be making available a convincing and very accurate witness to everything that's going on around you. One that is available twenty-four hours a day, everyday, without hesitation.
That's why it's not surprising that you'll find our cameras at work in places like convenience stores, airports, banks, and casinos. Places that rely heavily on a security system to provide a detailed video description of any individual who is involved in criminal activity.
Now that you've had a few minutes to think about it, try to remember again, what the person on the other page looked like. If you still can't recall, turn back to the page and see for yourself. But not before you memorize this phone number: 1-905-238-2279. It's where you can get the name of the Panasonic Closed Circuit TV dealer nearest you. Someone you won't soon forget.
Panasonic
Security Systems

1

CONSUMER NEWSPAPER
OVER 600 LINES: SINGLE

AGENCY
Roche Macaulay & Partners/Toronto
CLIENT
Panasonic

Panasonic calls agency. Needs ad.
We work.
Come up with ad, along with others.
Present ads to Creative Director.
Two page ad doesn't make the cut.
We're disappointed.
We work some more.
Re-present to Creative Director.
Two page ad survives.
Ad goes to client.
Client likes ad.
Ad approved.
A week passes.
Client calls.
Client's husband doesn't like ad.
Ad dies.
We're crushed.
Ad becomes spec, portfolio piece.
A year passes.
Panasonic calls again. Needs another ad.
We remind Creative Director of original ad.
Ad makes second trip to client.
Ad approved. Again.
We wait.
We worry.
Ad runs.
We're happy.
Ad wins at the One Show.
We're really happy.

IAN MacKELLAR
HOWARD BEAUCHAMP
GERALD SCHOENHOFF

The most dependable fishing line in the world.
STREN
CLEAR/BLUE

27

CONSUMER MAGAZINE
B/W OR COLOR LESS THAN A PAGE: CAMPAIGN

AGENCY
Carmichael Lynch/Minneapolis
CLIENT
Stren

Merrill Wreden, our client at Stren, asked us for a campaign that would get people to notice Stren again. It was a well known brand that had kind of fallen asleep. We did these ads to get Stren back at the top of people's minds, to get them thinking about and liking Stren again. Merrill swallowed hard and ran them. Sales went up about 40 percent.

JIM NELSON
FRANK HAGGERTY

INTERACTIVE: WEB SITE

AGENCY
Foote Cone & Belding/True North Technologies, San Francisco
CLIENT
Levi Strauss & Company

It was April 1995 and everywhere I looked there were web experts, visionaries and gurus. We were none of the above. The Levi's brand web site was a first for my partner Sam and I. As the lead creative team on the project, we did our creating and our learning at the same time. We didn't want to mimic so-called web culture because we figured that as more and more people discovered the web, it's culture would change accordingly—look what happened to break dancing. So we approached the site's look and content as we would any project. We wanted to make it different and we wanted to make it beautiful. This approach helped us create a site that inspired a lot of traffic, opinion and e-mail. Lucky for us, most of it was good.

And, lucky for us, we had some serious talent on our team. Despite a lot of people's best efforts, no one can really claim full credit for this site. It was the combined talent and hard work of many people at LS & Co., FCB/SF, TNT, R/GA, Organic and others. And it continues to be. Levi.com is an on-going project, a monster we've created that demands to be fed. As we strive to improve it, we try not to believe the hype.

For all the "netiquette" experts floating around out there, for all the interactive panelists and new media marvels who've crawled out of the traditional advertising woodwork, all it really takes is what it's always taken: a willing client, a desire to do things differently, a great concept, and your absolute best.

Ask a guru, they'll tell you the same thing in different words.

MARTIN LAUBER
SAMANTHA OSSELAER
TIM PRICE
TRACY COHEN
CHRIS LISICK
PIETER VAN PRAAG

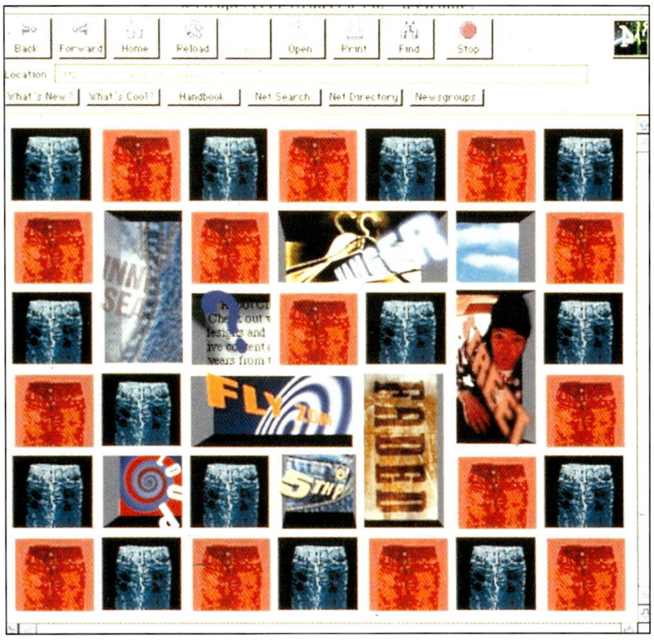

108

TRADE
B/W FULL PAGE OR SPREAD: SINGLE

AGENCY
Hunt/Adkins, Minneapolis
CLIENT
Dublin Productions

June, 1995, just outside of Giza. We are excavating a 4th dynasty Egyptian tomb, about to make an unparalleled discovery. Suddenly, after throwing several mummified Pharoahs out of the way, there they are: the Dublin manuscripts, neatly printed and stacked in boxes (although the logo is a bit large for our tastes). It proves quite little work for us to merely pick them up, dust them off and take all the credit for their creation. And being subsequently cursed with blindness, paralysis and dementia is a small price to pay for fame. Currently, we have archaeologists in 33 countries around the world looking for a campaign for a car account.

DOUG ADKINS
STEVE MITCHELL

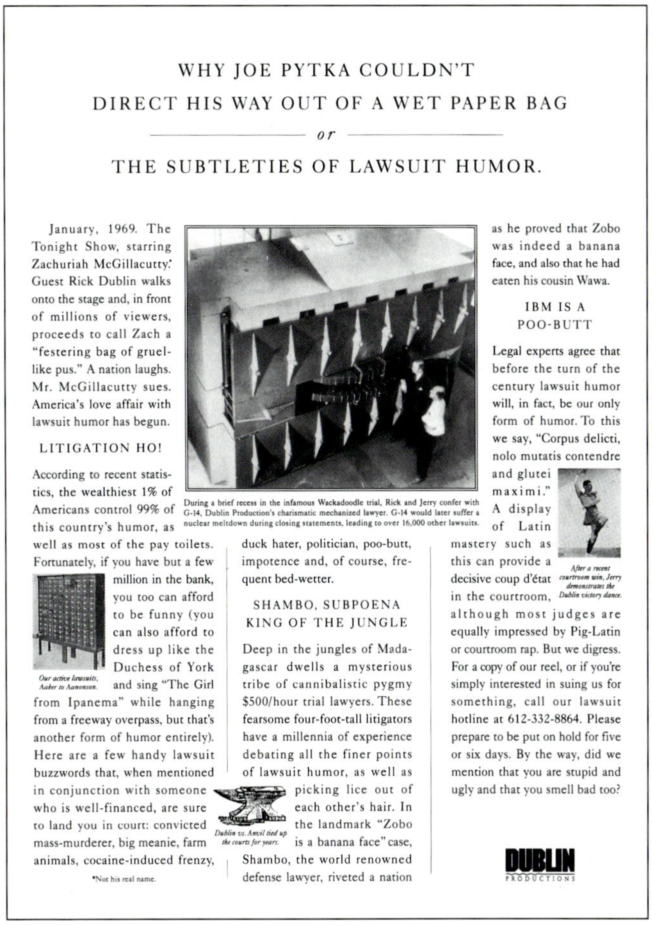

39

PUBLIC SERVICE/POLITICAL
NEWSPAPER OR MAGAZINE: CAMPAIGN

AGENCY
Fallon McElligott/Minneapolis
CLIENT
Minneapolis Animal Shelter

A volunteer once tape recorded the sounds animals make when they're kept at the shelter. He played it to his dog at home. The dog cowered in the corner.

Cages are so overcrowded that animals only get two days to be adopted. If one of them gets a contagious disease, every other animal has to be put to sleep. Only 20 percent of the cats are adopted.

The assignment was simple: find a home for the animals, fast. We both have pets from the pound, so we felt pretty strongly about it.

The ads ran a few days before the expiration date. People called the shelter, frantically asking if the dog or cat had been adopted. More importantly, they came to the shelter and took animals home.

SALLY HOGSHEAD
ROBB BURNHAM

OUTDOOR: CAMPAIGN

AGENCY
Cossette Communication-Marketing/Toronto
CLIENT
Nike Canada

When we were given this campaign to do for Nike we were very excited. We were also terrified because we didn't want to be the first creative team, probably ever, to drop the ball on a Nike assignment. Well, thanks to some really inspirational people and their inspirational stories we won a gold pencil and we're very excited about that. But mostly, we're just damn relieved we didn't drop the ball.

JIM GARBUTT
BRIAN HICKLING

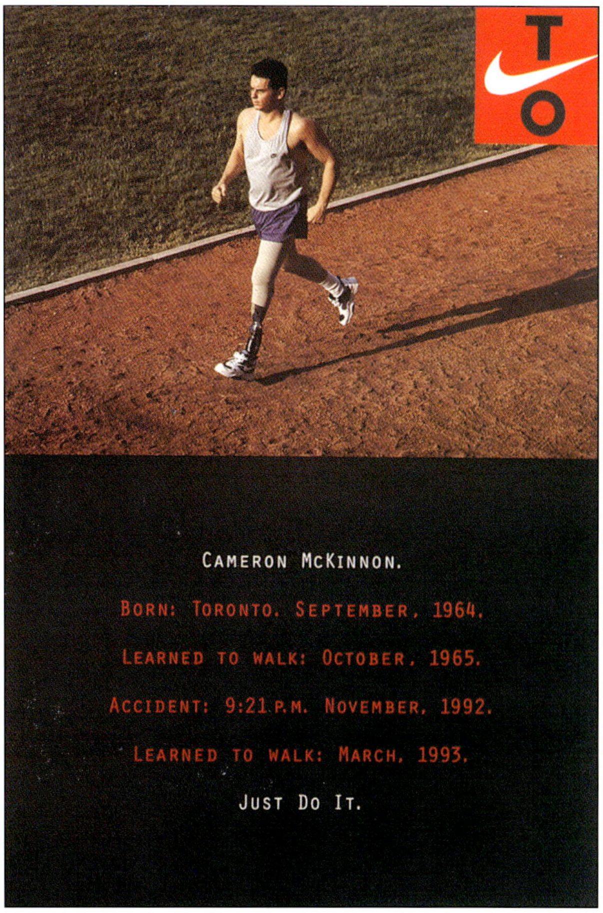

35

TRADE
B/W OR COLOR ANY SIZE: CAMPAIGN

AGENCY
Hunt Adkins/Minneapolis
CLIENT
Dublin Productions

It has come to our attention that our educational campaign has been tragically misunderstood. Imagine our dismay when we realized our efforts were provoking laughter rather than all-night, roundtable, intellectual discussions.

The Dublin manifestos should be enjoyed in the same somber, humorless spirit that they were conceived. They were meant to educate. They were not meant to entertain. If you are confused about when to laugh and when not to laugh, we strongly suggest the latter.

Obviously we have failed in our quest to enlighten the masses. However, we grudgingly accept this award because we are incredibly vain. Thank you for your time and remember: humor is nothing to laugh at.

DOUG ADKINS
STEVE MITCHELL

45

50

COLLATERAL
BROCHURES OTHER THAN BY MAIL

AGENCY
Fallon McElligott/Minneapolis
CLIENT
Flagstone Brewery

Obviously, there is no "magic" formula for winning a gold pencil. But formulas do exist and can prove to be quite useful in creating award-winning work. Here is the one we used:

$$\text{gold pencil} = \frac{\left[\dfrac{\text{Big Budget}}{\text{Civil War Imagery}} + \text{Copy Revision}^{10} \times \dfrac{(\text{12 bottles of product})^2}{\Delta t + 3} - x\right]}{\text{Luck}^{12}}$$

DAN OLSON
RILEY KANE

59

COLLATERAL
POINT OF PURCHASE AND IN-STORE

AGENCY
Dalbey & Denight/Portland
CLIENT
Prison Blues/Big House

We wish we could say this was a tough product to work on. But the truth is, you don't get a much juicier assignment than a fashion product made by prisoners.

And we wish we could say we came to the concept through long, hard thought and discussion. But, really, we had no budget, so we were pretty much corralled conceptually into a headline-dominant, black and white poster using these pre-existing black and white photographs by Giovanni . . .

The photos were of actual prisoners. Real tough looking SOB's. So, naturally, we put funny quotes to our serious looking models and *bam* — in two days we were pretty much done.

All in all, it was the kind of experience that we will look back on with desperate fondness as we fight with all the humor-deficient, stuffed-shirt, bank clients of the world.

JOEL THOMAS
MARK SLOTEMAKER
ROGER BENTLEY

CONSUMER RADIO: SINGLE

AGENCY
Goodby Silverstein & Partners/San Francisco
CLIENT
Sega of America

"I'm, ah, calling about a Sega radio spot that's been running up here in St. Paul in which a man is tortured during brain surgery, and we're supposed to think that's hilariously funny. Ah, I'm going to see this thing pulled off the air, if you get my drift."

(Actual phone message from irate customer.)

AL KELLY

(SFX: DRILL, BEEPING OF LIFE-SUPPORT MACHINE)

DOC: Ever had brain surgery, Jim?

(SFX: "CRUNCH")

JIM: No . . . um, do I have to be awake?

DOC: Just try to relax, Jim . . . all right . . . we'll just snip this away . . .

(SFX: SNIPPING SOUND)

DOC: Say, Jim have you seen that new Sega Saturn?

JIM: Uh, yeah, the 3D graphics are cool.

DOC: You know, it sounds very impressive. Better than your home stereo in fact.

JIM: Oh, really?

DOC: See the Sega Saturn's 24-bit surround sound processor sends out this uh, sonic image, fooling your cerebral cortex . . . here . . .

(SFX: POKING SOUND)

JIM: Ooohhh . . .

DOC: . . . into thinking it's surrounded. This in turn activates the hypothalamus under here . . .

(SFX: "R-R-RIP")

JIM: Ouch!

DOC: . . . which in turn stimulates the pituitary behind here . . .

(SFX: POKING SOUND)

JIM: Ow! That hurts!

DOC: . . . sending hormones along your corpus collosum behind this gray thing. If I could just . . .

(SFX: GRUNTING, STRAINING)

JIM: Aaaaah! Okay! Okay! I believe you! Stop it!

DOC: . . . get around this reticular formation I could show you . . .

JIM: Aaaaaiiiieee!!!!! Stop it! Stop! Okay! You made your point! Aaaaahhh!

ANNCR: Sega Saturn. So real, it's kind of scary.

DOC: Okay. Jim, let's try this: bark like a dog.

JIM: I'm not gonna . . .

(SFX: "SQUISH")

JIM: Woof! Woof!

ANNCR 2: Sega Saturn!

79

PUBLIC SERVICE/POLITICAL
RADIO: SINGLE and CAMPAIGN

AGENCY
Houston Herstek Favat/Boston
CLIENT
Massachusetts Department of Public Health

Even after losing his voice, Bob Mehrman remains one of the most courageous and determined people I have ever met. The world could use more people like him. And if the tobacco industry has its way, we will have more people like him.

MARK NARDI

BOB MEHRMAN (WITH AID OF ELECTROLARYNX): What happened? What went wrong? My life was supposed to be fun and exciting, sexy and glamorous. I thought I'd always be laughing and smiling and riding horses into a beautiful sunset. I was supposed to live the life of those people in cigarette advertisements. But now I can't even breathe through my mouth, I can't taste food, I can't smell, and I sound like a damn robot.

My name is Bob Mehrman. After smoking cigarettes for many years I developed cancer and my larynx had to be removed. Now I can only talk by holding this electrolarynx to my throat. But have no pity on me. Pity the young people who must fight the terrible seduction of cigarettes. It's important to do what we can so another person doesn't end up like me. Please let the tobacco industry hear your voice. They certainly don't want to hear mine.

ANNCR: The Massachusetts Department of Public Health.

72

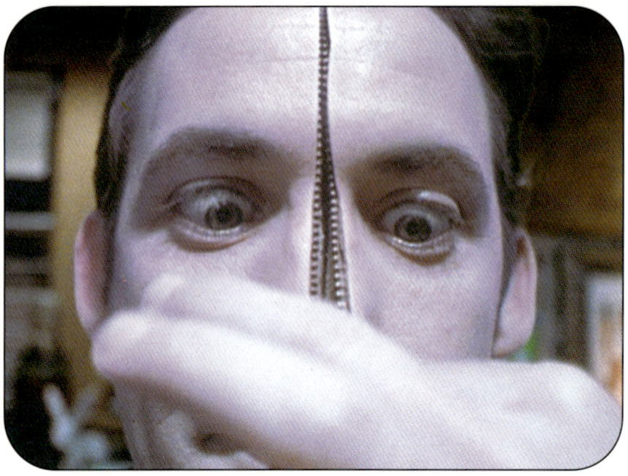

CONSUMER TELEVISION
OVER :30 SINGLE

AGENCY
Goodby Silverstein & Partners/San Francisco
CLIENT
California Fluid Milk Processor Advisory Board

We had never done a commercial with effects like this. We were in way over our heads. Fortunately we had Alan Scott, Alfred Urutia, Andy Traines, Anne Garefino, Betsy Flynn, Bill Perna, Bob Kerstetter, Brian Groves, Calabash Animations, Chris Hertsgaard, Cindy Epps, Daniel Robichaud, Danny Hulsizer, Deborah Ginnes, Debra Echard, Dennis Curtin, Dennis Hoey, Dennis Thomann, Denny Delk, Digital Domain, Don Lusby, Ed Neuman, Ed Ulbrich, Eric Press, Eric Edwards, Fred Ramondi, Fred Usher, Fritz Doddy, Gail Vance, Gloria Adams, Hannie Taglaar, Harlon Williams, Hollywood Digital, Isabel Ehringer, James Boorman, Jay Riddle, Jason Rowlett, Jais Lamarre, Jeff Goodby, Jeff Manning, Jill Heydorf, Jim Donahue, Jim Hawks, Jimmy Hite, Jim Stewart, John Ginnes, John Kilkinny, John Rosengrant, Jon Steele, Jonathan Elias, Josh Rich, Kathleen Cocciolo, Kellie Anderson, Kevin Locarro, Kinka Usher, Kristine Greco, Larry Schwartz, Lee Jimenez, Linda Harless, Margarita Mix, Mauricio Guitierez, Michele Donald, Michi Tomimatsu, Mike Pethel, Mike Smithson, Mike Trim, Mitch Kanner, Molly Prather, Monica Kendall, Neil Daniels, Nomad Editorial, Pacific Ocean Post, Paul Norman, Perry Blake, Rick Castro, Rose Kuo, Russell Horton, Saatchi & Saatchi/NY, Shane Mahan, Smillie Films, Stan Winston Studios, Steve Compas, Steve Lavy, Steve Seine, Stiles White, Stuart Stone Casting, Susan Keh, Susan Matveld, Susie Idema, Tara Crocitto, Tara the waitress at Shutters, Todd Isroelit, Tom Hollerbach, Tom Loewy, Tom Muldoon, Tom Routson, Tom Sing, Tony Cutrono and Tricia Pupel to help us.

HARRY COCCIOLO
SEAN EHRINGER

CONSUMER TELEVISION
OVER :30 CAMPAIGN

AGENCY
Cliff Freeman & Partners/New York
CLIENT
Prodigy

Barry White refused to leave his trailer. A pig named Petunia, from the "Pets" bus caught a bad case of heatstroke and had to be removed from the set. Moments later, the pig's lawyer (wearing suspenders emblazoned with dollar signs), pulls up in a gold Mercedes and threatens to sue. Byrdie, the banjo-slammin' starlet from the "Music" bus, silhouetted against a sunset a director would die for, gave the performance of a lifetime. Only to have one of her boobs pop out.

Good thing we were getting along with Tony Kaye.

DAVID ANGELO
JOHN LEU
TINA HALL
HAROLD EINSTEIN
CLIFF FREEMAN

89

CONSUMER TELEVISION
:30 CAMPAIGN

AGENCY
Wieden & Kennedy/Portland
CLIENT
Nike

My partner and I decided there was just too much pressure to write something really clever here. And, to be quite honest, we panicked. We're surrounded in this section by some of the biggest names in the business who are going to be writing painfully witty remarks—and we didn't want to be held to that standard. We're just two regular guys like you trying to make a living. And if that isn't good enough, sorry. Because that's all we can give. We did, however, want to take this opportunity to (1) thank the producer on this job, Kevin "Booger Lover" Diller and (2) somehow work in the phrase "Booger Lover."

ERIC SILVER
ANDREW CHRISTOU

94

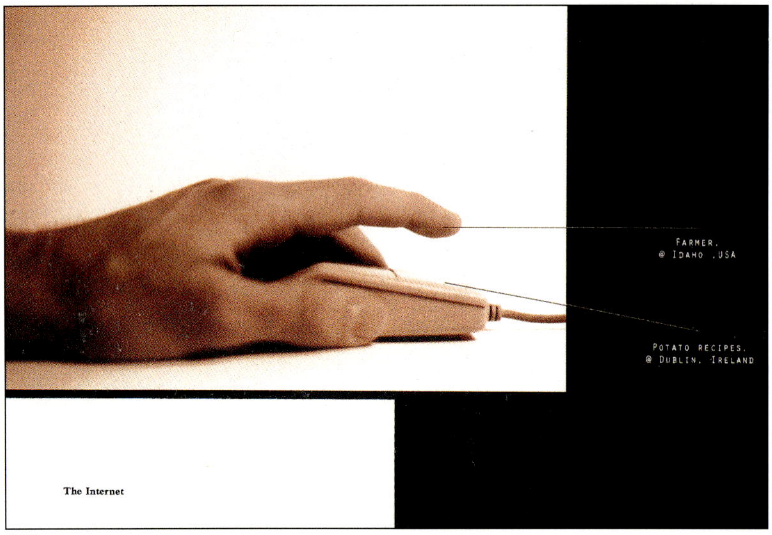
FARMER.
@ IDAHO .USA
POTATO RECIPES.
@ DUBLIN. IRELAND
The Internet

109

COLLEGE COMPETITION

COLLEGE
Art Center College of Design/Pasadena
ASSIGNMENT
The Internet

A few weeks ago, we got a letter from the One Show. They asked us to write a paragraph or two about our creative process. Since we both trusted our instincts and didn't show our work to any teachers or fellow students, we both laughed. To us, the creative process all comes down to loving your own point of view. It feels so much better winning the gold award this way, since our ad wasn't pre-approved by anyone.

FARIA RAJI
LISA BRINK

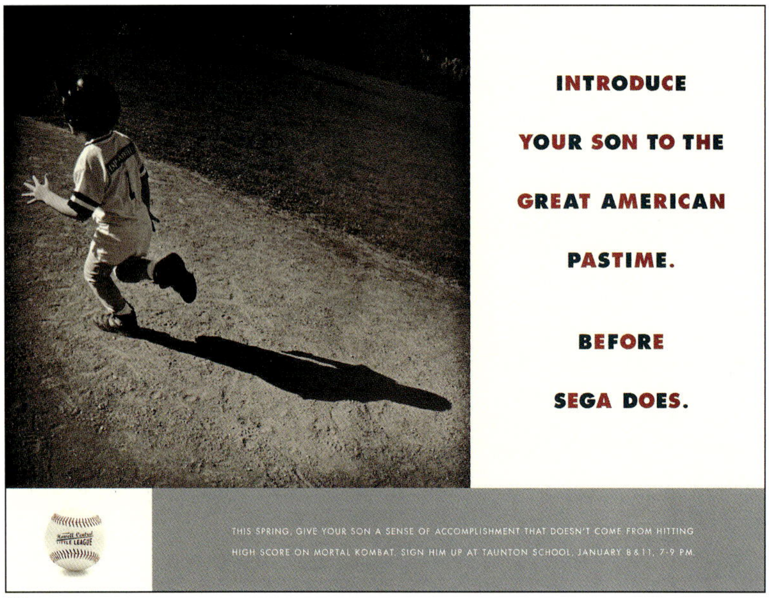
INTRODUCE
YOUR SON TO THE
GREAT AMERICAN
PASTIME.
BEFORE
SEGA DOES.
THIS SPRING, GIVE YOUR SON A SENSE OF ACCOMPLISHMENT THAT DOESN'T COME FROM HITTING
HIGH SCORE ON MORTAL KOMBAT. SIGN HIM UP AT TAUNTON SCHOOL, JANUARY 8&11, 7-9 PM.

68

PUBLIC SERVICE/POLITICAL
OUTDOOR AND POSTERS

AGENCY
Butler Shine & Stern/Sausalito
CLIENT
Howell Central Little League

We'd like to thank the judges for the great, high-profile recognition; and more importantly, for helping to eliminate any chance of us ever being asked to work on a video game account again.

For that, we are forever in your debt.

RYAN EBNER
PAUL RENNER

CONSUMER NEWSPAPER
600 LINES OR LESS: CAMPAIGN

AGENCY
Fallon McElligott/Minneapolis
CLIENT
Time International

The *Time* client killed two campaigns that we presented before they finally bought this one. It's amazing how smart a client can look in hindsight.

BOB BARRIE
DEAN BUCKHORN

TIME

Two warring African tribes.

Two million refugees.

Two minutes on the nightly news?

Understanding comes with TIME.

11

CONSUMER NEWSPAPER
OVER 600 LINES: CAMPAIGN

AGENCY
Ogilvy & Mather/Singapore
CLIENT
The British Council

A big thank you to the people of England, for having such a complex and difficult-to-master language. A huge salute to a very brave client, for not changing a single word or insisting on a bigger logo. And commiserations to everyone who said, "Gosh! This is such an obvious idea. Why didn't I think of this one before?"

The pencils are really beautiful. One of them even has a spelling mistake. Perfect.

SALLY OVERHEU
JACKIE HATHIRAMANI

WARNING!!
IT IS FORBIDDEN
TO ENTER A WOMAN
- BY ORDER

IMPROVE YOUR ENGLISH. We have over twenty part-time and full-time courses to help you read, write and speech (sorry, speak) correct English. Call 473 6661 for more information. The British Council

4

You are 2 months old. Your lungs are this tiny. You spend day after day around second-hand cigarette smoke. You breathe it in. You hack. You cough. You wheeze. Your lungs clog up with sticky fluid and thick mucous. You get bronchitis. Or pneumonia. If you have asthma, it will likely get worse. All together, up to 300,000 babies end up getting sick every year. 15,000 of them could end up hospitalized. Simply from being exposed to cigarette smoke. It's time we made smoking history. A message from The Massachusetts Department of Public Health.

63

PUBLIC SERVICE/POLITICAL
NEWSPAPER OR MAGAZINE: SINGLE

AGENCY
Houston Herstek Favat/Boston

CLIENT
Massachusetts Department of Public Health

Thank you for the gold award. This may be the only time we'd trade it for an Effie™.

TODD RIDDLE
MARK NARDI

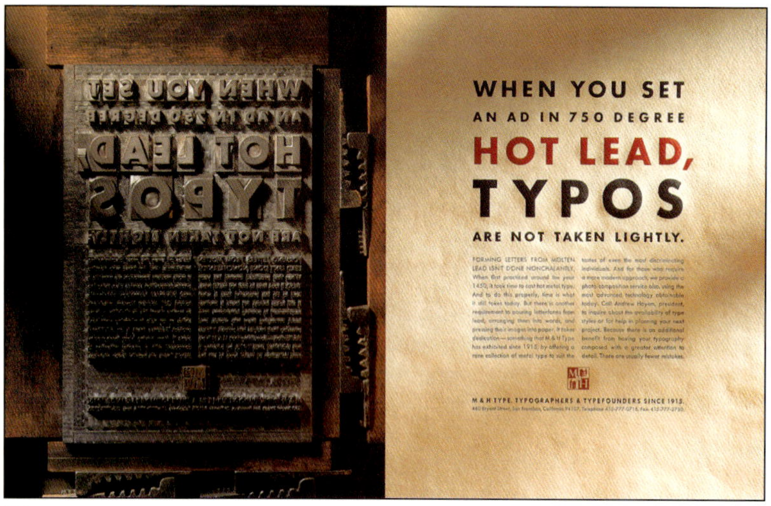
WHEN YOU SET
AN AD IN 750 DEGREE
HOT LEAD,
TYPOS
ARE NOT TAKEN LIGHTLY.

57

COLLATERAL
DIRECT MAIL: CAMPAIGN

AGENCY
Pagano Schenck & Kay/Boston

CLIENT
M&H Typography

The ancient alchemists were correct. You can turn lead into gold.

STEVE BAUTISTA
HAL CURTIS

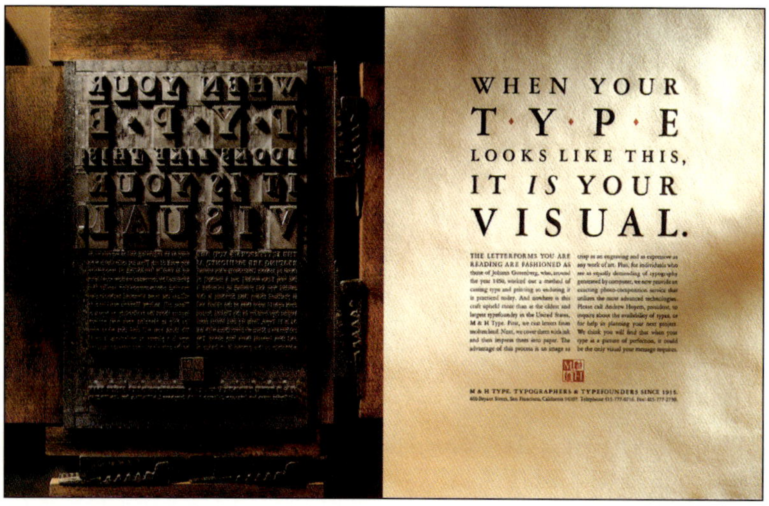
WHEN YOUR
T·Y·P·E
LOOKS LIKE THIS,
IT *IS* YOUR
VISUAL.

54

COLLATERAL
DIRECT MAIL: SINGLE

AGENCY
Pagano Schenck & Kay/Boston

CLIENT
M&H Typography

M&H Typography - ph.: 415-777-0716.
M&H Typography - fax: 415-777-2730.

STEVE BAUTISTA
HAL CURTIS

CONSUMER NEWSPAPER
600 LINES OR LESS: SINGLE

AGENCY
Price/McNabb, Charlotte, NC
CLIENT
East West Partners

I guess now we'll have to put it in our books.

SHARON McDANIEL AZULA
DAVID OAKLEY
SCOTT CORBETT

SPEND 69¢ FOR A BURGER AND YOU CAN HAVE IT YOUR WAY.
SPEND $169,000 FOR A HOME AND YOU CAN'T?
All together now: "Hold the bay windows, hold the crown molding, special orders don't upset us." OK, so it doesn't rhyme. But it does make sense. Give the people what they want.
A choice. That's what we're offering at Davis Lake. The flexibility for you to customize your own home. At any spending level.
Perhaps you want french doors instead of a bay window. No problem. Maybe you prefer hardwood to carpet. Consider it done. The way we see it, the home you buy should reflect your personality. Not some run-of-the-mill builder's.
Of course, everyone wants a community with amenities. And there are plenty at Davis Lake. An exclusive Swim and Tennis Club. A 14-acre stocked lake. Jogging trails, bike paths, and even an 88-foot waterslide. (Customized, no doubt).
What more could you possibly ask for? Maybe our phone number. It's (704) 598-0063. Please call us. Or come by for a visit. You just might find yourself shouting, "I love this place."
Customization available in the $130,000-$160,000 price range,
the $160,000-$210,000 range,
and the $210,000-$290,000 range.
DAVIS LAKE
A Better Way Of Life.
Harris Boulevard between I-85 & I-77. An East West Partners Community. 598-0063
8

CONSUMER MAGAZINE
B/W OR COLOR LESS THAN A PAGE: SINGLE

AGENCY
Carmichael Lynch/Minneapolis
CLIENT
Stren

Typical fishing magazine contents: Fish, boat, lake, fish, fishing rod, water, fish, fisherman, fisherman holding fish, fish fillets, dock, fish, fish.

Put something different in your ad, and people will notice it.

JIM NELSON
FRANK HAGGERTY

The most dependable fishing line in the world.
STREN
POWERBRAID
KEVLAR
24

Henry David Thoreau grew up in his father's pencil factory. While there, he developed a refining method that produced a superior grade of graphite. He also discovered that adjusting the proportion of clay to graphite created pencils of varying hardness. For many years, Thoreau Pencils were considered the finest in America. Henry became so successful, he could afford a house at the lake.

Print Finalists

CONSUMER NEWSPAPER
OVER 600 LINES: SINGLE

114
ART DIRECTOR:
John Gorse
WRITER:
Nick Worthington
TYPOGRAPHER:
Sid Russell
CLIENT:
Whitbread Beer Company
AGENCY:
Bartle Bogle Hegarty/
London

115
ART DIRECTOR:
John Gorse
WRITER:
Nick Worthington
TYPOGRAPHER:
Sid Russell
CLIENT:
Whitbread Beer Company
AGENCY:
Bartle Bogle Hegarty/
London

116
ART DIRECTOR:
Eric Houseknecht
WRITER:
Marcus Woolcott
PHOTOGRAPHER:
Jen Halim
CLIENT:
Gallery 13
AGENCY:
Bates/Hong Kong

117
ART DIRECTORS:
Paul Bennell
Mike Boekholt
Goh Wee Kim
WRITER:
Andy Flemming
PHOTOGRAPHER:
John Clang
CLIENT:
Bayer
AGENCY:
Bates/Singapore

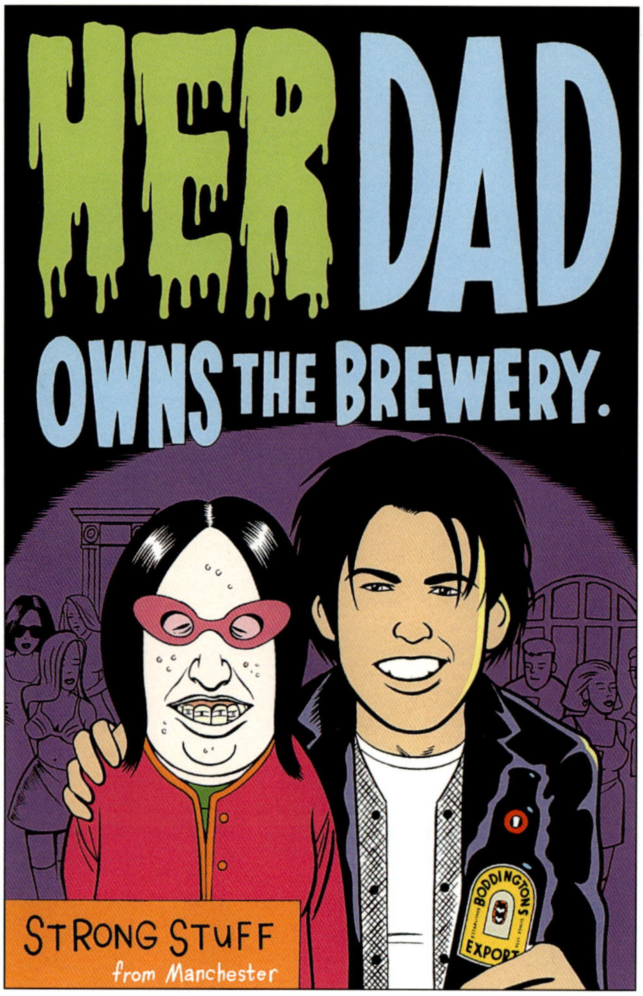

114

115

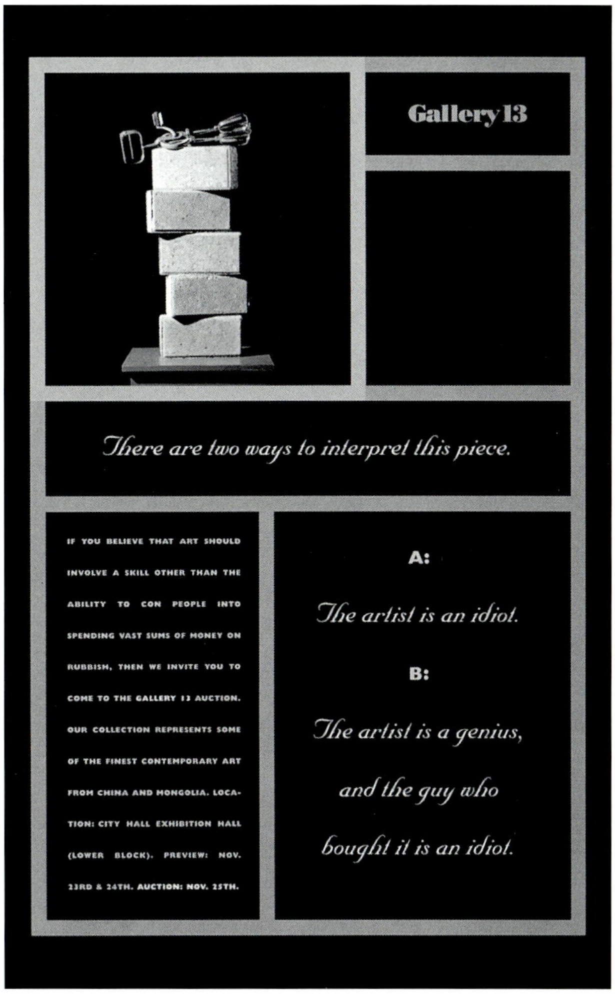
Gallery 13
There are two ways to interpret this piece.
IF YOU BELIEVE THAT ART SHOULD INVOLVE A SKILL OTHER THAN THE ABILITY TO CON PEOPLE INTO SPENDING VAST SUMS OF MONEY ON RUBBISH, THEN WE INVITE YOU TO COME TO THE GALLERY 13 AUCTION. OUR COLLECTION REPRESENTS SOME OF THE FINEST CONTEMPORARY ART FROM CHINA AND MONGOLIA. LOCATION: CITY HALL EXHIBITION HALL (LOWER BLOCK). PREVIEW: NOV. 23RD & 24TH. AUCTION: NOV. 25TH.
A:
The artist is an idiot.
B:
The artist is a genius, and the guy who bought it is an idiot.

116

Bayer
The fly killer

117

CONSUMER NEWSPAPER
OVER 600 LINES: SINGLE

118
ART DIRECTOR:
Jorge Lopez
WRITER:
Julio Wallovits
CLIENT:
Rover Espana
AGENCY:
Contrapunto/Madrid

119
ART DIRECTORS:
Markham Cronin
Tony Calcao
Alex Bogusky
WRITER:
Scott Linnen
PHOTOGRAPHERS:
Jose Molina
Tony Calcao
CLIENT:
Shimano American
Corporation
AGENCY:
Crispin & Porter/Miami

120
ART DIRECTOR:
Peter Rose
WRITERS:
Pedro Soler
Peter Rose
CLIENT:
Mercedes-Benz
Espana, S.A.
AGENCY:
Delvico Bates/Madrid

121
ART DIRECTORS:
Mark Schruntek
Dan Kelleher
Vinny Tulley
WRITERS:
Dan Kelleher
Mark Schruntek
Vinny Tulley
PHOTOGRAPHER:
Cailor/Resnick
CLIENT:
Stein Mart
AGENCY:
DeVito/Verdi, New York

118

119

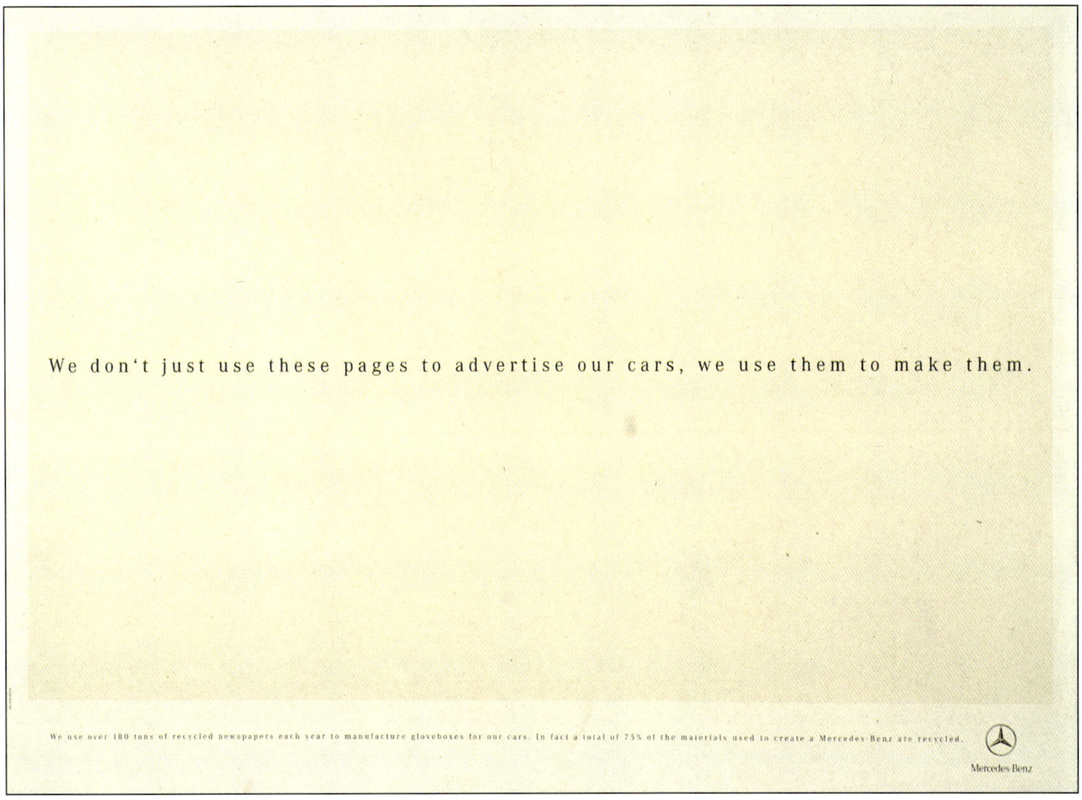
We don't just use these pages to advertise our cars, we use them to make them.
We use over 180 tons of recycled newspapers each year to manufacture gloveboxes for our cars. In fact a total of 75% of the materials used to create a Mercedes-Benz are recycled.
Mercedes-Benz

120

$185
Either way, someone gets $95.
$90
You decide. We sell the same cashmere sweater they sell. We just sell it for less. Up to 60% off every single thing, every single day. You Could Pay More, But You'll Have To Go Somewhere Else.
Stein Mart

121

CONSUMER NEWSPAPER
OVER 600 LINES: SINGLE

122
ART DIRECTOR:
Leslie Sweet
WRITER:
Sal DeVito
CLIENT:
Time Out
AGENCY:
DeVito/Verdi, New York

123
ART DIRECTORS:
Michael Tan
Low Eng Hong
WRITER:
Eugene Cheong
PHOTOGRAPHER:
Poon Kin Thong
TYPOGRAPHER:
Low Eng Hong
CLIENT:
Cycle & Carriage
AGENCY:
Euro RSCG Ball
Partnership/Singapore

124
ART DIRECTOR:
Simon Chandler
WRITER:
Eric Springer
PHOTOGRAPHER:
Hunter Freeman
CLIENT:
Sunvalley Shopping Center
AGENCY:
Goldberg Moser O'Neill/
San Francisco

125
ART DIRECTOR:
Noam Murro
WRITER:
Dean Hacohen
CLIENT:
El Al Airlines
AGENCY:
Goldsmith/Jeffrey,
New York

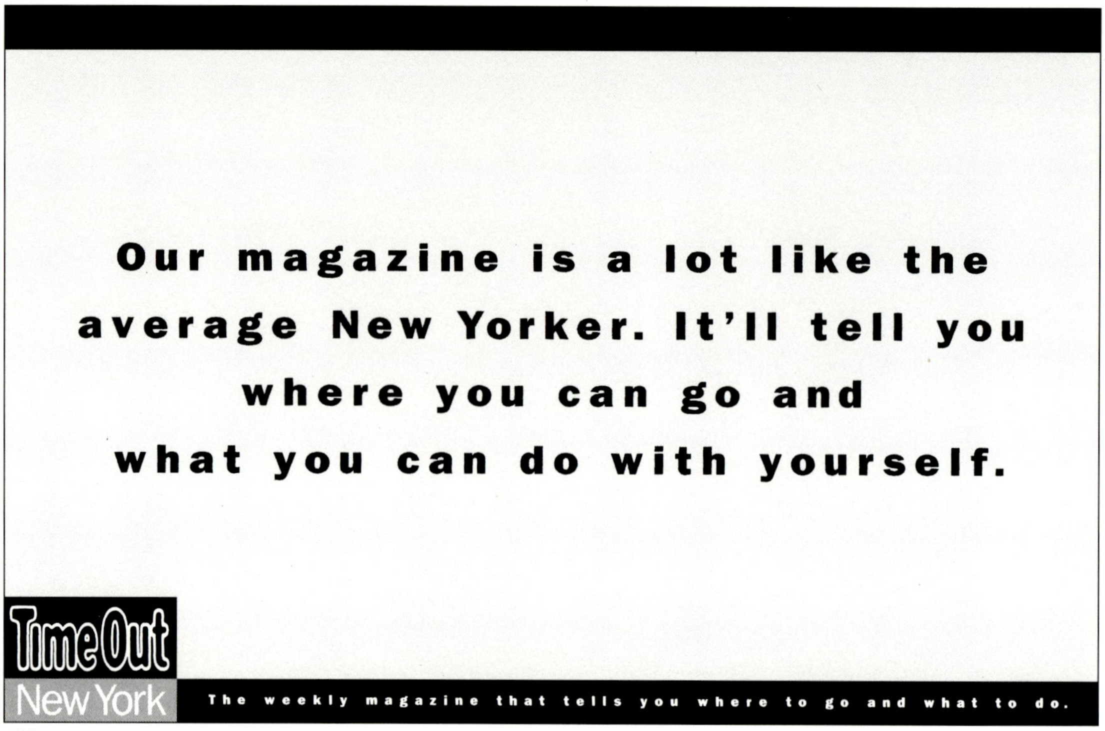

122

123

BANANA REPUBLIC–WILLIAMS-SONOMA–JOHNNY ROCKETS–THE BODY SHOP–CACHÉ–VICTORIA'S SECRET–EDDIE BAUER–THE BOMBAY COMPANY–HOLD EVERYTHING–POTTERY BARN–GREETINGS
Distant galaxies, far off constellations, new neighbors across the street.
Cast your eager eye heavenward with a Meade telescope from The Nature Company. Its powerful 90mm objective lens reveals fascinating details like the moons of Jupiter, the rings of Saturn and the kitchen of the O'Neills. We include a tripod and three eyepieces so you can truly go where no one has gone before. Except maybe Mrs. O'Neill.
THE NATURE COMPANY. ONE OF OVER 150 STORES. (510) 825-2042.
JCPENNEY–TROPICAL SQUEEZE HOT DOG & JUICE BAR–H2O PLUS–GANTOS
SUNVALLEY
THIS END UP–HUBERT BRAUN HAIRSTYLING–THINGS REMEMBERED–IMPOSTORS

On a trip to Israel, you try the local food.

Tap your foot to the local tunes.

Chat with the local folk.

Then the plane lands.

EL AL
The Airline of Israel

CONSUMER NEWSPAPER
OVER 600 LINES: SINGLE

126
ART DIRECTOR:
Gary Goldsmith
WRITER:
Dean Hacohen
ILLUSTRATOR:
Chris Wormell
CLIENT:
JP Morgan
AGENCY:
Goldsmith/Jeffrey,
New York

127
ART DIRECTOR:
Todd Grant
WRITER:
Bo Coyner
PHOTOGRAPHER:
Gil Smith
CLIENT:
American Isuzu Motors
AGENCY:
Goodby Silverstein &
Partners/San Francisco

128
ART DIRECTOR:
Todd Grant
WRITER:
Bo Coyner
PHOTOGRAPHER:
Gil Smith
CLIENT:
American Isuzu Motors
AGENCY:
Goodby Silverstein &
Partners/San Francisco

129
ART DIRECTOR:
Steve Luker
WRITER:
Steve Simpson
ILLUSTRATOR:
Mark Stearney
CLIENT:
Norwegian Cruise Line
AGENCY:
Goodby Silverstein &
Partners/San Francisco

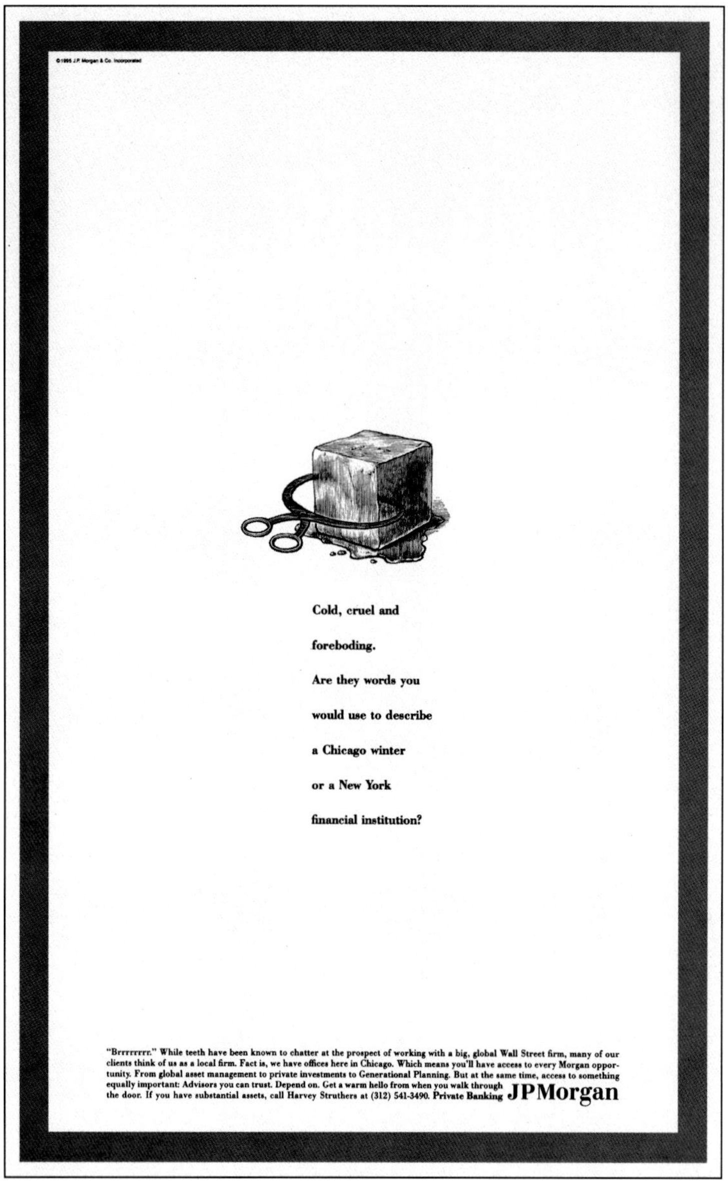

126

127

THIS MESSAGE IS
MADE POSSIBLE BY
THE TROOPER'S UNIQUE
CORNERING LIGHTS.
ISUZU
Practically / Amazing
What's more, the Isuzu Trooper is the only sport utility vehicle with such cornering lights. Which is nice, because recent studies indicate people like to see where they're going. For more information, call (800) 726-2700.

128

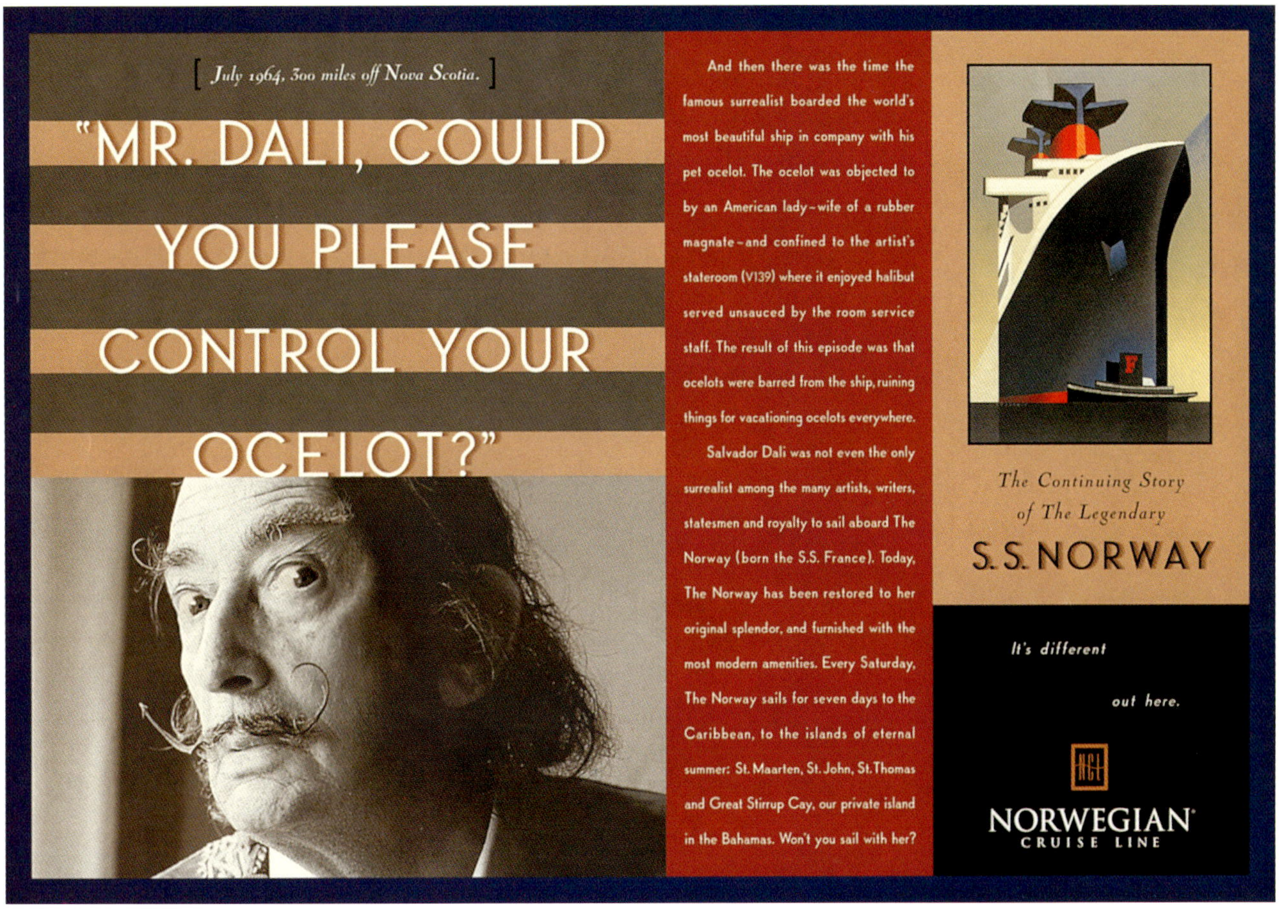
[July 1964, 300 miles off Nova Scotia.]
"MR. DALI, COULD YOU PLEASE CONTROL YOUR OCELOT?"
And then there was the time the famous surrealist boarded the world's most beautiful ship in company with his pet ocelot. The ocelot was objected to by an American lady–wife of a rubber magnate–and confined to the artist's stateroom (V139) where it enjoyed halibut served unsauced by the room service staff. The result of this episode was that ocelots were barred from the ship, ruining things for vacationing ocelots everywhere.
Salvador Dali was not even the only surrealist among the many artists, writers, statesmen and royalty to sail aboard The Norway (born the S.S. France). Today, The Norway has been restored to her original splendor, and furnished with the most modern amenities. Every Saturday, The Norway sails for seven days to the Caribbean, to the islands of eternal summer: St. Maarten, St. John, St. Thomas and Great Stirrup Cay, our private island in the Bahamas. Won't you sail with her?
The Continuing Story of The Legendary
S.S. NORWAY
It's different
out here.
NORWEGIAN
CRUISE LINE

129

CONSUMER NEWSPAPER
OVER 600 LINES: SINGLE

130
ART DIRECTOR:
Moe VerBrugge
WRITER:
Josh Miller
PHOTOGRAPHER:
Jeff Glancz
CLIENT:
New York Restaurant Group
AGENCY:
Hampel/Stefanides, New York

131
ART DIRECTOR:
Moe VerBrugge
WRITER:
Josh Miller
PHOTOGRAPHER:
Jeff Glancz
CLIENT:
New York Restaurant Group
AGENCY:
Hampel/Stefanides, New York

132
ART DIRECTOR:
David Dye
WRITER:
Sean Doyle
CLIENT:
The Guardian
AGENCY:
Leagas Delaney/London

133
ART DIRECTOR:
David Beverley
WRITER:
Robert Burleigh
CLIENT:
The Observer
AGENCY:
Leagas Delaney /London

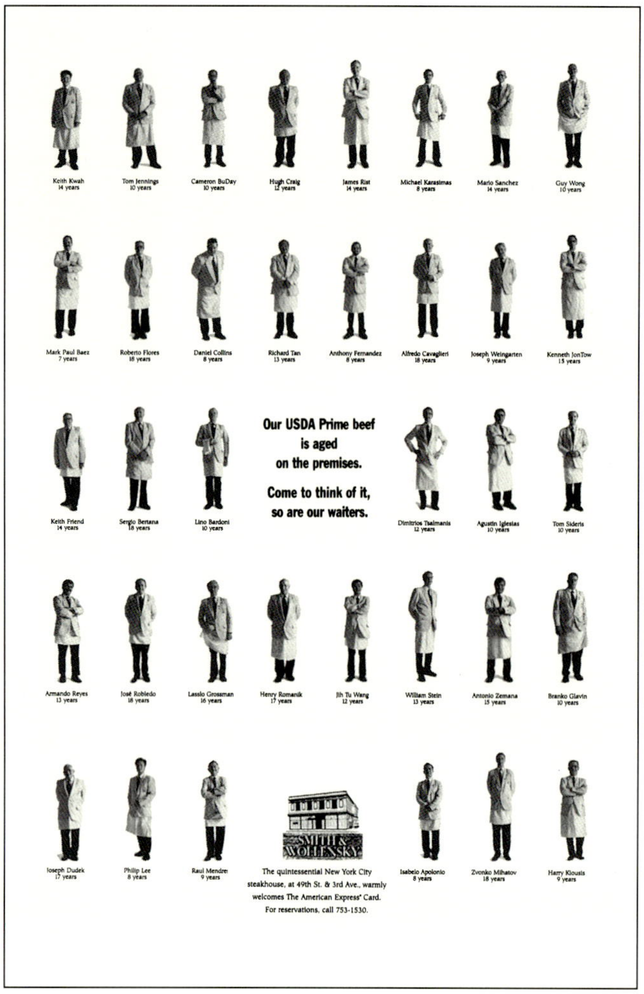

130

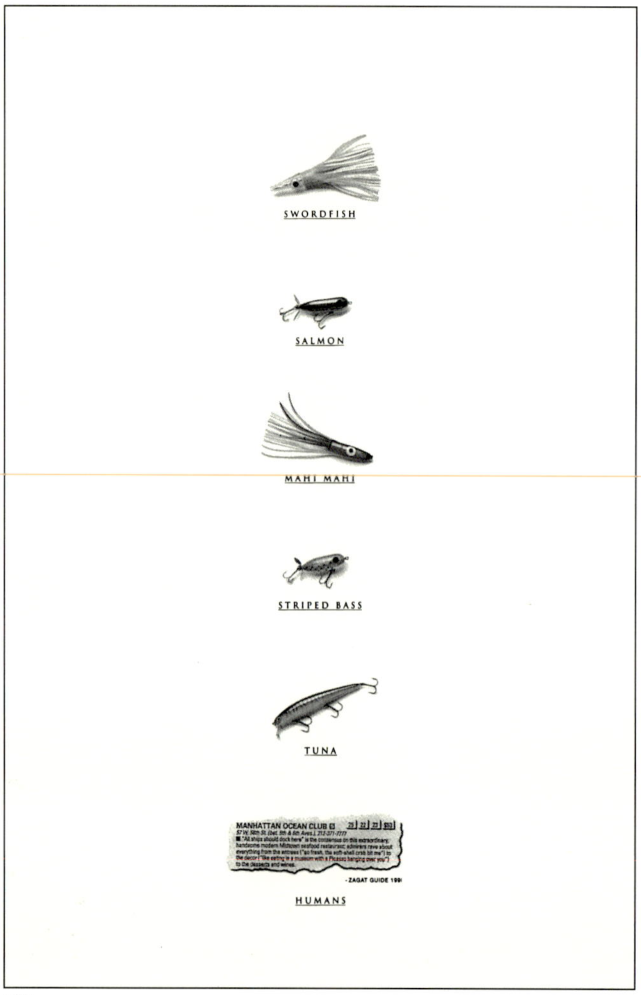

131

22 | 3 September 1995 the Observer

Today **273 people will go missing. This is the only mention it will get in a newspaper.**

Every day in Britain, people simply disappear without trace. They may be missing. But are they missed? Find out in 'The Missing', a 3 part serialisation of Andrew O'Hagan's new book. Tomorrow in The Guardian.

The **Guardian**

132

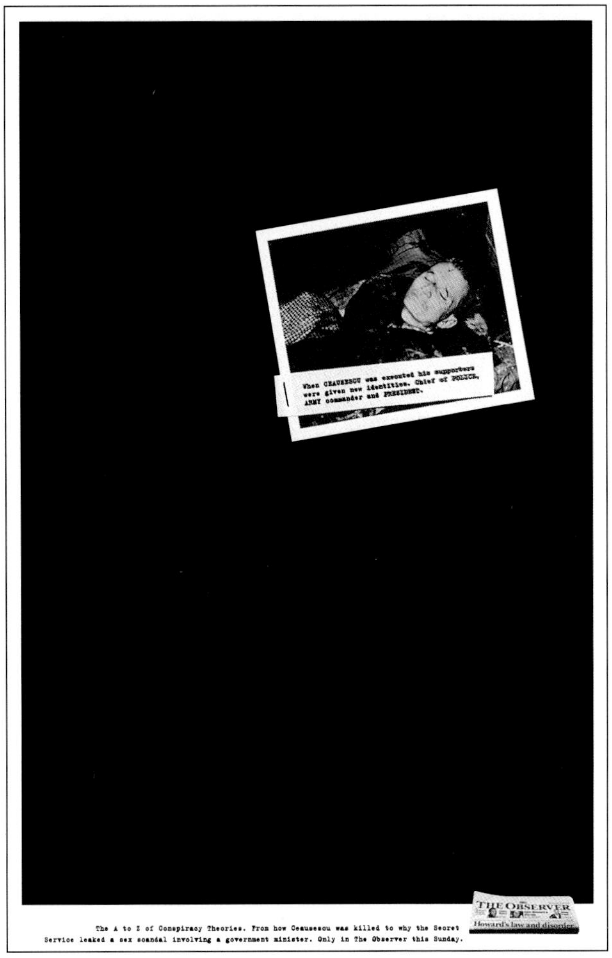

133

CONSUMER NEWSPAPER
OVER 600 LINES: SINGLE

134
ART DIRECTOR:
David Beverley
WRITER:
Robert Burleigh
CLIENT:
The Observer
AGENCY:
Leagas Delaney/London

135
ART DIRECTOR:
David Beverley
WRITER:
Robert Burleigh
CLIENT:
The Observer
AGENCY:
Leagas Delaney/London

136
ART DIRECTOR:
Tan Yew Leong
WRITER:
Yasmin Ahmad
PHOTOGRAPHER:
Barney Studio
CLIENT:
P. Lal Store
AGENCY:
Leo Burnett/Kuala Lumpur

137
ART DIRECTORS:
Yasmin Ahmad
Ali Mohamed
WRITER:
Yasmin Ahmad
ILLUSTRATOR:
Chan Lee Shon
CLIENT:
P. Lal Store
AGENCY:
Leo Burnett/Kuala Lumpur

134

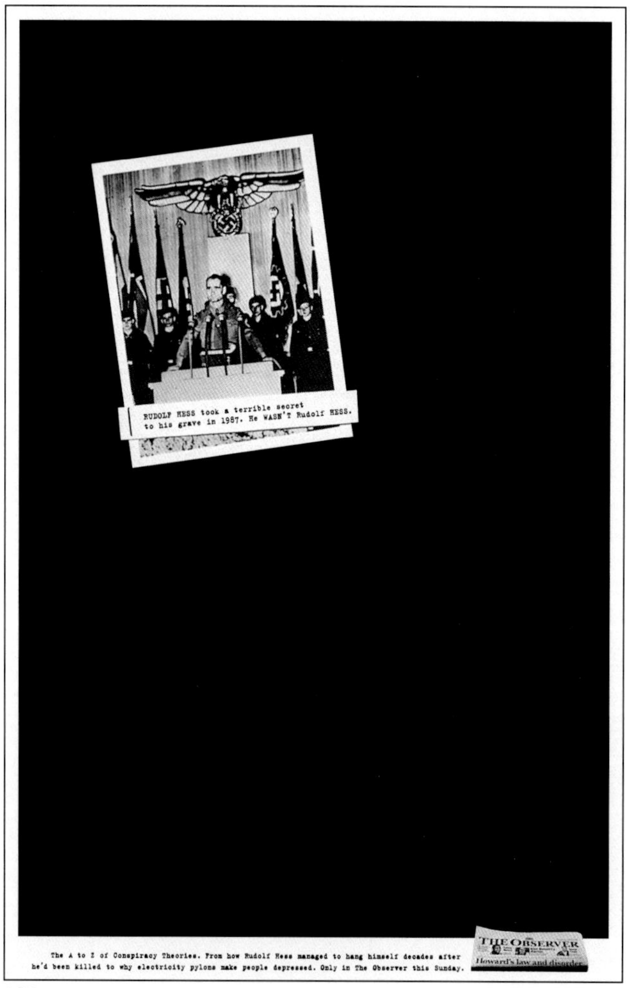

135

Why some of our shoe trees cost more than some people's shoes.

"One hundred ringgit for a pair of shoe trees?" I ask Mr.Doshi of P.Lal Store. "It's positively criminal. What view am I to take of this?"

"Yes, they're a steal, aren't they?" he answers casually. "I fancy we could make quite a bundle on them, if we abandoned our *guaranteed lowest fixed price* policy."

The shoe trees I am currently putting on trial were made by *Allen-Edmonds*. Their shoes are meticulously hand-made in Wisconsin; their shoe trees hand-carved from fragrant Wisconsinian cedar wood.

"Nothing quite like aromatic cedar for absorbing foot perspiration," says Mr.Doshi, "and nothing quite like perspiration for ruining the insides of a shoe."

I run my thumb against the grain of one shoe tree and bring the other one closer to my nose. I must say they are about as smooth as a baby's bottom, and they smell a damned sight better, too.

"They really are quite remarkable," I whisper, "and so they should be, if they are going to cost one hundred bloody ringgit."

"Mind you, they *are* cheaper at my store than in most parts of the world," he boasts. "I buy them straight from the factory, you see.

"Besides," he adds, "we're not lumbered with the sort of overheads that the West is."

"Hmmm," I hmmm-ed. "Tell me more about these *Allen-Edmonds* folks. They seem rather refined for Americans."

"Well," he says tapping his finger on his chin, "they go back even farther than us. Let's see. 1922, I believe it was. Seven years before P.Lal became the first established store in Kuala Lumpur. I don't know of any shoe craftsman more pernickety than them. Every pair comes with single oak leather soles, every stitch carried out by hand. Is it any wonder they're one of George Bush's favourite brands?

"And if you knew shoes like George knows shoes, you would know a lot about shoes," he mumbles mysteriously.

In any case, it figures, at least to me, that if *Allen-Edmonds* were that fussy about their shoes, they would probably be just as fussy about the maintenance of them. Hence, the slightly expensive shoe trees, I suppose.

"I can't stress enough the importance of utilising shoe trees," Mr.Doshi says.

"They keep good shoes looking good longer. They hold the shape of the shoe's upper, thus smoothing out the creases, and they keep the lining and insole soft and comfortable.

"Furthermore, shoe trees are a useful aid in the cleaning and shining of shoes. It saves you from having to stick your hands where your feet have been. Or worse, urghh," he adds grimacing, "where your *father's* feet have been.

"How often do you travel?" he asks clear out of the blue.

"Far too often," I reply woefully, "why do you ask?"

"Then you must know," he says, "how upsetting it is to pack a perfectly fine pair of shoes, only to discover that, at the end of your journey, they've transformed into some deflated bits of cow."

"Yes I see what you mean," I confess, looking down at the well-travelled deflated bits of deer presently wrapped around my feet.

"Quod erat demonstrandum," he crows triumphantly.

"Q.E.D.," I echo meekly as I check the contents of my purse. "So Mr.Doshi, how much did you say that pair of shoe trees was?"

P.Lal Store
GUARANTEED LOWEST FIXED PRICES
135, JALAN TUANKU ABDUL RAHMAN, 50100 KUALA LUMPUR TEL 2927062 & 2952341

Are pipes English *or* American?

An Indian shoe merchant explains.

You will rarely find a keener spokesman on the subject than Mr.Doshi of P.Lal Store.

Since 1929, P.Lal have been selling fine imported shoes in the main, and other hand-crafted items on the side.

Items such as pipes.

According to Mr.Doshi, the history of the pipe, riddled with adventure and scandal, traces all the way to China.

Back then, the pipe was mostly used for the consumption of intoxicating substances.

Which explains why it became a faithful travelling companion to Chinese sailors and slowly found its way to America.

"Mind you," stresses our Mr.Doshi, "all this happened way before Chris Columbus discovered America and her tobaccos in 1492.

"Chinese traders, you see. More eager than your average very eager person. They braved oceans in search of laundry business, only to find that the fashion of the day was, at best, minimalist.

"And so they left, leaving only some scalps, and the pipe, which then took on the much nobler form of tobacco-filled 'Peace pipes' among the American natives."

Or so Mr.Doshi's story goes.

In any case, by the early 17th century, pipe-smoking had crossed the Atlantic over to Europe, where it became all the rage.

This would not have been possible if it weren't for the entrepreneurial spirit of one English pioneer: Sir Walter Raleigh.

Sadly, Sir Walter's career as a tobacco trader was short-lived as he succumbed to the amorous demands of Elizabeth I; England's toughest, not to mention baldest, queen.

However in 1612, his efforts were continued by John Rolfe. An Englishman who, in spite of his agronomic achievements in Virginia and trading success in Europe, is today best known for his marriage to Pocahontas (of 'Pocahontas' fame).

Curiously enough, when Rolfe's trade first reached Europe, he discovered that the French were already using clay pipes to smoke medicinal herbs.

With the arrival of his fine Virginian tobacco, pipe-smoking soon became a pleasure instead of a prescription.

The European pipe was made of costly, yet fragile Turkish clay called *meerschaum*.

"Ah yes, the meerschaum," Mr.Doshi reflects, "too precious for its own good. It soon became more of an objet d'art than an objet d'decent-smoke."

Predictably, the meerschaum quickly lost out in popularity to pipes carved from the root of the *briar*, a tough shrub of the Mediterranean region.

Today, nearly ninety percent of all pipes are made from the resilient, and often very elegant, briar.

You can purchase some of the world's most distinguished briar pipes, such as hand-made pipes from *Comoy's of London, BBB* and *Ganneval, Bondier and Donninger*, right here in Kuala Lumpur on Jalan Tuanku Abdul Rahman, at P.Lal Store.

Mr.Doshi's shoe shop.

P.Lal Store
GUARANTEED LOWEST FIXED PRICES
135, JALAN TUANKU ABDUL RAHMAN, 50100 KUALA LUMPUR. TEL: 2927062 & 2952341

CONSUMER NEWSPAPER
OVER 600 LINES: SINGLE

138
ART DIRECTORS:
Yasmin Ahmad
Chan Lee Shon
WRITER:
Yasmin Ahmad
CLIENT:
P. Lal Store
AGENCY:
Leo Burnett/Kuala Lumpur

139
ART DIRECTOR:
Kevin Stark
WRITER:
Nick Kidney
CLIENT:
Mercedes-Benz UK
AGENCY:
Leo Burnett/London

140
ART DIRECTORS:
Dave Cook
Carol Holsinger
Gina Fortunato
WRITER:
Steve Amick
PHOTOGRAPHER:
Joe Fornabio
CLIENT:
The Village Voice
AGENCY:
Mad Dogs & Englishmen/
New York

141
ART DIRECTORS:
Dave Cook
Carol Holsinger
Gina Fortunato
WRITER:
Mikal Reich
PHOTOGRAPHER:
Joe Fornabio
CLIENT:
The Village Voice
AGENCY:
Mad Dogs & Englishmen/
New York

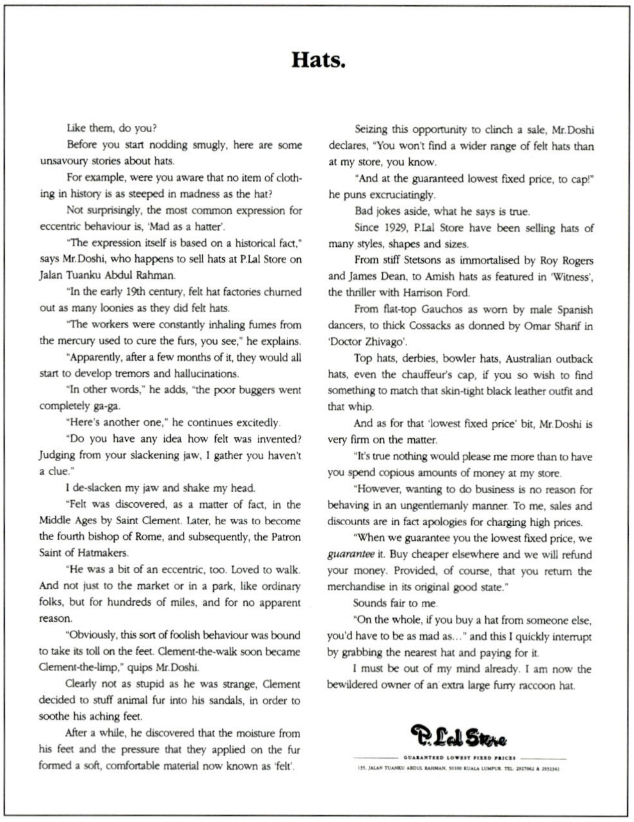

Hats.

Like them, do you?

Before you start nodding smugly, here are some unsavoury stories about hats.

For example, were you aware that no item of clothing in history is as steeped in madness as the hat?

Not surprisingly, the most common expression for eccentric behaviour is, 'Mad as a hatter'.

"The expression itself is based on a historical fact," says Mr.Doshi, who happens to sell hats at P.Lal Store on Jalan Tuanku Abdul Rahman.

"In the early 19th century, felt hat factories churned out as many loonies as they did felt hats.

"The workers were constantly inhaling fumes from the mercury used to cure the furs, you see," he explains.

"Apparently, after a few months of it, they would all start to develop tremors and hallucinations.

"In other words," he adds, "the poor buggers went completely ga-ga.

"Here's another one," he continues excitedly.

"Do you have any idea how felt was invented? Judging from your slackening jaw, I gather you haven't a clue."

I de-slacken my jaw and shake my head.

"Felt was discovered, as a matter of fact, in the Middle Ages by Saint Clement. Later, he was to become the fourth bishop of Rome, and subsequently, the Patron Saint of Hatmakers.

"He was a bit of an eccentric, too. Loved to walk. And not just to the market or in a park, like ordinary folks, but for hundreds of miles, and for no apparent reason.

"Obviously, this sort of foolish behaviour was bound to take its toll on the feet. Clement-the-walk soon became Clement-the-limp," quips Mr.Doshi.

Clearly not as stupid as he was strange, Clement decided to stuff animal fur into his sandals, in order to soothe his aching feet.

After a while, he discovered that the moisture from his feet and the pressure that they applied on the fur formed a soft, comfortable material now known as 'felt'.

Seizing this opportunity to clinch a sale, Mr.Doshi declares, "You won't find a wider range of felt hats than at my store, you know.

"And at the guaranteed lowest fixed price, to cap!" he puns excruciatingly.

Bad jokes aside, what he says is true.

Since 1929, P.Lal Store have been selling hats of many styles, shapes and sizes.

From stiff Stetsons as immortalised by Roy Rogers and James Dean, to Amish hats as featured in 'Witness', the thriller with Harrison Ford.

From flat-top Gauchos as worn by male Spanish dancers, to thick Cossacks as donned by Omar Sharif in 'Doctor Zhivago'.

Top hats, derbies, bowler hats, Australian outback hats, even the chauffeur's cap, if you so wish to find something to match that skin-tight black leather outfit and that whip.

And as for that 'lowest fixed price' bit, Mr.Doshi is very firm on the matter.

"It's true nothing would please me more than to have you spend copious amounts of money at my store.

"However, wanting to do business is no reason for behaving in an ungentlemanly manner. To me, sales and discounts are in fact apologies for charging high prices.

"When we guarantee you the lowest fixed price, we *guarantee* it. Buy cheaper elsewhere and we will refund your money. Provided, of course, that you return the merchandise in its original good state."

Sounds fair to me.

"On the whole, if you buy a hat from someone else, you'd have to be as mad as..." and this I quickly interrupt by grabbing the nearest hat and paying for it.

I must be out of my mind already. I am now the bewildered owner of an extra large furry raccoon hat.

P. Lal Store

GUARANTEED LOWEST FIXED PRICES

135, JALAN TUANKU ABDUL RAHMAN, 50100 KUALA LUMPUR. TEL: 2927062 & 2932341

138

139

Let's say an individual was approaching you, trying to sell you a subscription...you could drop that mother at 500 feet.
the village VOICE
NOT AMERICA'S FAVORITE PAPER

140

It's *so* nice that homosexuals, Jews and terrorists have a newspaper to read.
the village VOICE
NOT AMERICA'S FAVORITE PAPER

141

CONSUMER NEWSPAPER
OVER 600 LINES: SINGLE

142
ART DIRECTORS:
Dave Cook
Carol Holsinger
Gina Fortunato
WRITER:
Mikal Reich
PHOTOGRAPHERS:
Joe Fornabio
Mel Curtis
CLIENT:
The Village Voice
AGENCY:
Mad Dogs & Englishmen/
New York

143
ART DIRECTOR:
Mark Fuller
WRITER:
Ron Huey
PHOTOGRAPHER:
William Coupon
CLIENT:
Amgen
AGENCY:
The Martin Agency/
Richmond

144
ART DIRECTOR:
Mark Fuller
WRITER:
Joe Nagy
CLIENT:
Mercedes-Benz of
North America
AGENCY:
The Martin Agency/
Richmond

145
ART DIRECTOR:
Barney Goldberg
WRITER:
Anne Marie Floyd
PHOTOGRAPHER:
Brad Miller
CLIENT:
Mercedes-Benz of
North America
AGENCY:
The Martin Agency/
Richmond

I read it once
and I got all kinda
itchy-like...
THE MARINE
SUPPLY

the village VOICE

NOT AMERICA'S FAVORITE PAPER

142

THE HORROR STORIES YOU'VE
HEARD ABOUT CHEMOTHERAPY ARE TRUE.
THEY'RE ALSO A DECADE OLD.

Today, men and women are leading more active lives while undergoing chemotherapy treatment. And that's good news. Recent breakthroughs are helping reduce many of the common side effects of treatment including nausea and even more serious conditions that can develop like a low white blood cell count.

One drug, Neupogen (Filgrastim), is now being prescribed to help certain people on chemotherapy maintain a normal white blood cell count. Specifically, a normal neutrophil count. In short, neutrophils are white blood cells that help your body fight infection. Maintaining a normal neutrophil count during your chemotherapy treatment can be important for two reasons.

First, you have a much greater chance of staying on your chemotherapy schedule. And, that will mean getting your treatment behind you sooner. Secondly, maintaining a normal neutrophil count can help reduce your risk of infection. So you have a better chance of staying out of the hospital. Instead, you can spend more time at home where you belong with family and friends. Even daily activities like shopping and eating out can be more accessible.

Of course, Neupogen isn't appropriate for every patient. Ask your doctor if Neupogen should be a recommended part of your treatment. On the following page, you'll find an explanation of Neupogen and its possible side effects. The most common side effect that patients experience is mild-to-moderate bone pain, which can usually be controlled with a non-aspirin analgesic.

In closing, before we embarked on this educational campaign, we conducted extensive research with people undergoing chemotherapy and with doctors. Among those being treated, we found an overwhelming desire for more information concerning treatment. Doctors, many of whom had initial misgivings about any advertising at all, urged us to be candid and to point out that Neupogen isn't for everyone. We acted on their advice.

We realize that your medical care is a sensitive and personal matter. We'd like to know your feelings about the information presented here. If you would like to receive more information concerning Neupogen and how it might help in your treatment, please call us at 1-800-333-9777, extension 667.

NEUPOGEN

143

How the person who owns the snowplow company gets to the snowplow company.
You never know what sort of weather you'll face in the winter. Even so, some executives seem to get through it better than others. Maybe it's because they've got the advanced performance and safety features of the Mercedes-Benz S-Class. To see just how well-equipped the S-Class is, drive your current car to your nearest Mercedes dealer. But please stick to the plowed roads.
The S-Class

144

Priced so you can feel the wind in your hair while you still have your hair.
Don't be surprised to find yourself behind the wheel of your dream car a little ahead of schedule. With the Encore Program, you can buy or lease a pre-owned Mercedes that has passed a rigorous inspection. And includes a zero-deductible limited warranty and 24-hour roadside assistance. Take a test drive. And feel free to put the top down.
ENCORE
PRE-OWNED MERCEDES-BENZ

145

CONSUMER NEWSPAPER
OVER 600 LINES: SINGLE

146
ART DIRECTOR:
Leslie Ali
WRITER:
Carl Loeb
ILLUSTRATOR:
Michael Bull
CLIENT:
The Red Chip Review
AGENCY:
Moffatt/Rosenthal,
Portland

147
ART DIRECTOR:
Chris Nott
WRITER:
Roy Davimes
ILLUSTRATOR:
Scott Wright
CLIENT:
Maryview Medical Center
AGENCY:
Siddall Matus & Coughter/
Richmond

148
ART DIRECTOR:
Maria Kostyk-Petro
WRITER:
Lisa Lipkin-Balser
PHOTOGRAPHER:
Ellen Von Unwerth
CLIENT:
Sara Lee Intimates/
Wonderbra
AGENCY:
TBWA Chiat/Day, New York

149
ART DIRECTORS:
Stan Toyama
Robert Prins
WRITER:
Michael Folino
ILLUSTRATOR:
Raphael Montoliou
CLIENT:
America West Airlines
AGENCY:
Team One Advertising/
El Segundo, CA

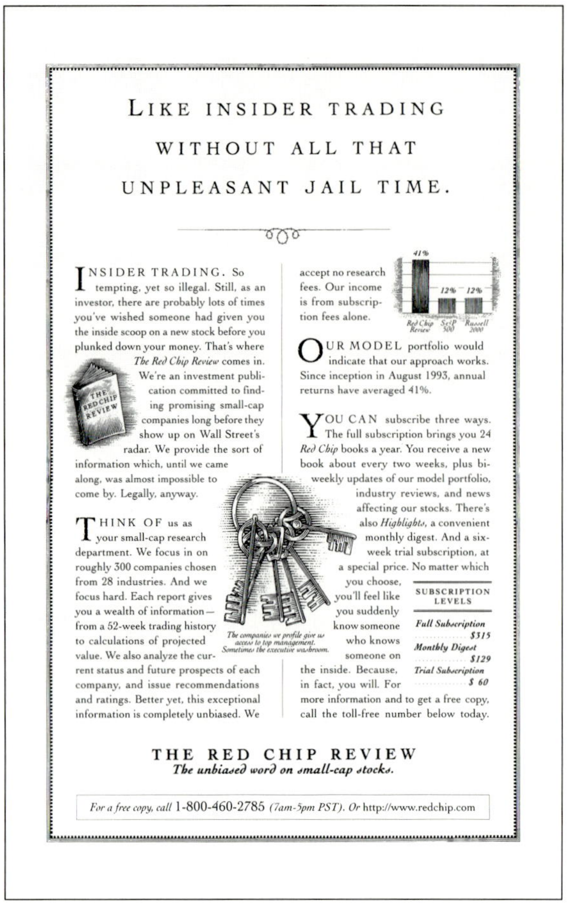

146

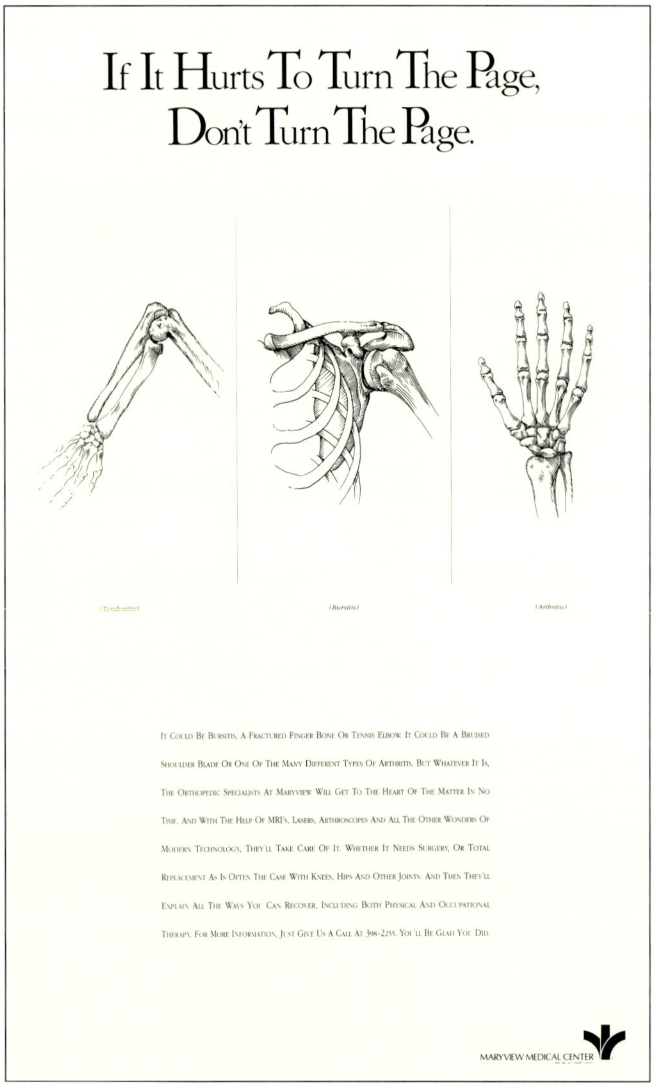

147

WINNER,
BEST SPECIAL EFFECTS.
THE ONE AND ONLY
wonderbra
THE PUSH-UP PLUNGE BRA

148

WE'VE REDUCED OUR FARES OUT OF ORANGE COUNTY.
NOT SURPRISINGLY, THE SEATS ON THE RIGHT WING ARE FILLING UP FIRST.

In today's fiscally conservative times it's reasonable to expect lower fares. Which is why America West is proud to announce that we've just reduced our fares out of Orange County Airport. And not simply bleeding heart fares to one location. We're talking lower fares, across the board, to most of our 70 destinations throughout the United States of America, Mexico and Canada. (Should you find yourself on the wrong side of the El Toro "Y," we also have low-fare service from LAX, Long Beach, Ontario and Burbank.) Along with our lower fares, we also offer extremely economical and convenient vacation packages (often referred to as "family values"). In addition to our incredible everyday low fares, we also have something that should appeal to the old-fashioned work ethic in everyone – our superior service. America West offers a wide array of amenities, such as pre-assigned seating and our worldwide frequent flyer program, called FlightFund.* We also take great pride in having one of the most modern fleets in the sky (next to our military, of course). All of which makes America West the airline with great service and low fares to and from Orange County. Conservatively speaking, that is. For reservations, call your travel agent, or America West at 1-800-235-9292.

$19
TO PHOENIX

$29
TO LAS VEGAS OR SACRAMENTO

HERE'S A SAMPLE OF OUR LOW FARES FROM ORANGE CO.

All fares one-way, no round-trip required

TO:	FOR:
Albuquerque	$ 69
Atlanta	$174
Baltimore	$179
Boston	$191
Chicago	$179
Columbus, OH	$139
Dallas/Ft. Worth	$184
Denver	$ 69
El Paso	$ 69
Houston	$129
Kansas City	$104
Milwaukee	$154
Minneapolis/St. Paul	$109
New York	$194
Newark	$186
Omaha	$ 99
Philadelphia	$177
St. Louis	$139
Vancouver, B.C.	$ 99
Washington, D.C.	$199
Wichita	$124

SOME OF OUR COMPLETE VACATION PACKAGES FROM ORANGE CO.

All packages include round-trip air, two nights' hotel, 500 bonus FlightFund miles and optional rental car where available.*

TO:	FROM:
Las Vegas	$ 79
Los Cabos, Mexico	$409
Mazatlan, Mexico	$374
Orlando	$389
Phoenix	$129
Reno	$ 99

America West Vacations
1-800-356-6611

We fly to over 70 destinations throughout the good old U.S. of A., not to mention our allies, Canada and Mexico.

America West Airlines.
IT SEEMS SILLY TO PAY MORE™

149

CONSUMER NEWSPAPER
OVER 600 LINES: SINGLE

150

ART DIRECTOR:
Jeff Williams

WRITER:
Craig Namba

CLIENT:
ESPN

AGENCY:
Wieden & Kennedy/
Portland

CONSUMER NEWSPAPER
OVER 600 LINES:
CAMPAIGN

151

ART DIRECTORS:
Paul Bennell
Mike Boekholt
Goh Wee Kim

WRITER:
Andy Flemming

PHOTOGRAPHERS:
Simon Harsent
John Clang

CLIENT:
Bayer

AGENCY:
Bates/Singapore

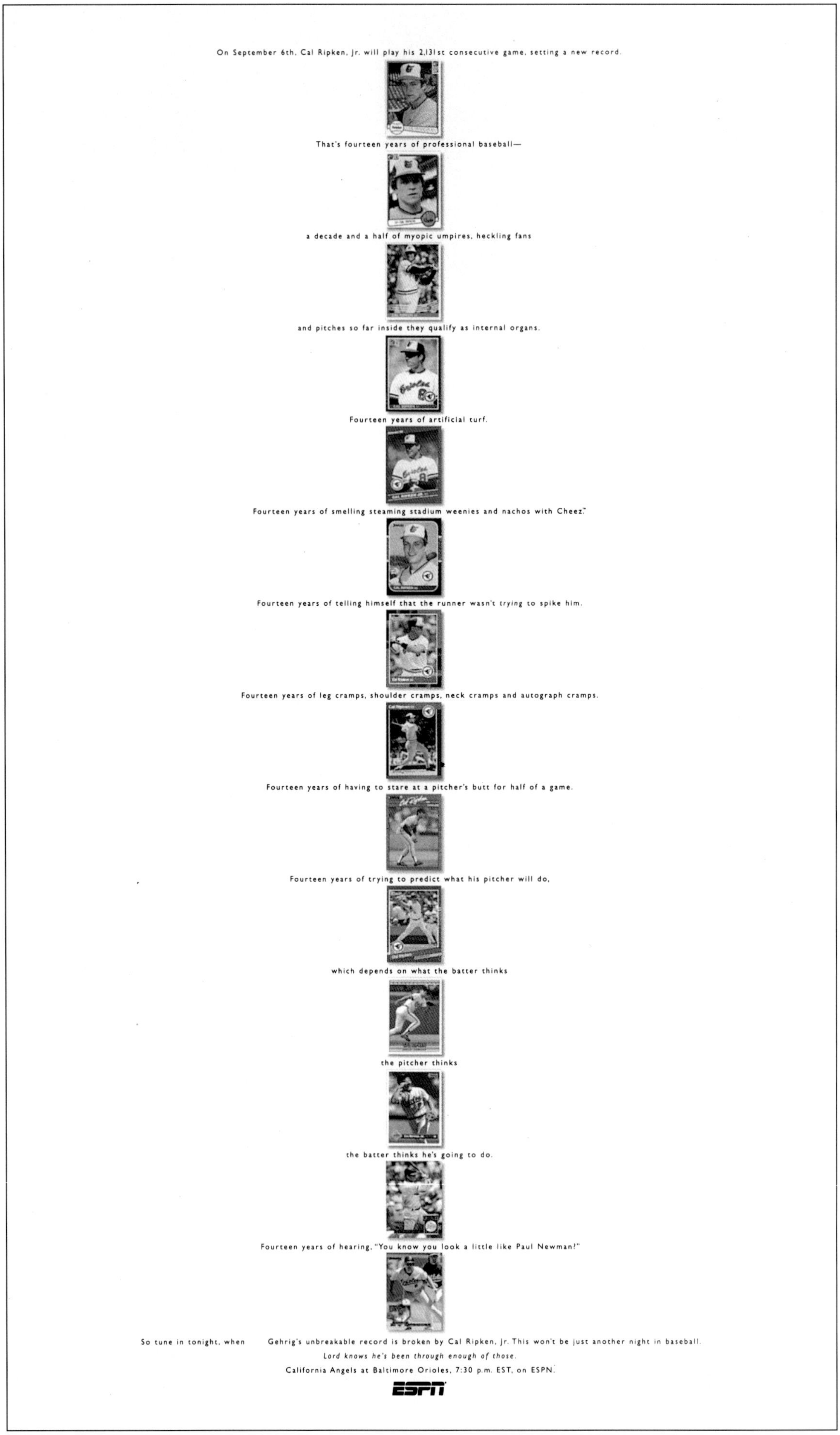
On September 6th, Cal Ripken, Jr. will play his 2,131st consecutive game, setting a new record.
That's fourteen years of professional baseball—
a decade and a half of myopic umpires, heckling fans
and pitches so far inside they qualify as internal organs.
Fourteen years of artificial turf.
Fourteen years of smelling steaming stadium weenies and nachos with Cheez.
Fourteen years of telling himself that the runner wasn't trying to spike him.
Fourteen years of leg cramps, shoulder cramps, neck cramps and autograph cramps.
Fourteen years of having to stare at a pitcher's butt for half of a game.
Fourteen years of trying to predict what his pitcher will do,
which depends on what the batter thinks
the pitcher thinks
the batter thinks he's going to do.
Fourteen years of hearing, "You know you look a little like Paul Newman?"
So tune in tonight, when Gehrig's unbreakable record is broken by Cal Ripken, Jr. This won't be just another night in baseball.
Lord knows he's been through enough of those.
California Angels at Baltimore Orioles, 7:30 p.m. EST, on ESPN.
ESPN

Bayer
The fly killer

Bayer
The fly killer

There was an old
lady who swallowed
a
Bayer
The fly killer

CONSUMER NEWSPAPER
OVER 600 LINES:
CAMPAIGN

152
ART DIRECTOR:
Mario Ricci
WRITER:
Bill Parker
PHOTOGRAPHER:
Michael MacDonald
CLIENT:
Upper Canada Brewing Company
AGENCY:
Bensimon Byrne/Toronto

153
ART DIRECTOR:
David Ayriss
WRITER:
Mark Waggoner
PHOTOGRAPHER:
Doug Petty
CLIENT:
The Oregonian
AGENCY:
Cole & Weber/Portland

REMEMBER
last
Weekend?
Yes.
No.
Dusted Hummel collection.
Alphabetized 8-track tapes.
Watched Murder, She Wrote. (Rerun.)
Why? Should I?
Over Edge
[Read A&E.]
The Oregonian
This should improve your memory. A weekly guide packed with info on music, movies, restaurants, clubs, galleries and more. Pick it up every Friday. You know, when you'd usually buy that new issue of Hummel Digest.
A&E. FRIDAYS.

DO YOU KNOW
more
about what's happening
IN THEIR NEIGHBORHOOD
than your own?
MP
MELROSE PLACE
The Oregonian
Every day, the Metro section brings you the latest community news. Specially zoned for your neighborhood. And on Thursdays, the Neighbors section delivers even more. Because when it comes to relationships, conspiracies and personal intrigue, who would you really rather know about: your next-door neighbors or theirs?
COMMUNITY NEWS. DAILY.

Child mauled
by
tiger.
(And other hilarious stories.)
The Oregonian
Every day, The Oregonian gives you two full pages of comics. Plus eight color pages every Sunday. Because what better way is there to start the day than with a sled crash, a spaceship explosion, or an attack by Tyrannosaurus Rex?
COMICS. DAILY.

CONSUMER NEWSPAPER
OVER 600 LINES:
CAMPAIGN

154

ART DIRECTORS:
David Swartz
Alex Bogusky

WRITERS:
Pieter Blikslager
T. Grand
Pat Harris

PHOTOGRAPHER:
Barry Rosenthal

CLIENT:
AvMed

AGENCY:
Crispin & Porter/Miami

155

ART DIRECTOR:
Joe Paprocki

WRITER:
Doug de Grood

CLIENT:
Star Tribune

AGENCY:
Fallon McElligott/
Minneapolis

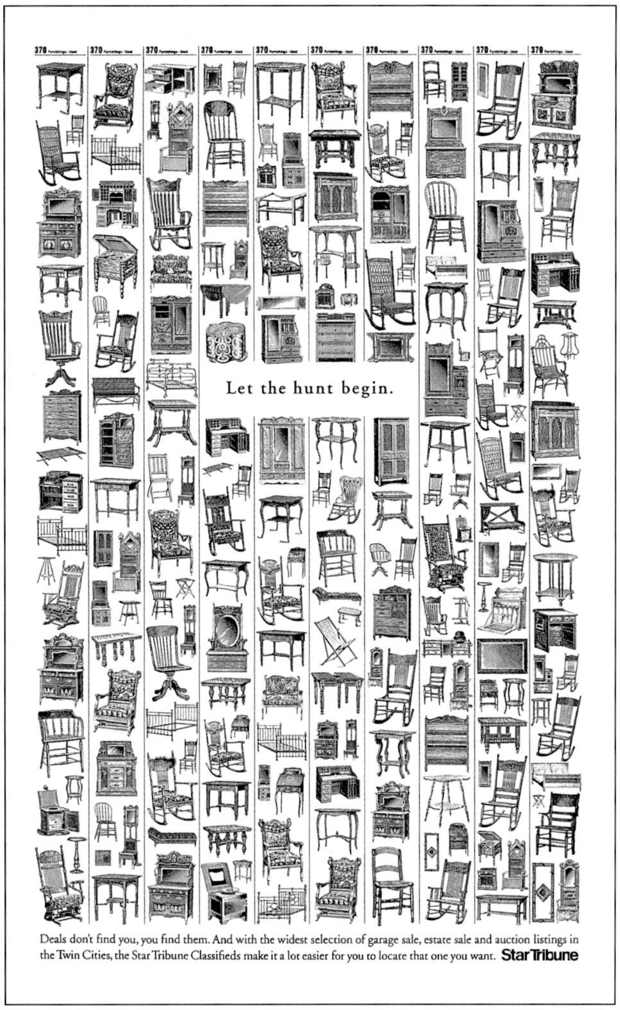
Let the hunt begin.
Deals don't find you, you find them. And with the widest selection of garage sale, estate sale and auction listings in the Twin Cities, the Star Tribune Classifieds make it a lot easier for you to locate that one you want.
StarTribune

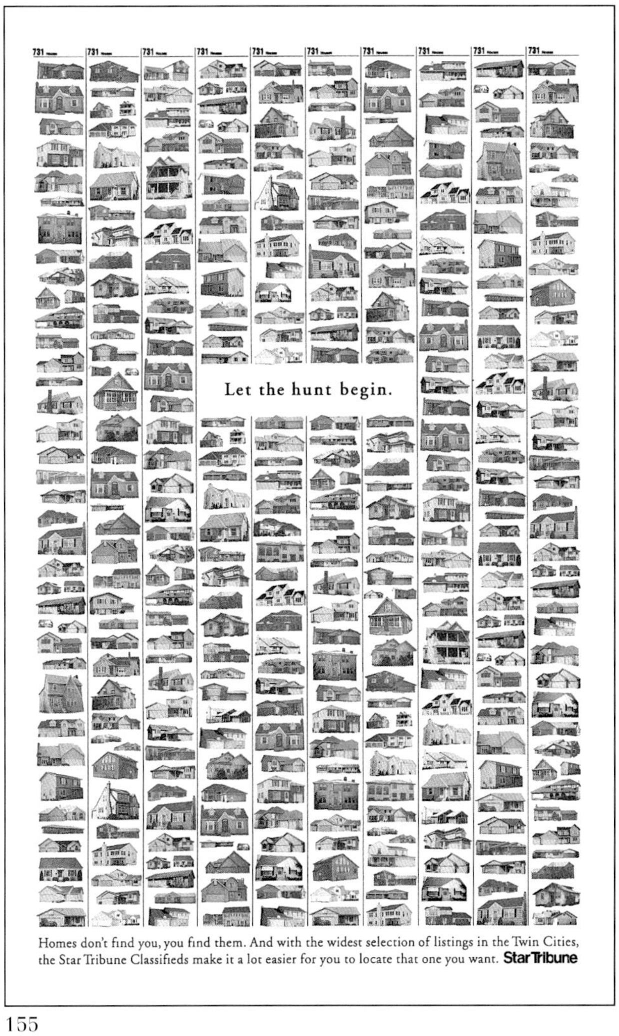
Let the hunt begin.
Homes don't find you, you find them. And with the widest selection of listings in the Twin Cities, the Star Tribune Classifieds make it a lot easier for you to locate that one you want.
StarTribune

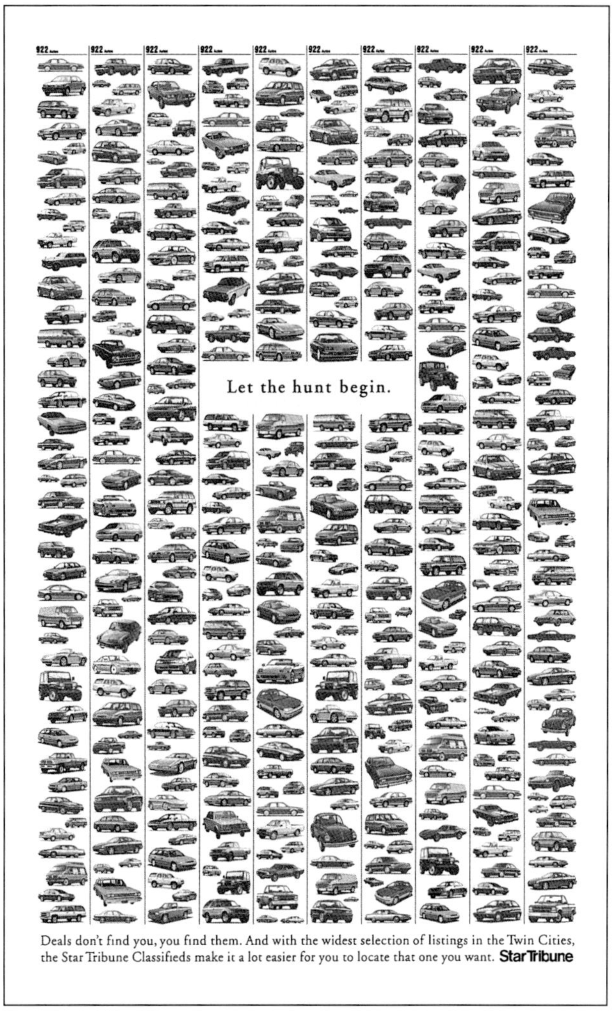
Let the hunt begin.
Deals don't find you, you find them. And with the widest selection of listings in the Twin Cities, the Star Tribune Classifieds make it a lot easier for you to locate that one you want.
StarTribune

CONSUMER NEWSPAPER
OVER 600 LINES:
CAMPAIGN

156

ART DIRECTOR:
Alan Davis

WRITER:
Jez Willy

PHOTOGRAPHER:
Elliott Erwitt

CLIENT:
Tesco

AGENCY:
Lowe Howard-Spink/
London

TO
MAJOR GENEF
WHATEVER YOU FORGET, REMEMBER WE OPEN ON MAY 29.
TESCO
Every little helps

Wine
WHATEVER YOU FORGET, REMEMBER WE OPEN ON FEB 13.
Cabot Place West, Canary Wharf. Open: Mon-Fri 7.30am-8pm, Sat 8am-6pm.
TESCO
Every little helps

CONSUMER NEWSPAPER
OVER 600 LINES:
CAMPAIGN

157

ART DIRECTORS:
Mark Fuller
Barney Goldberg

WRITERS:
Joe Nagy
Jeff Ross

CLIENT:
Mercedes-Benz of
North America

AGENCY:
The Martin Agency/
Richmond

When
wit and
charm
fail.
The SL-500: Legendary styling. 315 horses. Automatic soft top and removable hardtop. Multicontour leather seats. Burl walnut trim. Cellular phone. Alpine CD changer. 200-watt Bose sound system. Alas, there is still hope.
Mercedes-Benz

Taxicabs make pretty good slalom cones.
The new Mercedes-Benz E-Class: Rack-and-pinion steering. Double-wishbone front suspension. Bigger wheels. Wider tires. Even when you're just trying to make your way through traffic, it's a great way to get around.
Mercedes-Benz

Sends chills down your orthopedically supported spine.
The E320: 10-way adjustable leather seats with lumbar support. 217 horses. Double-wishbone front suspension. Stabilizer bars. Traction control. 10-hole alloy wheels. Xenon headlamps. The hair on your neck will stand straight up.
Mercedes-Benz

CONSUMER NEWSPAPER
OVER 600 LINES:
CAMPAIGN

158

ART DIRECTORS:
John Emmert
John Doyle

WRITER:
Dylan Lee

PHOTOGRAPHER:
Geoffrey Stein

CLIENT:
Shreve Crump & Low

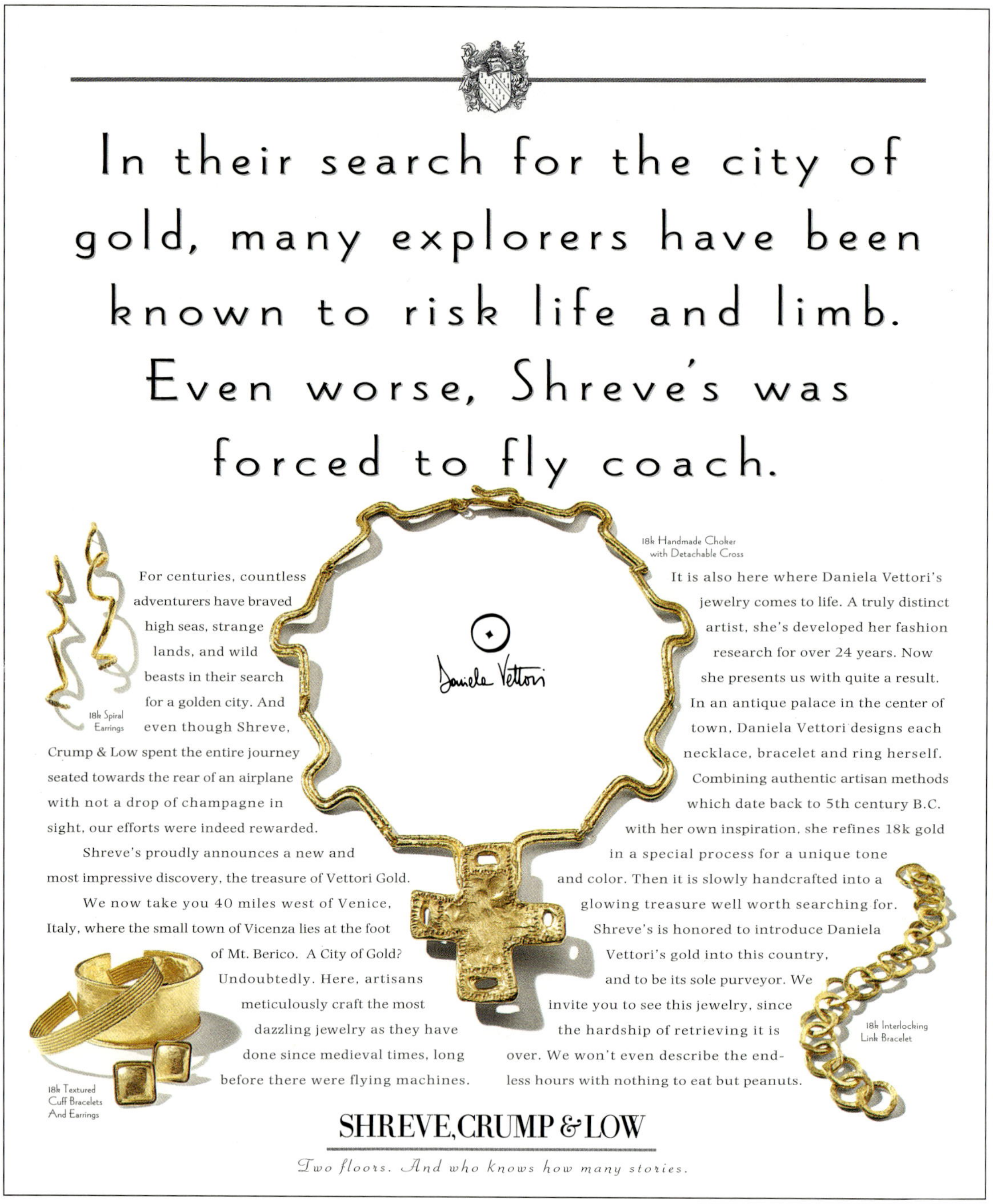

In their search for the city of gold, many explorers have been known to risk life and limb. Even worse, Shreve's was forced to fly coach.
18k Spiral Earrings
18k Handmade Choker with Detachable Cross
Daniela Vettori
For centuries, countless adventurers have braved high seas, strange lands, and wild beasts in their search for a golden city. And even though Shreve, Crump & Low spent the entire journey seated towards the rear of an airplane with not a drop of champagne in sight, our efforts were indeed rewarded.
Shreve's proudly announces a new and most impressive discovery, the treasure of Vettori Gold.
We now take you 40 miles west of Venice, Italy, where the small town of Vicenza lies at the foot of Mt. Berico. A City of Gold? Undoubtedly. Here, artisans meticulously craft the most dazzling jewelry as they have done since medieval times, long before there were flying machines.
It is also here where Daniela Vettori's jewelry comes to life. A truly distinct artist, she's developed her fashion research for over 24 years. Now she presents us with quite a result. In an antique palace in the center of town, Daniela Vettori designs each necklace, bracelet and ring herself. Combining authentic artisan methods which date back to 5th century B.C. with her own inspiration, she refines 18k gold in a special process for a unique tone and color. Then it is slowly handcrafted into a glowing treasure well worth searching for.
Shreve's is honored to introduce Daniela Vettori's gold into this country, and to be its sole purveyor. We invite you to see this jewelry, since the hardship of retrieving it is over. We won't even describe the endless hours with nothing to eat but peanuts.
18k Textured Cuff Bracelets And Earrings
18k Interlocking Link Bracelet
SHREVE, CRUMP & LOW
Two floors. And who knows how many stories.

6 years to create. 15 years to perfect. 100 years to arrive. Perhaps you've gone long enough without them.
Each one is perfectly round. Smooth. With brilliant lustre. What's that? You have none? By all means, we must do something about it.
The jewels we speak of are the pearls of Mikimoto. To create them, patience was indeed necessary.
They're cultured in Japan and in the warmer waters near Australia. The most precious are South Sea Pearls, which spend as long as six years inside an oyster. They are known as the Queen of Gems, and are featured in our centerpiece necklace.
You will find the criteria are unforgiving. Less than five of a hundred pearls harvested ever find their way onto the necklaces, bracelets and earrings of Mikimoto.
For you see, Kokichi Mikimoto was a man of the highest standards, and conviction. Refusing to bow to his family's opposition, damaging tides, debt, and failure time and time again, he cultured the world's first pearl in 1893. Fifteen years later, he perfected the process, creating perfectly round, iridescent gems - until then, a jewel only nature could produce.
The centennial of Mikimoto's triumph recently was celebrated, and Shreve, Crump & Low is honored to be the only store in Boston to offer his legacy. To be sure, it was a most rewarding wait.
Let us begin with a basic necklace. The pearls focus attention on the wearer, not themselves. And Shreve's has a vast selection of lengths and sizes. As with all Mikimoto pearls, they enhance not only formal wear, but casual as well.
For those who have been without, do visit us. We will promptly remedy the situation. If your patience is at its limit, you now only need wait until regular business hours.
18k Pearl & Diamond Drop Earrings
18k Mabe Pearl & Diamond Earrings
South Sea Pearl Necklace
18k Free Form Pin
Necklaces in a Wide Selection of Sizes all with 18k signature Mikimoto clasps
MIKIMOTO
SHREVE, CRUMP & LOW
Two floors. And who knows how many stories.

If you wish to enjoy the riches of Europe's Kings, you conquer them. If you wish them to enjoy yours, invite them over for dinner.
It is 1805, and Napoleon Bonaparte is conquering most of Europe. More than one king flees for his life, leaving unimaginable riches behind. The French royal treasury overflows.
Napoleon's reign, of course, did not last forever. And less than a century later, his nephew ascended to power. The new Emperor Napoleon aimed to boast an even grander court than his uncle.
But he needed no troops, only to appoint the factory of Christofle to be the royal silversmith. The final step was simple: invite the Kings of Europe to supper.
Presently, Shreve, Crump & Low offers an impressive treasury of Christofle, an honor few stores are allowed. The silver is crafted today just as when Christofle began. The silversmith works with many tools that are more than a century old, though the two most vital resources are still his hands. However, while the craftsmanship remains true to the original, the styles are always contemporary. Each year, new and unique silverware patterns, serving dishes and porcelain plates join the classic designs born in the Christofle workshop.
Shreve's invites you to inspect them yourself. You will find a bridal registry of Christofle is worthy of queens, empresses and princesses. Queens, empresses and princesses seem to agree, for it is the silver they have dined on for 165 years.
Ah, but we've neglected to inform you as to whether Napoleon was successful in his endeavor to impress. Well, when the Kings of Europe finished their meal, they inquired as to who made the silverware. Then they promptly ordered their own.
Silver Lace Elephant, $335
Christofle
Oceana, $215
Marly, $245
From The Flatware Collection (prices for five piece place settings)
Aria Gold, $395
"Vibrations" Wine Sleeve, $285
Caviar Server, $275
"Atlanta" Frame (5"x7"), $125
Christofle "Rubanea Blue" Five-Piece Place Setting, $149
Coordinating Service Plate, $55
SHREVE, CRUMP & LOW
Two floors. And who knows how many stories.

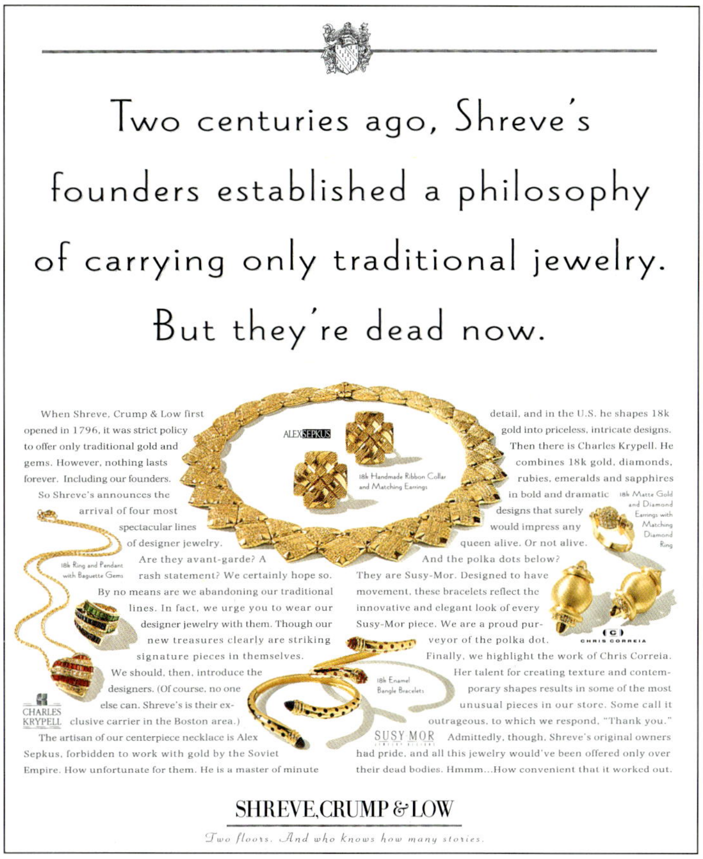
Two centuries ago, Shreve's founders established a philosophy of carrying only traditional jewelry. But they're dead now.
When Shreve, Crump & Low first opened in 1796, it was strict policy to offer only traditional gold and gems. However, nothing lasts forever. Including our founders.
So Shreve's announces the arrival of four most spectacular lines of designer jewelry.
Are they avant-garde? A rash statement? We certainly hope so. By no means are we abandoning our traditional lines. In fact, we urge you to wear our designer jewelry with them. Though our new treasures clearly are striking signature pieces in themselves.
We should, then, introduce the designers. (Of course, no one else can. Shreve's is their exclusive carrier in the Boston area.)
The artisan of our centerpiece necklace is Alex Sepkus, forbidden to work with gold by the Soviet Empire. How unfortunate for them. He is a master of minute detail, and in the U.S. he shapes 18k gold into priceless, intricate designs.
Then there is Charles Krypell. He combines 18k gold, diamonds, rubies, emeralds and sapphires in bold and dramatic designs that surely would impress any queen alive. Or not alive.
And the polka dots below? They are Susy-Mor. Designed to have movement, these bracelets reflect the innovative and elegant look of every Susy-Mor piece. We are a proud purveyor of the polka dot.
Finally, we highlight the work of Chris Correia. Her talent for creating texture and contemporary shapes results in some of the most unusual pieces in our store. Some call it outrageous, to which we respond, "Thank you."
Admittedly, though, Shreve's original owners had pride, and all this jewelry would've been offered only over their dead bodies. Hmmm...How convenient that it worked out.
ALEX SEPKUS
18k Handmade Ribbon Collar and Matching Earrings
18k Ring and Pendant with Baguette Gems
CHARLES KRYPELL
18k Matte Gold and Diamond Earrings with Matching Diamond Ring
CHRIS CORREIA
18k Enamel Bangle Bracelets
SUSY MOR
SHREVE, CRUMP & LOW
Two floors. And who knows how many stories.

CONSUMER NEWSPAPER
OVER 600 LINES:
CAMPAIGN

159

ART DIRECTOR:
John Emmert

WRITER:
Dylan Lee

PHOTOGRAPHER:
Geoffrey Stein

CLIENT:
Shreve Crump & Low

To discover our latest designer, Shreve, Crump & Low braved the most exotic and perilous lands. Yes, even Hoboken.
To Vicenza. To Sri Lanka. To Geneva, Athens, Madrid, and the South Sea. Shreve, Crump & Low quite literally searches the world over. No jungle is too savage. No sea, too treacherous.
And then there is Hoboken.
Shreve's would never ignore the treasures within our own time zone. Otherwise, creations such as those of Elizabeth Lindsay would go undiscovered.
You see, Ms. Lindsay is a dazzling find. Her studio lies in Hoboken, and inside she slowly turns sterling silver into precious adornments. She brings an extensive background of architectural study and interior design to her artistry. Ancient Mayan, Roman and Egyptian influences are interwoven with her own distinctive approach into necklaces, earrings and bracelets.
All of Lindsay's designs are individually crafted in America, painstakingly, we might add. Inspect them carefully. The silver is substantial in weight. And you will immediately notice each piece is detailed on both sides, some more intricately than would seem humanly possible. Elizabeth Lindsay prides herself on uniqueness, as well, and specializes in one-of-a-kind and limited-edition jewelry. Adorn yourself with her silver, and you could quite easily travel halfway around the world before you find someone doing the same.
Shreve's is honored to be the exclusive purveyor of Elizabeth Lindsay's sterling collection in Massachusetts. We invite you to travel here and visit us. After all, we've saved you the arduous journey to the land called New Jersey.
Scroll Earrings with Amethyst Drop, $215
Medallion Necklace with Pearl, $290
Necklace with Amethyst Beads, 42", $465
Scroll Ring with Iolite and 14k Accents, $310
Ring with 14k Accents, $145
Flower Bracelet with Green Tourmaline, $990
Earrings, $290
ELIZABETH LINDSAY
FINE JEWELRY
SHREVE, CRUMP & LOW
Two floors. And who knows how many stories.

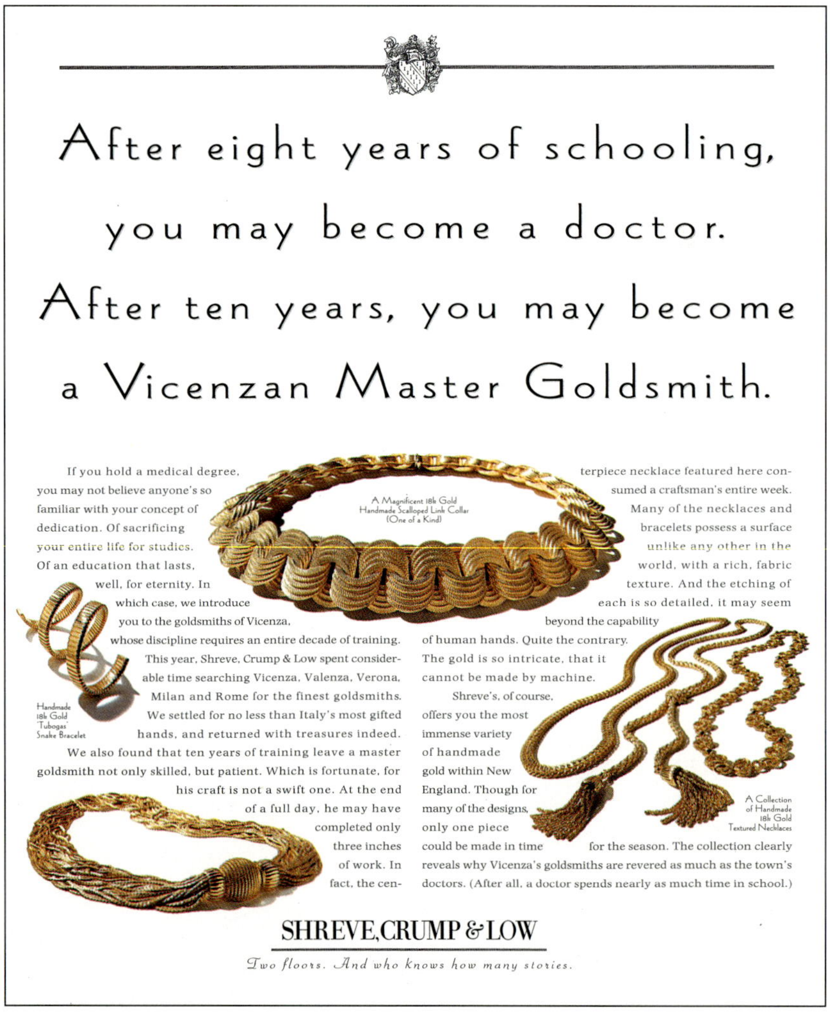
After eight years of schooling, you may become a doctor. After ten years, you may become a Vicenzan Master Goldsmith.
If you hold a medical degree, you may not believe anyone's so familiar with your concept of dedication. Of sacrificing your entire life for studies. Of an education that lasts, well, for eternity. In which case, we introduce you to the goldsmiths of Vicenza, whose discipline requires an entire decade of training.
This year, Shreve, Crump & Low spent considerable time searching Vicenza, Valenza, Verona, Milan and Rome for the finest goldsmiths. We settled for no less than Italy's most gifted hands, and returned with treasures indeed.
We also found that ten years of training leave a master goldsmith not only skilled, but patient. Which is fortunate, for his craft is not a swift one. At the end of a full day, he may have completed only three inches of work. In fact, the centerpiece necklace featured here consumed a craftsman's entire week.
Many of the necklaces and bracelets possess a surface unlike any other in the world, with a rich, fabric texture. And the etching of each is so detailed, it may seem beyond the capability of human hands. Quite the contrary. The gold is so intricate, that it cannot be made by machine.
Shreve's, of course, offers you the most immense variety of handmade gold within New England. Though for many of the designs, only one piece could be made in time for the season. The collection clearly reveals why Vicenza's goldsmiths are revered as much as the town's doctors. (After all, a doctor spends nearly as much time in school.)
A Magnificent 18k Gold Handmade Scalloped Link Collar (One of a Kind)
Handmade 18k Gold 'Tubogas' Snake Bracelet
A Collection of Handmade 18k Gold Textured Necklaces
SHREVE, CRUMP & LOW
Two floors. And who knows how many stories.

Shreve's is graciously invited to meet Europe's preeminent jewelry designer, and what do we do? Pillage.
18k Gold Diamond Pave' Heart Necklace
18k White Gold Diamond Pave' Key Pendant (below)
GIOIELMODA
Some might call it brash, uncivilized, even barbaric. Shreve, Crump & Low? Well, maybe.
Nonetheless, we unveil the jewelry of Pasquale Bruni Bossio. To be honest, once we laid eyes upon his diamonds and gold, we were quite ready to plunder. Nor did it take long to see why Bossio is not only on Europe's cutting edge, but the edge itself. His gift for designing 18k enamel jewelry is truly unrivaled.
Bossio's life has always been one of gold and gems. At 13 years of age, he took his first steps inside the factories of Valenza, Italy. Only 7 years later, his own workshop opened its doors. Within it today, the most wondrous collections are born.
Slowly, by hand, diamonds take the shape of a heart or moon or star. And they indeed shine. You also will notice they are very similar to nothing, for every design is original. His enamel designs are no less brilliant. Gem flowers bloom with vibrant yellow, green, turquoise, red and pink, reminiscent of the mod 60s. Rest assured, if imitation is the sincerest form of flattery, then Bossio is the most complimented designer in Europe.
During one of the regular trips Shreve's makes to Italy, we discovered Pasquale Bruni Bossio in Valenza. We also discovered we are the first and exclusive New England merchant to offer Bossio's jewelry. So you are ensured of being the first to wear it.
The treasure has been divided into two parts, and you will find it at the corner of Arlington and Boylston Streets, and in The Mall at Chestnut Hill. We, of course, are more than willing to share the booty.
18k Gold and Enamel Flower Collection
Diamond Stars on 18k White Gold Chains
SHREVE, CRUMP & LOW
Two floors. And who knows how many stories.

There's a place in Italy where gold is crafted into perhaps the world's most unique fashions. We will show you everything but the map.
It is in the city of Vicenza, west of Venice. But that is as much as we divulge. The part of town, the street, the shop number. They remain well-guarded details. However, the rest we gladly share. Shreve, Crump & Low is honored to introduce the latest fashions from Daniela Vettori.
From hands within her workshop spring forth the most unusual and dazzling treasures. Combining authentic artisan methods with her own inspiration, she refines 18k gold in a special process for a unique tone and color. All Vettori gold is required to be alloyed in her own shop, and is cast using the lost-wax method. (How lost? It's taken 700 years to be found.) Since all molds are handmade, their very nature ensures no two pieces are ever identical.
Daniela Vettori works with the rare and unusual as well, from baroque pearls to exotic stones. Often she labors many months with a solitary gem until completely satisfied with a priceless, truly original design. We can assure you, it is time extremely well spent.
Shreve's proudly serves as the exclusive purveyor of Vettori Gold in New England.
And now that it has just arrived in our store, we invite you to call us. We would be delighted to give you directions.
Daniela Vettori
18k Handmade Textured Collar and Earrings
18k Baroque Pearl Stick Pin
18k Multiple Strand Choker
18k and Tourmaline Collection
SHREVE, CRUMP & LOW
Two floors. And who knows how many stories.

CONSUMER NEWSPAPER
OVER 600 LINES:
CAMPAIGN

160

ART DIRECTORS:
Robert Prins
Stan Toyama

WRITERS:
Matthew Bogen
Michael Folino

ILLUSTRATORS:
John Craig
Raphael Montoliou
Geoff Grahn

CLIENT:
America West Airlines

AGENCY:
Team One Advertising/
El Segundo, CA

THERE ARE CHEAPER WAYS TO TRAVEL, BUT THEY ONLY OFFER RETURN FLIGHTS ONCE EVERY FOUR YEARS.

Sure, there are less expensive ways to get around the country. As long as you don't mind destinations that all begin with the word "Fort," or object to the occasional parachute jump. Of course, affordable air travel doesn't have to mean a tour of duty. Just fly America West. We offer everyday low fares (and even lower evening fares for those able to fly at night) to over 70 cities, coast-to-coast. But even at the height of a fare war, we wouldn't expect you to sacrifice. So, we always feature major-airline amenities like pre-assigned seating. A worldwide frequent flyer program called FlightFund.® And one of the most modern fleets in the sky. For reservations, just call your professional travel agent, or 1-800-235-9292. Because, after all, serving your country is noble, but it shouldn't be the only way you can afford to see it.

JUST A SAMPLE OF OUR LOW FARES.

Each way, based on round-trip purchase.

BETWEEN:	AND:	FOR:
Albuquerque	Orange Co.	$ 89
Albuquerque	Portland, OR	$109
Burbank	Atlanta	$179
Colorado Springs	Mazatlan, Mexico	$178
Las Vegas	Atlanta	$169
Las Vegas	New York	$179
Las Vegas	Vancouver, B.C.	$127
Las Vegas	Wichita	$149
Los Angeles	Newark	$150
Oakland	Atlanta	$179
Oakland	Houston	$120
Ontario, CA	Milwaukee	$164
Orange Co.	Newark	$194
Orange Co.	Phoenix	$ 54
Phoenix	Manzanillo, Mexico	$162
Phoenix	Minneapolis/St. Paul	$159
Phoenix	Vancouver, B.C.	$109
Reno/Lake Tahoe	Dallas/Ft. Worth	$179
San Francisco	Dallas/Ft. Worth	$ 85
San Francisco	Minneapolis/St. Paul	$199
San Francisco	New York	$150

One-way fares, round-trip not required.

Las Vegas	Colorado Springs	$ 49
Oakland	Tucson	$ 79
Phoenix	Chicago	$134
Phoenix	Colorado Springs	$ 49
Reno/Lake Tahoe	Houston	$139
Reno/Lake Tahoe	Tucson	$ 88

LOOK FOR OUR NEW SERVICE TO PUERTO VALLARTA AND MANZANILLO, MEXICO, STARTING OCTOBER 29TH.

JUST A FEW OF OUR COMPLETE VACATION PACKAGES.

All packages include round-trip air and two nights' hotel.

BETWEEN:	AND:	FROM:
Albuquerque	San Francisco	$279
Colorado Springs	San Diego	$294
Denver	Mazatlan, Mexico	$369
Las Vegas	Reno	$134
Los Angeles	Phoenix	$159
Oakland	Las Vegas	$ 99
Orange Co.	Los Cabos, Mexico	$389
Phoenix	Orlando	$404
Phoenix	Vancouver, B.C.	$349
Sacramento	Orange Co.	$149

All vacations include 500 FlightFund® bonus miles and an optional rental car where available. For more information on a complete vacation package, call your professional travel agent, or America West Vacations® at 1-800-356-6611.

America West Vacations®

America West Airlines®

IT SEEMS SILLY TO PAY MORE℠

*AIRFARES QUOTED ABOVE are subject to change, seats are limited and may not be available on all flights. Tickets are nonrefundable, but may be reissued for a $50 change fee. Passenger Facility Charges of $1 to $3 per airport, up to $12 per round-trip, and other restrictions apply, depending on itinerary. Most fares require: 7- to 21-day advance purchase, minimum stay, last day to purchase, travel completion dates, and travel at specific time of day and/or day of week may vary, depending on destination. Selected blackout dates apply. MEXICO FARES: U.S./Mexican taxes of up to $32 are additional. All fares, and new service to Puerto Vallarta and Manzanillo effective 10/29/95, subject to government approval.

PURCHASE ONE TICKET, AND GET THE SECOND FREE.
NOW IF YOU DON'T LIKE
WHO YOU'RE SITTING NEXT TO, IT'S YOUR FAULT.

Husband, wife, best friend, your chiropodist. Pick whomever you want. Because with America West's companion fares, two can now travel for the same exact price as one. Simply buy a ticket at one of our low domestic fares, and a companion of your choice flies for free. Of course, no matter who you choose to go with, you'll enjoy major airline amenities like assigned seating, our worldwide frequent flyer program, FlightFund®, and one of the most modern fleets in the sky. For reservations, just call your professional travel agent, or America West at 1-800-235-9292. Then call someone you'd love to travel with. That way, you won't have to worry about hearing the life story of the person sitting next to you, because you'll already know it.

A nonstop talker who can't wait to tell you all about his fascination with lettuce. Or, your significant other. You make the choice.

HERE'S A SAMPLE OF AMERICA WEST'S LOW COMPANION FARES.

Each way, based on round-trip purchase

BETWEEN:	AND:	YOU:	FRIEND:
Atlanta	Burbank	$312	FREE
Atlanta	Las Vegas	$307	FREE
Atlanta	Long Beach	$311	FREE
Atlanta	Los Angeles	$328	FREE
Atlanta	Oakland	$322	FREE
Atlanta	Ontario, CA	$294	FREE
Atlanta	Orange Co.	$304	FREE
Atlanta	Phoenix	$277	FREE
Atlanta	Portland, OR	$334	FREE
Atlanta	Reno/Lake Tahoe	$282	FREE
Atlanta	Sacramento	$304	FREE
Atlanta	San Diego	$294	FREE
Atlanta	San Francisco	$324	FREE
Atlanta	San Jose	$304	FREE
Atlanta	Seattle	$334	FREE
Baltimore	Chicago	$109	FREE
Baltimore	Phoenix	$339	FREE
Orlando	Columbus, OH	$161	FREE
Philadelphia	Columbus, OH	$164	FREE
Tampa/St. Petersburg	Columbus, OH	$161	FREE
Tampa/St. Petersburg	Phoenix	$341	FREE

LOOK FOR OUR NEW SERVICE TO PUERTO VALLARTA AND MANZANILLO, MEXICO, STARTING OCTOBER 29TH.

SOME OF OUR COMPLETE VACATION PACKAGES.

All packages include round-trip air, two nights' hotel, 500 bonus FlightFund® miles and optional rental car where available

BETWEEN:	AND:	FROM:
Atlanta	Orange Co.	$369
Atlanta	San Diego	$404
Boston	Orlando	$189
Newark	Las Vegas	$329
Newark	Phoenix	$409
New York/JFK	Los Cabos, Mexico	$549
New York/JFK	Reno	$364
Orlando	Las Vegas	$319
Orlando	Vancouver, B.C.	$469
Philadelphia	Tampa	$234

America West Vacations®
1-800-356-6611

America West Airlines.
IT SEEMS SILLY TO PAY MORE™

WE'VE REDUCED OUR FARES OUT OF ORANGE COUNTY.
NOT SURPRISINGLY, THE SEATS ON THE RIGHT WING ARE FILLING UP FIRST.

In today's fiscally conservative times it's reasonable to expect lower fares. Which is why America West is proud to announce that we've just reduced our fares out of Orange County Airport. And not simply bleeding heart fares to one location. We're talking lower fares, across the board, to most of our 70 destinations throughout the United States of America, Mexico and Canada. (Should you find yourself on the wrong side of the El Toro "Y," we also have low-fare service from LAX, Long Beach, Ontario and Burbank.) Along with our lower fares, we also offer extremely economical and convenient vacation packages (often referred to as "family values"). In addition to our incredible everyday low fares, we also have something that should appeal to the old-fashioned work ethic in everyone – our superior service. America West offers a wide array of amenities, such as pre-assigned seating and our worldwide frequent flyer program, called FlightFund®. We also take great pride in having one of the most modern fleets in the sky (next to our military, of course). All of which makes America West the airline with great service and low fares to and from Orange County. Conservatively speaking, that is. For reservations, call your travel agent, or America West at 1-800-235-9292.

$19
TO PHOENIX

$29
TO LAS VEGAS OR SACRAMENTO

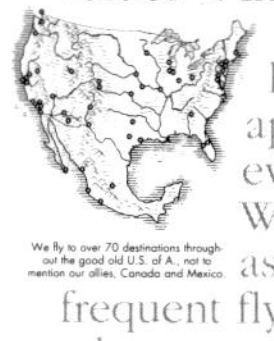

We fly to over 70 destinations throughout the good old U.S. of A., not to mention our allies, Canada and Mexico.

HERE'S A SAMPLE OF OUR LOW FARES FROM ORANGE CO.

TO:	FOR:
Albuquerque	$ 69
Atlanta	$174
Baltimore	$179
Boston	$191
Chicago	$179
Columbus, OH	$139
Dallas/Ft. Worth	$184
Denver	$ 69
El Paso	$ 69
Houston	$129
Kansas City	$104
Milwaukee	$154
Minneapolis/St. Paul	$109
New York	$194
Newark	$186
Omaha	$ 99
Philadelphia	$177
St. Louis	$139
Vancouver, B.C.	$ 99
Washington, D.C.	$199
Wichita	$124

SOME OF OUR COMPLETE VACATION PACKAGES FROM ORANGE CO.

TO:	FROM:
Las Vegas	$ 79
Los Cabos, Mexico	$409
Mazatlan, Mexico	$374
Orlando	$389
Phoenix	$129
Reno	$ 99

America West Vacations®
1-800-356-6611

America West Airlines.
IT SEEMS SILLY TO PAY MORE™

CONSUMER NEWSPAPER
OVER 600 LINES:
CAMPAIGN

161
ART DIRECTOR:
Danielle Lanz
WRITERS:
Hanspeter Schweizer
Andre Benker
PHOTOGRAPHER:
Felix Streuli
CLIENT:
Triumph International
AGENCY:
Wirz Werbeberatung AG/
Zurich

14th
February:
We
wish you
all
a lovely
Valentine's
night.
Jessica R, Jessica S, Jessica String
Triumph
INTERNATIONAL

Bra Fata Morgana
Today's
special offer:
3 for 2.
Triumph
INTERNATIONAL

Push-up Bra: Bijou D
This bra lifts a woman's heart. At least one or two inches.
Triumph
INTERNATIONAL

Do something for your husband's headache.
Corselet Amourette 143 TO N
Triumph
INTERNATIONAL

Bra: Amourette 158, Slip: Amourette 158 Tai
Jolly good, now the nights start to get longer.
Triumph
INTERNATIONAL

CONSUMER NEWSPAPER
600 LINES OR LESS:
SINGLE

162
ART DIRECTOR:
Dan Cohen
WRITER:
Paul Hartzell
PHOTOGRAPHER:
Kevin Logan
CLIENT:
Barron's
AGENCY:
Angotti Thomas
Hedge/New York

163
ART DIRECTOR:
Dan Cohen
WRITER:
Paul Hartzell
PHOTOGRAPHER:
Kevin Logan
CLIENT:
Barron's
AGENCY:
Angotti Thomas
Hedge/New York

164
ART DIRECTOR:
Ian Barry
WRITER:
Joan Shealy
CLIENT:
Virginia Power
AGENCY:
Arnold Finnegan
Martin/Richmond

165
ART DIRECTOR:
John Butler
WRITER:
Mike Shine
ILLUSTRATOR:
Mike Shine
DESIGNERS:
John Butler
Geordie Stephens
CLIENT:
Rasputin Records
AGENCY:
Butler Shine &
Stern/Sausalito

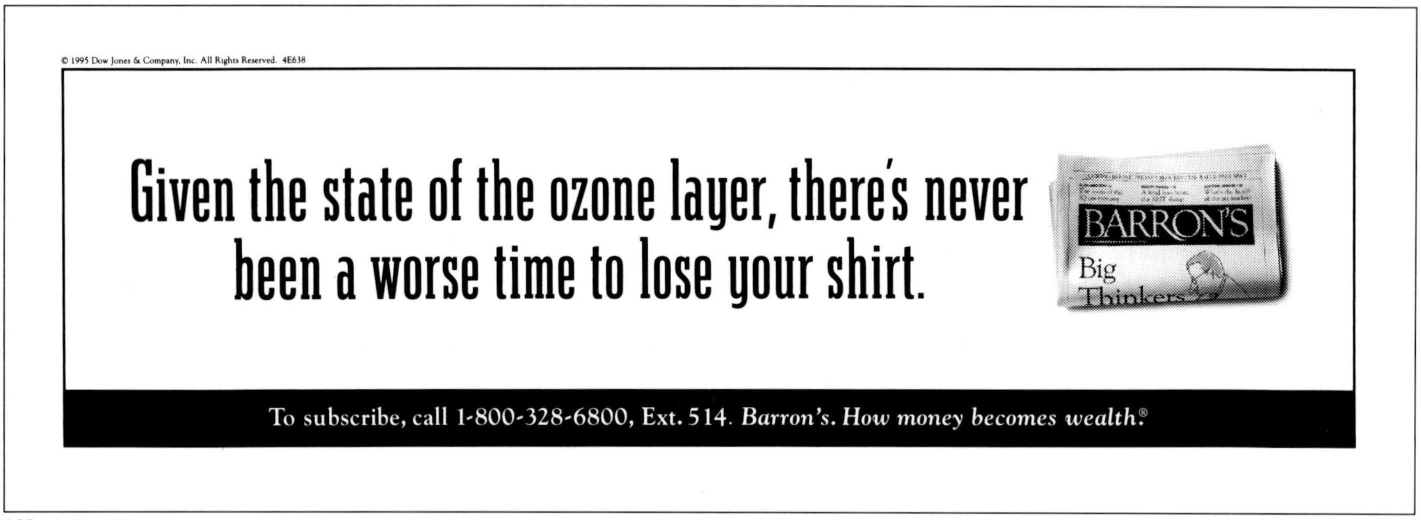
© 1995 Dow Jones & Company, Inc. All Rights Reserved. 4E638
Given the state of the ozone layer, there's never been a worse time to lose your shirt.
BARRON'S
Big
To subscribe, call 1-800-328-6800, Ext. 514. Barron's. How money becomes wealth.®
162

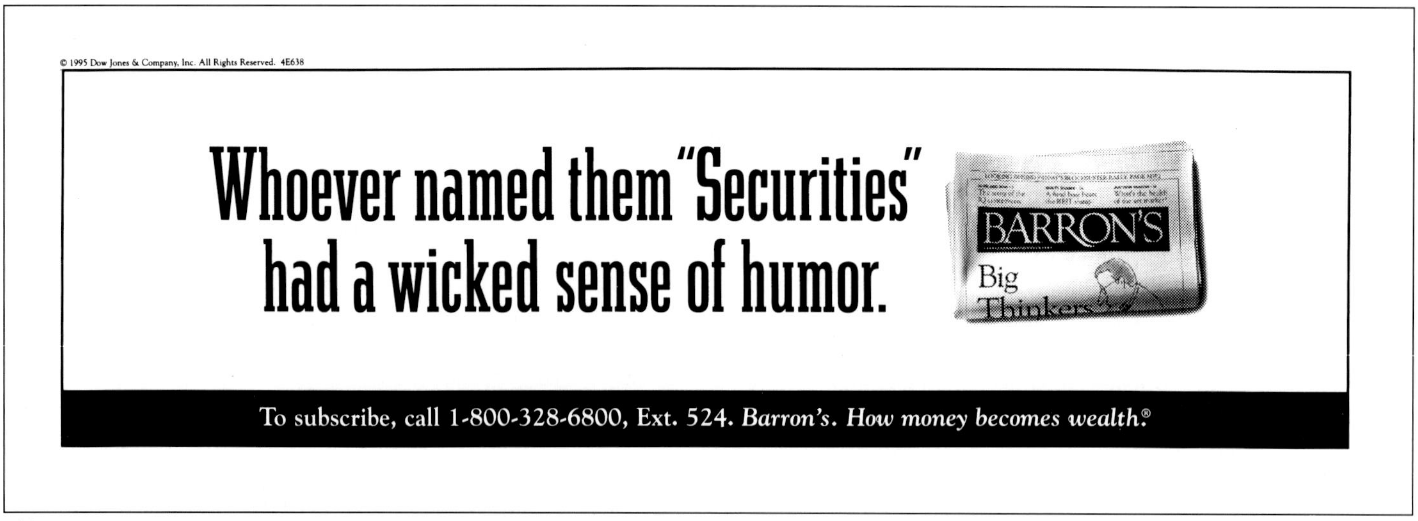
© 1995 Dow Jones & Company, Inc. All Rights Reserved. 4E638
Whoever named them "Securities" had a wicked sense of humor.
BARRON'S
Big
To subscribe, call 1-800-328-6800, Ext. 524. Barron's. How money becomes wealth.®
163

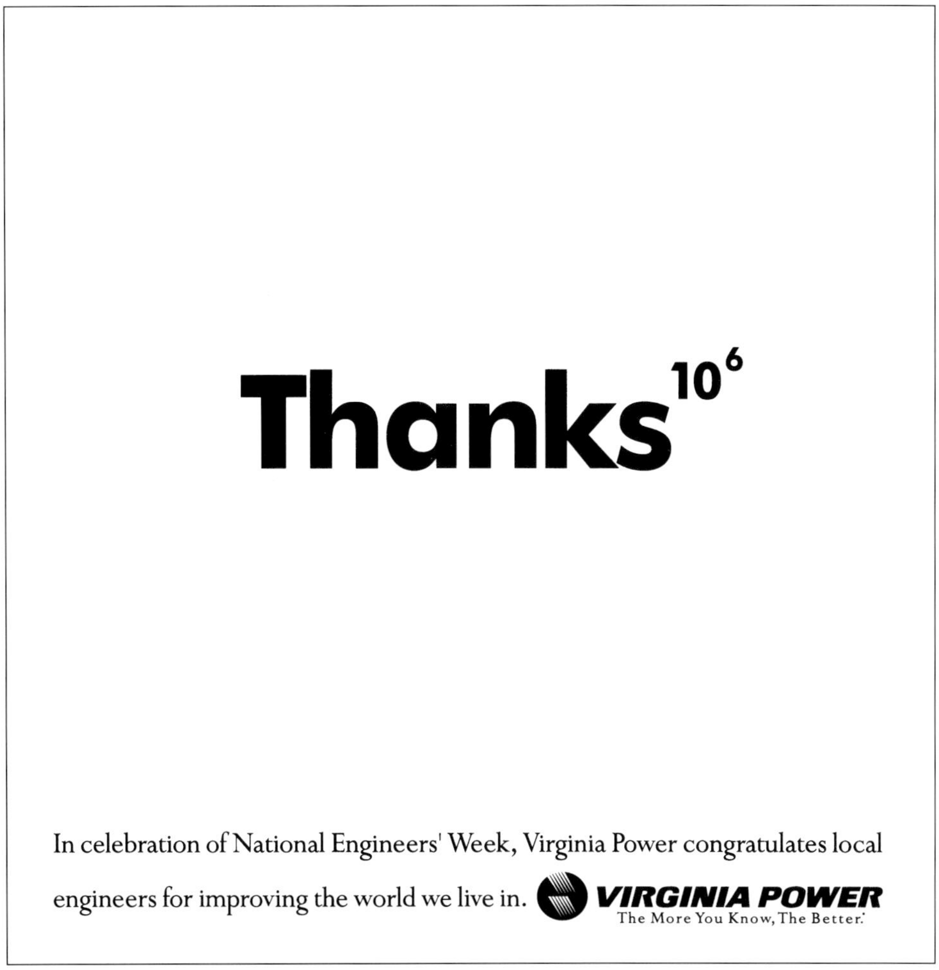
Thanks$^{10^6}$
In celebration of National Engineers' Week, Virginia Power congratulates local engineers for improving the world we live in.
VIRGINIA POWER
The More You Know, The Better.

164

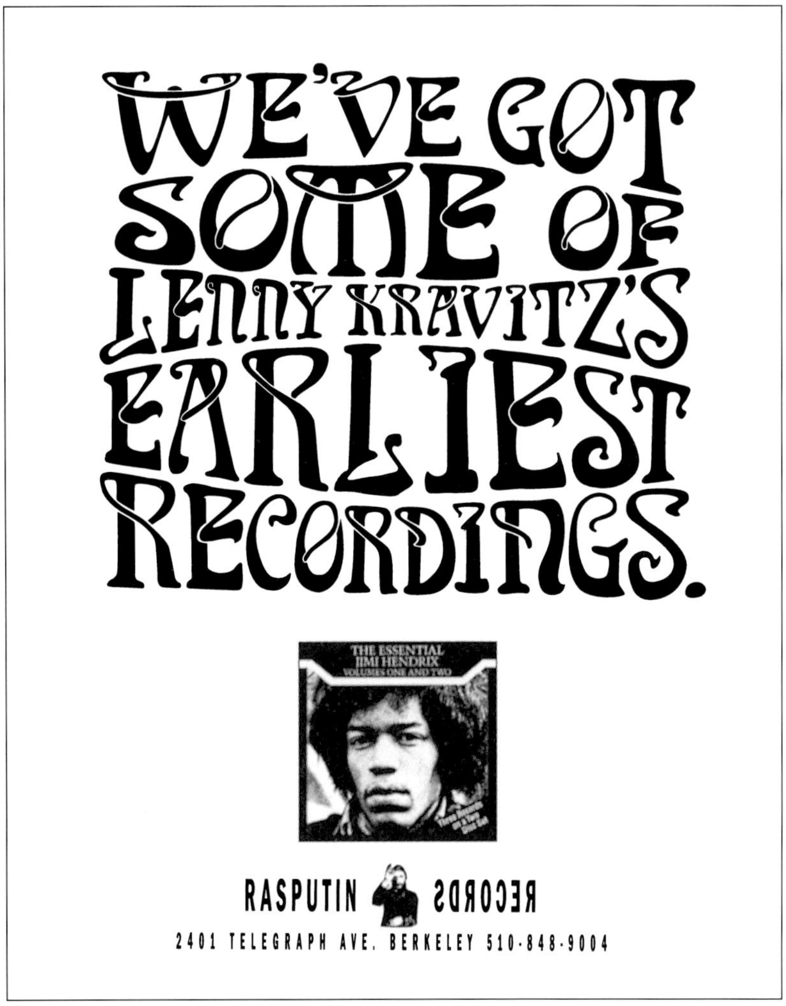
WE'VE GOT SOME OF LENNY KRAVITZ'S EARLIEST RECORDINGS.
THE ESSENTIAL JIMI HENDRIX VOLUMES ONE AND TWO
RASPUTIN RECORDS
2401 TELEGRAPH AVE. BERKELEY 510-848-9004

165

If you think other people's unwanted stuff isn't worth having, remember that someone once divorced Marilyn Monroe.

The Oregonian

The Classifieds. 221-8000.

166

CONSUMER NEWSPAPER
600 LINES OR LESS:
SINGLE

166
ART DIRECTOR:
Mike Sheen
WRITER:
John Heinsma
CLIENT:
The Oregonian
AGENCY:
Cole & Weber/Portland

167
ART DIRECTOR:
Andy Azula
WRITER:
Dave Pullar
CLIENT:
BMW of North America
AGENCY:
Fallon McElligott/
Minneapolis

168
ART DIRECTOR:
Dean Hanson
WRITER:
Mike Gibbs
CLIENT:
The Nikon School
AGENCY:
Fallon McElligott/
Minneapolis

THE M3 IS IN SUCH DEMAND, ADVERTISING IS UNNECESSARY.

(BELOW, A DISCUSSION ON WORLD PEACE.)

The fate of mankind rests in every individual's ability to co-exist in a nonviolent manner. For under the surface of disparity lies universal commonality. **THE ULTIMATE DRIVING MACHINE.®**

167

It's been said that to be a great photographer

you have to be in the right place at the right time.

(See below for upcoming times and places.)

THE NIKON SCHOOL 1995-1996 SCHEDULE

Here's your shot at greatness. In just one 8-hour day you'll learn everything from composition to the latest exposure techniques. And you'll even get the 157-page Nikon School Handbook–all for $90. Look for us in the following cities: Atlanta, Boston, Charlotte, Chicago, Cincinnati, Dallas, Denver, Detroit, Houston, Los Angeles, Miami, New York City, Philadelphia, Portland, San Diego, San Francisco, Seattle and Washington, D.C. And please call (516) 547-8666 or fax (516) 547-0309 for exact dates and times.

The Nikon School

CONSUMER NEWSPAPER
600 LINES OR LESS:
SINGLE

169
ART DIRECTOR:
Noam Murro
WRITER:
Dean Hacohen
ILLUSTRATORS:
Noam Murro
Dean Hacohen
CLIENT:
Identigene
AGENCY:
Goldsmith/Jeffrey,
New York

170
ART DIRECTOR:
Karin Onsager Birch
WRITER:
Josh Denberg
CLIENT:
Royal Cruise Line
AGENCY:
Goodby Silverstein &
Partners/San Francisco

171
ART DIRECTOR:
Tom Gianfagna
WRITER:
Gary Cohen
PHOTOGRAPHER:
Carl Furuta
CLIENT:
Land Rover North America
AGENCY:
Grace & Rothschild/
New York

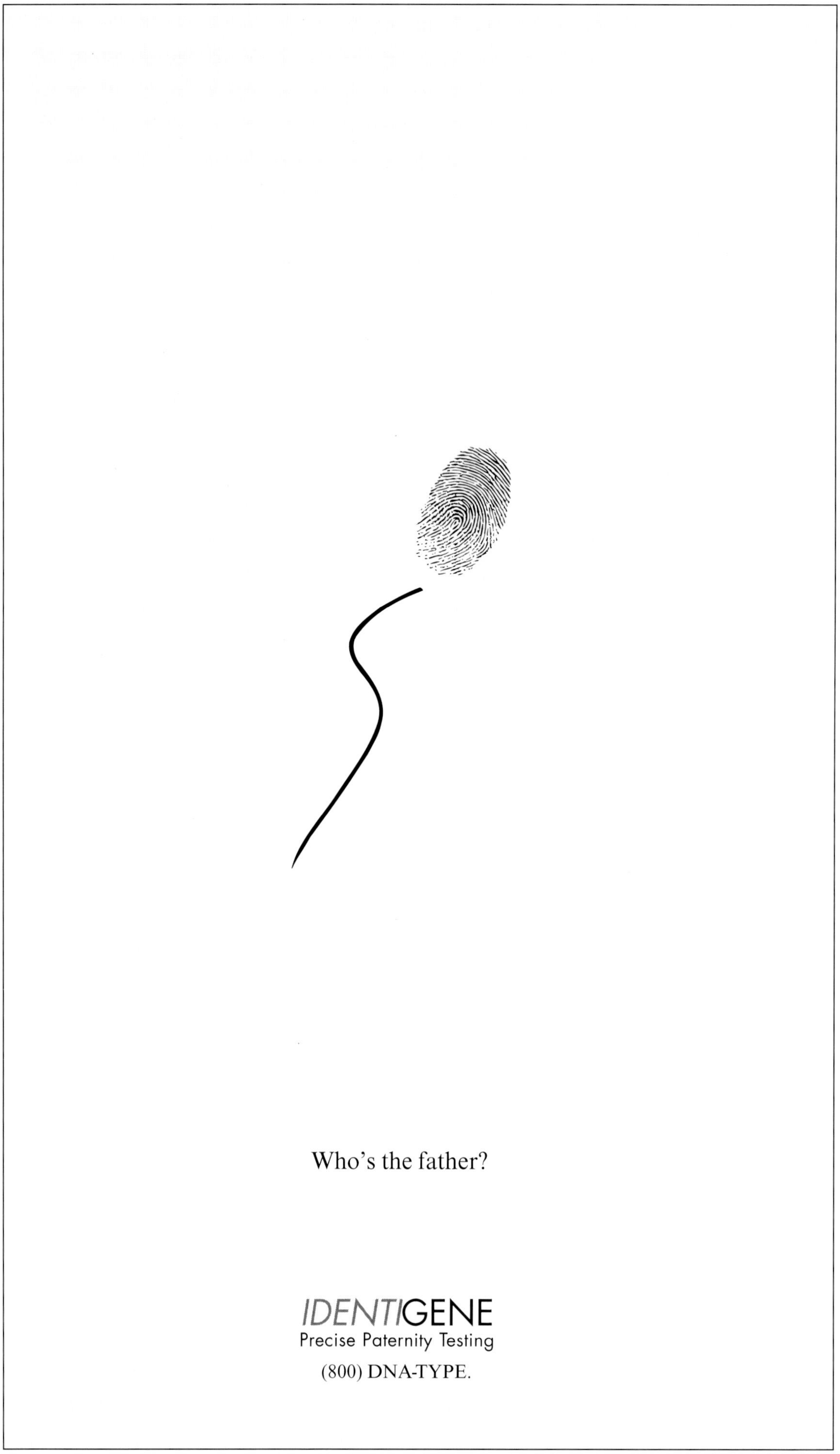
Who's the father?
IDENTIGENE
Precise Paternity Testing
(800) DNA-TYPE.

169

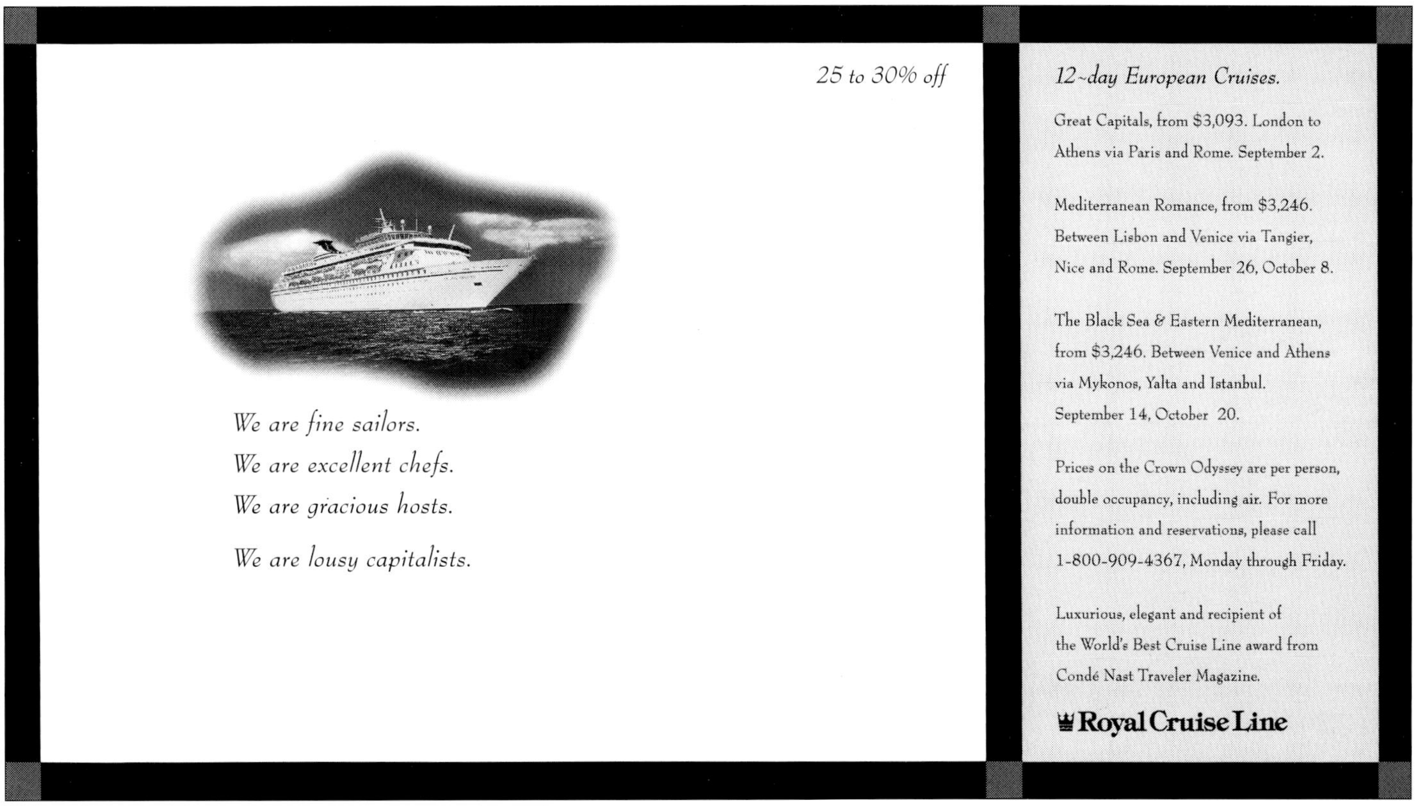

25 to 30% off
We are fine sailors.
We are excellent chefs.
We are gracious hosts.
We are lousy capitalists.
12-day European Cruises.
Great Capitals, from $3,093. London to Athens via Paris and Rome. September 2.
Mediterranean Romance, from $3,246. Between Lisbon and Venice via Tangier, Nice and Rome. September 26, October 8.
The Black Sea & Eastern Mediterranean, from $3,246. Between Venice and Athens via Mykonos, Yalta and Istanbul. September 14, October 20.
Prices on the Crown Odyssey are per person, double occupancy, including air. For more information and reservations, please call 1-800-909-4367, Monday through Friday.
Luxurious, elegant and recipient of the World's Best Cruise Line award from Condé Nast Traveler Magazine.
Royal Cruise Line

170

TREAD LIGHTLY·DRIVE RESPONSIBLY OFF ROAD.
PLEASE BUCKLE UP FOR SECURITY. © 1995 LAND ROVER NORTH AMERICA, INC.
If this is the new Range Rover, apparently England is more than five hours ahead.
LAND ROVER
RANGE ROVER
1-800-FINE-4WD

171

CONSUMER NEWSPAPER
600 LINES OR LESS:
SINGLE

172
ART DIRECTOR:
Allen Richardson
WRITER:
Ari Merkin
PHOTOGRAPHER:
Vic Huber
CLIENT:
Land Rover North America
AGENCY:
Grace & Rothschild/
New York

173
ART DIRECTOR:
Allen Richardson
WRITER:
Gary Cohen
PHOTOGRAPHER:
Vic Huber
CLIENT:
Land Rover North America
AGENCY:
Grace & Rothschild/
New York

174
ART DIRECTORS:
Jennifer Fleming-Balser
Holland Henton
WRITER:
Rich Tlapek
CLIENT:
Lennox
AGENCY:
GSD&M Advertising/
Austin

175
ART DIRECTOR:
David Beverley
WRITER:
Robert Burleigh
CLIENT:
Harrods
AGENCY:
Leagas Delaney/London

172

"My parents went on vacation and all I got was this stupid ceremonial tunic."
LAND ROVER
DISCOVERY

173

BUY THIS A/C AND
YOU CAN STILL AFFORD
THAT LA-Z-BOY.®
BEST OF ALL, YOU WON'T
STICK TO IT.
10 and 12 SEER Models
Why get stuck with any ordinary air conditioner when you can afford a Lennox? Plus, you're buying from an independent Lennox dealer you can count on. To see how easy it is to own a Lennox, just give us a call. And plop yourself down, instead of a lot of money.
LENNOX
ONE LESS THING TO WORRY ABOUT.™
[Dealer Insert]
LA-Z-BOY® IS A REGISTERED TRADEMARK OF LA-Z-BOY CHAIR COMPANY.
©LENNOX INDUSTRIES INC., 1995. LENNOX DEALERS ARE INDEPENDENTLY OWNED AND OPERATED BUSINESSES.

174

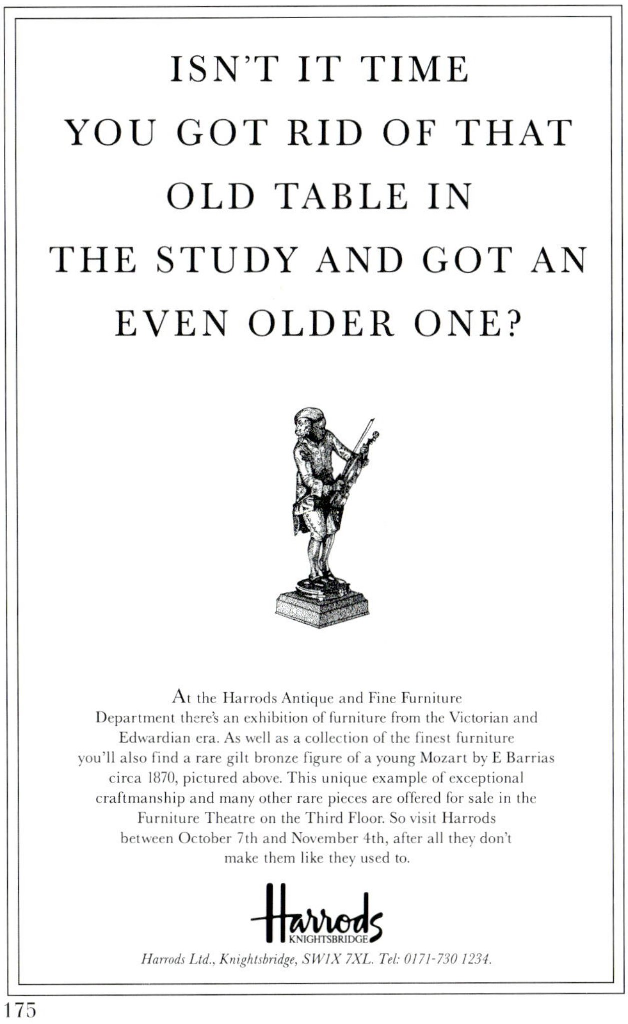
ISN'T IT TIME
YOU GOT RID OF THAT
OLD TABLE IN
THE STUDY AND GOT AN
EVEN OLDER ONE?
At the Harrods Antique and Fine Furniture Department there's an exhibition of furniture from the Victorian and Edwardian era. As well as a collection of the finest furniture you'll also find a rare gilt bronze figure of a young Mozart by E Barrias circa 1870, pictured above. This unique example of exceptional craftmanship and many other rare pieces are offered for sale in the Furniture Theatre on the Third Floor. So visit Harrods between October 7th and November 4th, after all they don't make them like they used to.
Harrods
KNIGHTSBRIDGE
Harrods Ltd., Knightsbridge, SW1X 7XL. Tel: 0171-730 1234.

175

CONSUMER NEWSPAPER
600 LINES OR LESS:
SINGLE

176
ART DIRECTOR:
Barney Goldberg
WRITER:
Jeff Ross
CLIENT:
Mercedes-Benz of
North America
AGENCY:
The Martin Agency/
Richmond

177
ART DIRECTOR:
Barney Goldberg
WRITER:
Jeff Ross
CLIENT:
Mercedes-Benz of
North America
AGENCY:
The Martin Agency/
Richmond

178
ART DIRECTOR:
Patrick Murray
WRITER:
Vinnie Chieco
PHOTOGRAPHER:
Robb Debenport
CLIENT:
Tabu Lingerie
AGENCY:
The Richards Group/Dallas

Sends chills
down your
orthopedically
supported
spine.
The E320: 10-way adjustable leather seats with lumbar support. 217 unbridled horses. The hair on your neck will stand straight up.
Mercedes-Benz

176

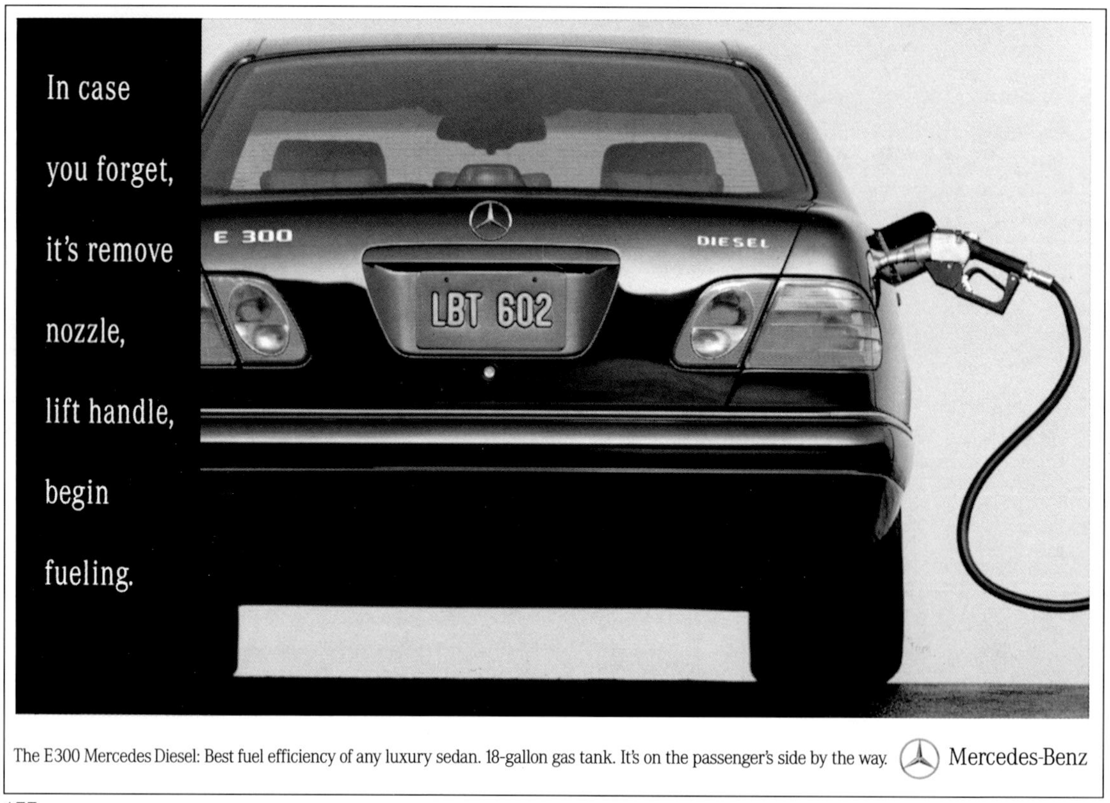
In case
you forget,
it's remove
nozzle,
lift handle,
begin
fueling.
E 300
DIESEL
LBT 602
The E300 Mercedes Diesel: Best fuel efficiency of any luxury sedan. 18-gallon gas tank. It's on the passenger's side by the way.
Mercedes-Benz

177

WHEN THE LIGHTS GO
OUT IT TURNS INTO
AN AEROBICS OUTFIT.

TABU
LINGERIE

CONSUMER NEWSPAPER
600 LINES OR LESS:
CAMPAIGN

179

ART DIRECTORS:
David Angelo
Greg Bell
John Leu

WRITER:
Cliff Freeman

PHOTOGRAPHERS:
Sean Michienzi
Craig Cutler

CLIENT:
Sauza Conmemorativo
Tequila

AGENCY:
Cliff Freeman & Partners/
New York

180

ART DIRECTORS:
Leslie Sweet
Abi Aron
Rob Carducci
Dan Kelleher
Mark Schruntek

WRITERS:
Rob Carducci
Abi Aron
Sal DeVito
Mark Schruntek
Dan Kelleher

CLIENT:
Time Out

AGENCY:
DeVito/Verdi, New York

Every week,
our writers watch
more movies
than Siskel & Ebert.
And eat at
more restaurants
than Ebert.
Time Out
New York
The weekly magazine that tells you where to go and what to do.

All the clubs
you'll never get into
in one magazine.
Time Out
New York
The weekly magazine that tells you where to go and what to do.

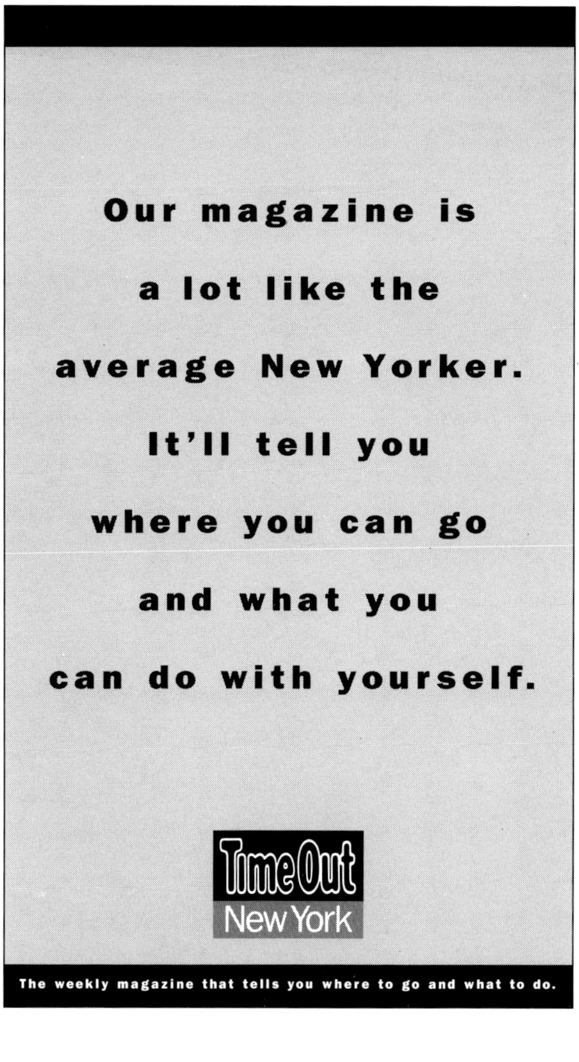
Our magazine is
a lot like the
average New Yorker.
It'll tell you
where you can go
and what you
can do with yourself.
Time Out
New York
The weekly magazine that tells you where to go and what to do.

CONSUMER NEWSPAPER
600 LINES OR LESS:
CAMPAIGN

181

ART DIRECTOR:
Dean Hanson

WRITER:
Mike Gibbs

PHOTOGRAPHER:
Parallel Productions

CLIENT:
Ameritech

AGENCY:
Fallon McElligott/
Minneapolis

CONSUMER MAGAZINE
B/W FULL PAGE OR
SPREAD: SINGLE

182

ART DIRECTORS:
Wendy Chan
Derrick Seah

WRITERS:
Todd Waldron
Liz Watson

ILLUSTRATOR:
Rita Cheung

CLIENT:
ITT Sheraton/Hong Kong

AGENCY:
Batey Ads/Hong Kong

183

ART DIRECTORS:
Dan Kelleher
Mark Schruntek

WRITERS:
Mark Schruntek
Dan Kelleher

CLIENT:
Daffy's

AGENCY:
DeVito/Verdi, New York

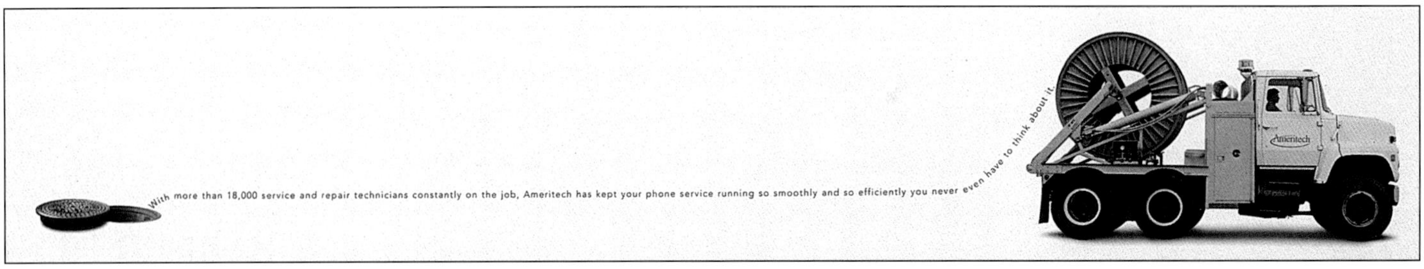

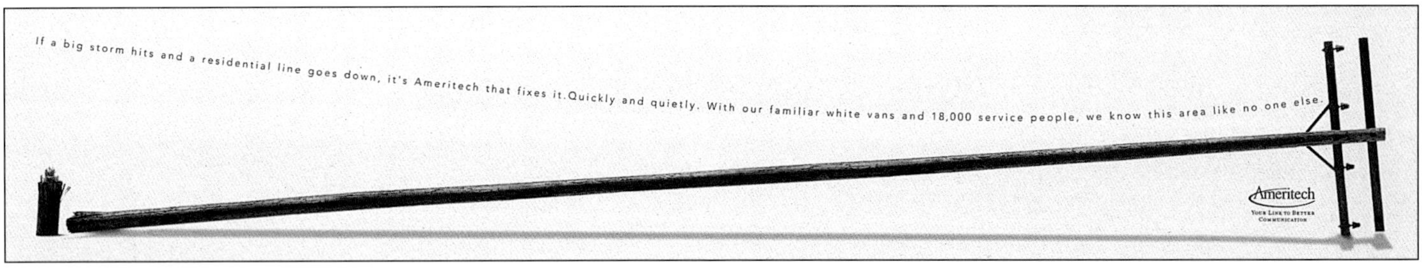

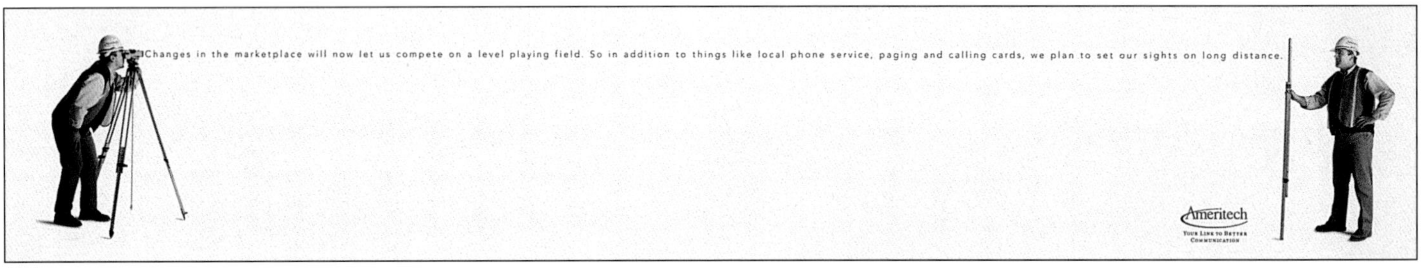

181

A WORLD OF CHOICE AT THE SHERATON HONG KONG HOTEL & TOWERS
Yet another Christmas ruined
because they forgot to make a reservation.
Grandstand
CONTINENTAL DINING
Great Wall
Bar
BUKHARA
Sky Lounge
FOR CHRISTMAS RESERVATIONS, PLEASE CALL OUR SEASONAL HOTLINE ON 2732 3777

182

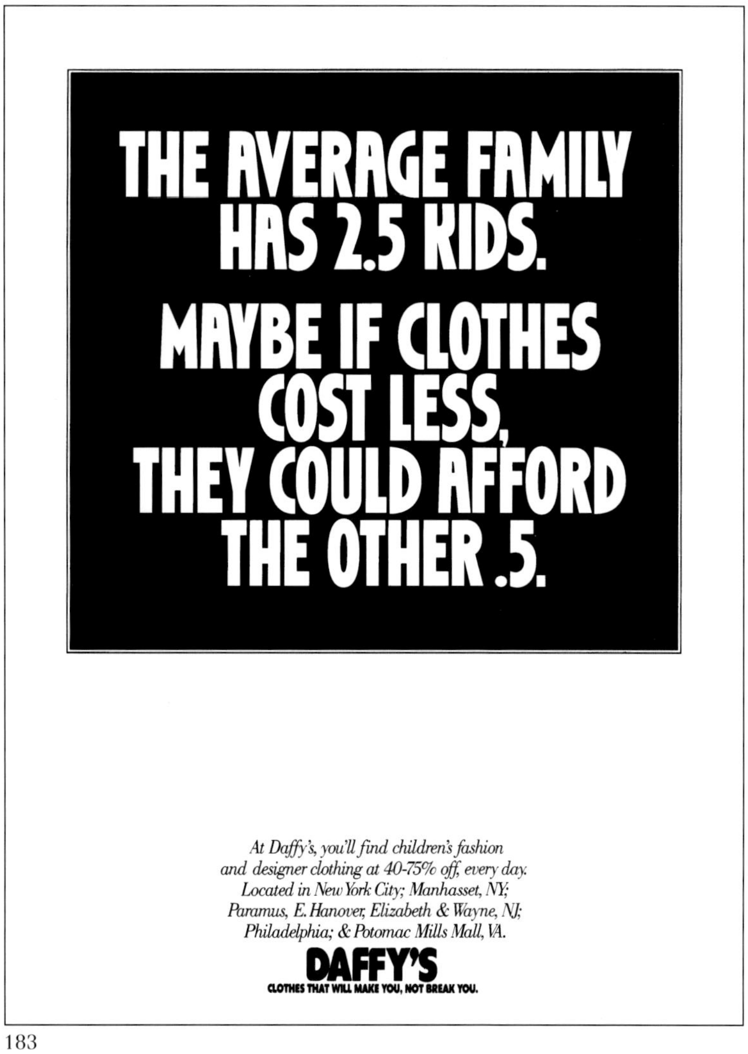
THE AVERAGE FAMILY HAS 2.5 KIDS.
MAYBE IF CLOTHES COST LESS, THEY COULD AFFORD THE OTHER .5.
At Daffy's, you'll find children's fashion and designer clothing at 40-75% off, every day. Located in New York City; Manhasset, NY; Paramus, E. Hanover, Elizabeth & Wayne, NJ; Philadelphia; & Potomac Mills Mall, VA.
DAFFY'S
CLOTHES THAT WILL MAKE YOU, NOT BREAK YOU.

183

CONSUMER MAGAZINE
B/W FULL PAGE OR
SPREAD: SINGLE

184
ART DIRECTORS:
Vinny Tulley
Rob Carducci
WRITERS:
Rob Carducci
Vinny Tulley
PHOTOGRAPHER:
Cailor/Resnick
CLIENT:
Stein Mart
AGENCY:
DeVito/Verdi, New York

185
ART DIRECTOR:
Mark Mizgala
WRITER:
Chris Staples
TYPOGRAPHER:
Karacters
CLIENT:
Ginsana
AGENCY:
Palmer Jarvis
Communications/
Vancouver

186
ART DIRECTOR:
Vanessa Rosser
WRITER:
Michael Campbell
ILLUSTRATOR:
Paul Higgins
CLIENT:
HarperCollins Publishers
AGENCY:
Saatchi & Saatchi/London

CONSUMER MAGAZINE
COLOR FULL PAGE OR
SPREAD: SINGLE

187
ART DIRECTOR:
Peter Gausis
WRITER:
Alfredo Marcantonio
PHOTOGRAPHER:
John Parker
CLIENT:
Sainsbury's
AGENCY:
Abbott Mead Vickers.
BBDO/London

184

185

UNBEATABLE DEALS ON TOP BRAND NUCLEAR WEAPONS
THE SALE TO END ALL SALES
AS SEEN ON RADAR
MEDVENEV SS-43 VIPER
● Liquid propelled intercontinental ballistic missile 36.5m long. ● Carries 10 independently targeted 500 kilotonne nuclear warheads. ● Accurate to within 125m radius of target. ● Silo-based with a range of 11,000km.
£7M £6M
SVERADNADZE SS-32 VULTURE
● Solid propelled short range ballistic missile 6.4m long. ● Carries one 100 kilotonne nuclear warhead. Adaptable also for high explosive, chemical and submunitions warheads. ● Accurate to within 15m radius of target. ● Road mobile with a range of 70km.
£2M £1M
DEVASTATION GUARANTEED OR YOUR MONEY BACK
ZORONIN SS-N-11 VINDICATOR
● Liquid propelled intercontinental ballistic missile 15.6m long. ● Carries seven independently targeted 100 kilotonne nuclear warheads. ● Accurate to within 450m radius of target. ● Submarine-launched with a range of 6500km
£5M £4M
SVERADNADZE SS-33 VANGUARD
● Solid propelled intercontinental ballistic missile 21.7m long. ● Carries one 750 kilotonne nuclear warhead. ● Accurate to within 900m radius of target. ● Silo-based with a range of 9400km.
£3M £2M
FREE DELIVERY IN MIDDLE EASTERN AREA
KRYKOV SS-N-13 VORTEX
● Solid propelled short range surface-to-surface missile 9.4m long. ● Carries one 200 kilotonne nuclear warhead. ● Target guidance is controlled by 'Band Stand' engagement radar on board ship. ● Accurate to within 10m radius of target. ● Ship-launched with a range of 120km.
£2M £1M
SVERADNADZE SS-49 VIGILANTE
● Solid propelled intercontinental ballistic missile 21.5m long. ● Carries one 550 kilotonne nuclear warhead. ● Accurate to within 100m radius of target. ● Rail mobile with a range of 10,500km.
£3M £2M
CHOMSKY SS-N-9 VIOLATOR
● Turbojet-powered short range surface to surface missile, 10.2m long. ● Carries one 350 kilotonne nuclear warhead. ● Mid course guidance is by radio command via 'Scoop Pair' radar. ● Final targeting is by infra-red homing device or active radar. ● Accurate to within 100m radius of target. ● Ship, submarine and ground launched with a range of 450km.
£15M £13M
MEDVENEV SS-47 VOLCANO
● Liquid propelled intercontinental ballistic missile 14.2m long. ● Carries a single 1000 kilotonne nuclear warhead. ● Accurate to within 200m radius of target. ● Submarine-launched with a range of 7800km.
£9M £8M
'WHICH NUCLEAR WEAPON?' BEST BUY
ZORONIN SS-45 VENOM
● Solid propelled intercontinental ballistic missile 23.8m long. ● Carries 10 independently targeted 500 kilotonne nuclear warheads. ● Accurate to within 100m radius of target. ● Rail mobile and silo-based with a range of 10,000km.
£4M £3M
ZORONIN SS-41 VANQUISHER
● Liquid propelled intercontinental ballistic missile 23.9m long. ● Carries 4 independently targeted 200 kilotonne nuclear warheads. ● Accurate to within 200m radius of target. ● Silo-based with a range of 10,000km.
£6M £5M
A ONCE IN A LIFETIME OFFER
KRYKOV AS-23 VENGEANCE
● Solid propelled short range air-to-surface missile. ● Carries 350 kilotonne nuclear warhead. ● Accurate to within 200m radius of target. ● Air-launched with a range of 300km.
£2M £1.7M
CRAIG THOMAS
A WILD JUSTICE
Harper Collins
ANYONE CAN BUY NUCLEAR ARMS AND TECHNOLOGY IN RUSSIA TODAY. IF YOU KNOW THE RIGHT PEOPLE.
READ ABOUT THE THREAT THE RUSSIAN MAFIA POSE TO THE WEST IN CRAIG THOMAS' NEW THRILLER 'A WILD JUSTICE'. £14.99.

186

Can you spot the fake tan?
You'll find the imposter in the bottom right hand corner.
Like most of the sugar sold in Britain it has been refined. A process that reduces it to pure sucrose.
The white granules, having been stripped of their natural molasses and trace elements, are then coated a suitably attractive shade of brown.
It is a pale imitation of the eight Sainsbury's Unrefined Brown Sugars alongside it. They owe their colouring to the field, more than the factory.
The sugar cane is cut, gathered, shredded and pressed at local mills on the islands of Mauritius and Barbados. Then clarified, boiled and crystallised. The sugars that result retain more of their natural flavour, as well as their colouring.
You'll find the subtle golden varieties make an ideal substitute for boring old white sugar. While the Demerara and Light Muscovado have echoes of creamy fudge. And the dark cooking sugars harbour a distinctive rich treacle toffee flavour. Each pack describes which sugar can be used where.
Whatever varieties you buy, you can be sure that it won't have been browned off. And nor will you be.
Sainsbury's. Everyone's favourite ingredient.

187

CONSUMER MAGAZINE COLOR FULL PAGE OR SPREAD: SINGLE

188
ART DIRECTOR:
Mike MacNeill
WRITER:
Keith Keith
PHOTOGRAPHER:
Brad Harris
CLIENT:
Aetna Retirement Services
AGENCY:
Ammirati Puris Lintas/New York

189
ART DIRECTOR:
Graham Watson
WRITER:
Bruce Crouch
TYPOGRAPHER:
Andy Bird
CLIENT:
Levi Strauss
AGENCY:
Bartle Bogle Hegarty/London

190
ART DIRECTOR:
Paul Jervis
WRITERS:
Mike Robertson
Stevie Pierson
PHOTOGRAPHER:
Robert Farber
CLIENT:
Cunard Sea Goddess
AGENCY:
Bates USA/New York

191
ART DIRECTOR:
Jamie Way
WRITER:
Randy Diplock
PHOTOGRAPHER:
Richard Picton
CLIENT:
Costa Rica Tourism
AGENCY:
BBDO Canada/Toronto

188

189

THE HEIGHT OF INDULGENCE IS THE BLISSFUL SOLITUDE THAT FLOATS ON A SLEEK WHITE YACHT SOMEWHERE BETWEEN TWO GLORIOUS PORTS AND ONE SERENE SEA. CALL YOUR TRAVEL COUNSELOR OR 1-800-7-CUNARD.

SEA GODDESS
CUNARD

190

THERE ARE VERY FEW ATHEISTS IN COSTA RICA.

If you didn't already, what would it take to make you believe?

Not necessarily in God, or a god, but a higher being.

For many of you who do, it was easy. It was the day you and your partner brought another human being into the world. The day you stared at your newborn and wondered what could possibly be going through their head.

For others, it was your first eclipse. Or, at the other end of the scale, watching an ant carrying what appeared to be a small loaf of bread up and down the crevices of a sidewalk.

For those who remain unconvinced there's Costa Rica.

In Costa Rica, you can't throw a dart without hitting something that makes you wonder who made it, how long it's existed or how it got here.

That's what happens when you take two large mountain ranges, dozens of volcanoes, two long beaches, hundreds of waterfalls, a rain forest and squeeze it all into a country the size of West Virginia.

But it's the other things that make you rub your eyes and look to the sky for answers.

Take for example, a single rock at the foot of Mount Chirripó. While the mountain itself, standing at 12,529 feet above sea level, leaves you breathless, it's a simple rock that makes you think.

Because this rock is a mirror image of Mount Chirripó itself.

Nobody knows how it got here. Nobody knows how it got this way. Some believe it was native Indians who carved it, others are convinced that the wind shaped it over millions of years, using Mount Chirripó as its model.

All we know for sure is that it sits near the town of San Gerardo, minding its own business, doing nothing more than provoking thought.

The same can be said for Costa Rica's stone spheres.

More than a thousand of them are spread over the flood plains of Río Térraba. Many more are buried. More impressive than their size, (some are as large as six feet in diameter) is how perfect they are.

There are as many theories on how they got here as there are stones themselves. The only thing the experts seem to agree on is that it's highly unlikely they'll ever figure them out.

If you decide to come to Costa Rica and spend some of your hard-earned money in our beautiful little country, we feel we should also tell you what you won't find here. Like a compass that works.

On certain parts of Mount Chirripó, as a result of energies that've been detected there, you'll find your compass will be more useful as a paper weight than to determine the direction you're heading. Some natives refer to Mount Chirripó as a "power place." And while they can't explain why it does what it does, their best guess is that the minerals and metals found in and around the mountain are responsible.

But when it comes to evidence of a higher being, you really need look no further than the living creatures who call Costa Rica their home. The sheer numbers alone are impressive enough.

At last count, Costa Rica was inhabited by 383 species of amphibians, 848 species of birds, 205 species of mammals, around 13,000 species of plants 400 species of butterflies and 1,500 species of fish.

Which brings us to something called a "gaspar."

Something that appears to be part fish and part alligator. Then there's the Costa Rican reptile that's affectionately known as a "Jesus Christ" lizard which can actually run on top of the water.

Whatever they are, they're two more things that'll make you scratch your head and, for a split second, reach for the remote control.

For every single thing seen in Costa Rica that makes people realize what a priviledge it is to be on this planet, there's something you can hear that'll bring you to the same conclusion.

The pounding of a waterfall, the howl of a monkey in the middle of the jungle. In Costa Rica, you'll find your senses so heightened, the smack of a single drop of rain hitting the leaf of a mangrove tree can be deafening.

The natives call it "pura vida." Pure life. And in Costa Rica, it's everywhere you turn.

It's all of the above, and things we haven't told you, that'll not only have you convinced in a higher being, but that they spent a little more time here than anywhere else.

We invite you to call your travel agent or Costa Rica Tourism at 1-800-343-6332.

And see for yourself why some things here are so incredible, you won't believe what you're seeing.

But you'll believe in something.

COSTA RICA
TAN YOUR SOUL

191

CONSUMER MAGAZINE
COLOR FULL PAGE OR
SPREAD: SINGLE

192

ART DIRECTOR:
Jamie Way

WRITER:
Randy Diplock

PHOTOGRAPHER:
Richard Picton

CLIENT:
Costa Rica Tourism

AGENCY:
BBDO Canada/Toronto

193

ART DIRECTOR:
Susan Westre

WRITER:
Greg Ketchum

PHOTOGRAPHER:
Michael O'Brien

CLIENT:
Apple Computer

AGENCY:
BBDO/Los Angeles

194

ART DIRECTOR:
Rob Palmer

WRITERS:
Kathy Hepinstall
David Lubars

PHOTOGRAPHERS:
Lars Topelmann
Helen Trotman

ILLUSTRATORS:
Joe Saputo
Antar Dayal

CLIENT:
Pioneer Electronics USA

AGENCY:
BBDO/Los Angeles

FINDING COSTA RICA IS EASY.
IT'S 180° FROM CLUB MED.

Now, that's not to say that one is any better than the other.

It just means that for many of you, a beach and a tan is all you're looking for in a vacation. And there's certainly nothing wrong with that.

But this ad is for the rest of you.

It's for those who want a vacation that does as much for your soul as it does for your skin. That's why we'd like to take this opportunity to tell you what you'll find, if you decide to spend your hard-earned money, in our country.

Essentially, what a Costa Rican vacation comes down to is having, within a day's drive, as many things to do and see as there are Costa Ricans anxious to show them to you.

It's tough to know where to start to tell someone about our country.

Nature might be a good place. Because 25% of our 19,700 square miles is protected rain forest, national parks and wildlife reserves. And while tourism may be our largest industry, our ecosystem is our most important asset.

We believe, the more people who have access to nature, the more educated they'll become about how important it is. Not only here, but around the world.

At last count, Costa Rica was inhabited by 383 species of amphibians, 848 species of birds, 205 species of mammals, around 13,000 species of plants, 400 species of butterflies and 1,500 species of fish.

Unfortunately, it's up to 1 species to ensure these numbers don't decrease.

All this and we haven't even touched on individual stories like the tens of thousands of leatherback turtles that come to Playa Grande like clockwork to lay their eggs. Then there's something called the gar. A creature that's not sure whether it's an alligator or a fish. And neither are we.

So, if you come here, we hope you'll understand if everyone seems to be a little over-zealous about the ecosystem here. As you can see, they've got a lot of reasons to be.

While there's nothing more important to us than the creatures that call Costa Rica home, there are many more reasons to visit.

About 90° worth.

In fact, many people who've come here, often refer to Costa Rica as an island. Despite the fact that it's not surrounded by water.

One of the reasons people think of Costa Rica that way, may have something to do with the fact that we've been a proud democracy since 1948. A country whose civil war lasted only 40 days. Which tells you a lot about the kind of people you'll find here.

It also goes a long way in explaining why Costa Ricans have, over the years, taken pride in their commitment to education instead of militarism. Today, you'll find more teachers here than police. So you won't be surprised when you learn that the literacy rate in our country is 92%.

Speaking of the military, we should also tell you that it's one more way Costa Rica is different.

In that we don't have one.

And we haven't had one for years. So, if you come to Costa Rica and hopefully our capital, San José, make sure you visit our old Army barracks.

Because today, it's one of 28 museums in the country.

A lot has happened since Columbus came here and called it "Rich Coast." But when we think about it, it's what hasn't happened here since then, that makes our country such a popular place to visit.

To this day, you'll find some of the world's most breath-taking sights, unspoiled by so-called progress.

Among them is Arenal Volcano which soars 5,358 feet above sea level and has been active since 1968. In one of the many other protected areas, you'll find rocks on the Santa Elena Peninsula that date back 150 million years. Then there's Mount Chirripó, Costa Rica's highest mountain and Barra Honda National Park on the Nicoya Peninsula. Where you'll find caves that have yet to be explored. By humans at least.

And on the world's largest uninhabited island, Cocos Island, there are more than 200 waterfalls.

As you can see, with all there is to tell you about our country, this ad could've been a lot bigger. To hear about what we've left out, call your travel agent or Costa Rica Tourism at 1-800-343-6332.

We'd be honored to have you.

By the way, we reluctantly inform you that you can also find 631 miles of beach on the Pacific coast and 131 on the Caribbean for you to relax and soak up some sun.

If you like that sort of thing.

COSTA RICA
TAN YOUR SOUL

192

What's on your PowerBook?
Wendy Finerman
Producer
Photographs of my kids
Script notes on all my films
Directors list
Writers list
Actors' credits and availability
Project status reports
My schedule for the next three months
School auction list
The Treehouse for my kids
Early Math for my kids
Putt-Putt's Fun Pack for my kids
FileMaker Pro
eWorld
My favorite Thanksgiving recipes
Our earthquake insurance policy
Fax modem
Contracts
Video clips from a movie I'm working on
Pediatric AIDS Foundation help list
Flight schedules from L.A. to New York
Our summer vacation itinerary
Samuel L. Jackson
Actor
Character biographies
Scene studies
Script changes
Potential film projects
My résumé, Rev. 16
My journal
A list of my favorite golf courses
All my golf scores
Links Pro
Final Draft 2.0
Hong Kong film library
My agent's phone numbers
My manager's phone number
My publicist's phone number
My daughter
Zoë's school schedule
A birthday card Zoe designed
New York house information
L.A. house information
My LoJack number
My wife's wish list
eWorld
Apple Remote Access
Ezekiel 25:17
MPL
MPL

193

PIONEER
The Art of Entertainment
The Road Kill Diaries
June 8
Wandered out into the road.
Heard music pounding.
Figured I had time to cross.
Didn't.
In no way does Pioneer advocate running over road critters. Every last one of us would swerve. © 1995 Pioneer Electronics (USA) Inc., Long Beach, CA.
PIONEER SUBWOOFERS. Nothing says "move it or lose it, varmint" like raw bass pounding out your window. Our subwoofers are designed with specially blended materials to handle up to 450 watts of pure power. They also come in a variety of car-friendly shapes and sizes. So, go ahead and put a ton of bass in your system. And give nature a chance to dig that crazy beat. Call 1-800-PIONEER for a dealer near you.

194

CONSUMER MAGAZINE
COLOR FULL PAGE OR
SPREAD: SINGLE

195
ART DIRECTOR:
Danny Brooke-Taylor
WRITER:
Steven Hanratty
PHOTOGRAPHER:
Jonathan Oakes
CLIENT:
Cussons
AGENCY:
BDH Advertising/
Manchester, England

196
ART DIRECTOR:
Frank Haggerty
WRITER:
Kerry Casey
PHOTOGRAPHER:
Jim Arndt
CLIENT:
Normark
AGENCY:
Carmichael Lynch/
Minneapolis

197
ART DIRECTOR:
Frank Haggerty
WRITER:
Jim Nelson
PHOTOGRAPHER:
Shawn Michienzi
CLIENT:
Stren
AGENCY:
Carmichael Lynch/
Minneapolis

198
ART DIRECTOR:
Frank Haggerty
WRITER:
Jim Nelson
PHOTOGRAPHER:
Shawn Michienzi
CLIENT:
Stren
AGENCY:
Carmichael Lynch/
Minneapolis

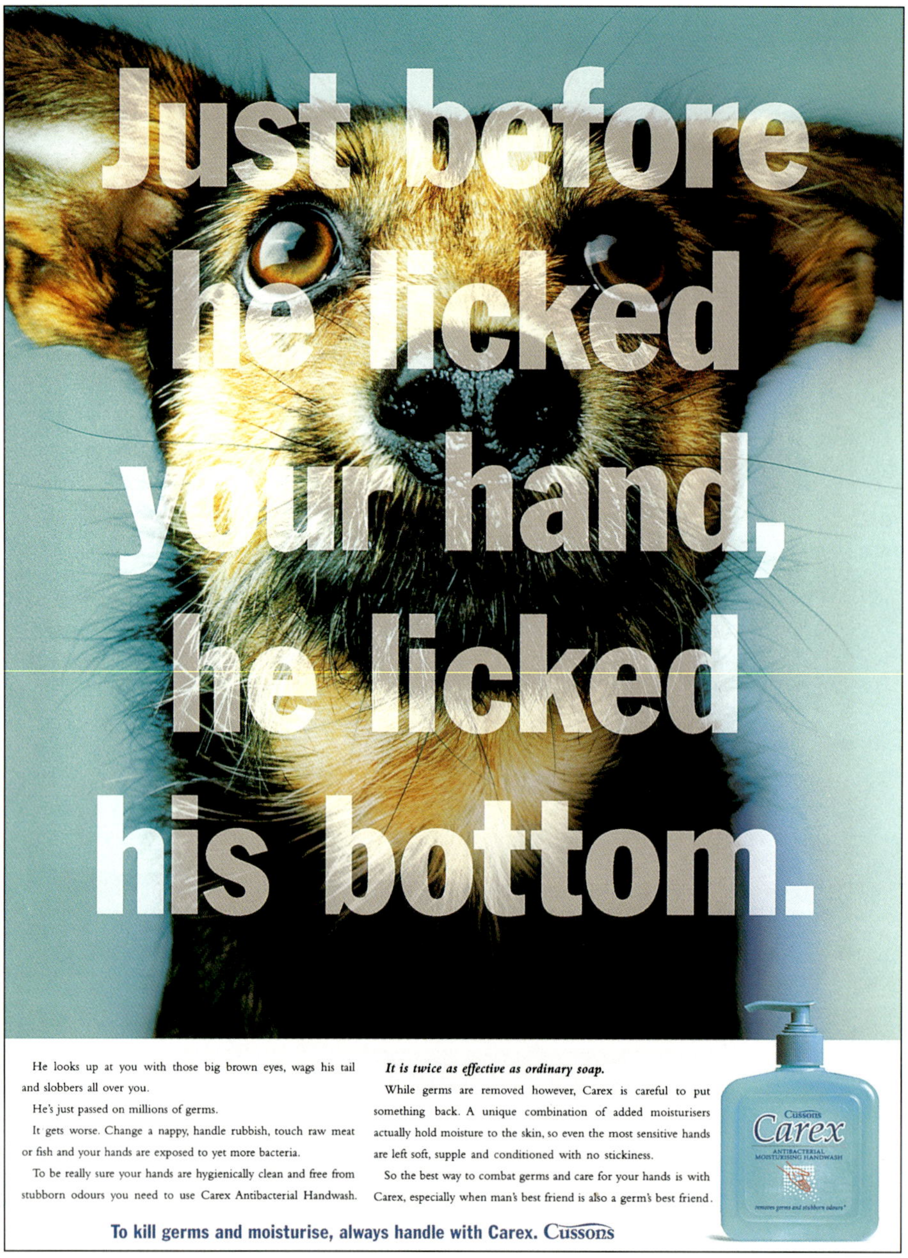

195

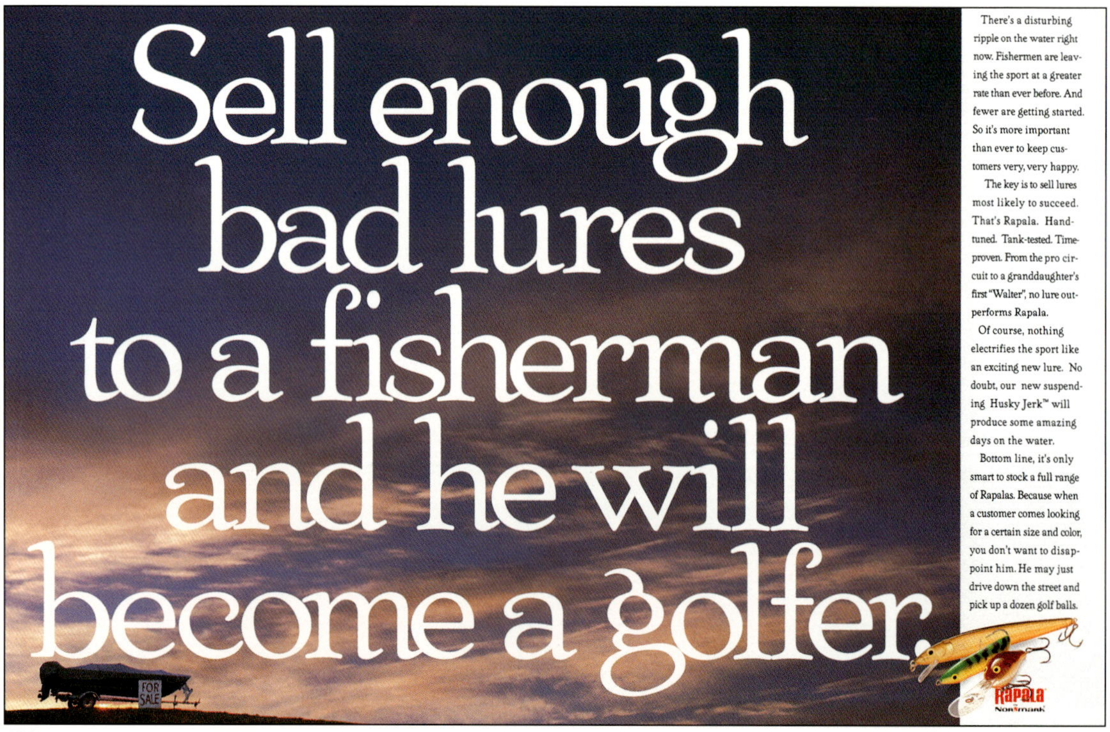

196

© 1995 Remington Arms Company, Inc.
The most dependable fishing line in the world.
STREN
POWERBRAID

197

© 1995 Remington Arms Company, Inc.
The most dependable fishing line in the world.
STREN
MAGNATHIN

198

CONSUMER MAGAZINE
COLOR FULL PAGE OR
SPREAD: SINGLE

199
ART DIRECTOR:
Frank Haggerty
WRITER:
Jim Nelson
PHOTOGRAPHER:
Shawn Michienzi
CLIENT:
Stren
AGENCY:
Carmichael Lynch/
Minneapolis

200
ART DIRECTOR:
Marc Gallucci
WRITER:
Maureen Begley
PHOTOGRAPHER:
Jim Erickson
CLIENT:
Eastpak
AGENCY:
Clarke Goward/Boston

201
ART DIRECTORS:
Markham Cronin
Tony Calcao
Alex Bogusky
WRITER:
Scott Linnen
PHOTOGRAPHERS:
Jose Molina
Tony Calcao
CLIENT:
Shimano American
Corporation
AGENCY:
Crispin & Porter/Miami

202
ART DIRECTOR:
Andrew Anema
WRITER:
Don Pogany
PHOTOGRAPHER:
Steve Bronstein
CLIENT:
Anheuser-Busch/
Budweiser
AGENCY:
DDB Needham/Chicago

199

200

The SD50 sport sandal
Shave your toes.
Introducing the world's first sandal specifically designed for the serious cyclist. Call 1-800-833-5540 for a free catalog. Power to the pedal.
SHIMANO
FOOTWEAR

201

©1995 Anheuser-Busch, Inc., Budweiser Beer, St. Louis, MO
Umpires,
this Bud's for you.

202

CONSUMER MAGAZINE
COLOR FULL PAGE OR
SPREAD: SINGLE

203
ART DIRECTOR:
Bob Barrie
WRITER:
Mike Lescarbeau
PHOTOGRAPHER:
E.J. Camp
CLIENT:
Sunset Marquis Hotel
AGENCY:
Fallon McElligott/
Minneapolis

204
ART DIRECTOR:
Bob Barrie
WRITER:
Dean Buckhorn
PHOTOGRAPHER:
P.F. Bentley
CLIENT:
Time
AGENCY:
Fallon McElligott/
Minneapolis

205
ART DIRECTOR:
Bob Barrie
WRITER:
Dean Buckhorn
PHOTOGRAPHER:
Gianni Giansanti
CLIENT:
Time
AGENCY:
Fallon McElligott/
Minneapolis

206
ART DIRECTOR:
Mike Mazza
WRITER:
Chuck McBride
PHOTOGRAPHER:
Graham Westmoreland
ILLUSTRATOR:
Alan Daniels
CLIENT:
American Isuzu Motors
AGENCY:
Goodby Silverstein &
Partners/San Francisco

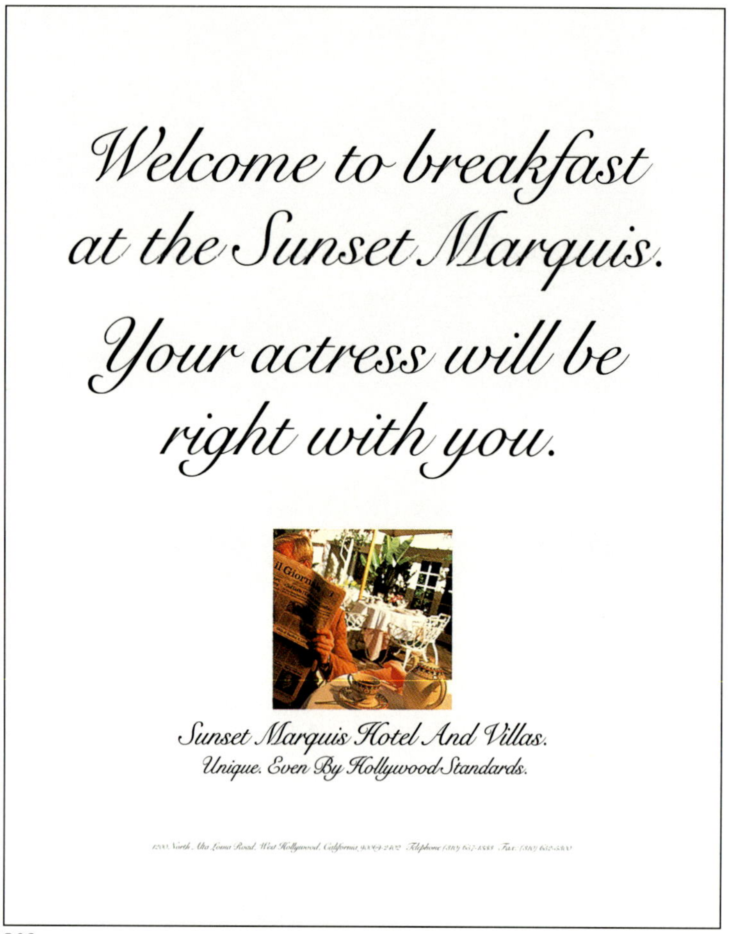

203

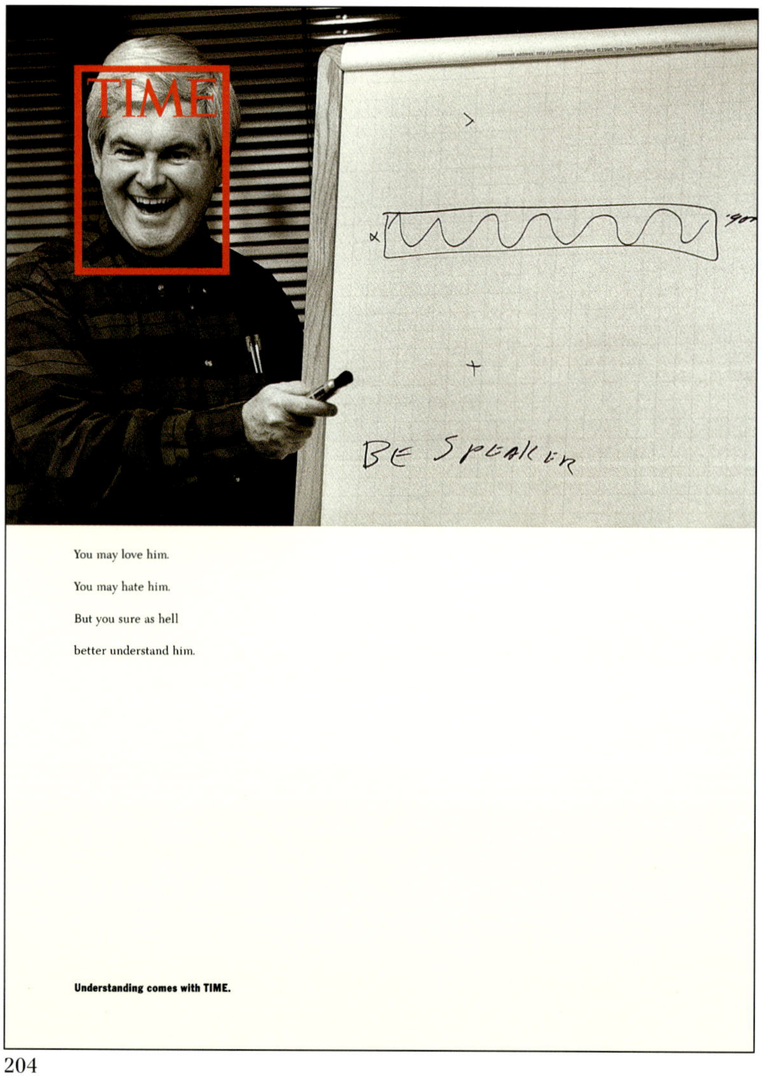

204

MAN OF THE YEAR
TIME
Even a man who addresses
billions of people a year
has a side that's rarely seen.
Understanding comes with TIME.

205

THE 60TH UNWRITTEN LAW OF DRIVING
CONCRETE PARKING BARRIERS
WERE INVENTED
TO TAKE OUT OIL PANS.
ALONG WITH 8.5 INCHES OF GROUND CLEARANCE. THE TROOPER LIMITED HAS MORE PROTECTIVE SKID PLATES THAN ANY OTHER IN ITS CLASS.
Ouch! That sound. That metal against concrete sound. It sends a flash of panic through your body as you visualize a pool of 10/30 weight slowly forming underneath you. You didn't mean to. Just like the curb the other day. And where did that mattress on the freeway come from, anyway? To get over these daily obstacles, we suggest a vehicle engineered to get you over mountain ranges and such. The new Trooper Limited. Call (800) 726-2700.
ISUZU
Practically/Amazing

206

CONSUMER MAGAZINE
COLOR FULL PAGE OR
SPREAD: SINGLE

207
ART DIRECTOR:
Jeremy Postaer
WRITER:
Paul Venables
PHOTOGRAPHERS:
Heimo
Gary Davis
CLIENT:
Bell Sports
AGENCY:
Goodby Silverstein &
Partners/San Francisco

208
ART DIRECTOR:
Joe Shands
WRITER:
Ron Saltmarsh
PHOTOGRAPHER:
Jim Erickson
CLIENT:
Haggar Clothing Company
AGENCY:
Goodby Silverstein &
Partners/San Francisco

209
ART DIRECTOR:
Steve Luker
WRITER:
Steve Simpson
PHOTOGRAPHERS:
Herb Ritts
Jim Erickson
CLIENT:
Norwegian Cruise Line
AGENCY:
Goodby Silverstein &
Partners/San Francisco

210
ART DIRECTORS:
Rich Silverstein
Todd Grant
WRITER:
Bo Coyner
PHOTOGRAPHER:
Clint Clemens
CLIENT:
Porsche Cars
North America
AGENCY:
Goodby Silverstein &
Partners/San Francisco

207

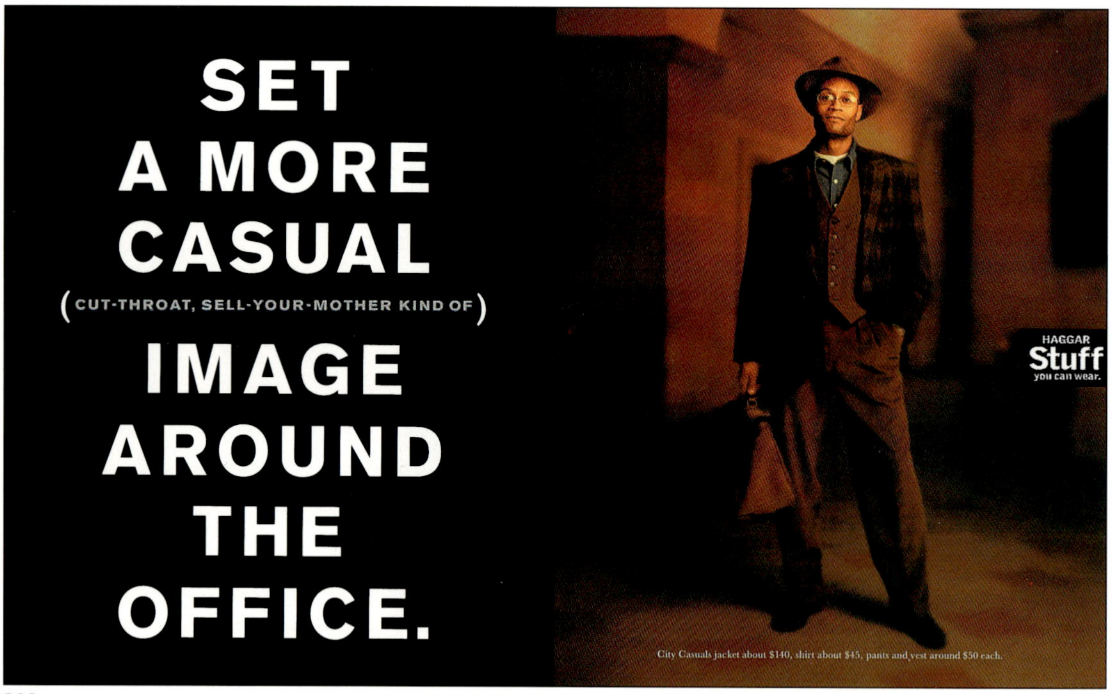

208

I live in a castle on the ocean floor. It is a roomy and convenient castle.
I like it.
My neighbors, fish, recently held an election. I was elected Emperor.
(Much to my surprise.)
I am the "Emperor of Fish." I think I will like this job.
NORWEGIAN
CRUISE LINE
It's
different
out
here.
My life has really changed since I put on a snorkel and mask.

209

turbo
Up to 181 mph, to be exact (if you've got
your own racetrack). Zero to sixty in just
over four heartbeats. 400 horses. Liquid all-
wheel drive. It's the new Nine Eleven Turbo.
Seriously bad news for the insect world.
Call 1-800-PORSCHE and find out why:
Porsche. There is no substitute.
Kills bugs fast.

210

CONSUMER MAGAZINE
COLOR FULL PAGE OR
SPREAD: SINGLE

211
ART DIRECTOR:
Erich Joiner
WRITER:
Steve Simpson
PHOTOGRAPHER:
Clint Clemens
CLIENT:
Porsche Cars
North America
AGENCY:
Goodby Silverstein &
Partners/San Francisco

212
ART DIRECTOR:
Sean Ehringer
WRITER:
Harry Cocciolo
CLIENT:
Unum Corporation
AGENCY:
Goodby Silverstein &
Partners/San Francisco

213
ART DIRECTORS:
Allen Richardson
Gerard Vaglio
WRITER:
Gary Cohen
PHOTOGRAPHER:
Vic Huber
CLIENT:
Land Rover North America
AGENCY:
Grace & Rothschild/
New York

214
ART DIRECTORS:
Eric Finkelstein
David Giles
WRITERS:
Robert Baiocco
Peter Iemma
PHOTOGRAPHER:
Todd Haiman
CLIENT:
House of Seagram
AGENCY:
Grey Advertising/New York

211

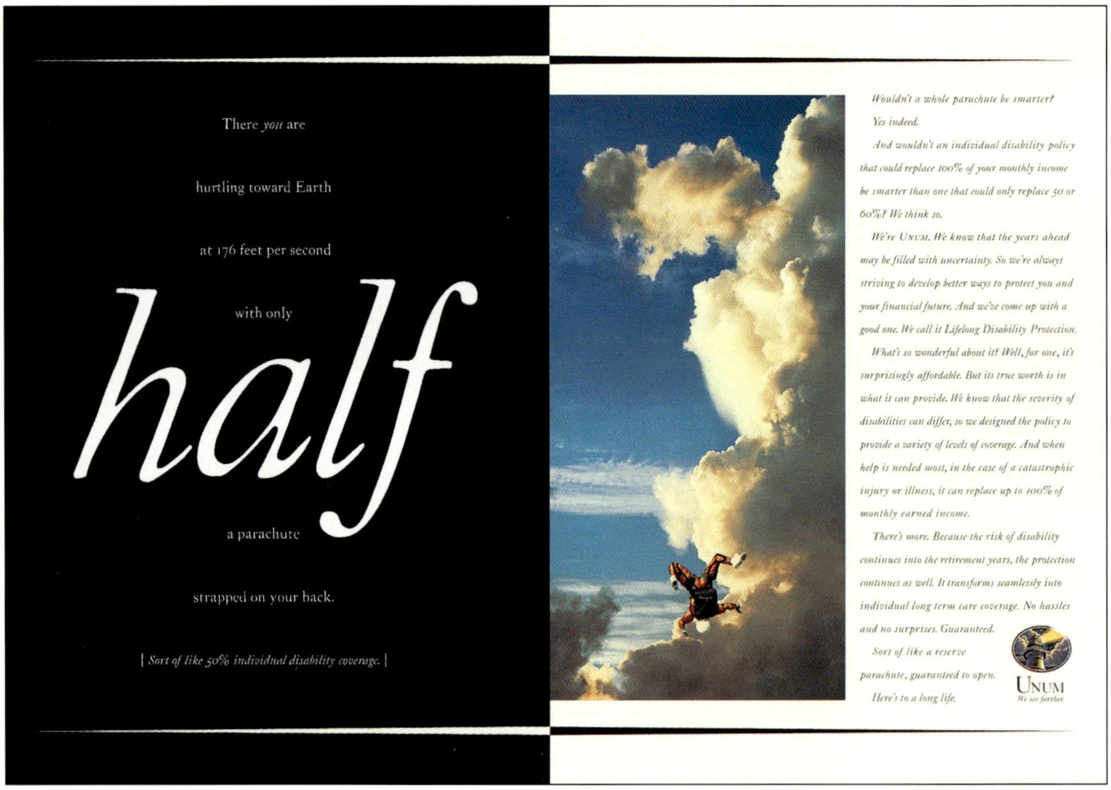

212

OPTIONAL EQUIPMENT SHOWN. TREAD LIGHTLY-DRIVE RESPONSIBLY OFF ROAD. BUCKLE UP FOR SECURITY. © 1994 LAND ROVER NORTH AMERICA, INC.
What to drive in places where you're the food.
The Defender 90 from Land Rover is one of the most sought-after vehicles in the world.
Which is why it's designed to keep whatever's out there, out there.
It offers the comfort of a front passenger safari cage, permanent four-wheel drive, and a brisk 3.9-liter V8 engine that can put just the right distance between you and a stomping, hungry, salivating who-knows-what.
With an immensely rugged 14-gauge steel chassis and phenomenally resilient coil spring suspension, it can climb over boulders, splash through a muddy gulch, power up a mountain, and curl down a twisted gorge.
Leaving a predator dumbstruck back at the gulch.
And now that the Defender comes with an optional removable hard top, a dangling green tree boa can't even drop in unannounced.
So why not call 1-800-FINE 4WD for the nearest dealer?
While it's not exactly the least expensive 4x4, the Defender offers you that invaluable old English option.
To be or not to be.
LAND ROVER
DEFENDER 90

213

Prenuptial Agreement
From the Law Offices of Giles, Finkelstein and Hart
To all to whom this may come to affect or may concern, know ye that it is understood that on the fourth day of February, Nineteen Hundred and Ninety-Five, that Jim Morrissey (hereafter known as the First Party) and Jeanne Fulton (hereafter known as the Second Party) are entering the contract of wedlock.
The following constitutes a full, legal and binding arrangement of said properties set before this date. This agreement shall be executed in multiple copies.
It is also to be understood that both the First Party and the Second Party are in complete agreement regarding the contents of this document and have stated so by signature and by witness on the fourth day of February, Nineteen Hundred and Ninety-Five. This agreement cannot be changed orally.
The following below is a full, detailed breakdown of said agreement regarding all properties of consequence shared by the First Party and the Second Party.
HIS
Season Tickets
Crown Royal
HERS
Everything else
If any provision of this Agreement shall later be found void or invalid in whole or in part, the remainder of this Agreement, and the remainder of that part of this Agreement not found void or invalid, shall remain in full force and effect.
In Witness Whereof, we the undersigned, on this date, the fourth day of February, Nineteen Hundred and Ninety-Five, are in complete agreement with the above arrangement and will abide by the contents of the document from the day of inception to the day the contract has been nullified by a court of law.
First Party
Signature Jim Morrissey Date 2/4/95
Second Party
Signature Jeanne Fulton Date 2/4/95
Notary Public Barbara McQuaid Date 2/4/95
Notary Public
No.00-000000
Certificate Filed in York County
Commission Expires April 8, 1999
NOTARY PUBLIC
Crown Royal
Those who appreciate quality enjoy it responsibly.
©1995 CROWN ROYAL • IMPORTED IN THE BOTTLE • BLENDED CANADIAN WHISKY • 40% ALCOHOL BY VOLUME (80 PROOF) • JOSEPH E. SEAGRAM & SONS, NEW YORK, NY

214

CONSUMER MAGAZINE COLOR FULL PAGE OR SPREAD: SINGLE

215
ART DIRECTOR:
Kirk Mosel
WRITER:
Chris Jacobs
CLIENT:
ITT Hartford
AGENCY:
Hampel/Stefanides, New York

216
ART DIRECTOR:
Ian Harding
WRITER:
Shaun McIlrath
PHOTOGRAPHER:
Alan McPhail
CLIENT:
Mauritius Government Tourist Board
AGENCY:
Impact FCA!/London

217
ART DIRECTOR:
David Dye
WRITER:
Will Awdry
CLIENT:
Adidas
AGENCY:
Leagas Delaney/London

218
ART DIRECTOR:
David Dye
WRITER:
David Dye
CLIENT:
Adidas
AGENCY:
Leagas Delaney/London

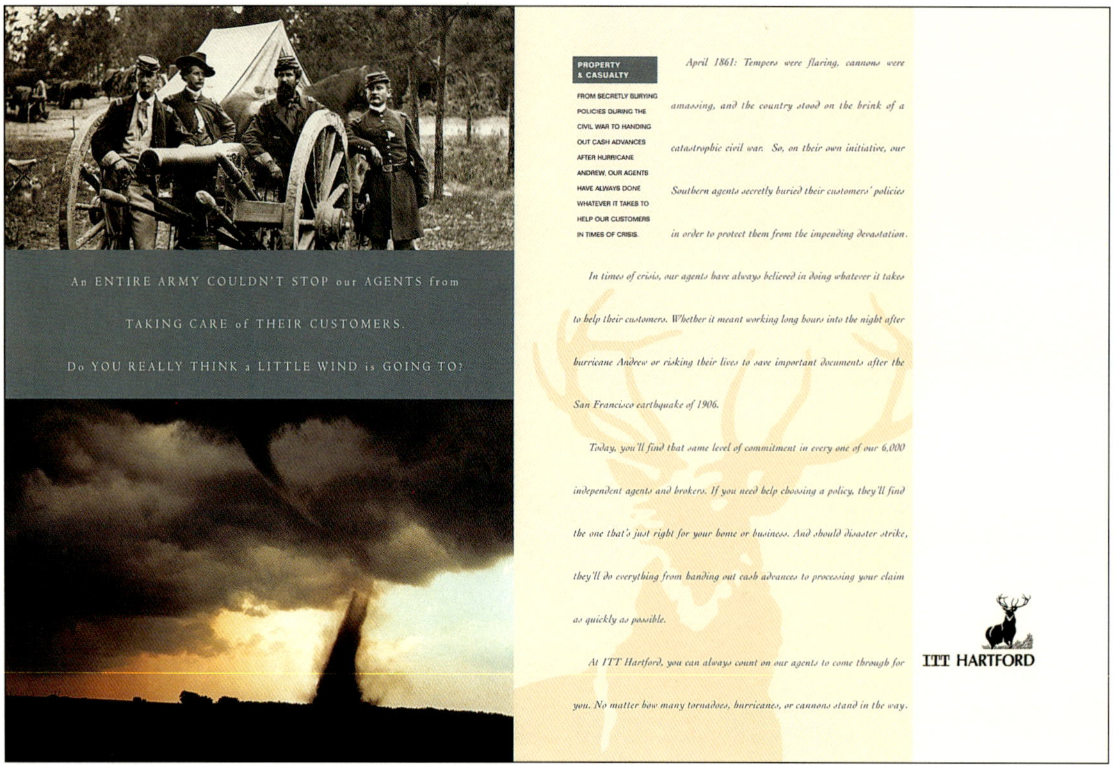

215

216

LINES
STRAIGHT
I
STAND
CAN'T
The Claw. Zig zagging around the mountains, you need two qualities. Traction comes with the shoe. Finding the guts is up to you.
adidas

217

JUST TO THE SIGNPOST...
JUST TO THE TRUCK.
JUST TO THE KERB.
JUST TO THE CROSSROADS.
JUST TO THE CAR.
JUST TO THE SIGNPOST.
adidas
RUNNING

218

CONSUMER MAGAZINE COLOR FULL PAGE OR SPREAD: SINGLE

219
ART DIRECTOR:
Paul Belford
WRITERS:
Nigel Roberts
Will Awdry
CLIENT:
Harrods
AGENCY:
Leagas Delaney/London

220
ART DIRECTOR:
Martin Galton
WRITER:
Tim Delaney
CLIENT:
Harrods
AGENCY:
Leagas Delaney/London

221
ART DIRECTOR:
Martin Galton
WRITER:
Tom Hudson
CLIENT:
Pepe
AGENCY:
Leagas Delaney/London

222
ART DIRECTOR:
Martin Galton
WRITER:
Tim Delaney
CLIENT:
Pepe
AGENCY:
Leagas Delaney/London

219

220

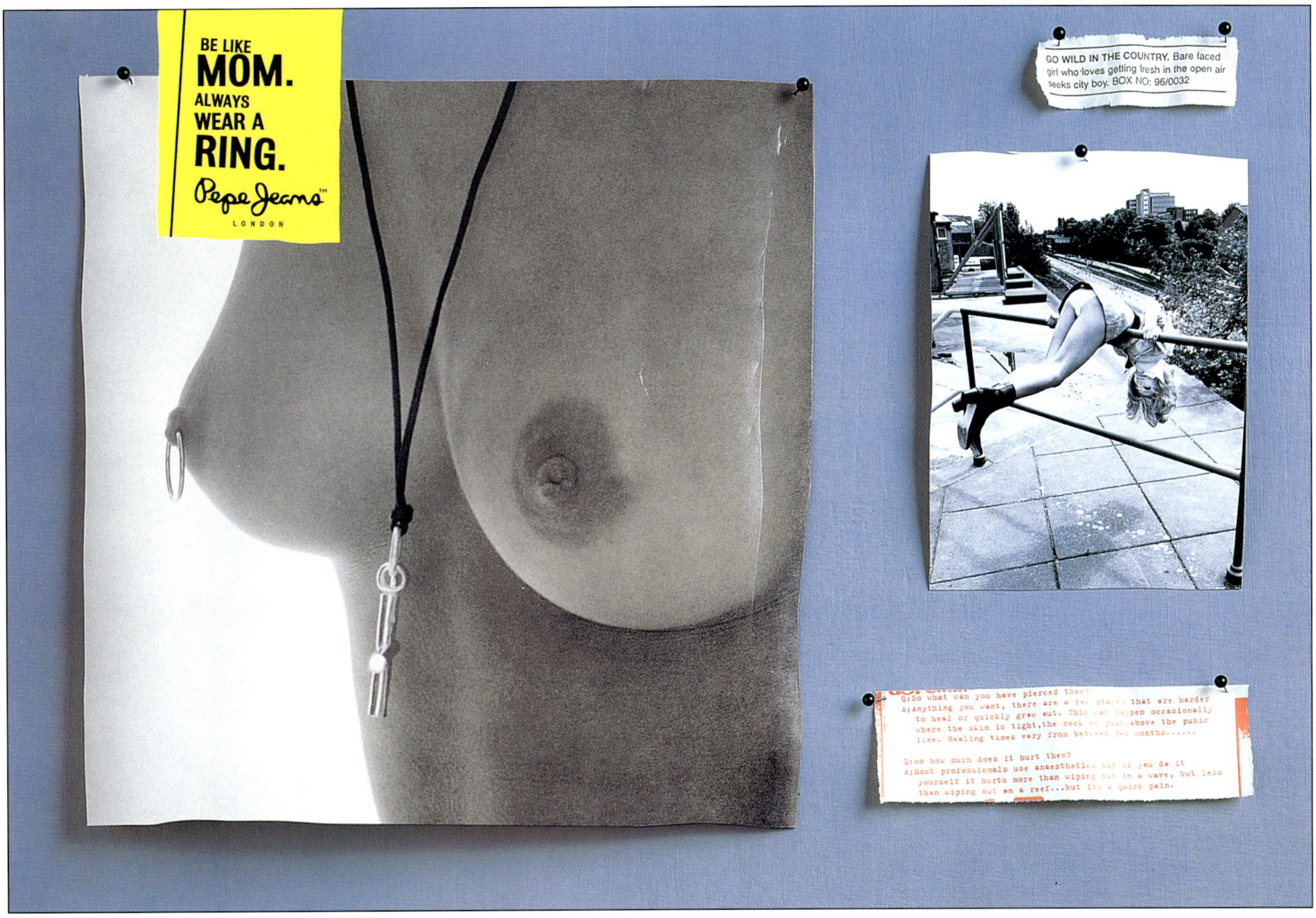
BE LIKE
MOM.
ALWAYS
WEAR A
RING.
Pepe Jeans
LONDON
GO WILD IN THE COUNTRY. Bare faced girl who loves getting fresh in the open air seeks city boy. BOX NO: 96/0032
Q:So what can you have pierced then?
A:Anything you want, there are a few places that are harder to heal or quickly grew out. This can happen occasionally where the skin is tight,the neck or just above the pubic line. Healing times vary from between 3-4 months......
Q:so how much does it hurt then?
A:Most professionals use anaesthetics but if you do it yourself it hurts more than wiping out in a wave, but less than wiping out on a reef...but its a quick pain.

221

HELPLINES
FOR confidential advice, day or night, phone my advice lines:
Where to touch a man to turn him on 0839 070 721
Where to touch a woman to turn her on 0839 070 723
How to achieve orgasm 0839 446 646
Put sparkle back into your sex life 0839 070 733
Sex with a man with a big penis 0839 66 44 17
Oral sex - advice for women 0839 664 462
Oral sex - advice for men 0839 664 453
Oral sex - how to do it 0839 664 452
Forbidden sex - the dangers 0839 446 645
How to measure a penis 0839 664 461
Size - how important is it? 0839 446 647
Can you make your penis larger? 0839 070 744
How to turn a woman on 0839 446 648
How to turn a man on 0839 446 649
Sexual exercises for women 0839 446 650
Conquer premature ejaculation 0839 446 653
How to overcome impotence 0839 446 661
Dealing with depression 0839 446 662
How to overcome stress 0839 446 663
Hidden power to make you slim 0839 446 670
How to put on weight 0839 446 671
Controlling high blood pressure without drugs 0839 446 675
How to deal with panic attacks 0839 070 734
How to look sexy 0839 070 740
Irritable Bowel Syndrome 0839 664 459
How to deal with flatulence/wind 0839 664 478
Advice for transvestites 0839 333 124
How to deal with sagging breasts 0839 333 122
How to conquer cramp at night 0839 333 123
Calls cost 39p per minute cheap rate, 49p at other times
For a leaflet with details of 100 Helpline numbers, write to: Dr Vernon Coleman, PO Box 3000, London N20 9RB
ALWAYS
CARRY
CHANGE
FOR THE
TELEPHONE.
Pepe Jeans
LONDON

222

CONSUMER MAGAZINE
COLOR FULL PAGE OR
SPREAD: SINGLE

223
ART DIRECTOR:
Paul Belford
WRITER:
Nigel Roberts
CLIENT:
Pepe
AGENCY:
Leagas Delaney/London

224
ART DIRECTOR:
John Knight
WRITER:
Richard Cook
PHOTOGRAPHER:
Trevor Key
CLIENT:
McDonald's
AGENCY:
Leo Burnett/London

225
ART DIRECTOR:
Greg Bokor
WRITER:
Kara Goodrich
PHOTOGRAPHER:
Jim Erickson
CLIENT:
Canstar
AGENCY:
Leonard/Monahan,
Providence

226
ART DIRECTOR:
Michaela LaRosse
WRITER:
Adrian Lim
PHOTOGRAPHERS:
Paul Arden
Laurie Haskell
CLIENT:
Tesco
AGENCY:
Lowe Howard-Spink/
London

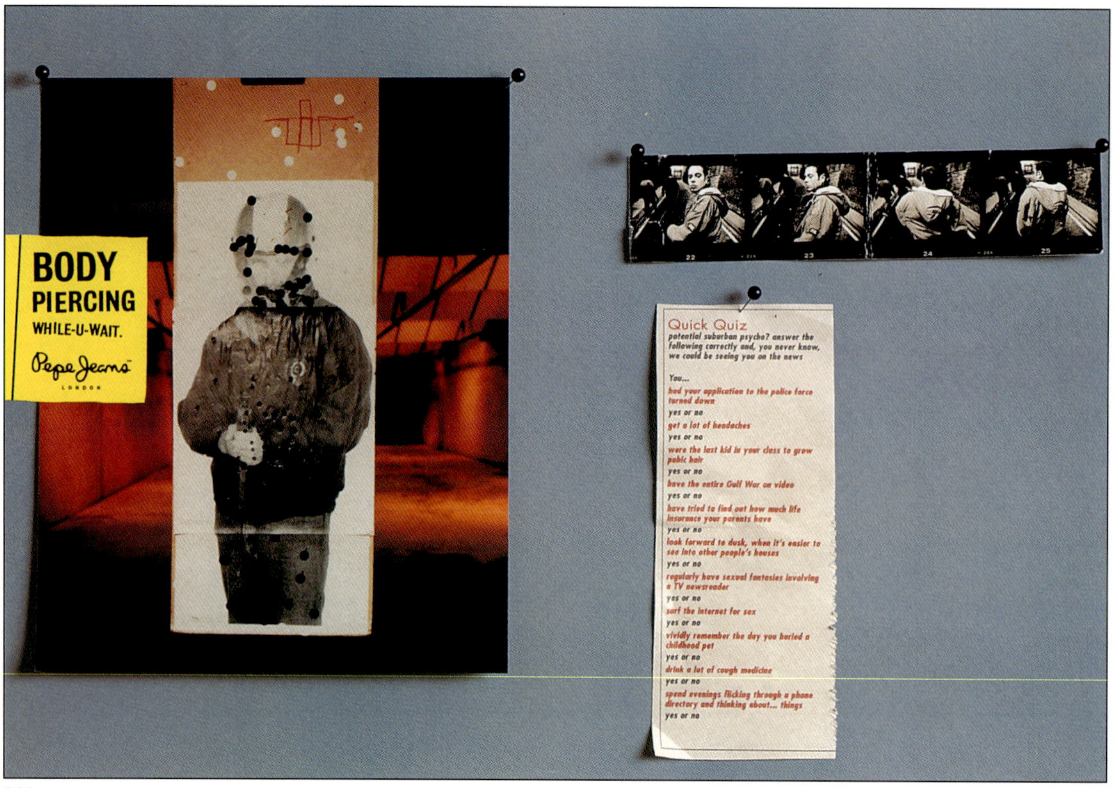

223

224

It's exercise.
FOR THE FIRST 15 MILES.
THEN IT'S
SOME KIND OF
SICK
COMPULSION
FUELED BY
GOD KNOWS WHAT.
Bauer

225

CAN WE INTEREST YOU IN A DELIGHTFUL GLASS OF BURNT TOAST, NEWLY MOWN GRASS, AND OLD SOCKS?
SOME GREAT NEWS FOR ALL BUDDING OZ CLARKES AND JILLY GOOLDENS.
A CHANCE FOR YOU TO SWIRL, SNIFF, SIP AND SLURP AT OUR SUNDAY WINE TASTING SESSIONS.
WE'LL BE UNCORKING A DIFFERENT BOTTLE EVERY WEEK, AND THERE'LL EVEN BE ADVICE ON HAND IF YOU HAVE ANY QUESTIONS.
SO MAKE SURE YOU'RE FREE THIS SUNDAY, OUR WINE WILL BE.
FREE WINE TASTING EVERY SUNDAY AT SELECTED STORES.
TESCO
Every little helps.

226

CONSUMER MAGAZINE
COLOR FULL PAGE OR
SPREAD: SINGLE

227
ART DIRECTOR:
Charles Inge
WRITER:
Phil Dearman
PHOTOGRAPHER:
Andy Green
CLIENT:
Vauxhall Motors
AGENCY:
Lowe Howard-Spink/
London

228
ART DIRECTOR:
Charles Inge
WRITER:
Phil Dearman
PHOTOGRAPHER:
Andy Green
CLIENT:
Vauxhall Motors
AGENCY:
Lowe Howard-Spink/
London

229
ART DIRECTOR:
Charles Inge
WRITER:
Phil Dearman
PHOTOGRAPHER:
Andy Green
CLIENT:
Vauxhall Motors
AGENCY:
Lowe Howard-Spink/
London

230
ART DIRECTOR:
Mark Fuller
WRITER:
Ron Huey
PHOTOGRAPHER:
William Coupon
CLIENT:
Amgen
AGENCY:
The Martin Agency/
Richmond

227

228

Mudmen from Papua New Guinea get their first glimpse of a Frontera, thanks to its powerful new engine and anti-clog brakes.
See a different world. THE 1995 FRONTERA FROM VAUXHALL

229

Today, men and women are leading more active lives while undergoing chemotherapy treatment. And that's good news. Recently, breakthroughs are helping reduce many of the common side effects of treatment including nausea and even more serious conditions that can develop like a low white blood cell count.

One drug, Neupogen (Filgrastim), is being prescribed to help certain people on chemotherapy maintain a more normal white blood cell count. Specifically, a normal neutrophil count. In short,

THE HORROR STORIES YOU'VE HEARD ABOUT CHEMOTHERAPY ARE TRUE. THEY'RE ALSO A DECADE OLD.

neutrophils are a type of white blood cell that helps your body fight infection. Maintaining a normal neutrophil count during treatment can be important for two reasons.

First, you have a much greater chance of staying on your recommended chemotherapy schedule. That means getting your treatment behind you sooner. Secondly, maintaining a normal neutrophil count can help reduce your risk of infection. So you have a better chance of staying out of the hospital. Instead, you can spend more time at home where you belong with family and friends. Even daily activities like shopping, going to movies and eating out at restaurants can be more accessible.

Of course, Neupogen isn't right for every patient. Ask your doctor if Neupogen should be a part of your treatment. On the following page, you'll find an explanation of Neupogen and its possible side effects. These may include mild-to-moderate bone pain, which can often be controlled with a non-aspirin analgesic.

As a final note, before we embarked on this educational campaign, we conducted extensive research in cities across the country. We talked with people who were currently undergoing, or had undergone chemotherapy treatment in the past. We also met with doctors, nurses and other cancer specialists. Among chemotherapy patients, we found an overwhelming desire for more information about cancer and chemotherapy treatment. Doctors and nurses, many of whom had initial misgivings about any advertising at all, urged us to please be candid in all of our communications. They also asked that we point out that Neupogen isn't for everyone. We acted on their advice.

We realize that your medical care is a sensitive and very personal matter. We'd like to know your feelings about the information presented here. If you would like to receive more information concerning Neupogen and how it might help in your treatment, call us at 1-800-333-9777.

NEUPOGEN

230

CONSUMER MAGAZINE COLOR FULL PAGE OR SPREAD: SINGLE

231
ART DIRECTOR:
Carolyn McGeorge
WRITER:
Raymond McKinney
PHOTOGRAPHER:
Dublin Productions
CLIENT:
Healthtex
AGENCY:
The Martin Agency/ Richmond

232
ART DIRECTOR:
Carolyn McGeorge
WRITER:
Raymond McKinney
PHOTOGRAPHER:
Dublin Productions
CLIENT:
Healthtex
AGENCY:
The Martin Agency/ Richmond

233
ART DIRECTOR:
Carolyn McGeorge
WRITER:
Raymond McKinney
PHOTOGRAPHER:
Dublin Productions
CLIENT:
Healthtex
AGENCY:
The Martin Agency/ Richmond

234
ART DIRECTOR:
Jamie Mahoney
WRITER:
Joe Alexander
PHOTOGRAPHER:
Dublin Productions
CLIENT:
Healthtex
AGENCY:
The Martin Agency/ Richmond

231

232

Here are Beth, Ellen and Jimmy showing off their new clothes. (Ellen and Jimmy are imaginary friends. Just play along.)
Aren't they cute? Beth in her plaid flannel jumper and matching turtleneck. Ellen in her leggings and apple-plaid top. And little Jimmy in his flannel romper with quilted patches. Call our toll-free number to find out more about our fall playwear like colorful denims and fun coveralls. We'll answer any questions, as well as give you some fashion tips for your child and her, er, friends.
Healthtex
1-800-554-7637
Call us toll-free at 1-800-554-7637 for the store nearest you, or if you simply have questions.

233

Paint and ketchup and glue and mud and juice and markers and chalk and ravioli. Now that's what little girls are made of.
Sugar and spice and everything nice?!?!? We don't think so. These days, little girls get into just about anything. (Isn't it great?) Which is why here at Healthtex, we suggest you get your child into something that's easy to wash. Like the outfit shown here. Or the dozens of other really cute new styles we have this spring. Just call us at 1-800-554-7637 to find out more. As for snakes, snails and puppy dog tails, no problem. All of our boys' clothes are just as easy to wash.
Healthtex
1-800-554-7637
Questions? Call 1-800-554-7637. Look for Healthtex at The Bon Marche, Boscov's and Lazarus.

234

CONSUMER MAGAZINE COLOR FULL PAGE OR SPREAD: SINGLE

235
ART DIRECTOR:
Jamie Mahoney
WRITER:
Joe Alexander
PHOTOGRAPHER:
Dublin Productions
CLIENT:
Healthtex
AGENCY:
The Martin Agency/ Richmond

236
ART DIRECTOR:
Jamie Mahoney
WRITER:
Raymond McKinney
PHOTOGRAPHER:
Dublin Productions
CLIENT:
Healthtex
AGENCY:
The Martin Agency/ Richmond

237
ART DIRECTOR:
Sean Riley
WRITER:
Raymond McKinney
CLIENT:
VF Corporation
AGENCY:
The Martin Agency/ Richmond

238
ART DIRECTOR:
Hunt Clark
WRITER:
Larry Silberfein
PHOTOGRAPH:
Auto Sport Magazine
CLIENT:
Volvo
AGENCY:
Messner Vetere Berger McNamee Schmetterer/ Euro RSCG, New York

235

236

VF CORPORATION. PROUD SPONSOR OF THE U.S. OPEN TENNIS CHAMPIONSHIPS.
Vanity Fair, JanSport, Jantzen, Lee, Riders, Rustler, Healthtex, Cutler, Nutmeg, Red Kap, Vassarette, Wrangler, Barbizon and Marithé and François Girbaud* are just some of the VF brands. *Under license agreement.

237

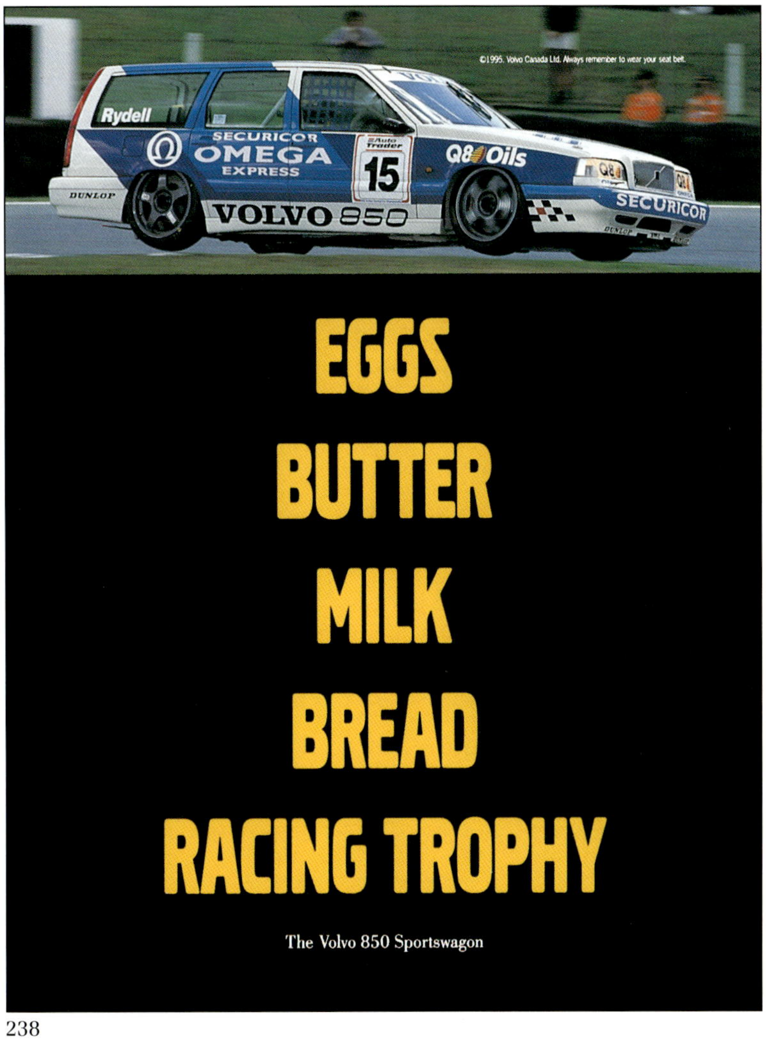
©1995. Volvo Canada Ltd. Always remember to wear your seat belt.
Rydell
SECURICOR
OMEGA
EXPRESS
15
Q8 Oils
VOLVO 850
SECURICOR
DUNLOP
EGGS
BUTTER
MILK
BREAD
RACING TROPHY
The Volvo 850 Sportswagon

238

CONSUMER MAGAZINE
COLOR FULL PAGE OR
SPREAD: SINGLE

239
ART DIRECTOR:
Keith Weinman
WRITER:
Jack Fund
PHOTOGRAPHER:
Garry Owens
CLIENT:
BMW of North America
AGENCY:
Mullen/Wenham, MA

240
ART DIRECTOR:
Bob Needleman
WRITER:
Frank Fleizach
PHOTOGRAPHER:
Chris Lawrence
CLIENT:
Reader's Digest/
American Health
AGENCY:
Needleman Fleizach Pilla/
New York

241
ART DIRECTOR:
Theo Ferreira
WRITER:
Bryn Puchert
PHOTOGRAPHER:
Mark Lanning
CLIENT:
Nissan S.A.
AGENCY:
Net#work/Benmore,
South Africa

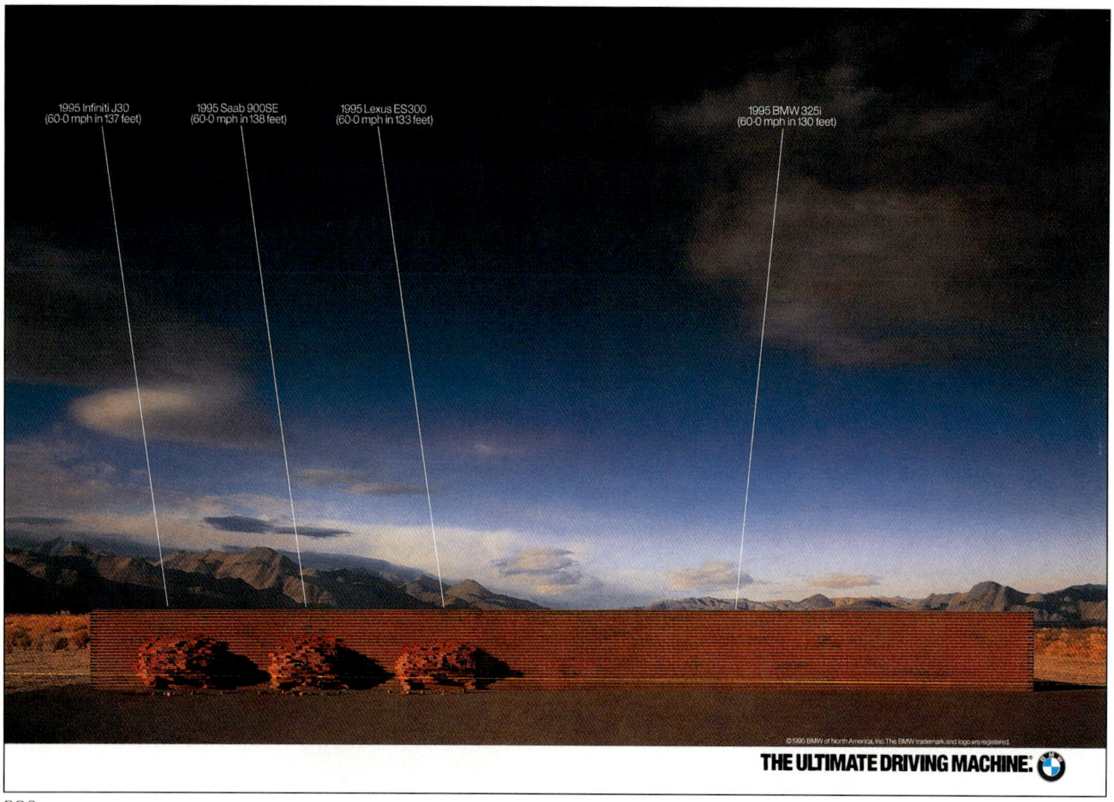

239

240

WITH LOOKS LIKE THESE,
THE MUDPACK IS OPTIONAL.
NISSAN
YOU CAN WITH A NISSAN
NEW SANI

CONSUMER MAGAZINE COLOR FULL PAGE OR SPREAD: SINGLE

242
ART DIRECTOR:
Hal Curtis
WRITER:
Steve Bautista
PHOTOGRAPHERS:
Harry DeZitter
Susie Cushner
Paul Clancy
ILLUSTRATOR:
Peter Hall
CLIENT:
Dexter Shoe Company
AGENCY:
Pagano Schenck & Kay/Boston

243
ART DIRECTOR:
Hal Curtis
WRITER:
Steve Bautista
PHOTOGRAPHERS:
Harry DeZitter
Susie Cushner
Paul Clancy
ILLUSTRATOR:
Peter Hall
CLIENT:
Dexter Shoe Company
AGENCY:
Pagano Schenck & Kay/Boston

244
ART DIRECTOR:
Terence Reynolds
WRITER:
Todd Tilford
PHOTOGRAPHER:
Duncan Sim
CLIENT:
AM General Corporation
AGENCY:
R&D/The Richards Group, Dallas

245
ART DIRECTOR:
Curt Detweiler
WRITER:
Curt Detweiler
CLIENT:
Limited Edition Fragrances
AGENCY:
Steamhouse Advertising/Singapore

242

243

HUMMER
YES, IT'S STREET LEGAL. YES, IT WILL GO THROUGH THE BANK DRIVE-THRU. NO, YOU CAN'T GET IT WITH A MACHINE GUN TURRET.
Hummer's off-road prowess is legendary. However, it is perfectly capable of performing admirably on the road as well. In fact, you'll find weaving in and out of traffic, parallel parking, and navigating your way through the city's parking garages a breeze. You'll also find eighteen-wheelers and New York cabbies more than willing to give you the right of way.
It wasn't created for the masses. It wasn't created for the average driver. Or some faceless common denominator. It was, instead, created for the United States Military. And save for some additional creature comforts, a new available gas engine, and the absence of optional equipment like missile launchers, the civilian Hummer is basically unchanged from its military counterpart. With 16 inches of ground clearance (twice that of any 4X4), steep approach and departure angles, a stable 72-inch track width, a 4-wheel fully independent suspension system with hydraulic shock absorbers and heavy-duty springs, and a unique geared hub assembly, a Hummer can go places no other vehicle can. Scale an 18-inch vertical wall. Ford two feet of water. Plow through three-foot snowdrifts. Traverse a 40% side-slope. Climb a 60% grade. Navigate even the deepest sand. Stand defiantly in the face of categorization, conformity, and boredom.
For more information, call 1-800-732-5493.

244

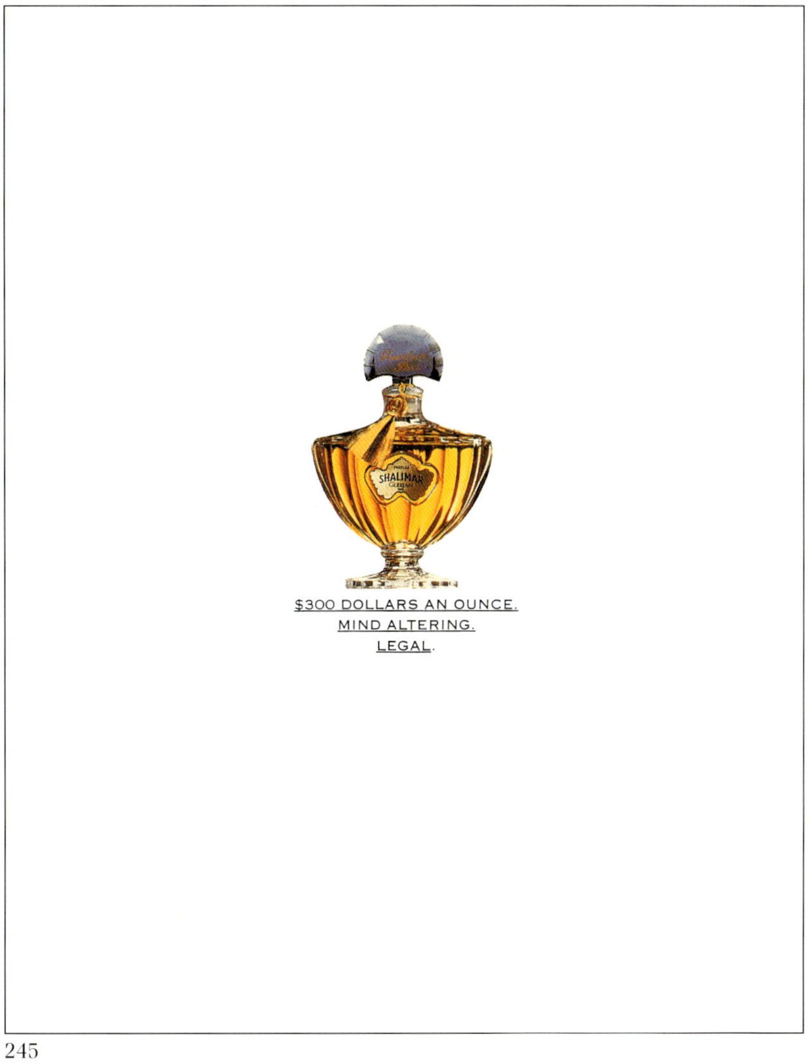
SHALIMAR
GUERLAIN
$300 DOLLARS AN OUNCE.
MIND ALTERING.
LEGAL.

245

CONSUMER MAGAZINE
COLOR FULL PAGE OR
SPREAD: SINGLE

246
ART DIRECTOR:
Alix Botwin
WRITER:
Jeff Kosakow
CLIENT:
V&S Vin & Sprit AB
AGENCY:
TBWA Chiat/Day, New York

247
ART DIRECTOR:
John Vitro
WRITER:
John Robertson
PHOTOGRAPHER:
Chris Wimpey
CLIENT:
Taylor Guitars
AGENCY:
VitroRobertson/San Diego

248
ART DIRECTOR:
John Vitro
WRITER:
John Robertson
ILLUSTRATOR:
Mark Fredrickson
CLIENT:
Thermoscan
AGENCY:
VitroRobertson/San Diego

249
ART DIRECTOR:
Darryl McDonald
WRITER:
James LeMaitre
PHOTOGRAPHER:
Duncan Sim
CLIENT:
Nike
AGENCY:
Wieden & Kennedy/
Portland

ABSOLUT HOUDINI.
ABSOLUT® VODKA. PRODUCT OF SWEDEN. 40 AND 50% ALC/VOL (80 AND 100 PROOF). 100% GRAIN NEUTRAL SPIRITS. ABSOLUT COUNTRY OF SWEDEN VODKA & LOGO, ABSOLUT, ABSOLUT BOTTLE DESIGN AND ABSOLUT CALLIGRAPHY ARE TRADEMARKS OWNED BY V&S VIN & SPRIT AB. ©1995 V&S VIN & SPRIT AB. IMPORTED BY THE HOUSE OF SEAGRAM, NEW YORK, NY. PHOTOGRAPHED BY STEVE BRONSTEIN.
THOSE WHO APPRECIATE QUALITY ENJOY IT RESPONSIBLY.

246

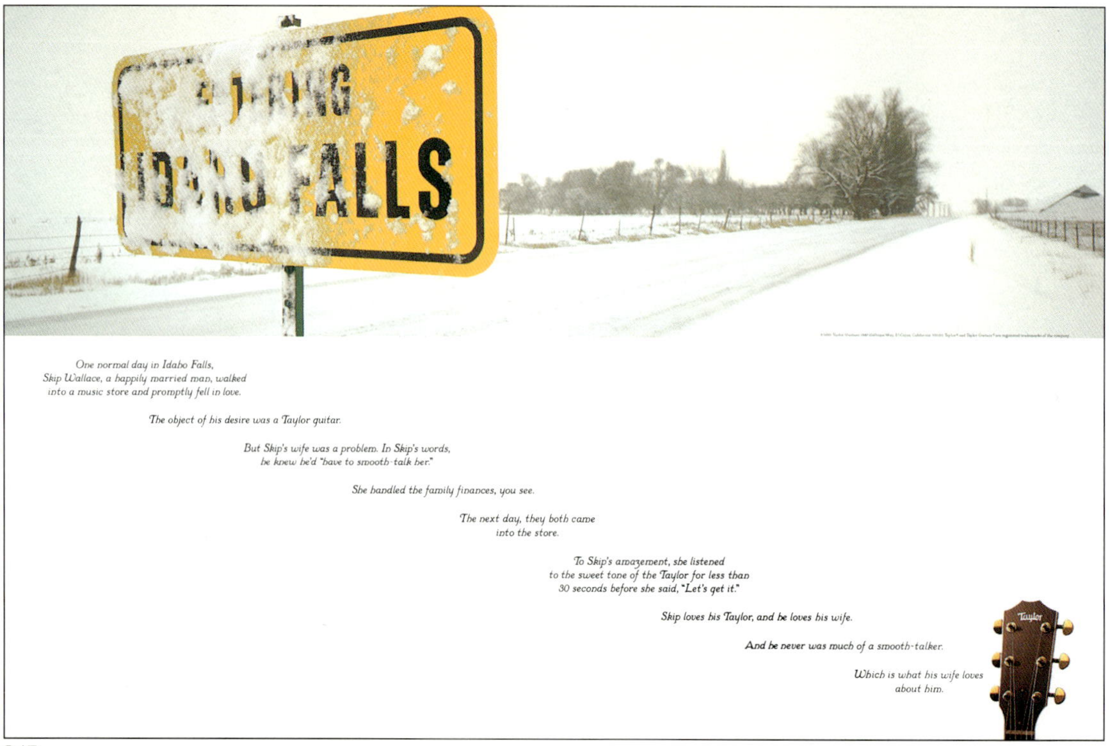

FALLS
One normal day in Idaho Falls,
Skip Wallace, a happily married man, walked
into a music store and promptly fell in love.
The object of his desire was a Taylor guitar.
But Skip's wife was a problem. In Skip's words,
he knew he'd "have to smooth-talk her."
She handled the family finances, you see.
The next day, they both came
into the store.
To Skip's amazement, she listened
to the sweet tone of the Taylor for less than
30 seconds before she said, "Let's get it."
Skip loves his Taylor, and he loves his wife.
And he never was much of a smooth-talker.
Which is what his wife loves
about him.
Taylor

247

THE GREAT THING
ABOUT THIS
THERMOMETER
IS THAT CHILDREN
HAVE YET TO LEARN
HOW TO CLENCH THEIR
EARS SHUT.
If there's one thing kids are good at, it's figuring out how to make it difficult to take their temperature.
They squirm. They wiggle. They whine. They even cry. But don't give up hope. Just throw out your old thermometer. And replace it with a Thermoscan® Instant Thermometer.
In one short second, it takes a temperature at the ear. It's easy. It's accurate. It's safe. (No wonder over a half-billion temperatures are being taken this way every year in doctors' offices and hospitals.)
And now you can get it for a new lower price. Which means the perfect family thermometer just got better.
The first name in fast temperatures
THERMOSCAN
INSTANT THERMOMETER

248

DAN O'BRIEN · POLE VAULT

249

CONSUMER MAGAZINE COLOR FULL PAGE OR SPREAD: SINGLE

250

ART DIRECTOR:
Darryl McDonald
WRITER:
James LeMaitre
PHOTOGRAPHER:
Duncan Sim
CLIENT:
Nike
AGENCY:
Wieden & Kennedy/ Portland

CONSUMER MAGAZINE COLOR FULL PAGE OR SPREAD: CAMPAIGN

251

ART DIRECTOR:
David Ruiz
WRITER:
Gustavo Caldas
PHOTOGRAPHERS:
Arara Pelegrin
Horrillo y Riola
Carlos Suarez
CLIENT:
Levi Strauss Espana, S.A.
AGENCY:
Bassat Ogilvy & Mather/ Barcelona

250

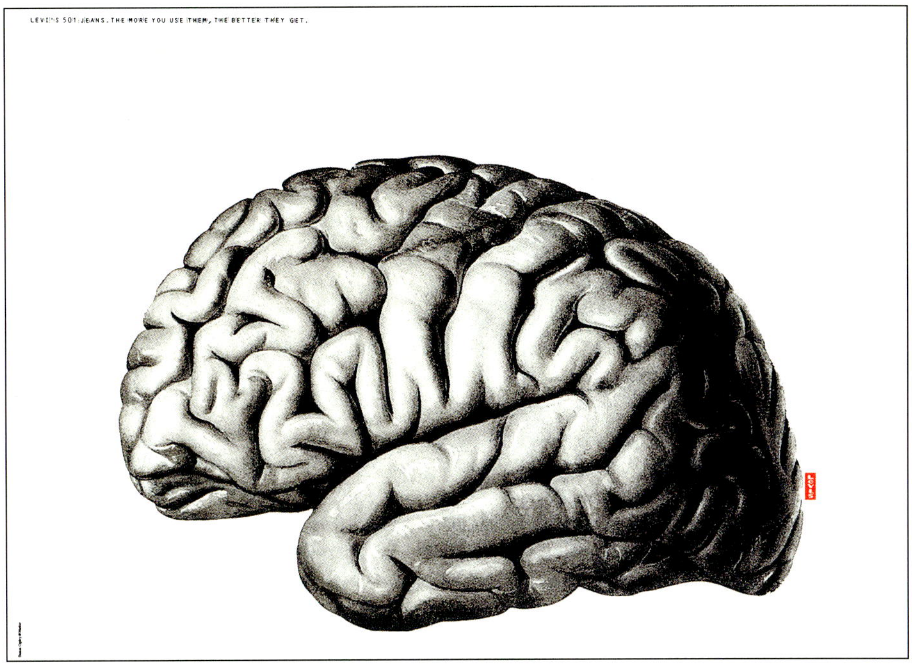
LEVI'S 501 JEANS. THE MORE YOU USE THEM, THE BETTER THEY GET.

LEVI'S 501 JEANS. BORN TO RESIST.

LEVI'S 501 JEANS. THE MORE YOU WASH THEM, THE BETTER THEY LOOK.

CONSUMER MAGAZINE
COLOR FULL PAGE OR
SPREAD: CAMPAIGN

252

ART DIRECTOR:
Rob Palmer

WRITERS:
Kathy Hepinstall
David Lubars

PHOTOGRAPHERS:
Lars Topelmann
Helen Trotman

ILLUSTRATORS:
Joe Saputo
Antar Dayal

CLIENT:
Pioneer Electronics USA

AGENCY:
BBDO/Los Angeles

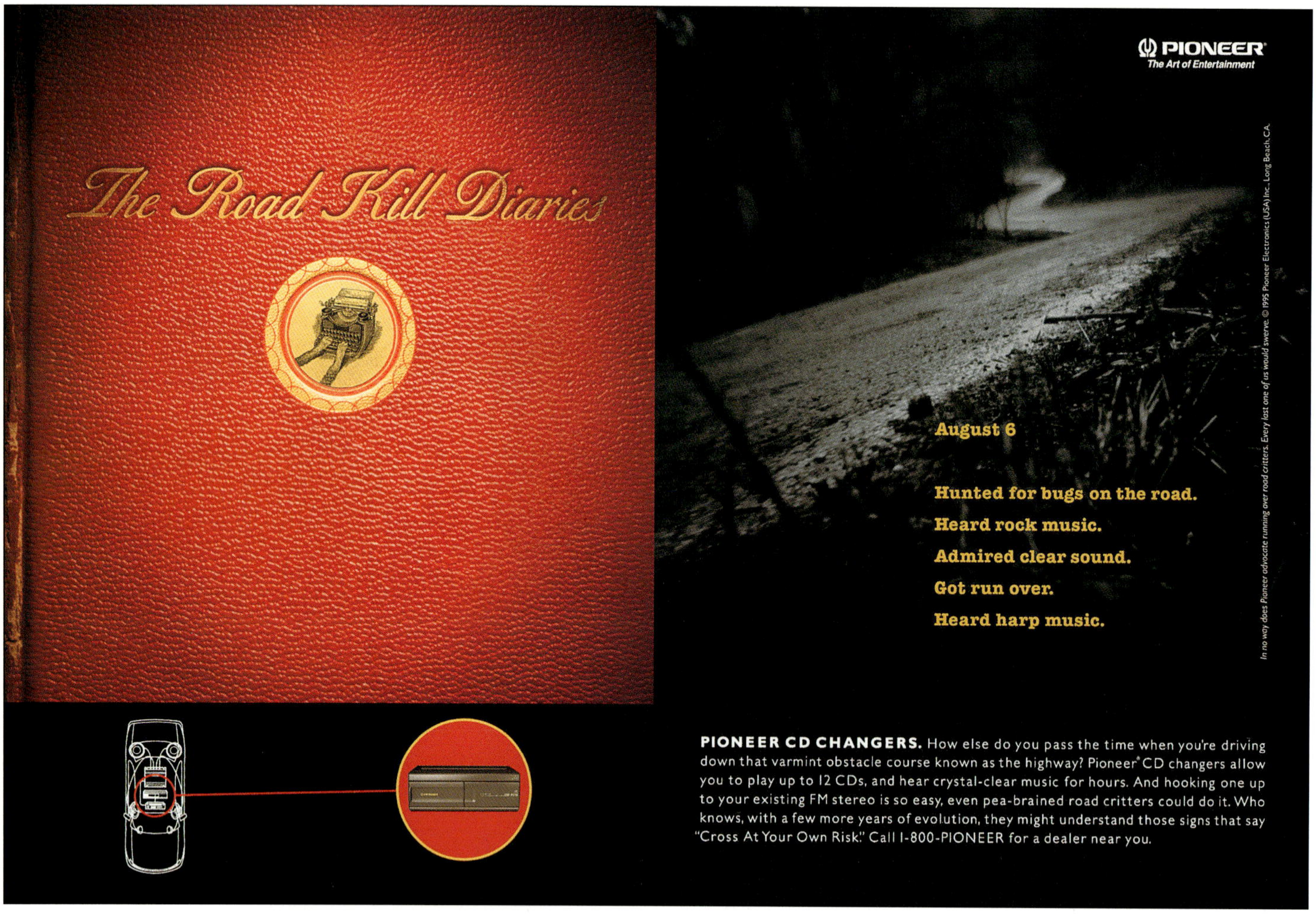

PIONEER
The Art of Entertainment
The Road Kill Diaries
May 3
Hung out with the other rodents.
Ran out in the road.
Whatever nailed me sounded awesome.
PIONEER CD PLAYERS. Even the smallest scampering critter, with barely a brain to register awe, will be impressed by our crystal clear CD sound and four-channel high power design. And our wide line of CD players, with Pioneer-invented Detachable Face Security,™ will fit any car you're driving. So take your CD collection, hit the road, and please brake for our furry little flea-bitten rock-and-roll friends. Call 1-800-PIONEER for the dealer nearest you.
In no way does Pioneer advocate running over road critters. Every last one of us would swerve. © 1995 Pioneer Electronics (USA) Inc., Long Beach, CA.

PIONEER
The Art of Entertainment
The Road Kill Diaries
June 29
Got up.
Sat in the road cleaning fur.
Heard a car coming.
Great speakers.
Bad brakes.
PIONEER SPEAKERS. Tiny ears ravaged by mites and fleas take notice when you upgrade your car stereo with Pioneer.® We make speakers to fit any car you're driving. And they're crafted from a unique blend of materials for lower distortion, higher sensitivity, and the earth-shaking bass you've grown to love. Try them out, and you'll get a clear, powerful sound guaranteed to amaze just about anything that darts in front of your car. Call 1-800-PIONEER for the dealer nearest you.
In no way does Pioneer advocate running over road critters. Every last one of us would swerve. © 1995 Pioneer Electronics (USA) Inc., Long Beach, CA.

CONSUMER MAGAZINE
COLOR FULL PAGE OR
SPREAD: CAMPAIGN

253

ART DIRECTOR:
Jamie Way

WRITER:
Randy Diplock

PHOTOGRAPHER:
Richard Picton

CLIENT:
Costa Rica Tourism

AGENCY:
BBDO Canada/Toronto

THERE ARE VERY FEW ATHEISTS IN COSTA RICA.

If you didn't already, what would it take to make you believe?

Not necessarily in God, or a god, but a higher being.

For many of you who do, it was easy. It was the day you and your partner brought another human being into the world. The day you stared at your newborn and wondered what could possibly be going through their head.

For others, it was your first eclipse. Or, at the other end of the scale, watching an ant carrying what appeared to be a small loaf of bread up and down the crevices of a sidewalk.

For those who remain unconvinced there's Costa Rica.

In Costa Rica, you can't throw a dart without hitting something that makes you wonder who made it, how long it's existed or how it got here.

That's what happens when you take two large mountain ranges, dozens of volcanoes, two long beaches, hundreds of waterfalls, a rain forest and squeeze it all into a country the size of West Virginia.

But it's the other things that make you rub your eyes and look to the sky for answers.

Take for example, a single rock at the foot of Mount Chirripó. While the mountain itself, standing at 12,529 feet above sea level, leaves you breathless, it's a simple rock that makes you think.

Because this rock is a mirror image of Mount Chirripó itself.

Nobody knows how it got here. Nobody knows how it got this way. Some believe it was native Indians who carved it, others are convinced that the wind shaped it over millions of years, using Mount Chirripó as its model.

All we know for sure is that it sits near the town of San Gerardo, minding its own business, doing nothing more than provoking thought.

The same can be said for Costa Rica's stone spheres.

More than a thousand of them are spread over the flood plains of Río Térraba. Many more are buried. More impressive than their size, (some are as large as six feet in diameter) is how perfect they are.

There are as many theories on how they got here as there are stones themselves. The only thing the experts seem to agree on is that it's highly unlikely they'll ever figure them out.

If you decide to come to Costa Rica and spend some of your hard-earned money in our beautiful little country, we feel we should also tell you what you won't find here. Like a compass that works.

On certain parts of Mount Chirripó, as a result of energies that've been detected there, you'll find your compass will be more useful as a paper weight than to determine the direction you're heading. Some natives refer to Mount Chirripó as a "power place." And while they can't explain why it does what it does, their best guess is that the minerals and metals found in and around the mountain are responsible.

But when it comes to evidence of a higher being, you really need look no further than the living creatures who call Costa Rica their home. The sheer numbers alone are impressive enough.

At last count, Costa Rica was inhabited by 383 species of amphibians, 848 species of birds, 205 species of mammals, around 13,000 species of plants 400 species of butterflies and 1,500 species of fish.

Which brings us to something called a "gaspar."

Something that appears to be part fish and part alligator. Then there's the Costa Rican reptile that's affectionately known as a "Jesus Christ" lizard which can actually run on top of the water.

Whatever they are, they're two more things that'll make you scratch your head and, for a split second, reach for the remote control.

For every single thing seen in Costa Rica that makes people realize what a priviledge it is to be on this planet, there's something you can hear that'll bring you to the same conclusion.

The pounding of a waterfall, the howl of a monkey in the middle of the jungle. In Costa Rica, you'll find your senses so heightened, the smack of a single drop of rain hitting the leaf of a mangrove tree can be deafening.

The natives call it "pura vida." Pure life. And in Costa Rica, it's everywhere you turn.

It's all of the above, and things we haven't told you, that'll not only have you convinced in a higher being, but that they spent a little more time here than anywhere else.

We invite you to call your travel agent or Costa Rica Tourism at 1-800-343-6332.

And see for yourself why some things here are so incredible, you won't believe what you're seeing.

But you'll believe in something.

COSTA RICA
TAN YOUR SOUL

FINDING COSTA RICA IS EASY.
IT'S 180° FROM CLUB MED.

Now, that's not to say that one is any better than the other.

It just means that for many of you, a beach and a tan is all you're looking for in a vacation. And there's certainly nothing wrong with that.

But this ad is for the rest of you.

It's for those who want a vacation that does as much for your soul as it does for your skin. That's why we'd like to take this opportunity to tell you what you'll find, if you decide to spend your hard-earned money, in our country.

Essentially, what a Costa Rican vacation comes down to is having, within a day's drive, as many things to do and see as there are Costa Ricans anxious to show them to you.

It's tough to know where to start to tell someone about our country.

Nature might be a good place. Because 25% of our 19,700 square miles is protected rain forest, national parks and wildlife reserves. And while tourism may be our largest industry, our ecosystem is our most important asset.

We believe, the more people who have access to nature, the more educated they'll become about how important it is. Not only here, but around the world.

At last count, Costa Rica was inhabited by 383 species of amphibians, 848 species of birds, 205 species of mammals, around 13,000 species of plants, 400 species of butterflies and 1,500 species of fish.

Unfortunately, it's up to 1 species to ensure these numbers don't decrease.

All this and we haven't even touched on individual stories like the tens of thousands of leatherback turtles that come to Playa Grande like clockwork to lay their eggs. Then there's something called the gar. A creature that's not sure whether it's an alligator or a fish. And neither are we.

So, if you come here, we hope you'll understand if everyone seems to be a little over-zealous about the ecosystem here. As you can see, they've got a lot of reasons to be.

While there's nothing more important to us than the creatures that call Costa Rica home, there are many more reasons to visit.

About 90° worth.

In fact, many people who've come here, often refer to Costa Rica as an island. Despite the fact that it's not surrounded by water.

One of the reasons people think of Costa Rica that way, may have something to do with the fact that we've been a proud democracy since 1948. A country whose civil war lasted only 40 days. Which tells you a lot about the kind of people you'll find here.

It also goes a long way in explaining why Costa Ricans have, over the years, taken pride in their commitment to education instead of militarism. Today, you'll find more teachers here than police. So you won't be surprised when you learn that the literacy rate in our country is 92%.

Speaking of the military, we should also tell you that it's one more way Costa Rica is different.

In that we don't have one.

And we haven't had one for years. So, if you come to Costa Rica and hopefully our capital, San José, make sure you visit our old Army barracks.

Because today, it's one of 28 museums in the country.

A lot has happened since Columbus came here and called it "Rich Coast." But when we think about it, it's what hasn't happened here since then, that makes our country such a popular place to visit.

To this day, you'll find some of the world's most breath-taking sights, unspoiled by so-called progress.

Among them is Arenal Volcano which soars 5,358 feet above sea level and has been active since 1968. In one of the many other protected areas, you'll find rocks on the Santa Elena Peninsula that date back 150 million years. Then there's Mount Chirripó, Costa Rica's highest mountain and Barra Honda National Park on the Nicoya Peninsula. Where you'll find caves that have yet to be explored. By humans at least.

And on the world's largest uninhabited island, Cocos Island, there are more than 200 waterfalls.

As you can see, with all there is to tell you about our country, this ad could've been a lot bigger. To hear about what we've left out, call your travel agent or Costa Rica Tourism at 1-800-343-6332.

We'd be honored to have you.

By the way, we reluctantly inform you that you can also find 631 miles of beach on the Pacific coast and 131 on the Caribbean for you to relax and soak up some sun.

If you like that sort of thing.

COSTA RICA
TAN YOUR SOUL

COSTA RICA HAS NO MILITARY.

Don't laugh.

This 68 year-old teacher has without a doubt, shaped more lives, had more effect on people in this part of the world than anyone ever has in a uniform.

Come to think of it, she has probably struck more fear in the hearts of more Costa Ricans too. If you've ever been in one of her classrooms, you'll know why.

We understand that unless you're related to her, Mrs. Sánchez, as wonderful as she is, isn't reason enough to rush to the airport, buy an airline ticket and hop on the next flight to Costa Rica.

But the kind of country that allows Mrs. Sánchez to be Mrs. Sánchez, might be.

It's been said by many that while Costa Rica is not surrounded by water it is, philosophically speaking, an island. We're a 174 year-old democracy right in the middle of things in Central America.

Costa Ricans first heard the news of their independence by horseback. Three years later, we had our first president. Back then, he was called Chief of State and his name was Juan Mora Fernández. It should come as no surprise for you to learn that Mr. Fernández was, that's right, a teacher.

It seems to make sense that a country whose first leader was a teacher would turn out the way it has. If Juan Mora Fernández was an Army General, a blacksmith, or a lawyer, we'd hazard a guess that Costa Rica would be a very different country than it is today.

BUT THERE'S ALWAYS MRS. SÁNCHEZ.

We know for sure we wouldn't find ourselves with more teachers than police officers as we do today.

It starts to make us wonder about other things. If our Army barracks in San José would be in the state they're in now. That state being a museum. Or, would we find ourselves in a country that, while it condones bullfighting, rewards the bull for its efforts rather than kill it?

Would Costa Rica still have more government-protected rain forest, parks and wildlife reserves per acre than anyone else on the planet? And would thousands of leatherback turtles still be welcome to virtually take over the beach at Playa Grande and lay their eggs in peace?

We're happy to say that we'll never find out. That all these things and everything else that makes our beautiful little country what it is, will stay the same.

We'd be honored if you called us at 1-800-343-6332. So we can tell you the other things that make Costa Rica such a nice place to visit, you might want to live here.

That's if Mrs. Sánchez likes you of course.

COSTA RICA

TAN YOUR SOUL

YOU HAVE TO BE A BIRD WATCHER TO COME TO COSTA RICA. IT'S NOT LIKE YOU HAVE A CHOICE.

With 840 species, you'll see what we mean.

To fully understand how Costa Rica and Costa Ricans became blessed with so many species of birds, you really have to look back millions of years.

To understand how we've kept them, you need look no further than a minute ago.

Our country started as a chain of volcanic islands. Through centuries of eruptions, earthquakes and erosion, Costa Rica became a continuous isthmus linking North and South America about 3 million years ago.

As a result, hundreds of different types of birds took advantage of this new link between North and South America. Combine that with our diverse geography, and it's impossible not to have a wealth of birds.

In Costa Rica, we have two coasts very close in proximity. And, wedged in between, are mountains towering as high as 12,000 feet above sea level.

As a result, the climate changes in Costa Rica almost as much as the land. Which, in turn, creates a wide range of vegetation and insects that support so many species of birds. Another 200 or so species migrate each year. Some from as far away as New Zealand.

Costa Rican birds are also renowned for being superb songsters. Birds like warblers, wrens and finches are especially so. During the rainy season, they can be positively deafening. It's been said, as many people come to Costa Rica every year to listen to our birds as to watch them.

When you're blessed with a country this rich in birds, there's only one thing to do. Protect them.

That's why, when you come to Costa Rica, you'll find that 25% of the land here is protected rain forest, national parks and wildlife reserves.

It's a commitment that both the government of Costa Rica and our people believe deeply in.

Which is why, if you come to Costa Rica, you'll still find birds like the laughing falcon eating snakes and little else; a resplendent quetzal cackling as it takes flight; a keel-billed toucan tossing its food from bill tip to throat with an effortless toss of its head.

We'd love to tell you all the things we're doing to keep things this way. So, feel free to call Costa Rica Tourism at 1-800-343-6332.

But we'd much rather see you in person.

As all Costa Ricans would.

Whether they have feathers or not.

COSTA RICA

TAN YOUR SOUL

HOW TO EXPLORE SIX COUNTRIES AND BE BACK IN TIME FOR DINNER.

And be there before it gets cold.

The only thing more impressive than having so many distinctly different areas, is the fact that it happens in a country that's about the size of West Virginia.

From the top of Irazú Volcano, you can see both coasts. Which means both beaches are closer than you thought. As are all the things you can do when you get there.

Like snorkeling, scuba diving, surfing, sailing, water skiing and fishing.

At the other end of the spectrum, is the rain forest. In Costa Rica, we're proud to say that we have the largest percentage of protected rain forest, parks and wildlife reserves in the world. So it's not surprising that at last count, Costa Rica was inhabited by 383 species of amphibians, 848 species of birds, 205 species of mammals, around 13,000 species of plants and 400 species of butterflies and over 1,500 species of fish.

When you're tired of counting, there's Arenal Volcano. It soars 5,358 feet above sea level and its crater is 459 feet deep. It's also one of the most active in the world.

Legend has it, the sound Arenal makes when it erupts, is almost as intimidating as the lava it spews.

There are few things capable of making a human being feel like a mere tenant on this planet. Staring down, way down, into the crater of a Costa Rican volcano is one of them.

Another one is a Costa Rican mountain. You don't have to drive very far to reach a major mountain range here. Or a major mountain like Mount Chirripó. It stands an incredible 12,529 feet above sea level and has places so remote, compasses refuse to work.

Another great example of how disparate a country Costa Rica is, is when you consider the range of temperatures in a country as tiny as ours. While the average high reaches 92°F in some areas, you may be surprised to know you can also find frost and ice at the top of a mountain like Chirripó.

The lowest recorded temperature? 16° F.

Or, just 40 miles from San José is the town of Turrialba. Where you can go white-water rafting or kayaking on the Reventazón River. On the way, expect to find the usual natives there to encourage you. Not guides, but monkeys, birds and other wildlife you'll encounter along the way.

Having said all this, there are still many things we haven't told you.

That's why we'd like you to call us at 1-800-343-6332.

So we can tell you about all the things you can do after dinner.

COSTA RICA

TAN YOUR SOUL

CONSUMER MAGAZINE
COLOR FULL PAGE OR
SPREAD: CAMPAIGN

254

ART DIRECTOR:
Bob Barrie

WRITER:
Dean Buckhorn

PHOTOGRAPHERS:
P.F. Bentley
Jean Marie Chauvet
Gianni Giansanti
Gotham Studio
Sasa Radic

CLIENT:
Time

AGENCY:
Fallon McElligott/
Minneapolis

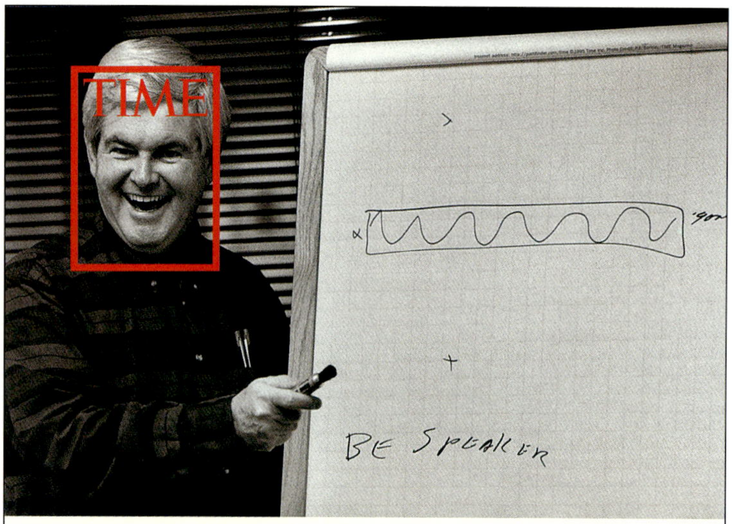

You may love him.

You may hate him.

But you sure as hell

better understand him.

Understanding comes with TIME.

Somehow, the networks

managed to edit 20,000 years

down to just 45 seconds.

Understanding comes with TIME.

MAN OF THE YEAR
TIME
Even a man who addresses
billions of people a year
has a side that's rarely seen.
Understanding comes with TIME.

TIME
You can understand computers
now. Or wait for your children
to explain them to you later.
Understanding comes with TIME.

TIME
In Sarajevo, the killing hasn't diminished.
Only the network coverage.
Understanding comes with TIME.

CONSUMER MAGAZINE
COLOR FULL PAGE OR
SPREAD: CAMPAIGN

255

ART DIRECTOR:
Mike Mazza

WRITERS:
Chuck McBride
Dave O'Hare

ILLUSTRATOR:
Alan Daniels

PHOTOGRAPHER:
Graham Westmoreland

CLIENT:
American Isuzu Motors

AGENCY:
Goodby Silverstein &
Partners/San Francisco

THE 60TH UNWRITTEN LAW OF DRIVING
CONCRETE PARKING BARRIERS WERE INVENTED TO TAKE OUT OIL PANS.
ALONG WITH 8.5 INCHES OF GROUND CLEARANCE, THE TROOPER LIMITED HAS MORE PROTECTIVE SKID PLATES THAN ANY OTHER IN ITS CLASS.
Ouch! That sound. That metal against concrete sound. It sends a flash of panic through your body as you visualize a pool of 10/30 weight slowly forming underneath you. You didn't mean to. Just like the curb the other day. And where did that mattress on the freeway come from, anyway? To get over these daily obstacles, we suggest a vehicle engineered to get you over mountain ranges and such. The new Trooper Limited. Call (800) 726-2700.
ISUZU
Practically/Amazing
Always wear a seat belt. And please treat the environment with respect. ©1995 American Isuzu Motors Inc.

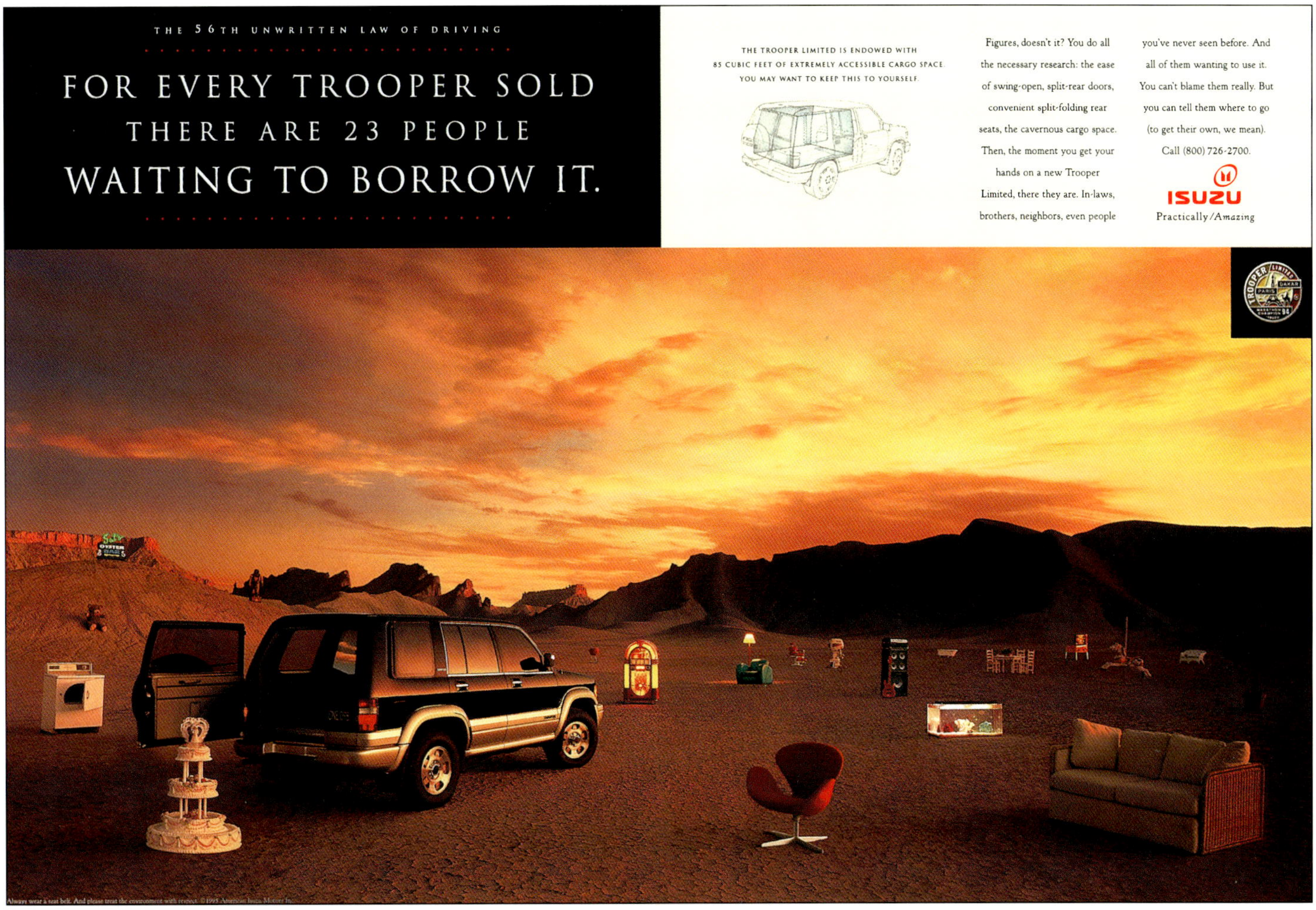

THE 56TH UNWRITTEN LAW OF DRIVING
FOR EVERY TROOPER SOLD THERE ARE 23 PEOPLE WAITING TO BORROW IT.
THE TROOPER LIMITED IS ENDOWED WITH 85 CUBIC FEET OF EXTREMELY ACCESSIBLE CARGO SPACE. YOU MAY WANT TO KEEP THIS TO YOURSELF.
Figures, doesn't it? You do all the necessary research: the ease of swing-open, split-rear doors, convenient split-folding rear seats, the cavernous cargo space. Then, the moment you get your hands on a new Trooper Limited, there they are. In-laws, brothers, neighbors, even people you've never seen before. And all of them wanting to use it. You can't blame them really. But you can tell them where to go (to get their own, we mean). Call (800) 726-2700.
ISUZU
Practically/Amazing
Always wear a seat belt. And please treat the environment with respect. ©1995 American Isuzu Motors Inc.

THE 58TH UNWRITTEN LAW OF DRIVING
THE ROAD IS PAVED WITH IDIOTS.
UNLIKE MOST 4WD VEHICLES, DUAL AIR BAGS COME STANDARD.
HIGH GROUND CLEARANCE FOR A BETTER OVERALL VIEW.
THE ONLY 4WD WITH STANDARD 4-WHEEL VENTILATED DISC ABS BRAKES.
IMPACT ABSORBING STRUCTURE DESIGNED TO PROTECT THE CABIN.
HEAD LAMP WIPERS. CLEARLY A BENEFIT, ESPECIALLY IN MUD.
They're out there, those runners of stop signs, those no-signal lane changers. And while we can do little to stop them, we've gone to great lengths to make them less of a threat. Presenting the new Trooper Limited. For more information please call (800) 726-2700.
ISUZU
Practically/Amazing

CONSUMER MAGAZINE
COLOR FULL PAGE OR
SPREAD: CAMPAIGN

256

ART DIRECTOR:
Peter Holmes

WRITERS:
Peter Holmes
Greg Freir

PHOTOGRAPHER:
George Simhoni

CLIENT:
Krinos Foods

AGENCY:
Holmes Donin Alloul/
Toronto

Contrary to grade school history, the ancient Greeks are still around.

Perhaps it's time we forgot a lot of what we've learned. Especially about the way we eat. For example, many of the people who live in the mountains of Crete live past ninety. The reason why is simple. It's what they eat. So it's little wonder that the World Health Organization as well as Harvard University recommend everybody eat like them. Not surprisingly so do we. That's exactly why we import these very foods to Canada. In fact, the whole range of Krinos Premium Quality beans, grains and legumes are now available at your favourite store. All of which makes it easy for you to enjoy both the flavours and the benefits of a wide variety of bean dishes. Care to know more? Just call 1-800-668-1470. We'll be glad to send you our Bean Book. It's full of information, delicious recipes and more. Because the sooner you learn the old world way of eating, the longer you can enjoy it.

Krinos
Foods from the cradle *of* civilization

George, Anton and Kiron Tsagarakis are brothers. So genes may explain why they've all lived past 85. But they'll tell you enjoying life, working hard and good food, like beans, grains and legumes also have a lot to do with it.

At 54 pounds, the sack Chrisoula Papoutsidaki is carrying is almost half her weight. Where does she get the strength at 87 years of age? The sack just happens to be full of beans, grains and legumes. A large part of her diet.

What can you learn about nutrition from Chrisoula? To begin with, she's 87 and the sack weighs 54 pounds.

Even more impossible, the hill she's walking up is a very steep two miles. So how does Chris climb hills every day at an age when most people have difficulty simply climbing out of bed? It's the food she eats. Food that enables most of the Mediterranean people to live healthy, active lives well past ninety. Food that could very well help you do the same. So concluded the World Health Organization after thirty years of study. It's called the Mediterranean diet. A diet mainly consisting of beans, grains and legumes. All of which are now available from Krinos. If you'd like to know more about this delicious, healthy food, just phone 1-800-268-3771 and ask for the Krinos Bean Book. It's full of information and easy to cook recipes. So you can start eating like Chrisoula Papoutsidaki and live longer for it.

Krinos
Foods from the cradle *of* civilization

CONSUMER MAGAZINE
COLOR FULL PAGE OR
SPREAD: CAMPAIGN

257

ART DIRECTOR:
Damon Williams

WRITER:
Rudy Fernandez

DESIGNER:
Troy King

CLIENT:
Sweet Bottom Plantation

AGENCY:
Hughes Advertising/
Atlanta

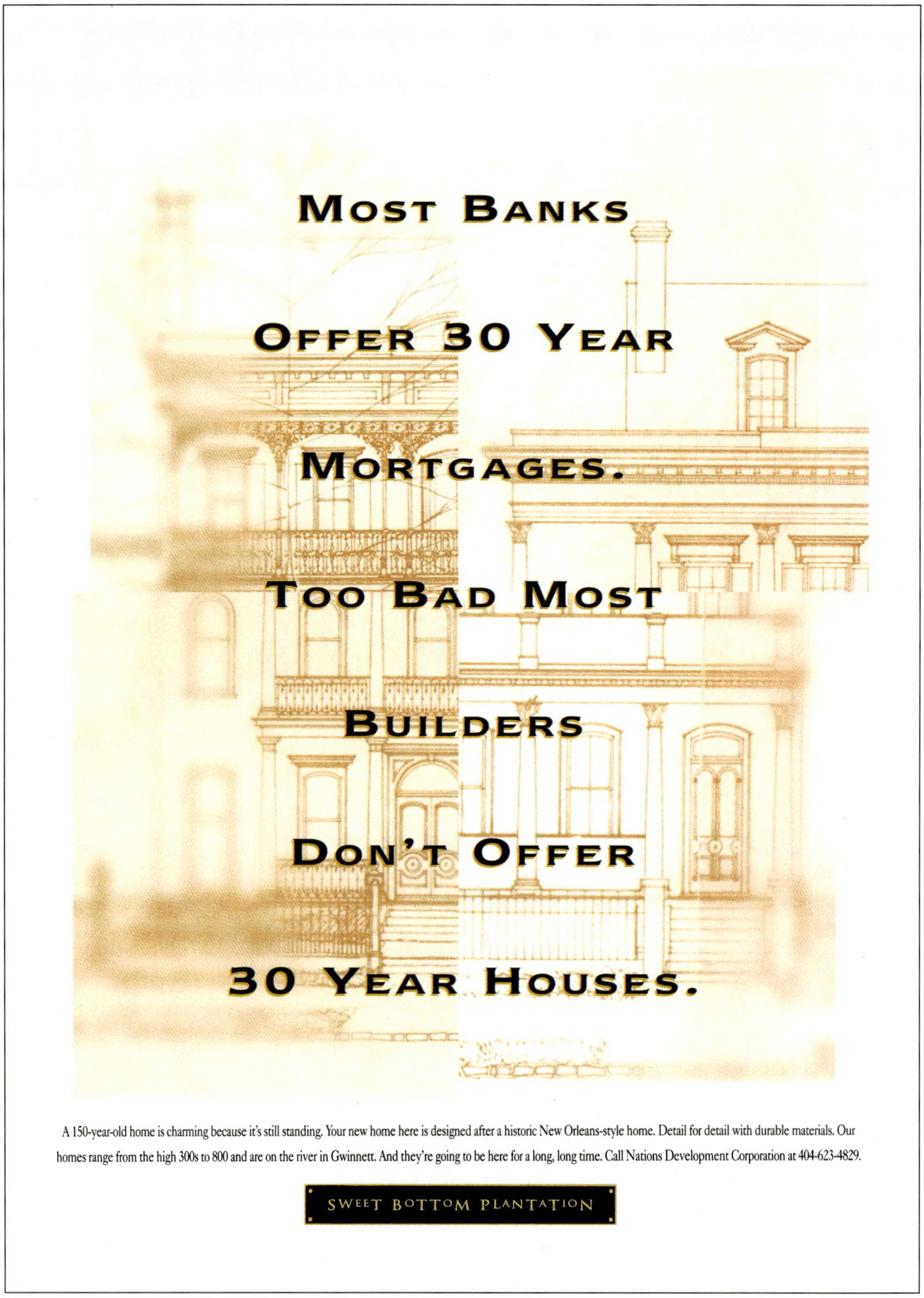
Most Banks Offer 30 Year Mortgages. Too Bad Most Builders Don't Offer 30 Year Houses.
A 150-year-old home is charming because it's still standing. Your new home here is designed after a historic New Orleans-style home. Detail for detail with durable materials. Our homes range from the high 300s to 800 and are on the river in Gwinnett. And they're going to be here for a long, long time. Call Nations Development Corporation at 404-623-4829.
Sweet Bottom Plantation

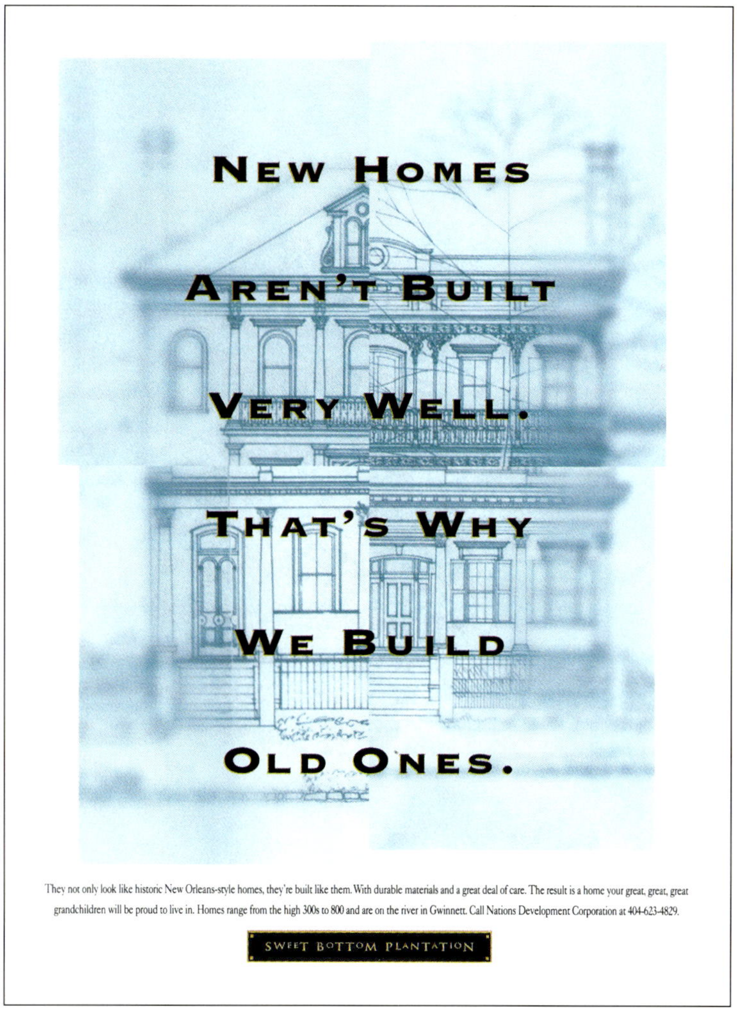
New Homes
Aren't Built
Very Well.
That's Why
We Build
Old Ones.
They not only look like historic New Orleans-style homes, they're built like them. With durable materials and a great deal of care. The result is a home your great, great, great grandchildren will be proud to live in. Homes range from the high 300s to 800 and are on the river in Gwinnett. Call Nations Development Corporation at 404-623-4829.
Sweet Bottom Plantation

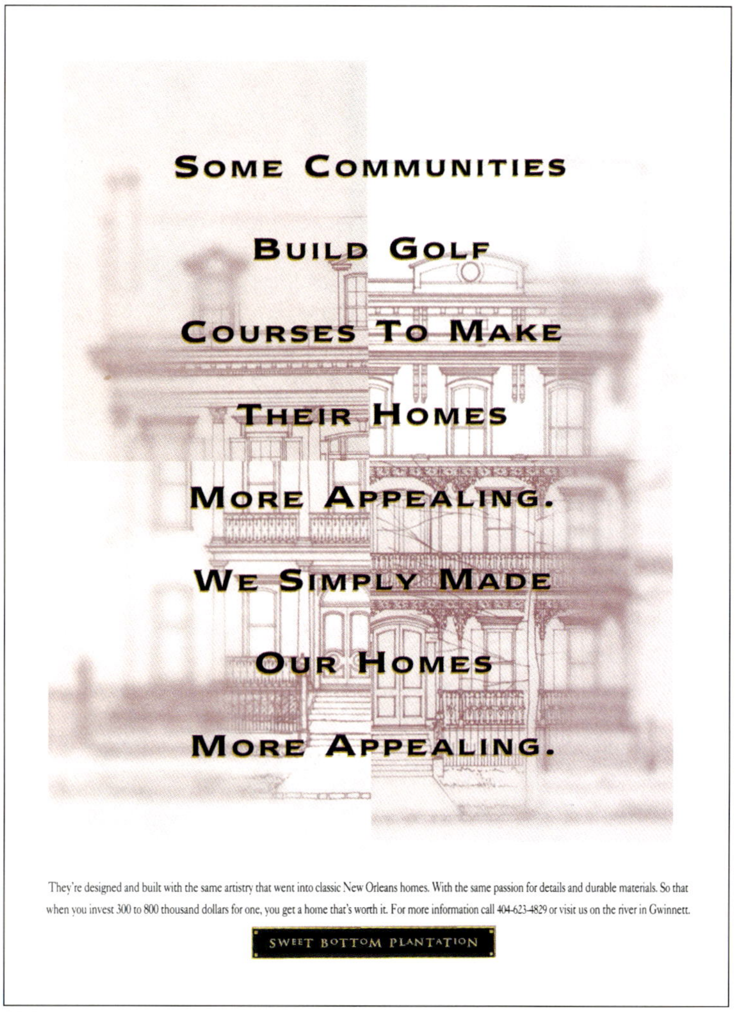
Some Communities
Build Golf
Courses To Make
Their Homes
More Appealing.
We Simply Made
Our Homes
More Appealing.
They're designed and built with the same artistry that went into classic New Orleans homes. With the same passion for details and durable materials. So that when you invest 300 to 800 thousand dollars for one, you get a home that's worth it. For more information call 404-623-4829 or visit us on the river in Gwinnett.
Sweet Bottom Plantation

CONSUMER MAGAZINE
COLOR FULL PAGE OR
SPREAD: CAMPAIGN

258

ART DIRECTOR:
Brian Hughes
WRITER:
Tim Godsall
PHOTOGRAPHER:
Hans Gissinger
CLIENT:
Olympus USA
AGENCY:
Kirshenbaum Bond &
Partners/New York

ATTENTION
Bouncers and Security Personnel
Lately, there have been reports of people gaining free entry to cultural events by posing as professional photographers. Capitalizing on the common knowledge that many professionals use the Olympus® Infinity Stylus Zoom as their personal snapshot camera, these gate-crashers merely flash their Stylus Zoom at Security and walk in boldly without paying. It is a sleazy scheme, and it has already cost venues and events around the country untold amounts of money. Olympus America Inc. does not condone these activities and we urge Security personnel to seek proof of professional status – merely carrying a Stylus Zoom does not confer professional status. The only reason professionals are so attached to the Stylus Zoom in the first place is because it's simple to use, takes great snapshots and looks stylish. And remember, real professionals use the Stylus Zoom for their personal snapshots – on the job they usually carry a telltale bag of cumbersome equipment. Use common sense and STOP THIS EPIDEMIC BEFORE IT GOES ANY FURTHER!
OLYMPUS®
How the Big Shots take Snapshots.™
WHAT TO LOOK OUT FOR!
The Infinity Stylus Zoom:
35-70mm Zoom, weatherproof, precise autofocus, 5 automatic flash modes including red-eye reduction.
©1995 Olympus America Inc. In USA call 1.800.6.CAMERA or write Olympus America Inc., 2 Corporate Center Drive, Melville, NY 11747. In Canada: Carsen Group, Inc., Toronto. Internet: http://www.olympusamerica.com

Use it
RESPONSIBLY
Recently there have been reports of people posing as professional photographers to gain entry to sporting events. Capitalizing on the common knowledge that many professionals use the Olympus® Infinity Stylus Zoom as their personal snapshot camera, these phony professionals show a Stylus to Security, then saunter past. Sadly, the people who end up paying the price are the honest patrons, as venues raise prices to recover lost income. Olympus America Inc. does not condone these activities, and we wish to state categorically that carrying a Stylus Zoom does not confer professional status. The only reason so many professionals own this camera is because it's simple, takes great snapshots and costs little. Unfortunately, the few people who are taking advantage of this situation are deeply affecting the rest of us. To help nip this problem in the bud, we urge you to immediately report anyone you see carrying a Stylus Zoom and acting suspiciously professional. We believe GOOD JUDGMENT AND A LITTLE PATIENCE WILL SEE US ALL THROUGH.
OLYMPUS®
How the Big Shots take Snapshots.™
THE CAMERA BEHIND THE CONFUSION
The Infinity Stylus Zoom:
35-70mm Zoom, weatherproof, precise autofocus, 5 automatic flash modes including red-eye reduction.
©1995 Olympus America Inc. In USA call 1.800.6.CAMERA or write Olympus America Inc., 2 Corporate Center Drive, Melville, NY 11747. In Canada: Carsen Group, Inc., Toronto. Internet: http://www.olympusamerica.com

!WARNING!
There have been reported instances of tourists abroad being mistaken for professional photographers because they were carrying Olympus® cameras. The confusion stems from the widely held belief that professionals use the Olympus IS-10 for their personal snapshots – hence anyone carrying the IS-10 is assumed to be a professional. Unfortunately, there are circumstances where being mistaken for a member of the press can mean being detained for questioning, or occasionally, well, no need to go into details.... The fact that professionals only use the IS-10 because it's simple, has a wide zoom and takes great snapshots, is of no consequence. Regrettably, there is not always time to explain this to your captors. So, in the interest of public safety, Olympus America Inc. is advising any tourists going abroad to exercise caution, and if you must bring your Olympus,* MAKE AN EFFORT TO DISGUISE THE CAMERA'S DISTINCTIVE APPEARANCE WITH ELECTRICAL TAPE.
OLYMPUS®
How the Big Shots take Snapshots.™
THE CAMERA BEHIND THE CONFUSION
The IS-10: 28 Wide Angle – 110mm Zoom lens, highly advanced autofocus system, 4 creative exposure modes, 4 automatic flash modes, including red-eye reduction.
*While we would never suggest not using your Olympus for capturing vacation memories, there may be extreme circumstances where a sketch pad and a decent palette of watercolors would serve admirably.
©1995 Olympus America Inc. In USA call 1.800.6.CAMERA or write Olympus America Inc., 2 Corporate Center Drive, Melville, NY 11747. In Canada: Carsen Group, Inc., Toronto. Internet: http://www.olympusamerica.com

Handle with
CAUTION!
The fact that professional photographers use the Olympus® Infinity SuperZoom 3500 as their personal snapshot camera has been a source of confusion lately. People are making the erroneous assumption that anyone carrying an Olympus SuperZoom is a professional, and this leads to potentially awkward situations. Being mistaken for a member of the press can mean offers of hotel or airline discounts, preferential treatment at restaurants and even free admission to cultural events. Finding yourself wrongfully whisked into a VIP lounge, or cornered by some fame-addicted celebrity can be a disorienting experience – but luckily it is avoidable. In the event that you are mistaken for a professional because of your SuperZoom, simply explain that the only reason so many professionals are attached to it in the first place is that it's easy to use and takes great snapshots. Point out that the majority of SuperZoom owners are, in fact, just amateurs like yourself.* We at Olympus believe we'll all get through this difficult time, IF WE JUST USE A LITTLE COMMON SENSE.
OLYMPUS®
How the Big Shots take Snapshots.
THE CAMERA BEHIND THE CONFUSION
The Infinity SuperZoom 3500: 35-120mm Zoom, 4 automatic flash modes including red-eye reduction, weatherproof, precise autofocus, continuous shooting mode for 4 frames per second.
*As a precaution, avoid using words like 'ciao' or 'babe' since this might only aggravate the situation.
©1995 Olympus America Inc. In USA call 1.800.6.CAMERA or write Olympus America Inc., 2 Corporate Center Drive, Melville, NY 11747. In Canada: Carsen Group, Inc., Toronto. Internet: http://www.olympusamerica.com

CONSUMER MAGAZINE
COLOR FULL PAGE OR
SPREAD: CAMPAIGN

259

ART DIRECTORS:
Martin Galton
Steve Paskin

WRITERS:
Tom Hudson
Sean Doyle

CLIENT:
Pepe

AGENCY:
Leagas Delaney/London

260

ART DIRECTORS:
Paul Belford
Martin Galton

WRITERS:
Nigel Roberts
Tom Hudson

CLIENT:
Pepe

AGENCY:
Leagas Delaney/London

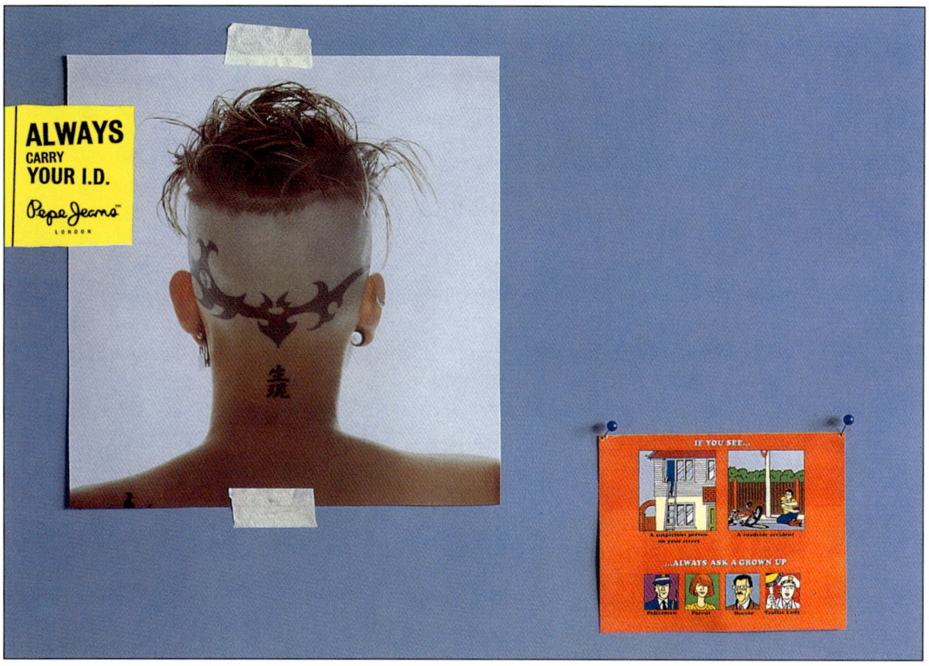

259

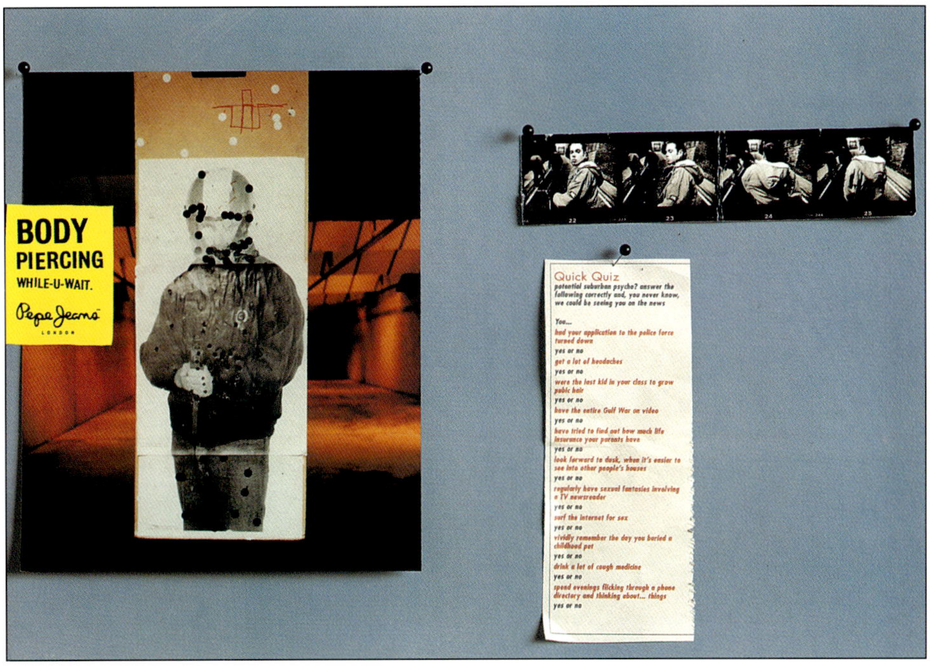
BODY
PIERCING
WHILE-U-WAIT.
Pepe Jeans
LONDON
Quick Quiz
potential suburban psycho? answer the following correctly and, you never know, we could be seeing you on the news
You...
had your application to the police force turned down
yes or no
get a lot of headaches
yes or no
were the last kid in your class to grow pubic hair
yes or no
have the entire Gulf War on video
yes or no
have tried to find out how much life insurance your parents have
yes or no
look forward to dusk, when it's easier to see into other people's houses
yes or no
regularly have sexual fantasies involving a TV newsreader
yes or no
surf the internet for sex
yes or no
vividly remember the day you buried a childhood pet
yes or no
drink a lot of cough medicine
yes or no
spend evenings flicking through a phone directory and thinking about... things
yes or no

THREE ANTI~WORK BOOKS
SABOTAGE
IN THE AMERICAN WORKPLACE
BE A
DISAPPOINTMENT.
AT LEAST
YOU'LL
HAVE ACHIEVED
SOMETHING.
Pepe Jeans
LONDON

LIFE
WITHOUT
DANGER
IS A WASTE OF
OXYGEN.
Pepe Jeans
LONDON

CONSUMER MAGAZINE
COLOR FULL PAGE OR
SPREAD: CAMPAIGN

261

ART DIRECTORS:
David Hernandez
Andrew Day

WRITERS:
George Gier
Ted Xistris

PHOTOGRAPHER:
Ben Kende

CLIENT:
Tommy Armour

AGENCY:
The Leap Partnership/
Chicago

262

ART DIRECTORS:
Whit Friese
Steve Haack

WRITERS:
John Coveny
Joe Bardetti

PHOTOGRAPHER:
Robert Whitman

CLIENT:
Schieffelin & Somerset/
Dewar's

AGENCY:
Leo Burnett Company/
Chicago

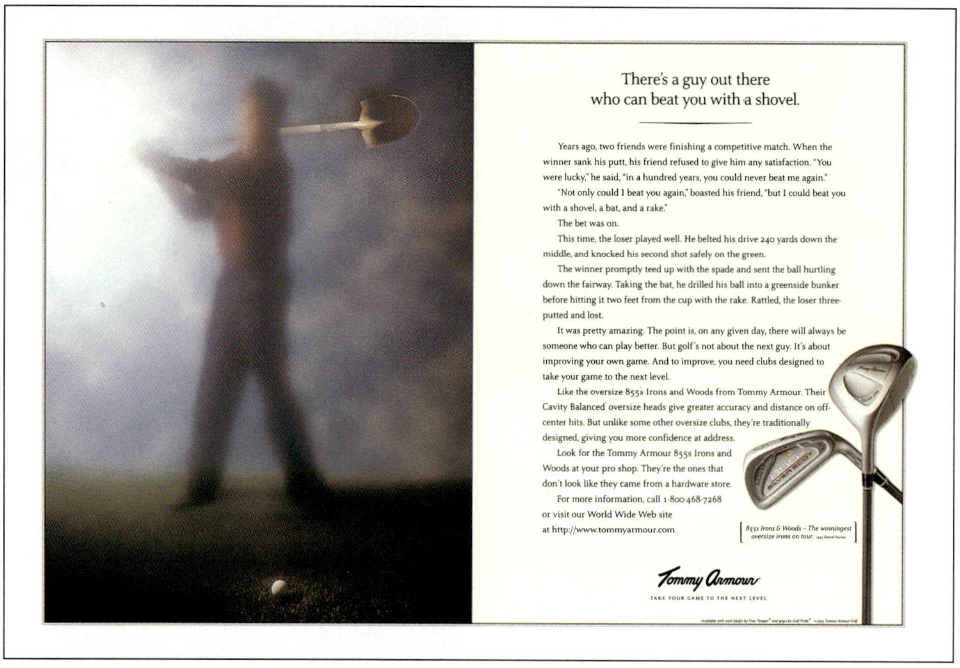

Do you really want to ask this guy to give you a "Screaming Orgasm"?
Dewar's.

Trust us, she does not want to hear the story about you and your friend Danny doing watermelon shooters in Daytona.
Dewar's.

Grape Vodka
Peach Schnapps
Cinnamon Shooter
Need we say more?
Dewar's.

CONSUMER MAGAZINE
COLOR FULL PAGE OR
SPREAD: CAMPAIGN

263
ART DIRECTOR:
Charles Inge
WRITER:
Phil Dearman
PHOTOGRAPHER:
Andy Green
CLIENT:
Vauxhall Motors
AGENCY:
Lowe Howard-Spink/
London

264
ART DIRECTOR:
Kevin Dailor
WRITER:
Steve Howard
PHOTOGRAPHER:
Harry DeZitter
CLIENT:
Hi-Tec Sports USA
AGENCY:
Mandelbaum Mooney
Ashley/San Francisco

Mudmen from Papua New Guinea get their first glimpse of a Frontera, thanks to its powerful new engine and anti-clog brakes.
See a different world. THE 1995 FRONTERA FROM VAUXHALL

Nao Xuan Hao of the Tien Giang Province is bowled over by the 1995 Frontera's torquier new engine and improved ground clearance.
See a different world. THE 1995 FRONTERA FROM VAUXHALL

A fisherman on Lake Tanganyika catches sight of the 1995 Frontera demonstrating its powerful new engine and up-rated coil suspension.
See a different world. THE 1995 FRONTERA FROM VAUXHALL

263

HI-TEC
GO PLACES. DO THINGS.

© 1995 Hi-Tec Sports USA, Inc. (800) 521-1698
HI-TEC
GO PLACES. DO THINGS.

© 1995 Hi-Tec Sports USA, Inc. (800) 521-1698
HI-TEC
GO PLACES. DO THINGS.

CONSUMER MAGAZINE
COLOR FULL PAGE OR
SPREAD: CAMPAIGN

265

ART DIRECTORS:
Jamie Mahoney
Carolyn McGeorge
WRITER:
Raymond McKinney
PHOTOGRAPHER:
Dublin Productions
CLIENT:
Healthtex
AGENCY:
The Martin Agency/
Richmond

266

ART DIRECTORS:
Steve Juliusson
Per Jacobson
Marcus Fernandez
Susan Westre
WRITERS:
Mark Ledermann
Brian Millar
PHOTOGRAPHERS:
Kenji Toma
Russel Porcas
Rolph Gobitz
CLIENT:
International Business
Machines
AGENCY:
Ogilvy & Mather/New York

IN A QUIET CORNER OF SOUTHWESTERN Ohio, the conflicting pressures of medical care and medical cost are being worked out in a very healthy way.
Thanks to a new Health Data Network, doctors in seven Dayton area hospitals are now spending more time with patients, and almost no time looking for records.
The network, spearheaded by IBM, lets authorized doctors look up medical histories within seconds, no matter where their patients were treated. Test results are also included, so repetitive testing has dropped.
In all, the network is helping the Greater Dayton Area Hospital Association better manage the big issues in health care today. While allowing doctors to focus on the little ones, too.
To learn how networking can help your business, call us at 1800 426-2808, ext. 5510. Or visit us on the World Wide Web at http://www.ibm.com
IBM.
Solutions for a small planet™
Change

TAKE A WALK AROUND LEGAL AND GENERAL today, and you'll find peace, harmony and a range of advanced micro-marketing techniques.
Since the '60s, this leading British insurance company has been keeping detailed records on all their customers – nearly 3 million of them in the life and pensions division alone.
Still, to stay ahead of the competition, they realized that they needed to, like, really dig where those customers were coming from.
Had their needs changed since the heady days when they first took out life insurance policies and pension plans? Were they still flower children or did they have grandchildren?
Being a pretty hip company, Legal and General called IBM. Together we used a range of data mining techniques to process a mountain of customer histories in only eight weeks.
Thanks to this mind-expanding performance, Legal and General has been able to attract new customers, get closer to existing ones, and thus offer them a wider range of services.
How can IBM consultants help you get more from what you already know?
Visit us on the World Wide Web at http://www.ibm.com or call 1 800 IBM-3333, ext. HA034.
IBM.
Solutions for a small planet™
Update file

IN THE TRADITION-RICH NEIGHBORHOODS of New Orleans, a global network unites a passionate love of china with the centuries-old home of Wedgwood.
The IBM Global Network lets Wedgwood keep its master craftspeople working together in Britain, while still servicing customers in cities and towns in seventy countries.
Customer questions about patterns and availability can be quickly answered. Orders can be placed. Quality control for the handcrafted china is more easily maintained.
In all, the IBM Global Network lets Wedgwood keep their traditional home while giving them the reach of a global corporation.
Want to see what IBM can do to improve your competitiveness?
Visit our home page on the World Wide Web at http://www.ibm.com/globalnetwork or call us at 1 800 IBM-3333, ext. HA035.
IBM.
Solutions for a small planet™
Settings

CONSUMER MAGAZINE COLOR FULL PAGE OR SPREAD: CAMPAIGN

267

ART DIRECTOR:
John Vitro

WRITER:
John Robertson

PHOTOGRAPHER:
Chris Wimpey

CLIENT:
Taylor Guitars

AGENCY:
VitroRobertson/San Diego

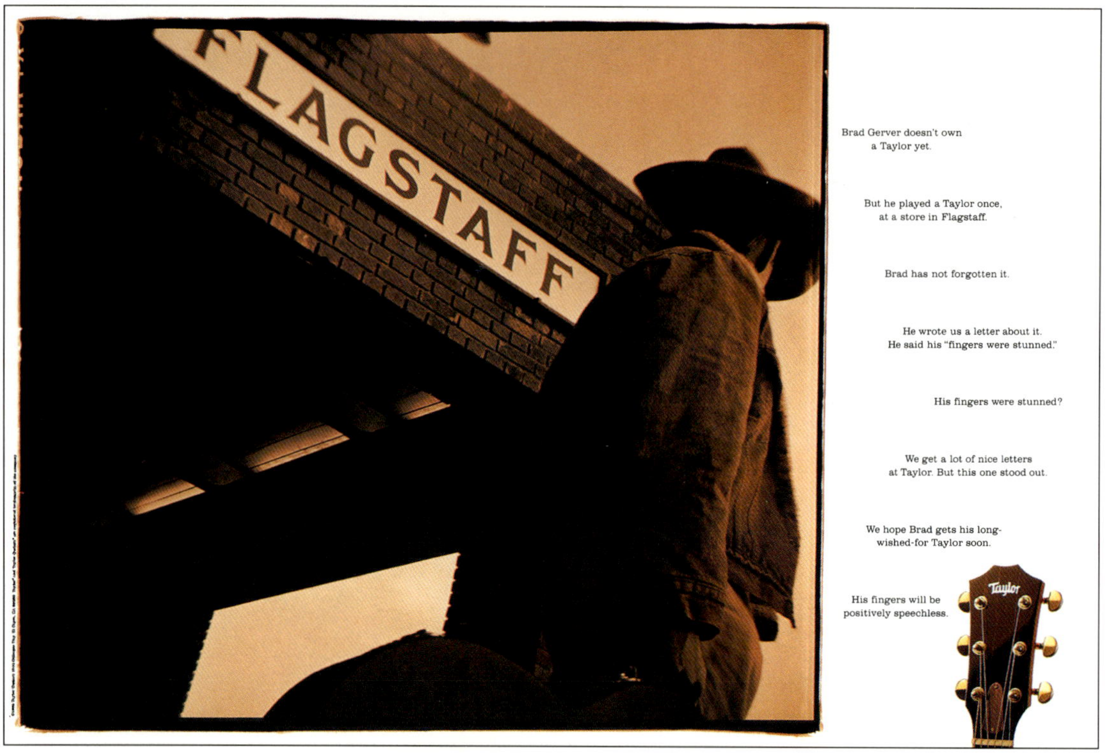
FLAGSTAFF
Brad Gerver doesn't own a Taylor yet.
But he played a Taylor once, at a store in Flagstaff.
Brad has not forgotten it.
He wrote us a letter about it. He said his "fingers were stunned."
His fingers were stunned?
We get a lot of nice letters at Taylor. But this one stood out.
We hope Brad gets his long-wished-for Taylor soon.
His fingers will be positively speechless.
Taylor

FALLS
One normal day in Idaho Falls, Skip Wallace, a happily married man, walked into a music store and promptly fell in love.
The object of his desire was a Taylor guitar.
But Skip's wife was a problem. In Skip's words, he knew he'd "have to smooth-talk her."
She handled the family finances, you see.
The next day, they both came into the store.
To Skip's amazement, she listened to the sweet tone of the Taylor for less than 30 seconds before she said, "Let's get it."
Skip loves his Taylor, and he loves his wife.
And he never was much of a smooth-talker.
Which is what his wife loves about him.
Taylor

©1995 Taylor Guitars 1940 Gillespie Way, El Cajon, CA 92020. Taylor® and Taylor Guitars® are registered trademarks of the company

Harlan Howard already had five guitars.

But one day he walked into a music store in Nashville.

I have a problem, he told Richard, the owner. All my guitars have dried up.

Richard started to talk about the low humidity.

No, not that, said Harlan. There aren't any more songs left in them. They're dry.

I need a guitar with some fresh songs in it.

A few hours later, he walked out with a new Taylor.

We're glad to say that each Taylor comes with a lifetime supply of new songs.

Provided, of course, that your lifetime is filled with fair amounts of joy, pain, tenderness and heartache.

©1996 Taylor Guitars 1940 Gillespie Way, El Cajon, CA 92020. Taylor® and Taylor Guitars® are registered trademarks of the company. Sign courtesy of Rock Block Guitars.

Andy Markel first laid eyes on his Taylor at a music store on Long Island.

He wrote us a letter about it, and admitted that he doesn't usually write letters to companies.

But he had to tell us that his Taylor guitar was more than a guitar.

It was like a good friend.

He also admitted he was a little embarrassed to tell us something else.

When he brought his Taylor home that first night, he kissed it before he put it in the case.

Kissed it twice, in fact.

That's the thing about friends. Some of them are friends, right from the beginning.

CONSUMER MAGAZINE
COLOR FULL PAGE OR
SPREAD: CAMPAIGN

268

ART DIRECTOR:
John Vitro
WRITER:
John Robertson
PHOTOGRAPHER:
Chris Wimpey
CLIENT:
Taylor Guitars
AGENCY:
VitroRobertson/San Diego

©1995 Taylor Guitars 1940 Gillespie Way, El Cajon, CA 92020. Taylor® and Taylor Guitars® are registered trademarks of the company.

There are a lot of music stores between Virginia and Missouri.

For two years, in 1988 and 1989, Ray Roberts began "poking his nose" into a lot of them.

He was looking for a guitar he could fall in love with.

Finally, at a store in Charlotte, North Carolina, he found his Taylor.

He could finally stop visiting music stores.

Well, not quite. Two stores in Lynchburg did ask him to come by.

They asked if he could bring in his Taylor. They wanted to see if everything they had heard was true.

©1995 Taylor Guitars 1940 Gillespie Way, El Cajon, CA 92020. Taylor® and Taylor Guitars® are registered trademarks of the company.

David Pearl remembers playing a Taylor for the first time.

He had strolled into a local music store, with a few hours of spare time on his hands.

And, just for the heck of it, he started playing his way through their entire inventory.

David wrote us about it. "I left my romantic period behind me years ago. Nevertheless, as I played your instrument I fell in love."

He played, and kept playing, and kept playing, until, in his words, "They had to ask me to leave at closing time."

He even came back the next day, hoping it wasn't just a one-time feeling, a fluke.

And just to be safe, he even made a point of getting there early.

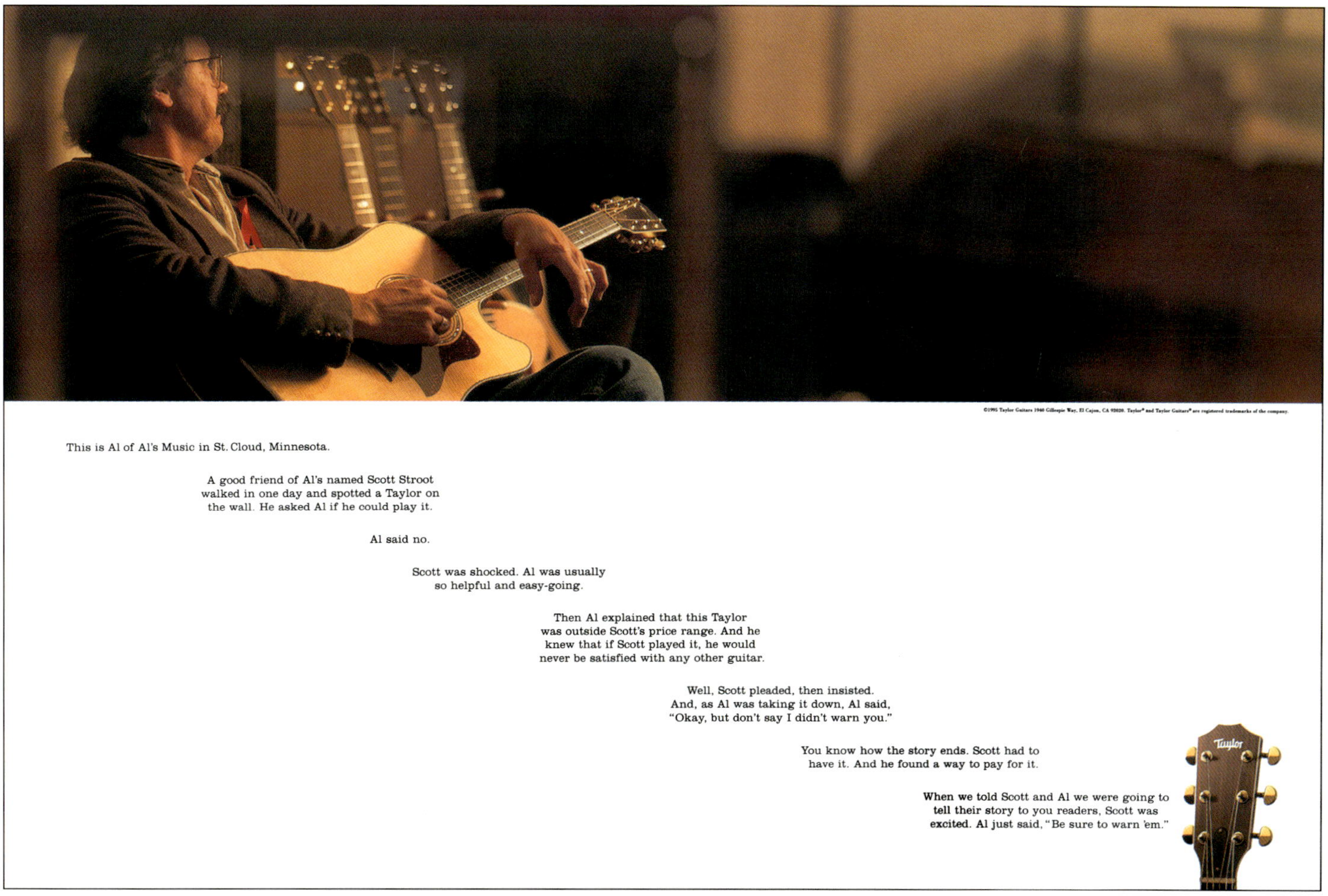
©1995 Taylor Guitars 1940 Gillespie Way, El Cajon, CA 92020. Taylor® and Taylor Guitars® are registered trademarks of the company.
This is Al of Al's Music in St. Cloud, Minnesota.
A good friend of Al's named Scott Stroot walked in one day and spotted a Taylor on the wall. He asked Al if he could play it.
Al said no.
Scott was shocked. Al was usually so helpful and easy-going.
Then Al explained that this Taylor was outside Scott's price range. And he knew that if Scott played it, he would never be satisfied with any other guitar.
Well, Scott pleaded, then insisted. And, as Al was taking it down, Al said, "Okay, but don't say I didn't warn you."
You know how the story ends. Scott had to have it. And he found a way to pay for it.
When we told Scott and Al we were going to tell their story to you readers, Scott was excited. Al just said, "Be sure to warn 'em."
Taylor

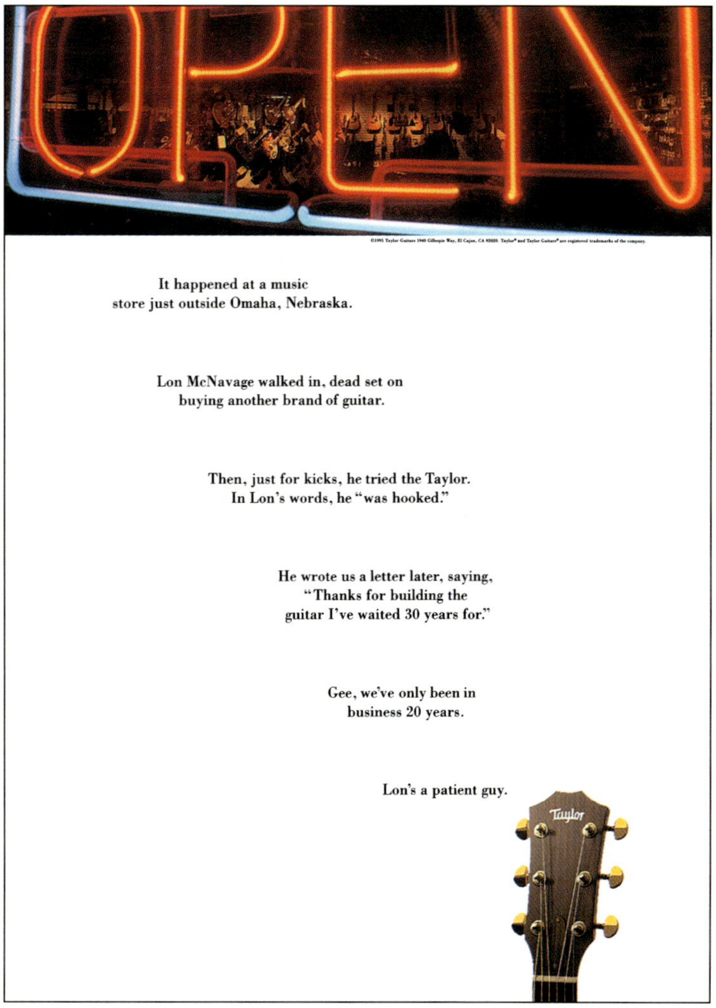
OPEN
It happened at a music store just outside Omaha, Nebraska.
Lon McNavage walked in, dead set on buying another brand of guitar.
Then, just for kicks, he tried the Taylor. In Lon's words, he "was hooked."
He wrote us a letter later, saying, "Thanks for building the guitar I've waited 30 years for."
Gee, we've only been in business 20 years.
Lon's a patient guy.
Taylor

CONSUMER MAGAZINE
COLOR FULL PAGE OR
SPREAD: CAMPAIGN

269

ART DIRECTOR:
Robert Nakata

WRITER:
Bob Moore

PHOTOGRAPHER:
John Huet

CLIENT:
Nike Europe

AGENCY:
Wieden & Kennedy/
Amsterdam

203 beautiful days
162 ugly ones
nike
running

running
nike
Bad days
tell more than
good days

CONSUMER MAGAZINE
COLOR FULL PAGE OR
SPREAD: CAMPAIGN

270

ART DIRECTOR:
Robert Nakata

WRITER:
Bob Moore

PHOTOGRAPHER:
John Huet

CLIENT:
Nike Europe

AGENCY:
Wieden & Kennedy/
Amsterdam

Test
your
faith
daily
nike
running

26
miles,
385
yards
and
15
feet
nike
running

CONSUMER MAGAZINE
COLOR FULL PAGE OR
SPREAD: CAMPAIGN

271
ART DIRECTOR:
Darryl McDonald
WRITER:
James LeMaitre
PHOTOGRAPHERS:
Duncan Sim
Marc Gouby
CLIENT:
Nike
AGENCY:
Wieden & Kennedy/
Portland

CONSUMER MAGAZINE
B/W OR COLOR LESS THAN
A PAGE: SINGLE

272
ART DIRECTOR:
Shelley Stout
WRITER:
Jim Haven
PHOTOGRAPH:
Semi-Ah-Moo Resort
CLIENT:
Semi-Ah-Moo Resort
AGENCY:
Borders Perrin &
Norrander/Portland

273
ART DIRECTOR:
Paul Asao
WRITER:
Jim Nelson
PHOTOGRAPHER:
Jim Marvy
CLIENT:
Normark
AGENCY:
Carmichael Lynch/
Minneapolis

271

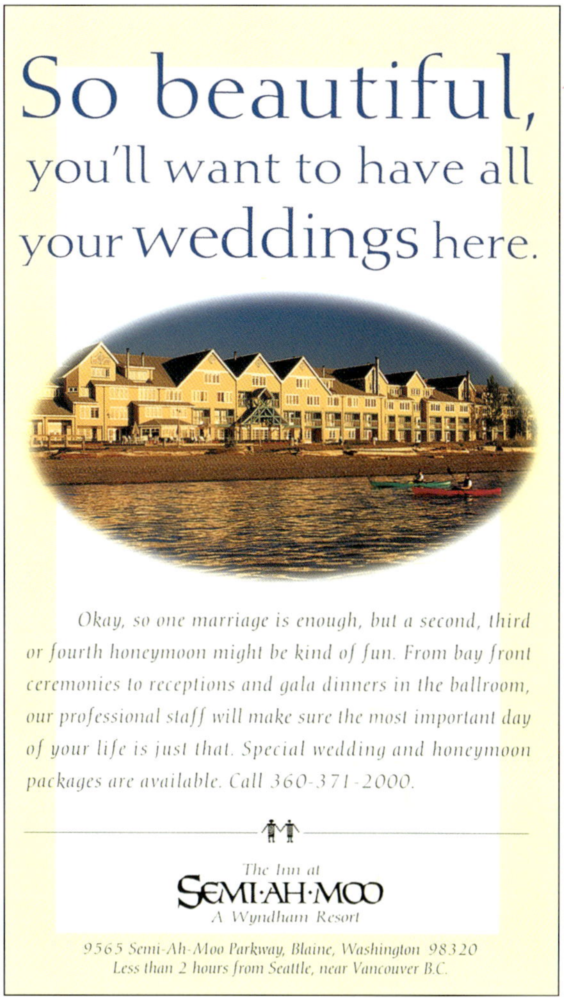
So beautiful,
you'll want to have all
your weddings here.
Okay, so one marriage is enough, but a second, third or fourth honeymoon might be kind of fun. From bay front ceremonies to receptions and gala dinners in the ballroom, our professional staff will make sure the most important day of your life is just that. Special wedding and honeymoon packages are available. Call 360-371-2000.
The Inn at
SEMI·AH·MOO
A Wyndham Resort
9565 Semi-Ah-Moo Parkway, Blaine, Washington 98320
Less than 2 hours from Seattle, near Vancouver B.C.

272

The neutrally buoyant, suspending Husky Jerk.
Oh my. Someone let the floating Rapalas spawn with the sinking Rapalas.
Rapala
Normark
©1995 Normark Corp., 10395 Yellow Circle Dr. Mpls., MN 55343

CONSUMER MAGAZINE
B/W OR COLOR LESS THAN
A PAGE: SINGLE

274
ART DIRECTOR:
Paul Asao
WRITER:
Tom Camp
PHOTOGRAPHER:
Jerry Stebbins
CLIENT:
Normark
AGENCY:
Carmichael Lynch/
Minneapolis

275
ART DIRECTOR:
Frank Haggerty
WRITER:
Jim Nelson
PHOTOGRAPHER:
Shawn Michienzi
CLIENT:
Stren
AGENCY:
Carmichael Lynch/
Minneapolis

276
ART DIRECTOR:
Heidi Flora
WRITER:
Kevin Jones
PHOTOGRAPHER:
Robert Whitman
CLIENT:
Westin Hotels & Resorts
AGENCY:
Cole & Weber/Seattle

274

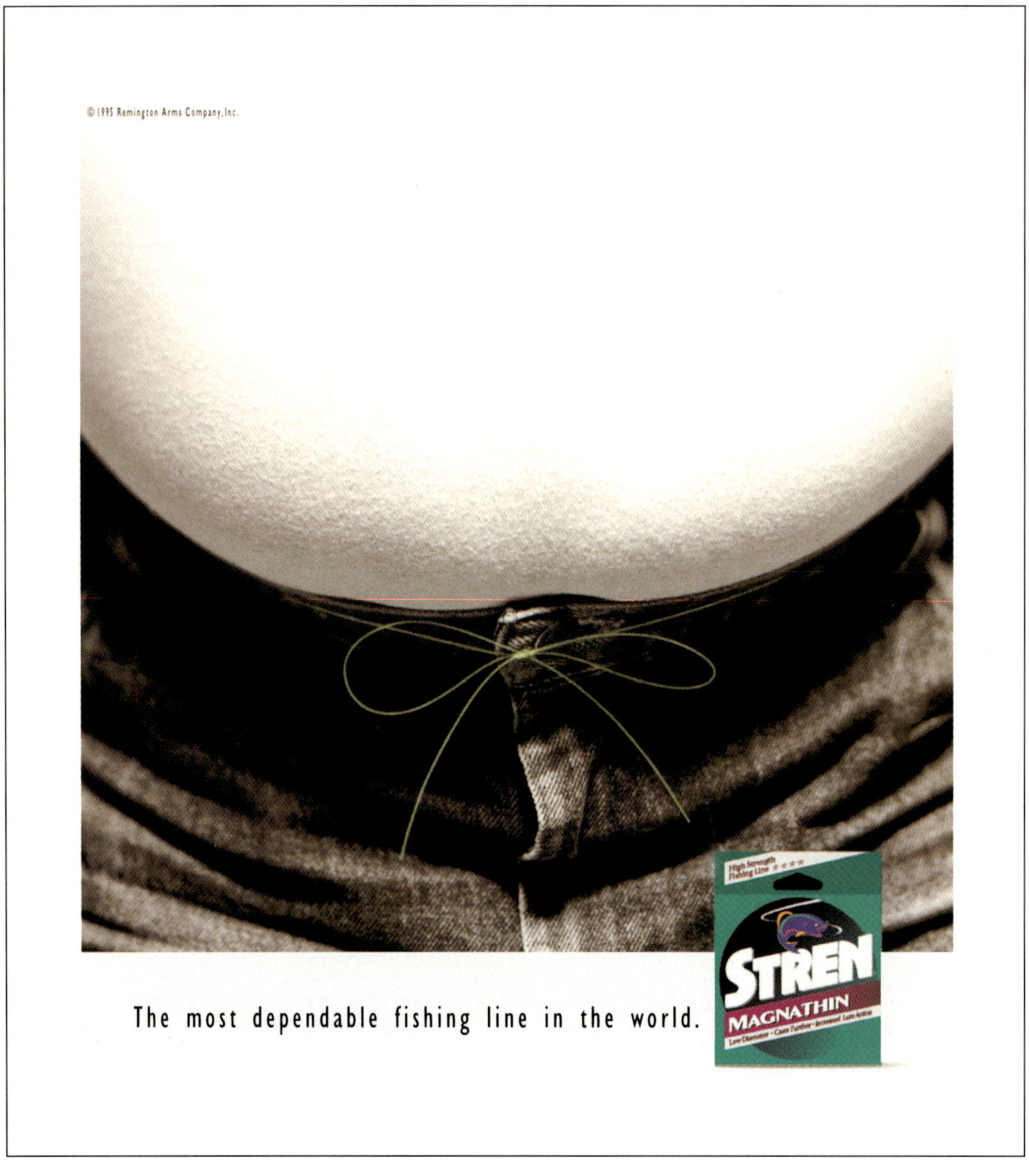

275

Where children
are seldom
seen,
but often created.
It's been called the most romantic resort in the world. If further instructions are necessary, you're probably too young. For reservations call your travel consultant or (800) 228-3000
The Leading Hotels of the World®
las brisas
acapulco
Westin Hotels & Resorts®

CONSUMER MAGAZINE
B/W OR COLOR LESS THAN
A PAGE: SINGLE

277
ART DIRECTORS:
Markham Cronin
Tony Calcao
Alex Bogusky
WRITER:
Scott Linnen
PHOTOGRAPHERS:
Jose Molina
Tony Calcao
CLIENT:
Shimano American
Corporation
AGENCY:
Crispin & Porter/Miami

278
ART DIRECTOR:
Leslie Sweet
WRITER:
Sal DeVito
CLIENT:
Time Out
AGENCY:
DeVito/Verdi, New York

279
ART DIRECTOR:
Gary Goldsmith
WRITER:
Tom Miller
CLIENT:
Barneys New York
AGENCY:
Goldsmith/Jeffrey,
New York

280
ART DIRECTOR:
Todd Grant
WRITER:
Bo Coyner
PHOTOGRAPHER:
Gil Smith
ILLUSTRATOR:
Patrick Mullins
CLIENT:
American Isuzu Motors
AGENCY:
Goodby Silverstein &
Partners/San Francisco

277

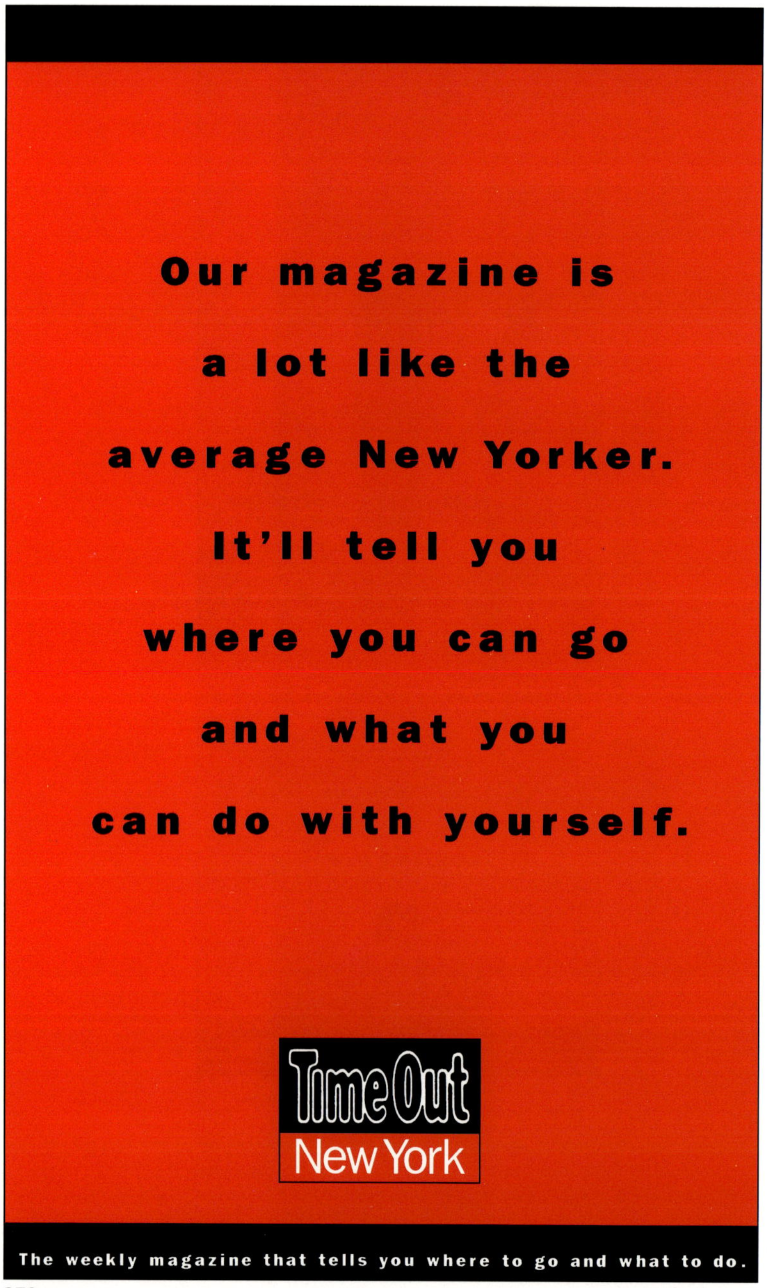

278

The End
Of cocoa-butter stained paperbacks
flying kites in the dunes
and lighter-fluid tinged hamburgers.
Junk drawers fill with seashells.
Volleyballs hibernate.
Fahrenheit goes from plus to minus.
Say goodbye to cheap sunglasses
bar-car Friday friendships
and the feeling of tan skin
with sand in the bed.
The best remedy for this depressing news?
New clothes.
Come see the new Fall Collection.
BARNEYS
NEW YORK

279

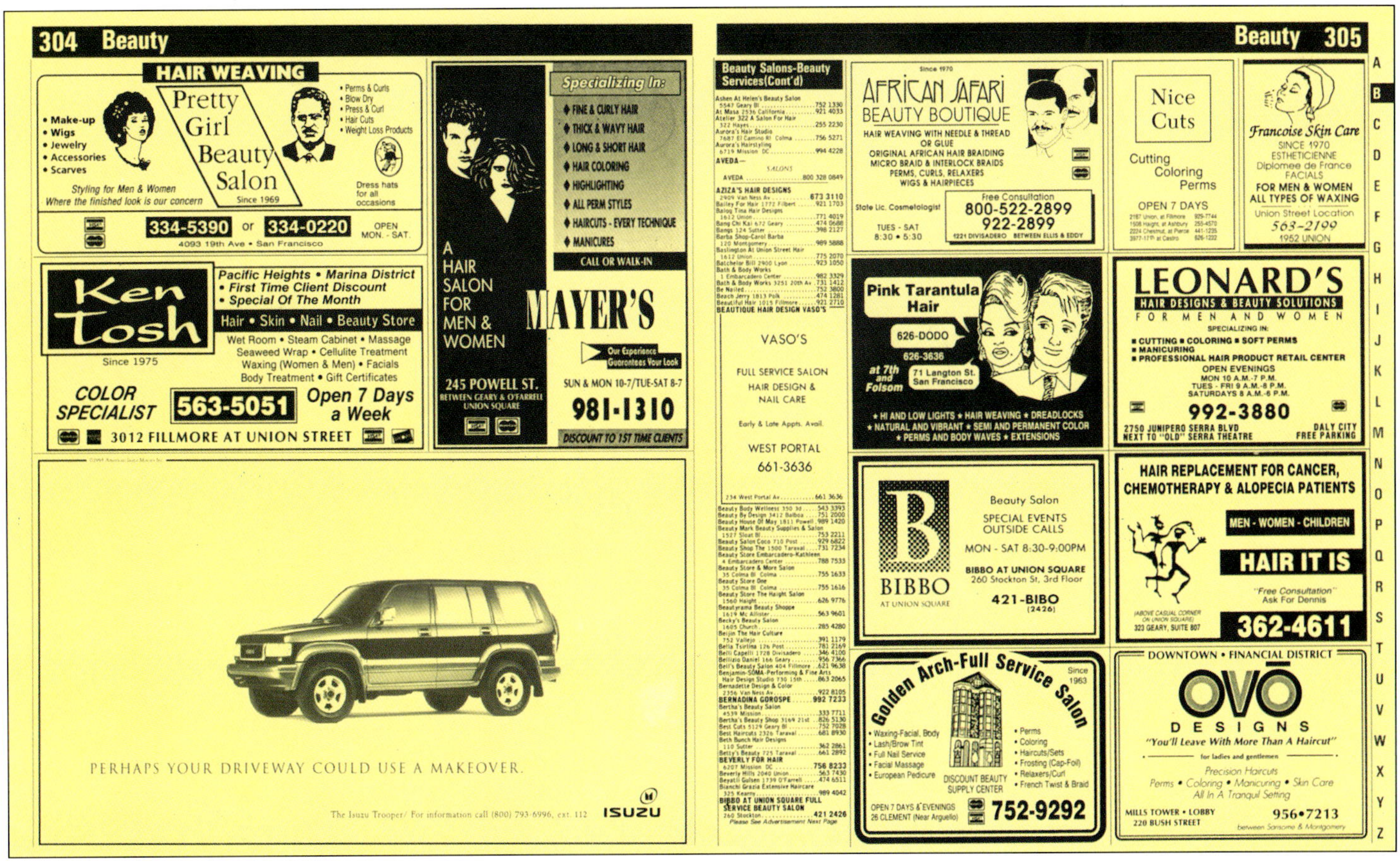
304 Beauty
HAIR WEAVING
Pretty Girl Beauty Salon
Make-up
Wigs
Jewelry
Accessories
Scarves
Styling for Men & Women
Where the finished look is our concern
Since 1969
334-5390 or 334-0220
OPEN MON. - SAT.
4093 19th Ave • San Francisco
Ken Tosh
Since 1975
Pacific Heights • Marina District
First Time Client Discount
Special Of The Month
Hair • Skin • Nail • Beauty Store
Wet Room • Steam Cabinet • Massage
Seaweed Wrap • Cellulite Treatment
Waxing (Women & Men) • Facials
Body Treatment • Gift Certificates
COLOR SPECIALIST
563-5051
Open 7 Days a Week
3012 FILLMORE AT UNION STREET
Specializing In:
FINE & CURLY HAIR
THICK & WAVY HAIR
LONG & SHORT HAIR
HAIR COLORING
HIGHLIGHTING
ALL PERM STYLES
HAIRCUTS - EVERY TECHNIQUE
MANICURES
CALL OR WALK-IN
A HAIR SALON FOR MEN & WOMEN
MAYER'S
Our Experience Guarantees Your Look
245 POWELL ST.
BETWEEN GEARY & O'FARRELL UNION SQUARE
SUN & MON 10-7/TUE-SAT 8-7
981-1310
DISCOUNT TO 1ST TIME CLIENTS
PERHAPS YOUR DRIVEWAY COULD USE A MAKEOVER.
ISUZU
Beauty 305
Beauty Salons-Beauty Services(Cont'd)
VASO'S
FULL SERVICE SALON
HAIR DESIGN & NAIL CARE
WEST PORTAL
661-3636
AFRICAN SAFARI BEAUTY BOUTIQUE
HAIR WEAVING WITH NEEDLE & THREAD OR GLUE
ORIGINAL AFRICAN HAIR BRAIDING
MICRO BRAID & INTERLOCK BRAIDS
PERMS, CURLS, RELAXERS
WIGS & HAIRPIECES
Free Consultation
800-522-2899
922-2899
TUES - SAT 8:30 - 5:30
Nice Cuts
Cutting
Coloring
Perms
OPEN 7 DAYS
Françoise Skin Care
SINCE 1970
FOR MEN & WOMEN
ALL TYPES OF WAXING
Union Street Location
563-2199
Pink Tarantula Hair
626-DODO
626-3636
at 7th and Folsom
71 Langton St. San Francisco
HI AND LOW LIGHTS • HAIR WEAVING • DREADLOCKS
NATURAL AND VIBRANT • SEMI AND PERMANENT COLOR
PERMS AND BODY WAVES • EXTENSIONS
LEONARD'S
HAIR DESIGNS & BEAUTY SOLUTIONS
FOR MEN AND WOMEN
CUTTING • COLORING • SOFT PERMS
MANICURING
PROFESSIONAL HAIR PRODUCT RETAIL CENTER
OPEN EVENINGS
992-3880
2750 JUNIPERO SERRA BLVD NEXT TO "OLD" SERRA THEATRE
DALY CITY FREE PARKING
BIBBO
Beauty Salon
SPECIAL EVENTS
OUTSIDE CALLS
MON - SAT 8:30-9:00PM
BIBBO AT UNION SQUARE
260 Stockton St. 3rd Floor
421-BIBO
HAIR REPLACEMENT FOR CANCER, CHEMOTHERAPY & ALOPECIA PATIENTS
MEN - WOMEN - CHILDREN
HAIR IT IS
"Free Consultation" Ask For Dennis
323 GEARY, SUITE 807
362-4611
Golden Arch-Full Service Salon
Since 1963
752-9292
DOWNTOWN • FINANCIAL DISTRICT
OVO DESIGNS
"You'll Leave With More Than A Haircut"
MILLS TOWER • LOBBY
220 BUSH STREET
956•7213

280

CONSUMER MAGAZINE
B/W OR COLOR LESS THAN
A PAGE: SINGLE

281
ART DIRECTOR:
Nikolas Studzinski
WRITER:
Alex Grieve
CLIENT:
UK Bungee Club
AGENCY:
Saatchi & Saatchi/London

282
ART DIRECTOR:
Denis Faye
WRITERS:
David Nobay
Stephen Beckett
CLIENT:
Minotaur Comics
AGENCY:
Wells Nobay McDowall/
Victoria, Australia

CONSUMER MAGAZINE
B/W OR COLOR LESS THAN
A PAGE: CAMPAIGN

283
ART DIRECTOR:
Gary Goldsmith
WRITER:
Tom Miller
CLIENT:
Barneys New York
AGENCY:
Goldsmith/Jeffrey,
New York

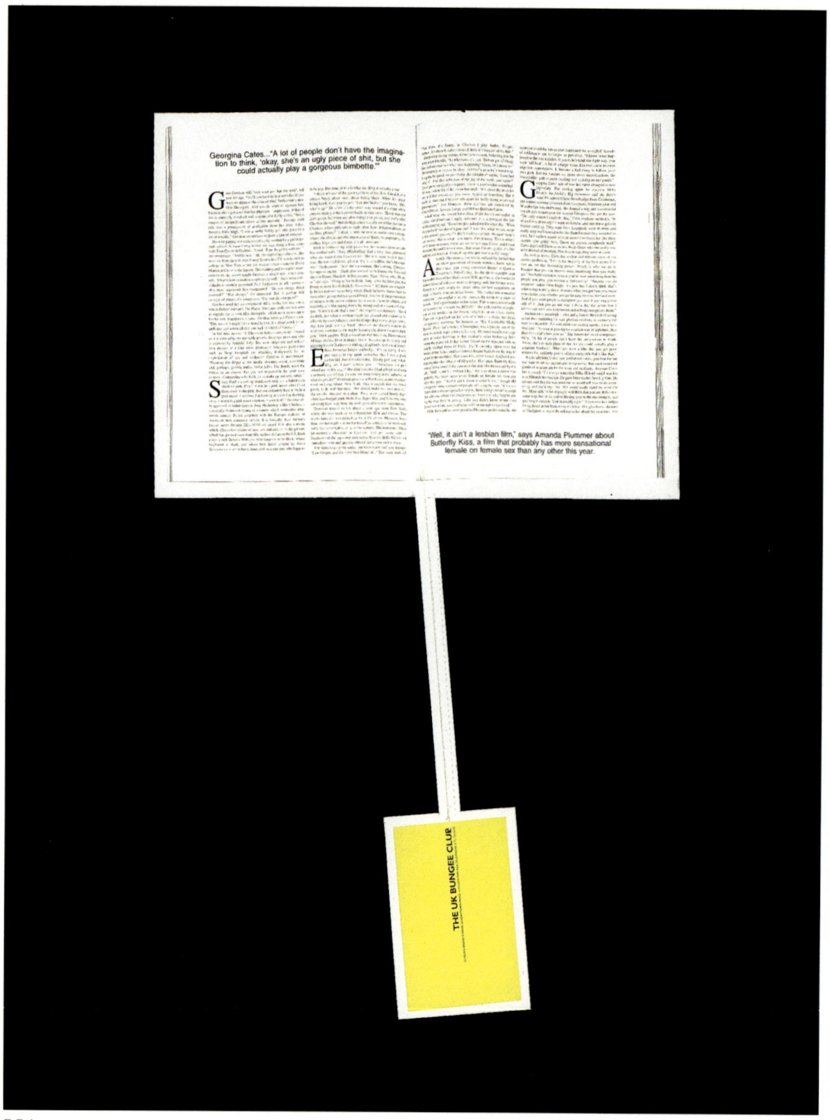

281

282

SPF 0
Blonde hair darkens.
Visine sales plummet.
Lifeguard whistles fall silent.
The signs are obvious.
Summer is over.
Once again baby oil is for babies.
Pool men take up roofing.
And towels migrate to bathrooms.
Slowly, the healthy glow is fading.
A milky luminescence returns.
But all is not lost.
You can still look good without a tan.
Come see the new Fall Collection.
BARNEYS
NEW YORK

Here comes the leash
It couldn't last forever.
When you were a child it was "Field Day."
Now it's "Summer Friday."
Those mystical two words.
It's get out of jail early.
Once a week.
12 days a year.
And it's ending.
Here comes the starch.
Five days of jackets.
High polish shoes.
Neckties.
Putting the leash back on is no fun.
Then again, that depends on where you buy it.
Come see the new Fall Collection.
BARNEYS
NEW YORK

The End
Of cocoa-butter stained paperbacks
flying kites in the dunes
and lighter-fluid tinged hamburgers.
Junk drawers fill with seashells.
Volleyballs hibernate.
Fahrenheit goes from plus to minus.
Say goodbye to cheap sunglasses
bar-car Friday friendships
and the feeling of tan skin
with sand in the bed.
The best remedy for this depressing news?
New clothes.
Come see the new Fall Collection.
BARNEYS
NEW YORK

CONSUMER MAGAZINE
B/W OR COLOR LESS THAN
A PAGE: CAMPAIGN

284

ART DIRECTOR:
Hal Curtis

WRITER:
Tim Cawley

PHOTOGRAPHER:
Jack Richmond

CLIENT:
Sterilite

AGENCY:
Pagano Schenck & Kay/
Boston

285

ART DIRECTOR:
Chris Schlegel

WRITER:
Andrew Payton

PHOTOGRAPHER:
RJ Muna

CLIENT:
Eveready Battery
Company

AGENCY:
Tausche Martin Lonsdorf/
Atlanta

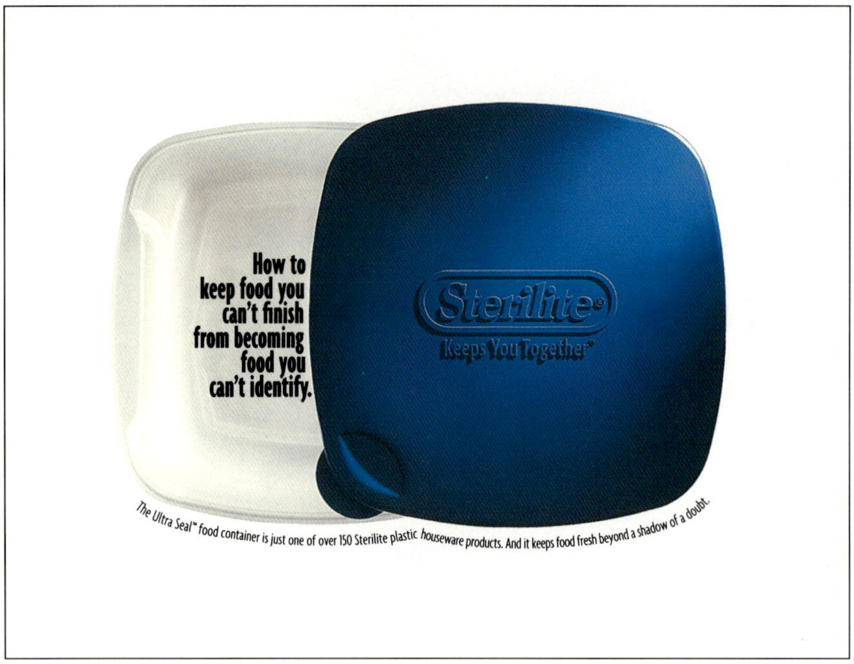

[12:07 pm]
Groom's ex-girlfriend sobs uncontrollably during vows.
[12:42 pm]
A small melee during the bouquet tossing.
[1:14 pm]
Bride's choice of polka for first dance promises a strange future.
If your battery stops, did it happen?
Energizer
Energizer® keeps camcorders going & going.™
For an Energizer Rechargeable Power Systems retailer near you, call 1.800.950.0151

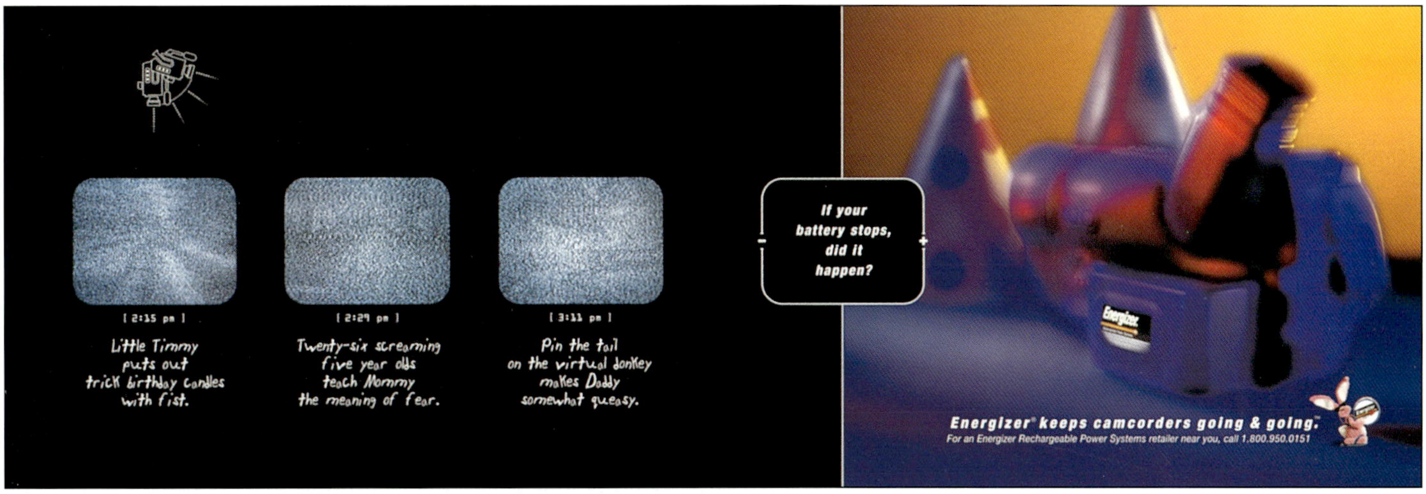
[2:15 pm]
Little Timmy puts out trick birthday candles with fist.
[2:29 pm]
Twenty-six screaming five year olds teach Mommy the meaning of fear.
[3:11 pm]
Pin the tail on the virtual donkey makes Daddy somewhat queasy.
If your battery stops, did it happen?
Energizer
Energizer® keeps camcorders going & going.™
For an Energizer Rechargeable Power Systems retailer near you, call 1.800.950.0151

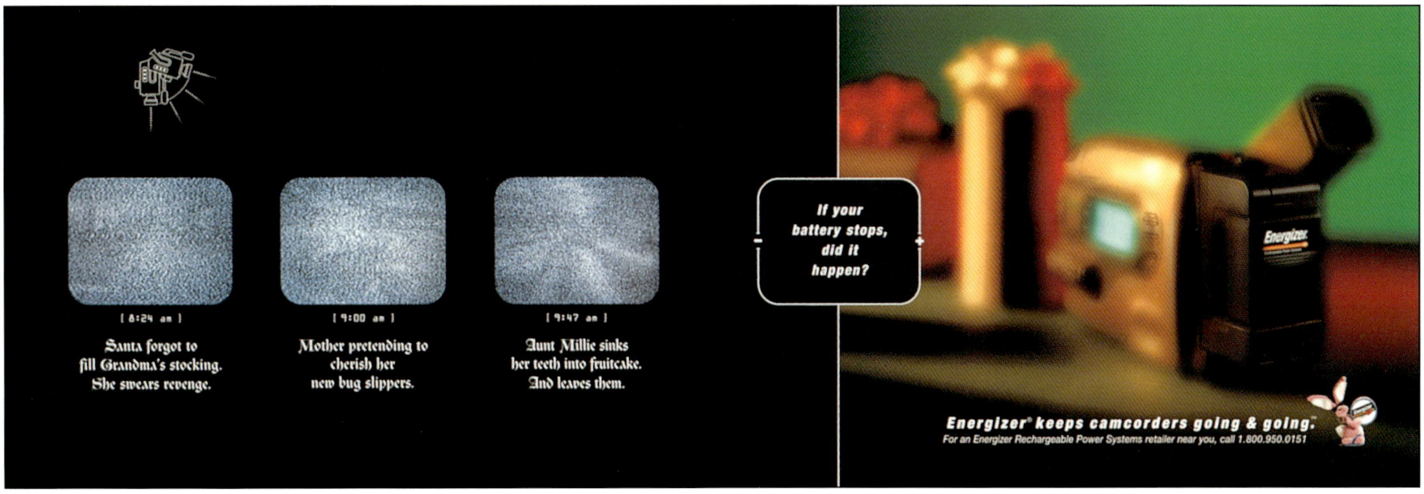
[8:24 am]
Santa forgot to fill Grandma's stocking. She swears revenge.
[9:00 am]
Mother pretending to cherish her new bug slippers.
[9:47 am]
Aunt Millie sinks her teeth into fruitcake. And leaves them.
If your battery stops, did it happen?
Energizer
Energizer® keeps camcorders going & going.™
For an Energizer Rechargeable Power Systems retailer near you, call 1.800.950.0151

CONSUMER MAGAZINE
B/W OR COLOR LESS THAN
A PAGE: CAMPAIGN

286
ART DIRECTORS:
David Stephens
Richard Edwards
WRITER:
David Nobay
PHOTOGRAPHER:
Tat Ming Yu
CLIENT:
Peter Wright Cars
AGENCY:
Wells Nobay McDowall/
Victoria, Australia

OUTDOOR: SINGLE

287
ART DIRECTOR:
Paul Briginshaw
WRITER:
Malcolm Duffy
TYPOGRAPHER:
Joe Hoza
CLIENT:
The Economist
AGENCY:
Abbott Mead Vickers.
BBDO/London

288
ART DIRECTOR:
Adam Francis
WRITER:
Andrew Foote
CLIENT:
Mutual Community
AGENCY:
Clemenger Adelaide/
Eastwood, Australia

Owner's manual.

The Economist

287

288

OUTDOOR: SINGLE

289
ART DIRECTOR:
Heidi Flora
WRITER:
Kevin Jones
PHOTOGRAPHER:
Robert Whitman
CLIENT:
Westin Hotels & Resorts
AGENCY:
Cole & Weber/Seattle

290
ART DIRECTOR:
Simon Winterflood
WRITER:
Sion Scott-Wilson
CLIENT:
McDonald's System
of New Zealand
AGENCY:
DDB Needham
New Zealand/Auckland

291
ART DIRECTOR:
Christine Ivers
WRITER:
Sarah Walter
CLIENT:
Ford Drivers School
AGENCY:
DDB Needham
New Zealand/Auckland

292
ART DIRECTOR:
Shane Gibson
WRITERS:
Mark Ringer
Ben Bradley
CLIENT:
McDonald's
AGENCY:
DDB Needham Sydney/
North Sydney

289

290

MAKE SURE
THIS IS
THE ONLY
THING
WRAPPED
AROUND
THIS POLE.
FORD ADVANCED DRIVERS SCHOOL
PH 486 4775
291

E
292

OUTDOOR: SINGLE

293
ART DIRECTOR:
Bob Barrie
WRITER:
Sally Hogshead
PHOTOGRAPHER:
Joe Lampi
CLIENT:
J. D. Hoyt's
AGENCY:
Fallon McElligott/
Minneapolis

294
ART DIRECTOR:
John Liegey
WRITER:
Sally Hogshead
CLIENT:
Star Tribune
AGENCY:
Fallon McElligott/
Minneapolis

295
ART DIRECTOR:
Sean Ehringer
WRITER:
Harry Cocciolo
PHOTOGRAPHER:
Hunter Freeman
CLIENT:
California Fluid Milk
Processor Advisory Board
AGENCY:
Goodby Silverstein &
Partners/San Francisco

296
ART DIRECTOR:
Paul MacFarlane
WRITER:
Paul MacFarlane
PHOTOGRAPHER:
Bill Mathis
CLIENT:
St. Louis Volvo Dealers
AGENCY:
Jacobsen Advertising/
St. Louis

293

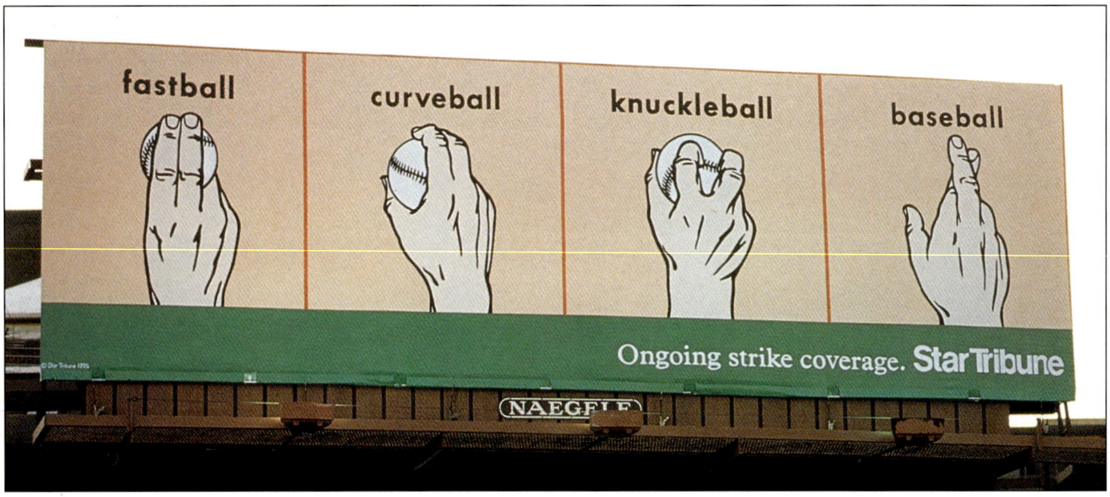

294

295

296

OUTDOOR: SINGLE

297
ART DIRECTOR:
David Beverley
WRITER:
Robert Burleigh
CLIENT:
The Guardian
AGENCY:
Leagas Delaney/London

298
ART DIRECTOR:
Matt Hazell
WRITER:
Jane Atkinson
CLIENT:
United Airlines
AGENCY:
Leo Burnett/London

299
ART DIRECTOR:
Barney Goldberg
WRITER:
Joe Nagy
PHOTOGRAPHER:
Chris Bailey
CLIENT:
Mercedes-Benz of
North America
AGENCY:
The Martin Agency/
Richmond

300
ART DIRECTORS:
Taras Wayner
Vicky Stolberg
WRITER:
Kevin Roddy
PHOTOGRAPHER:
Jim Lund
CLIENT:
Sierra Expressway
AGENCY:
Odiorne Wilde Narraway
Groome/San Francisco

297

298

Soon.

299

REST AREA
25,000 FEET ABOVE
$59. Fly Oakland to Sacramento.
Sierra Expressway

300

OUTDOOR: SINGLE

301
ART DIRECTOR:
Sally Overheu
WRITER:
Jackie Hathiramani
PHOTOGRAPHER:
Sally Overheu
CLIENT:
The British Council
AGENCY:
Ogilvy & Mather/
Singapore

302
ART DIRECTOR:
Sally Overheu
WRITER:
Jackie Hathiramani
PHOTOGRAPHER:
Sally Overheu
CLIENT:
The British Council
AGENCY:
Ogilvy & Mather/
Singapore

303
ART DIRECTOR:
Monique Kelley
WRITER:
Paul Ruta
PHOTOGRAPHER:
Dave Sloan
CLIENT:
Ikea Canada
AGENCY:
Roche Macaulay &
Partners/Toronto

304
ART DIRECTOR:
Graham Lee
WRITER:
Dave Crichton
PHOTOGRAPHER:
Phillip Rostron
CLIENT:
Maple Leaf Foods
AGENCY:
Roche Macaulay &
Partners/Toronto

301

302

Met that special someone?
IKEA
$399
$449
$539
$499
$339

303

EXTRA LONG HOT DOGS.
NEW FROM MAPLE LEAF.
MAPLE LEAF
EXTRA
LONGS
WIENERS

304

OUTDOOR: SINGLE

305
ART DIRECTOR:
Duncan Milner
WRITER:
John Stingley
PHOTOGRAPHER:
Rick Rusing
CLIENT:
Infiniti Division of Nissan
AGENCY:
TBWA Chiat/Day,
Venice, CA

306
ART DIRECTOR:
Steve Levit
WRITER:
Rich Siegel
PHOTOGRAPHER:
Michael Ruppert
CLIENT:
Lion Nathan International,
Castlemaine XXXX
AGENCY:
Team One Advertising/
El Segundo, CA

OUTDOOR: CAMPAIGN

307
ART DIRECTORS:
Dean Hore
Paul Hains
WRITER:
Dean Hore
PHOTOGRAPHER:
Shin Sugino
CLIENT:
Labatt Breweries of
Canada
AGENCY:
Bozell Palmer Bonner/
Toronto

305

306

GREAT PRIDE MAKES
A GREAT BEER.
THERE'S SIMPLY MORE TO IT.
Carlsberg
light

G E T M E
A BEER
Carlsberg
light

OUTDOOR: CAMPAIGN

307

ART DIRECTORS:
Dean Hore
Paul Hains

WRITER:
Dean Hore

PHOTOGRAPHER:
Shin Sugino

CLIENT:
Labatt Breweries of Canada

AGENCY:
Bozell Palmer Bonner/ Toronto

307 II

URBAN LITES
THERE'S SIMPLY MORE TO IT. THERE'S SIMPLY MORE TO IT. THERE'S SIMPLY MORE
Carlsberg Light
UNMATCHED BREWING SKILLS.

URBAN LITES
THERE'S SIMPLY MORE TO IT. THERE'S SIMPLY MORE TO IT. THERE'S SIMPLY MORE
Carlsberg Light
UNMATCHED BREW SKI

OUTDOOR: CAMPAIGN

308

ART DIRECTOR:
Marcus Fernandez

WRITER:
Brian Millar

PHOTOGRAPHER:
David Scheinmann

CLIENT:
IBM Corporation

AGENCY:
Ogilvy & Mather/Paris

e-mail to:popejohn@vatican.
OS/2 Warp Internet
Solutions for a small planet
IBM

Data added. New elephant population: 4,764.
DB2 Database
Solutions for a small planet
IBM

TRADE
B/W FULL PAGE OR SPREAD: SINGLE

309
ART DIRECTOR:
Steve Mitchell
WRITER:
Doug Adkins
CLIENT:
Dublin Productions
AGENCY:
Hunt Adkins/Minneapolis

310
ART DIRECTOR:
Steve Mitchell
WRITER:
Doug Adkins
CLIENT:
Dublin Productions
AGENCY:
Hunt Adkins/Minneapolis

311
ART DIRECTOR:
Roger Wong
WRITER:
Kevin Rathgeber
PHOTOGRAPHER:
Brad Stringer
CLIENT:
Kaizen Media Services
AGENCY:
Palmer Jarvis Communications/ Vancouver

312
ART DIRECTOR:
John Boiler
WRITER:
Glenn Cole
CLIENT:
Oregon Film & Video Office
AGENCY:
Wieden & Kennedy/ Portland

309

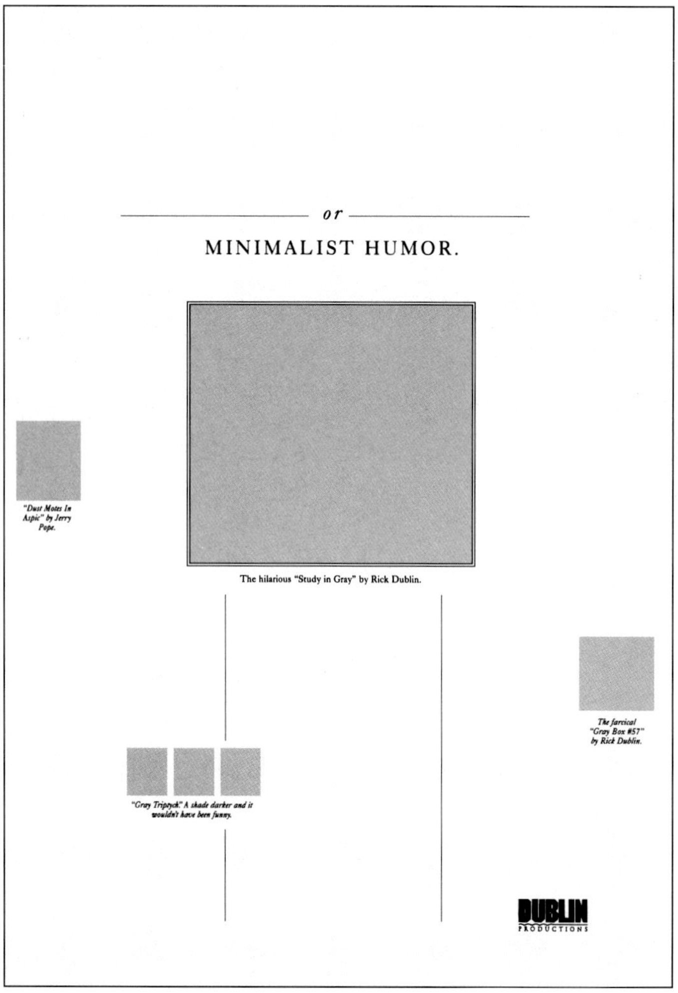

310

DR. MILLER
PSYCHIATRIST
640-4336
Creative media solutions.
KAIZEN
BRITISH COLUMBIA (604) 640-4336
ALBERTA (403) 421-1010
SASKATCHEWAN (306) 757-1044
MANITOBA (204) 925-8525

311

Oregon
Script Idea
No. 11
Open on black. Stay in black. The whole film is completely black. It's a film noir thing. About pre-creation. A Brief History of Time meets the lens cap. We get that Darth Vader guy to narrate. It's swooshing sounds. It's space noises. It's black holes in an inky black abyss. Fade to black.
Or, if you decide to shoot with the lens cap off, film the diverse post-creation landscapes in Oregon. The crews are sharp, the locations are fresh, the scouting is thorough, and it's light most of the time. Call David Woolson at the Oregon Film & Video Office, (503) 229-5832.
Oregon. Things look different here.

312

TRADE
COLOR FULL PAGE OR
SPREAD: SINGLE

313
ART DIRECTOR:
Jason Stinsmuehlen
WRITER:
Scott Habetz
PHOTOGRAPHER:
Ilan Rubin
CLIENT:
The Stanley Works
AGENCY:
Ammirati Puris Lintas/
New York

314
ART DIRECTOR:
Jason Stinsmuehlen
WRITER:
Scott Habetz
PHOTOGRAPHER:
Gary McGuire
CLIENT:
Apple Computer
AGENCY:
BBDO/Los Angeles

315
ART DIRECTOR:
Richard Mirabelli
WRITER:
Dan Burrier
CLIENT:
Apple Computer
AGENCY:
BBDO/Los Angeles

316
ART DIRECTOR:
Geordie Stephens
WRITER:
Ryan Ebner
PHOTOGRAPHER:
Heimo
CLIENT:
Bolt Products
AGENCY:
Butler Shine & Stern/
Sausalito

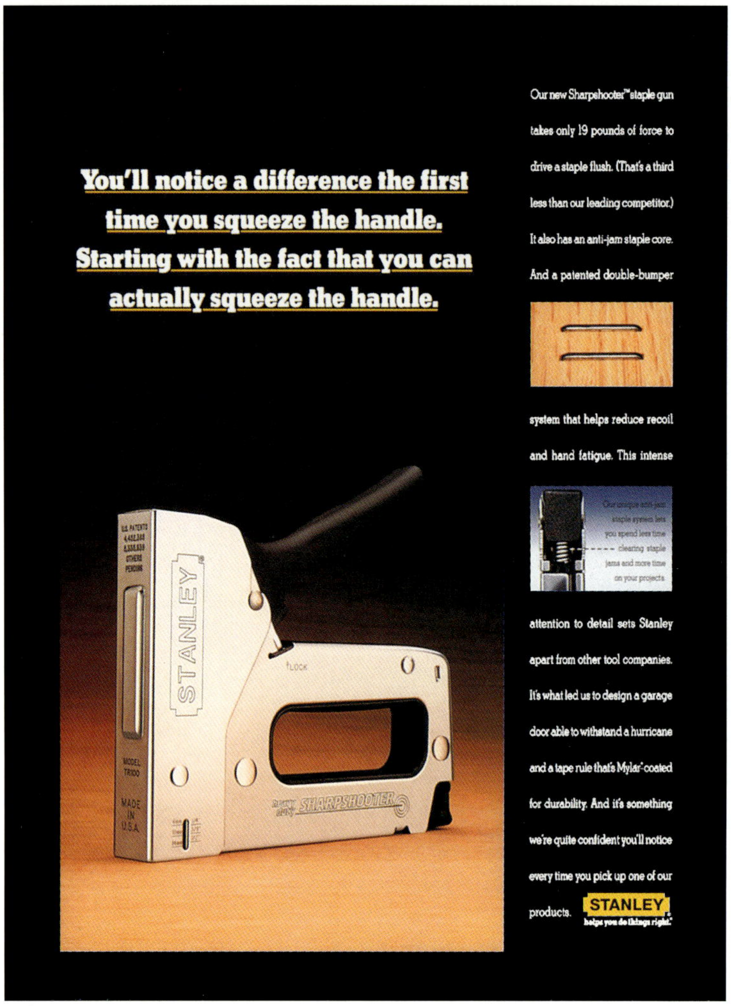

313

314

Introducing Windows 95.
It has a trash can you can open
and take things back out of again.
Imagine that.

315

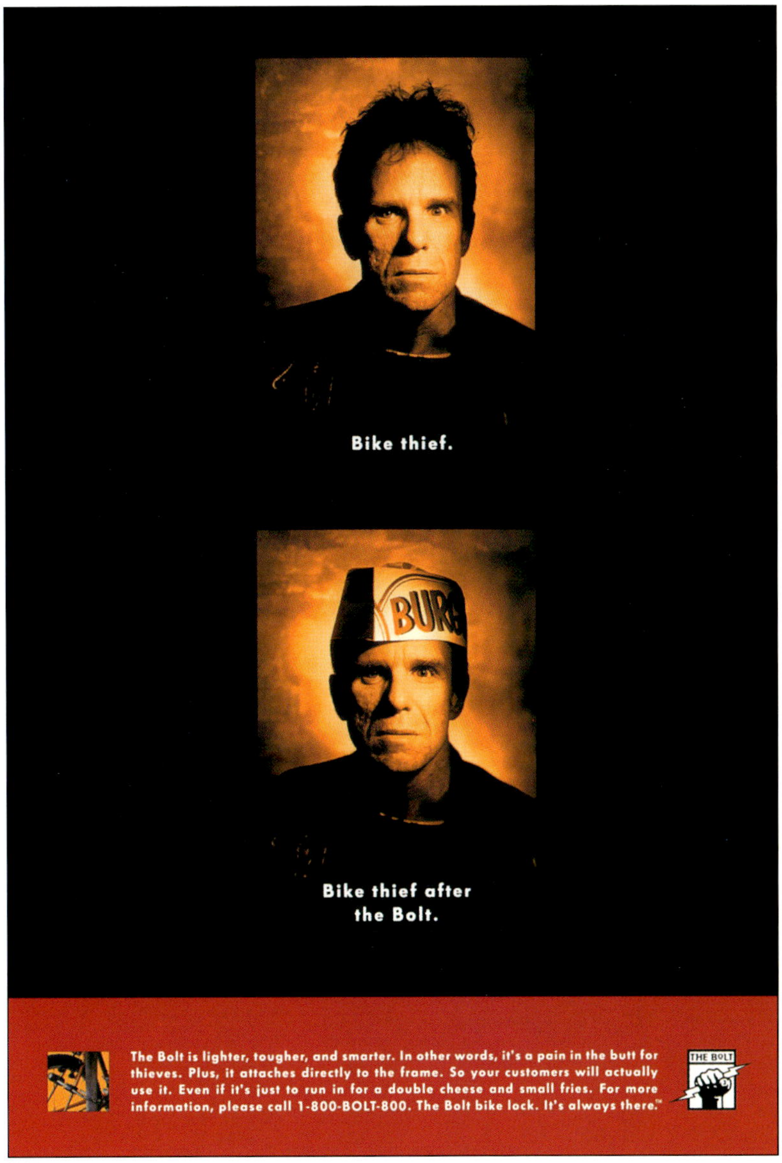
Bike thief.
Bike thief after
the Bolt.
The Bolt is lighter, tougher, and smarter. In other words, it's a pain in the butt for thieves. Plus, it attaches directly to the frame. So your customers will actually use it. Even if it's just to run in for a double cheese and small fries. For more information, please call 1-800-BOLT-800. The Bolt bike lock. It's always there.™
THE BOLT

316

TRADE
COLOR FULL PAGE OR SPREAD: SINGLE

317
ART DIRECTOR:
Geordie Stephens
WRITER:
Ryan Ebner
PHOTOGRAPHER:
Gordon Edwardes
CLIENT:
Bolt Products
AGENCY:
Butler Shine & Stern/Sausalito

318
ART DIRECTORS:
Tim Tone
Kelly Gothier
WRITER:
Randy T. Gosda
PHOTOGRAPHER:
Jim Arndt
CLIENT:
Andersen Windows
AGENCY:
Campbell Mithun Esty/Minneapolis

319
ART DIRECTORS:
Vinny Matassa
WRITER:
John Neumann
PHOTOGRAPHER:
Patrick Fox
CLIENT:
American Standard
AGENCY:
Carmichael Lynch/Minneapolis

320
ART DIRECTOR:
Bob Pullum
WRITER:
Dylan Lee
PHOTOGRAPHER:
Gary Hush
CLIENT:
Kenwood
AGENCY:
Citron Haligman Bedecarre/San Francisco

317

318

IF ONLY OUR WIVES COULD SHARE THIS MOMENT.
We now christen the world's most advanced urinal. Our Innsbrook.™ It flushes with just half a gallon, which may soon become the legal limit. You get the clean efficiency of proximity flushing, yet it's very easy to install. The electronics are inside the porcelain. Just a half-inch line hookup and you're done. Cheers. Call 1-800-752-6292, ext. 910.
American Standard

319

Don't you sometimes just want to jump in your car and drive far away where it's quiet, and you can listen to the wind blow, and the birds sing, and maybe, just maybe, even your own heartbeat?
KENWOOD

320

TRADE
COLOR FULL PAGE OR SPREAD: SINGLE

321
ART DIRECTOR:
Kim Wright
WRITER:
David Garzotto
PHOTOGRAPHER:
Byll Williams
CLIENT:
Masland Carpets
AGENCY:
Cole Henderson Drake/
Atlanta

322
ART DIRECTOR:
Christopher Cole
WRITER:
Eric Sorensen
ILLUSTRATOR:
Jerry Gale
CLIENT:
Great Faces
AGENCY:
Cole Sorensen/
Birmingham, AL

323
ART DIRECTOR:
Bill Winchester
WRITER:
Tom Evans
PHOTOGRAPHER:
Curtis Johnson
CLIENT:
Pfizer Animal Health
AGENCY:
Colle & McVoy/
Minneapolis

324
ART DIRECTOR:
Bill Winchester
WRITER:
Tom Evans
PHOTOGRAPHER:
Curtis Johnson
CLIENT:
Pfizer Animal Health
AGENCY:
Colle & McVoy/
Minneapolis

321

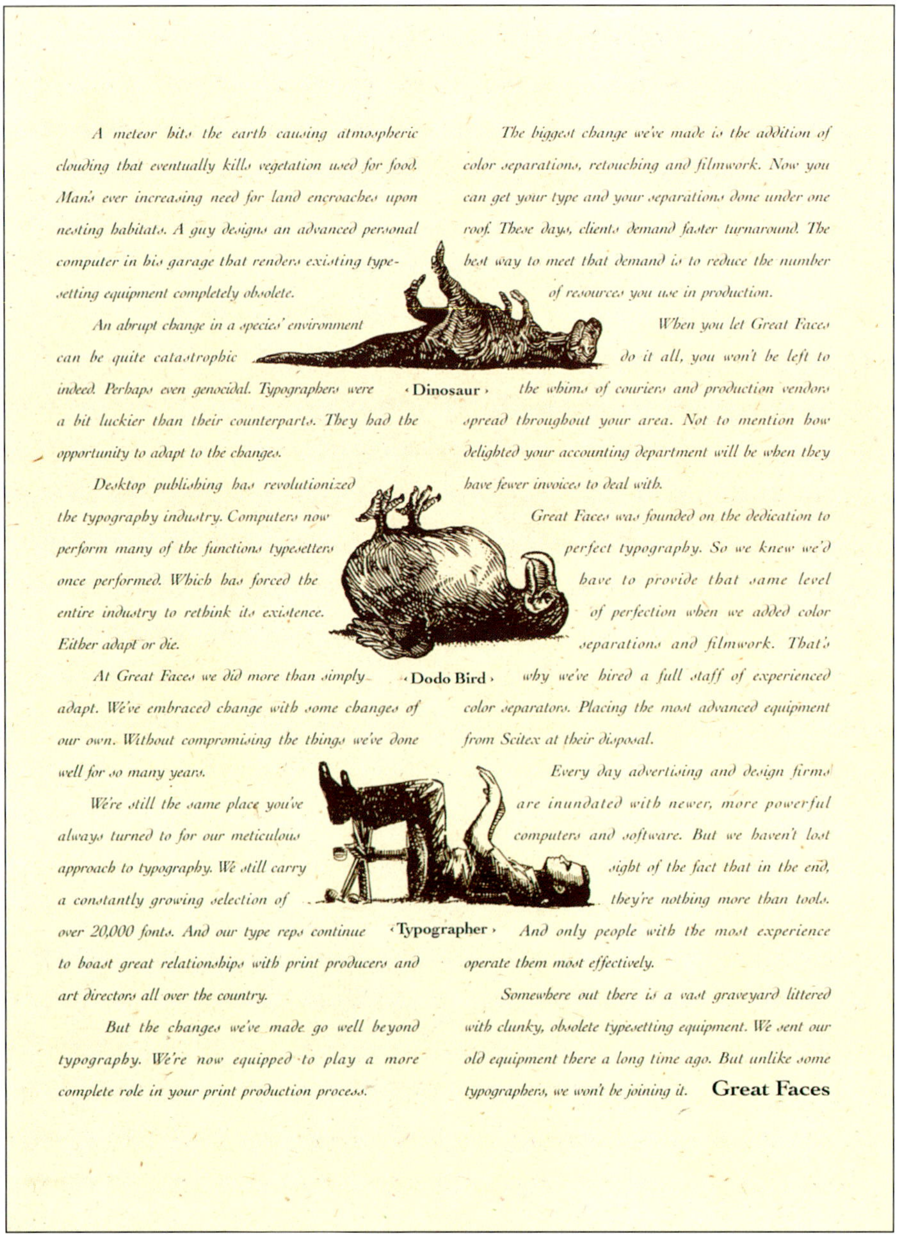

322

ADAMS™
FLEA AND TICK MIST
KILLS
CAUTION
Who cares if it's an ugly bottle?
Dogs are color blind anyway.
Veterinarians have recommended Adams for twenty years,
so dog and cat owners who know what works know to look for our
distinctive blue bottle. No matter how ugly it is.
Adams. The really strong stuff in the ugly blue bottle.

323

ADAMS™
FLEA AND TICK MIST
KILLS
CAUTION
We were gonna put a
doggy and kitty on the label but the
science dept. laughed at us.
When you're ready to get serious about flea and tick control,
look for Adams. It's the professional formula in the not-so-pretty package.
The way we see it, killing fleas and ticks is an ugly job.
Adams. The really strong stuff in the ugly blue bottle.

324

TRADE
COLOR FULL PAGE OR SPREAD: SINGLE

325

ART DIRECTOR:
Bill Winchester

WRITER:
Tom Evans

PHOTOGRAPHER:
Curtis Johnson

CLIENT:
Pfizer Animal Health

AGENCY:
Colle & McVoy/ Minneapolis

326

ART DIRECTOR:
Fernando Planelles

WRITERS:
Arturo Tollesson
Juan Pablo Caja

TYPOGRAPHER:
Eva Conesa

CLIENT:
Laboratorios Salvat

AGENCY:
Euro RSCG/Barcelona

327

ART DIRECTOR:
Bob Barrie

WRITER:
Dean Buckhorn

PHOTOGRAPHER:
John McGrail

CLIENT:
Time

AGENCY:
Fallon McElligott/ Minneapolis

328

ART DIRECTOR:
Bob Barrie

WRITER:
Doug de Grood

CLIENT:
Time

AGENCY:
Fallon McElligott/ Minneapolis

325

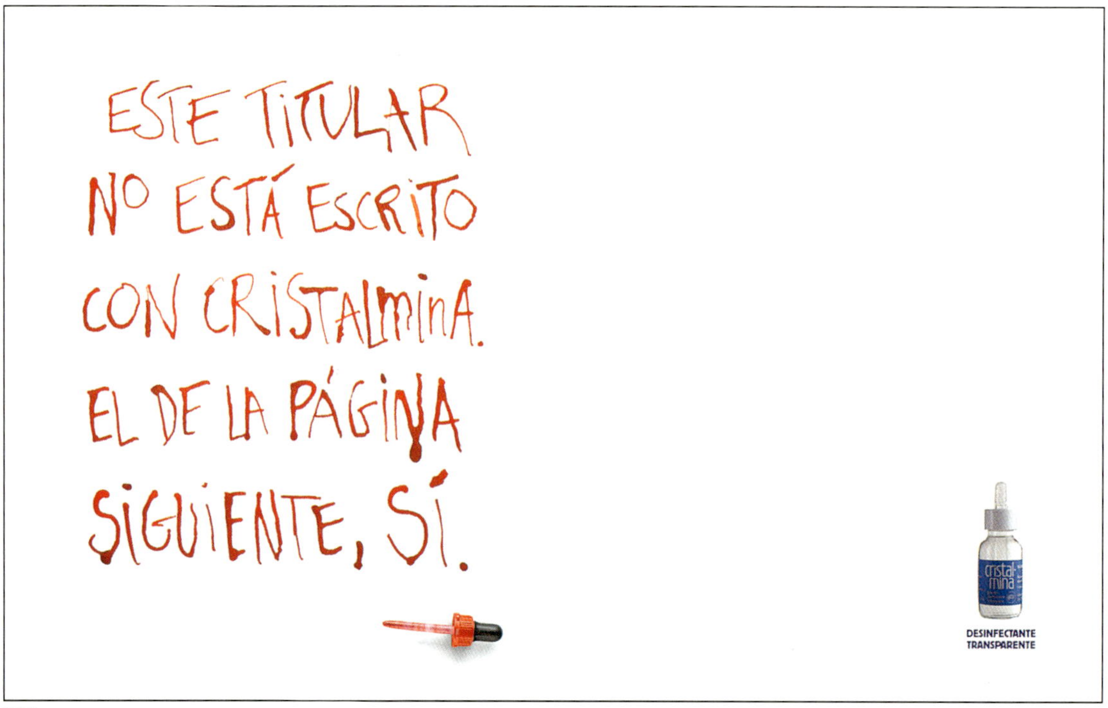

326

Telecommunications.

Cyberspace. The Internet.

Ironically, you can keep up

with them by reading words

printed on actual paper.

Understanding comes with TIME.

327

©1995 Time Inc.

MAN OF THE YEAR

TIME

☐ **A man?**

☐ **A woman?**

☐ **A computer?**

☐ **A great ad opportunity?**

So far, only one thing is certain.

The big winner will be advertisers, regardless of who is named TIME's Man of the Year. After all, this one issue offers the rare combination of media publicity, outstanding newsstand performance and a quality of readership that is unparalleled. This double issue breaks Dec. 18 with a cover date of Dec. 25. The closing date is Nov. 27. If you'd like to take advantage of this opportunity, contact your TIME sales representative today. We promise, this is one media decision you'll never question.

328

TRADE
COLOR FULL PAGE OR
SPREAD: SINGLE

329
ART DIRECTOR:
Bob Barrie
WRITER:
Dean Buckhorn
PHOTOGRAPHER:
Brian Snyder
CLIENT:
Time
AGENCY:
Fallon McElligott/
Minneapolis

330
ART DIRECTOR:
Jeremy Postaer
WRITER:
Steve Johnston
PHOTOGRAPHER:
Heimo
CLIENT:
DHL Airways
AGENCY:
Goodby Silverstein &
Partners/San Francisco

331
ART DIRECTOR:
Emil Wilson
WRITER:
Blake Daley
CLIENT:
Haggar Clothing Company
AGENCY:
Goodby Silverstein &
Partners/San Francisco

332
ART DIRECTOR:
Gene Brenek
WRITER:
Peter Berta
PHOTOGRAPHER:
Eric Pearle
ILLUSTRATOR:
Edd Patton
CLIENT:
Farah
AGENCY:
GSD&M Advertising/
Austin

329

330

HAGGAR
Stuff
you can wear.
MORE HAGGAR RETAILERS ARE BUYING SMALL, PRIVATE ISLANDS. (THE LARGE ONES ARE SO OSTENTATIOUS.) Sell more Haggar and you can make more money. It's as simple as that. Our low wholesale prices* (as compared to Dockers®) and excellent rate of sale practically guarantee it. With that in mind, if you think you might be interested in replacing some of your Dockers with Haggar clothes, then give our President, Frank Bracken a call at (214) 956-4356. Hurry, those private islands are going fast.
*Based on a comparison of wholesale price lists. Dockers® is a registered trademark of Levi Strauss and Co. Haggar® and Stuff You Can Wear™ are proprietary trademarks of Haggar Clothing Co. ©1996 Haggar Clothing Co.

331

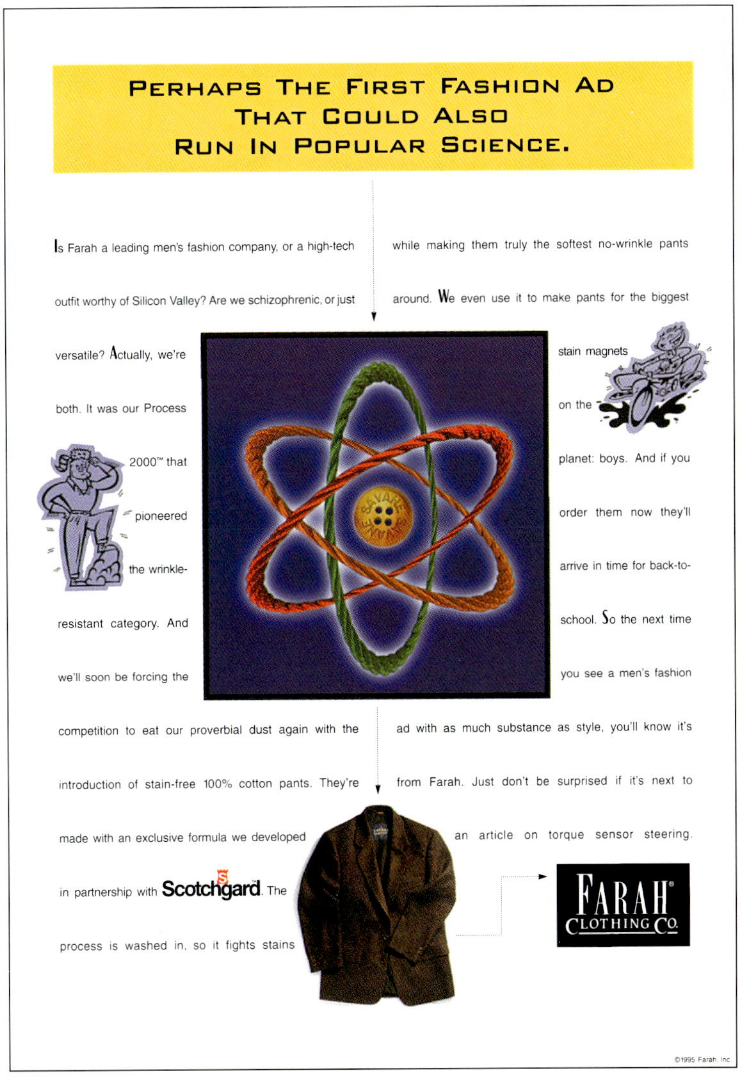
PERHAPS THE FIRST FASHION AD THAT COULD ALSO RUN IN POPULAR SCIENCE.
Is Farah a leading men's fashion company, or a high-tech outfit worthy of Silicon Valley? Are we schizophrenic, or just versatile? Actually, we're both. It was our Process 2000™ that pioneered the wrinkle-resistant category. And we'll soon be forcing the competition to eat our proverbial dust again with the introduction of stain-free 100% cotton pants. They're made with an exclusive formula we developed in partnership with Scotchgard. The process is washed in, so it fights stains while making them truly the softest no-wrinkle pants around. We even use it to make pants for the biggest stain magnets on the planet: boys. And if you order them now they'll arrive in time for back-to-school. So the next time you see a men's fashion ad with as much substance as style, you'll know it's from Farah. Just don't be surprised if it's next to an article on torque sensor steering.
FARAH CLOTHING CO.
©1995 Farah, Inc.

332

TRADE
COLOR FULL PAGE OR SPREAD: SINGLE

333
ART DIRECTOR:
Tom Kane
WRITER:
Josh Miller
PHOTOGRAPHER:
Steve Hellerstein
CLIENT:
Sun Apparel
AGENCY:
Hampel/Stefanides, New York

334
ART DIRECTOR:
Mark Cohen
WRITER:
David Locascio
PHOTOGRAPHER:
Richard Dailey
CLIENT:
No Touch Tire Care
AGENCY:
Kresser Stein Robaire/ Santa Monica

335
ART DIRECTORS:
Rob Rich
Ted Royer
WRITER:
Kara Goodrich
PHOTOGRAPHER:
Kerry Peterson
ILLUSTRATOR:
Brad Palm
CLIENT:
Polaroid
AGENCY:
Leonard/Monahan, Providence

336
ART DIRECTORS:
Rob Rich
Ted Royer
WRITER:
Kara Goodrich
PHOTOGRAPHER:
Kerry Peterson
ILLUSTRATOR:
Brad Palm
CLIENT:
Polaroid
AGENCY:
Leonard/Monahan, Providence

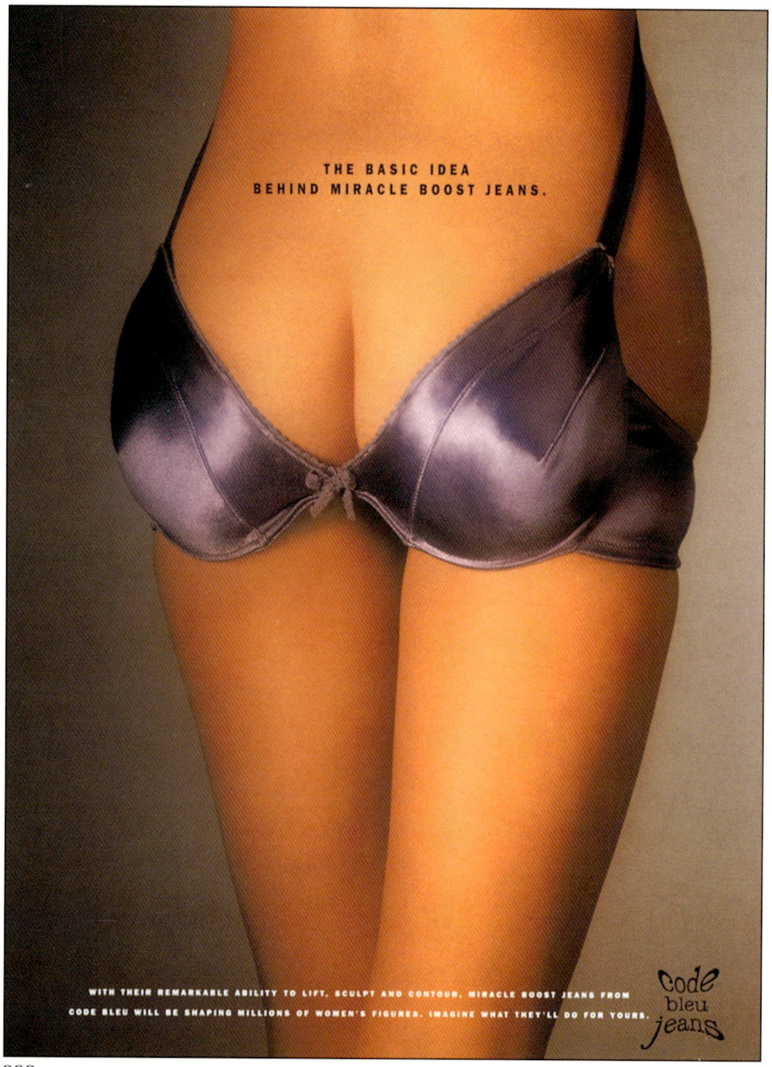

333

334

Criminals always leave a trail. This one leads to a jail cell. With Polaroid instant cameras and film, investigators can easily document evidence and be sure they have it before the crime scene is disturbed. That means building a case quicker. In court, instant pictures also act as excellent witnesses providing irrefutable evidence. Call 1-800-662-8337, ext. 916 to order a Spectra Law Enforcement Kit or a product catalog. Instant evidence.
Polaroid

335

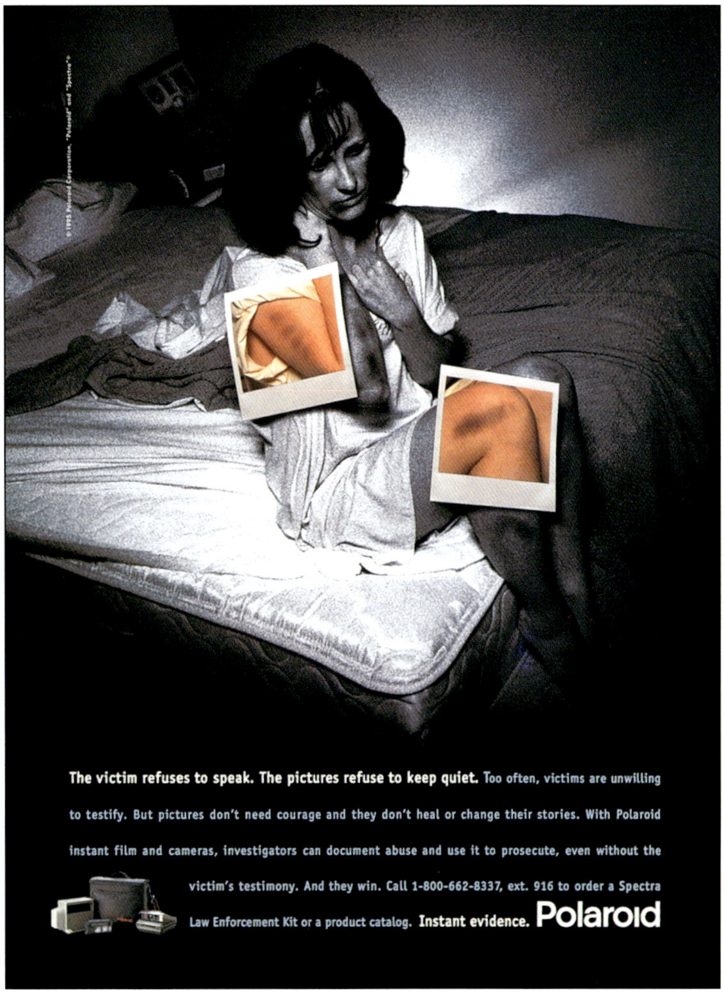
The victim refuses to speak. The pictures refuse to keep quiet. Too often, victims are unwilling to testify. But pictures don't need courage and they don't heal or change their stories. With Polaroid instant film and cameras, investigators can document abuse and use it to prosecute, even without the victim's testimony. And they win. Call 1-800-662-8337, ext. 916 to order a Spectra Law Enforcement Kit or a product catalog. Instant evidence.
Polaroid

336

TRADE
COLOR FULL PAGE OR SPREAD: SINGLE

337
ART DIRECTOR:
Jim Mountjoy
WRITER:
Ed Jones
PHOTOGRAPHER:
Steve Murray
CLIENT:
North Carolina Business and Industry
AGENCY:
Loeffler Ketchum Mountjoy/Charlotte, NC

338
ART DIRECTOR:
Jim Mountjoy
WRITER:
Ed Jones
PHOTOGRAPHER:
George Humphries
CLIENT:
North Carolina Business and Industry
AGENCY:
Loeffler Ketchum Mountjoy/Charlotte, NC

339
ART DIRECTOR:
Jim Mountjoy
WRITER:
Ed Jones
PHOTOGRAPHER:
Harry DeZitter
CLIENT:
North Carolina Film Commission
AGENCY:
Loeffler Ketchum Mountjoy/Charlotte, NC

340
ART DIRECTOR:
Carolyn McGeorge
WRITER:
Raymond McKinney
PHOTOGRAPHER:
Dublin Productions
CLIENT:
Healthtex
AGENCY:
The Martin Agency/Richmond

337

338

YOU WON'T HAVE TO YELL "QUIET ON THE SET!"
Fade up. Killer location. Something's got to be wrong with this picture. Everything's going too easy. Crew's too bleeping nice. Cut to face of location scout. She whispers,"Wait'll you see the other 5 locations." Dailies roll in. Boffo. You're already thinking sequel. You dial (919) 733-9900 to set it up. You show rough cut. Everybody applauds. Even clueless studio executives. (This worries you slightly.) You remember why you got into films in the first place. Life is good. The end.
North Carolina Film Commission

339

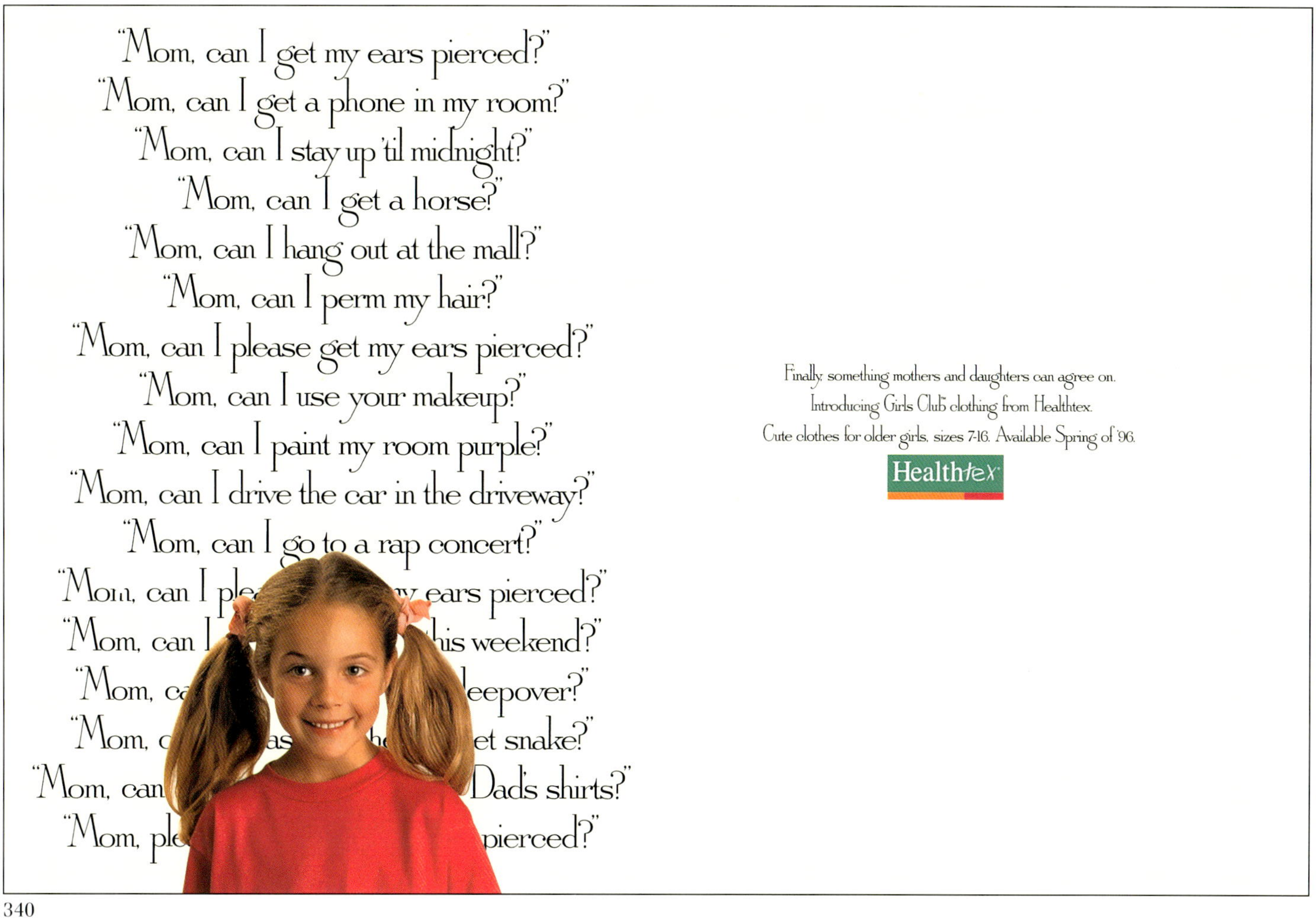

"Mom, can I get my ears pierced?"
"Mom, can I get a phone in my room?"
"Mom, can I stay up 'til midnight?"
"Mom, can I get a horse?"
"Mom, can I hang out at the mall?"
"Mom, can I perm my hair?"
"Mom, can I please get my ears pierced?"
"Mom, can I use your makeup?"
"Mom, can I paint my room purple?"
"Mom, can I drive the car in the driveway?"
"Mom, can I go to a rap concert?"
"Mom, can I ple … ears pierced?"
"Mom, can I … his weekend?"
"Mom, ca … leepover?"
"Mom, c … et snake?"
"Mom, can … Dad's shirts?"
"Mom, ple … pierced?"
Finally, something mothers and daughters can agree on.
Introducing Girls Club™ clothing from Healthtex.
Cute clothes for older girls, sizes 7-16. Available Spring of '96.
Healthtex

340

TRADE
COLOR FULL PAGE OR
SPREAD: SINGLE

341
ART DIRECTOR:
Doug Trapp
WRITER:
Tom Kelly
PHOTOGRAPHER:
Tom Connors
CLIENT:
Flyshacker
AGENCY:
Martin/Williams,
Minneapolis

342
ART DIRECTOR:
Wayne Thompson
WRITER:
Lyle Wedemeyer
PHOTOGRAPHER:
Paul Westbrook
CLIENT:
Fredrickson & Byron
AGENCY:
Martin/Williams,
Minneapolis

343
ART DIRECTOR:
Wayne Thompson
WRITER:
Tom Kelly
PHOTOGRAPHER:
Eric Emmings
CLIENT:
3M
AGENCY:
Martin/Williams,
Minneapolis

344
ART DIRECTOR:
Wayne Thompson
WRITER:
Tom Kelly
PHOTOGRAPHER:
Eric Emmings
CLIENT:
3M
AGENCY:
Martin/Williams,
Minneapolis

341

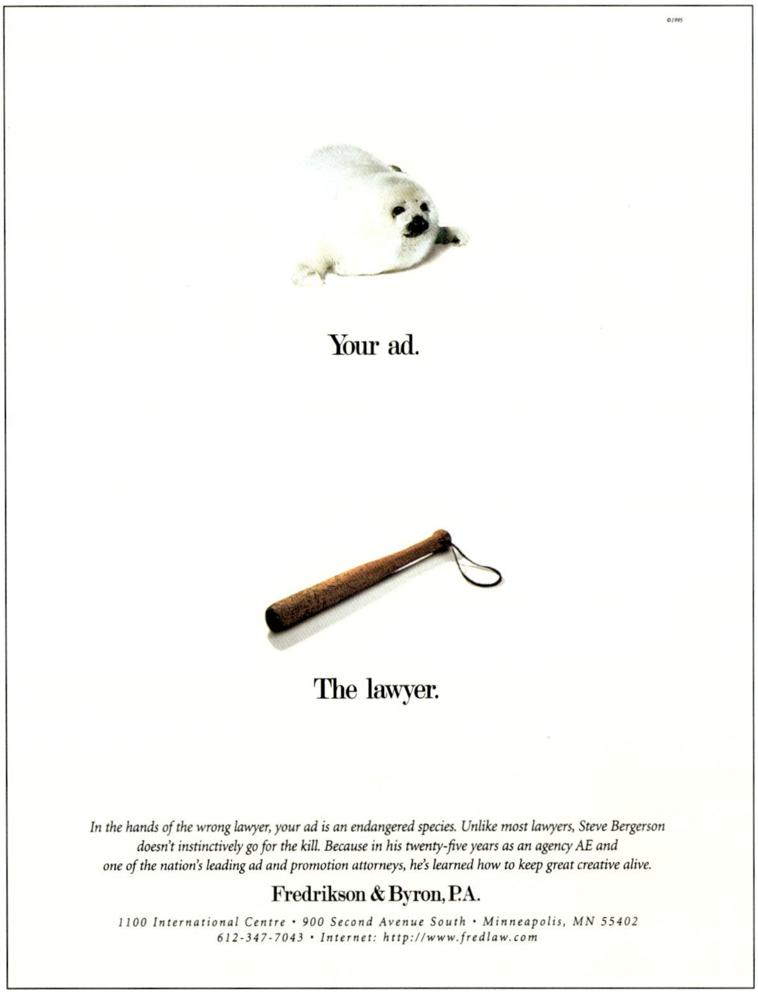

342

©1995, 3M.
Cinta De Pintor Para Cubrir
De Calidad Professional
3M
Translation: "Cha-Ching."
The new trilingual packaging on all 3M DIY products can translate into more profit for you. Why? Because if you're expanding into Mexico or Canada, our products can now go with you. They can also help you tap into the burgeoning Hispanic market here at home. Call your 3M Representative to find out more.
3M Reliability

343

©1995, 3M.
3M
Customer
• Friendly
• Loves to do it himself
• Brand loyal
• No harmful fumes
Contains: 1 repeat customer
It's about the only thing we don't package.
At 3M, we don't package customers. But we do deliver them. Because consumers know and trust the 3M name. A name on a line over 5000 products strong. Find out how a relationship with us can benefit your business. Contact your sales representative today.
3M Reliability

344

TRADE
COLOR FULL PAGE OR
SPREAD: SINGLE

345
ART DIRECTOR:
Scott Stefan
WRITER:
Chris D'Rozario
PHOTOGRAPHER:
Robert Tardio
CLIENT:
Hammermill Papers
AGENCY:
Messner Vetere Berger
McNamee Schmetterer/
Euro RSCG, New York

346
ART DIRECTOR:
Peter Judd
WRITER:
Jason Siciliano
PHOTOGRAPHER:
Pete West
CLIENT:
Wiedman Arabians
AGENCY:
mmm...funkalicious
advertising/San Francisco

347
ART DIRECTOR:
Sharon McDaniel Azula
WRITER:
David Oakley
CLIENT:
Weyerhaeuser
AGENCY:
Price/McNabb,
Charlotte, NC

345

346

To find out how your company can save thousands of dollars a year, turn to the next page.

To find out how your company can save thousands of dollars a year, turn to the previous page.

A company of 50 people that uses both sides of the page on just 20% of its paperwork can save around $2000 a year in paper costs.
A message from North Carolina's leading paper recycler.

Weyerhaeuser

TRADE
COLOR FULL PAGE OR
SPREAD: SINGLE

348
ART DIRECTOR:
Jim Baldwin
WRITER:
Mike Renfro
CLIENT:
Siplast Roofing
AGENCY:
The Richards Group/Dallas

349
ART DIRECTOR:
Kenny Sink
WRITER:
Tommy Thompson
CLIENT:
Fairfax County Economic
Development Authority
AGENCY:
Siddall Matus & Coughter/
Richmond

350
ART DIRECTOR:
Scott MacGregor
WRITER:
Eric Grunbaum
PHOTOGRAPHER:
Vic Huber
CLIENT:
Nissan Motor Corporation
AGENCY:
TBWA Chiat/Day,
Venice, CA

351
ART DIRECTOR:
John Vitro
WRITER:
John Robertson
PHOTOGRAPHER:
Chris Wimpey
CLIENT:
Taylor Guitars
AGENCY:
VitroRobertson/San Diego

348

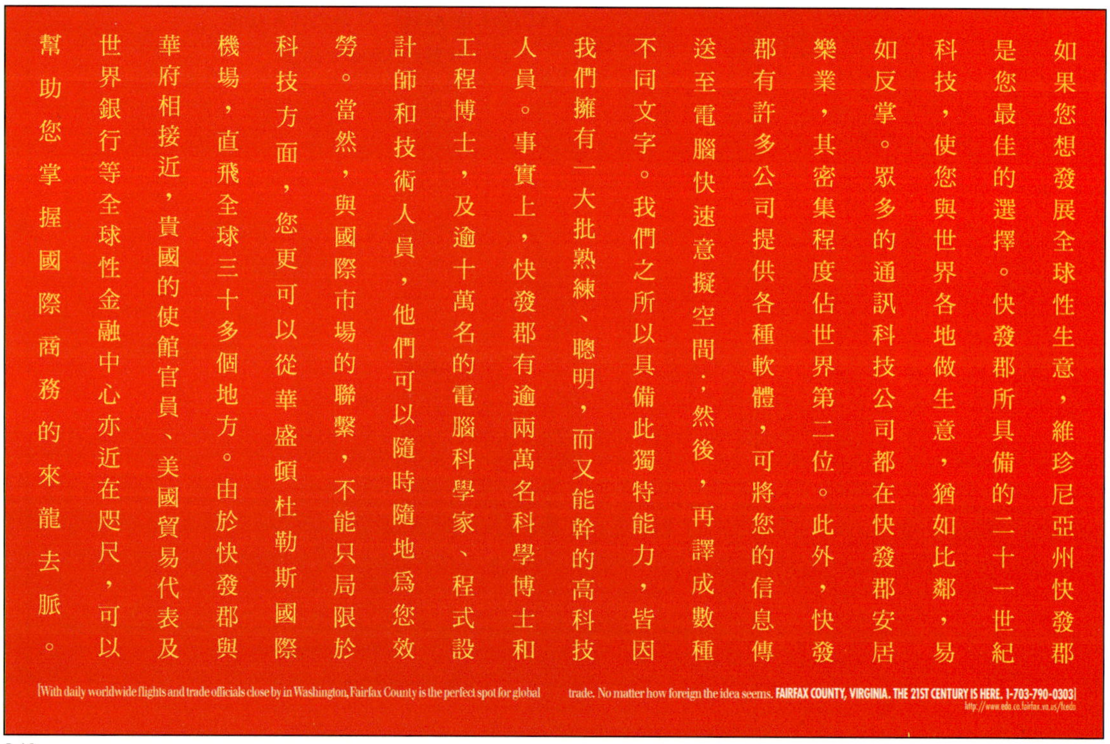

349

IT EATS UP THE ROAD, BUT CHEWS WITH ITS MOUTH CLOSED.
THE NISSAN 240SX SE
On one hand, it's a hard-charging, corner-carving sports coupe with a distinct taste for long stretches of twisty asphalt. On the other hand, it's a luxurious two-door cocoon that pampers its passengers in available 6-speaker CD sound and leather appointments. The Nissan® 240SX® It's like a sterling silver fork at an all-you-can-eat buffet. Call 1-800-NISSAN-3 for details. *It's time to expect more from a car.*®
NISSAN
Nissan Motor Corp. U.S.A. In Canada, call 1-800-387-0122. Buckle up.

THE STORY OF A COUPLE OF GUYS WITH SKINNY NECKS, A BEAT-UP VOLVO, AND A DREAM.
The name of the place actually was the American Dream.
It was a small guitar shop in San Diego, back in 1973, where Bob Taylor got his first job building guitars. Bob was 18.
There was another new employee there named Kurt Listug. Once they started talking to each other–which took about three months–they knew they'd be friends.
For a while, life was as good as it gets. Bob and Kurt spent their entire day around guitars, going home each night covered in sawdust and lacquer.
Then, one day, the owner of the American Dream had decided he'd had enough of running a small guitar shop. His lucky red socks had apparently stopped generating income.
So Bob and Kurt scrambled and gathered up about $10,000 from their parents, and they became the proud but completely baffled owners of their very own American Dream.
And then the fun started.
Within the next few months, they had sunk another several thousand dollars into the business with very little results. There was a lot more to learn than what they had learned in 11th grade wood shop.
This story could have easily ended here and they could have moved on to other things and this ad could have been a lot shorter.
But they kept going.
Bob and Kurt moved in with their families, kept suppliers at arm's length as long as they could, and kept on.
Let Kurt tell it. "We were a bunch of teenage hippies trying to run a business. We knew absolutely nothing. When I called on the first store and found out that guitars have to wholesale for a lot less than the retail price, I was totally depressed."
Wow. Bummer, man.
But when you're young and you love guitars and you've fallen asleep many nights with a guitar book on your chest, you can't very well give up, can you? After all, that would mean getting a real job.
So they dedicated themselves to learning more and figuring it out.
They decided to put the name "Taylor" on their guitars because it sounded good, it sounded American, it was nice and short and besides, "Listug" sounded funny.
And because they were two young kids starting out with no great history or experience behind them, they were able to find new ways to do things.
"We've never been the captive of a long and distinguished tradition," Bob says, which is another way of saying, "We pretty much had no idea what we were doing."
As time went on, they got better. And things got better.
For one thing, people that bought their guitars really, really liked them.
Bob had figured out a way to make a slimmer, "skinnier" neck, and people loved the way it felt and played.
Bob says, "Because I'd never studied guitar making, I was too ignorant to know that a neck should be fat and clunky. I just kept filing until the neck was slim and felt good."
"Also, I was too unskilled to make a dovetail joint, so I *bolted* the neck onto the body."
At the time, this was considered an unspeakable act.
Years later, it would seem like perfect good sense, since the neck could be removed and repaired quickly, without ruining the finish.
One day, several years later, they sold a number of guitars to a single dealer, and they used the extra money to put Kurt on the road in search of more dealers.
Kurt filled up his old Volvo with gas and hit the highway, traveling from California to Maine. When his car broke down during a bad snowstorm in Wisconsin, he had some second thoughts. But, by that time, second thoughts weren't listened to that much.
Second thoughts. Third thoughts. Fourth thoughts. It didn't matter. It was going to work.
Luckily, the dealers liked the guitars a whole lot, and he even sold his samples on the way back, so there was cash for Christmas.
Maybe you were one of those original dealers Kurt visited a long time ago in that Volvo.
Then again, maybe we didn't meet up with you until a few years later.
Today, there are 450 dealers in the U.S. and Canada, and hundreds more around the world.
And we're still the only major guitar company in America where a good old-fashioned guitar builder–a luthier–is in charge, who doesn't always do things the good old-fashioned way.
We hope that people continue to enjoy the guitars we build. We hope you have a good time selling them. And if a customer ever walks in and hasn't heard much about Taylor, we hope you'll tell him or her a little bit of this story.
It's still the American Dream. Today, it just goes by another name.
Taylor Guitars,® 1940 Gillespie Way, El Cajon, CA 92020. (619) 258-1207.
If you'd like to write or call us, we'd love to hear from you.
Taylor

TRADE
COLOR FULL PAGE OR SPREAD: SINGLE

352
ART DIRECTOR:
Randy Gerda
WRITERS:
Bill Swanston
Sims Boulware
CLIENT:
Fila USA
AGENCY:
W.B. Doner & Company/
Baltimore

353
ART DIRECTOR:
John Boiler
WRITER:
Glenn Cole
PHOTOGRAPHER:
Ray Atkeson
CLIENT:
Oregon Film & Video Office
AGENCY:
Wieden & Kennedy/
Portland

TRADE
B/W OR COLOR LESS THAN A PAGE: SINGLE

354
ART DIRECTOR:
David Stephens
WRITER:
David Nobay
CLIENT:
DirectWorks
AGENCY:
Wells Nobay McDowall/
Victoria, Australia

SOME TIME AGO, WE SENT OLYMPIC SKIER MANUELA DI CENTA OUT TO TEST THE LIMITS OF FILA'S NEW OUTDOOR LINE.
IF YOU SEE HER, TELL HER WE'D LIKE OUR CLOTHES BACK.
She's Italian. Fairly tall. About thirty years old. With dark brown hair. Of course the dead give-away is that she's wearing some really cool stuff from Fila's new Outdoor line. A complete line that includes everything for both casual outdoor enthusiasts and hard-core Manuela types. So for information about fabrics, colors, designs, prices, or if you just happen to spot Manuela, call 1-800-787-FILA for the name and number of your Fila Outdoor and Winter Sports Rep.
FILA
OUTDOOR

352

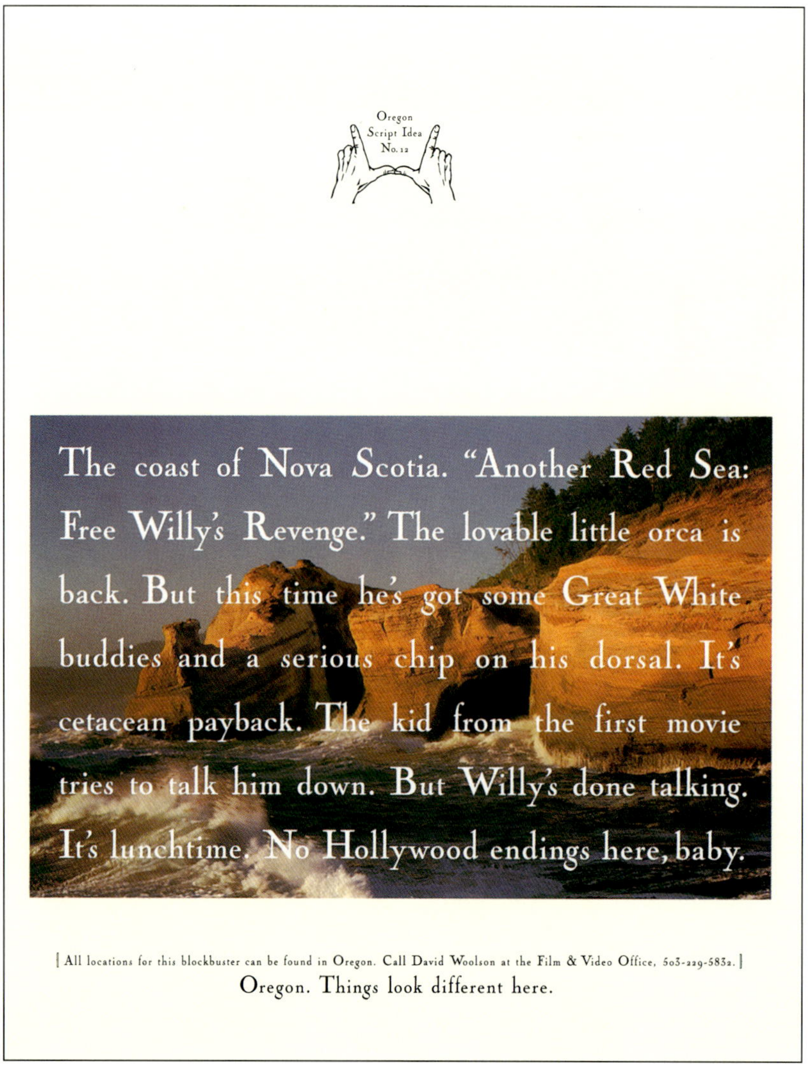
Oregon Script Idea No. 12
The coast of Nova Scotia. "Another Red Sea: Free Willy's Revenge." The lovable little orca is back. But this time he's got some Great White buddies and a serious chip on his dorsal. It's cetacean payback. The kid from the first movie tries to talk him down. But Willy's done talking. It's lunchtime. No Hollywood endings here, baby.
[All locations for this blockbuster can be found in Oregon. Call David Woolson at the Film & Video Office, 503-229-5832.]
Oregon. Things look different here.

353

ASSUMING WE SLOUCHED HOME LAST NIGHT EMPTY HANDED:

It has to be said (without the slightest whiff of bitterness, mind you) that in the great scheme of things, direct marketing awards rank somewhere between Tofu and nasal hair clippers.

Their very existence, it could be argued, is perpetuated by blatant narcissism and the desire by creative types to justify their jet-set lifestyle and passion for all things expensable.

With this in mind, our lack of success at last night's ADMA awards, far from reflecting any lacking on our part, actually represents a brave statement. A lone voice of discontent, if you will. In short, we're proud of our lack of success last night. Damn proud.

So, if you're looking for the kind of agency that's more interested in winning business for their clients than trophies for their shelves, call Julie McDowall or David Nobay on (03) 9349 2700.

DIRECTWORKS

ASSUMING WE DANCED HOME LAST NIGHT LADEN WITH GOLD:

Ever notice how the very people who claim awards are worthless are invariably the same talentless souls incapable of ever winning one?

It's a common enough theme (though given the number of talentless souls masquerading as direct marketing gurus, hardly surprising).

Not us, mind you. We're over the moon about our resounding success at last night's ADMA awards. After all, we view the trophies we lugged home in a wheelbarrow not as shallow gimmicks, but rather irrefutable confirmation of our growing stature among Australia's direct marketing fraternity.

More important still, proof positive that the same work which is winning praise among our peers is winning business for our clients.

If that sounds like the kind of agency you want to award some business to, call Julie McDowall or David Nobay on (03) 9349 2700.

DIRECTWORKS

TRADE
B/W OR COLOR
ANY SIZE: CAMPAIGN

355

ART DIRECTOR:
Rob Palmer
WRITER:
Max Godsil
ILLUSTRATOR:
Howard Lim
CLIENT:
Northrop Grumman Corporation
AGENCY:
BBDO/Los Angeles

Surveillance
Precision
* Stealth
Superlative range combined with absolute stealth enables the B-2 Spirit to fly anywhere on earth on a moment's notice, penetrate even the most advanced air defenses and strike hardened targets with utmost precision, all of which simultaneously ensures a swift, successful strike, and a rather uneventful night's journey for its crew of two.
NORTHROP GRUMMAN
*

Surveillance
* Precision
Stealth
The "brilliant" antiarmor submunition (BAT) possesses advanced acoustic and infrared sensors enabling it to seek, locate and destroy targets from great distances with utmost stealth and precision, meaning not only that fewer of our people ever need be placed in harm's way, but that everyone will be going home much sooner than expected.
NORTHROP GRUMMAN
*

* Surveillance
Precision
Stealth
The E-8A (JSTARS) aircraft has a search area of 35,000 square miles. (An area somewhat larger than South Carolina.) From a distance of 150 miles, it can detect, track and classify fixed and moving targets as small as a jeep. Data can then be relayed to command posts and attack aircraft in real time. Such as: Objectives unequivocally achieved. Go home.
NORTHROP GRUMMAN
*

TRADE
B/W OR COLOR
ANY SIZE: CAMPAIGN

356

ART DIRECTORS:
Tim Tone
Kelly Gothier

WRITERS:
Randy T. Gosda
John Lutter

PHOTOGRAPHER:
Joe Michl

CLIENT:
Andersen Windows

AGENCY:
Campbell Mithun Esty/
Minneapolis

NO MATTER
WHO LIVES THERE,
IT'LL ALWAYS
BE YOUR HOUSE.

You don't live in it. You live with it. Every day. Referrals. Reputation. Callbacks, or worse. Houses don't forget. So remember Andersen® Windows. Whether you build a hundred, a dozen or one, one thing's sure. If you built it, it's yours.

WHAT GOOD
IS A WARRANTY IF
IT DOESN'T COVER
YOUR BUTT?

Let it rain. Let it snow. Let the wind blow like hello 20-year window glass warranty. Good-bye worry. Pack up the tools. Look back once. Gotta move on. No matter who lives there, it'll always be your house.

HOMES THAT MAKE
A STATEMENT NEED AN
EXCLAMATION POINT.

With the Andersen Art Glass™ Collection, one look says it all.
Beauty. Quality. Variety. In one easy installation, nothing builds a better reputation.
No matter who lives there, it'll always be your house.

Andersen
AW
Windows·Patio Doors

WON'T FIND A
WINDOW THAT OPENS
MORE DOORS.

Andersen® Tilt-Wash. The window people want. People look for. For good reasons, too.
Easy to open. Easy to clean. And closes weathertight. Andersen® It's an easy sell, all right.
No matter who lives there, it'll always be your house.

Andersen
AW
Windows·Patio Doors

TRADE
B/W OR COLOR
ANY SIZE: CAMPAIGN

357
ART DIRECTOR:
Jim Mountjoy
WRITER:
Steve Lasch
PHOTOGRAPHER:
Jim Arndt
CLIENT:
Shakespeare
AGENCY:
Loeffler Ketchum
Mountjoy/Charlotte, NC

358
ART DIRECTOR:
Emil Wilson
WRITER:
Blake Daley
CLIENT:
Haggar Clothing Company
AGENCY:
Goodby Silverstein &
Partners/San Francisco

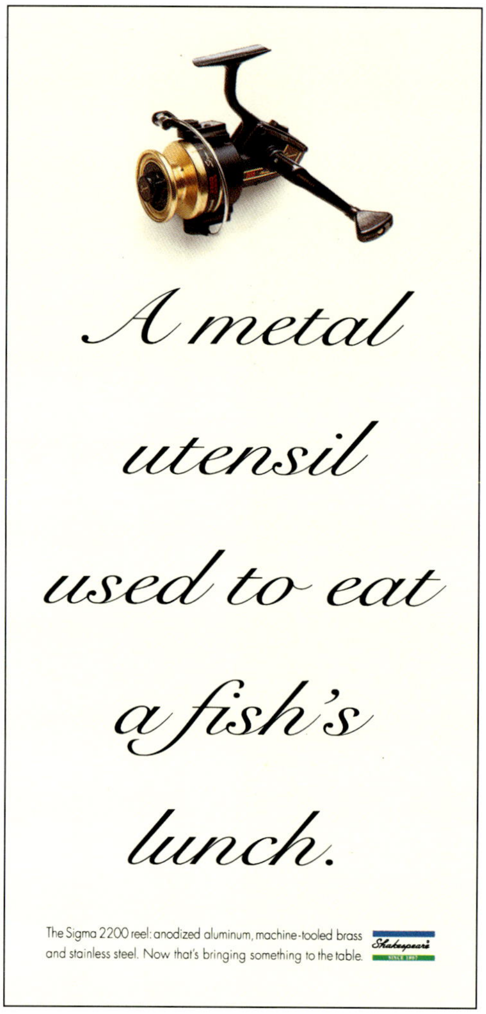
A metal utensil used to eat a fish's lunch.
The Sigma 2200 reel: anodized aluminum, machine-tooled brass and stainless steel. Now that's bringing something to the table.
Shakespeare

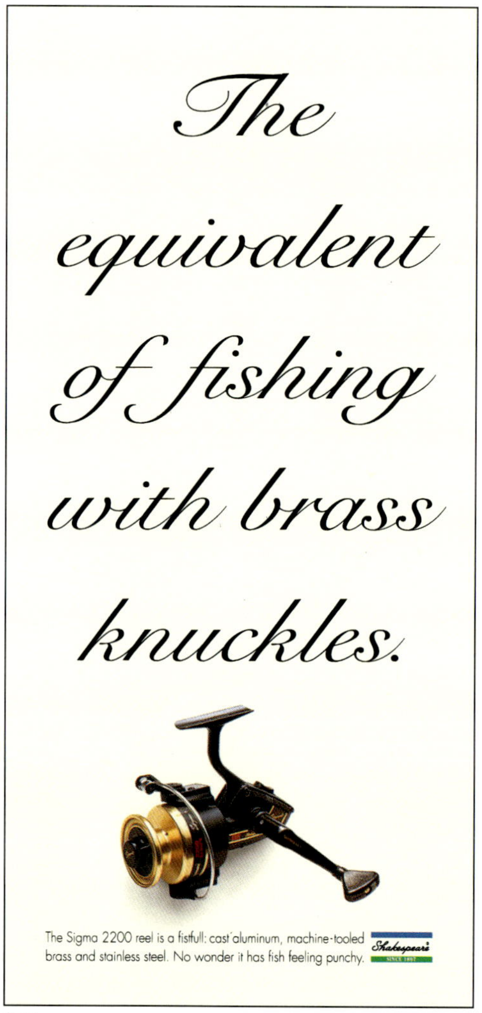
The equivalent of fishing with brass knuckles.
The Sigma 2200 reel is a fistfull: cast aluminum, machine-tooled brass and stainless steel. No wonder it has fish feeling punchy.
Shakespeare

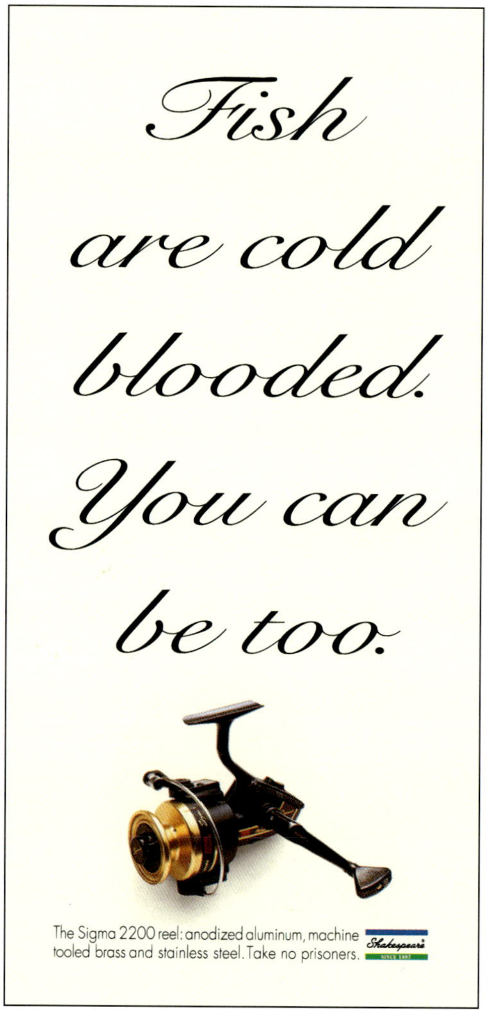
Fish are cold blooded. You can be too.
The Sigma 2200 reel: anodized aluminum, machine tooled brass and stainless steel. Take no prisoners.
Shakespeare

HAGGAR
Stuff
you can wear.
MORE HAGGAR RETAILERS ARE BUYING SMALL, PRIVATE ISLANDS. (THE LARGE ONES ARE SO OSTENTATIOUS.) Sell more Haggar and you can make more money. It's as simple as that. Our low wholesale prices* (as compared to Dockers*) and excellent rate of sale practically guarantee it. With that in mind, if you think you might be interested in replacing some of your Dockers with Haggar clothes, then give our President, Frank Bracken a call at (214) 956-4356. Hurry, those private islands are going fast.
Based on a comparison of wholesale price lists. Dockers is a registered trademark of Levi Strauss and Co. Haggar* and Stuff You Can Wear* are proprietary trademarks of Haggar Clothing Co. ©1996 Haggar Clothing Co.

TO CIRCUMVENT EXORBITANT LUXURY TAXES, MOST HAGGAR RETAILERS REGISTER THEIR YACHTS IN BERMUDA. If you're really interested in making money, simply replace some of the Dockers* on your sales floor with Haggar clothes. Curious? Give our President, Frank Bracken a call at (214) 956-4356. He'll personally explain how Haggar's low wholesale prices* and excellent rate of sale could put you in your own yacht in no time.
HAGGAR
Stuff
you can wear.
Based on a comparison of wholesale price lists. Dockers is a registered trademark of Levi Strauss and Co. Haggar* and Stuff You Can Wear* are proprietary trademarks of Haggar Clothing Co. © 1995 Haggar Clothing Co.

HAGGAR
Stuff
you can wear.
A HELPFUL HINT: WHEN VISITING THE HOME OF A HAGGAR RETAILER, ALWAYS REFER TO IT AS AN "ESTATE," RATHER THAN A "MANSION." Sell Haggar clothes and you're bound to make more money. Just take a look at our low wholesale prices* and excellent rate of sale, and you'll begin to see why. In fact, with numbers this good, you may decide to replace some of your Dockers* with Haggar clothes. Give our president, Frank Bracken a call at (214) 956-4356. He'll have details on making the switch, as well as some excellent real estate tips.

TRADE
B/W OR COLOR
ANY SIZE: CAMPAIGN

359

ART DIRECTOR:
Dave Cook

WRITER:
Mikal Reich

TYPOGRAPHER:
Graham Clifford

CLIENT:
DX

AGENCY:
Mad Dogs & Englishmen/
New York

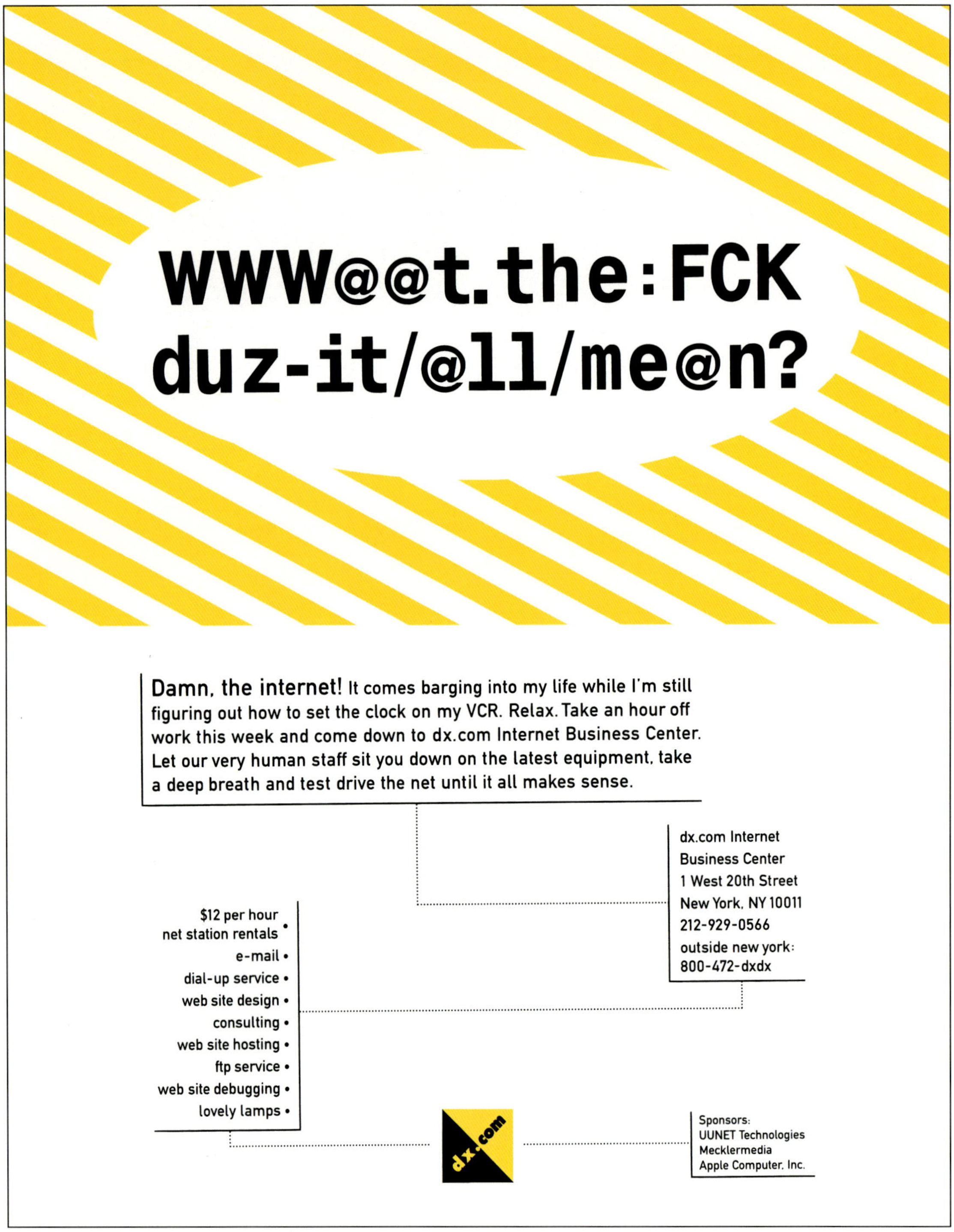
WWW@@t.the:FCK
duz-it/@ll/me@n?
Damn, the internet! It comes barging into my life while I'm still figuring out how to set the clock on my VCR. Relax. Take an hour off work this week and come down to dx.com Internet Business Center. Let our very human staff sit you down on the latest equipment, take a deep breath and test drive the net until it all makes sense.
dx.com Internet
Business Center
1 West 20th Street
New York, NY 10011
212-929-0566
outside new york:
800-472-dxdx
$12 per hour net station rentals •
e-mail •
dial-up service •
web site design •
consulting •
web site hosting •
ftp service •
web site debugging •
lovely lamps •
dx.com
Sponsors:
UUNET Technologies
Mecklermedia
Apple Computer, Inc.

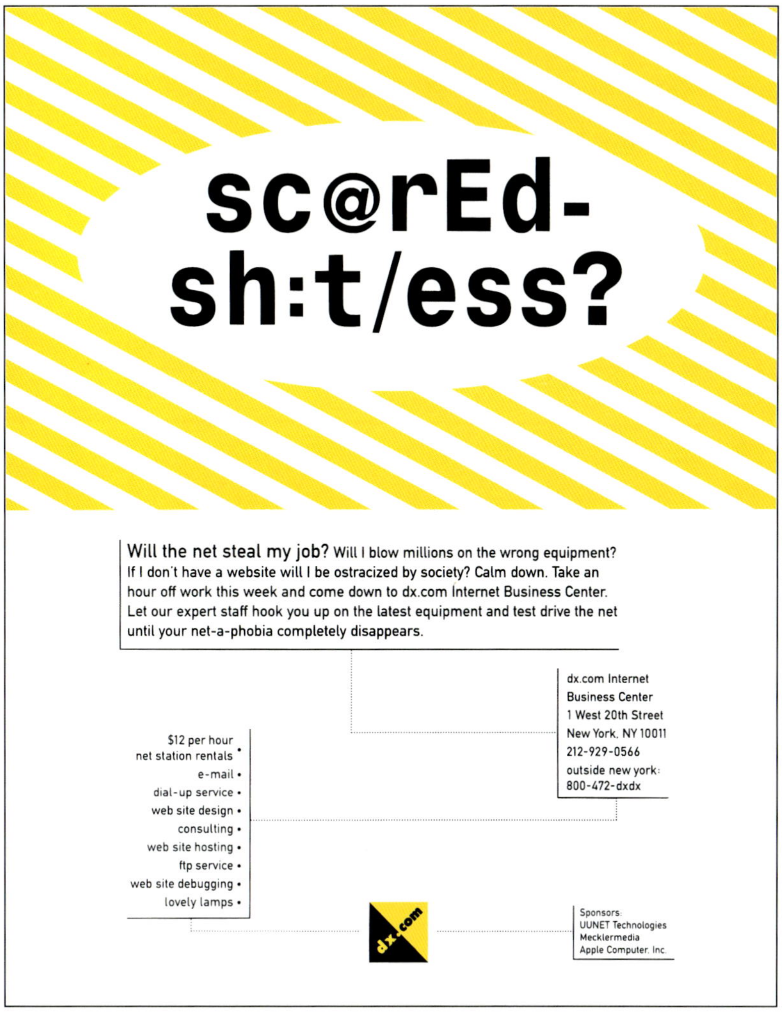
sc@rEd-
sh:t/ess?
Will the net steal my job? Will I blow millions on the wrong equipment? If I don't have a website will I be ostracized by society? Calm down. Take an hour off work this week and come down to dx.com Internet Business Center. Let our expert staff hook you up on the latest equipment and test drive the net until your net-a-phobia completely disappears.
dx.com Internet
Business Center
1 West 20th Street
New York, NY 10011
212-929-0566
outside new york:
800-472-dxdx
$12 per hour
net station rentals •
e-mail •
dial-up service •
web site design •
consulting •
web site hosting •
ftp service •
web site debugging •
lovely lamps •
dx.com
Sponsors:
UUNET Technologies
Mecklermedia
Apple Computer, Inc.

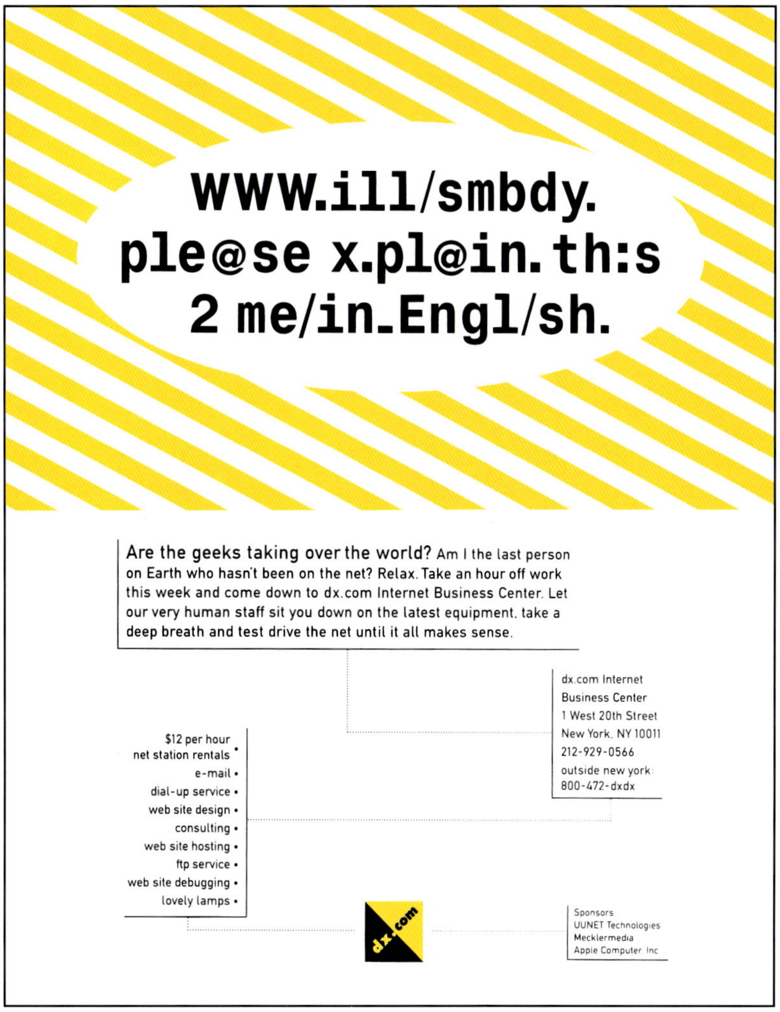
www.ill/smbdy.
ple@se x.pl@in.th:s
2 me/in.Engl/sh.
Are the geeks taking over the world? Am I the last person on Earth who hasn't been on the net? Relax. Take an hour off work this week and come down to dx.com Internet Business Center. Let our very human staff sit you down on the latest equipment, take a deep breath and test drive the net until it all makes sense.
dx.com Internet
Business Center
1 West 20th Street
New York, NY 10011
212-929-0566
outside new york:
800-472-dxdx
$12 per hour
net station rentals •
e-mail •
dial-up service •
web site design •
consulting •
web site hosting •
ftp service •
web site debugging •
lovely lamps •
dx.com
Sponsors
UUNET Technologies
Mecklermedia
Apple Computer, Inc.

TRADE
B/W OR COLOR
ANY SIZE: CAMPAIGN

360

ART DIRECTOR:
Kenny Sink

WRITER:
Tommy Thompson

CLIENT:
Fairfax County Economic Development Authority

AGENCY:
Siddall Matus & Coughter/ Richmond

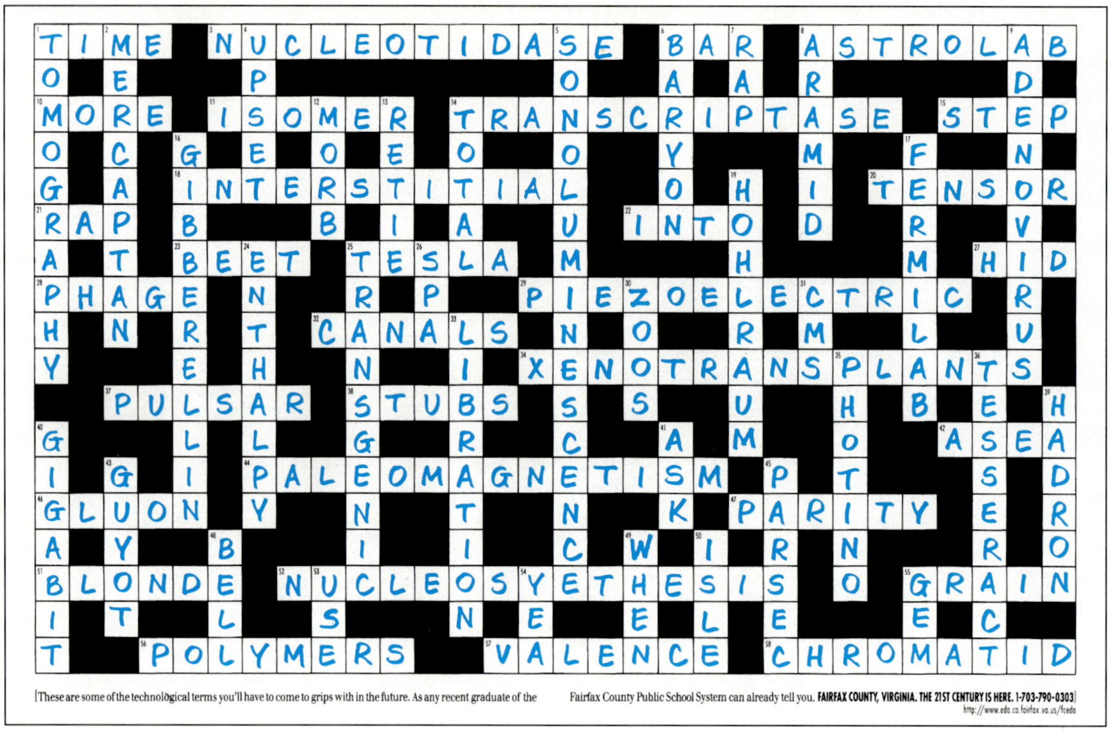

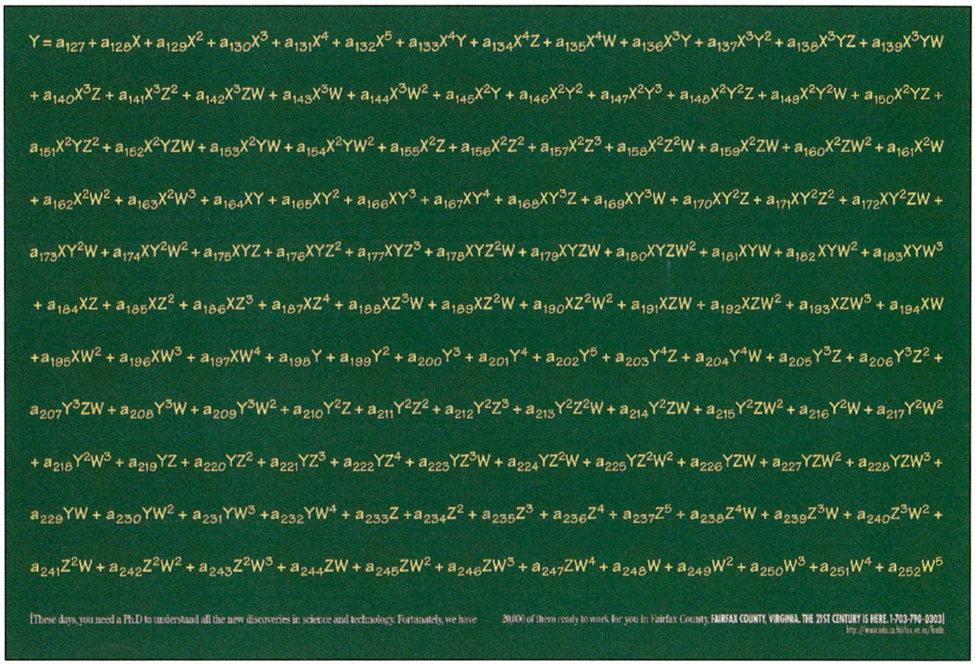
$Y = a_{127} + a_{128}X + a_{129}X^2 + a_{130}X^3 + a_{131}X^4 + a_{132}X^5 + a_{133}X^4Y + a_{134}X^4Z + a_{135}X^4W + a_{136}X^3Y + a_{137}X^3Y^2 + a_{138}X^3YZ + a_{139}X^3YW$
$+ a_{140}X^3Z + a_{141}X^3Z^2 + a_{142}X^3ZW + a_{143}X^3W + a_{144}X^3W^2 + a_{145}X^2Y + a_{146}X^2Y^2 + a_{147}X^2Y^3 + a_{148}X^2Y^2Z + a_{149}X^2Y^2W + a_{150}X^2YZ +$
$a_{151}X^2YZ^2 + a_{152}X^2YZW + a_{153}X^2YW + a_{154}X^2YW^2 + a_{155}X^2Z + a_{156}X^2Z^2 + a_{157}X^2Z^3 + a_{158}X^2Z^2W + a_{159}X^2ZW + a_{160}X^2ZW^2 + a_{161}X^2W$
$+ a_{162}X^2W^2 + a_{163}X^2W^3 + a_{164}XY + a_{165}XY^2 + a_{166}XY^3 + a_{167}XY^4 + a_{168}XY^3Z + a_{169}XY^3W + a_{170}XY^2Z + a_{171}XY^2Z^2 + a_{172}XY^2ZW +$
$a_{173}XY^2W + a_{174}XY^2W^2 + a_{175}XYZ + a_{176}XYZ^2 + a_{177}XYZ^3 + a_{178}XYZ^2W + a_{179}XYZW + a_{180}XYZW^2 + a_{181}XYW + a_{182}XYW^2 + a_{183}XYW^3$
$+ a_{184}XZ + a_{185}XZ^2 + a_{186}XZ^3 + a_{187}XZ^4 + a_{188}XZ^3W + a_{189}XZ^2W + a_{190}XZ^2W^2 + a_{191}XZW + a_{192}XZW^2 + a_{193}XZW^3 + a_{194}XW$
$+ a_{195}XW^2 + a_{196}XW^3 + a_{197}XW^4 + a_{198}Y + a_{199}Y^2 + a_{200}Y^3 + a_{201}Y^4 + a_{202}Y^5 + a_{203}Y^4Z + a_{204}Y^4W + a_{205}Y^3Z + a_{206}Y^3Z^2 +$
$a_{207}Y^3ZW + a_{208}Y^3W + a_{209}Y^3W^2 + a_{210}Y^2Z + a_{211}Y^2Z^2 + a_{212}Y^2Z^3 + a_{213}Y^2Z^2W + a_{214}Y^2ZW + a_{215}Y^2ZW^2 + a_{216}Y^2W + a_{217}Y^2W^2$
$+ a_{218}Y^2W^3 + a_{219}YZ + a_{220}YZ^2 + a_{221}YZ^3 + a_{222}YZ^4 + a_{223}YZ^3W + a_{224}YZ^2W + a_{225}YZ^2W^2 + a_{226}YZW + a_{227}YZW^2 + a_{228}YZW^3 +$
$a_{229}YW + a_{230}YW^2 + a_{231}YW^3 + a_{232}YW^4 + a_{233}Z + a_{234}Z^2 + a_{235}Z^3 + a_{236}Z^4 + a_{237}Z^5 + a_{238}Z^4W + a_{239}Z^3W + a_{240}Z^3W^2 +$
$a_{241}Z^2W + a_{242}Z^2W^2 + a_{243}Z^2W^3 + a_{244}ZW + a_{245}ZW^2 + a_{246}ZW^3 + a_{247}ZW^4 + a_{248}W + a_{249}W^2 + a_{250}W^3 + a_{251}W^4 + a_{252}W^5$
[These days, you need a Ph.D to understand all the new discoveries in science and technology. Fortunately, we have 20,000 of them ready to work for you in Fairfax County. FAIRFAX COUNTY, VIRGINIA. THE 21ST CENTURY IS HERE. 1-703-790-0303]

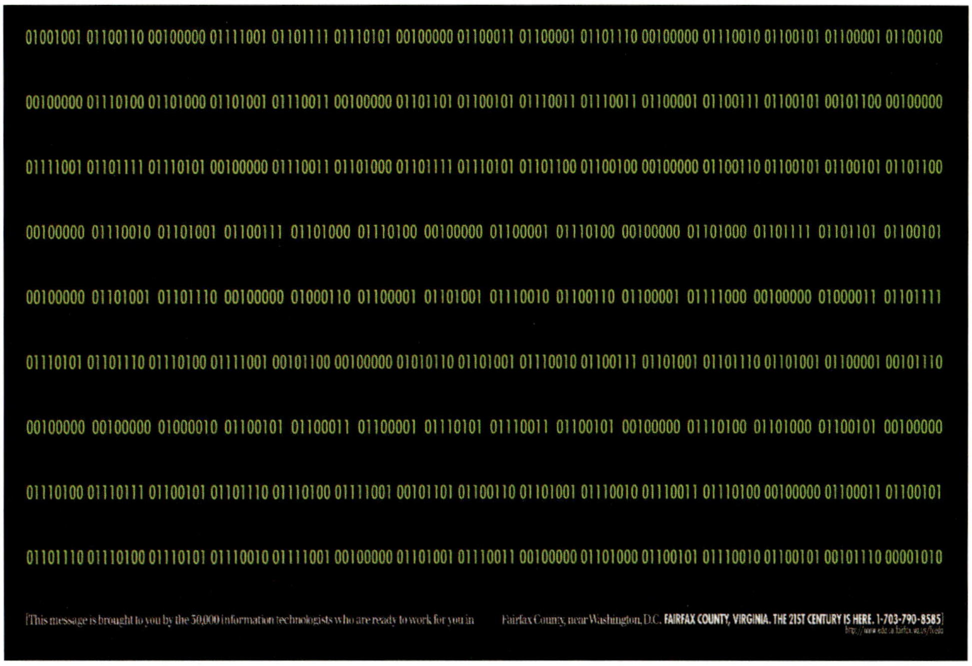
01001001 01100110 00100000 01111001 01101111 01110101 00100000 01100011 01100001 01101110 00100000 01110010 01100101 01100001 01100100
00100000 01110100 01101000 01101001 01110011 00100000 01101101 01100101 01110011 01110011 01100001 01100111 01100101 00101100 00100000
01111001 01101111 01110101 00100000 01110011 01101000 01101111 01110101 01101100 01100100 00100000 01100110 01100101 01100101 01101100
00100000 01110010 01101001 01100111 01101000 01110100 00100000 01100001 01110100 00100000 01101000 01101111 01101101 01100101
00100000 01101001 01101110 00100000 01000110 01100001 01101001 01110010 01100110 01100001 01111000 00100000 01000011 01101111
01110101 01101110 01110100 01111001 00101100 00100000 01010110 01101001 01110010 01100111 01101001 01101110 01101001 01100001 00101110
00100000 00100000 01000010 01100101 01100011 01100001 01110101 01110011 01100101 00100000 01110100 01101000 01100101 00100000
01110100 01110111 01100101 01101110 01110100 01111001 00101101 01100110 01101001 01110010 01110011 01110100 00100000 01100011 01100101
01101110 01110100 01110101 01110010 01111001 00100000 01101001 01110011 00100000 01101000 01100101 01110010 01100101 00101110 00001010
[This message is brought to you by the 50,000 information technologists who are ready to work for you in Fairfax County, near Washington, D.C. FAIRFAX COUNTY, VIRGINIA. THE 21ST CENTURY IS HERE. 1-703-790-8585]

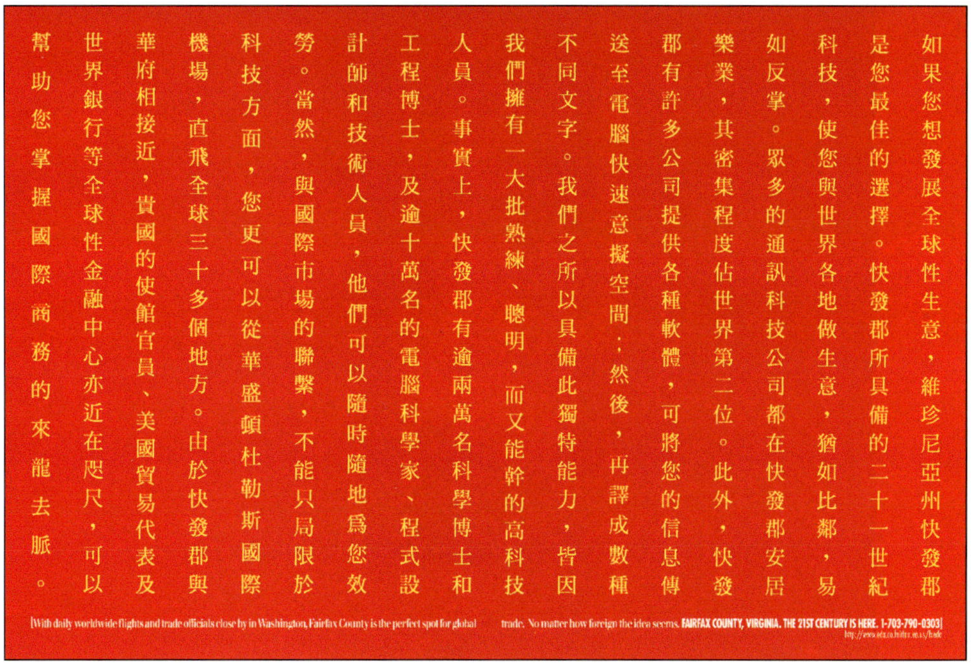
如果您想發展全球性生意，維珍尼亞州快發郡
是您最佳的選擇。快發郡所具備的二十一世紀
科技，使您與世界各地做生意，猶如比鄰，易
如反掌。眾多的通訊科技公司都在快發郡安居
樂業，其密集程度佔世界第二位。此外，快發
郡有許多公司提供各種軟體，可將您的信息傳
送至電腦快速意擬空間；然後，再譯成數種
不同文字。我們之所以具備此獨特能力，皆因
我們擁有一大批熟練、聰明，而又能幹的高科技
人員。事實上，快發郡有逾兩萬名科學博士和
工程博士，及逾十萬名的電腦科學家、程式設
計師和技術人員，他們可以隨時隨地爲您效
勞。當然，與國際市場的聯繫，不能只局限於
科技方面，您更可以從華盛頓杜勒斯國際
機場，直飛全球三十多個地方。由於快發郡與
華府相接近，貴國的使館官員、美國貿易代表及
世界銀行等全球性金融中心亦近在咫尺，可以
幫助您掌握國際商務的來龍去脈。
[With daily worldwide flights and trade officials close by in Washington, Fairfax County is the perfect spot for global trade. No matter how foreign the idea seems. FAIRFAX COUNTY, VIRGINIA. THE 21ST CENTURY IS HERE. 1-703-790-0303]

TRADE
B/W OR COLOR
ANY SIZE: CAMPAIGN

361

ART DIRECTOR:
Larry Frey

WRITER:
Scott Wild

PHOTOGRAPHERS:
Larry Frey
Jim Appleton

CLIENT:
ESPN

AGENCY:
Wieden & Kennedy/
Portland

COLLATERAL
BROCHURES OTHER
THAN BY MAIL

362

ART DIRECTOR:
Terry Schneider

WRITER:
Simeon Roane

PHOTOGRAPHER:
Pete Stone

CLIENT:
Fight Team USA

AGENCY:
Borders Perrin &
Norrander/Portland

OUR CLOTHES ARE
MADE
IN A
SWEAT
SHOP.
THE
ANIMAL
WE
TEST
OUR
PRODUCTS
ON.
FIGHT TEAM
USA
FIGHT TEAM
USA

COLLATERAL
BROCHURES OTHER
THAN BY MAIL

363

ART DIRECTORS:
Georgina Lee
Frank Kofsuske

WRITER:
Eric Osterhaus

PHOTOGRAPHERS:
Jim Erickson
Daniel Proctor

CLIENT:
Haggar Clothing Company

AGENCY:
Goodby Silverstein & Partners/San Francisco

364

ART DIRECTOR:
Georgina Lee

WRITER:
Eric Osterhaus

ILLUSTRATOR:
Paul Cox

CLIENT:
Haggar Clothing Company

AGENCY:
Goodby Silverstein & Partners/San Francisco

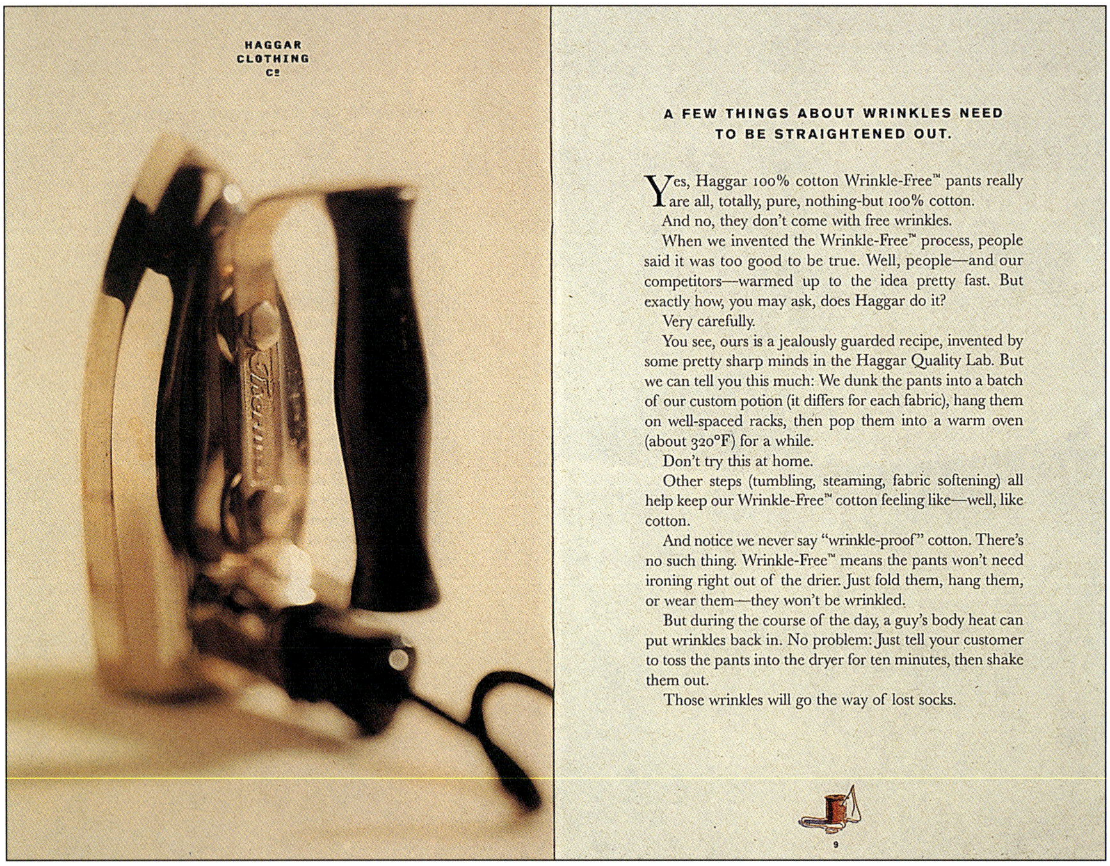

HAGGAR CLOTHING Cº
A FEW THINGS ABOUT WRINKLES NEED TO BE STRAIGHTENED OUT.
Yes, Haggar 100% cotton Wrinkle-Free™ pants really are all, totally, pure, nothing-but 100% cotton.
And no, they don't come with free wrinkles.
When we invented the Wrinkle-Free™ process, people said it was too good to be true. Well, people—and our competitors—warmed up to the idea pretty fast. But exactly how, you may ask, does Haggar do it?
Very carefully.
You see, ours is a jealously guarded recipe, invented by some pretty sharp minds in the Haggar Quality Lab. But we can tell you this much: We dunk the pants into a batch of our custom potion (it differs for each fabric), hang them on well-spaced racks, then pop them into a warm oven (about 320°F) for a while.
Don't try this at home.
Other steps (tumbling, steaming, fabric softening) all help keep our Wrinkle-Free™ cotton feeling like—well, like cotton.
And notice we never say "wrinkle-proof" cotton. There's no such thing. Wrinkle-Free™ means the pants won't need ironing right out of the drier. Just fold them, hang them, or wear them—they won't be wrinkled.
But during the course of the day, a guy's body heat can put wrinkles back in. No problem: Just tell your customer to toss the pants into the dryer for ten minutes, then shake them out.
Those wrinkles will go the way of lost socks.
9

363

HAGGAR
CLOTHING
Co

Turning a Hello into a Good Buy.

Your daily sales reports are out-of-date daily.

2

HAGGAR
CLOTHING
Co

Okay, let's assume that you're already a fairly good salesperson. And let's also assume you have more than a passing interest in becoming an even better one.

What's going to help you get there?

Forget about those daily sales reports. They might have some recordkeeping value to the folks who run your store, but they don't really tell you anything useful that'll help you sell more.

No, what you need is feedback that shows you—at any given moment—exactly what you need to focus on in order to sell more.

Which leads us to "company secrets" we'd like to share with you.

3

365
ART DIRECTORS:
Tom Saputo
Peter di Grazia
WRITER:
Linda Bradford
PHOTOGRAPHERS:
Rick Rusing
Jeff Nadler
Jock MacDonald
ILLUSTRATOR:
Joe Saputo
CLIENT:
Saturn Corporation
AGENCY:
Hal Riney & Partners/
San Francisco

366
ART DIRECTORS:
Tom Saputo
Steve Stone
WRITER:
Linda Bradford
PHOTOGRAPHER:
Holly Stewart
ILLUSTRATORS:
Kent Leach
Tom Saputo
CLIENT:
Saturn Corporation
AGENCY:
Hal Riney & Partners/
San Francisco

367
ART DIRECTOR:
Joe Ivey
WRITER:
David Parson
PHOTOGRAPHER:
Buck Holzemer
CLIENT:
Ciba-Geigy
AGENCY:
Howard Merrell &
Partners/Raleigh, NC

368
ART DIRECTORS:
Kel Andersen
Bill Bonomo
Dave Martin
WRITERS:
Todd Heyman
Tony Macchia
Nancy Vecilla
PHOTOGRAPHER:
Chip Forelli
CLIENT:
American Express
AGENCY:
Ogilvy & Mather Direct/
New York

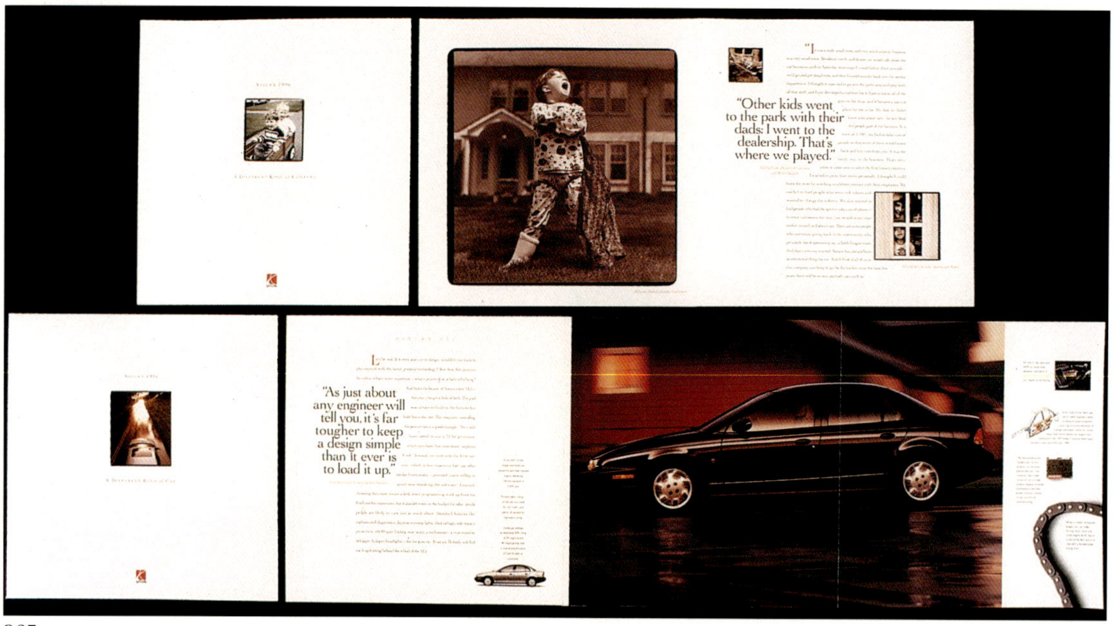

365

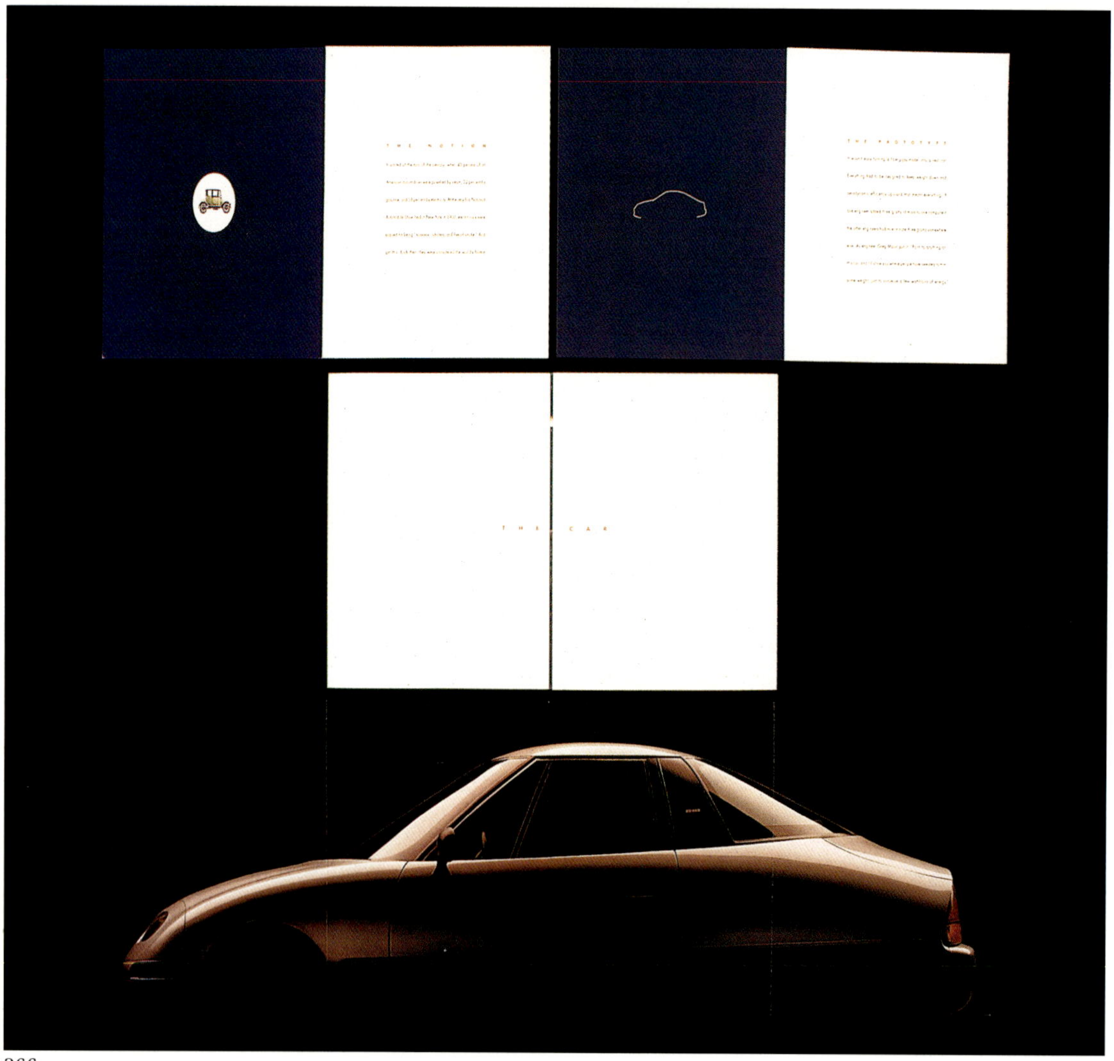
366

This Is A Product Demonstration.
Introducing The World's First
Fungicide That's Invisible To The Naked Eye:
New Clear Liquid Banner Maxx.
We'd like to make one thing perfectly clear: next to new Banner® MAXX,® no other broad spectrum fungicide even compares. It's the first transparent fungicide. And the benefits of this revolutionary formula are as clear as the product itself.
Simply put, Banner MAXX is the best tank-mix partner. It looks like water, pours like water, and has the same properties as water. It won't clog filters and has no odor. And unlike competitors who offer only wettable powders or granules, Banner MAXX will never settle out.
Even more impressive is the fact that Banner MAXX controls 18 turf diseases, including dollar spot and summer patch. It contains no petroleum solvents, so there's no potential for phytotoxicity. And it's available in closed system containers, minimizing worker and environmental exposure.
For more details, call 1-800-395-TURF. Because no matter how you look at it, Banner MAXX isn't like any fungicide on earth. But you can see that for yourself.

367

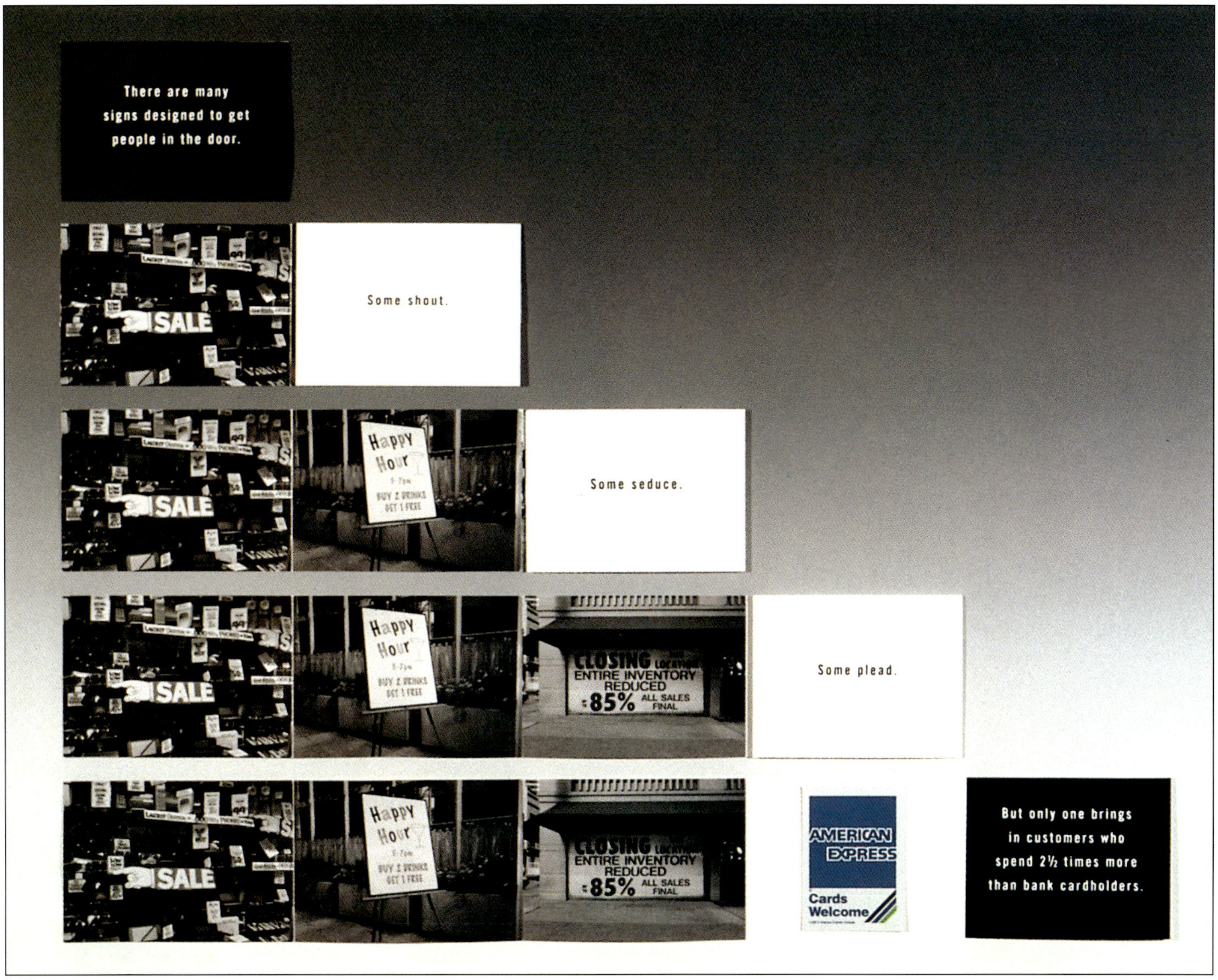
There are many
signs designed to get
people in the door.
SALE
Some shout.
Happy
Hour
BUY 2 DRINKS
GET 1 FREE
Some seduce.
CLOSING
ENTIRE INVENTORY
REDUCED
85%
ALL SALES
FINAL
Some plead.
AMERICAN
EXPRESS
Cards
Welcome
But only one brings
in customers who
spend 2½ times more
than bank cardholders.

368

COLLATERAL
BROCHURES OTHER
THAN BY MAIL

369
ART DIRECTORS:
Kelly O'Keefe
Jeff Schaich
WRITER:
Tracy Lynn Tierney
PHOTOGRAPHERS:
Jon Hood
Sonny Bowyer
CLIENT:
VCU Ad Center
AGENCY:
O'Keefe Marketing/
Richmond

COLLATERAL
SALES KITS

370
ART DIRECTORS:
David Haifleigh
Janelle Aune
Monique Coco McCall
WRITER:
David Haifleigh
PHOTOGRAPHERS:
Priscilla Montoya
Jim Erickson
CLIENT:
Haggar Clothing Company
AGENCY:
The Hibbert Group/Denver

371
ART DIRECTOR:
Rich Kohnke
WRITER:
Steve Koeneke
PHOTOGRAPHER:
Dave Giloy
ILLUSTRATOR:
Cathy Holly
CLIENT:
Sherpa Snowshoes
AGENCY:
Kohnke Koeneke/
Milwaukee

372
ART DIRECTOR:
Alyssa D'Arienzo
WRITER:
Kara Goodrich
PHOTOGRAPHER:
Jim Erickson
ILLUSTRATOR:
Robert Tretrainier
CLIENT:
Canstar
AGENCY:
Leonard/Monahan,
Providence

369

370

The company that started it all is starting it all over again.
We kept the name. Everything else was subject to change.
We're pleased to announce that you're no longer bound by Sherpa bindings.
On the surface, they're great looking snowshoes. Only after you turn them over do things start to get ugly.
They come complete with their own shocks. Struts are provided by the owner.
The snowshoe of choice for people who don't want to get in over their head.
Perfect for those who want to get away from everyone who wants to get away from it all.
You may have thought we dropped off the face of the earth. Actually we were just testing snowshoes on the other side of it.

371

Bauer 1996
It's freedom.
YOU JUST HAPPEN TO BE A POWERLESS SLAVE TO IT. Bauer
Bauer 1996 The Products.

372

COLLATERAL
DIRECT MAIL: SINGLE

373
ART DIRECTOR:
David Houghton
WRITER:
Brian Howlett
CLIENT:
Star Protection
AGENCY:
Axmith McIntyre Wicht/
Toronto

374
ART DIRECTOR:
Christopher Cole
WRITER:
Eric Sorensen
ILLUSTRATOR:
Jerry Gale
CLIENT:
Great Faces
AGENCY:
Cole Sorensen/
Birmingham, AL

375
ART DIRECTOR:
Eric Bute
WRITER:
David Morring
CLIENT:
Habitat For Humanity
AGENCY:
FJCandN/Salt Lake City

376
ART DIRECTOR:
Gary Goldsmith
WRITER:
Tom Miller
CLIENT:
Barneys New York
AGENCY:
Goldsmith/Jeffrey,
New York

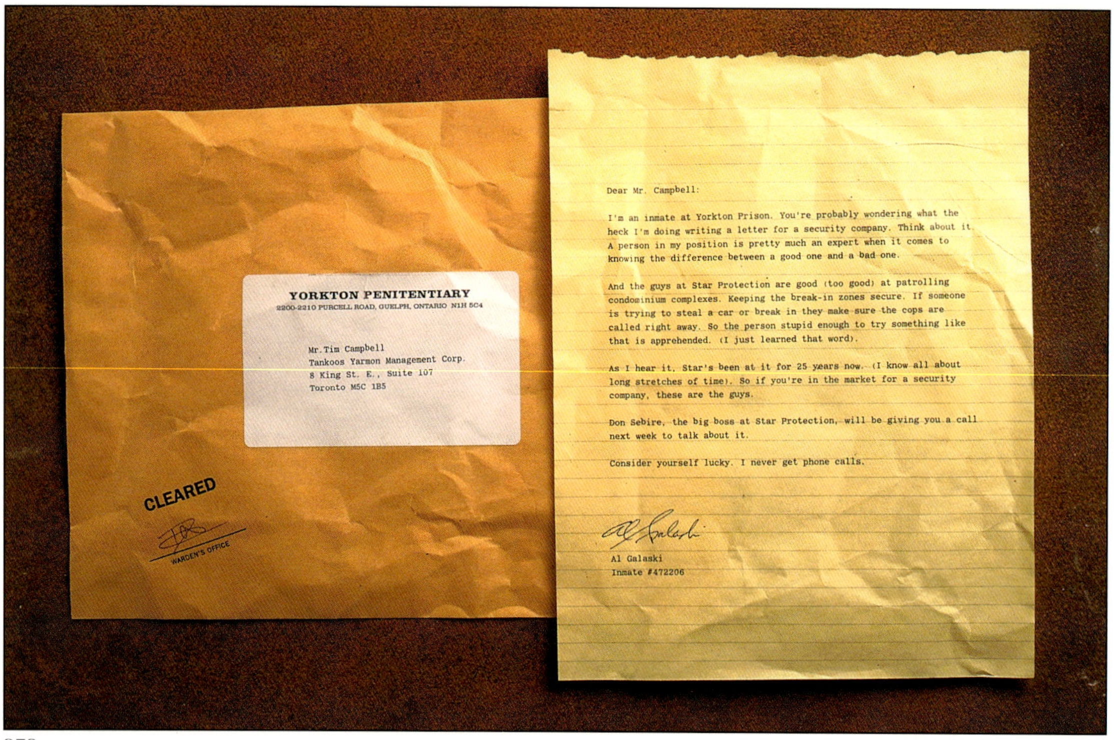

373

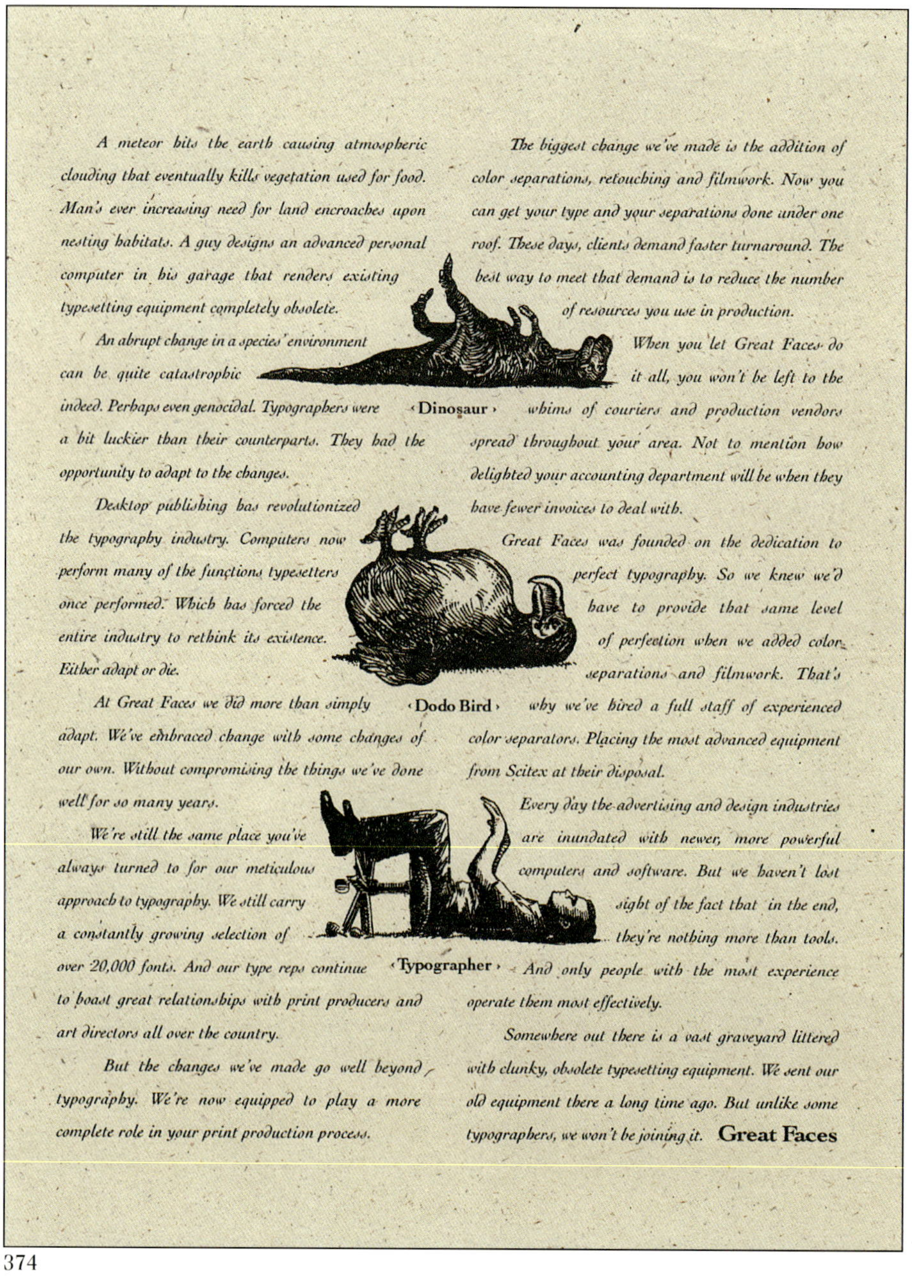

374

EVERY CENT RAISED AT OUR DINNER GOES INTO BUILDING NEW HOMES.
REALLY, WE DON'T WASTE ANYTHING.
Join Habitat for Humanity for our annual Fundraising Dinner and Auction.
Saturday, April 29, 1995
Northwest Pipeline Corporation
295 Chipeta Way
Research Park, Salt Lake City
6:30 p.m.
Refreshments and Silent Auction
(Cash Bar available)
8:00 p.m.
Dinner and Live Auction
Semiformal Dress
R.S.V.P. by April 14, 1995
HABITAT FOR HUMANITY
Salt Lake Valley
For more information call 262-3751

375

SPF 0
Blonde hair darkens.
Visine sales plummet.
Lifeguard whistles fall silent.
The signs are obvious.
Summer is over.
Once again baby oil is for babies.
Pool men take up roofing.
And towels migrate to bathrooms.
Slowly, the healthy glow is fading.
A milky luminescence returns.
But all is not lost.
You can still look good without a tan.
Come see the new Fall Collection.
BARNEYS NEWYORK

376

COLLATERAL
DIRECT MAIL: SINGLE

377
ART DIRECTOR:
Mike Proctor
WRITER:
Ian Cohen
PHOTOGRAPHER:
Chris Noble
CLIENT:
The North Face
AGENCY:
Hammerquist & Saffel/
Seattle

378
ART DIRECTOR:
Rich Kohnke
WRITER:
Steve Koeneke
CLIENT:
West Allis Memorial
Hospital
AGENCY:
Kohnke Koeneke/
Milwaukee

379
ART DIRECTOR:
Dave Cook
WRITER:
Mikal Reich
TYPOGRAPHER:
Graham Clifford
CLIENT:
DX
AGENCY:
Mad Dogs & Englishmen/
New York

380
ART DIRECTOR:
Dave Cook
WRITER:
Mikal Reich
TYPOGRAPHER:
Graham Clifford
CLIENT:
DX
AGENCY:
Mad Dogs & Englishmen/
New York

377

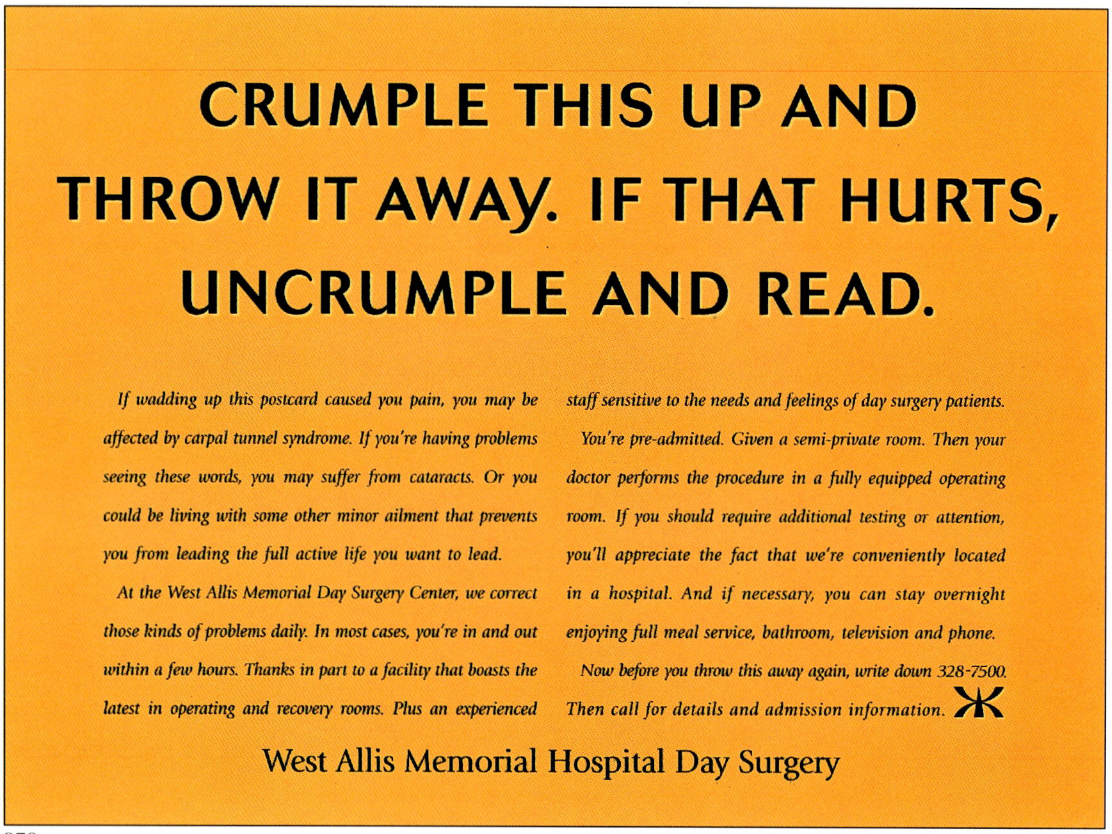

CRUMPLE THIS UP AND THROW IT AWAY. IF THAT HURTS, UNCRUMPLE AND READ.
If wadding up this postcard caused you pain, you may be affected by carpal tunnel syndrome. If you're having problems seeing these words, you may suffer from cataracts. Or you could be living with some other minor ailment that prevents you from leading the full active life you want to lead.
At the West Allis Memorial Day Surgery Center, we correct those kinds of problems daily. In most cases, you're in and out within a few hours. Thanks in part to a facility that boasts the latest in operating and recovery rooms. Plus an experienced staff sensitive to the needs and feelings of day surgery patients.
You're pre-admitted. Given a semi-private room. Then your doctor performs the procedure in a fully equipped operating room. If you should require additional testing or attention, you'll appreciate the fact that we're conveniently located in a hospital. And if necessary, you can stay overnight enjoying full meal service, bathroom, television and phone.
Now before you throw this away again, write down 328-7500. Then call for details and admission information.
West Allis Memorial Hospital Day Surgery

378

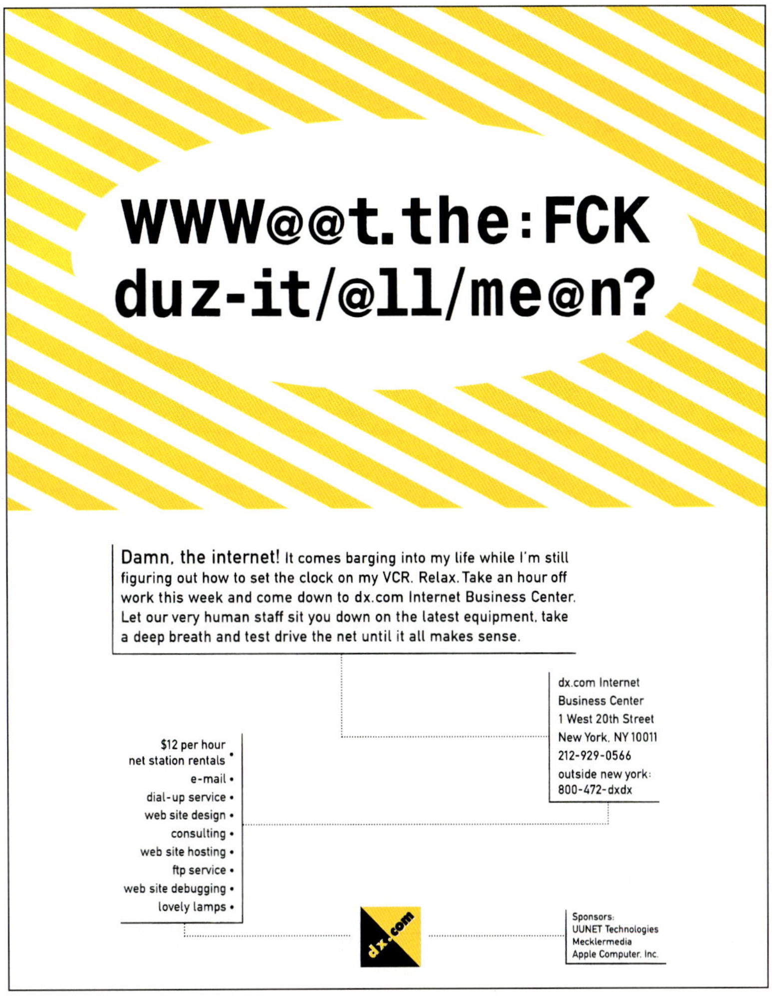
WWW@@t.the:FCK
duz-it/@ll/me@n?
Damn, the internet! It comes barging into my life while I'm still figuring out how to set the clock on my VCR. Relax. Take an hour off work this week and come down to dx.com Internet Business Center. Let our very human staff sit you down on the latest equipment, take a deep breath and test drive the net until it all makes sense.
dx.com Internet
Business Center
1 West 20th Street
New York, NY 10011
212-929-0566
outside new york:
800-472-dxdx
$12 per hour net station rentals •
e-mail •
dial-up service •
web site design •
consulting •
web site hosting •
ftp service •
web site debugging •
lovely lamps •
dx.com
Sponsors:
UUNET Technologies
Mecklermedia
Apple Computer, Inc.

379

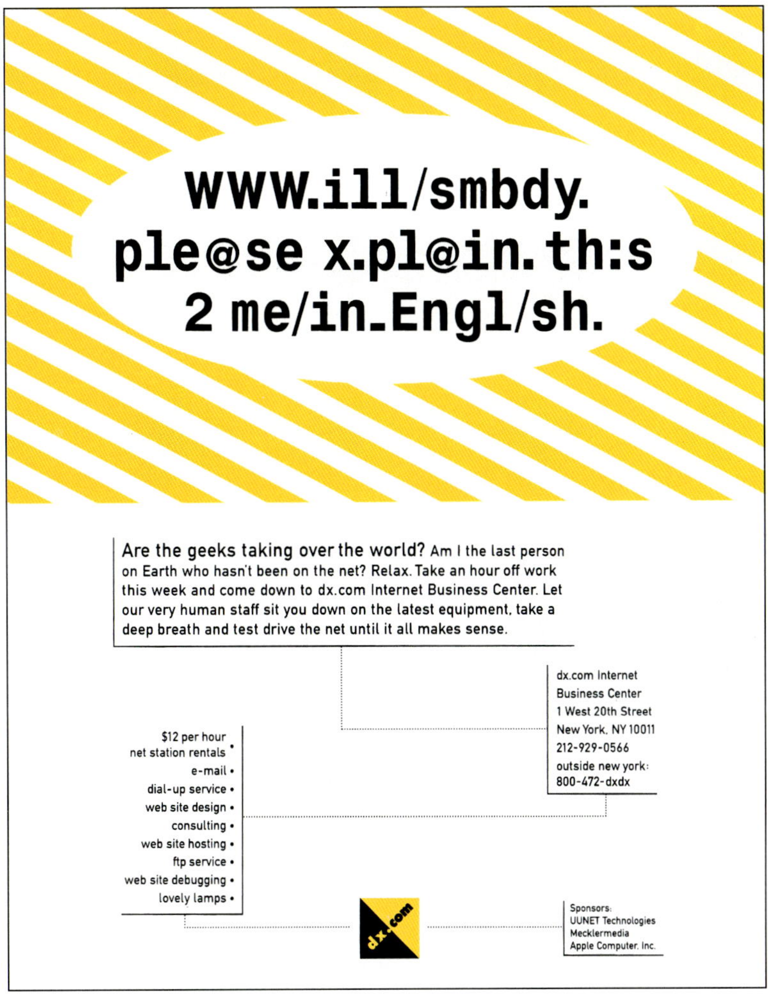
WWW.ill/smbdy.
ple@se x.pl@in.th:s
2 me/in_Engl/sh.
Are the geeks taking over the world? Am I the last person on Earth who hasn't been on the net? Relax. Take an hour off work this week and come down to dx.com Internet Business Center. Let our very human staff sit you down on the latest equipment, take a deep breath and test drive the net until it all makes sense.
dx.com Internet
Business Center
1 West 20th Street
New York, NY 10011
212-929-0566
outside new york:
800-472-dxdx
$12 per hour net station rentals •
e-mail •
dial-up service •
web site design •
consulting •
web site hosting •
ftp service •
web site debugging •
lovely lamps •
dx.com
Sponsors:
UUNET Technologies
Mecklermedia
Apple Computer, Inc.

380

COLLATERAL
DIRECT MAIL: SINGLE

381
ART DIRECTOR:
Taras Wayner
WRITER:
Kevin Roddy
PHOTOGRAPHER:
Tom Seawell
CLIENT:
The San Francisco Ad Club
AGENCY:
Odiorne Wilde Narraway Groome/San Francisco

382
ART DIRECTOR:
Hal Curtis
WRITER:
Steve Bautista
PHOTOGRAPHER:
Michele Clement
CLIENT:
M&H Typography
AGENCY:
Pagano Schenck & Kay/ Boston

383
ART DIRECTOR:
Daniel Vendramin
WRITER:
Paul Evans
ILLUSTRATOR:
Kam Yu
CLIENT:
Kam Yu Medical Illustration
AGENCY:
Rage Advertising/Toronto

384
ART DIRECTOR:
Chris Nott
WRITER:
Roy Davimes
PHOTOGRAPHER:
John Henley
CLIENT:
John Henley Photography
AGENCY:
Siddall Matus & Coughter/ Richmond

381

382

Happy Valentine's Day
Kam Yu • Medical Illustration • 416 ~ 929 ~ 7894

383

UNEVEN RIPPLE
To you, it's a beautiful picture. To him, it's an embarrassment worthy of intense self-flagellation.
JOHN HENLEY
THE PORTRAIT OF A LANDSCAPE PHOTOGRAPHER 804 649 1400 FAX 804 649 8012

384

COLLATERAL
DIRECT MAIL: SINGLE

385

ART DIRECTOR:
Chris Nott
WRITER:
Roy Davimes
PHOTOGRAPHER:
John Henley
CLIENT:
John Henley Photography
AGENCY:
Siddall Matus & Coughter/
Richmond

386

ART DIRECTOR:
Chris Nott
WRITER:
Roy Davimes
PHOTOGRAPHER:
John Henley
CLIENT:
John Henley Photography
AGENCY:
Siddall Matus & Coughter/
Richmond

COLLATERAL
DIRECT MAIL: CAMPAIGN

387

ART DIRECTOR:
Gary Goldsmith
WRITER:
Tom Miller
CLIENT:
Barneys New York
AGENCY:
Goldsmith/Jeffrey,
New York

385

386

SPF 0
Blonde hair darkens.
Visine sales plummet.
Lifeguard whistles fall silent.
The signs are obvious.
Summer is over.
Once again baby oil is for babies.
Pool men take up roofing.
And towels migrate to bathrooms.
Slowly, the healthy glow is fading.
A milky luminescence returns.
But all is not lost.
You can still look good without a tan.
Come see the new Fall Collection.
BARNEYS
NEWYORK

Here comes the leash
It couldn't last forever.
When you were a child it was "Field Day."
Now it's "Summer Friday."
Those mystical two words.
It's get out of jail early.
Once a week.
12 days a year.
And it's ending.
Here comes the starch.
Five days of jackets.
High polish shoes.
Neckties.
Putting the leash back on is no fun.
Then again, that depends on where you buy it.
Come see the new Fall Collection.
BARNEYS
NEWYORK

The End
Of cocoa-butter stained paperbacks
flying kites in the dunes
and lighter-fluid tinged hamburgers.
Junk drawers fill with seashells.
Volleyballs hibernate.
Fahrenheit goes from plus to minus.
Say goodbye to cheap sunglasses
bar-car Friday friendships
and the feeling of tan skin
with sand in the bed.
The best remedy for this depressing news?
New clothes.
Come see the new Fall Collection.
BARNEYS
NEWYORK

COLLATERAL
DIRECT MAIL: CAMPAIGN

388

ART DIRECTOR:
Chris Harrison
WRITER:
Michael O'Reilly
CLIENT:
Vince the Mover
AGENCY:
Michael O'Reilly Advertising/Toronto

COLLATERAL
POINT OF PURCHASE
AND IN-STORE

389

ART DIRECTOR:
Andy Fackrell
WRITER:
Kash Sree
CLIENT:
Raffles Hotel
AGENCY:
Batey Ads/Singapore

390

ART DIRECTOR:
Andy Fackrell
WRITER:
Kash Sree
PHOTOGRAPHER:
Charles Liddall
CLIENT:
Raffles Hotel
AGENCY:
Batey Ads/Singapore

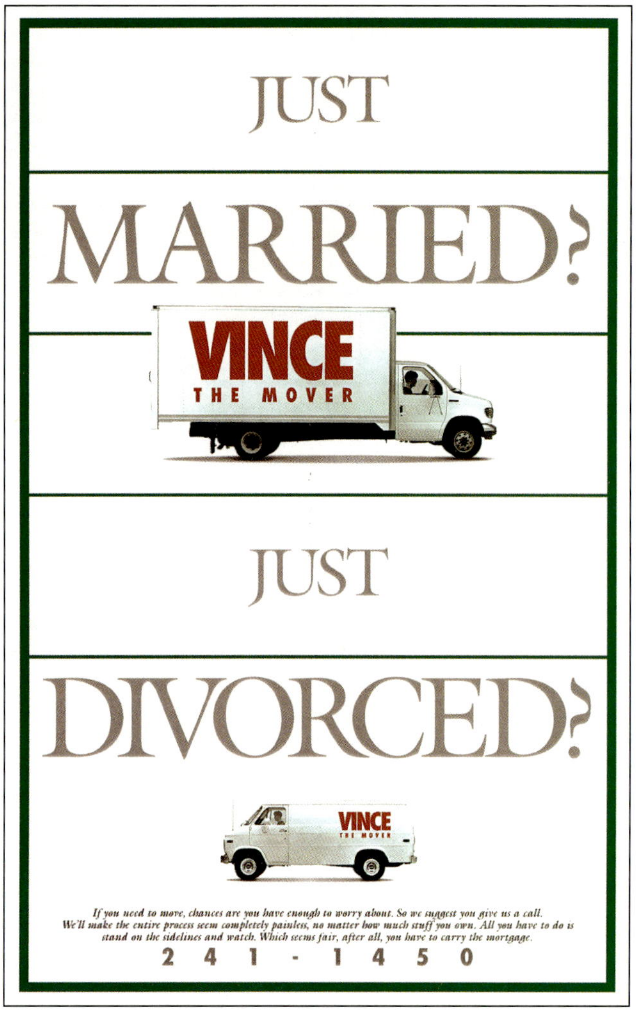

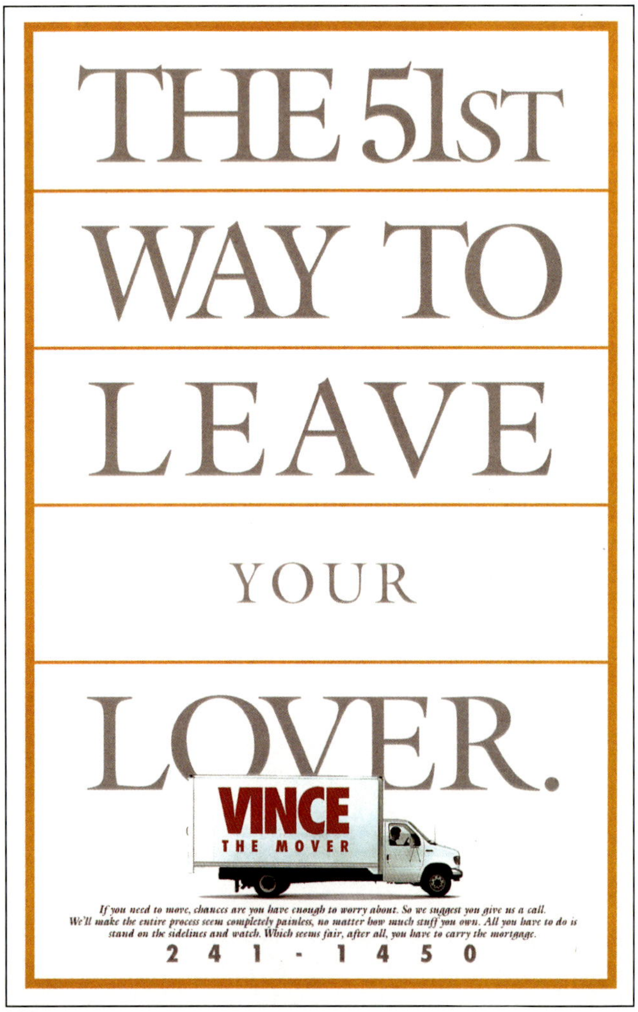

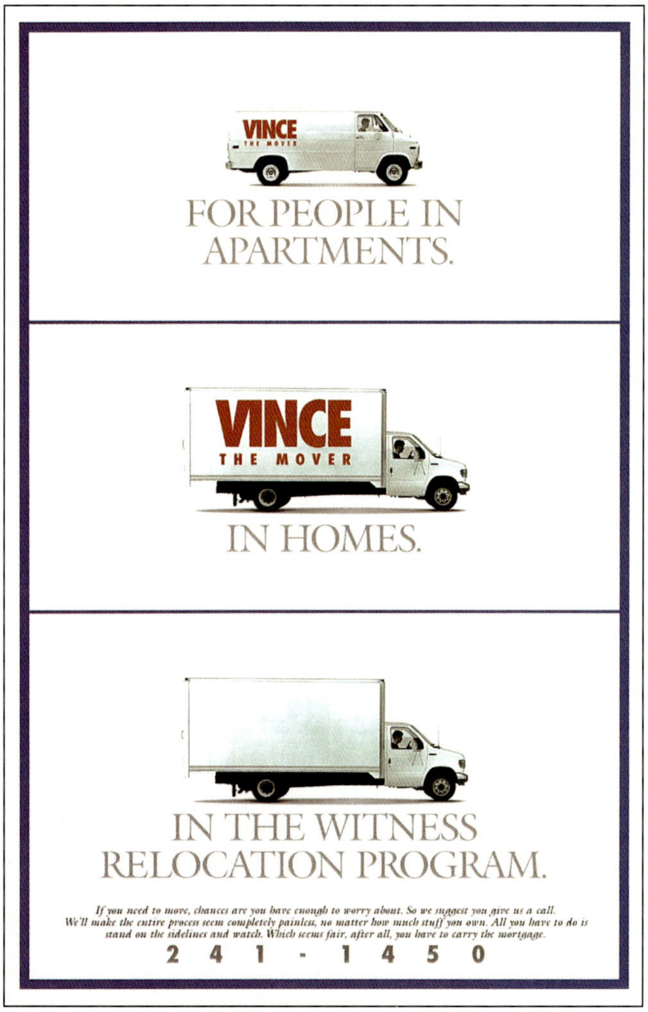

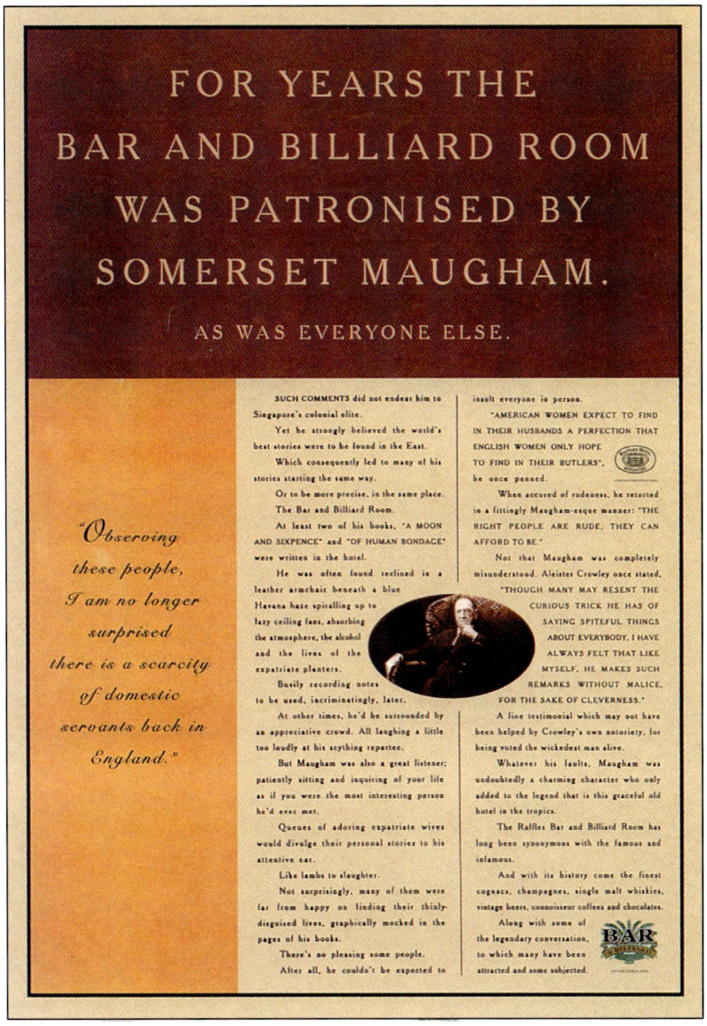

FOR YEARS THE BAR AND BILLIARD ROOM WAS PATRONISED BY SOMERSET MAUGHAM.
AS WAS EVERYONE ELSE.
"Observing these people, I am no longer surprised there is a scarcity of domestic servants back in England."
SUCH COMMENTS did not endear him to Singapore's colonial elite.
Yet he strongly believed the world's best stories were to be found in the East.
Which consequently led to many of his stories starting the same way.
Or to be more precise, in the same place.
The Bar and Billiard Room.
At least two of his books, "A MOON AND SIXPENCE" and "OF HUMAN BONDAGE" were written in the hotel.
He was often found reclined in a leather armchair beneath a blue Havana haze spiralling up to lazy ceiling fans, absorbing the atmosphere, the alcohol and the lives of the expatriate planters.
Busily recording notes to be used, incriminatingly, later.
At other times, he'd be surrounded by an appreciative crowd. All laughing a little too loudly at his scything repartee.
But Maugham was also a great listener; patiently sitting and inquiring of your life as if you were the most interesting person he'd ever met.
Queues of adoring expatriate wives would divulge their personal stories to his attentive ear.
Like lambs to slaughter.
Not surprisingly, many of them were far from happy on finding their thinly-disguised lives, graphically mocked in the pages of his books.
There's no pleasing some people.
After all, he couldn't be expected to insult everyone in person.
"AMERICAN WOMEN EXPECT TO FIND IN THEIR HUSBANDS A PERFECTION THAT ENGLISH WOMEN ONLY HOPE TO FIND IN THEIR BUTLERS", he once penned.
When accused of rudeness, he retorted in a fittingly Maugham-esque manner: "THE RIGHT PEOPLE ARE RUDE. THEY CAN AFFORD TO BE."
Not that Maugham was completely misunderstood. Aleister Crowley once stated, "THOUGH MANY MAY RESENT THE CURIOUS TRICK HE HAS OF SAYING SPITEFUL THINGS ABOUT EVERYBODY, I HAVE ALWAYS FELT THAT LIKE MYSELF, HE MAKES SUCH REMARKS WITHOUT MALICE, FOR THE SAKE OF CLEVERNESS."
A fine testimonial which may not have been helped by Crowley's own notoriety, for being voted the wickedest man alive.
Whatever his faults, Maugham was undoubtedly a charming character who only added to the legend that is this graceful old hotel in the tropics.
The Raffles Bar and Billiard Room has long been synonymous with the famous and infamous.
And with its history come the finest cognacs, champagnes, single malt whiskies, vintage beers, connoisseur coffees and chocolates.
Along with some of the legendary conversation, to which many have been attracted and some subjected.
BAR

389

ENTRY WAS DENIED TO THOSE NOT WEARING A JACKET, TIE OR A GOOD CHICKEN CURRY.
The compulsory white linen jacket and public school tie were largely successful in keeping out undesirables. The nouveau riche, Americans, chartered accountants and the like.
THERE WERE standards to maintain, after all. One couldn't allow patrons to dress for tropics just because they were in the tropics.
So it may come as a surprise to find a twenty-four stone, bearded giant wandering around the Bar and Billiard Room, barefooted in curry-stained pyjamas.
But Professor Peiter van Stein Callenfels was exceptional in more than just his attire.
The original model for Sir Arthur Conan Doyle's 'PROFESSOR CHALLENGER', Callenfels was a noted archaeologist and historian turned coffee planter. (The more cynical might consider that a natural progression).
And like many of the region's planters, he would while away the hours nursing a few beers in the splendour of the Bar and Billiard Room.
Unlike many planters though, he would do so speaking fluently in four different languages.
For Raffles was a place where he could find what he considered the rarest of commodites.
Civilised conversation.
To Callenfels, this consisted of the fruits of his intellect bombastically thrust upon a preferably female audience.
After all, he did consider himself somewhat of a ladies man.
This could be attributed to his impressive physique, which spilled gloriously out of the gaps in his pyjamas and cascaded over the sides of his reinforced armchair.
Was it his fine head of hair and whiskers, which he proudly groomed only once a year?
Or perhaps it was his impeccable taste in curry, enshrined in a pastiche of stains down the front of his pyjamas.
Whatever it was, it cannot be denied that he did possess a certain charm.
And if one missed his stentorian boom, by some strange quirk of deafness, Callenfels could always be identified by the steady stream of serving staff briskly gliding between him and the bar, in an attempt to keep pace with his insatiable thirst.
Legend has it that he could consume up to thirty-five beers or ten bottles of gin in a sitting. And they soon learned not to insult him by serving less than a quart at a time.
(If only he'd been around during the thirties, his excessive consumption could have single-handedly seen the hotel through the recession.)
Not that his gargantuan appetite was limited to alcohol. He could voraciously devour his way through the entire Raffles Dining Room menu and had done so on many occasions.
It is even rumoured that Callenfels may have once eaten human flesh while living with cannibals in Sumatra.
Entirely possible, when you consider he ate everything else that wasn't fast enough to escape.
The Bar and Billiard Room has long been dedicated to the ageless pleasure of self indulgence.
The finest selection of champagnes, cognacs, single malt whiskies, vintage beers, connoisseur coffees and chocolates can all be secured in quantity (if need be).
Along with the legendary conversation that has long been associated with the place.
BAR

390

COLLATERAL
POINT OF PURCHASE
AND IN-STORE

391
ART DIRECTORS:
Scott Kaplan
Tom Kraemer
WRITERS:
Tom Kraemer
Scott Kaplan
PHOTOGRAPHER:
Steven Harris
CLIENT:
The Clog Factory
AGENCY:
Big & Tall Advertising/
New York

392
ART DIRECTORS:
Mark Slotemaker
Roger Bentley
WRITER:
Joel Thomas
PHOTOGRAPHERS:
Giovanni Stephano
Mark Slotemaker
CLIENT:
Big House
AGENCY:
Dalbey & Denight
Advertising/Portland

393
ART DIRECTOR:
Jeff Ford
WRITER:
Matthew Vandermark
ILLUSTRATOR:
Jeff Ford
CLIENT:
Mosman Wharf
Bootmakers
AGENCY:
D'OH Advertising/
Surry Hills, Australia

394
ART DIRECTOR:
Joe Paprocki
WRITER:
Dave Pullar
ILLUSTRATOR:
Bob Blewett
CLIENT:
Burnsville Pistol Range
AGENCY:
Fallon McElligott/
Minneapolis

391

392

SHOE REPAIRS
393

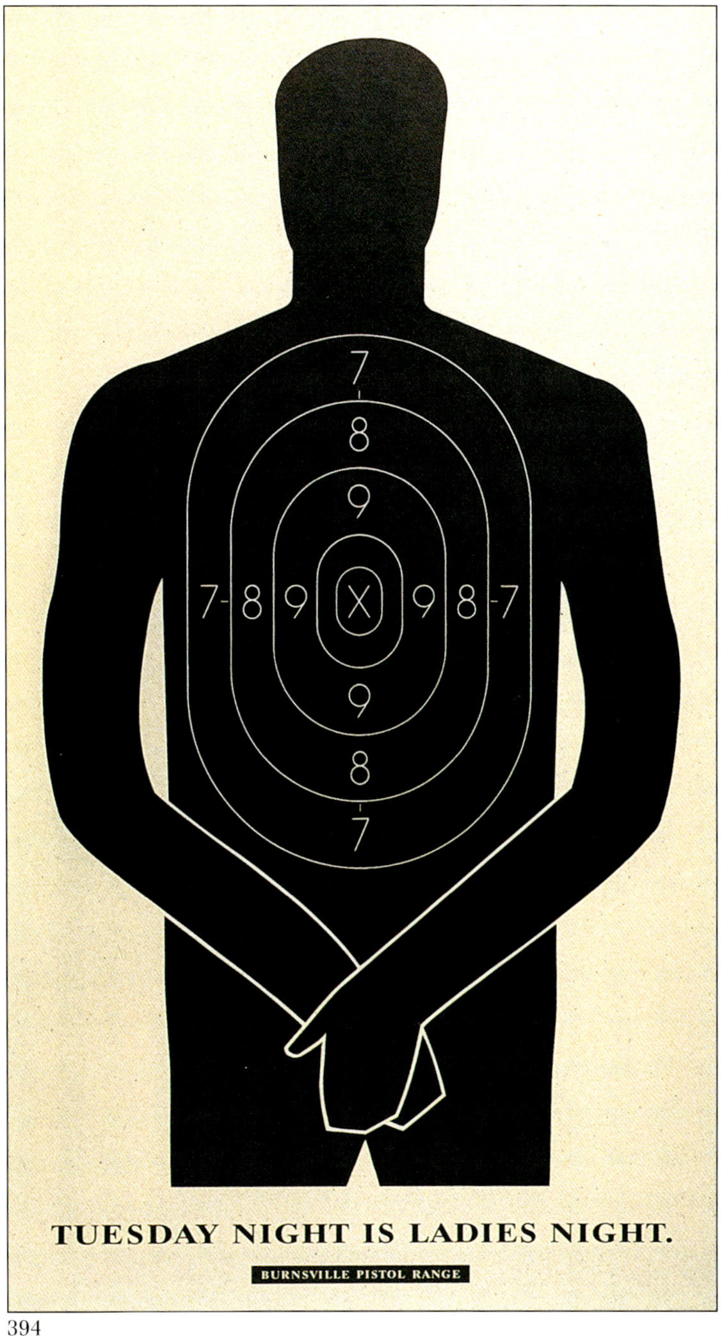
7
8
9
7 8 9 X 9 8 7
9
8
7
TUESDAY NIGHT IS LADIES NIGHT.
BURNSVILLE PISTOL RANGE
394

395
ART DIRECTOR:
Bob Barrie
WRITER:
Sally Hogshead
ILLUSTRATOR:
Bob Barrie
CLIENT:
J. D. Hoyt's
AGENCY:
Fallon McElligott/
Minneapolis

396
ART DIRECTOR:
Bob Barrie
WRITER:
Sally Hogshead
CLIENT:
J. D. Hoyt's
AGENCY:
Fallon McElligott/
Minneapolis

397
ART DIRECTOR:
Brent Ladd
WRITER:
Brian Brooker
PHOTOGRAPHER:
Dennis Fagan
CLIENT:
Rootin' Ridge
AGENCY:
GSD&M Advertising/
Austin

398
ART DIRECTOR:
Steve Stone
WRITER:
Dave O'Hare
CLIENT:
Pepsi/Starbuck's Coffee
Partnership
AGENCY:
Hal Riney & Partners/
San Francisco

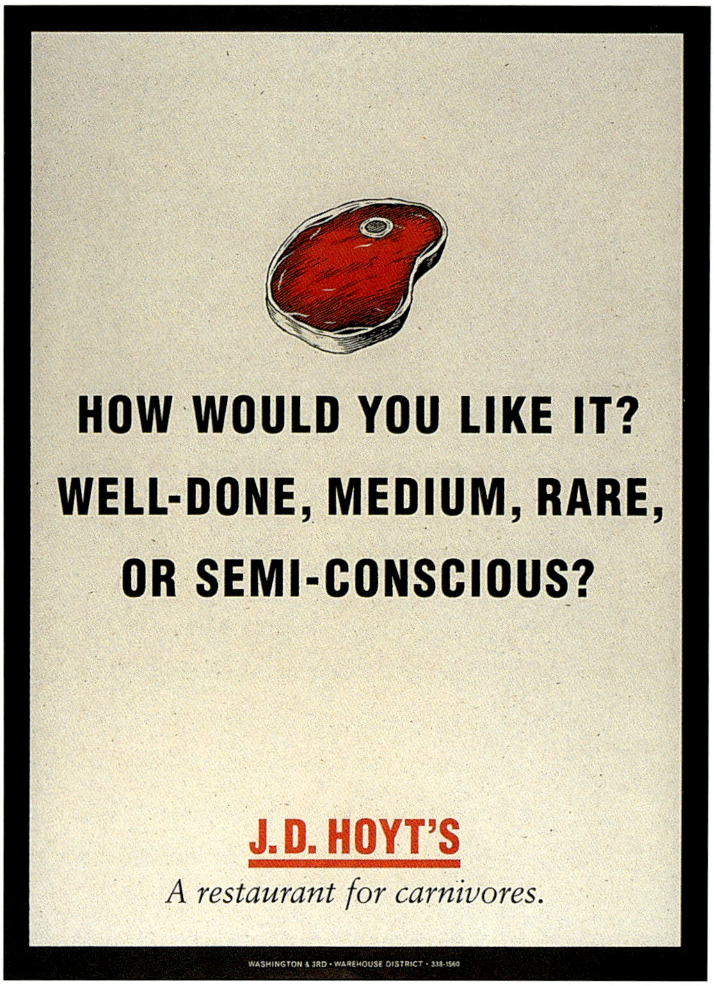
HOW WOULD YOU LIKE IT?
WELL-DONE, MEDIUM, RARE,
OR SEMI-CONSCIOUS?
J.D. HOYT'S
A restaurant for carnivores.
WASHINGTON & 3RD • WAREHOUSE DISTRICT • 338-1560

395

THE MOST SACRED
HINDU BEING.
AND A DAMN TASTY
T-BONE.
J.D. HOYT'S
A restaurant for carnivores.
WASHINGTON & 3RD • WAREHOUSE DISTRICT • 338-1560

396

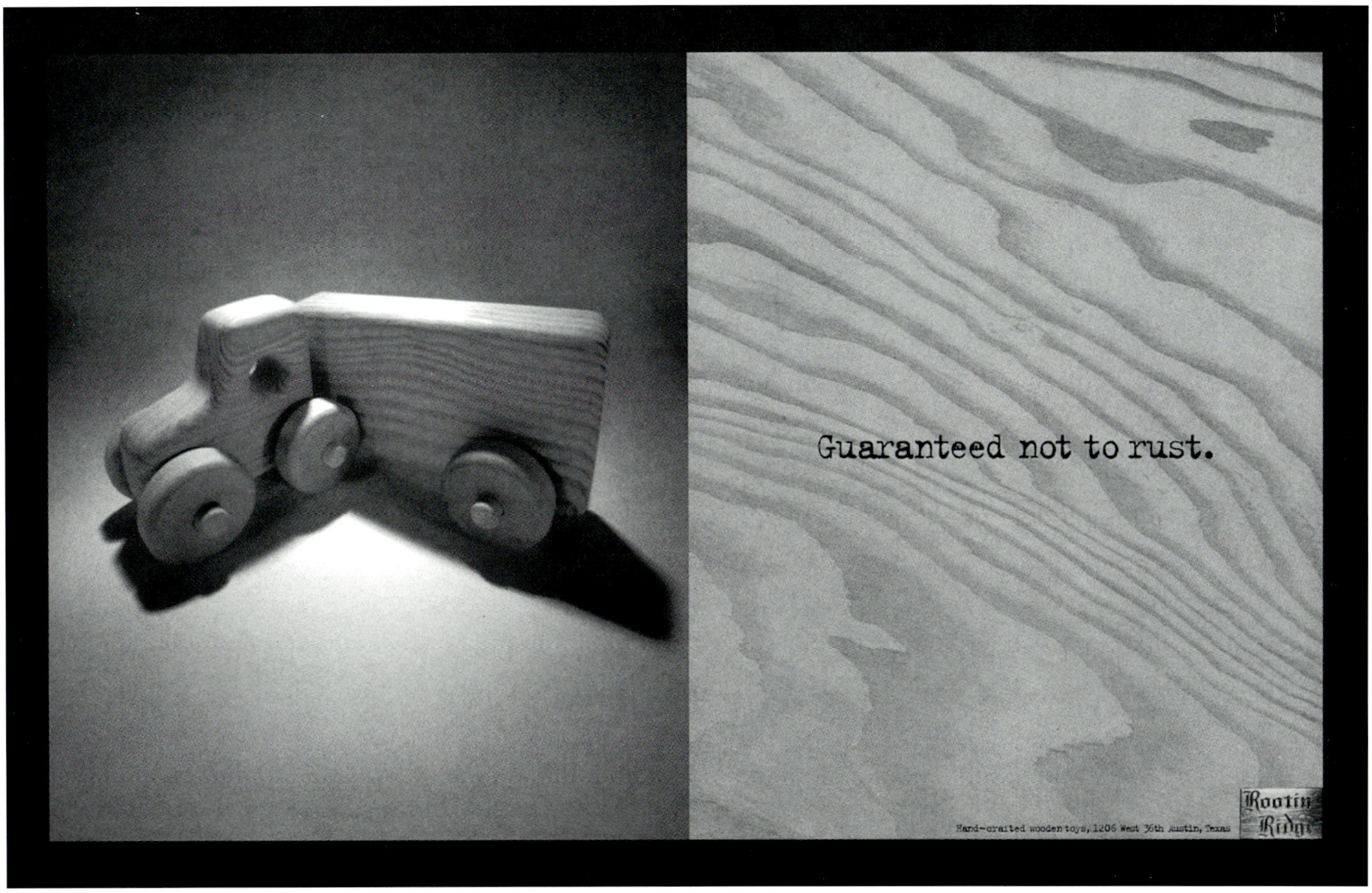
Guaranteed not to rust.
Hand-crafted wooden toys, 1206 West 36th Austin, Texas
Rootin Ridge

397

A refresher course on the appropriateness of Mazagran
DO YOU REALLY NEED TO BE TOLD [APPARENTLY SO] WHEN TO DRINK THIS ?
It seems rather presumptuous, us telling you when to enjoy something. However, it is quite conceivable that Mazagran, a refreshing beverage quaffed by French Legionnaires in the arid corners of northwest Africa over 150 years ago, will, in fact, raise a few usage questions for a modern person such as yourself. ✱ Let us begin to clear up any perplexities by first telling you that Mazagran is, in essence, a lightly carbonated coffee. Oh dear, does that confound you even more? [*Faites attention, s'il vous plaît.*] Those very same Legionnaires discovered that by adding cool, sparkling mineral water to freshly brewed coffee and then adding a pinch or two, depending upon the generosity of the lender, of sugar, they could create a decidedly different, yet remarkably quenching, beverage, which they came to call Mazagran, named, unspectacularly, after the fortress they were posted in. [Obviously the average Legionnaire was creative up to a point.] ✱ Now, to the matter of when: Certainly a Legionnaire would enjoy a Mazagran after a march across the desert. [You may substitute a 10K road race, or a round of tennis if you like.] He'd definitely want a refreshing pick-me-up while manning the ramparts. [How about during an afternoon break at work?] And again, he might enjoy a Mazagran after dinner, while discussing *les événements du monde* with friends. ✱ You see, you have much more in common with Mazagran than you might have thought. So why not ask the barista to make you one? Now, perhaps.
Tennis, cycling, roast turkey. There are many appropriate times to enjoy Mazagran.
MAZAGRAN
"JE CROIS QUE JE VAIS PRENDRE LA MIENNE AVEC DINER."
("I'M THINKING OF HAVING MINE WITH DINNER.")
"VRAIMENT?!?"
("REALLY?!?")

398

COLLATERAL
POINT OF PURCHASE
AND IN-STORE

399
ART DIRECTOR:
Steve Stone
WRITER:
Dave O'Hare
CLIENT:
Pepsi/Starbuck's Coffee Partnership
AGENCY:
Hal Riney & Partners/ San Francisco

400
ART DIRECTOR:
Steve Mitchell
WRITER:
Matt Elhardt
PHOTOGRAPHER:
Curtis Johnson
CLIENT:
Rohol
AGENCY:
Hunt Adkins/Minneapolis

401
ART DIRECTOR:
Greg Bokor
WRITER:
Kara Goodrich
PHOTOGRAPHER:
Jim Erickson
CLIENT:
Canstar
AGENCY:
Leonard/Monahan, Providence

402
ART DIRECTOR:
Greg Bokor
WRITER:
John Simpson
PHOTOGRAPHER:
Bruce Deboer
ILLUSTRATOR:
John William Casilear
CLIENT:
FX Matt Brewing Company
AGENCY:
Leonard/Monahan, Providence

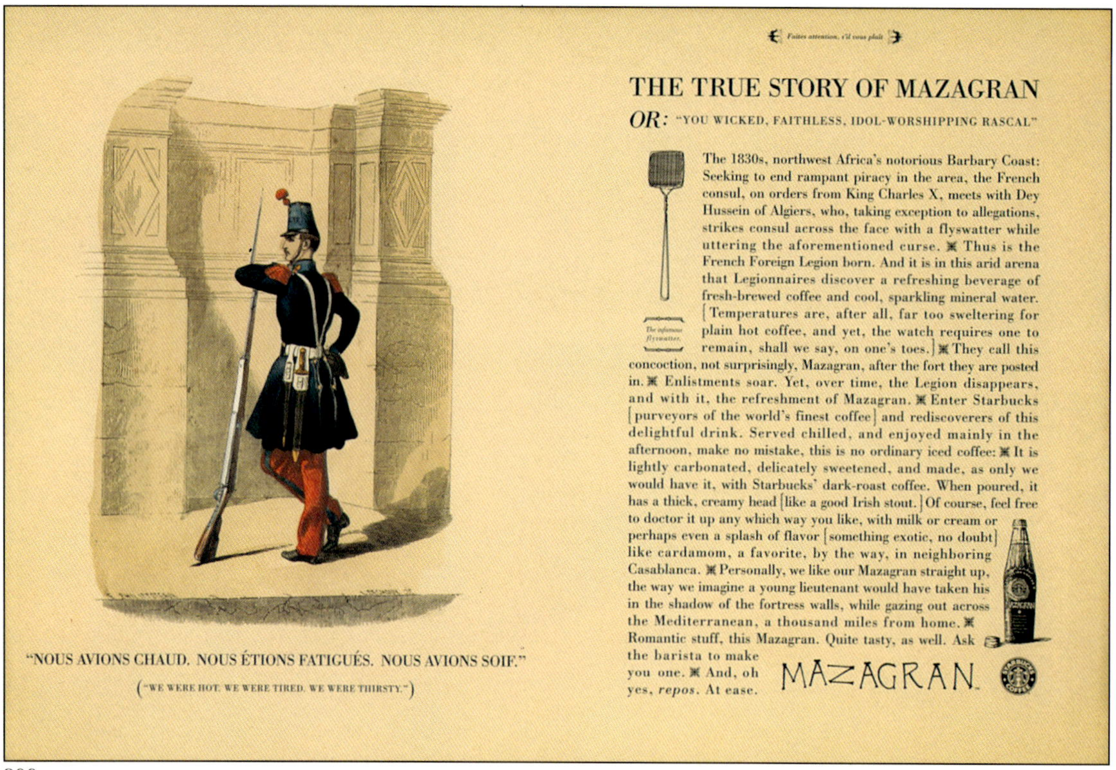

399

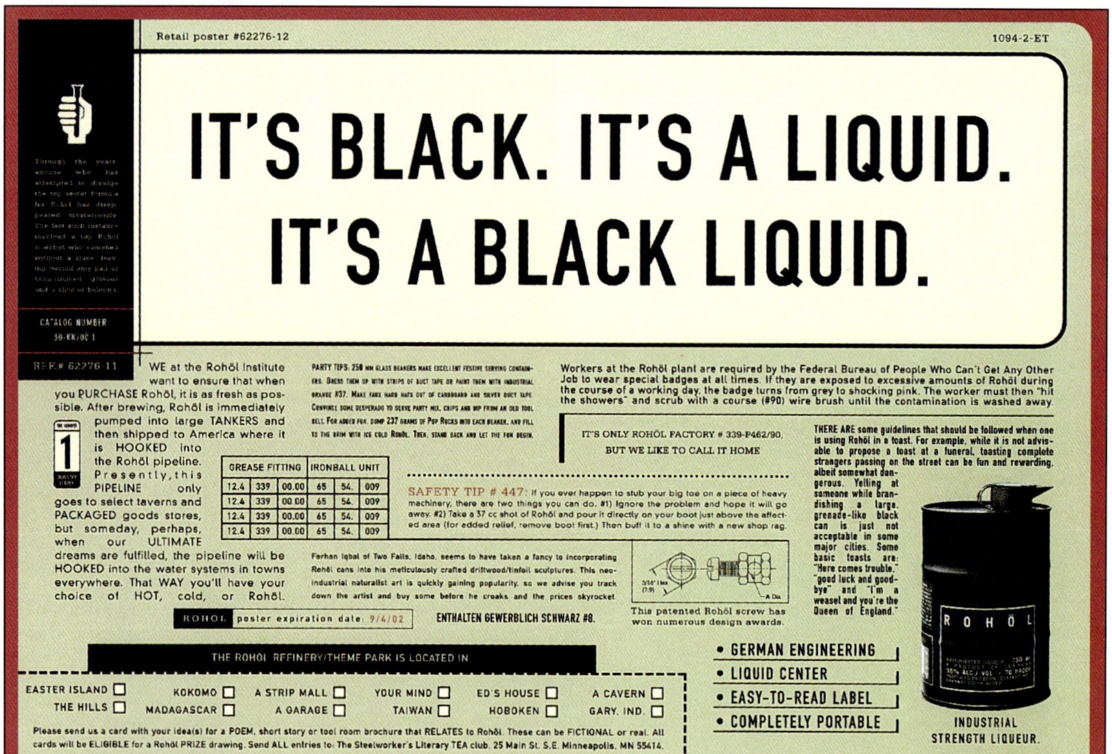

400

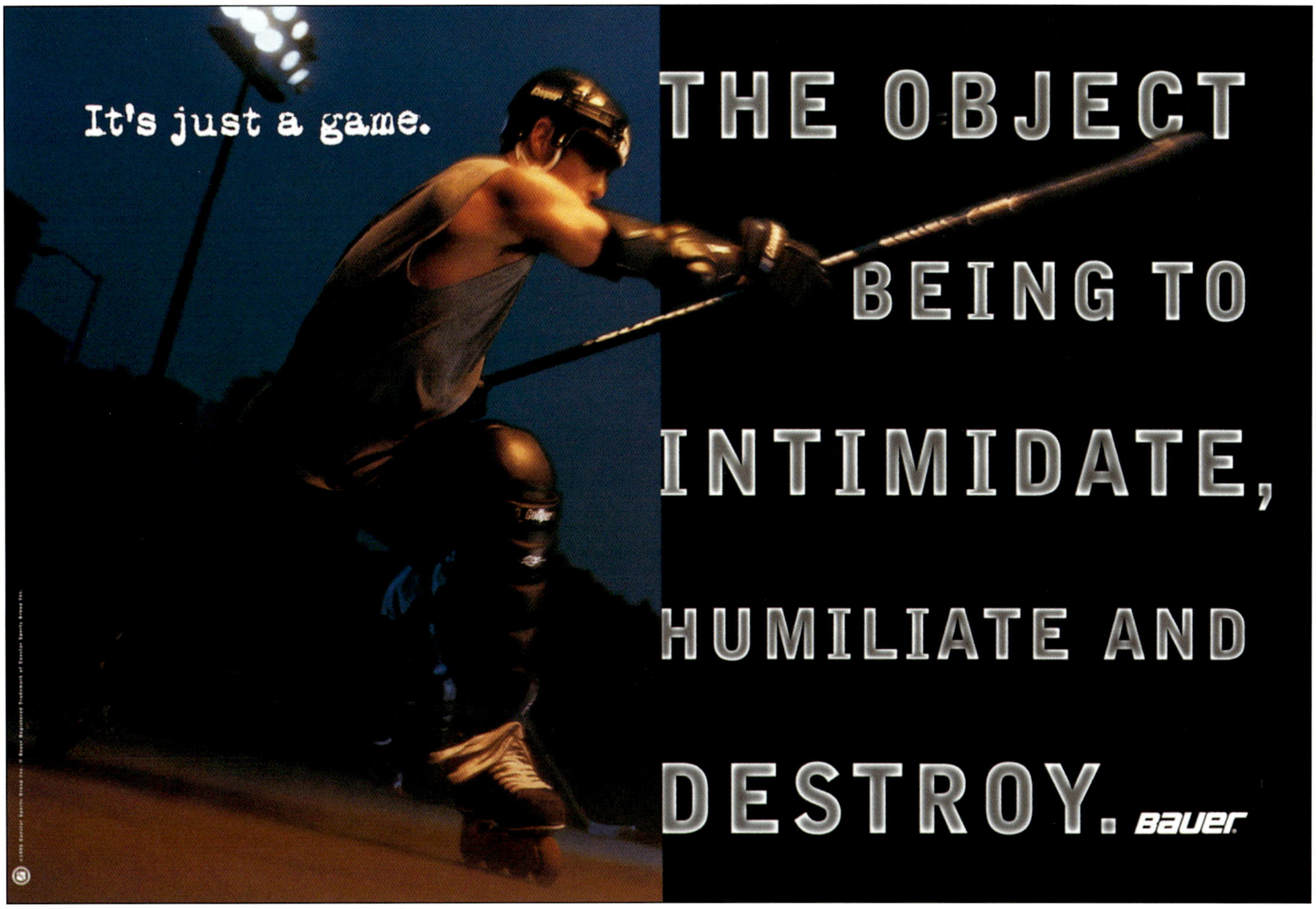
It's just a game.
THE OBJECT BEING TO INTIMIDATE, HUMILIATE AND DESTROY.
Bauer

401

THE ADIRONDACK WILDERNESS. UNTOUCHED. NATURAL. FREE. JUST LIKE OUR BEER, EXCEPT THE FREE PART.
WITHOUT QUESTION, HOPS AND BARLEY ARE THE TWO MOST PRECIOUS THINGS ON EARTH. LOVE COMES IN THIRD. TIED WITH YEAST.
WHEN THE FIRST VISITORS CAME TO THE ADIRONDACKS, THEY FOUND A BREATHTAKING LAND WHERE NATURE RAN WILD. ANCIENT MOUNTAINS ROSE UP TOWARDS THE SKY. CRYSTAL LAKES LAY HIDDEN IN THEIR VALLEYS LIKE JEWELS FROM GOD'S HOARD. THEY FOUND, IN FACT, EVERYTHING A WEARY CITY DWELLER COULD HOPE FOR. WITH ONE NOTABLE EXCEPTION: A GOOD BEER. FORTUNATELY, THE ADIRONDACKS HAVEN'T CHANGED. EQUALLY FORTUNATE, THE BEER SITUATION HAS. TODAY THERE'S SARANAC ADIRONDACK AMBER, BLACK & TAN, PALE ALE AND GOLDEN. A FAMILY OF BEERS FROM A FAMILY-OWNED BREWERY. EACH TASTED FIVE TIMES DURING OUR PAINSTAKING BREWING PROCESS. EACH MADE IN SMALL BATCHES WITH THE FINEST NATURAL INGREDIENTS, INCLUDING A UNIQUE VARIETY OF HOPS AND MALTED BARLEY THAT MAKES SARANAC UNLIKE ANY OTHER BEER. A FACT WHICH, UPON TASTING ONE, YOU WILL DISCOVER FOR YOURSELF.
THIS IS THE COMPLETE LINE OF SARANAC BEERS. AS YOU CAN SEE, THEY ARE IN A LINE.
SARANAC BEER. THE SPIRIT OF THE ADIRONDACKS.
SARANAC
ADIRONDACK AMBER

402

COLLATERAL
POINT OF PURCHASE
AND IN-STORE

403
ART DIRECTOR:
Jim Mountjoy
WRITER:
Ed Jones
PHOTOGRAPHER:
Jim Arndt
CLIENT:
Arthur's
AGENCY:
Loeffler Ketchum
Mountjoy/Charlotte, NC

404
ART DIRECTOR:
Jimmy Olson
WRITER:
Jim Schmidt
CLIENT:
Oscar Isberian Rugs
AGENCY:
McConnaughy Stein
Schmidt Brown/Chicago

405
ART DIRECTOR:
Karen Lynch
WRITER:
Spencer Deadrick
PHOTOGRAPHER:
David Benoit
CLIENT:
Chelsea Clock
AGENCY:
Mullen/Wenham, MA

406
ART DIRECTOR:
Michael Wilde
WRITER:
Jeff Odiorne
PHOTOGRAPHER:
Bob Mizono
CLIENT:
The McKenzie River
Corporation
AGENCY:
Odiorne Wilde Narraway
Groome/San Francisco

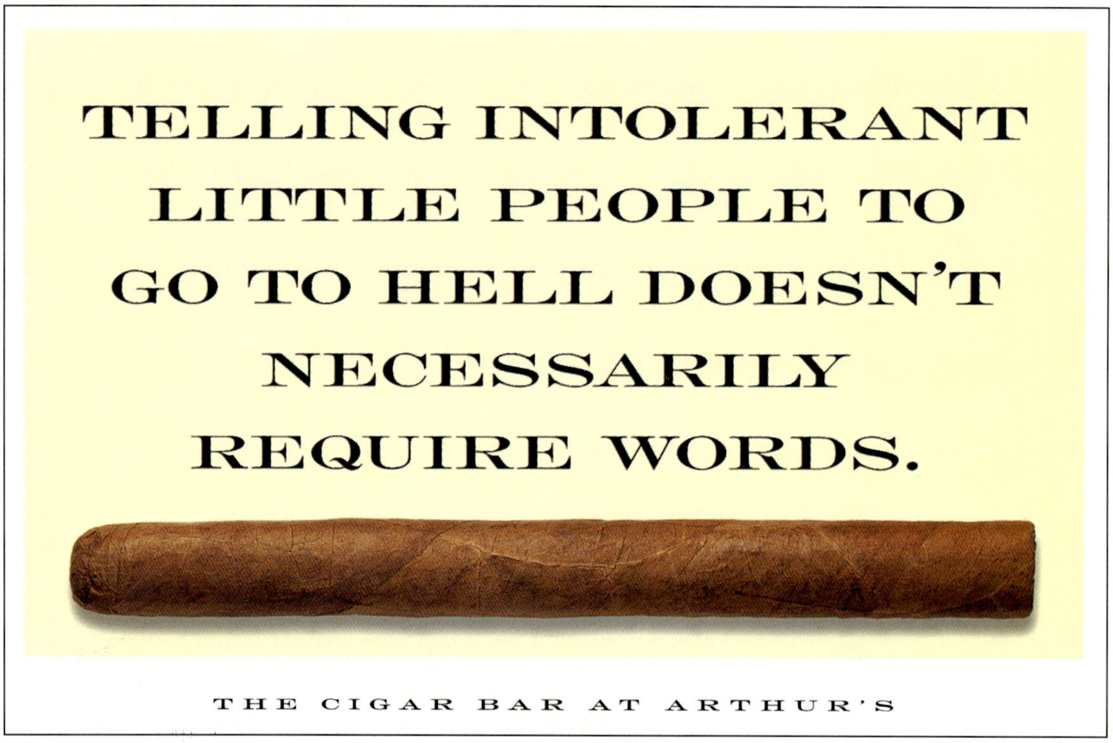

403

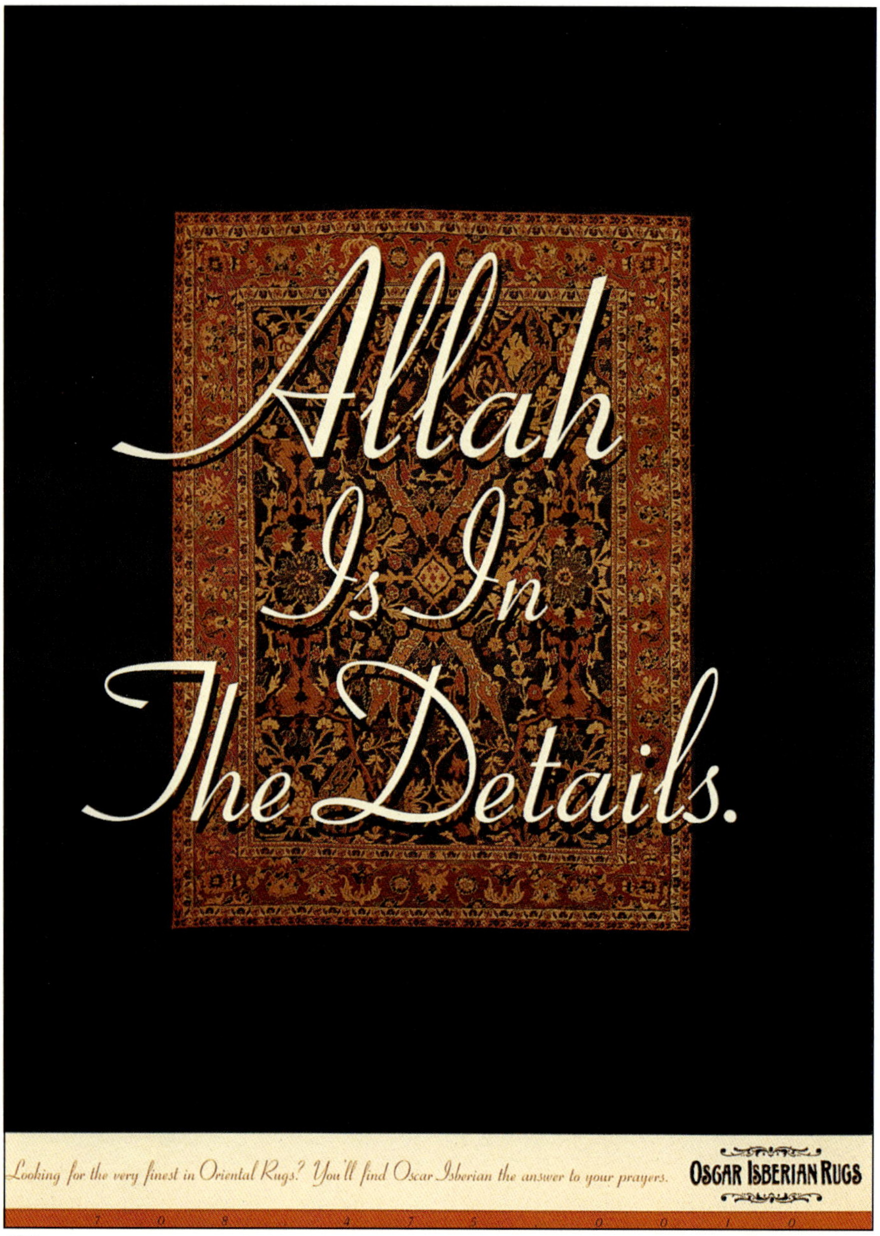

404

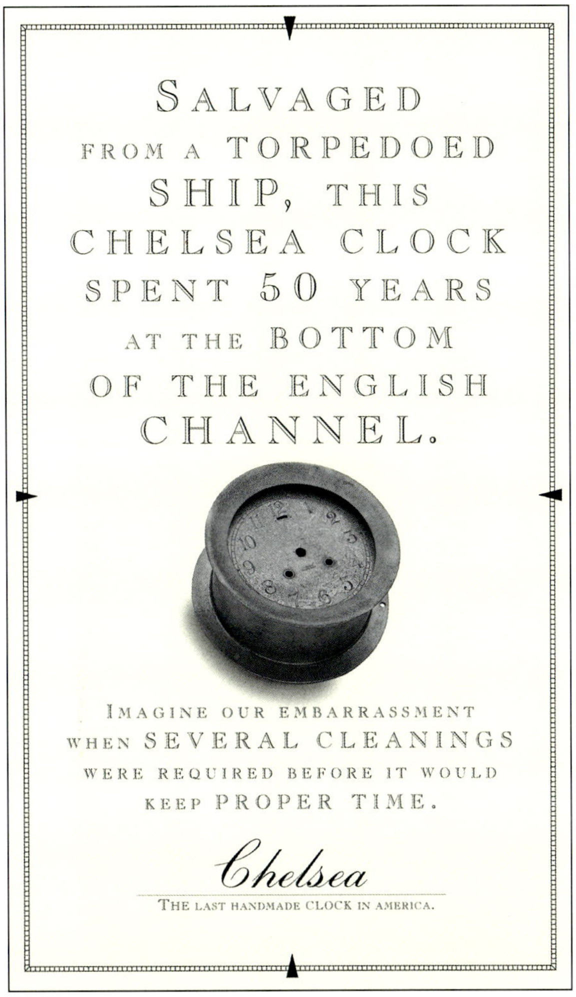
SALVAGED FROM A TORPEDOED SHIP, THIS CHELSEA CLOCK SPENT 50 YEARS AT THE BOTTOM OF THE ENGLISH CHANNEL.
IMAGINE OUR EMBARRASSMENT WHEN SEVERAL CLEANINGS WERE REQUIRED BEFORE IT WOULD KEEP PROPER TIME.
Chelsea
THE LAST HANDMADE CLOCK IN AMERICA.

405

MR./ MRS. CAB DRIVER
MY NAME IS
MY ADDRESS IS
PLEASE TAKE ME HOME.
STEEL RESERVE.
THE NOT-TOO-SERIOUS
HIGH GRAVITY LAGER.
STEEL RESERVE
HIGH GRAVITY LAGER
211

406

COLLATERAL
POINT OF PURCHASE
AND IN-STORE

407
ART DIRECTOR:
Cody Spinadel
WRITER:
Mike Collado
PHOTOGRAPHER:
Tim Schaedler
ILLUSTRATOR:
Allan Davidson
CLIENT:
American Firearms
AGENCY:
Paradigm
Communications/Tampa

408
ART DIRECTOR:
David Nien-Li Yang
WRITERS:
David Nien-Li Yang
Eric Weltner
Rich Wolchock
CLIENT:
Hunan Garden Restaurant
AGENCY:
The Puckett Group/
St. Louis

409
ART DIRECTORS:
Terence Reynolds
Christian Wojciechowski
WRITER:
Todd Tilford
PHOTOGRAPHER:
Richard Reens
CLIENT:
AM General Corporation
AGENCY:
R&D/The Richards Group,
Dallas

410
ART DIRECTOR:
Christian Wojciechowski
WRITER:
Mark Ronquillo
ILLUSTRATOR:
Brandy-Redd Smith
CLIENT:
Sunshine Miniature Trees
AGENCY:
R&D/The Richards Group,
Dallas

407

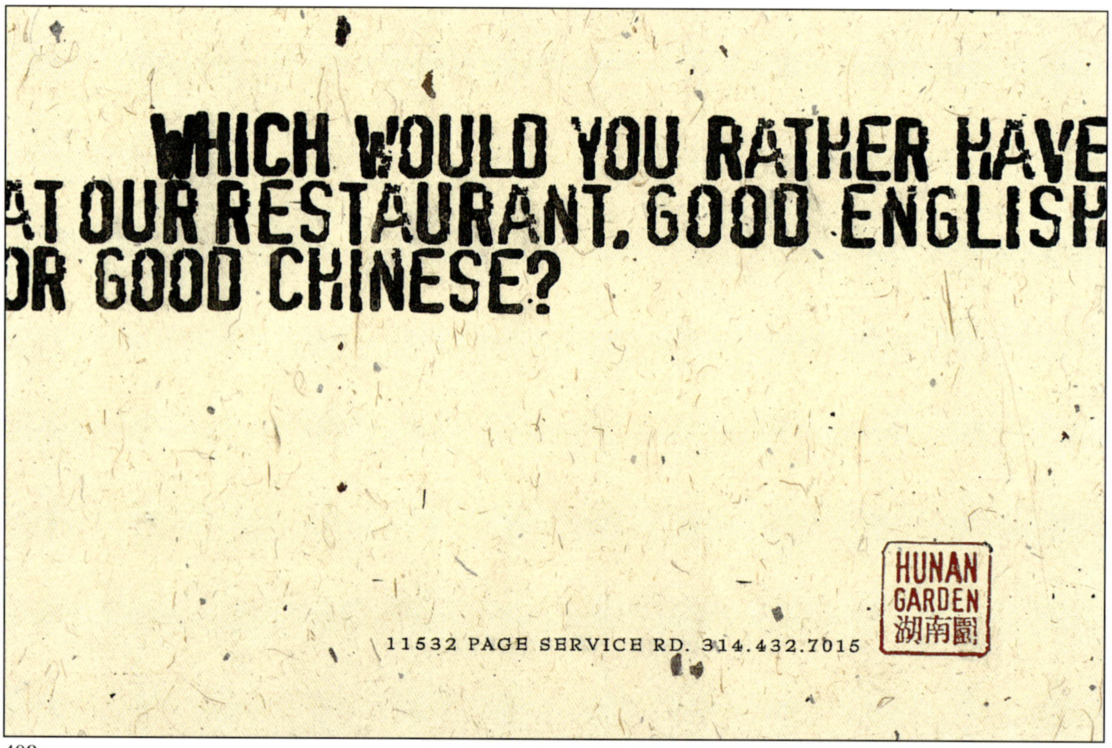

408

IT'S NOT A MATTER OF NO ONE ELSE BEING ABLE TO KEEP UP. IT'S A MATTER OF NO ONE ELSE BEING ABLE TO FOLLOW.
HUMMER

409

斜幹
a bonsai can live over one hundred years.
be sure to leave watering instructions with your grandchildren.
SUNSHINE MINIATURE TREES
718 GREENVILLE AVENUE

410

COLLATERAL
POINT OF PURCHASE
AND IN-STORE

411
ART DIRECTOR:
Patrick Murray
WRITER:
Vinnie Chieco
PHOTOGRAPHER:
Robb Debenport
CLIENT:
Tabu Lingerie
AGENCY:
R&D/The Richards Group, Dallas

412
ART DIRECTORS:
Jim Baldwin
Ron Henderson
WRITERS:
Ron Henderson
Jim Baldwin
PHOTOGRAPHER:
Pat Haverfield
CLIENT:
Yegua Creek Brewing Company
AGENCY:
The Richards Group/Dallas

413
ART DIRECTOR:
Steve Levit
WRITER:
Rich Siegel
CLIENT:
Lion Nathan International, Castlemaine XXXX
AGENCY:
Team One Advertising/ El Segundo, CA

COLLATERAL
SELF-PROMOTION

414
ART DIRECTOR:
Penny Duerr
WRITER:
Kerry Casey
PHOTOGRAPHER:
Doug Snyder
CLIENT:
Carmichael Lynch
AGENCY:
Carmichael Lynch/ Minneapolis

411

412

CASTLEMAINE
XXXX
"Satisfies an outback thirst."
WHAT DO WE DO IN THE OUTBACK FOR ENTERTAINMENT?
(OVER)
CASTLEMAINE
XXXX
"Satisfies an outback thirst."
WHAT DO WE DO IN THE OUTBACK FOR ENTERTAINMENT?
(OVER)

413

Listen. Find the heartbeat. We are a culture of listeners. It's how we find the place for your brand. The perfect place. We comb the competitive landscape with your strengths, your hopes, your vision as our compass. Then it happens. There is this tingle. This certainty. It's you. Your place. At Carmichael Lynch, positioning is a passion. We listen to your heartbeat. We find a position as unique as your fingerprint.
THE SUMMER SHE WAS 200 FRECKLES OLD.
Welcome to Carmichael Lynch. May we take your coat?

414

COLLATERAL
SELF-PROMOTION

415
ART DIRECTOR:
Mark Gettner
WRITER:
Patrick Knoll
PHOTOGRAPHER:
Doug Synder
CLIENT:
DDB Needham/Chicago
AGENCY:
DDB Needham/Chicago

416
ART DIRECTOR:
Rob Reilly
WRITER:
Rob Reilly
PHOTOGRAPHER:
Doug Synder
CLIENT:
Rob Reilly
AGENCY:
Harris Drury Cohen/
Ft. Lauderdale

417
ART DIRECTORS:
Karen Kwan
Kenny Chan
WRITER:
Tim Cohrs
PHOTOGRAPHER:
John Huet
CLIENT:
Lai Venuti & Lai
AGENCY:
Lai Venuti & Lai/
Santa Clara

418
ART DIRECTOR:
Cameron Bridges
WRITERS:
Kim Genkinger
Aaron Stern
PHOTOGRAPHER:
Todd Droy
CLIENT:
McClain Finlon
Advertising
AGENCY:
McClain Finlon
Advertising/Denver

415

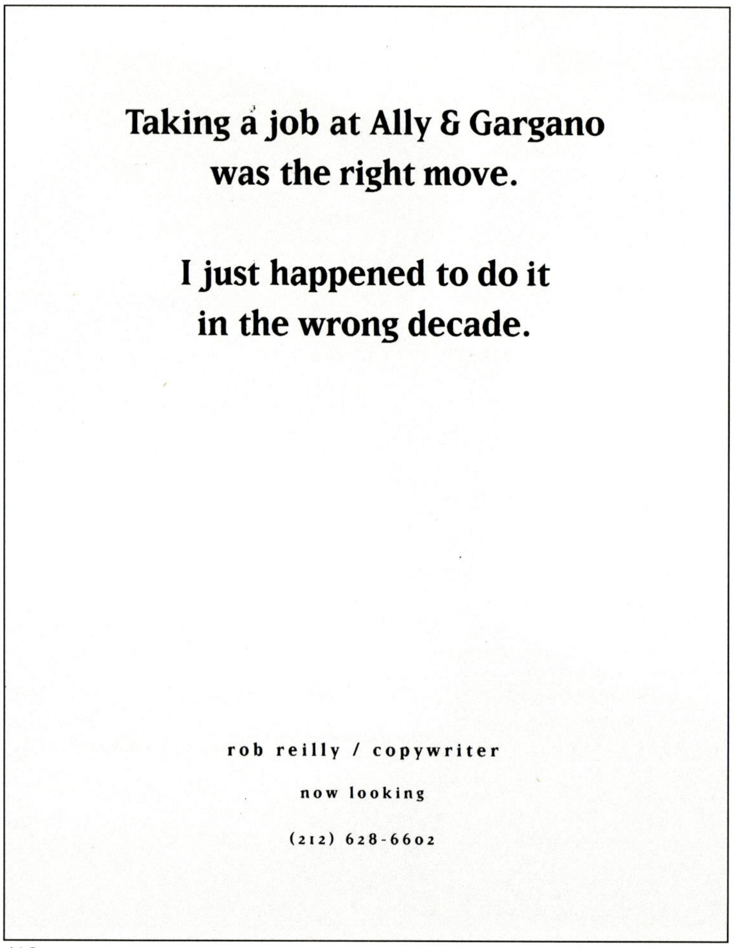

416

COMPETITION

417

PART OF YOU WILL LEARN.
PART OF YOU WILL CLEAN.
THE McCLAIN FINLON INTERNSHIP PROGRAM. IT'S FOR THOSE OF YOU INTERESTED IN EXPLORING CREATIVE, ACCOUNT SERVICES OR MEDIA. BUT NOT FOR FOR THOSE OF YOU ABOVE TITLES LIKE WHIPPING BOY, COPY CLOWN OR GO-FER. WANNA PLAY? CALL (303) 436 9400

418

COLLATERAL
SELF-PROMOTION

419
ART DIRECTORS:
Jeffrey Keyton
Stacy Drummond
ILLUSTRATOR:
David Sandlin
CLIENT:
MTV
AGENCY:
MTV/New York

420
ART DIRECTOR:
Thomas Walmrath
WRITER:
Guido Heffels
CLIENT:
Appel Grafik GmbH
AGENCY:
Springer & Jacoby
Werbung GmbH/Hamburg

421
ART DIRECTORS:
Gavin Bradley
Len Cheeseman
WRITER:
Damien Wilkins
ILLUSTRATOR:
Evan Purdie
TYPOGRAPHERS:
Len Cheeseman
Gavin Bradley
Carl Kennard
Eric de Vries
PHOTOGRAPHERS:
Bill Binzen
Matt Blamires
Ross Brown
Malcolm Burdan
Judy Darragh
Gideon Mendel
Bill Paynter
George Simhoni
Heinz Sobiecki
Tony Squares
John Swannell
Lee Tamahori
Arno Wirtz
CLIENT:
Saatchi & Saatchi/
New Zealand
AGENCY:
Saatchi & Saatchi/
Wellington, New Zealand

419

420

SAATCHI & SAATCHI
ADVERTISING
101-103 COURTENAY PLACE, PO BOX 6540, TE ARO, WELLINGTON
TEL: +64-4-385 6524. FAX: +64-4-385 4463
PETER CULLINANE

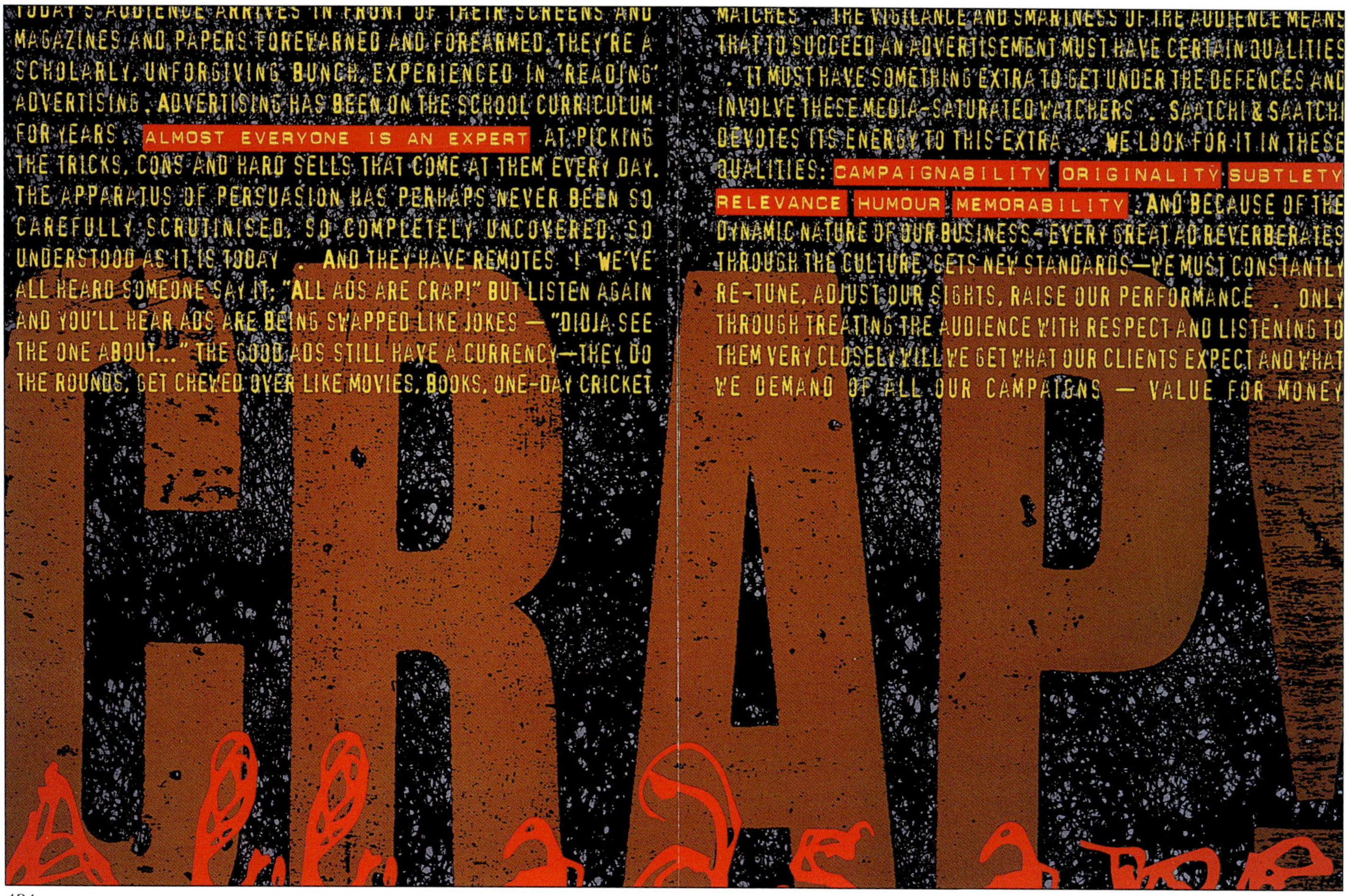
TODAY'S AUDIENCE ARRIVES IN FRONT OF THEIR SCREENS AND MAGAZINES AND PAPERS FOREWARNED AND FOREARMED. THEY'RE A SCHOLARLY, UNFORGIVING BUNCH, EXPERIENCED IN 'READING' ADVERTISING. ADVERTISING HAS BEEN ON THE SCHOOL CURRICULUM FOR YEARS. ALMOST EVERYONE IS AN EXPERT AT PICKING THE TRICKS, CONS AND HARD SELLS THAT COME AT THEM EVERY DAY. THE APPARATUS OF PERSUASION HAS PERHAPS NEVER BEEN SO CAREFULLY SCRUTINISED, SO COMPLETELY UNCOVERED, SO UNDERSTOOD AS IT IS TODAY. AND THEY HAVE REMOTES! WE'VE ALL HEARD SOMEONE SAY IT: "ALL ADS ARE CRAP!" BUT LISTEN AGAIN AND YOU'LL HEAR ADS ARE BEING SWAPPED LIKE JOKES — "DIDJA SEE THE ONE ABOUT..." THE GOOD ADS STILL HAVE A CURRENCY—THEY DO THE ROUNDS, GET CHEWED OVER LIKE MOVIES, BOOKS, ONE-DAY CRICKET
MATCHES. THE VIGILANCE AND SMARTNESS OF THE AUDIENCE MEANS THAT TO SUCCEED AN ADVERTISEMENT MUST HAVE CERTAIN QUALITIES. IT MUST HAVE SOMETHING EXTRA TO GET UNDER THE DEFENCES AND INVOLVE THESE MEDIA-SATURATED WATCHERS. SAATCHI & SAATCHI DEVOTES ITS ENERGY TO THIS EXTRA. WE LOOK FOR IT IN THESE QUALITIES: CAMPAIGNABILITY ORIGINALITY SUBTLETY RELEVANCE HUMOUR MEMORABILITY. AND BECAUSE OF THE DYNAMIC NATURE OF OUR BUSINESS - EVERY GREAT AD REVERBERATES THROUGH THE CULTURE, SETS NEW STANDARDS—WE MUST CONSTANTLY RE-TUNE, ADJUST OUR SIGHTS, RAISE OUR PERFORMANCE. ONLY THROUGH TREATING THE AUDIENCE WITH RESPECT AND LISTENING TO THEM VERY CLOSELY WILL WE GET WHAT OUR CLIENTS EXPECT AND WHAT WE DEMAND OF ALL OUR CAMPAIGNS — VALUE FOR MONEY
CRAP

COLLATERAL
POSTERS

422
ART DIRECTOR:
Jason Bramley
WRITERS:
Jonathan Biggins
Andrew Flemming
PHOTOGRAPHER:
John Clang
CLIENT:
Air New Zealand
AGENCY:
Bates/Singapore

423
ART DIRECTORS:
Elvio Sanchez
Fabian Lynch
WRITER:
Julio Wallovits
CLIENT:
Madame Sol
AGENCY:
BDDP Mancebo Kaye/
Madrid

424
ART DIRECTOR:
Michael Caguin
WRITER:
Stephen Etzine
CLIENT:
The Blarney Touch
AGENCY:
The Campbell Group/
Baltimore

425
ART DIRECTOR:
Lee Hester
WRITER:
Scott Boswell
PHOTOGRAPHER:
James Archambeault
CLIENT:
Kentucky Tourism
AGENCY:
Creative Alliance/
Louisville

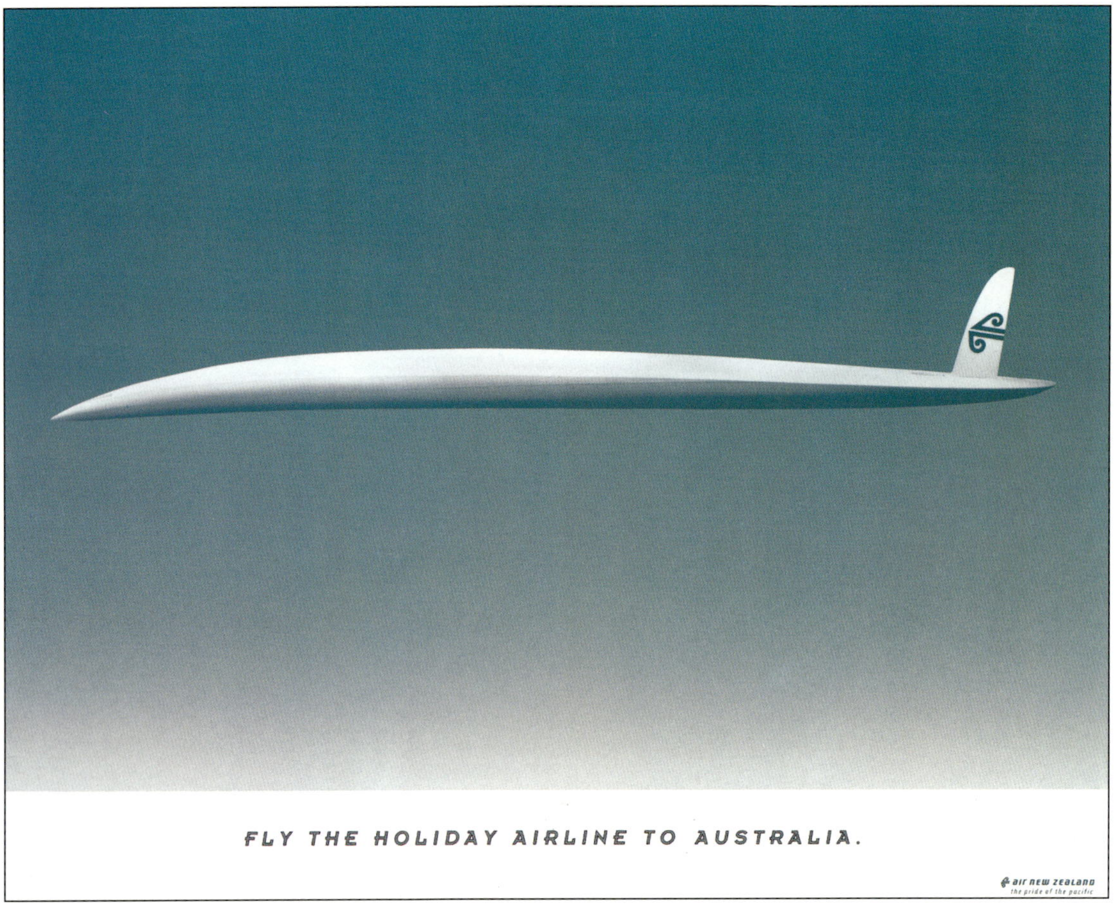

422

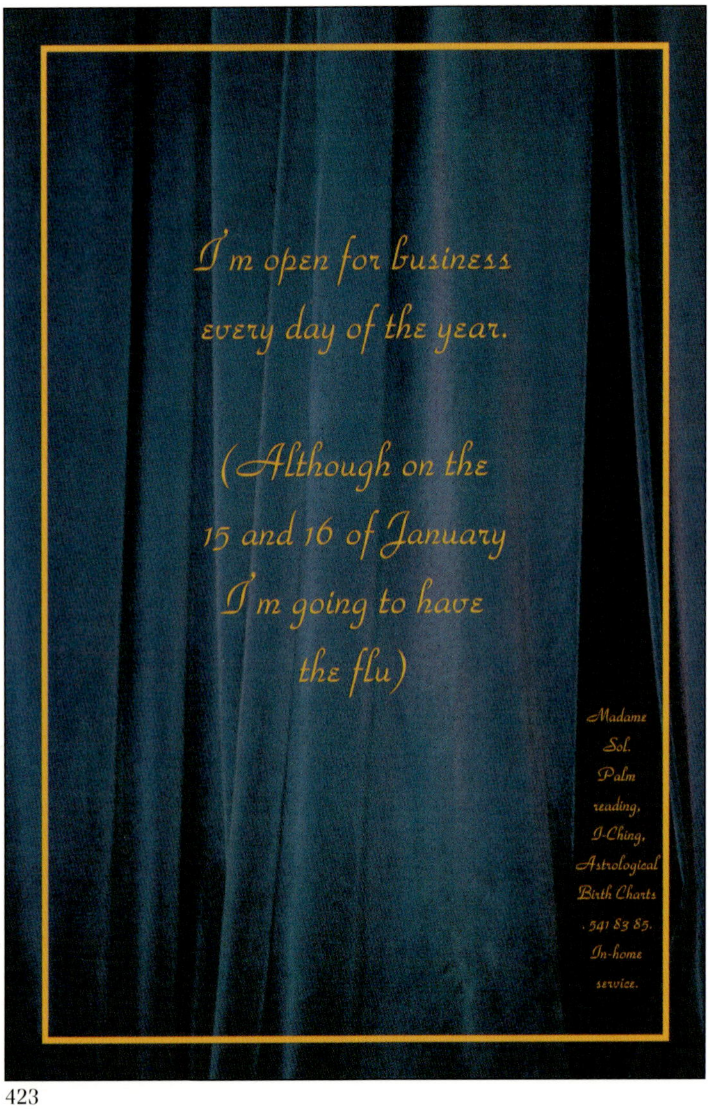

423

"I'm no
Michelangelo,
but at least I won't take
4 years to paint
your ceiling."
Tommy Doonan
The Blarney Touch
House Painting
954) 969-8653

424

From the historic homes and meeting places to the simplistic beauty of Shaker furniture and crafts, nearly everything at the Shaker Village of Pleasant Hill remains as it was 200 years ago. Except for the peaceful Shakers themselves.
As practicing celibates, their order died out in 1923. But their past, along with the rest of Kentucky's rich history, is alive and well. And equally inspiring is a trip to My Old Kentucky Home in Bardstown.
There are also any number of fascinating museums and guided tours through many of Kentucky's beautiful and historic homes. Take yourself back in time. Explore Kentucky.
For your free Kentucky Vacation Guide, call 1-800-225-TRIP.
THE SHAKERS. EXPERTS IN PRESERVING EVERYTHING BUT THEMSELVES.
Kentucky
What You've Been Looking For

425

COLLATERAL
POSTERS

426
ART DIRECTORS:
Markham Cronin
Tony Calcao
Alex Bogusky
WRITER:
Scott Linnen
PHOTOGRAPHERS:
Jose Molina
Tony Calcao
CLIENT:
Shimano American Corporation
AGENCY:
Crispin & Porter/Miami

427
ART DIRECTOR:
Braden Bickle
WRITER:
Braden Bickle
PHOTOGRAPHER:
Robbie Capps
CLIENT:
Big Ride
AGENCY:
Dally/Dallas

428
ART DIRECTOR:
Ellen Steinberg
WRITER:
Luke Sullivan
PHOTOGRAPHER:
Shawn Michienzie
ILLUSTRATOR:
Ellen Steinberg
CLIENT:
BMW of North America
AGENCY:
Fallon McElligott/Minneapolis

429
ART DIRECTOR:
Jennifer Fleming-Balser
WRITER:
Dylan Lee
CLIENT:
The Comedy Connection
AGENCY:
Hey, They Copied That Out of C.A./Austin

426

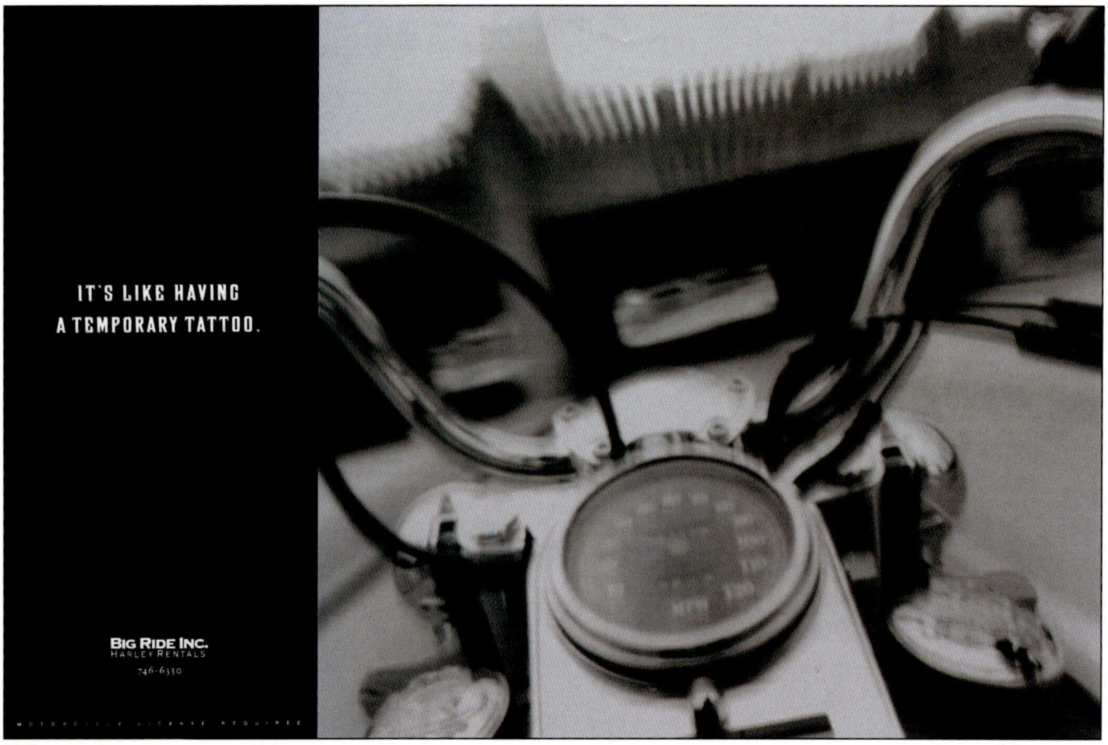

427

BMW
All BMWs are cut from the same cloth.
Which may explain why 4 out of the top 5 finishers at LeMans,
including the winner, were racecars powered by BMW.

428

Tonight's material may be offensive to:

Blacks, whites, Asians, Italians, people who think Elvis is alive, people who think they're Elvis, Elvis, Baptists, Catholics, the KKK, Tammy Faye, Satanists, white trash, recycled trash, he or she who is politically correct, ugly people, pretty people, homosexuals, heterosexuals, nuns, asexuals, rabid dogs, dog lovers, rabid dog lovers, rabid lovers, lawyers, waste management technicians, people who actually feel a tingling sensation when using shampoo on one half of their hair, young people, old people, dead people, democrats, republicans, anarchists, politicians' girlfriends, politicians' boyfriends, models, scientists, model scientists, the butcher, the baker, the candlestick maker, you and what army, rock groups, anyone who's ever line danced to "Achy Breaky Heart," Trekkies, nerds, fat brain surgeons, those who like their toilet paper with the sheets coming over the top, vegetables, minerals, stoics, people who say "duh" a lot, intellectuals, men who dress like women, women who dress like men, men who dress like women who dress like men, those who like their toilet paper with the sheets coming under the bottom, *Not Me* from "The Family Circus," PBS, the MTV generation, baby boomers, the Kabyles tribe of North Africa, hookers, fleas, ducks, mice, and the people who make commercials with women smiling about feminine hygiene products.

comedy CONNECTION

*Views expressed by comedians may not necessarily reflect those of management.

429

COLLATERAL
POSTERS

430
ART DIRECTOR:
Ginger Hood
WRITER:
Rich Tlapek
CLIENT:
Hill Holliday
AGENCY:
Hill Holliday Connors
Cosmopulos/Boston

431
ART DIRECTOR:
Mark Fuller
WRITER:
Joe Nagy
PHOTOGRAPHER:
Michael Rausch
CLIENT:
Mercedes-Benz of
North America
AGENCY:
The Martin Agency/
Richmond

432
ART DIRECTOR:
Mark Fuller
WRITER:
Joe Nagy
PHOTOGRAPHER:
Oli Tennet
CLIENT:
Moto Europa
AGENCY:
The Martin Agency/
Richmond

433
ART DIRECTOR:
Mark Fuller
WRITER:
Joe Nagy
PHOTOGRAPHER:
Kyoichi Nakamura
CLIENT:
Moto Europa
AGENCY:
The Martin Agency/
Richmond

IT'S THE NEXT
BEST THING
TO LEAVING
ADVERTISING
FOR GOOD.
And you thought there was no way out. Take a sabbatical with full pay for up to 4 months as a public service volunteer in the field of your choice. To qualify you need 5 years of experience with the agency. Which is long enough to make you want to quit for a while. For details call Margaret at ext. 3473.
HILL HOLLIDAY SABBATICAL

430

Taxicabs make pretty good slalom cones.
The Next Generation E-Class

431

SO, LUST IS
ONE OF THE SEVEN
DEADLY SINS.
SEE YOU IN HELL.
804-355-0550, 1220 North Boulevard, Richmond, Virginia
moto europa
THE EUROPEAN MOTORCYCLE CENTER

THIS MACHINE MIGHT
OFFEND SENSITIVE,
POLITICALLY CORRECT TYPES.
HERE'S WHERE TO GET ONE.
804-355-0550, 1220 North Boulevard, Richmond, Virginia
moto europa
THE EUROPEAN MOTORCYCLE CENTER

434
ART DIRECTOR:
Bob Meagher
WRITER:
Joe Nagy
PHOTOGRAPHER:
Michael Waine
CLIENT:
Wrangler Company
AGENCY:
The Martin Agency/
Richmond

435
ART DIRECTOR:
Dave Piatkowski
WRITER:
Jon Krevolin
PHOTOGRAPHER:
Joel Markman
CLIENT:
Accounting Partners
AGENCY:
ODBB Advertising/
New York

436
ART DIRECTOR:
Dave Piatkowski
WRITER:
Jon Krevolin
PHOTOGRAPHER:
Joel Markman
CLIENT:
Accounting Partners
AGENCY:
ODBB Advertising/
New York

It's like a trailer hitch for your jeans.
If you're looking for a great pair of jeans, look for the loop. It's there to tell you that you've found the only jeans built specifically for the great outdoors.
Wrangler RUGGED WEAR
Geared For The Outdoors
434

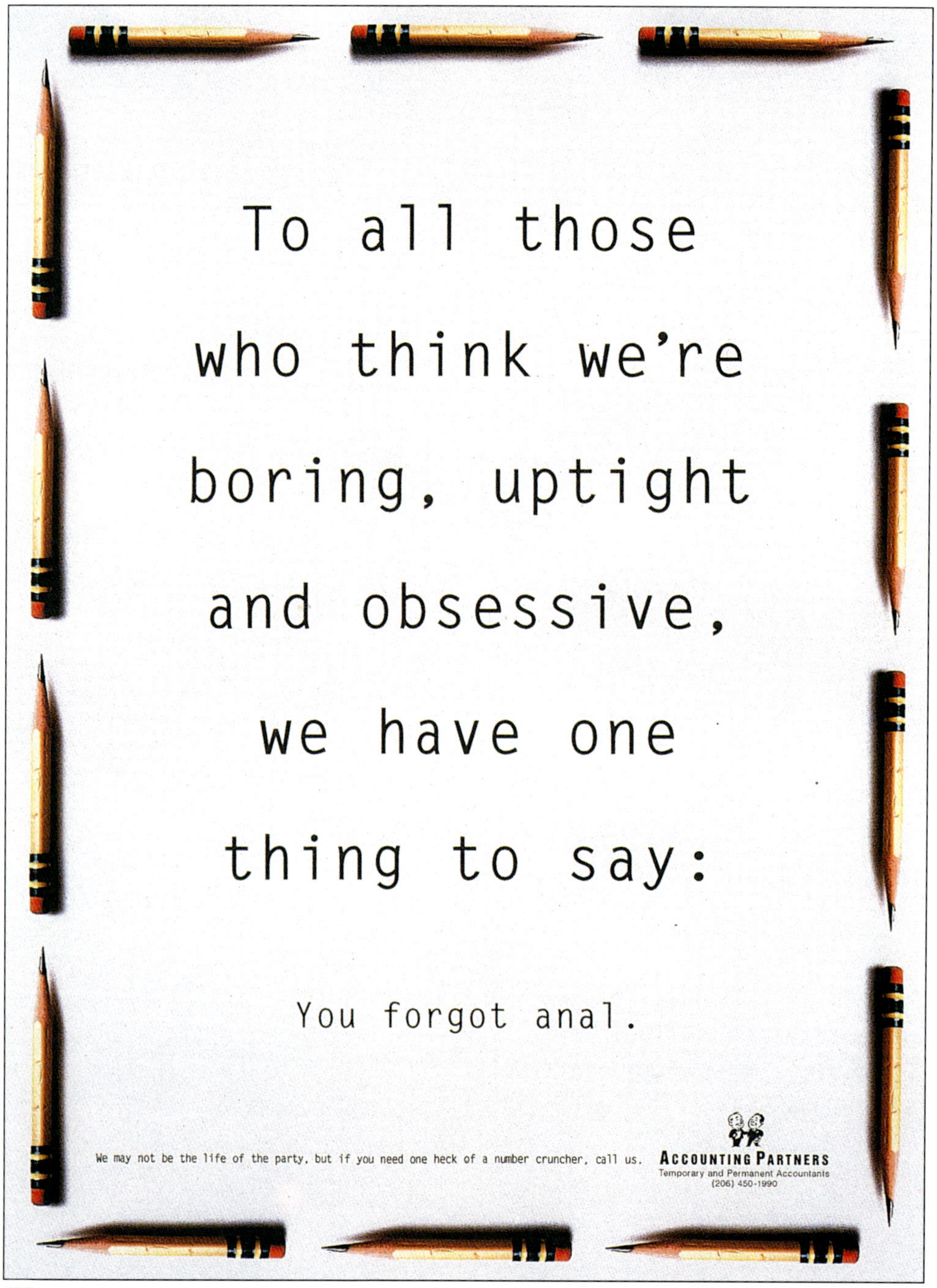

To all those who think we're boring, uptight and obsessive, we have one thing to say:
You forgot anal.
We may not be the life of the party, but if you need one heck of a number cruncher, call us.

435

Remember that kid you used to copy off in math class?
Now he's got a day rate.
If you need a little help with your accounting, call us. It's not cheating anymore.
ACCOUNTING PARTNERS
Temporary and Permanent Accountants
(206) 450-1990

Some of history's most enduring official documents were drafted with pencils. The Gettysburg Address, for example. Small wonder then, the largest consumer of pencils today is the U.S. government. They buy 45 million a year. Probably for as little as $20 each, with their bulk discount.

Public Service & Political Finalists

PUBLIC SERVICE/
POLITICAL NEWSPAPER
OR MAGAZINE: SINGLE

437
ART DIRECTOR:
Elvio Sanchez
WRITER:
Julio Wallovits
TYPOGRAPHER:
Fabian Lynch
CLIENT:
International Blind Sports Association
AGENCY:
BDDP Mancebo Kaye/ Madrid

438
ART DIRECTOR:
Fabian Lynch
WRITER:
Julio Wallovits
PHOTOGRAPHER:
Francois Labastie
CLIENT:
Nou Raco
AGENCY:
BDDP Mancebo Kaye/ Madrid

439
ART DIRECTORS:
George Capuano
Glenn Price
WRITER:
Larry Cadman
PHOTOGRAPHER:
Steve Hellerstein
CLIENT:
Boy Scouts of America
AGENCY:
Bozell/New York

440
ART DIRECTORS:
Norman Alcuri
Fiona Chen
WRITER:
Andrew Bruck
CLIENT:
Asia Watch
AGENCY:
DMB&B Tokyu/Singapore

437

438

NASA DIDN'T JUST
SAY TO JIM LOVELL,
"HEY, YOU LOOK LIKE
A GOOD
GUY, WANT TO
GO TO THE MOON?"
FOR THE COMMANDER OF APOLLO 13,
THE COUNTDOWN STARTED EARLY.
WHEN HE JOINED TROOP 60 AT AGE TWELVE.
EAGLE SCOUT
SCOUTING
For Life.

439

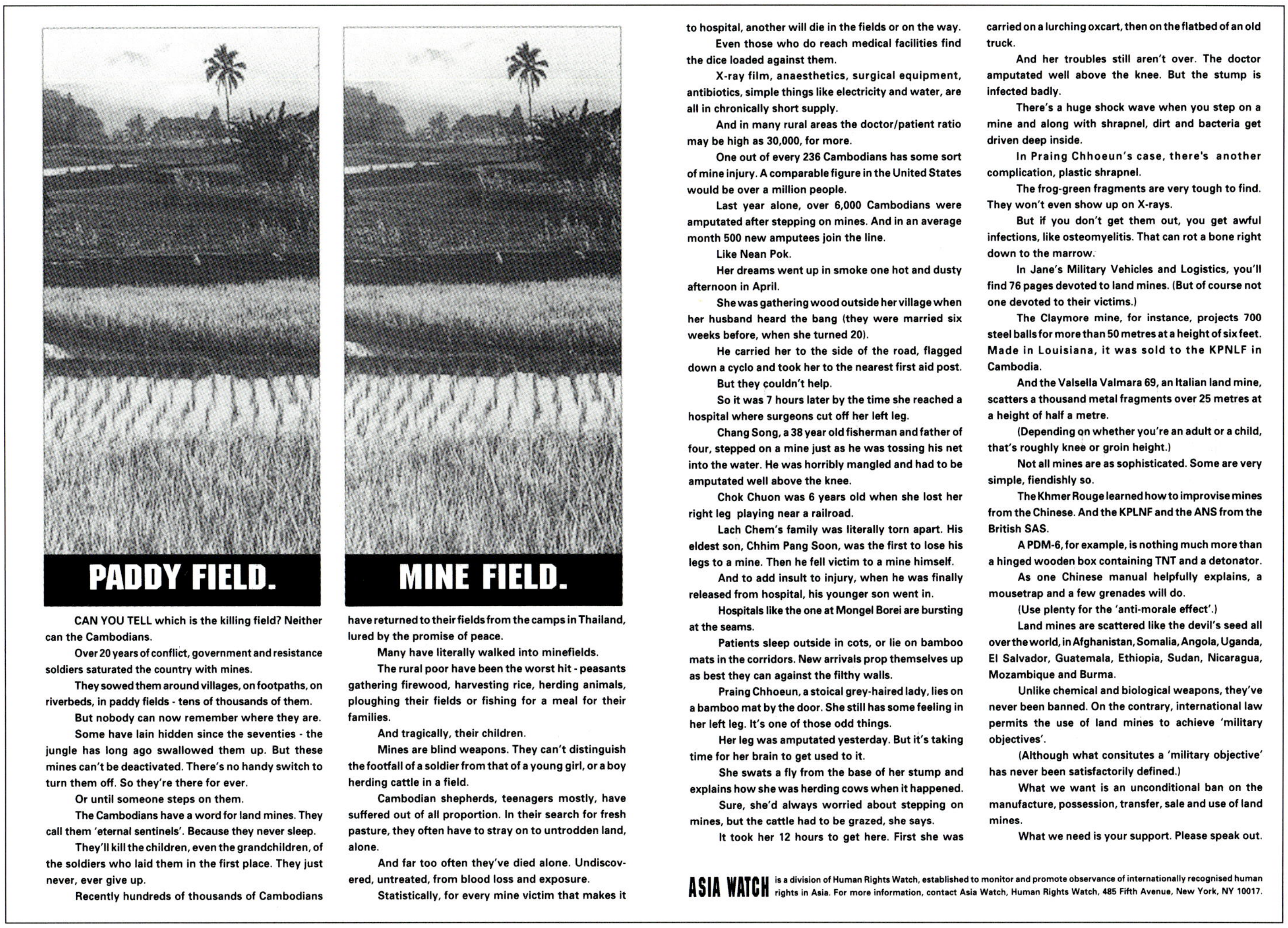
PADDY FIELD.
MINE FIELD.
CAN YOU TELL which is the killing field? Neither can the Cambodians.
Over 20 years of conflict, government and resistance soldiers saturated the country with mines.
They sowed them around villages, on footpaths, on riverbeds, in paddy fields - tens of thousands of them.
But nobody can now remember where they are.
Some have lain hidden since the seventies - the jungle has long ago swallowed them up. But these mines can't be deactivated. There's no handy switch to turn them off. So they're there for ever.
Or until someone steps on them.
The Cambodians have a word for land mines. They call them 'eternal sentinels'. Because they never sleep.
They'll kill the children, even the grandchildren, of the soldiers who laid them in the first place. They just never, ever give up.
Recently hundreds of thousands of Cambodians have returned to their fields from the camps in Thailand, lured by the promise of peace.
Many have literally walked into minefields.
The rural poor have been the worst hit - peasants gathering firewood, harvesting rice, herding animals, ploughing their fields or fishing for a meal for their families.
And tragically, their children.
Mines are blind weapons. They can't distinguish the footfall of a soldier from that of a young girl, or a boy herding cattle in a field.
Cambodian shepherds, teenagers mostly, have suffered out of all proportion. In their search for fresh pasture, they often have to stray on to untrodden land, alone.
And far too often they've died alone. Undiscovered, untreated, from blood loss and exposure.
Statistically, for every mine victim that makes it to hospital, another will die in the fields or on the way.
Even those who do reach medical facilities find the dice loaded against them.
X-ray film, anaesthetics, surgical equipment, antibiotics, simple things like electricity and water, are all in chronically short supply.
And in many rural areas the doctor/patient ratio may be high as 30,000, for more.
One out of every 236 Cambodians has some sort of mine injury. A comparable figure in the United States would be over a million people.
Last year alone, over 6,000 Cambodians were amputated after stepping on mines. And in an average month 500 new amputees join the line.
Like Nean Pok.
Her dreams went up in smoke one hot and dusty afternoon in April.
She was gathering wood outside her village when her husband heard the bang (they were married six weeks before, when she turned 20).
He carried her to the side of the road, flagged down a cyclo and took her to the nearest first aid post.
But they couldn't help.
So it was 7 hours later by the time she reached a hospital where surgeons cut off her left leg.
Chang Song, a 38 year old fisherman and father of four, stepped on a mine just as he was tossing his net into the water. He was horribly mangled and had to be amputated well above the knee.
Chok Chuon was 6 years old when she lost her right leg playing near a railroad.
Lach Chem's family was literally torn apart. His eldest son, Chhim Pang Soon, was the first to lose his legs to a mine. Then he fell victim to a mine himself.
And to add insult to injury, when he was finally released from hospital, his younger son went in.
Hospitals like the one at Mongel Borei are bursting at the seams.
Patients sleep outside in cots, or lie on bamboo mats in the corridors. New arrivals prop themselves up as best they can against the filthy walls.
Praing Chhoeun, a stoical grey-haired lady, lies on a bamboo mat by the door. She still has some feeling in her left leg. It's one of those odd things.
Her leg was amputated yesterday. But it's taking time for her brain to get used to it.
She swats a fly from the base of her stump and explains how she was herding cows when it happened.
Sure, she'd always worried about stepping on mines, but the cattle had to be grazed, she says.
It took her 12 hours to get here. First she was carried on a lurching oxcart, then on the flatbed of an old truck.
And her troubles still aren't over. The doctor amputated well above the knee. But the stump is infected badly.
There's a huge shock wave when you step on a mine and along with shrapnel, dirt and bacteria get driven deep inside.
In Praing Chhoeun's case, there's another complication, plastic shrapnel.
The frog-green fragments are very tough to find. They won't even show up on X-rays.
But if you don't get them out, you get awful infections, like osteomyelitis. That can rot a bone right down to the marrow.
In Jane's Military Vehicles and Logistics, you'll find 76 pages devoted to land mines. (But of course not one devoted to their victims.)
The Claymore mine, for instance, projects 700 steel balls for more than 50 metres at a height of six feet. Made in Louisiana, it was sold to the KPNLF in Cambodia.
And the Valsella Valmara 69, an Italian land mine, scatters a thousand metal fragments over 25 metres at a height of half a metre.
(Depending on whether you're an adult or a child, that's roughly knee or groin height.)
Not all mines are as sophisticated. Some are very simple, fiendishly so.
The Khmer Rouge learned how to improvise mines from the Chinese. And the KPLNF and the ANS from the British SAS.
A PDM-6, for example, is nothing much more than a hinged wooden box containing TNT and a detonator.
As one Chinese manual helpfully explains, a mousetrap and a few grenades will do.
(Use plenty for the 'anti-morale effect'.)
Land mines are scattered like the devil's seed all over the world, in Afghanistan, Somalia, Angola, Uganda, El Salvador, Guatemala, Ethiopia, Sudan, Nicaragua, Mozambique and Burma.
Unlike chemical and biological weapons, they've never been banned. On the contrary, international law permits the use of land mines to achieve 'military objectives'.
(Although what consitutes a 'military objective' has never been satisfactorily defined.)
What we want is an unconditional ban on the manufacture, possession, transfer, sale and use of land mines.
What we need is your support. Please speak out.
ASIA WATCH is a division of Human Rights Watch, established to monitor and promote observance of internationally recognised human rights in Asia. For more information, contact Asia Watch, Human Rights Watch, 485 Fifth Avenue, New York, NY 10017.

440

PUBLIC SERVICE/
POLITICAL NEWSPAPER
OR MAGAZINE: SINGLE

441
ART DIRECTOR:
Bob Barrie
WRITER:
Phil Calvit
PHOTOGRAPHER:
Rick Dublin
CLIENT:
Cease Fire
AGENCY:
Fallon McElligott/
Minneapolis

442
ART DIRECTOR:
Robb Burnham
WRITER:
Sally Hogshead
PHOTOGRAPHER:
Marc Norberg
CLIENT:
Minneapolis Animal
Shelter
AGENCY:
Fallon McElligott/
Minneapolis

443
ART DIRECTOR:
Robb Burnham
WRITER:
Sally Hogshead
PHOTOGRAPHER:
Marc Norberg
CLIENT:
Minneapolis Animal
Shelter
AGENCY:
Fallon McElligott/
Minneapolis

444
ART DIRECTOR:
Jennifer Ward
WRITER:
Kevin Lynch
ILLUSTRATOR:
Kent Barton
CLIENT:
Partnership for a
Drug-Free America
AGENCY:
Four Walls and a Roof/
Chicago

441

442

Expiration Date:
MON. SEPT 25
He's long haired, litter-trained, playful and affectionate (for a cat). He's also one of 60 animals scheduled to be put to sleep on Monday, unless he finds a home. *Adopt. Fast. 348-4250.* MINNEAPOLIS ANIMAL SHELTER

443

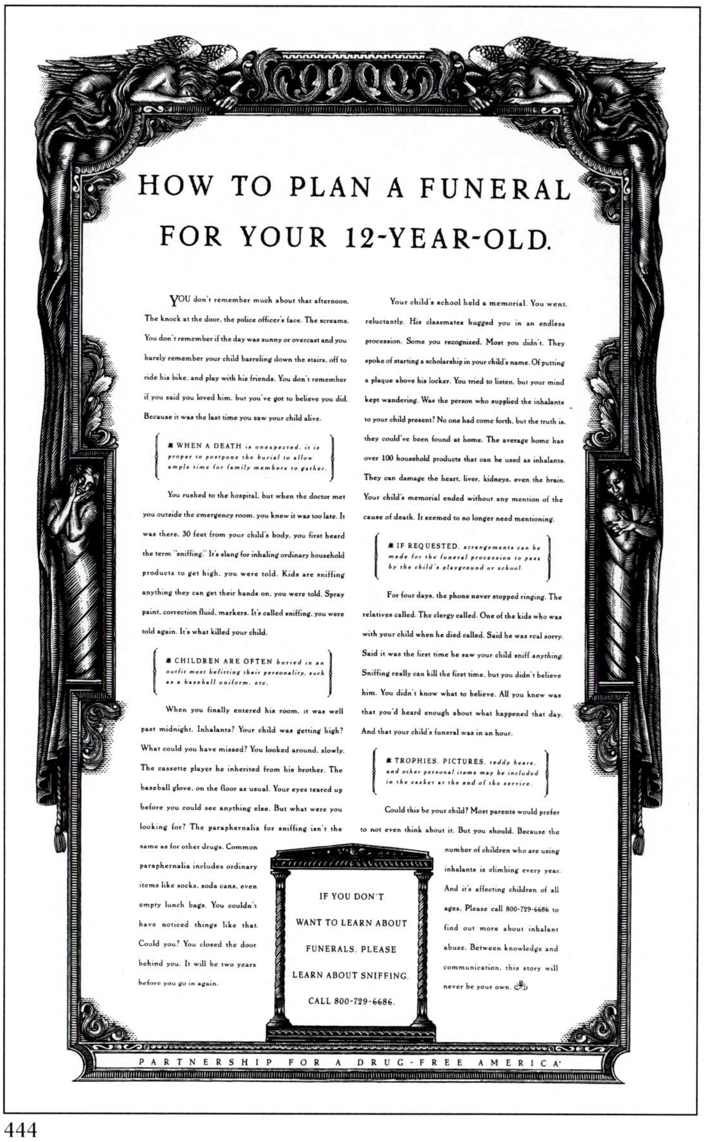
HOW TO PLAN A FUNERAL FOR YOUR 12-YEAR-OLD.
YOU don't remember much about that afternoon. The knock at the door, the police officer's face. The screams. You don't remember if the day was sunny or overcast and you barely remember your child barreling down the stairs, off to ride his bike, and play with his friends. You don't remember if you said you loved him, but you've got to believe you did. Because it was the last time you saw your child alive.
* WHEN A DEATH *is unexpected, it is proper to postpone the burial to allow ample time for family members to gather.*
You rushed to the hospital, but when the doctor met you outside the emergency room, you knew it was too late. It was there, 30 feet from your child's body, you first heard the term "sniffing." It's slang for inhaling ordinary household products to get high, you were told. Kids are sniffing anything they can get their hands on, you were told. Spray paint, correction fluid, markers. It's called sniffing, you were told again. It's what killed your child.
* CHILDREN ARE OFTEN *buried in an outfit most befitting their personality, such as a baseball uniform, etc.*
When you finally entered his room, it was well past midnight. Inhalants? Your child was getting high? What could you have missed? You looked around, slowly. The cassette player he inherited from his brother. The baseball glove, on the floor as usual. Your eyes teared up before you could see anything else. But what were you looking for? The paraphernalia for sniffing isn't the same as for other drugs. Common paraphernalia includes ordinary items like socks, soda cans, even empty lunch bags. You couldn't have noticed things like that. Could you? You closed the door behind you. It will be two years before you go in again.
Your child's school held a memorial. You went, reluctantly. His classmates hugged you in an endless procession. Some you recognized. Most you didn't. They spoke of starting a scholarship in your child's name. Of putting a plaque above his locker. You tried to listen, but your mind kept wandering. Was the person who supplied the inhalants to your child present? No one had come forth, but the truth is, they could've been found at home. The average home has over 100 household products that can be used as inhalants. They can damage the heart, liver, kidneys, even the brain. Your child's memorial ended without any mention of the cause of death. It seemed to no longer need mentioning.
* IF REQUESTED, *arrangements can be made for the funeral procession to pass by the child's playground or school.*
For four days, the phone never stopped ringing. The relatives called. The clergy called. One of the kids who was with your child when he died called. Said he was real sorry. Said it was the first time he saw your child sniff *anything*. Sniffing really can kill the first time, but you didn't believe him. You didn't know what to believe. All you knew was that you'd heard enough about what happened that day. And that your child's funeral was in an hour.
* TROPHIES, PICTURES, *teddy bears, and other personal items may be included in the casket at the end of the service.*
Could this be your child? Most parents would prefer to not even think about it. But you should. Because the number of children who are using inhalants is climbing every year. And it's affecting children of all ages. Please call 800-729-6686 to find out more about inhalant abuse. Between knowledge and communication, this story will never be your own.
IF YOU DON'T WANT TO LEARN ABOUT FUNERALS, PLEASE LEARN ABOUT SNIFFING. CALL 800-729-6686.
PARTNERSHIP FOR A DRUG-FREE AMERICA

444

PUBLIC SERVICE/
POLITICAL NEWSPAPER
OR MAGAZINE: SINGLE

445
ART DIRECTOR:
Jennifer Fleming-Balser
WRITERS:
Rich Tlapek
Chuck Meehan
CLIENT:
Babe Ruth Museum
AGENCY:
GSD&M Advertising/
Austin

446
ART DIRECTOR:
Ted Royer
WRITER:
John Simpson
CLIENT:
Roger Williams Park Zoo
AGENCY:
Leonard/Monahan,
Providence

447
ART DIRECTOR:
Derrick Haas
WRITER:
Justin Rogers
PHOTOGRAPHER:
Jack Bankhead
TYPOGRAPHER:
Rob Wallis
CLIENT:
Guide Dogs For The Blind
Association
AGENCY:
McCann-Erickson/London

448
ART DIRECTOR:
Cliff Sorah
WRITER:
Joe Alexander
CLIENT:
John F. Kennedy Library
Foundation
AGENCY:
The Martin Agency/
Richmond

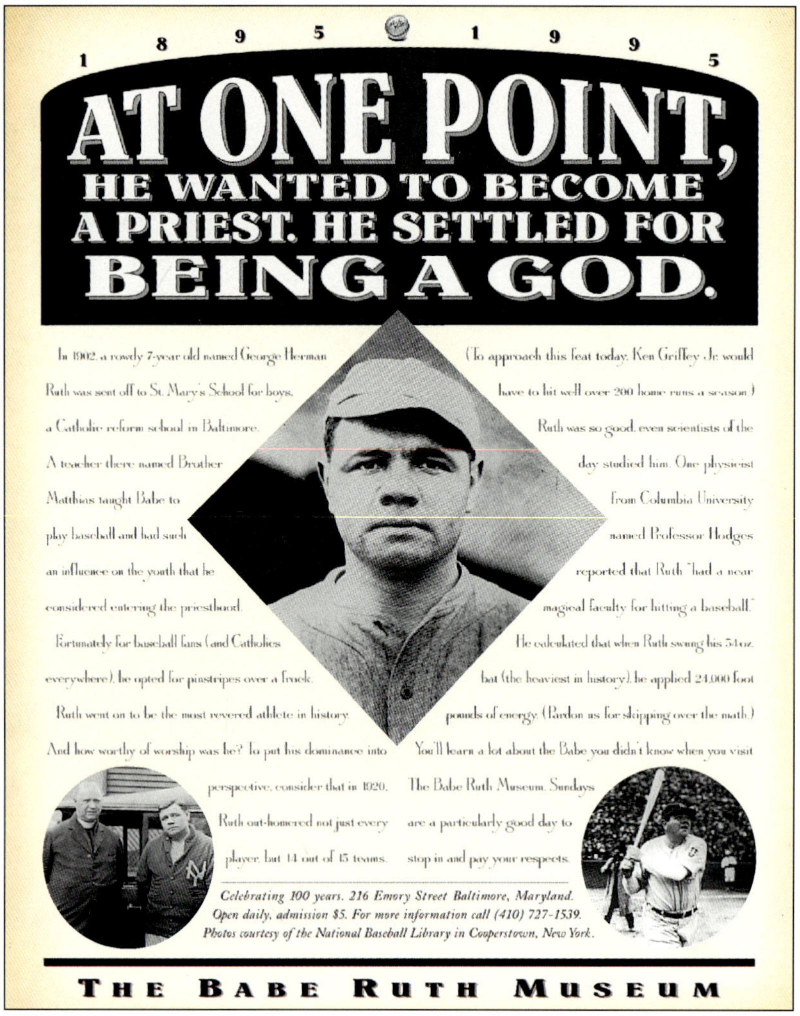

445

446

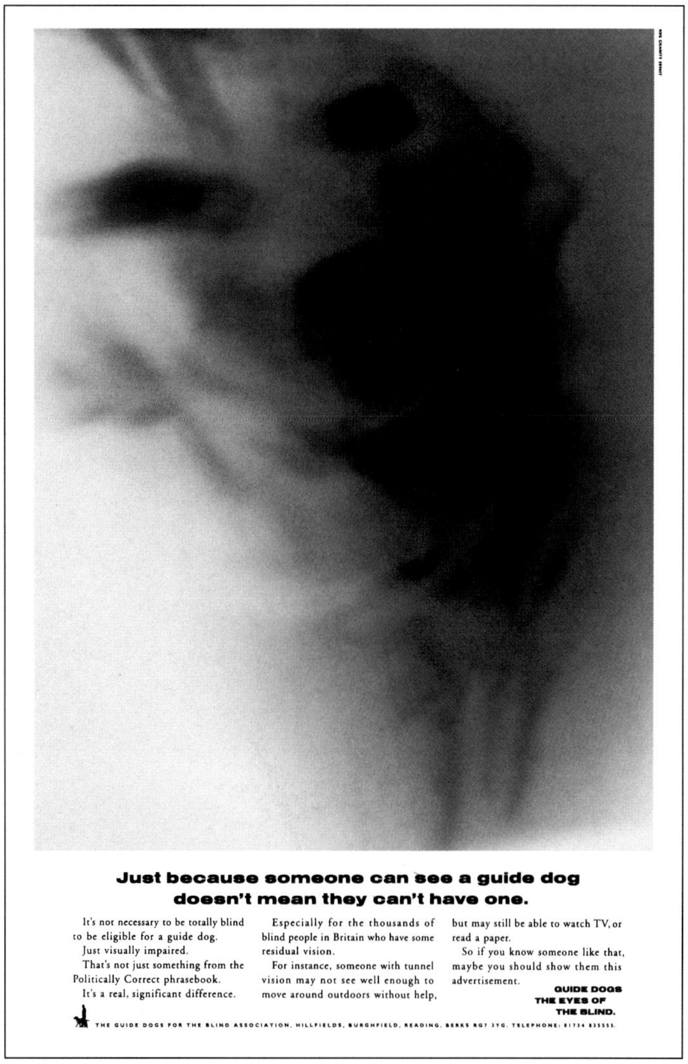
Just because someone can see a guide dog doesn't mean they can't have one.
It's not necessary to be totally blind to be eligible for a guide dog.
Just visually impaired.
That's not just something from the Politically Correct phrasebook.
It's a real, significant difference.
Especially for the thousands of blind people in Britain who have some residual vision.
For instance, someone with tunnel vision may not see well enough to move around outdoors without help, but may still be able to watch TV, or read a paper.
So if you know someone like that, maybe you should show them this advertisement.
GUIDE DOGS THE EYES OF THE BLIND.
THE GUIDE DOGS FOR THE BLIND ASSOCIATION, HILLFIELDS, BURGHFIELD, READING, BERKS RG7 3YG. TELEPHONE: 01734 835555.

447

COMMUNISM. NUCLEAR WAR.
THE STRUGGLE FOR CIVIL RIGHTS.
NO WONDER HIS BACK HURT.
From the moment he took office in January of 1961, John F. Kennedy wrestled with one history-making issue after another. Cuba. Segregation in the South. Space. Berlin. Southeast Asia. At The New Museum at the John F. Kennedy Library, you'll retrace every one of these vital moments. Through video, interviews, and period re-creations, you'll debate Richard Nixon. Face off with Fidel Castro. Challenge Khrushchev. Cheer for astronaut John Glenn. As you step into the past, an interesting thing will happen. You'll step into the present and future, too. Because as you learn how John Kennedy handled critical issues, you'll develop a keener perspective on how national leaders handle foreign affairs. And how past issues are still playing out today. So plan to visit us soon. Or just call 617-929-4523 today to learn more. After all, as JFK said, "we celebrate the past to awaken the future."
THE NEW MUSEUM AT THE JFK LIBRARY

448

PUBLIC SERVICE/
POLITICAL NEWSPAPER
OR MAGAZINE: SINGLE

449
ART DIRECTOR:
Tom McMahon
WRITER:
Tim Wallis
PHOTOGRAPH:
America's Black
Holocaust Museum
Yuenkel Studios
CLIENT:
America's Black
Holocaust Museum
AGENCY:
Meyer & Wallis/Milwaukee

450
ART DIRECTOR:
Nick Schon
WRITER:
Maxine Baker
PHOTOGRAPHER:
Leo Regan
TYPOGRAPHER:
Roger Kennedy
CLIENT:
Joint Israel Appeal
AGENCY:
Saatchi & Saatchi/London

451
ART DIRECTORS:
Len Cheeseman
Evan Purdie
WRITERS:
Ken Double
Steve Cooper
PHOTOGRAPHER:
Tony Squares
ILLUSTRATOR:
Evan Purdie
TYPOGRAPHERS:
Len Cheeseman
Carl Kennard
CLIENT:
New Zealand Red Cross
AGENCY:
Saatchi & Saatchi/
Wellington, New Zealand

449

450

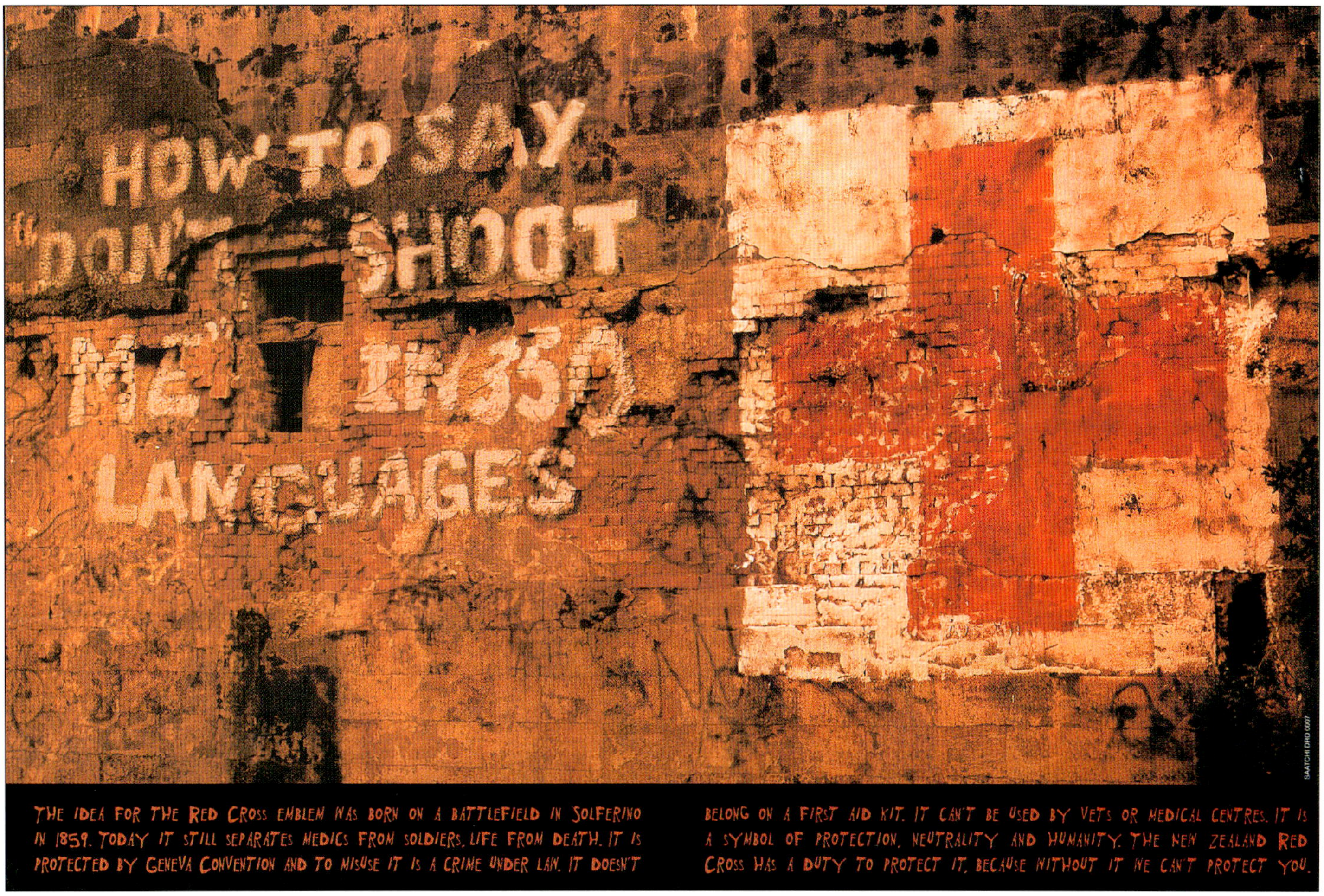
HOW TO SAY
"DON'T SHOOT
ME" IN 350
LANGUAGES
SAATCHI DRD 0007
THE IDEA FOR THE RED CROSS EMBLEM WAS BORN ON A BATTLEFIELD IN SOLFERINO IN 1859. TODAY IT STILL SEPARATES MEDICS FROM SOLDIERS, LIFE FROM DEATH. IT IS PROTECTED BY GENEVA CONVENTION AND TO MISUSE IT IS A CRIME UNDER LAW. IT DOESN'T BELONG ON A FIRST AID KIT. IT CAN'T BE USED BY VETS OR MEDICAL CENTRES. IT IS A SYMBOL OF PROTECTION, NEUTRALITY AND HUMANITY. THE NEW ZEALAND RED CROSS HAS A DUTY TO PROTECT IT, BECAUSE WITHOUT IT WE CAN'T PROTECT YOU.

PUBLIC SERVICE/ POLITICAL NEWSPAPER OR MAGAZINE: CAMPAIGN

452
ART DIRECTOR:
Doug Chapman
WRITER:
Mick O'Brien
PHOTOGRAPHERS:
Al Fisher
Herman Leonard
Bruce Peterson
CLIENT:
Jazz Foundation of America
AGENCY:
Allen & Gerritsen/ Watertown, MA

453
ART DIRECTOR:
John Butler
WRITER:
Ryan Ebner
PHOTOGRAPHER:
Heimo
CLIENT:
Homeward Bound of Marin
AGENCY:
Butler Shine & Stern/ Sausalito

ALWAYS THROW GARBAGE IN THE PROPER
TRASH RECEPTACLES.
MARIN'S HOMELESS NEED TO EAT, TOO.
PLEASE HELP MAKE A DIFFERENCE. MAKE A DONATION.
HOMEWARD BOUND OF MARIN 415-457-2157

THE AVERAGE HOME IN MARIN COSTS $382,000.
AND YOU'RE SURPRISED WE HAVE A HOMELESS PROBLEM?
PLEASE HELP MAKE A DIFFERENCE. MAKE A DONATION.
HOMEWARD BOUND OF MARIN 415-457-2157

MARIN HAS SOME OF THE NICEST
STREETS IN THE COUNTRY.
JUST ASK THE 1200 PEOPLE WHO SLEEP
ON THEM EVERY NIGHT.
PLEASE HELP MAKE A DIFFERENCE. MAKE A DONATION.
HOMEWARD BOUND OF MARIN 415-457-2157

PUBLIC SERVICE/
POLITICAL NEWSPAPER
OR MAGAZINE: CAMPAIGN

454
ART DIRECTOR:
Bhupesh Luther
WRITER:
Vidur Vohra
PHOTOGRAPHER:
Gaurav Bharadwaj
CLIENT:
The Doon School
AGENCY:
Contract Advertising/
New Delhi

455
ART DIRECTOR:
Bob Barrie
WRITER:
Phil Calvit
PHOTOGRAPHER:
Rick Dublin
CLIENT:
Cease Fire
AGENCY:
Fallon McElligott/
Minneapolis

THERE'S A LADY WHO DRIVES ABOUT IN AN OLD HERALD EVERY EVENING FEEDING COWS AND STRAY DOGS. RUMOUR HAS IT SHE'S MAD.
It must be true. She hangs around the butcher's shop all afternoon picking up scraps and innards. She collects stale bread, and scavenges for half-rotten fruit too. She puts them into little plastic bags as if they were gifts. Then she drives off in her rickety old car, humming tunelessly. She takes exactly the same route everyday. (They say the animals wait for her, and fret if she's late.) But if she's so concerned, why doesn't she feed hungry people instead? Maybe she does. Or maybe she's left that for sane people like us?
SMALL ACTS OF KINDNESS CAN CHANGE YOUR WORLD.
TRY IT.
DLK 4542
Issued in the interest of public kindness by the Doon School.

GO AWAY YOU HORRIBLE, LAZY WOMAN, FIND SOME HONEST WORK.
She lives in a deserted, crumbling ruin. She's a hundred years old. She's nearly blind. She can barely stand on her aching legs. And she hasn't eaten in days. Now, what is it you wanted her to do? Well, when she rings your doorbell, she has a pretty good idea of what she wants from you. She wants that stale bread you're going to throw into the bin. She wants the *katori* of *daal* that's been lying in your fridge for three days. She wants you to show her you can see the difference between someone who's greedy and someone who's just tired, weak and helpless. She thinks you can do it. And she sits down to wait.
SMALL ACTS OF KINDNESS CAN CHANGE YOUR WORLD.
TRY IT.
Issued in the interest of public kindness by the Doon School.

BUY SOMEONE ELSE'S CHILD A CHOCOLATE FOR A CHANGE.
Some children haven't seen a chocolate in their lives. They wouldn't know what to do if you gave them one. You'd have to show them how to take the wrapper off and coax them to take a bite. Then stand back and wait for their faces to break out into a smile. (As much from the taste of chocolate, as from the taste of unexpected kindness.) At this point you may find that you're smiling too (you may even notice tears welling up in your eyes). The children will probably run off to play. But, the look you saw on their faces will make you try it again sometime. With old toys perhaps. Or books. Or clothes. They all work just as well. For, as someone said, it is more fun to give than to receive, even though it isn't always tax deductible.
SMALL ACTS OF KINDNESS CAN CHANGE YOUR WORLD.
TRY IT.
Issued in the interest of public kindness by the Doon School.

West Monroe, LA.
Matilda Crabtree, 14. Shot and killed by father when she jumped from closet and yelled "Boo" to scare parents. Last words: "I love you, daddy."
A gun in the home is much more likely to kill a family member than to kill an intruder.
CEASE FIRE
Think about your family before you think about getting a handgun.

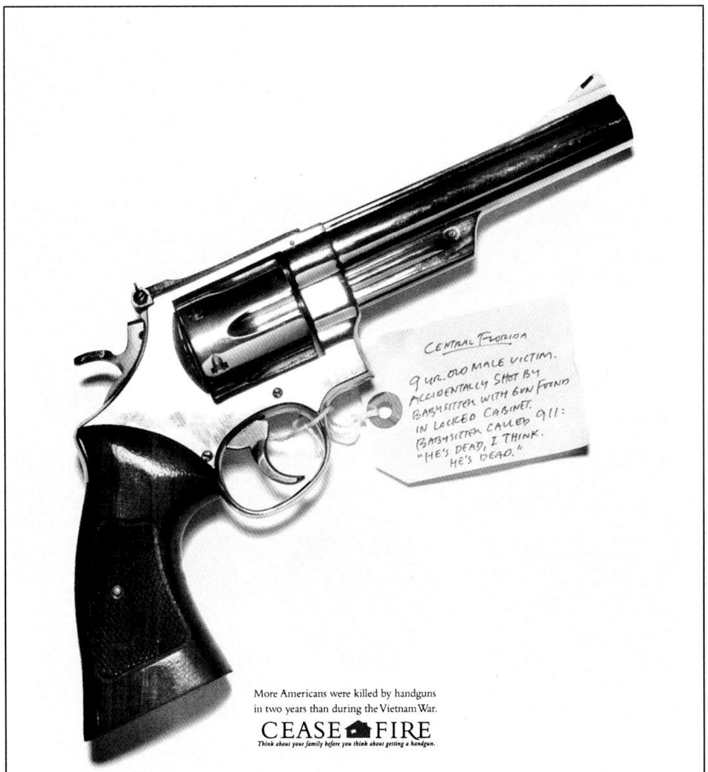
CENTRAL FLORIDA
9 YR. OLD MALE VICTIM. ACCIDENTALLY SHOT BY BABYSITTER WITH GUN FOUND IN LOCKED CABINET. BABYSITTER CALLED 911: "HE'S DEAD, I THINK. HE'S DEAD."
More Americans were killed by handguns in two years than during the Vietnam War.
CEASE FIRE
Think about your family before you think about getting a handgun.

Glenwood Springs, CO
Carl Midland, 13. Killed while he and a friend acted out scenes from a movie. Boys found gun in drawer while looking for a ski hat.
In 1992, gun deaths were the second leading cause of death for children aged 10-14.
CEASE FIRE
Think about your family before you think about getting a handgun.

PUBLIC SERVICE/
POLITICAL NEWSPAPER
OR MAGAZINE: CAMPAIGN

456
ART DIRECTOR:
Tom Lichtenheld
WRITER:
Sally Hogshead
PHOTOGRAPHER:
Buck Holzemer
CLIENT:
Children's Defense Fund
AGENCY:
Fallon McElligott/
Minneapolis

457
ART DIRECTORS:
Ron Harper
Don Schramek
WRITER:
Jim Lansbury
CLIENT:
National Archives
AGENCY:
Gray Kirk VanSant/
Baltimore

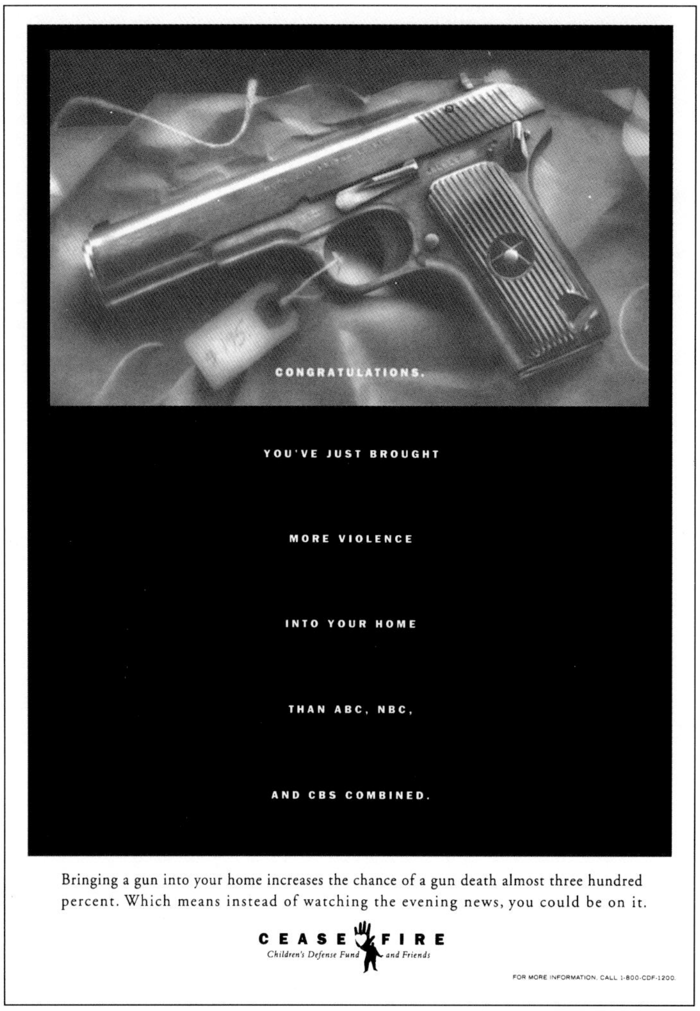

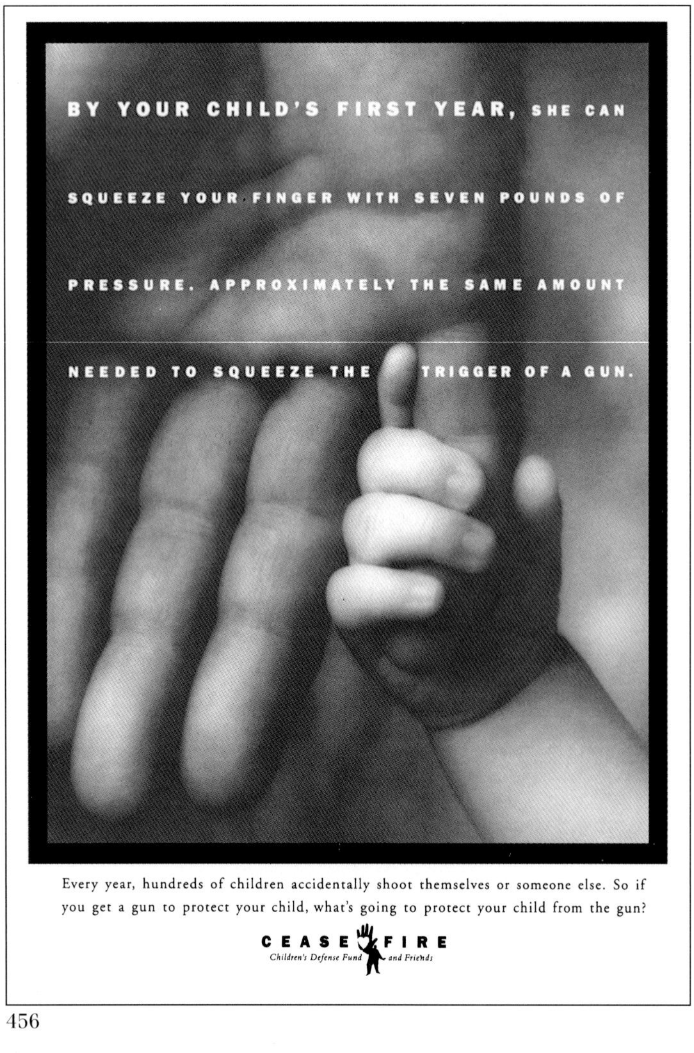

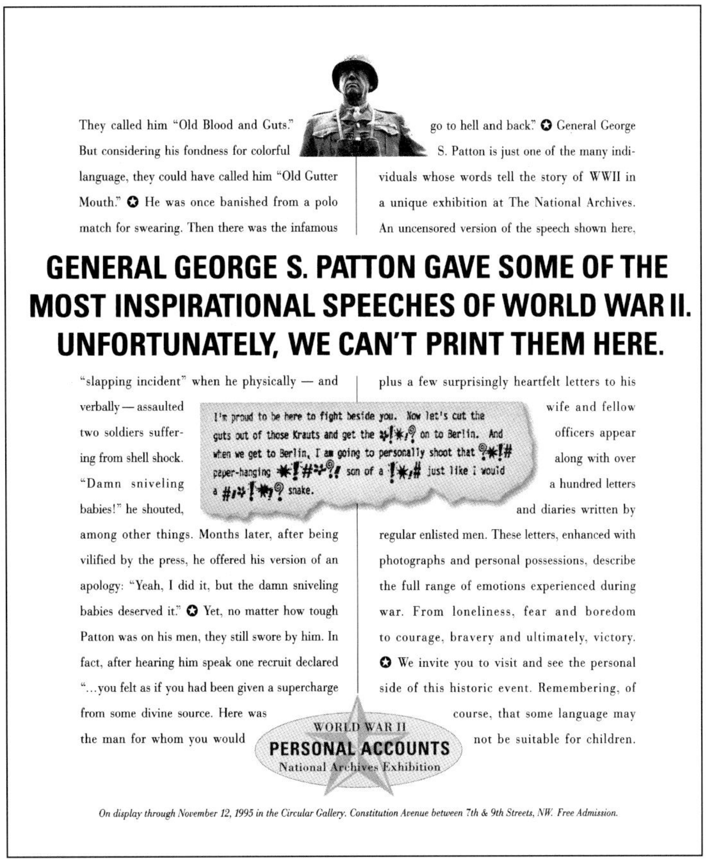

They called him "Old Blood and Guts." But considering his fondness for colorful language, they could have called him "Old Gutter Mouth." ✪ He was once banished from a polo match for swearing. Then there was the infamous "slapping incident" when he physically — and verbally — assaulted two soldiers suffering from shell shock. "Damn sniveling babies!" he shouted, among other things. Months later, after being vilified by the press, he offered his version of an apology: "Yeah, I did it, but the damn sniveling babies deserved it." ✪ Yet, no matter how tough Patton was on his men, they still swore by him. In fact, after hearing him speak one recruit declared "...you felt as if you had been given a supercharge from some divine source. Here was the man for whom you would go to hell and back." ✪ General George S. Patton is just one of the many individuals whose words tell the story of WWII in a unique exhibition at The National Archives. An uncensored version of the speech shown here, plus a few surprisingly heartfelt letters to his wife and fellow officers appear along with over a hundred letters and diaries written by regular enlisted men. These letters, enhanced with photographs and personal possessions, describe the full range of emotions experienced during war. From loneliness, fear and boredom to courage, bravery and ultimately, victory. ✪ We invite you to visit and see the personal side of this historic event. Remembering, of course, that some language may not be suitable for children.
GENERAL GEORGE S. PATTON GAVE SOME OF THE MOST INSPIRATIONAL SPEECHES OF WORLD WAR II. UNFORTUNATELY, WE CAN'T PRINT THEM HERE.
I'm proud to be here to fight beside you. Now let's cut the guts out of those Krauts and get the *!*,? on to Berlin. And when we get to Berlin, I am going to personally shoot that ?*!# paper-hanging *!#*?! son of a !*,# just like I would a #,*!*? snake.
WORLD WAR II
PERSONAL ACCOUNTS
National Archives Exhibition
On display through November 12, 1995 in the Circular Gallery. Constitution Avenue between 7th & 9th Streets, NW. Free Admission.

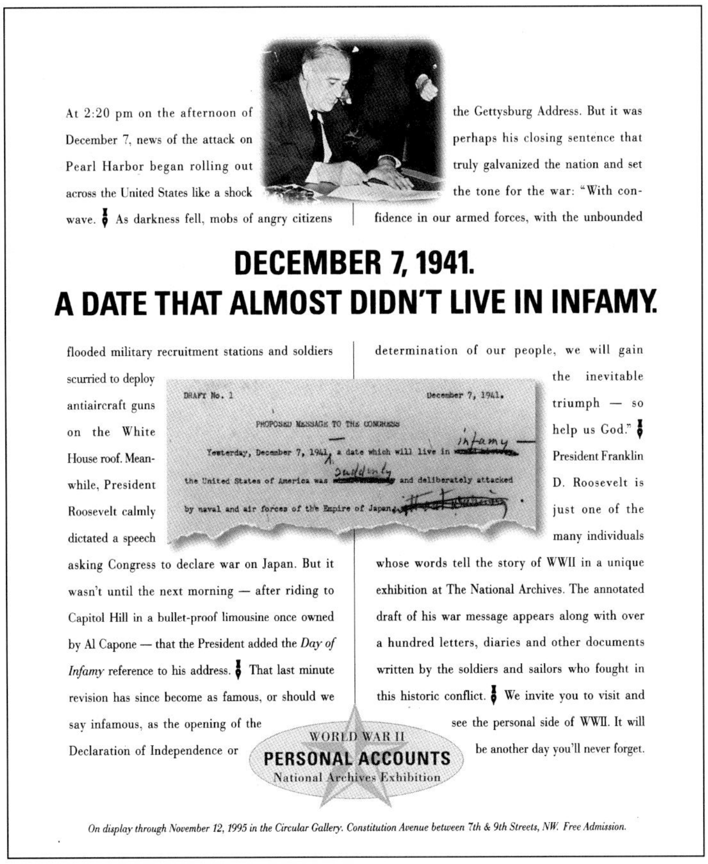

At 2:20 pm on the afternoon of December 7, news of the attack on Pearl Harbor began rolling out across the United States like a shock wave. As darkness fell, mobs of angry citizens flooded military recruitment stations and soldiers scurried to deploy antiaircraft guns on the White House roof. Meanwhile, President Roosevelt calmly dictated a speech asking Congress to declare war on Japan. But it wasn't until the next morning — after riding to Capitol Hill in a bullet-proof limousine once owned by Al Capone — that the President added the *Day of Infamy* reference to his address. That last minute revision has since become as famous, or should we say infamous, as the opening of the Declaration of Independence or the Gettysburg Address. But it was perhaps his closing sentence that truly galvanized the nation and set the tone for the war: "With confidence in our armed forces, with the unbounded determination of our people, we will gain the inevitable triumph — so help us God." President Franklin D. Roosevelt is just one of the many individuals whose words tell the story of WWII in a unique exhibition at The National Archives. The annotated draft of his war message appears along with over a hundred letters, diaries and other documents written by the soldiers and sailors who fought in this historic conflict. We invite you to visit and see the personal side of WWII. It will be another day you'll never forget.
DECEMBER 7, 1941. A DATE THAT ALMOST DIDN'T LIVE IN INFAMY.
DRAFT No. 1
December 7, 1941.
PROPOSED MESSAGE TO THE CONGRESS
Yesterday, December 7, 1941, a date which will live in infamy
the United States of America was suddenly and deliberately attacked
by naval and air forces of the Empire of Japan.
WORLD WAR II
PERSONAL ACCOUNTS
National Archives Exhibition
On display through November 12, 1995 in the Circular Gallery. Constitution Avenue between 7th & 9th Streets, NW. Free Admission.

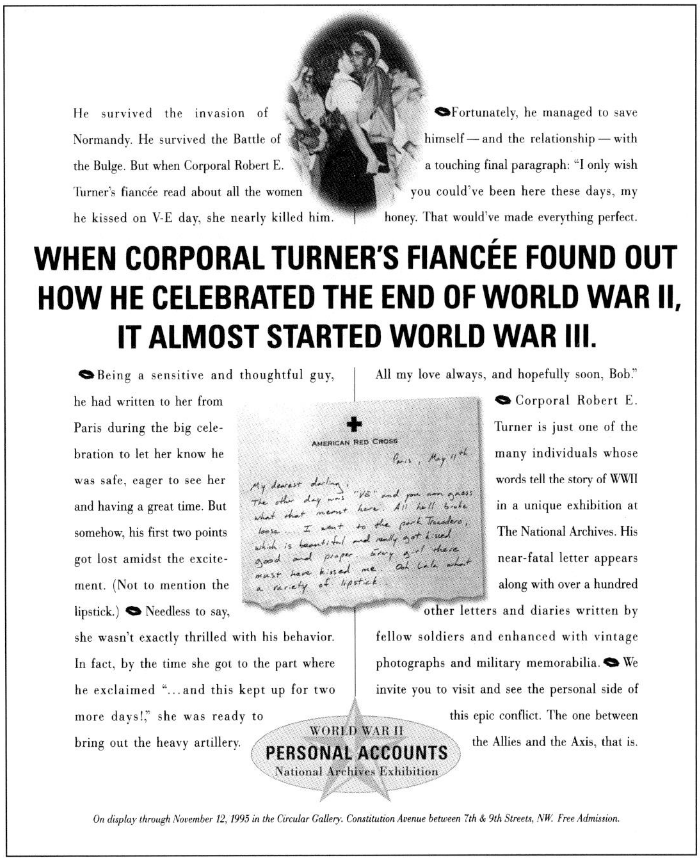

He survived the invasion of Normandy. He survived the Battle of the Bulge. But when Corporal Robert E. Turner's fiancée read about all the women he kissed on V-E day, she nearly killed him. Being a sensitive and thoughtful guy, he had written to her from Paris during the big celebration to let her know he was safe, eager to see her and having a great time. But somehow, his first two points got lost amidst the excitement. (Not to mention the lipstick.) Needless to say, she wasn't exactly thrilled with his behavior. In fact, by the time she got to the part where he exclaimed "...and this kept up for two more days!," she was ready to bring out the heavy artillery. Fortunately, he managed to save himself — and the relationship — with a touching final paragraph: "I only wish you could've been here these days, my honey. That would've made everything perfect. All my love always, and hopefully soon, Bob." Corporal Robert E. Turner is just one of the many individuals whose words tell the story of WWII in a unique exhibition at The National Archives. His near-fatal letter appears along with over a hundred other letters and diaries written by fellow soldiers and enhanced with vintage photographs and military memorabilia. We invite you to visit and see the personal side of this epic conflict. The one between the Allies and the Axis, that is.
WHEN CORPORAL TURNER'S FIANCÉE FOUND OUT HOW HE CELEBRATED THE END OF WORLD WAR II, IT ALMOST STARTED WORLD WAR III.
AMERICAN RED CROSS
Paris, May 11th
My dearest darling,
The other day was "VE" and you can guess what that meant here. All hell broke loose... I went to the park Trocadero, which is beautiful and really got kissed good and proper. Every girl there must have kissed me. Ooh La La what a variety of lipstick.
WORLD WAR II
PERSONAL ACCOUNTS
National Archives Exhibition
On display through November 12, 1995 in the Circular Gallery. Constitution Avenue between 7th & 9th Streets, NW. Free Admission.

PUBLIC SERVICE/
POLITICAL NEWSPAPER
OR MAGAZINE: CAMPAIGN

458

ART DIRECTOR:
Jennifer Fleming-Balser

WRITERS:
Rich Tlapek
Chuck Meehan

CLIENT:
Babe Ruth Museum

AGENCY:
GSD&M Advertising/
Austin

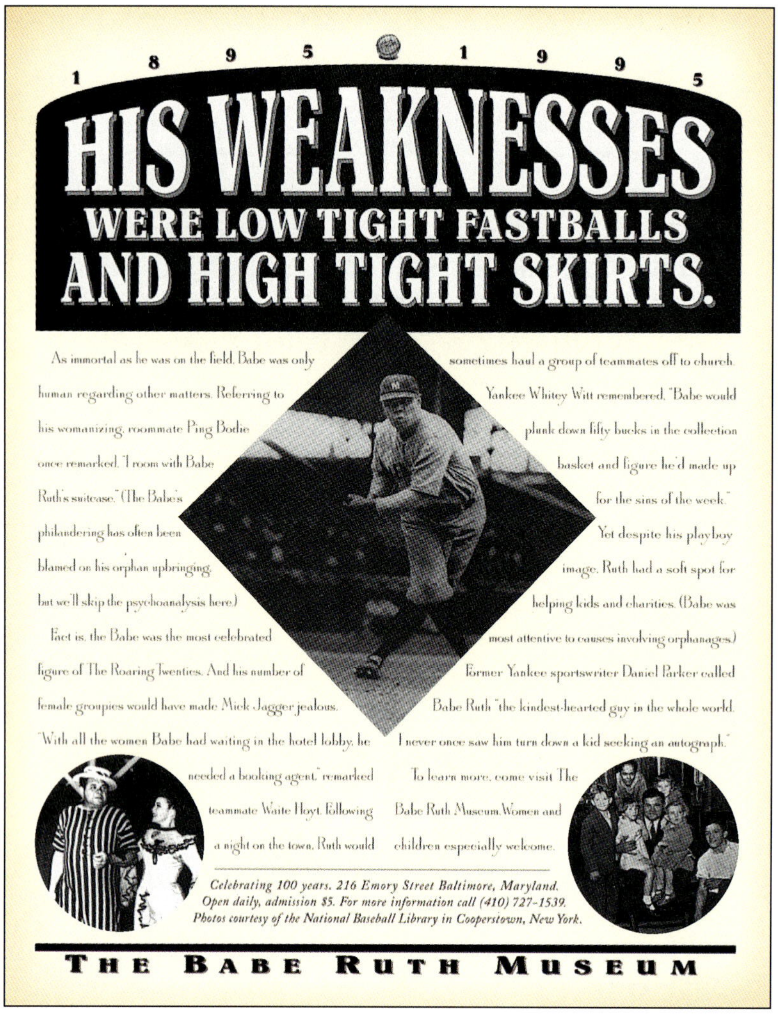

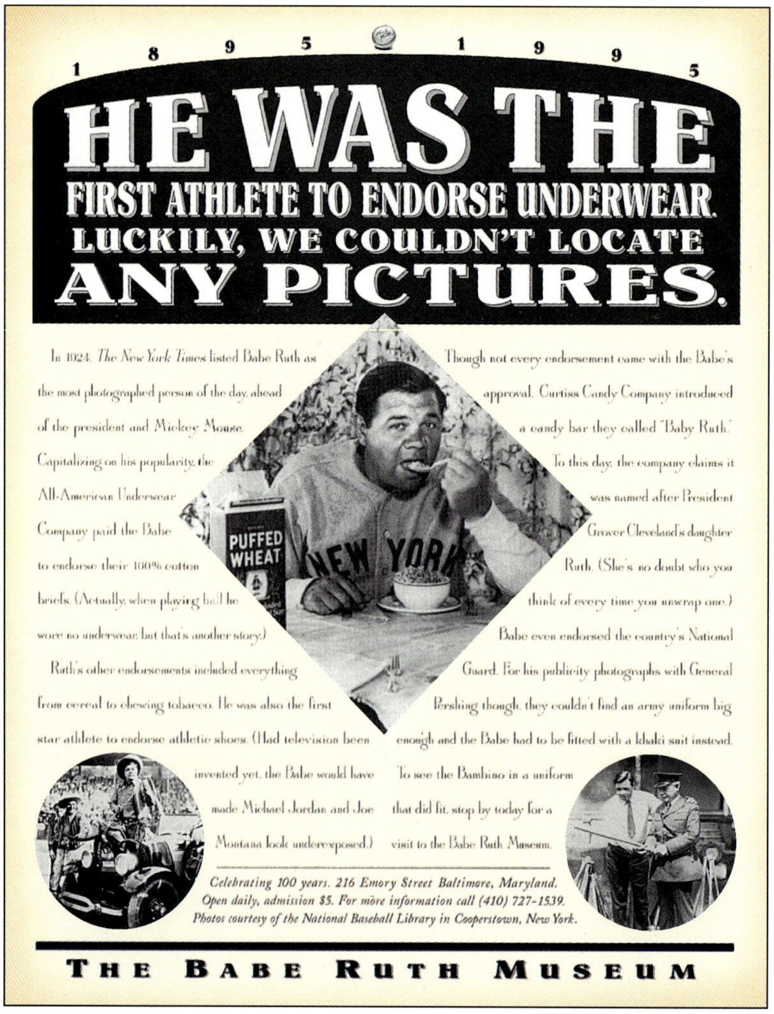

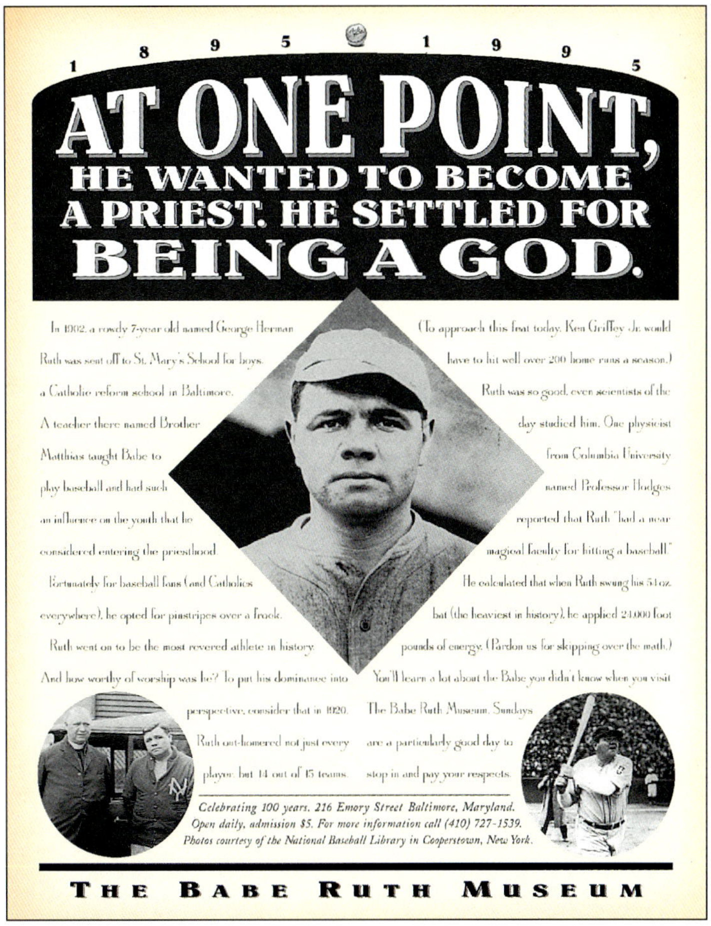
1 8 9 5 1 9 9 5
AT ONE POINT, HE WANTED TO BECOME A PRIEST. HE SETTLED FOR BEING A GOD.
In 1902, a rowdy 7-year old named George Herman Ruth was sent off to St. Mary's School for boys, a Catholic reform school in Baltimore.
A teacher there named Brother Matthias taught Babe to play baseball and had such an influence on the youth that he considered entering the priesthood.
Fortunately for baseball fans (and Catholics everywhere), he opted for pinstripes over a frock.
Ruth went on to be the most revered athlete in history. And how worthy of worship was he? To put his dominance into perspective, consider that in 1920, Ruth out-homered not just every player, but 14 out of 15 teams. (To approach this feat today, Ken Griffey Jr. would have to hit well over 200 home runs a season.)
Ruth was so good, even scientists of the day studied him. One physicist from Columbia University named Professor Hodges reported that Ruth "had a near magical faculty for hitting a baseball." He calculated that when Ruth swung his 54 oz. bat (the heaviest in history), he applied 24,000 foot pounds of energy. (Pardon us for skipping over the math.)
You'll learn a lot about the Babe you didn't know when you visit The Babe Ruth Museum. Sundays are a particularly good day to stop in and pay your respects.
Celebrating 100 years. 216 Emory Street Baltimore, Maryland.
Open daily, admission $5. For more information call (410) 727-1539.
Photos courtesy of the National Baseball Library in Cooperstown, New York.
THE BABE RUTH MUSEUM

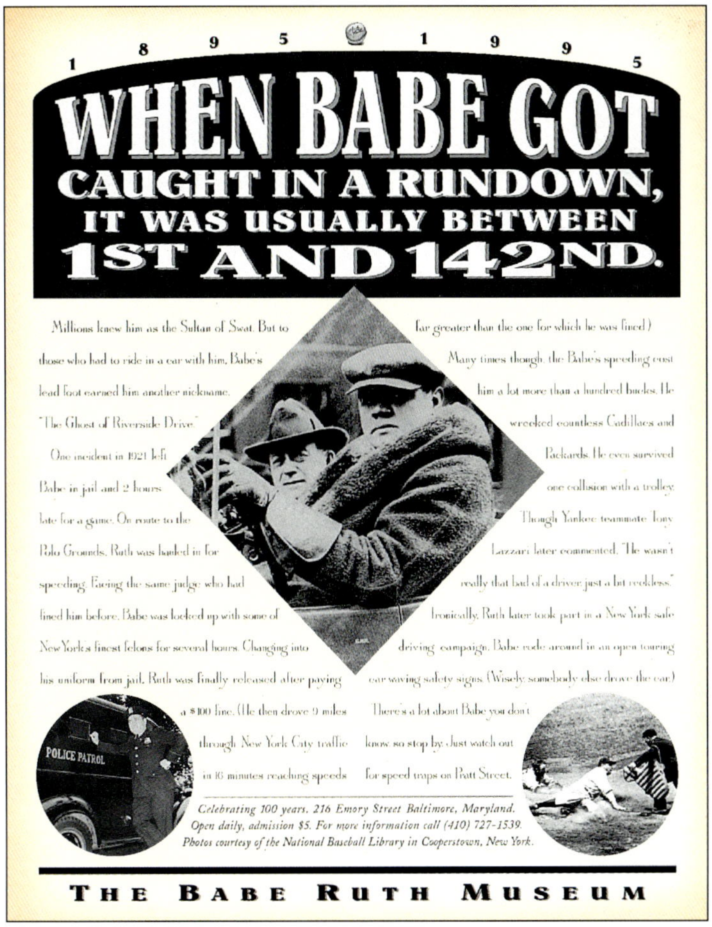
1 8 9 5 1 9 9 5
WHEN BABE GOT CAUGHT IN A RUNDOWN, IT WAS USUALLY BETWEEN 1ST AND 142ND.
Millions knew him as the Sultan of Swat. But to those who had to ride in a car with him, Babe's lead foot earned him another nickname, "The Ghost of Riverside Drive."
One incident in 1921 left Babe in jail and 2 hours late for a game. On route to the Polo Grounds, Ruth was hauled in for speeding. Facing the same judge who had fined him before, Babe was locked up with some of New York's finest felons for several hours. Changing into his uniform from jail, Ruth was finally released after paying a $100 fine. (He then drove 9 miles through New York City traffic in 16 minutes reaching speeds far greater than the one for which he was fined.)
Many times though, the Babe's speeding cost him a lot more than a hundred bucks. He wrecked countless Cadillacs and Packards. He even survived one collision with a trolley. Though Yankee teammate Tony Lazzari later commented, "He wasn't really that bad of a driver, just a bit reckless."
Ironically, Ruth later took part in a New York safe driving campaign. Babe rode around in an open touring car waving safety signs. (Wisely, somebody else drove the car.)
There's a lot about Babe you don't know, so stop by. Just watch out for speed traps on Pratt Street.
POLICE PATROL
Celebrating 100 years. 216 Emory Street Baltimore, Maryland.
Open daily, admission $5. For more information call (410) 727-1539.
Photos courtesy of the National Baseball Library in Cooperstown, New York.
THE BABE RUTH MUSEUM

1 8 9 5 1 9 9 5
HIS BIGGEST DAY EVER AT THE PLATE? 18 HOT DOGS.
You won't find this statistic in any official box score. But the Babe did wolf down 18 wieners once at a New Jersey State Fair eating contest.
Yankee reporter Art Robinson recalled another time Babe stayed up all night playing cards and "probably ate 14 sirloin sandwiches with some odds and ends thrown in." The next day on just two hours of sleep, he hit two homers over the center field wall.
Of course, the Bambino didn't always wait until after games to indulge. He was known to order hot dogs and ice cream from a vendor right in the middle of a game when his hearty appetite beckoned. (Babe kept a jar of bicarbonate soda handy in the dugout just in case of any unexpected gastronomical emergencies.)
His legendary eating habits even led to the creation of "Yankee pinstripes." In spring of 1925, Yankee team owner Colonel Jacob Ruppert requested pinstripes be added to the Yankee uniform, reportedly to make Ruth look thinner to the team's fans.
Amazingly enough, while the Bambino's waistline topped out at a whopping 49 3/4 inches in 1932, his most impressive career numbers came from the end of a bat, not a fork.
To see those numbers for yourself, stop by. Our sincere apologies to Babe, but no food allowed.
Celebrating 100 years. 216 Emory Street Baltimore, Maryland.
Open daily, admission $5. For more information call (410) 727-1539.
Photos courtesy of the National Baseball Library in Cooperstown, New York.
THE BABE RUTH MUSEUM

PUBLIC SERVICE/ POLITICAL NEWSPAPER OR MAGAZINE: CAMPAIGN

459

ART DIRECTORS:
Terry Finley
Chris Chaffin

WRITERS:
Joe Perry
Rocky Botts

PHOTOGRAPHERS:
Karl Petzke
Michael O'Neil
Wil Mosgrove

CLIENT:
Independent Sector/
Advertising Council

AGENCY:
Hal Riney & Partners/
San Francisco

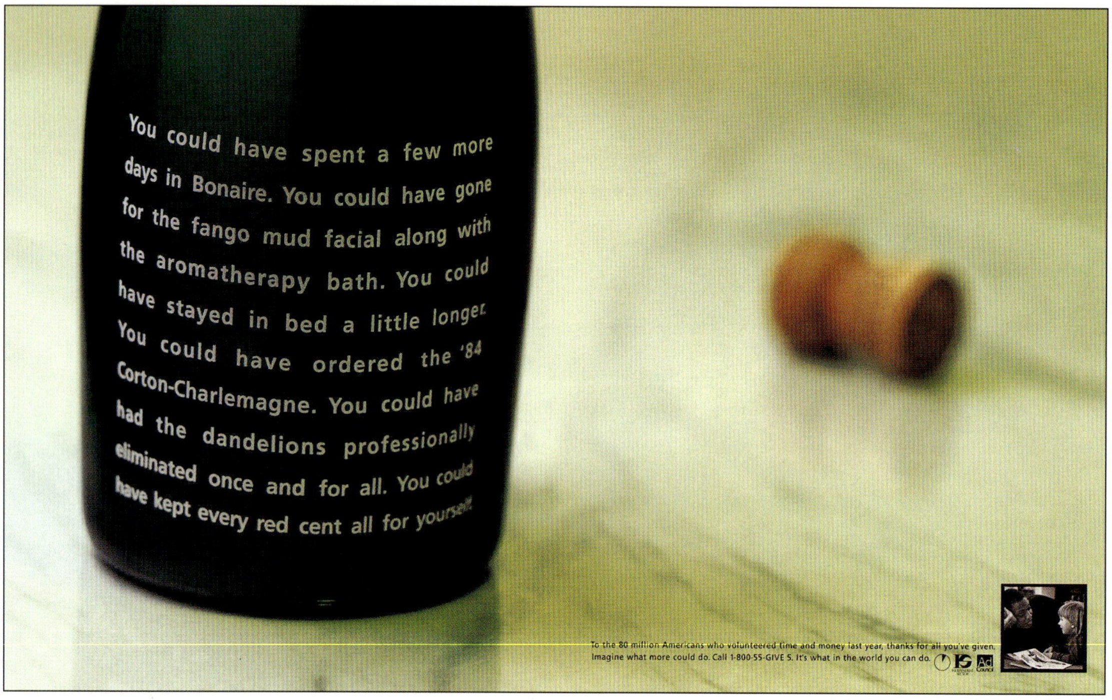

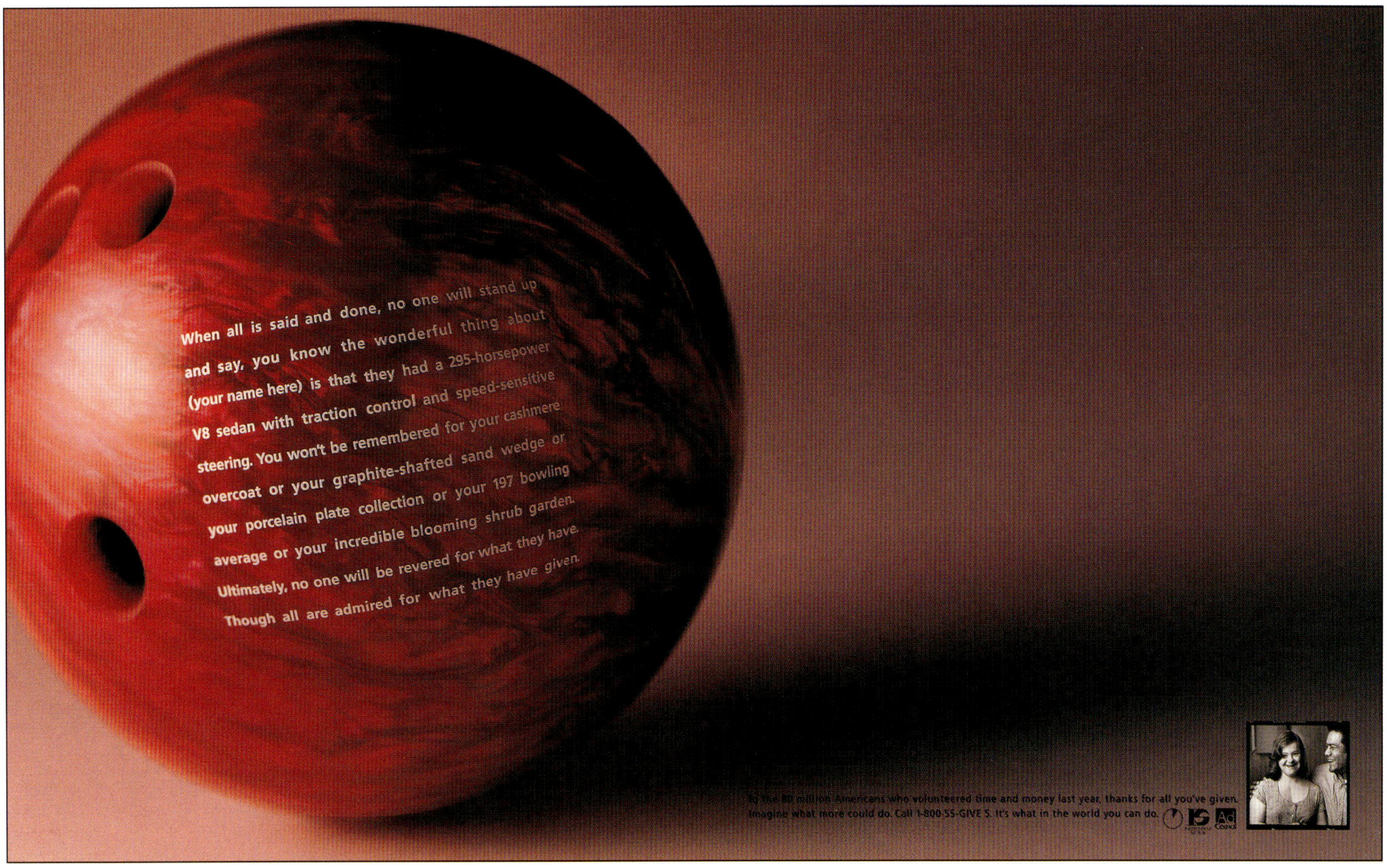
When all is said and done, no one will stand up and say, you know the wonderful thing about (your name here) is that they had a 295-horsepower V8 sedan with traction control and speed-sensitive steering. You won't be remembered for your cashmere overcoat or your graphite-shafted sand wedge or your porcelain plate collection or your 197 bowling average or your incredible blooming shrub garden. Ultimately, no one will be revered for what they have. Though all are admired for what they have given.
To the 80 million Americans who volunteered time and money last year, thanks for all you've given.
Imagine what more could do. Call 1-800-55-GIVE 5. It's what in the world you can do.
Ad Council

In America, you are not required to offer food to the hungry. Or shelter to the homeless. There is no ordinance forcing you to visit the lonely, or comfort the infirm. Nowhere in the Constitution does it say you have to provide clothing for the poor. In fact, one of the nicest things about living here in America is that you really don't have to do anything for anybody.
To the 80 million Americans who volunteered time and money last year, thanks for all you've given.
Imagine what more could do. Call 1-800-55-GIVE 5. It's what in the world you can do.
Ad Council

PUBLIC SERVICE/
POLITICAL NEWSPAPER
OR MAGAZINE: CAMPAIGN

460

ART DIRECTOR:
Troy King

WRITERS:
Rudy Fernandez
Zach Watkins

CLIENT:
Atlanta History Center

AGENCY:
Hughes Advertising/
Atlanta

DON'T BE SHOCKED THAT THIS IS IN OUR MUSEUM.
BE SHOCKED THAT IT'S OUTSIDE OUR MUSEUM.
Our history is both beautiful and horrifying. Here, you'll find everything from the terrors of war to peaceful historical gardens. Come experience the power of our history. Because the only way to become the city of the future is to take an honest look at our past. For information call 814-4000.
ATLANTA HISTORY CENTER

HE OWNED THE LARGEST BARBER SHOP IN ATLANTA.
HE JUST WASN'T ALLOWED TO GET HIS HAIR CUT THERE.
We share a history that's both beautiful and tragic. And you'll find it all here. The beauty of historic homes, the horrors of war, the serenity of gardens and even the reasons why Atlanta's first black millionaire never rose above second-class status. For information call 814-4000.
ATLANTA HISTORY CENTER

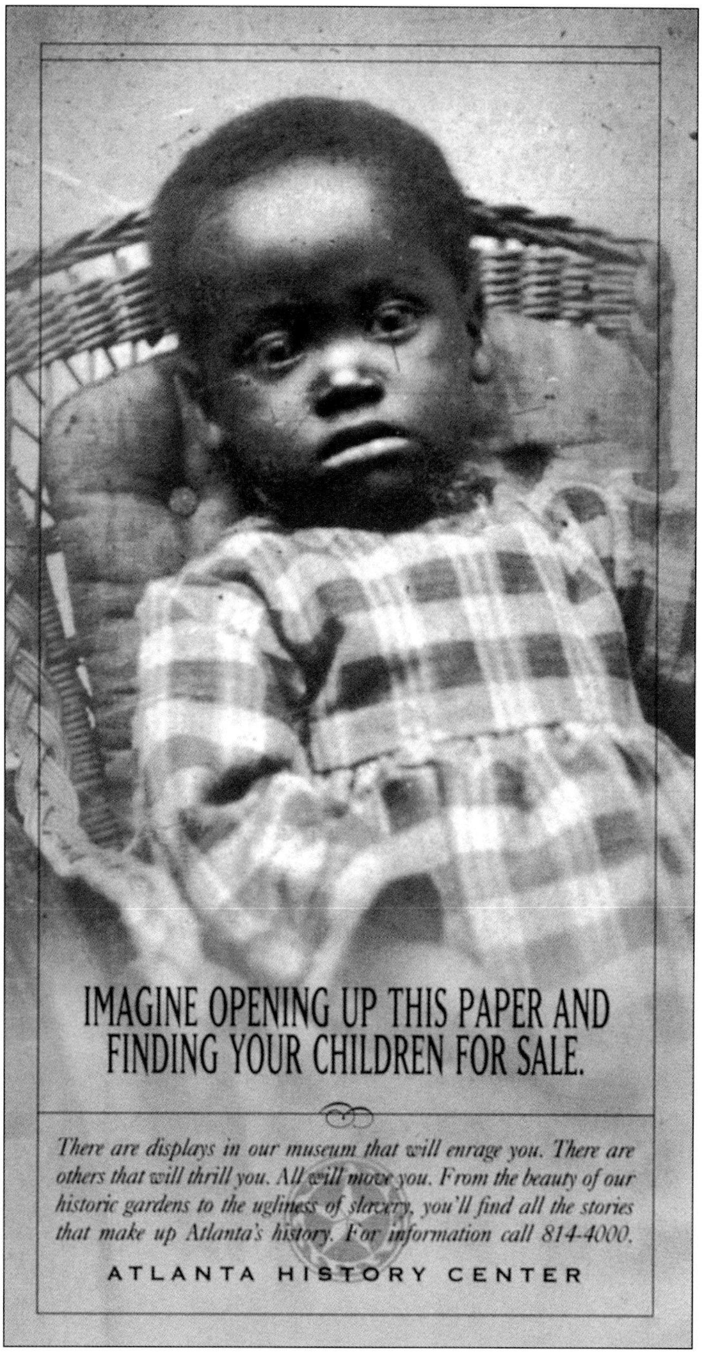
IMAGINE OPENING UP THIS PAPER AND FINDING YOUR CHILDREN FOR SALE.
There are displays in our museum that will enrage you. There are others that will thrill you. All will move you. From the beauty of our historic gardens to the ugliness of slavery, you'll find all the stories that make up Atlanta's history. For information call 814-4000.
ATLANTA HISTORY CENTER

PUBLIC SERVICE/
POLITICAL NEWSPAPER
OR MAGAZINE: CAMPAIGN

461

ART DIRECTOR:
Julie Topetzes
WRITER:
Alex Mohler
PHOTOGRAPHER:
Steve Grubman
CLIENT:
Wisconsin Humane Society
AGENCY:
Laughlin/Constable, Milwaukee

He can't tell his rawhide tuggie from your $300 Italian loafers. And you expect him to find his way home?
License Your Pet
Let's face it, man's best friend isn't always the world's greatest problem solver. Particularly when the problem is finding his way home. With a license, pets can be identified and returned to their owners the same day. For your free pet licensing kit, call the Wisconsin Humane Society at 961-0310, ext. 177.
Wisconsin Humane Society

SHE CAN SIT. SHE CAN SPEAK. WHAT SHE CAN'T DO IS PICK UP A PHONE AND CALL YOU FROM THE CORNER OF 4TH & PULASKI.
License Your Pet
ANY DOG CAN SPEAK. INFORMING YOU WHEN THEY'RE LOST IS THE TRICKY PART. WITH A LICENSE, YOUR PET CAN BE IDENTIFIED AND RETURNED HOME THE SAME DAY. FOR YOUR FREE PET LICENSING KIT, CALL THE WISCONSIN HUMANE SOCIETY AT 961-0310, EXT. 177.
Wisconsin Humane Society

Remember when you were four and lost somewhere between Better Sportswear and Fine China?
License Your Pet
Or was it in the vast expanse of the Small Electrics department? After that experience, they pinned a name and address on you. Remember? Same idea here. For your free pet licensing kit, call the Wisconsin Humane Society at 961-0310, ext. 177.
Wisconsin Humane Society
Photo: Steve Grubman

Unlike other commitments that involve a license, you're not stuck with the in-laws for life.
License Your Pet
There's no reason why a good relationship should end in separation. When you license your pet, you're helping ensure you'll be reunited with your loved one should he or she wander astray. For your free pet licensing kit, call the Wisconsin Humane Society at 961-0310, ext. 177.
Wisconsin Humane Society
Photo: Steve Grubman

PUBLIC SERVICE/
POLITICAL NEWSPAPER
OR MAGAZINE: CAMPAIGN

462
ART DIRECTOR:
Jim Mountjoy
WRITER:
Ed Jones
PHOTOGRAPHERS:
Curtis Johnson
Dan Guravich
CLIENT:
North Carolina Zoo
AGENCY:
Loeffler Ketchum
Mountjoy/Charlotte, NC

463
ART DIRECTOR:
Cliff Sorah
WRITER:
Joe Alexander
CLIENT:
John F. Kennedy Library
Foundation
AGENCY:
The Martin Agency/
Richmond

TO A CHILD USED TO SEEING THINGS ON A 19" TV SCREEN, IT CAN BE QUITE AN EXPERIENCE.
Polar Bears at the North Carolina Zoo, Asheboro

BE ONE OF THE FEW TO MEET HIM FACE TO FACE AND NOT LEAVE A YELLOW TRAIL IN THE SNOW.
Polar Bears at the North Carolina Zoo, Asheboro

CAN YOU SPOT THE POLAR BEAR IN THIS PICTURE?
NEITHER COULD THE PENGUIN IN HIS BELLY.
Polar Bears at the North Carolina Zoo, Asheboro

IT'S LIKE A RIDE ON PT 109. MINUS THE SHARKS, TORPEDOES AND FOURTEEN-HOUR SWIM.
John F. Kennedy's life and the sea are inseparable. He crossed the Atlantic as a young boy. Commanded a PT boat in the South Pacific during World War II. And spent many weekends at Hyannis Port during his Presidency piloting his 26' sloop "Victura." So it only seems appropriate that visitors to The New Museum at the JFK Library can come by boat. Here, after you come ashore, you'll walk back into time. Through footage, interviews, and re-creations of places and events that marked important times in the life of our 35th President. Just call 617-929-4523 today to find out how you can enjoy a Boston Harbor cruise on your way to the Museum. You'll not only enjoy a nice relaxing ride. You'll feel the passion that inspired an entire generation. Who knows, maybe you'll feel the call for public service and test the political waters yourself.
DAILY BOAT RIDES TO THE JFK LIBRARY

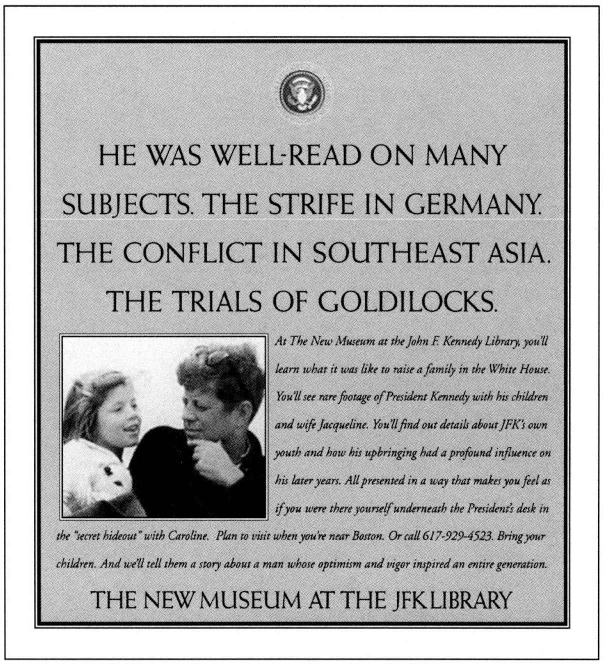
HE WAS WELL-READ ON MANY SUBJECTS. THE STRIFE IN GERMANY. THE CONFLICT IN SOUTHEAST ASIA. THE TRIALS OF GOLDILOCKS.
At The New Museum at the John F. Kennedy Library, you'll learn what it was like to raise a family in the White House. You'll see rare footage of President Kennedy with his children and wife Jacqueline. You'll find out details about JFK's own youth and how his upbringing had a profound influence on his later years. All presented in a way that makes you feel as if you were there yourself underneath the President's desk in the "secret hideout" with Caroline. Plan to visit when you're near Boston. Or call 617-929-4523. Bring your children. And we'll tell them a story about a man whose optimism and vigor inspired an entire generation.
THE NEW MUSEUM AT THE JFK LIBRARY

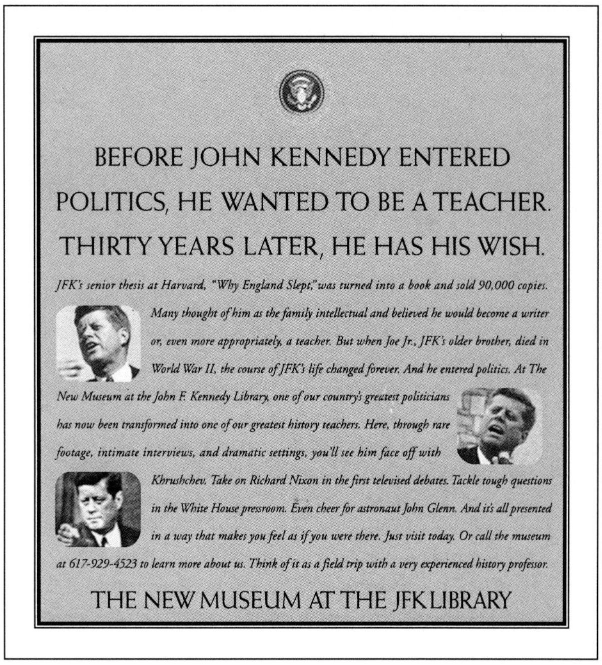
BEFORE JOHN KENNEDY ENTERED POLITICS, HE WANTED TO BE A TEACHER. THIRTY YEARS LATER, HE HAS HIS WISH.
JFK's senior thesis at Harvard, "Why England Slept," was turned into a book and sold 90,000 copies. Many thought of him as the family intellectual and believed he would become a writer or, even more appropriately, a teacher. But when Joe Jr., JFK's older brother, died in World War II, the course of JFK's life changed forever. And he entered politics. At The New Museum at the John F. Kennedy Library, one of our country's greatest politicians has now been transformed into one of our greatest history teachers. Here, through rare footage, intimate interviews, and dramatic settings, you'll see him face off with Khrushchev. Take on Richard Nixon in the first televised debates. Tackle tough questions in the White House pressroom. Even cheer for astronaut John Glenn. And it's all presented in a way that makes you feel as if you were there. Just visit today. Or call the museum at 617-929-4523 to learn more about us. Think of it as a field trip with a very experienced history professor.
THE NEW MUSEUM AT THE JFK LIBRARY

PUBLIC SERVICE/
POLITICAL NEWSPAPER
OR MAGAZINE: CAMPAIGN

464

ART DIRECTOR:
Cliff Sorah

WRITER:
Joe Alexander

CLIENT:
John F. Kennedy Library Foundation

AGENCY:
The Martin Agency/
Richmond

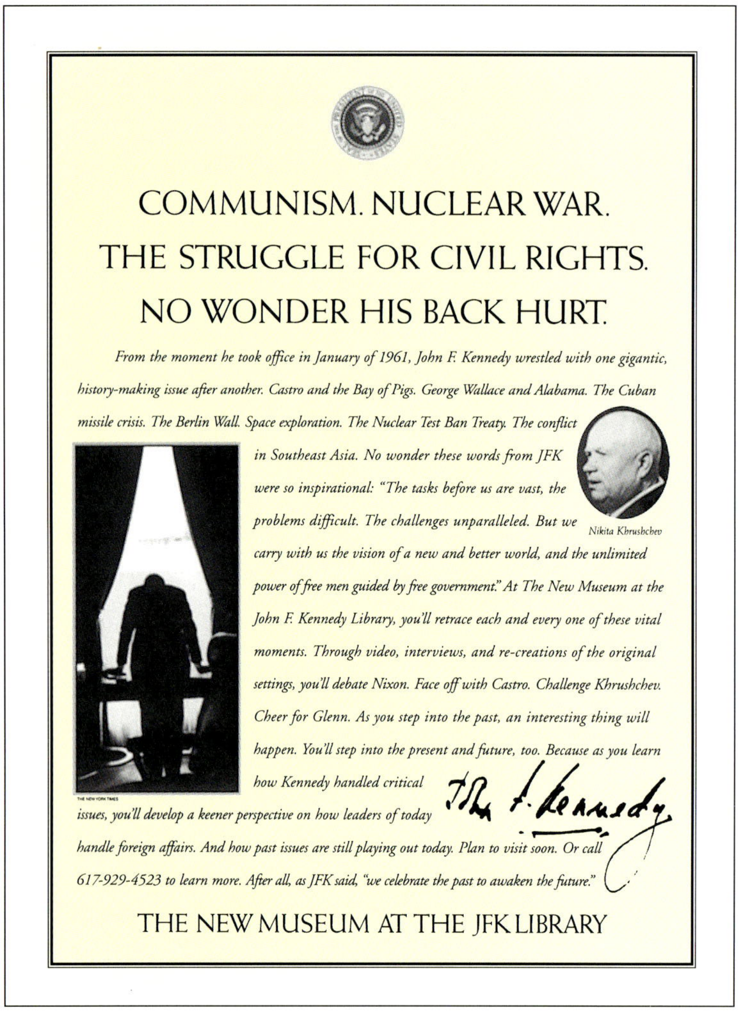

COMMUNISM. NUCLEAR WAR.
THE STRUGGLE FOR CIVIL RIGHTS.
NO WONDER HIS BACK HURT.
From the moment he took office in January of 1961, John F. Kennedy wrestled with one gigantic, history-making issue after another. Castro and the Bay of Pigs. George Wallace and Alabama. The Cuban missile crisis. The Berlin Wall. Space exploration. The Nuclear Test Ban Treaty. The conflict in Southeast Asia. No wonder these words from JFK were so inspirational: "The tasks before us are vast, the problems difficult. The challenges unparalleled. But we carry with us the vision of a new and better world, and the unlimited power of free men guided by free government." At The New Museum at the John F. Kennedy Library, you'll retrace each and every one of these vital moments. Through video, interviews, and re-creations of the original settings, you'll debate Nixon. Face off with Castro. Challenge Khrushchev. Cheer for Glenn. As you step into the past, an interesting thing will happen. You'll step into the present and future, too. Because as you learn how Kennedy handled critical issues, you'll develop a keener perspective on how leaders of today handle foreign affairs. And how past issues are still playing out today. Plan to visit soon. Or call 617-929-4523 to learn more. After all, as JFK said, "we celebrate the past to awaken the future."
Nikita Khrushchev
THE NEW MUSEUM AT THE JFK LIBRARY

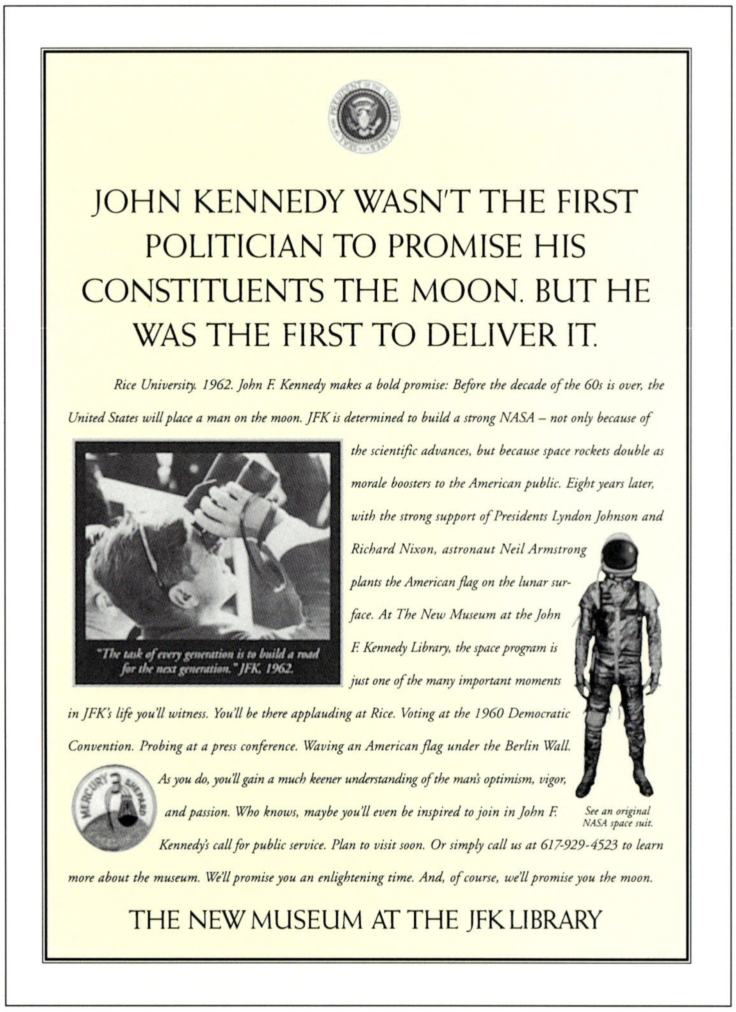

JOHN KENNEDY WASN'T THE FIRST
POLITICIAN TO PROMISE HIS
CONSTITUENTS THE MOON. BUT HE
WAS THE FIRST TO DELIVER IT.
Rice University. 1962. John F. Kennedy makes a bold promise: Before the decade of the 60s is over, the United States will place a man on the moon. JFK is determined to build a strong NASA – not only because of the scientific advances, but because space rockets double as morale boosters to the American public. Eight years later, with the strong support of Presidents Lyndon Johnson and Richard Nixon, astronaut Neil Armstrong plants the American flag on the lunar surface. At The New Museum at the John F. Kennedy Library, the space program is just one of the many important moments in JFK's life you'll witness. You'll be there applauding at Rice. Voting at the 1960 Democratic Convention. Probing at a press conference. Waving an American flag under the Berlin Wall. As you do, you'll gain a much keener understanding of the man's optimism, vigor, and passion. Who knows, maybe you'll even be inspired to join in John F. Kennedy's call for public service. Plan to visit soon. Or simply call us at 617-929-4523 to learn more about the museum. We'll promise you an enlightening time. And, of course, we'll promise you the moon.
"The task of every generation is to build a road for the next generation." JFK, 1962.
See an original NASA space suit.
THE NEW MUSEUM AT THE JFK LIBRARY

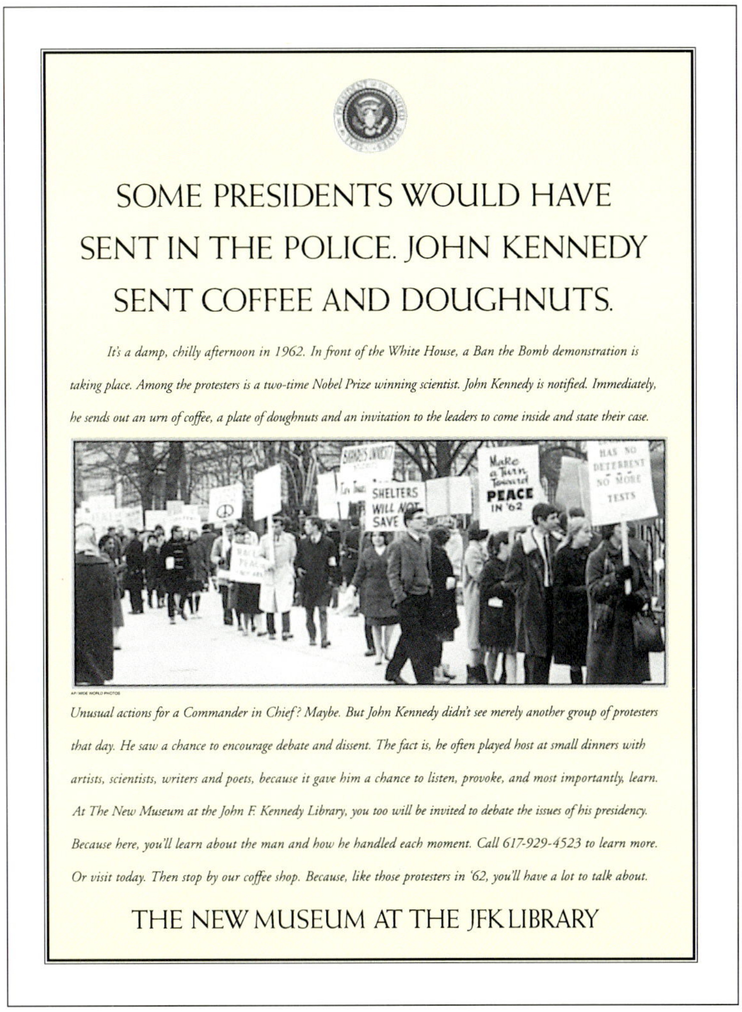
SOME PRESIDENTS WOULD HAVE SENT IN THE POLICE. JOHN KENNEDY SENT COFFEE AND DOUGHNUTS.
It's a damp, chilly afternoon in 1962. In front of the White House, a Ban the Bomb demonstration is taking place. Among the protesters is a two-time Nobel Prize winning scientist. John Kennedy is notified. Immediately, he sends out an urn of coffee, a plate of doughnuts and an invitation to the leaders to come inside and state their case.
SHELTERS WILL NOT SAVE
PEACE IN '62
Unusual actions for a Commander in Chief? Maybe. But John Kennedy didn't see merely another group of protesters that day. He saw a chance to encourage debate and dissent. The fact is, he often played host at small dinners with artists, scientists, writers and poets, because it gave him a chance to listen, provoke, and most importantly, learn.
At The New Museum at the John F. Kennedy Library, you too will be invited to debate the issues of his presidency. Because here, you'll learn about the man and how he handled each moment. Call 617-929-4523 to learn more. Or visit today. Then stop by our coffee shop. Because, like those protesters in '62, you'll have a lot to talk about.
THE NEW MUSEUM AT THE JFK LIBRARY

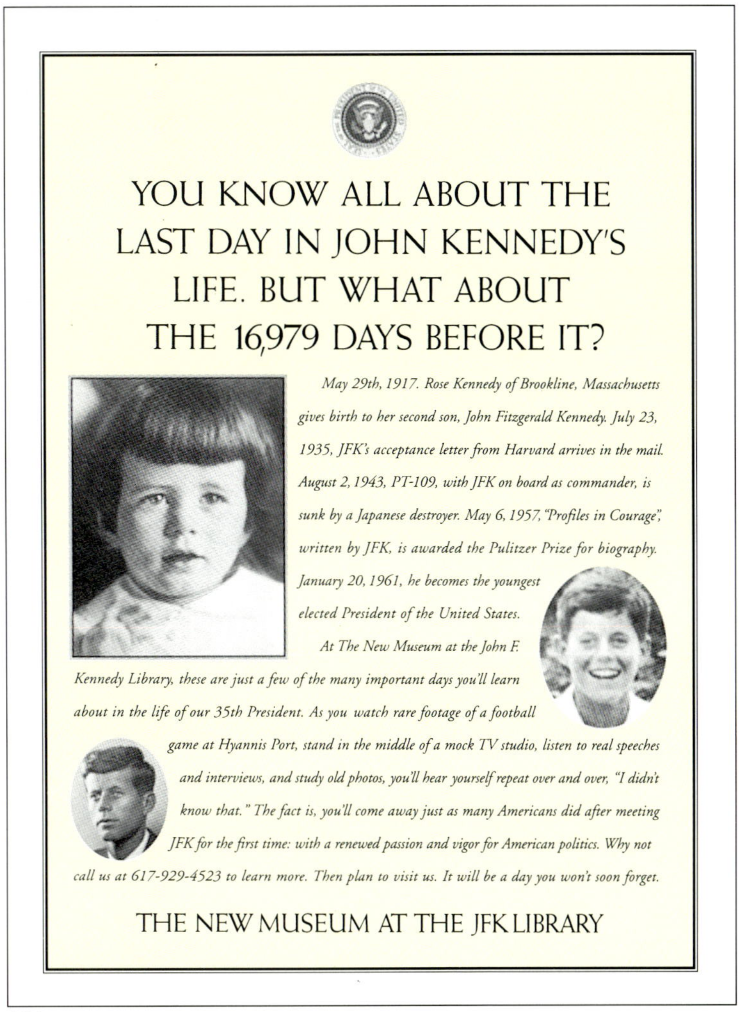
YOU KNOW ALL ABOUT THE LAST DAY IN JOHN KENNEDY'S LIFE. BUT WHAT ABOUT THE 16,979 DAYS BEFORE IT?
May 29th, 1917. Rose Kennedy of Brookline, Massachusetts gives birth to her second son, John Fitzgerald Kennedy. July 23, 1935, JFK's acceptance letter from Harvard arrives in the mail. August 2, 1943, PT-109, with JFK on board as commander, is sunk by a Japanese destroyer. May 6, 1957, "Profiles in Courage", written by JFK, is awarded the Pulitzer Prize for biography. January 20, 1961, he becomes the youngest elected President of the United States.
At The New Museum at the John F. Kennedy Library, these are just a few of the many important days you'll learn about in the life of our 35th President. As you watch rare footage of a football game at Hyannis Port, stand in the middle of a mock TV studio, listen to real speeches and interviews, and study old photos, you'll hear yourself repeat over and over, "I didn't know that." The fact is, you'll come away just as many Americans did after meeting JFK for the first time: with a renewed passion and vigor for American politics. Why not call us at 617-929-4523 to learn more. Then plan to visit us. It will be a day you won't soon forget.
THE NEW MUSEUM AT THE JFK LIBRARY

PUBLIC SERVICE/
POLITICAL NEWSPAPER
OR MAGAZINE: CAMPAIGN

465

ART DIRECTOR:
Sean Riley

WRITER:
Joe Alexander

CLIENT:
Science Museum
of Virginia

AGENCY:
The Martin Agency/
Richmond

SHUTTLE
MEAL TRAY
THE·REAL·REASON
PEOPLE·WEIGH
LESS·IN·SPACE.
DESTINY IN SPACE·FILMED IN IMAX
SCIENCE MUSEUM OF VIRGINIA·367-0000

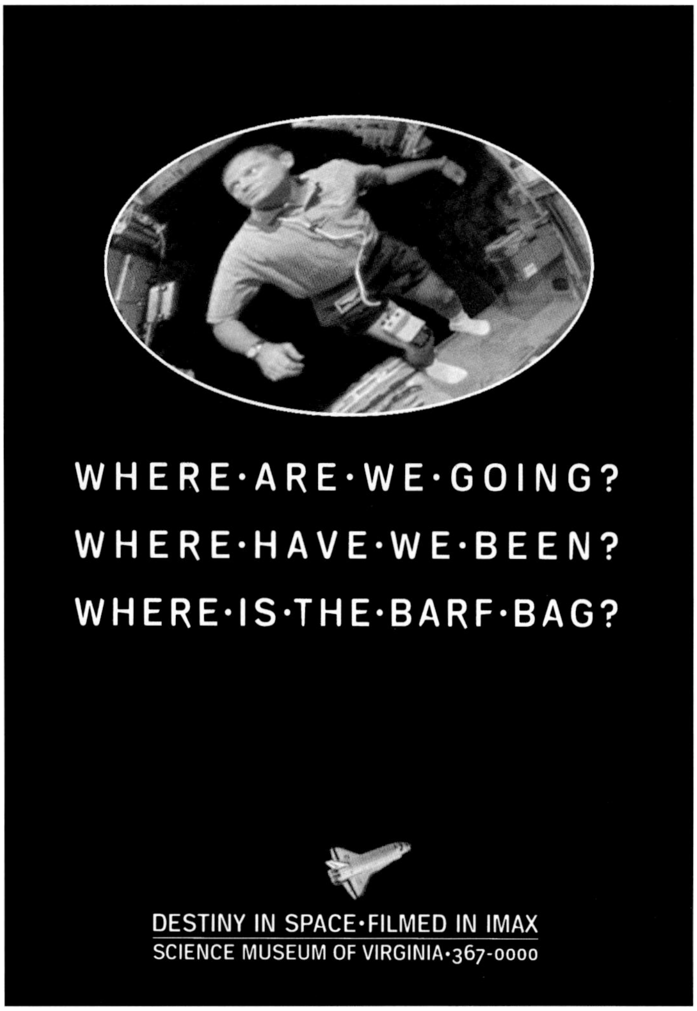
WHERE·ARE·WE·GOING?
WHERE·HAVE·WE·BEEN?
WHERE·IS·THE·BARF·BAG?
DESTINY IN SPACE·FILMED IN IMAX
SCIENCE MUSEUM OF VIRGINIA·367-0000

PUBLIC SERVICE/
POLITICAL NEWSPAPER
OR MAGAZINE: CAMPAIGN

466

ART DIRECTORS:
Len Cheeseman
Evan Purdie

WRITERS:
Ken Double
Steve Cooper

PHOTOGRAPHER:
Tony Squares

ILLUSTRATOR:
Evan Purdie

TYPOGRAPHERS:
Len Cheeseman
Carl Kennard

CLIENT:
New Zealand Red Cross

AGENCY:
Saatchi & Saatchi/
Wellington, New Zealand

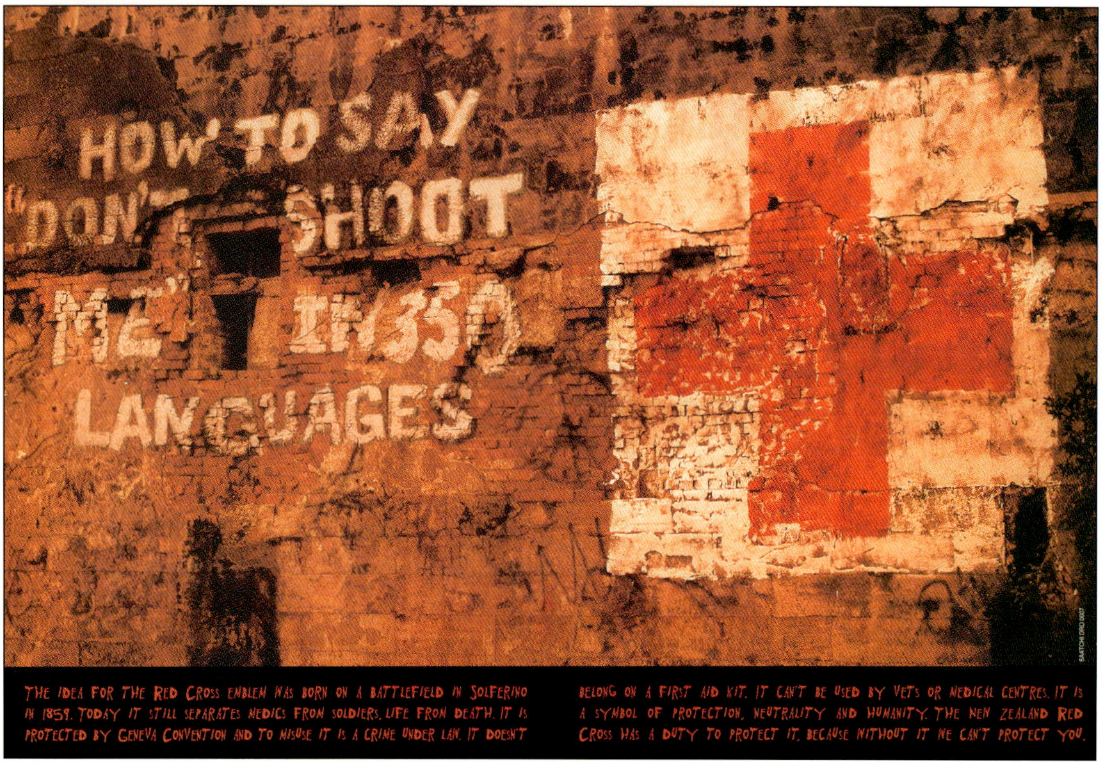

WE TEACH THEM HOW TO FIGHT
NEW ZEALAND RED CROSS
ALL'S FAIR IN LOVE AND WAR? NO IT ISN'T. EVEN IN BATTLE THERE ARE RULES. IN THE COURSE OF HUMANITARIAN WORK IN WAR ZONES ALL OVER THE WORLD, THE RED CROSS ENCOUNTERS SOLDIERS WHO HAVE NO IDEA WHAT THEIR OBLIGATIONS ARE TO PRISONERS, TO CIVILIANS OR TO THE ENEMY. IF WE CAN TEACH THOSE SOLDIERS ABOUT THE CONDUCT REQUIRED OF THEM BY THE GENEVA CONVENTIONS, THEN WE CAN SAVE LIVES. YOU MAY BE SURPRISED BY SOME OF THE WORK RED CROSS DOES, BUT WHATEVER IT IS AND WHEREVER IT TAKES US WE STILL NEED YOUR HELP TO DO IT.

A TRAINED USED CAR SALESMAN COULD SAVE YOUR LIFE
ONE OWNER
N.Z. new
Easy finance
LOW K's
MANY EXTRAS
CASH for CARS
OPEN FOOD
NEW ZEALAND RED CROSS
IN AN EMERGENCY, ANYONE AT ALL TRAINED IN THE BASIC SKILLS OF FIRST AID COULD SAVE YOUR LIFE. EVERY YEAR, RED CROSS PUTS THOUSANDS OF NEW ZEALANDERS THROUGH FIRST AID COURSES, TEACHING THEM SIMPLE PROCEDURES LIKE RESUSCITATION AND THE DRESSING OF WOUNDS. DISCIPLINES THAT COULD MEAN THE DIFFERENCE BETWEEN A LIFE AND A DEATH. TEACHING FIRST AID IS A CRUCIAL PART OF PREPARING PEOPLE TO COPE WITH THE CONSEQUENCES OF A DISASTER. AT RED CROSS WE'VE LEARNED THAT IF YOU PREPARE FOR THE WORST, IT OFTEN DOESN'T HAPPEN.

WHEREVER WE GO IT'S A DISASTER
NEW ZEALAND RED CROSS
AVOIDING DISASTER IS NOT SOMETHING WE CARE TO THINK ABOUT. WE NEED TO BE PREPARED FOR CATASTROPHES THAT CAN SUDDENLY HAPPEN ANYWHERE AT ANY TIME, BE IT A WAR IN RWANDA OR A PLANE GOING DOWN IN THE RUAHINES. FOR MILLIONS THE RED CROSS EMBLEM HAS BECOME A FAMILIAR AND REASSURING SIGHT IN THE AFTERMATH OF A DISASTER. WE PREPARE OURSELVES FOR AN INSTANT RESPONSE, AND THROUGH OUR FIRST AID AND RESCUE COURSES, WE ALSO PREPARE YOU. ALTHOUGH WE MAY ASK FOR YOUR HELP NOW AND THEN, ONE DAY YOU MIGHT NEED OURS.

PUBLIC SERVICE/
POLITICAL NEWSPAPER
OR MAGAZINE: CAMPAIGN

467
ART DIRECTOR:
Tom McMahon
WRITER:
Mike Lear
DESIGNER:
Valerie Homan
CLIENT:
Lowry Park Zoo
AGENCY:
WestGroup/Tampa

PUBLIC SERVICE/
POLITICAL OUTDOOR
AND POSTERS

468
ART DIRECTOR:
Rick Paynter
WRITER:
Larry Cadman
PHOTOGRAPHER:
Michael Weinstein
CLIENT:
Rabbi Marc H.
Tannenbaum Foundation
AGENCY:
Bozell/New York

469
ART DIRECTOR:
Paul Renner
WRITER:
Ryan Ebner
PHOTOGRAPHERS:
Marko Lavrisha
Gareth Hopson
CLIENT:
Howell Central Little
League
AGENCY:
Butler Shine & Stern/
Sausalito

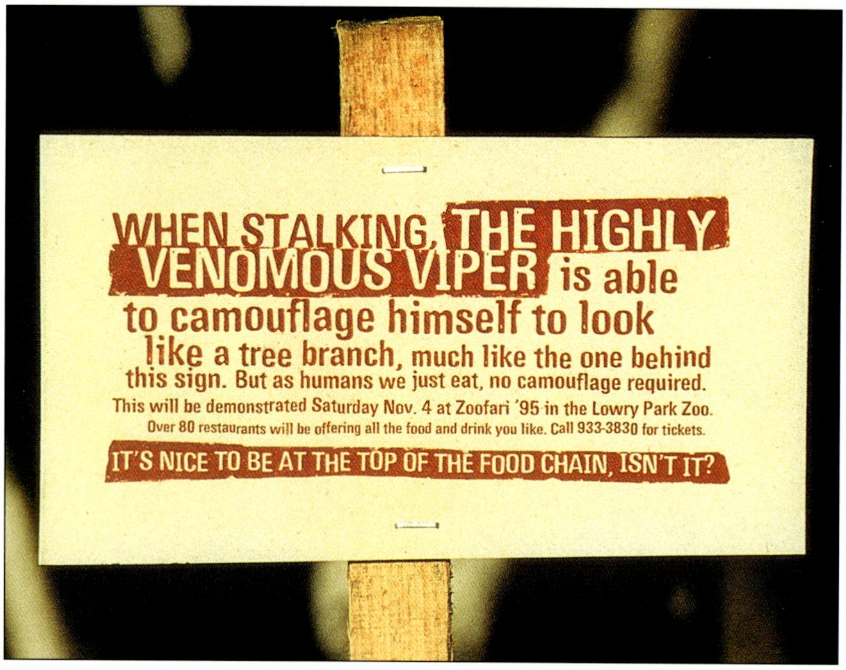

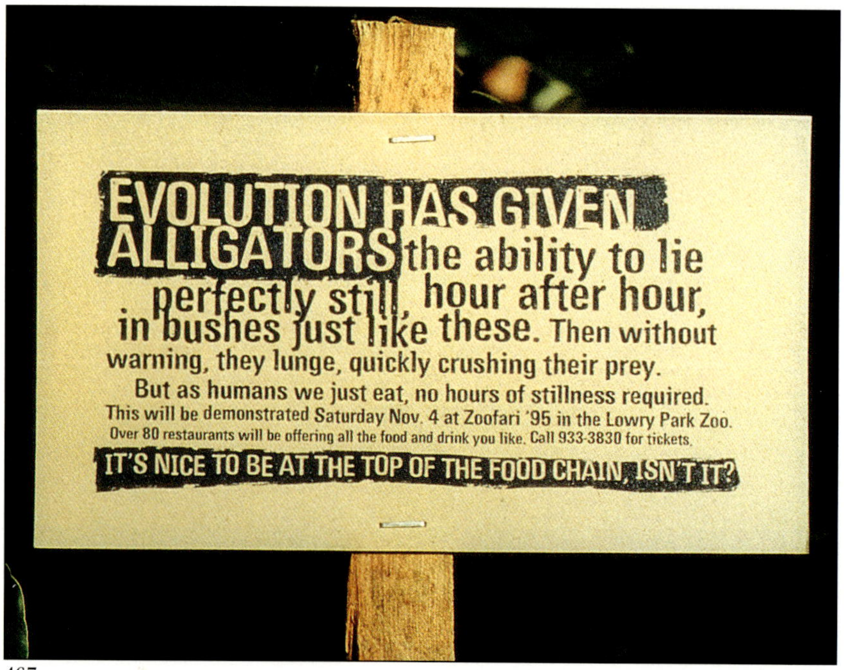

467

It's going to take three of the world's great religions to get them to start hating each other.
Karima Shah
Peter Baldwin
Dianne Lazarus
Photo Credit: Michael Weinstein
Children aren't born hating each other. But they learn quickly enough. These days, too many Muslims, Christians and Jews are being taught to fear and hate each other based simply on who they are. Carried to its extreme, this misuse of religion leads to "final solutions" and "ethnic cleansings."
RABBI MARC H. TANENBAUM FOUNDATION, INC.
The Rabbi Marc H. Tanenbaum Foundation was set up to fight religious bigotry and foster tolerance among religions. We're beginning to see results. To find out more and to join us in the fight, write the Rabbi Marc H. Tanenbaum Foundation, 575 Madison Avenue, Suite 400, New York, N.Y., 10022.

468

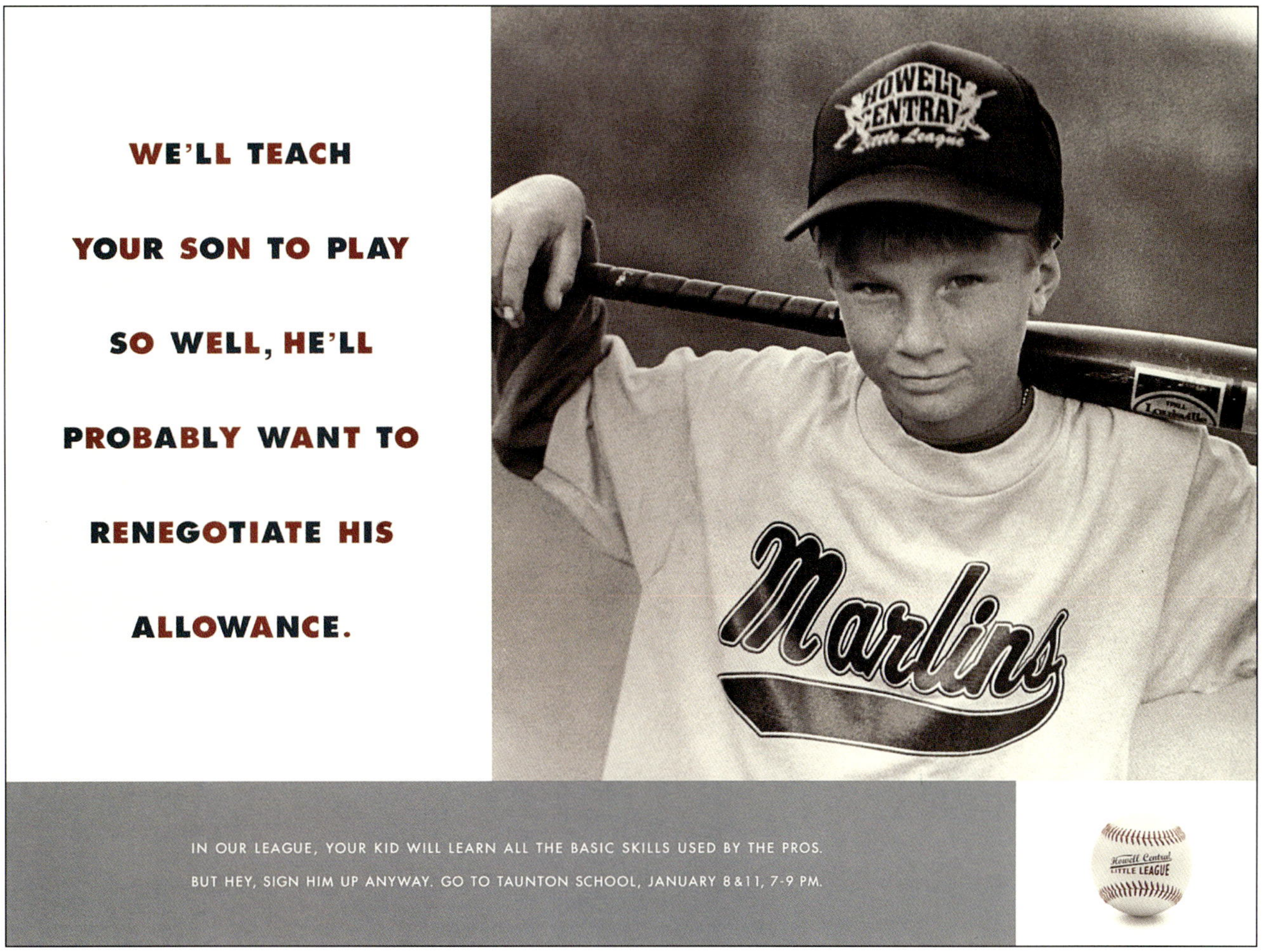
WE'LL TEACH YOUR SON TO PLAY SO WELL, HE'LL PROBABLY WANT TO RENEGOTIATE HIS ALLOWANCE.
Marlins
IN OUR LEAGUE, YOUR KID WILL LEARN ALL THE BASIC SKILLS USED BY THE PROS.
BUT HEY, SIGN HIM UP ANYWAY. GO TO TAUNTON SCHOOL, JANUARY 8 & 11, 7-9 PM.
Howell Central LITTLE LEAGUE

469

PUBLIC SERVICE/
POLITICAL OUTDOOR
AND POSTERS

470
ART DIRECTOR:
Paul Renner
WRITER:
Ryan Ebner
PHOTOGRAPHERS:
Marko Lavrisha
Gareth Hopson
CLIENT:
Howell Central Little League
AGENCY:
Butler Shine & Stern/
Sausalito

471
ART DIRECTOR:
John Butler
WRITER:
Mike Shine
DESIGNERS:
John Butler
Geordie Stephens
CLIENT:
Marin Museum of American Indians
AGENCY:
Butler Shine & Stern/
Sausalito

472
ART DIRECTOR:
John Butler
WRITER:
Mike Shine
DESIGNERS:
John Butler
Geordie Stephens
CLIENT:
Marin Museum of American Indians
AGENCY:
Butler Shine & Stern/
Sausalito

473
ART DIRECTOR:
John Butler
WRITER:
Mike Shine
DESIGNERS:
John Butler
Geordie Stephens
CLIENT:
Marin Museum of American Indians
AGENCY:
Butler Shine & Stern/
Sausalito

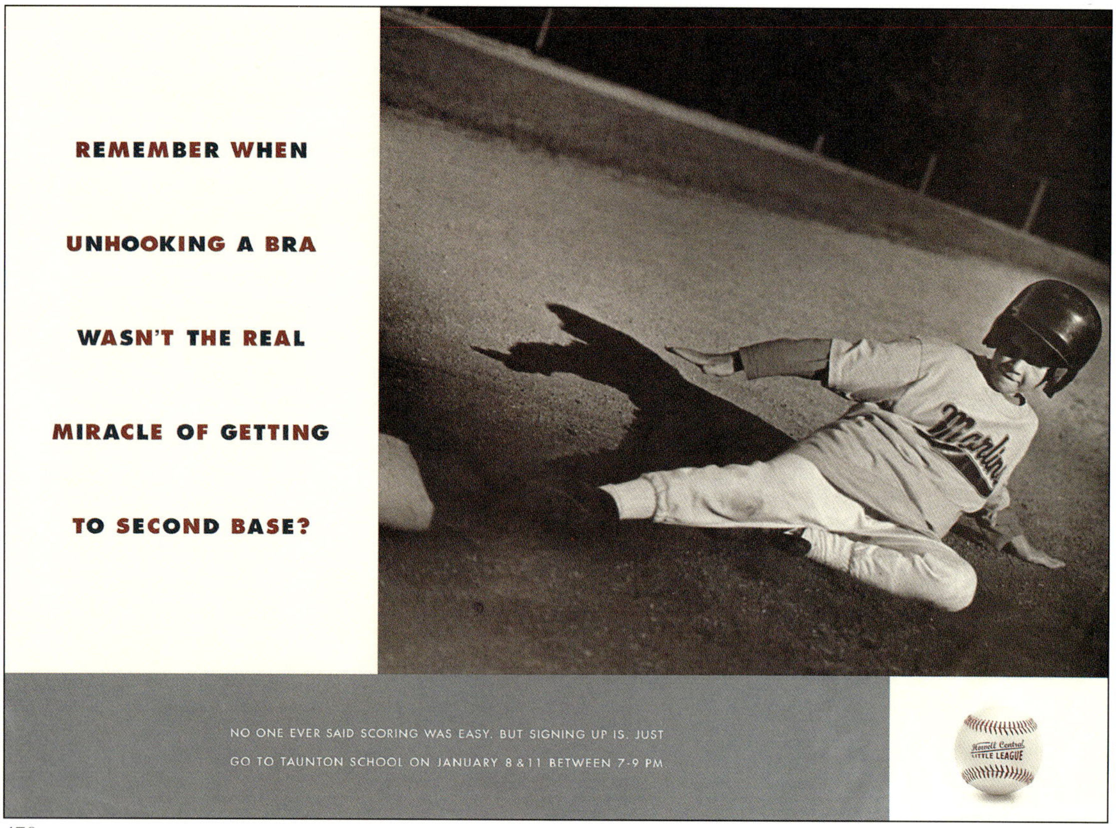

470

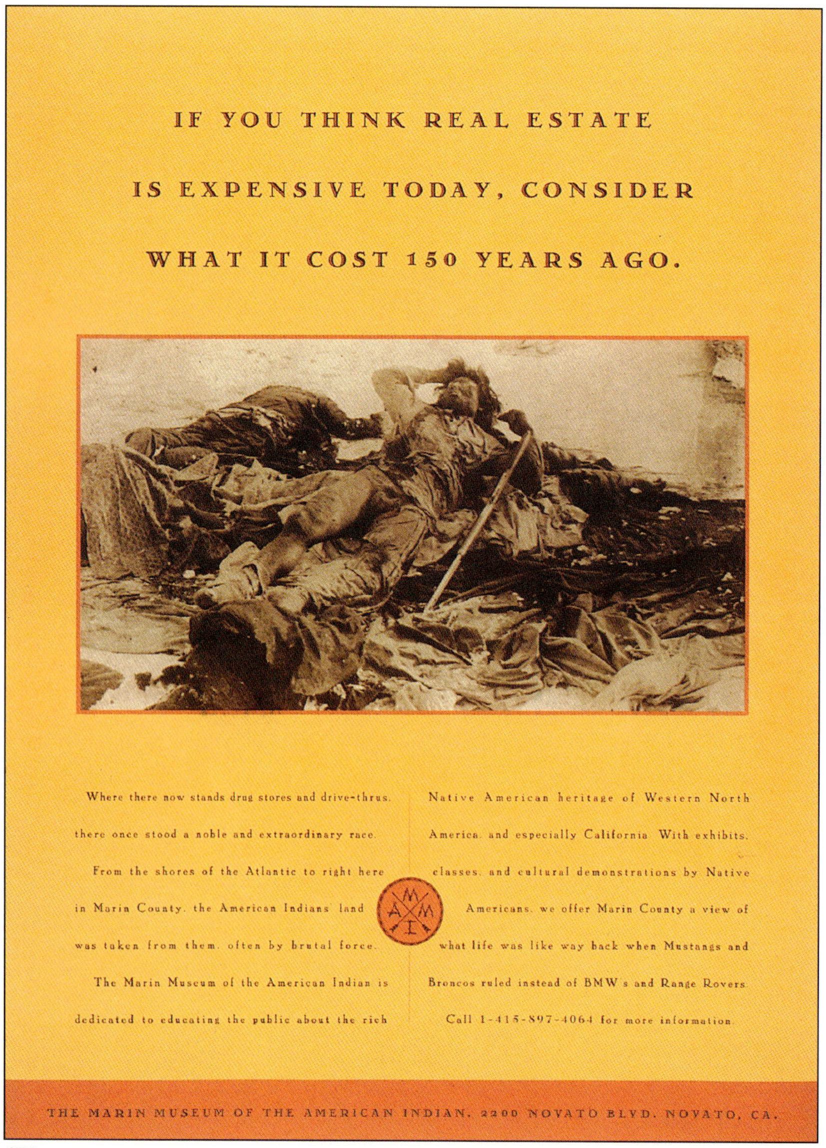

471

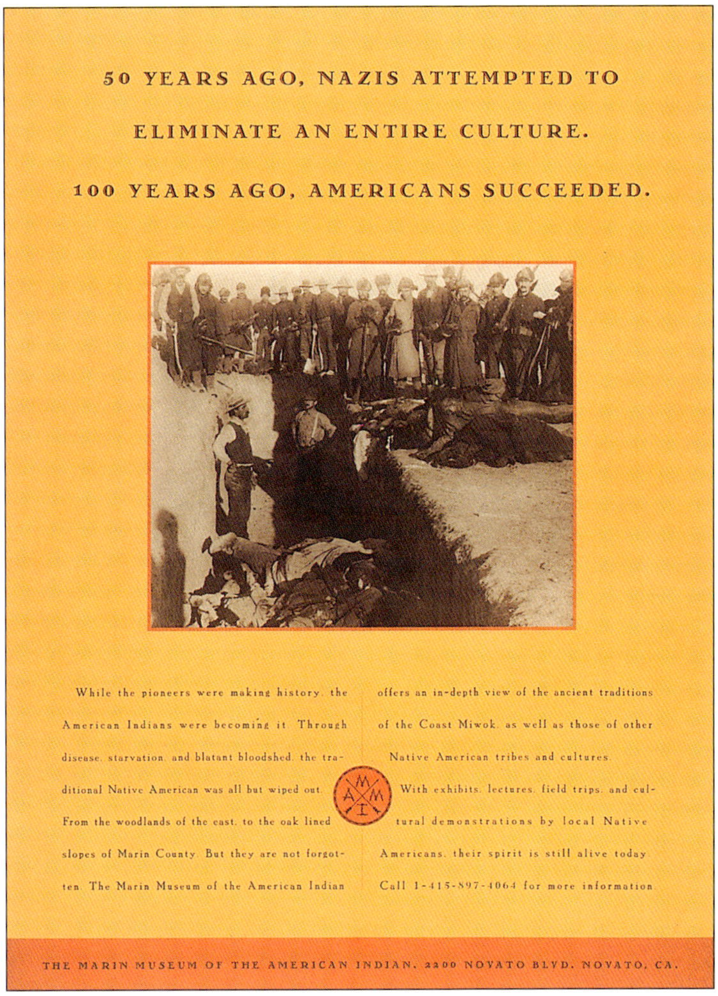
50 YEARS AGO, NAZIS ATTEMPTED TO
ELIMINATE AN ENTIRE CULTURE.
100 YEARS AGO, AMERICANS SUCCEEDED.
While the pioneers were making history, the American Indians were becoming it. Through disease, starvation, and blatant bloodshed, the traditional Native American was all but wiped out. From the woodlands of the east, to the oak lined slopes of Marin County. But they are not forgotten. The Marin Museum of the American Indian offers an in-depth view of the ancient traditions of the Coast Miwok, as well as those of other Native American tribes and cultures.
With exhibits, lectures, field trips, and cultural demonstrations by local Native Americans, their spirit is still alive today. Call 1-415-897-4064 for more information.
THE MARIN MUSEUM OF THE AMERICAN INDIAN. 2200 NOVATO BLVD. NOVATO, CA.

472

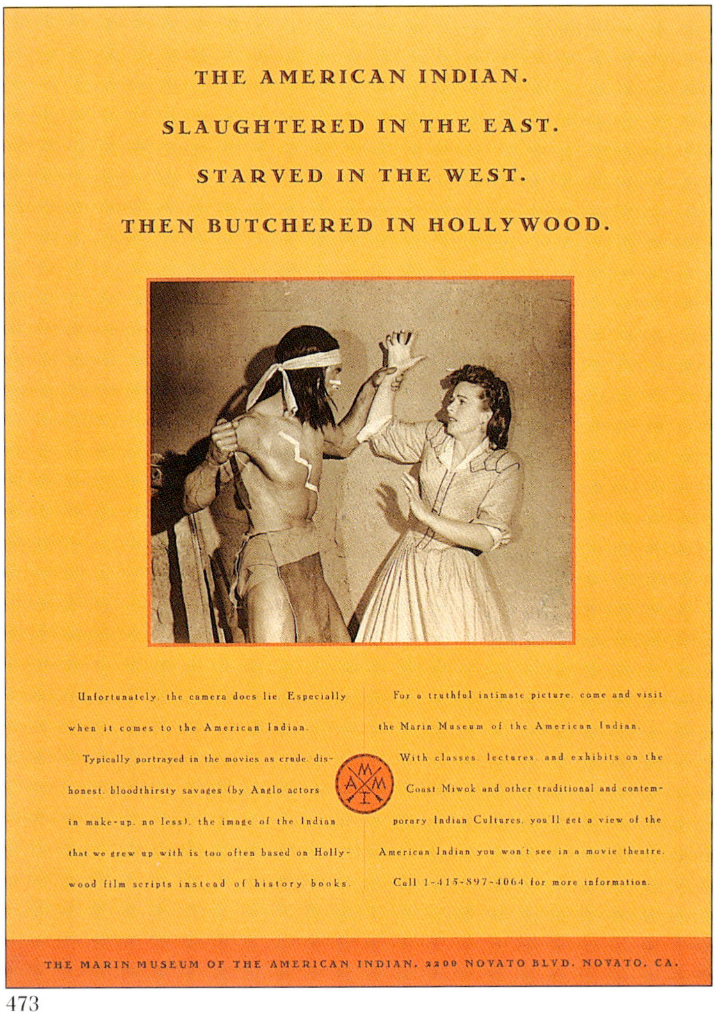
THE AMERICAN INDIAN.
SLAUGHTERED IN THE EAST.
STARVED IN THE WEST.
THEN BUTCHERED IN HOLLYWOOD.
Unfortunately, the camera does lie. Especially when it comes to the American Indian.
Typically portrayed in the movies as crude, dishonest, bloodthirsty savages (by Anglo actors in make-up, no less), the image of the Indian that we grew up with is too often based on Hollywood film scripts instead of history books.
For a truthful intimate picture, come and visit the Marin Museum of the American Indian.
With classes, lectures, and exhibits on the Coast Miwok and other traditional and contemporary Indian Cultures, you'll get a view of the American Indian you won't see in a movie theatre.
Call 1-415-897-4064 for more information.
THE MARIN MUSEUM OF THE AMERICAN INDIAN. 2200 NOVATO BLVD. NOVATO, CA.

473

PUBLIC SERVICE/
POLITICAL OUTDOOR
AND POSTERS

474
ART DIRECTOR:
Chris Do
WRITER:
Colleen Mathis
PHOTOGRAPHER:
William Mercer McLeod
CLIENT:
Childhaven
AGENCY:
Cole & Weber/Seattle

475
ART DIRECTOR:
Christopher Gyorgy
WRITER:
Marshall Twinam
PHOTOGRAPHER:
John Katz
CLIENT:
Circle Ten Council/
Boy Scouts of America
AGENCY:
DDB Needham Worldwide
Dallas Group

476
ART DIRECTOR:
Marcy Levey
WRITER:
David Neale
CLIENT:
Virginia Coalition
For The Homeless
AGENCY:
Earle Palmer Brown/
Richmond

477
ART DIRECTOR:
Ed Tajon
WRITER:
Hugh Carson
PHOTOGRAPHER:
Dave Wilson Studios
CLIENT:
The Baltimore Zoo
AGENCY:
Eisner & Associates/
Baltimore

474

475

THE MORE BLACK INK ON A PAGE, THE MORE HEAT IT ABSORBS. THE MORE HEAT IT ABSORBS, THE WARMER THE PAGE. THE WARMER THE PAGE THE BETTER INSULATION IT MAKES WHEN HOMELESS PEOPLE STUFF IT INSIDE THEIR SHIRTS.

VIRGINIA COALITION FOR THE HOMELESS

644 5527

476

It's
A
Girl
The Baltimore Zoo is proud to announce the birth of a beautiful, bouncing baby chimpanzee.
Swing by the Chimpanzee Forest and wish her a Happy Birthday.
THE BALTIMORE ZOO
Home of the #1 rated Children's Zoo. Admission $7.50 adults, $4.00 children (ages 2-15) and seniors. Daily:10am-4pm. Free parking. Call 366-LION. Exit 7 off I-83.

477

PUBLIC SERVICE/
POLITICAL OUTDOOR
AND POSTERS

478
ART DIRECTOR:
Dick Brown
WRITER:
Dick Brown
CLIENT:
Humane Society of Utah
AGENCY:
EvansGroup/Salt Lake City

479
ART DIRECTOR:
Tom Lichtenheld
WRITER:
Sally Hogshead
PHOTOGRAPHER:
Buck Holzemer
CLIENT:
Children's Defense Fund
AGENCY:
Fallon McElligott/
Minneapolis

480
ART DIRECTOR:
Robb Burnham
WRITER:
Sally Hogshead
PHOTOGRAPHER:
Marc Norberg
CLIENT:
Minneapolis Animal
Shelter
AGENCY:
Fallon McElligott/
Minneapolis

481
ART DIRECTOR:
Robb Burnham
WRITER:
Sally Hogshead
PHOTOGRAPHER:
Marc Norberg
CLIENT:
Minneapolis Animal
Shelter
AGENCY:
Fallon McElligott/
Minneapolis

Our vet
will be back
shortly.
Sit.
Stay.
HUMANE
SOCIETY
OF UTAH
SHOTS, SPAYS, NEUTERS AND GREAT VETERINARIANS ARE JUST NEXT DOOR.
478

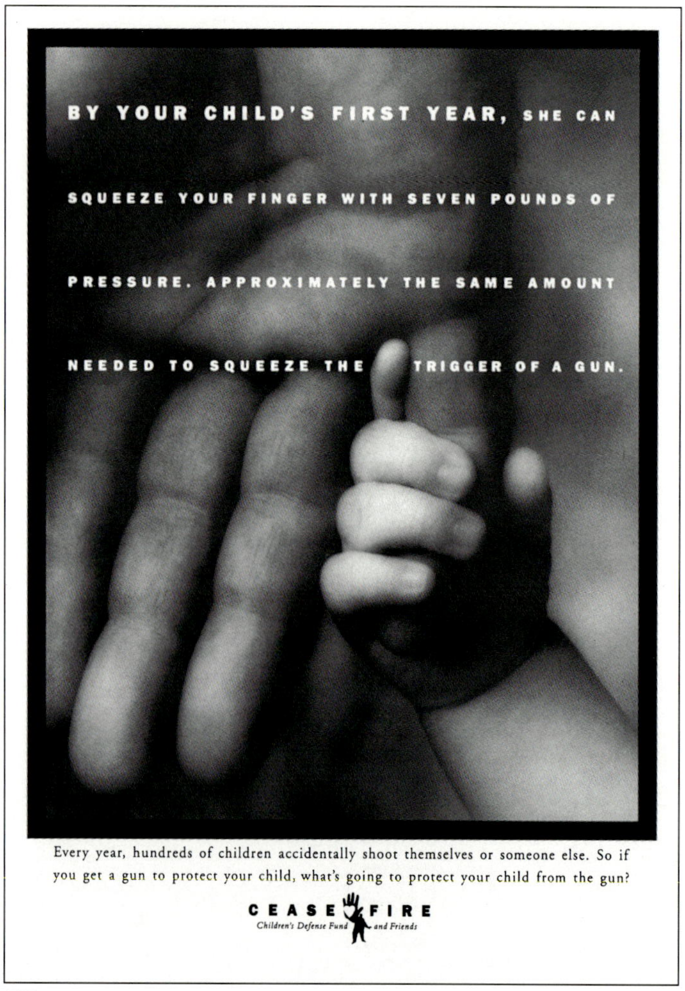
BY YOUR CHILD'S FIRST YEAR, SHE CAN
SQUEEZE YOUR FINGER WITH SEVEN POUNDS OF
PRESSURE. APPROXIMATELY THE SAME AMOUNT
NEEDED TO SQUEEZE THE TRIGGER OF A GUN.
Every year, hundreds of children accidentally shoot themselves or someone else. So if you get a gun to protect your child, what's going to protect your child from the gun?
CEASE FIRE
Children's Defense Fund and Friends
479

Expiration Date:
MON. JULY 24
He's about half German Shepherd, he's housebroken, and he knows how to shake hands. If he's your kind of dog, come get him quick. This offer expires soon. Adopt. Fast. 348-4250. MINNEAPOLIS ANIMAL SHELTER

480

Expiration Date:
MON. MAY 29
Ever since we've had her, she's been wagging her tail like crazy. Unfortunately her owner couldn't keep her any longer, and now, neither can we. Can you? Adopt. Fast. 348-4250. MINNEAPOLIS ANIMAL SHELTER

481

PUBLIC SERVICE/ POLITICAL OUTDOOR AND POSTERS

482
ART DIRECTOR:
Robb Burnham
WRITER:
Sally Hogshead
PHOTOGRAPHER:
Marc Norberg
CLIENT:
Minneapolis Animal Shelter
AGENCY:
Fallon McElligott/ Minneapolis

483
ART DIRECTOR:
Jennifer Fleming-Balser
WRITERS:
Rich Tlapek
Chuck Meehan
CLIENT:
Babe Ruth Museum
AGENCY:
GSD&M Advertising/ Austin

484
ART DIRECTOR:
Larry Bowdish
WRITER:
Roger Baldacci
PHOTOGRAPHER:
Russ Quackenbush
CLIENT:
Group Against Smoking Pollution
AGENCY:
Houston Herstek Favat/ Boston

485
ART DIRECTOR:
Rob Rich
WRITER:
Jim Garaventi
PHOTOGRAPHER:
Harry DeZitter
CLIENT:
The Museum of Fine Arts/ Boston
AGENCY:
Ingalls/Boston

482

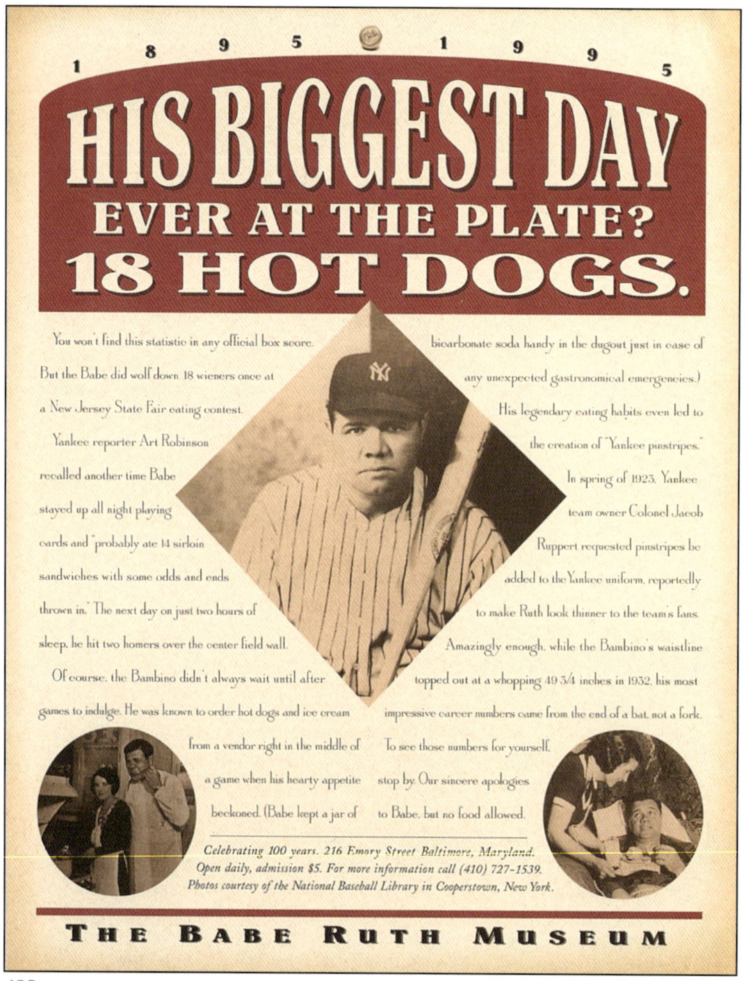

483

APPARENTLY, DR. KEVORKIAN
WASN'T THE FIRST TO INTRODUCE
SUICIDE MACHINES.
Come to Marlboro Country.
GASP
GROUP AGAINST SMOKING POLLUTION

484

Alpha-Pi, 1961 Morris Louis
Ken Moody, 1984 Robert Mapplethorpe
Abstract vs Representational. Join us for the debate.
Degrees of Abstraction: From Morris Louis to Mapplethorpe, March 11 thru October 22
MUSEUM of FINE ARTS

485

PUBLIC SERVICE/
POLITICAL TELEVISION:
SINGLE

486
ART DIRECTORS:
Chris Brignola
Jennifer Van Blarcom
WRITERS:
Jennifer Van Blarcom
Chris Brignola
AGENCY PRODUCER:
Linda Tesa
DIRECTOR:
Jerry Cailor
CLIENT:
Planned Parenthood
AGENCY:
DeVito/Verdi, New York

487
ART DIRECTOR:
Jan-Dirk Bouw
WRITER:
David Bell
PRODUCTION COMPANY:
De Schiettent
DIRECTOR:
Lex Brand
CLIENT:
St. Patrick's Church
AGENCY:
GGT Advertising/London

488
ART DIRECTOR:
Jonathan Grainger
WRITER:
David Wolff
AGENCY PRODUCER:
Katie Regan
PRODUCTION COMPANY:
Great Guns
DIRECTOR:
Richard Spence
CLIENT:
Refuge
AGENCY:
Grey Advertising/London

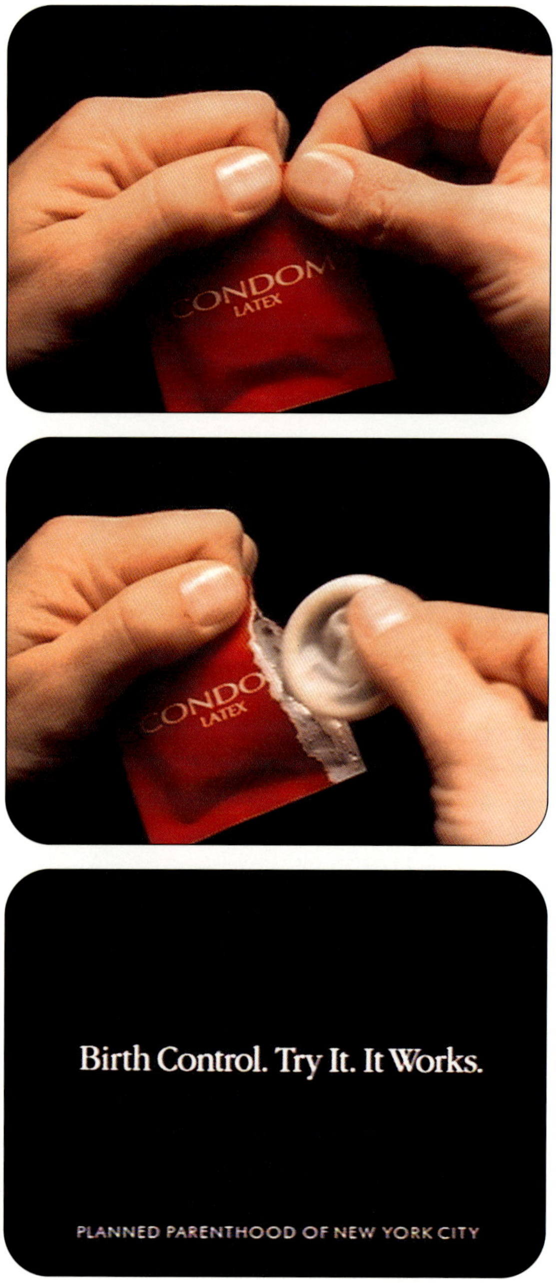

486

ANNCR: It's easier than putting on a diaper.
SUPER: BIRTH CONTROL. TRY IT. IT WORKS.

487

(SFX: WATER DRIPPING)
(SFX: RAIN)
SUPER: DONATIONS NEEDED FOR URGENT REPAIRS. 0171 437 2010.

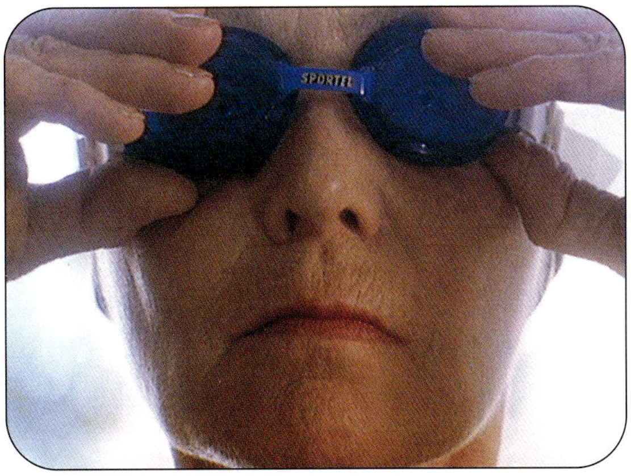

488

FEMALE ANNCR: One woman in ten . . .

(MUSIC: CLASSICAL)

FEMALE ANNCR: . . . is left-handed . . . one woman in nine . . .

(SFX: KIDS RUNNING AROUND A GARDEN)

FEMALE ANNCR: . . . reads *Good Housekeeping.* One woman in eight . . .

(SFX: SWIMMING POOL SOUNDS)

MALE ANNCR: . . . swims regularly.

FEMALE ANNCR: One woman in seven . . .

(MUSIC: "NEWS AT TEN" THEME)

MALE ANNCR: . . . watches the news at ten.

FEMALE ANNCR: One woman in six . . .

(SFX: SUPERMARKET SOUNDS)

MALE ANNCR: . . . shops on Saturday.

FEMALE ANNCR: One woman in five . . .

(SFX: CAFE SOUNDS)

MALE ANNCR: . . . has given up smoking.

FEMALE ANNCR: One woman in four . . .

(SFX: VIOLENT FIGHTING SOUNDS)

FEMALE ANNCR: . . . one woman in four is physically abused by her partner. Help us to change this frightening statistic. Give us your change.

SUPER: REFUGE. P.O BOX 855 CHISWICK LONDON W4 4JF.

PUBLIC SERVICE/
POLITICAL TELEVISION:
SINGLE

489

ART DIRECTORS:
Todd Riddle
Mark Nardi

WRITERS:
Mark Nardi
Todd Riddle

AGENCY PRODUCER:
Nancy McGraw

PRODUCTION COMPANY:
Picture Park

DIRECTOR:
Errol Morris

CLIENT:
Massachusetts Department of Public Health

AGENCY:
Houston Herstek Favat/ Boston

490

ART DIRECTOR:
Chris Bleackley

WRITER:
Maggie Mouat

AGENCY PRODUCER:
Brigid Howard

PRODUCTION COMPANY:
Silverscreen Productions

DIRECTOR:
Geoff Dixon

CLIENT:
Land Transport Safety Authority

AGENCY:
Saatchi & Saatchi/ Wellington, New Zealand

PUBLIC SERVICE/
POLITICAL TELEVISION:
CAMPAIGN

491

ART DIRECTOR:
Jeremy Postaer

WRITER:
Paul Venables

AGENCY PRODUCERS:
Betsy Flynn
Cindy Fluitt

PRODUCTION COMPANY:
In-House

DIRECTOR:
Jeremy Postaer

CLIENT:
San Francisco Jazz Festival

AGENCY:
Goodby Silverstein & Partners/San Francisco

489

(SFX: BABY CRYING AND COUGHING)

ANNCR: Every year 300,000 babies get sick from second-hand smoke. But the tobacco industry just doesn't want to hear it.

(SFX: MONITOR IS TURNED OFF, BABY SOUNDS STOP)

SUPER: IT'S TIME WE MADE SMOKING HISTORY.

SUPER: MASSACHUSETTS DEPARTMENT OF HEALTH.

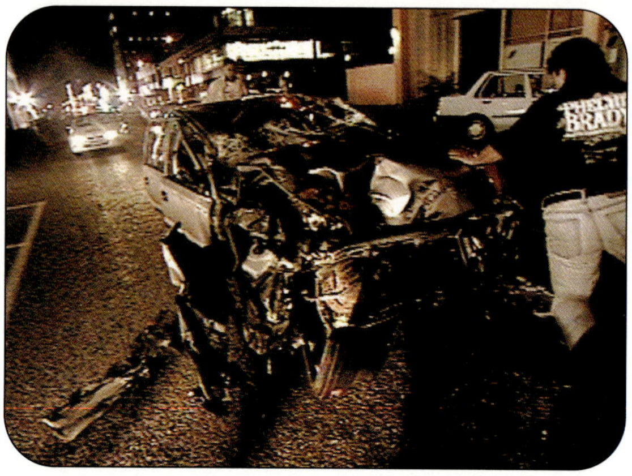

490

PAUL: Are you going to drive this?

SARAH: Well, you're not driving.

PAUL: I can drive.

SARAH: Just look at you, you can't even walk straight.

PAUL: Huh, look at you. We'll get a cab then. Taxi . . . taxi.

SARAH: There aren't any taxis. Just give me the keys.

PAUL: Taxi . . . taxi.

SARAH: Paul, give me the keys.

PAUL: We'll walk.

SARAH: No. Just get in the car.

PAUL: Check this out.

SARAH: Patsy Cline—no way!

(SFX: CAR CRASHING, HORN JAMMED ON)

(SFX: PAUL CRYING FOR HELP)

BYSTANDER: Call an ambulance.

(SFX: SIRENS)

SUPER: IF YOU DRINK THEN DRIVE, ONE WAY OR ANOTHER YOU'LL BE STOPPED.

SUPER: LAND TRANSPORT SAFETY AUTHORITY.

491

ANNCR: In 1961, two musicians at extreme ends of the jazz spectrum played together for the first time, here, at what used to be the Jazz Workshop. Wes Montgomery sat in with John Coltrane's revolutionary band. The music was breakthrough. The music was also never recorded. This time, we're telling you up front. We're not coming out with a CD.

SUPER: SAN FRANCISCO JAZZ FESTIVAL. OCTOBER 13 THROUGH 29.

William Faulkner refused to write without one. Thomas Edison's were custom made to fit horizontally in his shirt pockets. And John Steinbeck, who preferred the Mongol 480 #2 3/8 round, once said of the characters in his stories: "They cannot move until I pick up a pencil."

Radio Finalists

CONSUMER RADIO: SINGLE

492

WRITER:
Marianne Curtis
AGENCY PRODUCER:
Annie Tartaglia-Price
CLIENT:
Crystal Springs
AGENCY:
Cramer-Krasselt/Phoenix

493

WRITER:
Kim Porter
AGENCY PRODUCERS:
Heidi Molden
Jeri Vaughn
Anne Marie Canon
PRODUCTION COMPANY:
Clatter & Din
CLIENT:
Tosco Refining & Marketing Company
AGENCY:
Elgin Syferd DDB Needham/Seattle

494

WRITER:
Doug de Grood
AGENCY PRODUCER:
Mary Schultz
CLIENT:
Magnavox
AGENCY:
Fallon McElligott/ Minneapolis

495

WRITER:
Dean Hacohen
AGENCY PRODUCER:
Dean Hacohen
CLIENT:
Crain's New York Business
AGENCY:
Goldsmith/Jeffrey, New York

496

WRITER:
Dean Hacohen
AGENCY PRODUCER:
Dean Hacohen
CLIENT:
Crain's New York Business
AGENCY:
Goldsmith/Jeffrey, New York

492

ANNCR: From the mountains that reach up to the angels, it flows toward us as though on a mission to bring us joy. Through nature's wondrous, cleansing way, it trickles across Earth's rugged surface, bringing life to all it touches. Truly, this luminescent, magical liquid is a glorious gift from heaven itself. This is Crystal Springs water. This is also a bunch of crap. It would make a neat story if it were true. No. We take ordinary water and filter the daylights out of it at a non-mystical bottling plant. No mountain. No trickling stream. Just a chain-link fence and a guard named Ed. But it's better than it would be running out of the ground someplace where all the animals could come and stick their tounges right in it. Crystal Springs is the cleanest, most refreshing water there is. But if it helps to imagine it running across a bunch of mossy rocks as some other bottled waters claim, go right ahead. Just remember those animals. And their tongues.

ANNCR 2: Crystal Springs bottled water. Quite honestly the best you'll ever drink. It's what Ed drinks.

493

(SFX: RAIN AND THUNDER; WINDSHIELD WIPERS; CAR ENGINE)

(MUSIC: OMINOUS, SLOWLY TURNING POSITIVE, WHIMSICAL CRESCENDO)

MAN: The night was cold, dark and wet. Like an old cup of coffee on the desktop of a government worker. Alfonzo's hands gripped the steering wheel like a hairnet on a cafeteria lady. He glanced at his gas gauge. The red light was glowing like a schoolgirl fresh from the prom. "Should I stop?" he asked himself like a drunk at last call. After deliberating, Alfonzo obeyed the gleaming reminder like a henpecked husband on garbage night. And searched for a safe, bright place to fill up. Suddenly, there were lights. Hundreds of them. Like something, well . . . something . . . bright. He spotted a big blue sign: "Tosco!" it proclaimed like a TV evangelist. Alfonzo pulled in. This Tosco was more convenient than a live-in girlfriend, he thought. And clean. Clean like the jokes that nuns tell. And Tosco had food. Food as bountiful as hair in the ear of a middle-aged man. And the employees were helpful. As helpful as a good metaphor.

494

(SFX: PHONE RINGING)

GUY 1: Hello?

GUY 2: Hey, Mike.

GUY 1: What?

GUY 2: You wanna come over and watch my Magnavox big-screen TV?

GUY 1: Aaahh, what's on?

GUY 2: The Peruvian Croquet Finals.

GUY 1: Sure.

ANNCR: The 52-inch Magnavox big-screen TV . . . with SmartScreen . . . and a picture so sharp even boring sports seem cool.

(SFX: CROQUET SOUNDS)

GUY 1: He touched the wicket!

GUY 2: Yeah! He touched the wicket!

GUY 1: Did you see that?

GUY 2: Oh, man!

ANNCR: Magnavox. Smart. Very smart.

495

(SFX: TUMBLERS IN WALL SAFE CLICKING SLOWLY BACK AND FORTH)

ANNCR: The average office safe in the New York area — replete with confidential marketing plans, pricing strategies, and detail on impending management shake-ups, can take up to six long hours of sweat and toil to break into.

But, of course, that's not really necessary. *Crain's New York Business* is available at newsstands now.

496

ANNCR: "Whoops." That's the term New York executives use when they realize they've missed an appointment. "Shoot"—the term most commonly used when they miss a cab. "For crying out loud"—now there's the term most often heard when they miss a golf putt.

But what about when New York executives miss a story in *Crain's New York Business* they should have read? Do you really think we want to pay a seven figure fine to the FCC?

497

(MUSIC: ROMANTIC)

MAN: I love you.

WOMAN: I love you, too.

MAN: And I love the rich, aromatic flavor of this Morning Blend, Coffee Time flavored coffee from World Wide food products.

WOMAN: Nothing compares to the feeling I get from a fresh, steaming cup of Apricot-Seasoned Herbal Potpourri.

MAN: Mmm, except for the Paprika-Scented, Double Dose Happy Time, French Manor Latte Light Blend.

WOMAN: Aw, I love it when you talk about coffee like that.

MAN: You know, if I could just get a little milk in my coffee, I'll have World Wide food products flavored coffees and you . . . pure heaven!

WOMAN: Mmph, you're so sweet . . . but I think we're out of milk.

(MUSIC: COMES TO SCRATCHING HALT)

MAN: There's no milk?

(SFX: CRASHING NOISE)

MAN: This coffee tastes like dirt without milk!

WOMAN: You're the one that drank it, Mr. Lovey-Dovey Coffee Freak!

MAN: Oh, I'm a freak!

WOMAN: Yeah, you are—

MAN: You know what you need? You need a pot of Laid-back, Take a Chill, I'm-Sorry-I'm-So-Greedy, Double Decaf.

(MUSIC: ROMANTIC AGAIN)

(SFX: BREAKING GLASS)

ANNCR: Got Milk?

ANNCR 2: Brought to you by America's Dairy Farmers.

498

ANNCR (SINGING):

Sprite can make you taller
Sprite can make you cool
Drinking Sprite will give you sex appeal
And make your dreams come true
It increases your upper body strength
Makes you faster and jump higher
Sprite will bring you inner peace
And cool your inner fire
Sprite helps people live together
Build a better world
Sprite can put a happy face
On every boy and girl

Sprite's the way to friendship
And looking the best you can
Drinking Sprite means you're okay
And that you understand

If you believe that all these things
Can be yours by drinking Sprite
You should really stop listening to this stupid song
and go out and get a life

Jingles are nothing
Thirst is everything
Obey your thirst
Sprite.

499

ANNCR: The human stomach. A miracle of science.

(SFX: STOMACH GURGLE)

ANNCR: And sound. But what are these sounds trying to tell us? If we listen carefully . . .

(SFX: STOMACH GURLE SLOWS)

ANNCR: . . . and slow this sound down.

(SFX: STOMACH GURGLE, ODD WORD SOUNDS)

ANNCR: We begin to hear something interesting.

(SFX: STOMACH GURGLE SOUNDING LIKE: "MMM . . . HAAAGEN-DAAZS")

ANNCR 2: Haagen-Dazs. It's not just ice cream.

ANNCR: It's Haagen-Dazs.

CONSUMER RADIO: SINGLE

497

WRITERS:
Al Kelly
Blake Daley
AGENCY PRODUCER:
Kim Noble
CLIENT:
California Fluid Milk Processor Advisory Board
AGENCY:
Goodby Silverstein & Partners/San Francisco

498

WRITERS:
Jay Sharfstein
Adam Seifer
AGENCY PRODUCER:
Laurie Leokum
PRODUCTION COMPANY:
Bang Music
CLIENT:
The Coca-Cola Company/ Sprite
AGENCY:
Lowe & Partners/SMS, New York

499

WRITER:
Chris Gerald
AGENCY PRODUCER:
Shawna McPeek
PRODUCTION COMPANY:
Prisma/Toronto
CLIENT:
Ault Foods
AGENCY:
Lowe SMS/Toronto

CONSUMER RADIO: SINGLE

500

WRITERS:
Andy Spade
Shalom Auslander
AGENCY PRODUCER:
Roxanne Karsch
CLIENT:
NYNEX Yellow Pages
AGENCY:
TBWA Chiat/Day, New York

501

WRITERS:
Michael Folino
Greg Collins
Matthew Bogen
Glen Wachowiak
AGENCY PRODUCERS:
Francesca Cohn
Amy Melikian
CLIENT:
America West Airlines
AGENCY:
Team One Advertising/
El Segundo, CA

CONSUMER RADIO: CAMPAIGN

502

WRITERS:
Michelle Roufa
Arthur Bijur
AGENCY PRODUCERS:
Mary Ellen O'Brien
Maresa Wickham
CLIENT:
Little Caesars Pizza
AGENCY:
Cliff Freeman & Partners/
New York

500

(SFX: "DING")

(SFX: TRUCK BACKING UP, STREET NOISES)

MAN: Okay, bring it back. Keep comin'. Plenty of room, come on back. Okay, a little bit more.

(SFX: CRASHING NOISE)

MAN: Plenty of room. Keep coming . . .

ANNCR: The Opticians heading in the NYNEX Yellow Pages. After Oil and before Outboard Motors. NYNEX. More information. More solutions. More stuff. And look in your local directory for NYNEX Consumer Tips.

ANNCR: Not available in all regions.

501

MATT BOGEN: Hi, Matt Bogen here for America West Airlines. Today we're calling a souvenir shop to see what they have for fans of the Phoenix Suns.

(SFX: PHONE RINGING)

VENDOR: Souvenir shack.

MATT: Hi, I'm looking for a model of that colorful America West Phoenix Suns plane. You have any in stock?

VENDOR: Ennnnnn!! Can't help you there, bub. But tell you what, how about a portrait of the Suns starting lineup strikingly rendered on lush, black velvet?

MATT: Mmm, nice . . .

VENDOR: Look at it just right, and their eyes seem to follow you around the room.

MATT: Really?

VENDOR: Hey, it's not just art. It's a conversation piece!

MATT: Uh, you sell a lot of those?

VENDOR: Not a one . . . which means yours would be what we call a "limited edition." How does that grab ya?

MATT: Painfully. But tell me, since the official airline of the Suns is America West, do you have any portraits of the America West spokesman.

VENDOR: Uh, no.

MATT: Want to buy some?

(SFX: PHONE DISCONNECTING, DIAL TONE)

MATT: While he thinks it over, this has been Matt Bogen for America West Airlines. The Official Airline of your Phoenix Suns.

502

(MUSIC: DRAMATIC, SUSPENSEFUL MUSIC)

(SFX: KEY IN LOCK, DOOR OPENS)

ANNCR: November 1st. Billy Smith came home from work early.

BILL: Honey, I'm ho—LY SMOKES, Carol!

WOMAN: Bill?!?

DELIVERY KID: Mr. Smith!

ANNCR: Yes. Bill had come home to find his wife . . . with the pizza delivery boy!

BILL: Carol, why?! Getting pizza delivered!

LITTLE GIRL: Pizza!!!

BILL: In front of the kids, too!

WOMAN: But you love pizza . . .

BILL: I only love Little Caesars pizza!

WOMAN: But . . . these are Little Caesars pizzas!

(MUSIC: EXTREMELY DRAMATIC CHORD)

BILL: Then how do you explain him? Little Caesars doesn't deliver!!!

(MUSIC: EVEN MORE DRAMATIC CHORD)

WOMAN: They do now!!! Now Little Caesars delivers!

BILL: Is this true? Say something, boy!

DELIVERY KID: Um . . . Pizza Pizza?

(MUSIC: INSANELY DRAMATIC CRESCENDO)

BILL: It is true!!!

(MUSIC: ROMANTIC)

BILL: Two Little Caesars pizzas . . . delivered! Carol (BIG KISS)—what can I ever do to thank you (KISS, KISS, KISS)?

CAROL: You could stop kissing the delivery boy . . .

(MUSIC: DRAMATIC AGAIN)

ANNCR: Little Caesars delivers! Get Supreme Supreme — two pizzas with six toppings for $9.98. And get them delivered for just $2.00 more—still about what you'd pay for just one pizza from those other guys!

LITTLE CAESAR: Pizza! Pizza!

CONSUMER RADIO: CAMPAIGN

503

(SFX: OUTDOOR SOUNDS)

MAN (THROUGH ROTTEN, TINNY SPEAKER): Welcome to Burger Land. May I take your order? Actually, before I do, I feel the need to point out here that I do have an Ivy League college degree. You belive that? Four years of work. A hundred grand. And here I am. . . . But I guess that's neither here nor there, is it? So . . . may I take your or —. See, the thing is I majored in Art Appreciation. Which qualifies me to do . . . what?

(SFX: CAR HONK)

MAN: Elbow my way through a crowd at the art museum? Goin', "Let me through, I am a professional." I don't think so. . . . Fortunately, I now minor in Romance Languages (FAKE LAUGH). So, uh, may I take your order, monsieur? (FAKE LAUGH) Actually, now's not really a good time. Could you just loop around and come back? I really think I need some time here alone.

ANNCR: For a degree you can actually use, call Dunwoody Technical Institute for training in careers like electronics, engineering, drafting, or automated manufacturing. Call Dunwoody at 374-5800. That's 374-5800.

504

ANNCR: If you've ever smiled as you watched a mosquito fly into a bug zapper, you're a Minnesotan. If you've ever said, "Boy, this is a nice fishing shack," you're a Minnesotan. If you've ever told anyone that snowplows are a blessing, you're a Minnesotan. If you've ever shown houseguests your tackle box, you're a Minnesotan.

If you think Minnesotans deserve their own beer, try Minnesota's Best. Brewed in St. Paul by the Stroh Brewery. Proud contributor to the Minnesota Parks and Trails Council. Minnesota's Best beer. You gotta be Minnesotan to get it.

503

WRITER:
Luke Sullivan
AGENCY PRODUCER:
Monika Prince
CLIENT:
Dunwoody Technical Institute
AGENCY:
Fallon McElligott/ Minneapolis

504

WRITER:
Lyle Wedemeyer
AGENCY PRODUCER:
Becky Anderson
CLIENT:
The Stroh Brewery Company
AGENCY:
Martin/Williams, Minneapolis

By 1890, consumers knew that the best graphite came from Asia. As a way to associate their product with this high quality, the Koh-I-Noor Pencil Co. painted their pencils yellow, a color of Asian royalty. Today 75% of all pencils are yellow. Color might sway consumers, but not pencil inspectors. Imperfect goods are cut in half and made into golf pencils.

Television Finalists

CONSUMER TELEVISION
OVER :30 SINGLE

505
ART DIRECTOR:
Walter Campbell
WRITER:
Tom Carty
AGENCY PRODUCER:
Frank Lieberman
PRODUCTION COMPANY:
Tony Kaye Films
DIRECTOR:
Tony Kaye
CLIENT:
Volvo Car UK
AGENCY:
Abbott Mead Vickers.
BBDO/London

506
ART DIRECTORS:
David Harner
David Johnson
WRITERS:
David Johnson
David Harner
AGENCY PRODUCERS:
Regina Ebel
Rani Vaz
PRODUCTION COMPANY:
Pytka
DIRECTOR:
Joe Pytka
CLIENT:
Pepsi Cola Company
AGENCY:
BBDO/New York

507
ART DIRECTOR:
George Gilewski
WRITER:
Jon Freir
AGENCY PRODUCER:
Mike Cooper
PRODUCTION COMPANY:
Imported Artists
DIRECTOR:
Richard D'Alessio
CLIENT:
Chrysler Canada
AGENCY:
BBDO Canada/Toronto

508
ART DIRECTORS:
David Angelo
John Leu
WRITERS:
Tina Hall
Harold Einstein
Cliff Freeman
AGENCY PRODUCER:
Mary Ellen Duggan
PRODUCTION COMPANY:
Tony Kaye Films
DIRECTOR:
Tony Kaye
CLIENT:
Prodigy
AGENCY:
Cliff Freeman & Partners/
New York

505

(SFX: THUNDER, WIND)

MAN (YELLING): Twister!

ANNCR: A tornado is a rapidly rotating column of air in contact with the ground. It comes from thunderstorms. You've got to get yourself there in the exact spot that the tornado forms. Sometimes rain and hail wrap around this region and envelop it and we call that "The Bear's Cage" and that's a very, very dangerous area to be in. We drop probes into the paths of tornadoes, trying to get an idea of what kind of force is contained within these vortices. We hope to be able to forecast these storms better . . . to save lives. Maneuverability is very important. It handles the road like it's on rails. We have to depend on the vehicle for our lives.

SUPER: A CAR YOU CAN BELIEVE IN. THE VOLVO 850 T-5.

506

PRODUCER: Push in camera three, pan right, pan right . . . cut to camera two.

ANNCR 1: Oh, what a shot. Time-out is called right now. Shaq has got to do something big to get back into this game.

PRODUCER: And roll commercial.

ANNCR 1: Shaq is leaving the court.

ANNCR 2: What do you mean he's leaving the court?

PRODUCER: Stay with him, just stay with him.

TECHNICIAN 1: Look, he's over there, he's on "Lucy"!

ALL TECHNICIANS: What!

CHIEF: Peking Duck.

TECHNICIAN 1: Where is he?

PRODUCER: He's on four, he's on four.

TECHNICIAN 2: What is going on here?

(MUSIC: "BONANZA" THEME)

TECHNICIAN 3: I didn't know Shaq could ride a horse.

SHAQ: Nice day, huh?

RALPH KRAMDEN: Hi ya, pal.

NEWSCASTER: New cars to generate . . .

ANNCR 1: Well, the time-out is over.

ANNCR 2: I wonder if he's going to get back . . .

(SFX: WOODY WOODPECKER'S LAUGH)

ANNCR 1: Hey, wait a minute, Shaq's back right now.

ANNCR 2: He's got it, how about that.

(SFX: CHEERING)

SHAQ: Who says there's nothing good on TV.

SUPER: NOTHING ELSE IS A PEPSI.

507

SUPER: THE NEW ORIGINALS FROM CHRYSLER CANADA.

508

(SFX: BANJO BEING SMASHED)

WOMAN 1: I . . . can't . . . play . . . this . . . thing!

(MUSIC: SEVENTIES-STYLE)

(SFX: BUS DOORS OPENING)

BARRY WHITE: Having problems, baby?

WOMAN 1: Hey?

BARRY WHITE: Beating up on your banjo?

(MUSIC: VARIOUS BANJO TUNES)

BARRY WHITE: Welcome aboard.

JAZZ MAN: Hey bro, you do weddings?

(MUSIC: "WEDDING MARCH" ON SITAR)

WOMAN 2 (SCREAMING): Who sang "Kung Foo Fighting?"

BARRY WHITE (THROUGH MICROPHONE): The answer . . . is Karl Douglas.

(MUSIC: VIOLIN)

HEADBANGER: Mosh pit!

(MUSIC: REALLY LOUD)

BARRY WHITE (THROUGH MICROPHONE): Next stop . . . Barry's world.

(MUSIC: DISCO)

GOSPEL SINGER: *Yeah . . . yeah, yeah, oh yeah, yeah . . .*

ANNCR: Music . . . just one of the many interest groups you'll find on the new Prodigy.

SUPER: PRODIGY.

SUPER: WHATEVER YOU'RE INTO.

CONSUMER TELEVISION
OVER :30 SINGLE

509
ART DIRECTOR:
Matt Vescovo
WRITERS:
Arthur Bijur
Cliff Freeman
Steve Dildarian
AGENCY PRODUCER:
Mary Ellen Duggan
PRODUCTION COMPANY:
Johns + Gorman Films
DIRECTOR:
Jeff Gorman
CLIENT:
Little Caesars Pizza
AGENCY:
Cliff Freeman & Partners/
New York

510
ART DIRECTOR:
Ken Woodard
WRITER:
Suzanne Finnamore
AGENCY PRODUCER:
Steve Neely
PRODUCTION COMPANY:
Satellite Films
DIRECTOR:
Peter Care
CLIENT:
Levi Strauss & Company
AGENCY:
Foote Cone & Belding/
San Francisco

511
ART DIRECTOR:
Jay Pond-Jones
WRITER:
Robert Saville
AGENCY PRODUCER:
Diane Croll
PRODUCTION COMPANY:
Paul Weiland Films
DIRECTOR:
Frank Budgen
CLIENT:
Holsten
AGENCY:
GGT Advertising/London

512
ART DIRECTOR:
Joe Shands
WRITER:
Ron Saltmarsh
AGENCY PRODUCER:
Cindy Epps
PRODUCTION COMPANY:
Smillie Films
DIRECTOR:
Kinka Usher
CLIENT:
Haggar Clothing Company
AGENCY:
Goodby Silverstein &
Partners/San Francisco

509

LITTLE CAESAR: Pizza! Pizza!
DIRECTOR: Cut! Caesar, you're introducing delivery. You've got to tell the world, "Delivery! Delivery!"
LITTLE CAESAR: Pizza! Pizza!
DIRECTOR: Delivery!
LITTLE CAESAR: Pizza!
DIRECTOR: Delivery!
LITTLE CAESAR: Pizza!
DIRECTOR: D-D . . .
LITTLE CAESAR: P-P . . . Pizza! Pizza!
SCRIPT GIRL: Maybe we should use one of the back-ups.
VOICE: Back-ups!
BACK-UP 1: Delivery. Delivery.
DIRECTOR: Thank you.
BACK-UP 2: (LOOKS IN PEEPHOLE AND FLIPS HAIR.)
DIRECTOR: Next!
BACK-UP 3: Delivery. Delivery.
DIRECTOR: No!
BACK-UP 4: Delivery. Delivery.
DIRECTOR: Why is he doing that?
BACK-UP 5: What was the line?
DIRECTOR: Get him out of there! Let's just go with what we've got.
LITTLE CAESAR: Delivery! Delivery!
DIRECTOR: Yes!
ANNCR: Now get the Pizza Pizza Salad Special. Two Little Caesars pizzas and a Fresh Express Farms Salad all for one low price. Little Caesars, the best pizza in America. Carry out or delivered.

510

SINGERS (OFF CAMERA): *Uh! Uh!*
SINGER: Rap, rap, rap. Check. Uh!
DRIVER: In Prague . . . you can trade them for a car.
SINGER: *Whatcha say? . . .*
SUPER: 501.
SUPER: LEVI'S.

511

DENNIS (SINGING):
He's just your average guy
With your average job
He's your average white
Suburbanite slob
He likes football and
Porno and films about war
He's got an average house
With a nice hardwood floor.
But sometimes that just ain't enough
To keep a man like him interested
Oh no, no way, uh-uh.
So he knocks back some drinks
As he props up the bar
Then he jangles his keys
As he gets in his car.
He's an asshole, he's an asshole, what an asshole
(yoddie yo-ho-ho—the world's biggest asshole)
He's an asshole, he's an asshole, such an asshole
(yoddie yo-ho-ho—the world's biggest asshole).
He drives drunk with his kids, drives pissed with
the lads, he couldn't care less
he's one hell of a dad.
He's an asshole, he's an asshole, what an asshole
(Yoddie yo-ho-ho-the worlds biggest asshole).
A-S-S-H-O-L-E, everybody, A-S-S-H-O-L-E, A-S-S-H-O-L-E.

SUPER: DRINK AND DRIVE? GET REAL.

512

(MUSIC: SUSPENSEFUL)

(SFX: DOOR CLOSING)

(SFX: BUZZ OF CAMERA TURNING)

GUARD: I'm gonna check something out . . . cover for me.

SPY: I've got the plans.

(SFX: BEEP OF WATCH)

MAN: Get to the roof. You've got your pill? You can't be . . .

(SFX: "CLICK")

MAN: . . . taken alive.

SPY: Check.

(SFX: ELEVATOR DOOR SLIDING OPEN)

(SFX: ELEVATOR HYDRAULICS)

GUARD: I saw you on the monitors . . .

(SFX: MAN SWALLOWING POISON PILL)

GUARD: . . . your clothes—they're very nice.

ANNCR: City casuals. Look good at the office no matter what kind of day you're having.

SUPER: HAGGAR. STUFF YOU CAN WEAR.

CONSUMER TELEVISION
OVER :30 SINGLE

513
ART DIRECTOR:
Todd Grant
WRITER:
Bo Coyner
AGENCY PRODUCER:
Barbro Eddy
PRODUCTION COMPANY:
Wild Scientific
DIRECTOR:
David Wild
CLIENT:
Sega of America
AGENCY:
Goodby Silverstein &
Partners/San Francisco

514
ART DIRECTOR:
Pat Harris
WRITER:
Pieter Blikslager
AGENCY PRODUCER:
Veronica Zelle
PRODUCTION COMPANY:
Johns + Gorman Films
DIRECTOR:
Rent Sidon
CLIENT:
Optometric Options
AGENCY:
Ground Zero/Venice, CA

515
ART DIRECTOR:
Charles Inge
WRITER:
Phil Dearman
AGENCY PRODUCER:
Claire Taylor
PRODUCTION COMPANY:
Spots Films
DIRECTOR:
Barry Myers
CLIENT:
The Pierre White Company
AGENCY:
Lowe Howard-Spink/
London

516
ART DIRECTOR:
Tom Notman
WRITER:
Alistair Wood
ILLUSTRATOR:
Mark Thomas
AGENCY PRODUCER:
Charles Crisp
PRODUCTION COMPANY:
Hibbert Ralph Animation
DIRECTOR:
Jerry Hibbert
CLIENT:
Whitbread Beer Company
AGENCY:
Lowe Howard-Spink/
London

513

ANNCR: Welcome . . . to the Theater of the Eye.
(SFX: WEIRD, QUIRKY NOISES)
(SFX: MOVIE PROJECTOR)
ANNCR: Rods and Cones, report to the orbital socket . . .
ROD: How nice . . . we're trimming the toe nails.
(SFX: CLIPPING SOUNDS)
ROD: What's that?
(SFX: SLIGHT SNORE)
(SFX: CLOSING OF A SATURN COMPONENT)
CONE: Uhhhh . . .
(SFX: FAST-PACED, HIGH-ENERGY GAME SOUNDS)
(SFX: SODA HITTING THE FLOOR, TELEPHONE RING)
ROD: Huhhh . . .
(SFX: TELEPHONE RINGING)
OPTIC NERVE: Optic Nerve.
MAN: This is the Brain . . . what's going on down there?
OPTIC NERVE: Uhhh . . . pfff . . .
GUY AT DOOR: The Ear Drum's going off . . . go get heelllp!!!
NERVOUS SYSTEM GUY 1: We're having a breakdown, we're having a breakdown, we're having a breakdown, we're having a breakdown . . .
NERVOUS SYSTEM GUY 2: Aaaaaaaaaaahhhhhhhhhhhhhhh!!!
BRAIN: What else can go wrong?
SECRETARY: Urgent, synapse on line two . . . it's the Sphincter.
(SFX: SLURPING NOISES)
SPHINCTER: What . . . is . . . going . . . on . . . up . . . there?!
(SFX: SOUNDS OF WALL CLOSING IN)
ANNCR: Sega . . .
(SFX: DOOR CLOSING)
ANNCR: Saturn.

514

(MUSIC: WESTERN-STYLE)
(SFX: DRAMATIC, EXAGGERATED GUN SHOTS)
SUPER: GLASSES STARTING AT 60 DOLLARS.
SUPER: OPTOMETRIC OPTIONS.

515

(MUSIC: RUSSIAN-STYLE)

GANG LEADER 1: We are the People's Army. All members of the aristocracy are to be arrested. Take him away.

GANG LEADER 2: We are the People's Army. All members of the aristocracy are to be arrested.

GANG LEADER 1: But comrades . . . I am People's Army too.

GANG LEADER 2: You expect us to believe that? Take him away.

GANG LEADER 3 (OFF CAMERA): We are the People's Army . . .

SUPER: SMIRNOFF BLACK.

ANNCR: The mellow taste of Smirnoff Black. Imperial Russia's best kept secret.

516

SUPER: MR. FLOWERS' GUIDE TO WALKING STICKS.

(SFX: OUTDOOR SOUNDS)

MR. FLOWERS: Yes. A good stick is the gentleman's scepter, Derek. With it he may probe suspicious hollows in trees and reed banks.

(SFX: BICYCLE SOUNDS)

MR. FLOWERS: Wait a minute—that man's been fishing without a license. This is where a good stick earns its keep. Wait . . . gently bently . . . and now!

(SFX: BICYCLE WHEEL SPINNING)

POLICEMAN: There'll be a reward for this . . . two pints of Flowers Original.

SUPER: MR. FLOWERS CLAIMS HIS REWARD.

DEREK: How did you know he didn't have a license?

MR. FLOWERS: Derek, my father hasn't had a fishing license for 40 years.

SUPER: DAMNED FINE ALE.

CONSUMER TELEVISION
OVER :30 SINGLE

517
ART DIRECTOR:
Tim Hanrahan
WRITER:
Hank Perlman
AGENCY PRODUCER:
Dan Duffy
PRODUCTION COMPANY:
@radical.media
DIRECTORS:
Bryan Buckley
Frank Todaro
CLIENT:
ESPN/National Hockey League
AGENCY:
Wieden & Kennedy/ Portland

518
ART DIRECTOR:
Rick McQuiston
WRITER:
Hank Perlman
AGENCY PRODUCER:
Dan Duffy
PRODUCTION COMPANY:
@radical.media
DIRECTORS:
Bryan Buckley
Frank Todaro
CLIENT:
ESPN
AGENCY:
Wieden & Kennedy/ Portland

519
ART DIRECTOR:
Eric C. King
WRITER:
Derek Barnes
AGENCY PRODUCER:
Jennifer Smieja
PRODUCTION COMPANY:
Satellite Films
DIRECTORS:
Spike Jonze
CLIENT:
Nike
AGENCY:
Wieden & Kennedy/ Portland

520
ART DIRECTOR:
Bret Ridgeway
WRITER:
Jim Riswold
AGENCY PRODUCER:
Diane Sittig
PRODUCTION COMPANY:
Pytka
DIRECTOR:
Joe Pytka
CLIENT:
Nike
AGENCY:
Wieden & Kennedy/ Portland

517

COACH COLIN CAMPBELL: The Stanley Cup hasn't changed us, we're still the same team . . . all the same old guys here, same thing.

TIM ROBBINS: You know how this works?

JIM RICHTER: Ummm . . .

COACH CAMPBELL: Tim . . . Tim's what you call an aggressive Ranger fan.

TIM: Can you get me tickets for the game on Friday?

MARK MESSIER: Arrr.

TIM: How 'bout tickets for Friday night, any extra ones?

MARK: No.

COACH CAMPBELL: He's been working with the guys, he likes the guys, the guys like him.

TIM: It's a cool mask.

JIM: Um, yeah.

TIM: It's cool.

COACH CAMPBELL: But he wants to be assistant coach.

TIM: You know, you don't really have to hit, 'cause sometimes . . . a good strong stare . . . hold on, hold on, try it again . . . no, no, no, try it again, one more time. That's, that's good, that's good . . . what's the big deal? I stand behind you at the bench, I'm the assistant, assistant, assistant coach . . . puck goes in, it's a goal . . . so you don't really want that. I could be the guy who opens the door, you know, I could be the guy that gives people water . . . you know, I just gotta be at that game, give me a shot.

SUPER: STANLEY CUP CHAMPION NEW YORK RANGERS VS. BUFFALO SABRES. NHL OPENING NIGHT ON ESPN.

518

BRETT HABER: So many people wonder where the theme for SportsCenter came from. David St. Hubbins from Spinal Tap, you've gotta tell me where this came from.

SUPER: DAVID ST. HUBBINS COMPOSER, "SPORTSCENTER THEME."

DAVID ST. HUBBINS: I don't really know. It's a mystery, you know, it sort of sprang from my forehead like Zeus and Penelope, or however that story goes . . . and I was sitting there watching SportsCenter . . . and I went . . .

(SFX: DAVID PLAYING GUITAR)

DAVID: Dah, dah, dah, daah . . . bump, bump, bump—and I liked it, but the bump, bump, bump bit sounded a bit wimpy then I thought da, da, da—which was much better than bump, bump, bump—which obviously sucks.

BRETT: Are you working on any other sports-related projects?

DAVID: Oh yeah, I've written some stings for various sports . . . like when a bloke hits a home run, we're gonna play:

(SFX: DAVID PLAYING HARD ROCK GUITAR)

DAVID: Like that, you know.

BRETT: Right, what about football maybe?

DAVID: Football . . . you know when the bloke goes across the line the music goes:

(SFX: DAVID PLAYING HARD ROCK GUITAR)

BRETT: What about if you wanted to go obscure, say maybe curling.

DAVID: Yeah, I got a curling piece, it goes like this . . . (SINGING) *Curling, curling, let's all go bloody curling, on ESPN.*

SUPER: THIS IS SPORTSCENTER.

519

PETE SAMPRAS: This looks pretty good. Stop . . . right here.

ANDRE AGASSI: This ought to wrinkle . . . someone's tennis whites.

(SFX: TENNIS GAME SOUNDS, CROWD CHEERING)

CROWD: Andre! Andre!

ANDRE: No, no, over the net!

CROWD: Pete! Pete!

SUPER: JUST DO IT.

SUPER: (NIKE LOGO).

520

ANNCR: Bottom of the seventh . . . Mattingly at bat . . . one out . . . runner on third . . . here's the pitch. Mattingly . . .

(SFX: BALL BEING HIT)

ANNCR: . . . hits it deep . . . to right center.

KEN GRIFFEY, JR.: I got it, I got it . . . I got it, I got it. I got it, I got it.

ANNCR: Runner tags . . . here's the throw . . . across the USA . . . and into Yankee Stadium. And it's going to be close . . . Mr. Umpire says he's going to be . . .

UMPIRE (OFF CAMERA): Oouutt!

SUPER: JUST DO IT.

ANNCR: The kid's got an arm.

SUPER: (NIKE LOGO).

CONSUMER TELEVISION OVER :30 SINGLE

521

ART DIRECTOR:
Darryl McDonald
WRITERS:
Jim Riswold
Jimmy Smith
AGENCY PRODUCER:
Donna Portaro
PRODUCTION COMPANY:
Propaganda Films
DIRECTOR:
Dominic Sena
CLIENT:
Nike
AGENCY:
Wieden & Kennedy/
Portland

522

ART DIRECTOR:
John Boiler
WRITER:
Stacy Wall
AGENCY PRODUCERS:
Bill Davenport
Jeff Selis
PRODUCTION COMPANY:
Pytka
DIRECTOR:
Joe Pytka
CLIENT:
Nike
AGENCY:
Wieden & Kennedy/
Portland

523

ART DIRECTOR:
Linda Knight
WRITER:
James LeMaitre
AGENCY PRODUCER:
Dan Duffy
PRODUCTION COMPANY:
Pytka
DIRECTOR:
Joe Pytka
CLIENT:
Nike
AGENCY:
Wieden & Kennedy/
Portland

CONSUMER TELEVISION :30 SINGLE

524

ART DIRECTOR:
Tim Dillingham
WRITER:
Tim Dillingham
PRODUCTION COMPANY:
GLC Productions
DIRECTORS:
Adam Schell
Jonathan Schell
CLIENT:
Skids
AGENCY:
The Ad Store/New York

521

MARSHALL FAULK: Is there a defense that can stop me? Maybe not. Maybe if they had cars . . .

(SFX: CARS CRASHING)

MARSHALL: . . . they could stop me. Maybe not. Maybe if they had trucks. Maybe not.

(SFX: HELICOPTERS)

MARSHALL: Maybe if they had helicopters. Helicopters . . . and Jets. Maybe, maybe. Maybe not.

SUPER: JUST DO IT.

SUPER: (NIKE LOGO).

522

STANLEY KRAVER: When I was a boy, I dreamed of playing football . . . but I was allergic to milk. And the soybean juice substitute my mother gave me made my bones weak. But I digress. My point is: I love football! Football: the ballet of bulldozers. The moment of grace in a sea of fury. The crowd, fickle, fanatical, faithful. Every kick-off a possibility. Every down a war. And every now and then it doesn't come down to fancy strategy, or speed, or strength. It comes down to who has more heart. You see, football is in my bones, and where goes the two point conversion, the on-side kick, or the TV time-out, so go I!

I've seen the locker room my friends . . . smelled the shoes, stormed the field, and sung the songs. And I have heard the footsteps, and they say to me, Stanley, is football the greatest game in the world? And I say, "Yes, footsteps. Yes it is."

523

(SFX: DOGS BARKING, KIDS PLAYING)

(SFX: CAR HORN BEEPS TWICE)

KID: Car!

(SFX: MOTORCYCLE REVVING)

KID: Motorcycle gang!

RIDER: Go Rangers!

KID: Marathon! Parade!

(MUSIC: MARCHING BAND PLAYING SOUSA'S "THE THUNDERER")

(SFX: EARTH RUMBLING)

KID: Stampede!

(SFX: CATTLE MOOING)

SUPER: JUST DO IT. STREET HOCKEY.

SUPER: (NIKE LOGO).

524

SKATER: I never thought it could happen to me. I guess no one ever really does. But I was out of control. I was hurting myself, people around me, everything was a blur. Sooner or later I had to crash. But then I got help.

ANNCR: Skids—a revolutionary front-mounted toe braking system. When you can't stop yourself, Skids will stop you. By Kryptonics.

CONSUMER TELEVISION
:30 SINGLE

525
ART DIRECTOR:
Dennis Lim
WRITER:
Harold Einstein
AGENCY PRODUCER:
Jackie Vidor
PRODUCTION COMPANY:
Gartner-Grasso
DIRECTOR:
James Gartner
CLIENT:
Apple Computer
AGENCY:
BBDO/Los Angeles

526
ART DIRECTOR:
Seiji Kishi
WRITER:
John Dullaghan
AGENCY PRODUCER:
Jackie Vidor
PRODUCTION COMPANY:
Pytka
DIRECTOR:
Joe Pytka
CLIENT:
Apple Computer
AGENCY:
BBDO/Los Angeles

527
ART DIRECTOR:
Donna Weinheim
WRITER:
Donna Weinheim
AGENCY PRODUCERS:
Bob Emerson
Hyatt Choate
PRODUCTION COMPANY:
Satellite Films
DIRECTOR:
Simon West
CLIENT:
Pepsi Cola Company
AGENCY:
BBDO/New York

528
ART DIRECTORS:
Greg Bell
David Angelo
WRITERS:
Tina Hall
Cliff Freeman
Harold Einstein
AGENCY PRODUCERS:
Mary Ellen Duggan
Maresa Wickham
PRODUCTION COMPANY:
Harmony Pictures
DIRECTOR:
Charles Wittenmeier
CLIENT:
Little Caesars Pizza
AGENCY:
Cliff Freeman & Partners/
New York

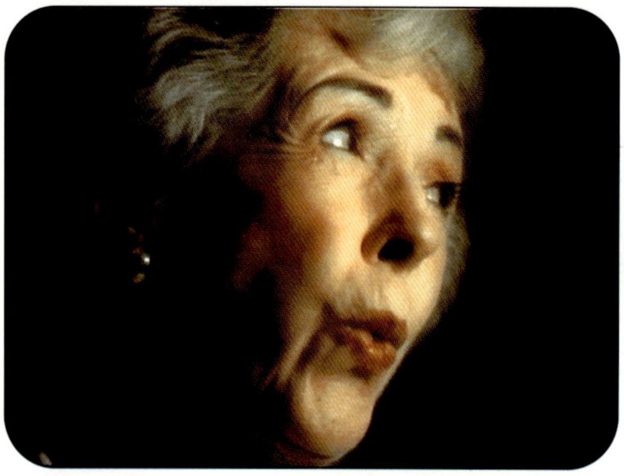

525

MAC: The northern female mockingbird.

(SFX: BIRD SOUNDS)

WIFE: (MAKES BIRD SOUNDS).

MAC: And here's her mate, the northern male mockingbird.

(SFX: BIRD SOUNDS AGAIN)

WIFE: (MAKES BIRD SOUNDS).

HUSBAND: (MAKES BIRD SOUNDS).

ANNCR: If you owned the world's easiest computer, what would you do with it?

SUPER: MACINTOSH.

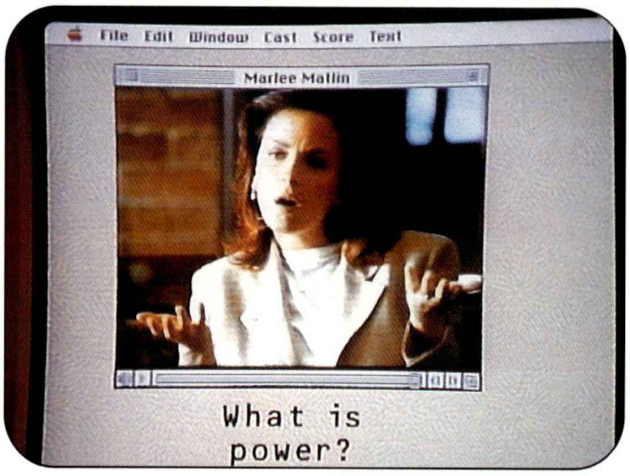

526

(INTERWEAVING OF MARLEE TYPING AND SIGNING WITH TEXT APPEARING ON SCREEN)

SUPER: MARLEE MATLIN, ACTRESS.

MARLEE/TEXT:

What is Power?

Power is communication.

Power is no limits.

No barriers, no restrictions.

Power is fighting stereotypes.

Power is proving them wrong.

Power is control, independence, confidence.

Power is the freedom of expression.

SUPER: POWER IS MACINTOSH.

527

(SFX: WAVES AND SEAGULLS SQUAWKING)

LITTLE GIRL: Mom, he's done it again!!

SUPER: NOTHING ELSE IS A PEPSI.

528

ANNCR: Over the years, Little Caesars has run promotions with many of its neighbors.

ANNCR: Two pizzas and a backrub. Two pizzas and a colorful fish.

(SFX: CHATTERING TEETH)

ANNCR: And some chattering teeth. And this thing. And one of our most popular, the perm.

MAN WITH PERM: They'll never top that one.

ANNCR: And finally, two pizzas and a movie.

MAN: Wow!

ANNCR: It's the Blockbuster Video Pizza Pizza Deal. Buy one Little Caesars Pleaser loaded with cheese and toppings, and a pizza with one topping all for a low, low price. And now get a free Blockbuster Video rental when you rent two.

LITTLE CAESAR: Pizza! Pizza!

CONSUMER TELEVISION
:30 SINGLE

529

ART DIRECTOR:
Brian Hickling
WRITER:
Jim Garbutt
AGENCY PRODUCER:
Sheila Sone
PRODUCTION COMPANIES:
Radke Films
Keen Music
CLIENT:
Nike Canada
AGENCY:
Cossette Communication-Marketing/Toronto

530

ART DIRECTOR:
Brad Cohn
WRITER:
Bill Lindsey
AGENCY PRODUCER:
Wil Wilcox
PRODUCTION COMPANY:
Fahrenheit Films
DIRECTOR:
Steve Chase
CLIENT:
Anheuser-Busch/Bud Light
AGENCY:
DDB Needham/Chicago

531

ART DIRECTOR:
John Staffen
WRITER:
Mike Rogers
AGENCY PRODUCER:
Eric Herrmann
PRODUCTION COMPANY:
BFCS
DIRECTOR:
John Lloyd
CLIENT:
New York State Lottery
AGENCY:
DDB Needham Worldwide/
New York

532

ART DIRECTOR:
Dean Hanson
WRITER:
Bruce Bildsten
PRODUCTION COMPANY:
Smillie Films
DIRECTOR:
Kinka Usher
CLIENT:
Timex
AGENCY:
Fallon McElligott/
Minneapolis

529

SUPER: ED BACON.

SUPER: AGE: 63.

SUPER: STARTED RUNNING: NOVEMBER, 1994.

SUPER: RAN TORONTO MARATHON: MAY, 1995.

SUPER: FINISHED: LAST.

SUPER: TIME: 5 HOURS, 48 MINUTES, 39 SECONDS.

SUPER: (NIKE TORONTO LOGO).

SUPER: JUST DO IT.

530

JOHNNY: Dad?

EARL: Yeah?

JOHNNY: There's something I've wanted to tell you . . .

EARL: What is it, son?

JOHNNY: Well, dad, you're my dad . . .

JOHNNY: . . . and . . . I love you, man.

EARL: You're not getting the Bud Light, Johnny.

ANNCR: For the great taste that won't fill you up and never lets you down, make it a Bud Light.

JOHNNY: Ray . . .

RAY: Forget it, Johnny.

JOHNNY: Where's the love, man? . . .

SUPER: MAKE IT A BUD LIGHT.

531

ANNCR 1: From New York it's "Late Evening Tonight." With world renowned magician Barry Hazelwood. Prima Ballerina . . . Isabella Hazelwood. Chef Stuart Hazelwood and his famous salad flambe. And featuring the Happy Hazelwood orchestra.

(SFX: AUDIENCE CLAPPING)

ANNCR 1: Now the woman who loved talk shows so much she went out and bought her own. Missssssus Hazelwood.

ANNCR 2: New York Lotto. Hey, you never know.

532

ANNCR: The revolutionary new Timex Data Link watch uses light beams . . . to transfer dates and data from your computer to your wrist . . . with just a touch of your paw.

(SFX: DOG TYPING)

ANNCR: Pretty smart, eh? The Timex Data Link Watch.

SUPER: DATA LINK BY TIMEX.

(SFX: CAT TYPING)

CONSUMER TELEVISION
:30 SINGLE

533
ART DIRECTOR:
Jason Peterson
WRITER:
Izzy DeBellis
AGENCY PRODUCER:
Lyn Roar
PRODUCTION COMPANY:
Johns + Gorman Films
DIRECTOR:
Jeff Gorman
CLIENT:
The Coca-Cola Company/
Diet Sprite
AGENCY:
Fallon McElligott Berlin/
New York

534
ART DIRECTOR:
Genji Handa
WRITER:
Paul Carek
AGENCY PRODUCERS:
Debra Trotz
Jan Frei
PRODUCTION COMPANY:
Giraldi/Suarez
DIRECTOR:
Bob Giraldi
CLIENT:
Dreyer's Grand Ice Cream
AGENCY:
Goldberg Moser O'Neill/
San Francisco

535
ART DIRECTOR:
Jason Gaboriau
WRITER:
Tom Miller
AGENCY PRODUCER:
Barbara Callihan
PRODUCTION COMPANY:
Reel Diehl
CLIENT:
Crain's New York Business
AGENCY:
Goldsmith/Jeffrey,
New York

536
ART DIRECTOR:
Chris Hooper
WRITER:
Chuck McBride
AGENCY PRODUCER:
Ben Latimer
PRODUCTION COMPANY:
Propaganda Films
DIRECTOR:
Michael Bay
CLIENT:
American Isuzu Motors
AGENCY:
Goodby Silverstein &
Partners/San Francisco

533

(SFX: RESTAURANT NOISES)

WOMAN: All men are liars. They say they love you, but they don't. They say they love kids, but they forget to mention they already have two. They tell you that the bandage on their right finger is from a fishing accident. Yeah!

MAN: Huh!

WOMAN: Sorry. . . . Do you mind? . . . I like it, what is it?

MAN: It's Diet Sprite.

WOMAN: Diet . . . Sprite?

MAN: Diet . . . Sprite!

WOMAN: Diet??

MAN: Diet!!

WOMAN: Liar.

SUPER: DIET SPRITE.

534

(SFX: BABY BABBLING, PADDING SOUNDS OF BABY CRAWLING)

MOM (OFF CAMERA): C'mon, honey. That's my big boy. Good! There you go! Now c'mon. C'mon. Mommy's gonna put you in your high chair . . .

MOM (OFF CAMERA): . . . and fix you some Dreyer's Cookies 'n' Cream.

(SFX: PACIFIER BEING SPIT OUT)

(SFX: MUSIC AND BABY GIGGLES)

ANNCR: Dreyer's. Evidently it's not your normal ice cream.

535

ANNCR: In the foot hills of Pennsylvania, in the Amish town of Minst, the people live a carefree life. They don't worry about hostile takeovers. They aren't concerned with being ambushed by competitors. Or blindsided by unexpected information. It is a town of joy, friendliness and boundless love. And when you move there . . . you can cancel your subscription to *Crain's*.

536

(SFX: NATURE SOUNDS)

(SFX: SOUND OF TURTLE WALKING)

(SFX: WINGS FLAPPING, SWOOPING NOISE)

(SFX: SHELL HITTING ROCK)

(SFX: ROCK STARTING TO SLIP, RUMBLING AS IT FALLS)

(SFX: TIRES ON MOUNTAIN ROAD)

GUY: We're not lost.

(SFX: SLIGHT RUMBLE OF ROCK)

(SFX: SOUND OF KEY CHAIN VIBRATING, INCREASED RUMBLING)

(MUSIC: BIG BAND)

SUPER: NOW WITH DUAL AIR BAGS.

SUPER: THE NEW RODEO.

SUPER: ISUZU. PRACTICALLY AMAZING.

CONSUMER TELEVISION
:30 SINGLE

537

ART DIRECTOR:
Jeremy Postaer
WRITER:
Paul Venables
AGENCY PRODUCERS:
Betsy Flynn
Greg Martinez
PRODUCTION COMPANY:
In-House
CLIENT:
Bell Sports
AGENCY:
Goodby Silverstein &
Partners/San Francisco

538

ART DIRECTOR:
Tom Routson
WRITER:
Bob Kerstetter
AGENCY PRODUCER:
Cindy Epps
PRODUCTION COMPANY:
Smillie Films
DIRECTOR:
Kinka Usher
CLIENT:
California Fluid Milk
Processor Advisory Board
AGENCY:
Goodby Silverstein &
Partners/San Francisco

539

ART DIRECTOR:
Sean Ehringer
WRITER:
Harry Cocciolo
AGENCY PRODUCER:
Cindy Epps
PRODUCTION COMPANY:
Crossroads Films
DIRECTOR:
Roger Tonry
CLIENT:
Major League Baseball
AGENCY:
Goodby Silverstein &
Partners/San Francisco

540

ART DIRECTOR:
Sean Ehringer
WRITER:
Harry Cocciolo
AGENCY PRODUCER:
Cindy Epps
PRODUCTION COMPANY:
Crossroads Films
DIRECTOR:
Roger Tonry
CLIENT:
Major League Baseball
AGENCY:
Goodby Silverstein &
Partners/San Francisco

537

(MUSIC: EERIE TUNE WHISTLING THROUGHOUT)

(SFX: ONE HEARTBEAT)

SUPER: HUMANS ARE THE ONLY SPECIES

(SFX: ONE HEARTBEAT)

SUPER: WITH THE ABILITY TO REASON.

(SFX: ONE HEARTBEAT)

SUPER: AND SOMETIMES

(SFX: ONE HEARTBEAT)

SUPER: THEY EVEN USE IT.

(SFX: SMASHING NOISE)

ANNCR: Bell Helmets.

(SFX: SQUISHING AND SNAPPING NOISE)

SUPER: COURAGE FOR YOUR HEAD.

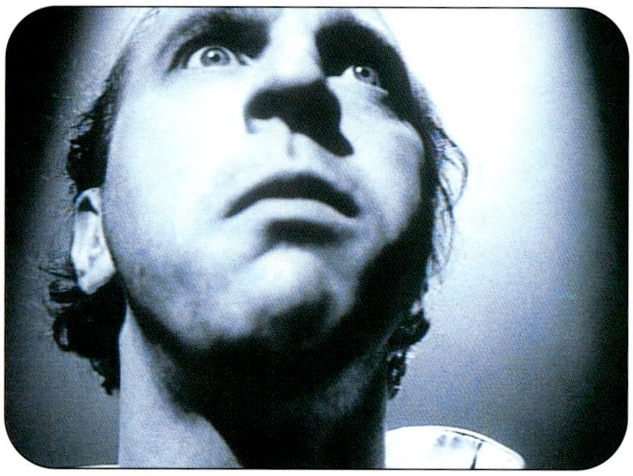

538

DAUGHTER (VOICE IMAGINED): Daddy, who drank all the milk?

(SFX: ECHOING SOUNDS OF COURTROOM, PEOPLE, JUDGE'S GAVEL)

JUDGE: Young lady, do you see the man in this courtroom?

DAUGHTER: That's him! He did it! My daddy!

(SFX: MURMURING IN COURTROOM)

JUDGE: Guilty!

MOTHER: How could you?

(SFX: SLAM OF GAVEL)

MOTHER: Guilty.

SON: Guilty!

DAUGHTER: Guilty!

(SFX: PRISON DOOR LOCKING)

DAD: Hhhmmmmm . . .

(SFX: "GULP")

SUPER: GOT MILK?

539

SUPER: BILL "SPACEMAN" LEE.

BILL LEE: We're playing here in Boston, and we have a runner at first base—his name is Julio Gotai. And Louis Apareechio knows that he believes in voodoo and he's really superstitious so he takes two tongue depressors, and he takes 'em and he puts a big cross on second base. And Julio Gotai goes into second base and he will not touch second base.

SUPER: WELCOME TO THE SHOW.

BILL: And he makes the out. Brilliant thought process in that respect.

SUPER: (MAJOR LEAGUE BASEBALL LOGO).

540

SUPER: WAVELAND AVENUE.

GUY: You know the apartment itself is—it's a small apartment. I'm not sitting here acting like it's a big apartment by any means.

I remember I got a new phone and a friend of mine saw it and he said, "Oh good, now it's like a real phone booth." (LAUGHS) You know . . . so, you know, it's small . . . it's a small apartment, and I pay way too much rent for it. But I like the view.

SUPER: WELCOME TO THE SHOW.

GUY (THROUGH A MEGAPHONE): Hey, umpire . . . I'm talking to you!

SUPER: (MAJOR LEAGUE BASEBALL LOGO).

GUY: I'm just practicing right now.

CONSUMER TELEVISION
:30 SINGLE

541
ART DIRECTOR:
Sean Ehringer
WRITER:
Harry Cocciolo
AGENCY PRODUCER:
Cindy Epps
PRODUCTION COMPANY:
Crossroads Films
DIRECTOR:
Roger Tonry
CLIENT:
Major League Baseball
AGENCY:
Goodby Silverstein & Partners/San Francisco

542
ART DIRECTOR:
Jamie Mambro
WRITER:
Ernie Schenck
AGENCY PRODUCER:
Diane Carlin
PRODUCTION COMPANY:
The End
DIRECTOR:
Zack Snyder
CLIENT:
Reebok International
AGENCY:
Hill Holliday Connors Cosmopulos/Boston

543
ART DIRECTOR:
Pamela Clinkard
WRITER:
Risa Mickenberg
AGENCY PRODUCER:
Tony Frere
PRODUCTION COMPANY:
Tony Kaye Films
DIRECTOR:
Tony Kaye
CLIENT:
Keds
AGENCY:
Kirshenbaum Bond & Partners/New York

544
ART DIRECTOR:
CJ Waldman
WRITER:
Todd Godwin
AGENCY PRODUCER:
Alice Mintzer
PRODUCTION COMPANY:
Gerard De Thame Films
DIRECTOR:
Gerard De Thame
CLIENT:
The Coca-Cola Company/ Sprite
AGENCY:
Lowe & Partners/SMS, New York

541

BILL LEE: The earth is a one-celled organism, and you reduce it down, and you put a seam on it and you got a baseball. And everything is round, it goes all the way around. This line goes around for infinity. It continues and continues and continues, it never stops. And that's the way the Earth is, it rotates on its axis and you have spring and summer and you have the baseball season.

SUPER: WELCOME TO THE SHOW.

BILL: And then it gets dormant and everybody goes to South America and you're down there . . . but it goes back.

SUPER: (MAJOR LEAGUE BASEBALL LOGO).

542

(MUSIC: LADYSMITH BLACK MAMBAZO'S "RAIN, RAIN BEAUTIFUL RAIN")

SUPER: RULE 86.

SUPER: RAIN-OUTS ARE FOR BASEBALL PLAYERS.

SUPER: REWRITE THE BOOK.

SUPER: REEBOK.

543

ANNCR: What size Keds were you wearing when they stopped delivering milk, when you got too big to be carried, when your mother was the prettiest woman on earth. . . . What size Keds were you wearing when you learned to take a compliment, and you started to hold your father's hand again.

What size Keds will you be wearing when the first of your friends gets married. . . . And, what size Keds will you be wearing when a woman walks on Mars.

Keds. Never stop growing.

544

(MUSIC: OPERA)

ANNCR (WITH FRENCH ACCENT): What do the really, really beautiful people drink when they get thirsty? The same thing as the rest of us.

SUPER: IMAGE IS NOTHING.

SUPER: THIRST IS EVERYTHING.

SUPER: OBEY YOUR THIRST.

ANNCR: Sprite.

CONSUMER TELEVISION
:30 SINGLE

545
ART DIRECTORS:
Randy Saitta
Andy Hirsch
WRITER:
Marty Orzio
AGENCY PRODUCER:
Gary Grossman
PRODUCTION COMPANY:
Bruce Dowad & Associates
DIRECTOR:
Bruce Dowad
CLIENT:
Mercedes-Benz of North America
AGENCY:
Lowe & Partners/SMS, New York

546
ART DIRECTOR:
Kurt Reifschneider
WRITER:
John Schofield
AGENCY PRODUCER:
Branson Veal
PRODUCTION COMPANY:
Blue Goose Productions
DIRECTOR:
Ron Gross
CLIENT:
Washington State Lottery
AGENCY:
McCann-Erickson/Seattle

547
ART DIRECTOR:
Deborah Prenger
WRITER:
Glen Hunt
AGENCY PRODUCER:
Dee Anderson
PRODUCTION COMPANY:
Zoo TV Productions
DIRECTOR:
Allen Mestel
CLIENT:
Canadian Recording Industry Association
AGENCY:
Roche Macaulay & Partners/Toronto

548
ART DIRECTOR:
Richard Bess
WRITER:
Jon Pearce
AGENCY PRODUCER:
Jack Epsteen
PRODUCTION COMPANY:
Stiefel & Company
DIRECTOR:
Craig Henderson
CLIENT:
American Honda Motor Company
AGENCY:
Rubin Postaer & Associates/Santa Monica

545

ANNCR: Yes, another morning, and another trek to the office. . . . But, in the new Mercedes-Benz E-Class you're in one of the safest cars on the road.

(SFX: SILVERWARE SHAKING, MANY RHINOS PASSING BY)

ANNCR: You're inside a protective cage, with front airbags and, get this, side airbags.

(SFX: RHINO CRASHING INTO CAR DOOR)

ANNCR: Heaven knows, there are animals on these roads.

SUPER: MERCEDES-BENZ. THE NEXT GENERATION E-CLASS STARTS AT $39,000.

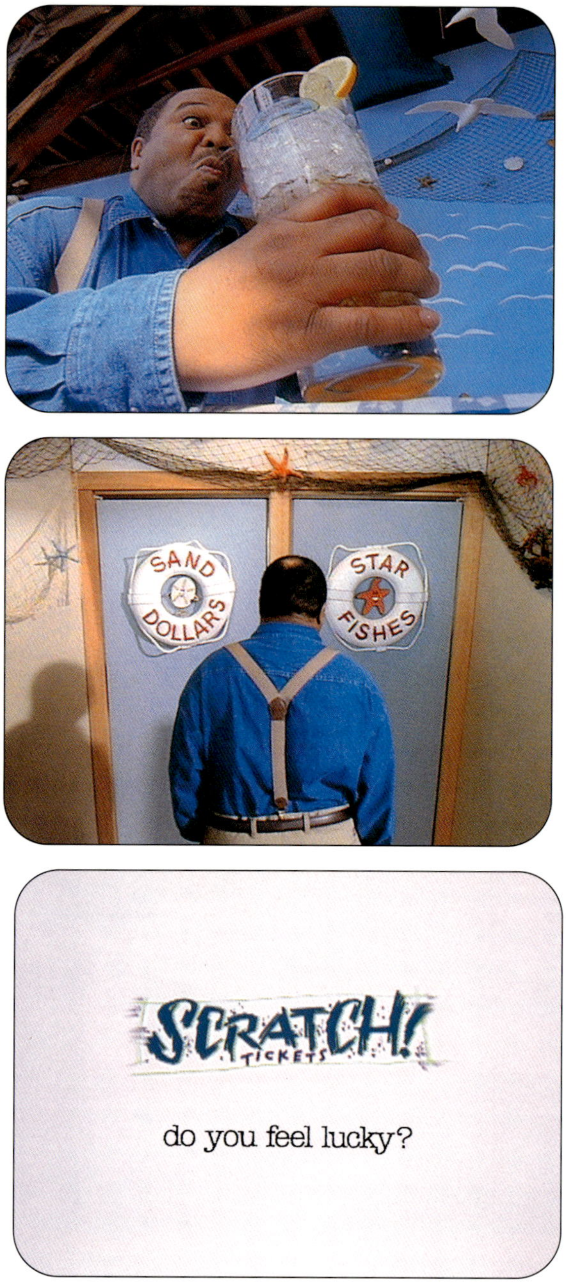

546

ANNCR: You win some. You lose some.

(SFX: TICKET BEING SCRATCHED)

ANNCR: But with a Lottery scratch ticket there's a one in five chance you'll win something. Wouldn't that be nice for a change?

(SFX: A SHRIEK)

ANNCR: DO YOU FEEL LUCKY?

547

(MUSIC: "CARMINA BURANA")

SUPER: MUSIC CAN MAKE ANYTHING MORE INTERESTING.

SUPER: PICK UP A NEW CD OR TAPE AND SEE WHAT IT CAN DO FOR YOU.

SUPER: IT'S BETTER WITH MUSIC.

548

(SFX: CAR WHIZZING BY)

(SFX: SIREN, CAR CHASE SOUNDS)

ANNCR: Remember, it's not only how fast you can go. It's also where you can go. The new Honda Passport. With standard dual airbags, and one powerful V-6 engine.

COP: Hello there. . . .

SUPER: HONDA. THE NEW PASSPORT.

CONSUMER TELEVISION
:30 SINGLE

549
ART DIRECTOR:
Vince Aamodt
WRITER:
Todd Carey
AGENCY PRODUCER:
Gary Paticoff
PRODUCTION COMPANY:
Colossal Pictures
DIRECTOR:
Richard Kizu-Blair
CLIENT:
American Honda Motor Company
AGENCY:
Rubin Postaer & Associates/Santa Monica

550
ART DIRECTOR:
Martin Tonnas
WRITER:
Dick Sittig
AGENCY PRODUCER:
Elaine Hinton
PRODUCTION COMPANY:
Coppos Films
DIRECTOR:
Brent Thomas
CLIENT:
Prince
AGENCY:
TBWA Chiat/Day, Venice, CA

551
ART DIRECTOR:
Jerry Gentile
WRITER:
Scott Vincent
AGENCY PRODUCER:
Michelle Burke
PRODUCTION COMPANY:
Johns + Gorman Films
DIRECTOR:
Jeff Gorman
CLIENT:
Sunkist California Pistachios
AGENCY:
TBWA Chiat/Day, Venice, CA

552
ART DIRECTOR:
Rick McQuiston
WRITER:
Hank Perlman
AGENCY PRODUCER:
Dan Duffy
PRODUCTION COMPANY:
@radical.media
DIRECTORS:
Bryan Buckley
Frank Todaro
CLIENT:
ESPN
AGENCY:
Wieden & Kennedy/Portland

549

(SFX: CAR HORNS, TRUCK ENGINES, SIRENS)

CAB DRIVER: What's the hold up? Move it!

(SFX: CAR HORN AND YELLING)

(SFX: ERASER AND NOISE SLOWLY FADING)

SUPER: SIMPLIFY. HONDA.

550

JIMMY CONNORS: Hi Patti, I'm home.

(SFX: RACQUET HITTING BALL)

(SFX: BALL HITTING LIGHT SWITCH)

(SFX: BALL BEING HIT REPEATEDLY)

(SFX: BALL HITTING MICROWAVE BUTTONS)

(SFX: RUNNING WATER)

PATTI CONNORS: Honey, can you help me with this?

(SFX: BALL HITTING CLASP, CLICKING)

(SFX: "WHACK" OF BALL FLIPPING CHANNELS)

(SFX: FLY BUZZING)

(SFX: WHACK OF BALL)

PATTI: Did you kill it?

JIMMY: No, but he'll be buzzing an octave higher.

ANNCR: The Prince Precision Series. It's how great players make the ball do what they want.

SUPER: PRINCE.

551

SUPER: ROMAYNE RIDDELL. TRANCE CHANNELER.

ROMAYNE: Well, I started trance channeling about six years ago. It's almost like my body was suddenly filled with love. (IN HIGH-PITCHED VOICE) Hello Peter, how are you today?

PETER: Very good, Neya. How are you?

ROMAYNE: Very fine thank you. So, what is it that you wanted to know.

SUPER: EVERYBODY KNOWS THE BEST NUTS COME FROM CALIFORNIA.

PETER: Where are you from?

ROMAUNE: I'm from Jupiter.

ANNCR: Sunkist California Pistachios. Now that's a nut.

SUPER: CALIFORNIA PISTACHIOS.

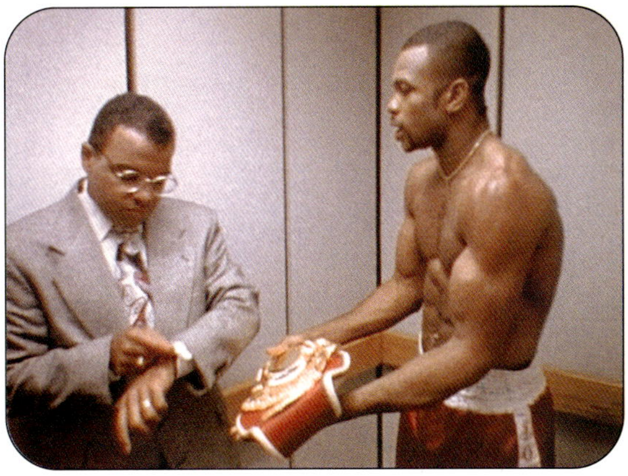

552

SUPER: CHARLEY STEINER, SPORTSCENTER ANCHOR.

CHARLEY STEINER: We have athletes hanging out at SportsCenter all the time. The one thing they have in common though, they all want their highlights on, they all want the publicity, they all want their names spelled right. But some of them tend to take it a little too far.

JUAN HOWARD: No really Karl, I want you to have the car. It's not enough room. Have the car.

CHEROKEE PARKS: Hey, is this your Rolex right here?

ROY JONES: C'mon, man, you can take it. It's much better than what you have on now. C'mon, man.

DAN PATRICK: Cherokee, I have a watch.

CHEROKEE: It's really nice.

DAN: Cherokee! I have a watch!

ROY: Take it man. C'mon, Mike.

MIKE: I can't do this . . .

ROY: C'mon, c'mon . . . Mike, Mike!

SUPER: THIS IS SPORTSCENTER. ESPN.

CONSUMER TELEVISION
:30 SINGLE

553
ART DIRECTOR:
Rick McQuiston
WRITER:
Hank Perlman
AGENCY PRODUCER:
Dan Duffy
PRODUCTION COMPANY:
@radical.media
DIRECTORS:
Bryan Buckley
Frank Todaro
CLIENT:
ESPN
AGENCY:
Wieden & Kennedy/
Portland

554
ART DIRECTOR:
Rick McQuiston
WRITER:
Hank Perlman
AGENCY PRODUCER:
Dan Duffy
PRODUCTION COMPANY:
@radical.media
DIRECTORS:
Bryan Buckley
Frank Todaro
CLIENT:
ESPN
AGENCY:
Wieden & Kennedy/
Portland

555
ART DIRECTOR:
Darryl McDonald
WRITER:
Jamie Barrett
AGENCY PRODUCER:
Jeff Selis
PRODUCTION COMPANY:
Optic Nerve
DIRECTOR:
Phil Morrison
CLIENT:
Nike
AGENCY:
Wieden & Kennedy/
Portland

556
ART DIRECTOR:
Andrew Christou
WRITER:
Evelyn Monroe
AGENCY PRODUCER:
Beth Harding
PRODUCTION COMPANY:
Mars Media
DIRECTOR:
Samuel Bayer
CLIENT:
Nike
AGENCY:
Wieden & Kennedy/
Portland

553

SUPER: BACKSTAGE, SPORTSCENTER STUDIOS.

DAN PATRICK: I don't know why Lindros has gotta drop the gloves . . . Nealy and Stevens, they don't fight anymore, they're respected around the league, and besides, penalty minutes don't equate to toughness in my book, I mean when I think tough, Doug Gilmore's tough, Mark Messier's tough.

KEITH OBERNANY: You need some more rouge.

DAN: Here, thanks. You know your foundation's looked great lately.

KEITH: Thanks.

SUPER: THIS IS SPORTSCENTER. ESPN.

554

SUPER: BARRY SACKS, SPORTSCENTER PRODUCER.

BARRY SACKS: I think the question I get asked most is: At the end of the show, when the music's playing, the anchors are talking to each other, what are they saying?

DAN PATRICK: I'm Dan Patrick.

KEITH OBERNANY: I'm Keith Obernany, see you later.

DAN: You phoney—do they sell men's clothes where you get that outfit?

BRETT HABER: I've got a wedgy like nobody's business right now.

KARL RAVECH: Thanks for sharing that.

KEITH: When's the last time your hair actually moved, like 1977?

DAN: When you put your fingers through it.

KARL: That wedgy didn't prevent that gas from coming out.

BRETT: Hey, that's the naugahide rubbing on the chair—don't make things up, huh?

DAN: I oughta kick your—

BRETT: I don't know what's on your teeth, but I assume you're saving it for later.

SUPER: THIS IS SPORTSCENTER. ESPN.

555

(MUSIC: ELEVATOR)

BELLHOP: Welcome to Detroit, home of . . . Barry Sanders! You're a big one, aren't ya? I'm not as big . . . I'm about "the Sandman's" size, as I say. Sanders! Low to the ground, much like me! Sanders, Nike Turf Trainers, just like me! Bellboy! Sanders! Boom . . . kaboom . . . It's Sanders back around! Aaargh! What seems to have happened to Barry Sanders? Right behind you, Largie! Oh! In between your legs!

SUPER: (NIKE LOGO).

556

(MUSIC: LOW, AGGRESSIVE)

(SFX: YELLING, VOLLEYBALL GAME SOUNDS)

ANNCR: They are not sisters. They are not classmates. They are not friends. They are not even the girls team. They're a pack of wolves.

(SFX: WOMAN SCREAMING)

ANNCR: Tend to your sheep.

SUPER: JUST DO IT.

SUPER: (NIKE LOGO).

CONSUMER TELEVISION
:30 SINGLE

557
ART DIRECTOR:
Andrew Christou
WRITER:
Eric Silver
AGENCY PRODUCER:
Kevin Diller
PRODUCTION COMPANY:
NFL Films
DIRECTOR:
Greg Kohs
CLIENT:
Nike
AGENCY:
Wieden & Kennedy/
Portland

558
ART DIRECTOR:
Andrew Christou
WRITER:
Eric Silver
AGENCY PRODUCER:
Kevin Diller
PRODUCTION COMPANY:
NFL Films
DIRECTOR:
Greg Kohs
CLIENT:
Nike
AGENCY:
Wieden & Kennedy/
Portland

559
ART DIRECTOR:
Chris Shipman
WRITER:
Jamie Barrett
AGENCY PRODUCER:
Dan Duffy
PRODUCTION COMPANY:
Mars Media
DIRECTOR:
Samuel Bayer
CLIENT:
Nike
AGENCY:
Wieden & Kennedy/
Portland

560
ART DIRECTOR:
Tim Hanrahan
WRITER:
Jamie Barrett
AGENCY PRODUCER:
Beth Harding
PRODUCTION COMPANY:
Palomar Pictures
DIRECTOR:
Gore Verbinsky
CLIENT:
Nike
AGENCY:
Wieden & Kennedy/
Portland

557

SUPER: NIKE PRESENTS THIS WEEK IN PEE WEE FOOTBALL.

ANNCR: It was crunch time in Elgin. As Cougars' quarterback, Ned Barnes, sought divine guidance, as he launched the desperation "Hail Mary."

Reaching into his pocket full of miracles number twelve tried to pull off one more magnificent moment, but it was not to be, as the Indians escape with the win.

SUPER: (NIKE LOGO).

558

SUPER: NIKE PRESENTS THIS WEEK IN PEE WEE FOOTBALL.

ANNCR: In Tahoe number 64, Bubba Wilkinson, remains a contradiction—the angel with a dirty face.

TEAMMATE: Yeah, Bubba come on.

ANNCR: Blessed with enormous body strength and uncommon quickness, Wilkinson doesn't tackle players, he buries them. Funk and flash are trademarks of a one-armed bandit, who yields a jackpot of big plays.

SUPER: (NIKE LOGO).

559

VARIOUS ATHLETES (SPEAKING INDIVIDUALLY):
I do not play bingo.
I am not shrinking.
I am not strong for my age . . . I am strong.
I will never say . . . I've fallen and I can't get up.
I am wrinkled and I am gray . . .
but I am not old.
SUPER: JUST DO IT.
SUPER: (NIKE LOGO).

560

(MUSIC: OMINOUS)
(SFX: BASKETBALL BOUNCING)
(MUSIC: ESCALATES)
(SFX: BALL SLAMMING THROUGH HOOP)
SUPER: JUST DO IT.
SUPER: (NIKE LOGO).
(SFX: CREAKING OF RIM)

CONSUMER TELEVISION
:30 SINGLE

561
ART DIRECTOR:
Vince Engel
WRITER:
Jim Riswold
AGENCY PRODUCER:
Derek Ruddy
PRODUCTION COMPANY:
Pytka
DIRECTOR:
Joe Pytka
CLIENT:
Nike
AGENCY:
Wieden & Kennedy/
Portland

CONSUMER TELEVISION
:30 CAMPAIGN

562
ART DIRECTOR:
Dennis Lim
WRITERS:
Harold Einstein
Greg Ketchum
David Lubars
AGENCY PRODUCER:
Jackie Vidor
PRODUCTION COMPANY:
Gartner-Grasso
DIRECTOR:
James Gartner
CLIENT:
Apple Computer
AGENCY:
BBDO/Los Angeles

561

MICHAEL JORDAN: I had this dream . . . I retired. I became a weak-hitting, Double A outfielder . . . with a below-average arm. I had a sixteen dollar meal per diem. I rode from small town to small town . . . on a bus.

SUPER (AS NEWSPAPER HEADLINE): I'M BACK.

MICHAEL: And then I returned . . . to the game I love . . . and shot 7 for 28. Can you imagine it? Nah. . . .

SUPER: (NIKE LOGO).

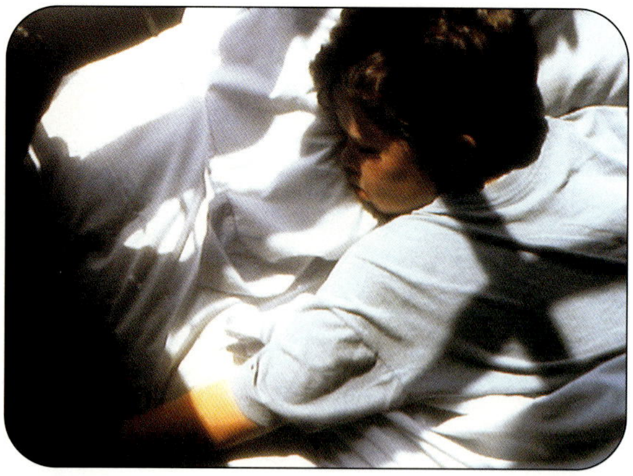

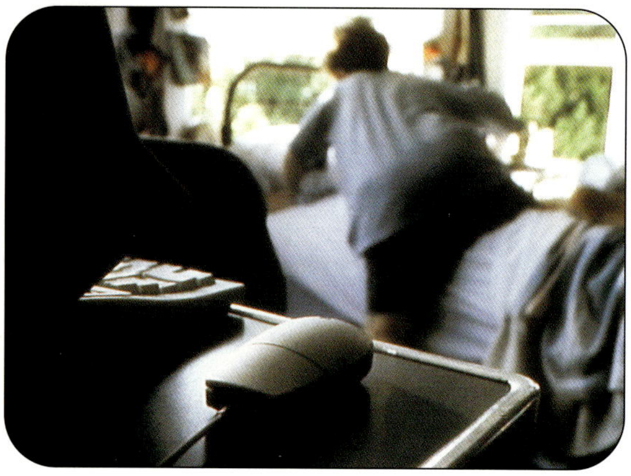

562

(SFX: CLOCK TICKING)

(SFX: RINGING)

CUT-OUT FIGURE: It's time to wake up, Tommy.

PURPLE BLOB: Tommy!

COWBOY: Hey, partner, it's time to get up.

TOMMY: Oh, no, here she comes.

SUPER (ON COMPUTER SCREEN): MOM ALERT.

MOM: Tommy, your oatmeal's getting cold.

TOUGH GUY: You asked for it, Tommy.

(MUSIC: MARCHING BAND BLARES FROM COMPUTER, THEN STOPS)

(SFX: CLOCK TICKING)

ANNCR: If you owned the world's easiest computer, what would you do with it?

SUPER: MACINTOSH.

CONSUMER TELEVISION
:30 CAMPAIGN

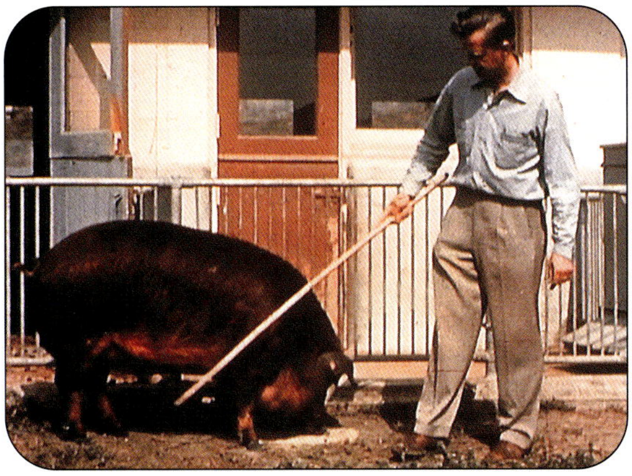

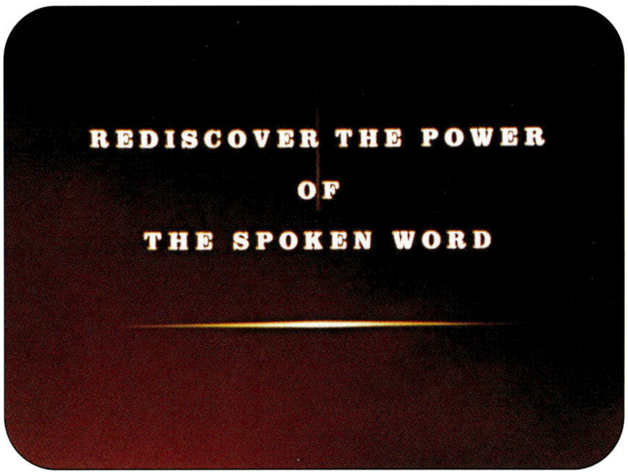

563

ART DIRECTORS:
Eric Pfieffer
John Butler
Mike Shine
WRITERS:
Jim DiPlazza
Ryan Ebner
AGENCY PRODUCER:
Adrienne Cummins
PRODUCTION COMPANY:
Backyard Productions
DIRECTOR:
Rob Pritts
CLIENT:
Cartoon Network
AGENCY:
Butler Shine & Stern/
Sausalito

564

ART DIRECTOR:
Lindsey Redding
WRITER:
Adrian Jeffrey
AGENCY PRODUCER:
Tim Maguire
PRODUCTION COMPANY:
HLA/London
DIRECTOR:
Tomato
CLIENT:
BBC Radio Scotland
AGENCY:
Faulds Advertising/
Edinburgh

563

(MUSIC: UPBEAT, FAST)

SUPER: PORKY VS. MR. PIG.

ANNCR:

This is Porky Pig.

This is Mr. Pig.

Porky has hooves.

Mr. Pig has hooves.

Porky has a blunt snout.

Mr. Pig has a blunt snout.

Porky likes the water.

Mr. Pig likes the water.

Porky can sustain large blows to the head.

Mr. Pig, well, cannot.

ANNCR: Nothing compares to Cartoon Network. The only place for all your favorite cartoons, 24 hard-hitting hours a day.

SUPER: CARTOON NETWORK. TOTALLY UNREAL.

PORKY: That's all folks.

564

ANNCR (FROM BBC SCOTLAND PROGRAM): Line out. Outside the French 22. Back to the main . . . oop . . . now the referee has called a halt to proceedings, it's now over the Scottish 22 and heading upfield. It's a magnificent fellow with a black underbelly, a gold-colored back and a red cockscomb and the cockerel's over the Scot's 5 meter line, heading for touch and the stewards are looking just a little bit flushed, perplexed, a little bit perplexed and flushed . . . just selling them a wee dummy and a wee side step and away he goes. Yes, he's over the touch line, now he's on the running track, and he's almost away.

SUPER: REDISCOVER THE POWER OF THE SPOKEN WORD.

(MUSIC: BBC SCOTLAND THEME)

SUPER: BBC SCOTLAND.

SUPER: UK NATIONAL STATION OF THE YEAR.

CONSUMER TELEVISION
:30 CAMPAIGN

565
ART DIRECTORS:
George Chadwick
Lisbeth Rokicki
WRITER:
Mary Dean
AGENCY PRODUCER:
Iliani Matisse
PRODUCTION COMPANIES:
Ginco
Olive Jar Studios
DIRECTORS:
Erica Russell
Tom Gasek
CLIENT:
Levi's Jeans For Women
AGENCY:
Foote Cone & Belding/
San Francisco

566
ART DIRECTOR:
Sean Ehringer
WRITER:
Harry Cocciolo
AGENCY PRODUCER:
Cindy Epps
PRODUCTION COMPANY:
Crossroads Films
DIRECTOR:
Roger Tonry
CLIENT:
Major League Baseball
AGENCY:
Goodby Silverstein &
Partners/San Francisco

567
ART DIRECTOR:
Steve Whittier
WRITER:
Jim Glynn
PHOTOGRAPHER:
Dan Sidor
PRODUCTION COMPANY:
Crosspoint Productions
DIRECTOR:
Steve Whittier
CLIENT:
Rocky Mountain College
of Art and Design
AGENCY:
Karsh & Hagan/
Englewood, CO

568
ART DIRECTOR:
Larry Frey
WRITER:
Jerry Cronin
AGENCY PRODUCER:
Jeff Selis
PRODUCTION COMPANY:
@radical.media
DIRECTORS:
Robert Leacock
Larry Frey
CLIENT:
ESPN
AGENCY:
Wieden & Kennedy/
Portland

565

(MUSIC: PROVOCATIVE)

SUPER: LEVI'S JEANS FOR WOMEN.

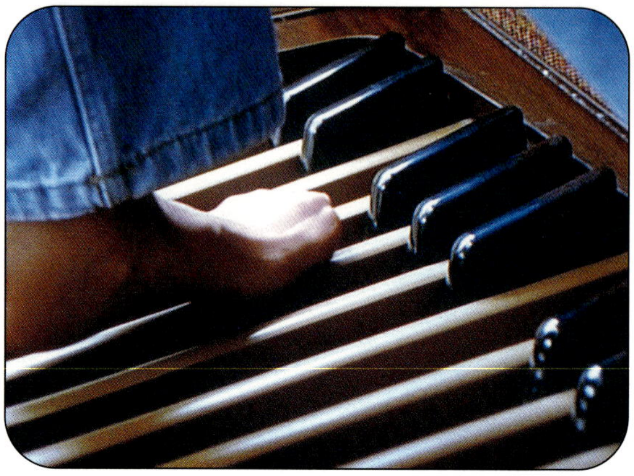

566

(SFX: BASEBALL GAME ORGAN MUSIC)

ORGAN PLAYER (OFF CAMERA): The old-timers like this one.

(MUSIC: "TAKE ME OUT TO THE BALL GAME")

ORGAN PLAYER: But if it were up to me . . .

(MUSIC: "JOY TO THE WORLD")

ORGAN PLAYER (SINGING): *Jeremiah was a bullfrog!! . . . Was a good friend of mine!!*

(MUSIC: "JOY TO THE WORLD" CONTINUES)

SUPER: WELCOME TO THE SHOW.

SUPER: MAJOR LEAGUE BASEBALL.

567

(SFX: SUPERMARKET MUZAK, CHECKOUT SOUNDS)

SUPER: CAMPBELL'S SELLS THEIR SOUP CANS FOR 49 CENTS.

SUPER: ANDY WARHOL SELLS HIS SOUP CANS FOR $250,000.

SUPER: THE DIFFERENCE IS . . . ART.

SUPER: WE CAN TEACH THAT.

SUPER: ROCKY MOUNTAIN COLLEGE OF ART & DESIGN. 753-6046.

568

SUPER: "FLUFF," TOUR CADDIE.

(MUSIC: JAZZ)

FLUFF: Grass tossing is an individual art. . . . If you want to do it correctly . . . it is simply raising it, and letting it go. There is none of this . . .

(SFX: CADDIES LAUGHING)

FLUFF: . . . 'cause then you can make it go, you know, anyway you want it. The wind could be blowing forty miles an hour that way, I'm gonna make it go that way and tell 'em it's into us.

You cannot make it go where it's not going. You just have to let go . . . kind of like life. You just have to let go once in awhile.

(SFX: CADDIES LAUGHING)

SUPER: ESPN GOLF.

CONSUMER TELEVISION
:30 CAMPAIGN

569

ART DIRECTORS:
Bryan Buckley
Frank Todaro

WRITERS:
Bryan Buckley
Frank Todaro

AGENCY PRODUCER:
Robert Fernandez

PRODUCTION COMPANY:
@radical.media

DIRECTORS:
Bryan Buckley
Frank Todaro

CLIENT:
ESPN/Major League Baseball

AGENCY:
Wieden & Kennedy/ Portland

570

ART DIRECTOR:
Rick McQuiston

WRITER:
Hank Perlman

AGENCY PRODUCER:
Dan Duffy

PRODUCTION COMPANY:
@radical.media

DIRECTORS:
Bryan Buckley
Frank Todaro

CLIENT:
ESPN

AGENCY:
Wieden & Kennedy/ Portland

569

JOEY: I hate to say this, but I think Boston's gonna hold the Yankees off, what do you think?

VINCE: (CHOKING).

JOEY: What's the matter, Vinny? Take some water.

VINCE: All right, cut it out.

JOEY: You okay?

VINCE: I was just doing my imitation of the Red Sox.

JOEY: You know, that's not funny.

VINCE: That's a little funny.

JOEY: Some day you're gonna be choking for real, and I'm not gonna be there to save you.

VINCE: How are you gonna save me, by busting my rib cage?

SUPER: BOSTON RED SOX VS. NEW YORK YANKEES.

JOEY: You know, you're a sick man.

VINCE: Hey, you've got no sense of humor.

JOEY: You're not right.

570

SUPER: GLEN JACOBS, SPORTSCENTER PRODUCTION ASSISTANT.

GLEN JACOBS: My name's Glen Jacobs, and I've been a P.A. here at SportsCenter for about three months, and it's been really great.

CRAIG KILBORN: You've embarassed me on national TV.

GLEN: I work long hours sure, but I get a lot of exercise . . . it's really cool when one of the guys reads something I've written on the air.

CRAIG: Nice try Sparky, nice try . . . maybe next time.

GLEN: Four months ago, I was writing a paper about my idol, Craig Kilborn.

CRAIG: Gary.

GLEN: Uh, Glen.

CRAIG: Okay.

GLEN: Here I am getting career advice from him.

CRAIG: Two words for you: pizza delivery.

GLEN: It's incredible.

SUPER: THIS IS SPORTSCENTER. ESPN.

CONSUMER TELEVISION
:30 CAMPAIGN

571

ART DIRECTOR:
Rick McQuiston

WRITER:
Hank Perlman

AGENCY PRODUCER:
Dan Duffy

PRODUCTION COMPANY:
@radical.media

DIRECTORS:
Bryan Buckley
Frank Todaro

CLIENT:
ESPN

AGENCY:
Wieden & Kennedy/
Portland

572

ART DIRECTORS:
John Jay
Young Kim

WRITER:
Jimmy Smith

AGENCY PRODUCER:
Jill Andreservic

PRODUCTION COMPANY:
@radical.media

DIRECTOR:
Robert Leacock

CLIENT:
Nike NYC

AGENCY:
Wieden & Kennedy/
Portland

571

(SFX: HELICOPTER NOISES)

SUPER: SPORTSCENTER NEWSROOM MAY 18, 1995.

DAN PATRICK: He's here. Make a hole people!

SUPER: SPORTSCENTER HELIPAD BRISTOL, CONNECTICUT.

JASON KIDD (SUBTITLED): Here's the highlights. You might want to check out the third quarter.

DAN (SUBTITLED): Sure you can't stay?

JASON (SUBTITLED): I got to get back. I have an early practice tomorrow.

(SFX: HELICOPTER NOISES AGAIN)

SUPER: THIS IS SPORTSCENTER. ESPN.

572

SUPER: JACKIE JACKSON

JACKIE JACKSON: Ed bet these guys that I was the highest jumper of all time, so we go to the park, we get a kid to climb the pole, to put the quarter on the top of the backboard; so, Ed looks at me and says, "Jack, get your quarter," so he was always my inspiration; so ah, I just jumped up, touched the top of it and got the quarter and came down, and that's how the legend started: Jackie Jackson, so nice had to name him twice.

SUPER: (NIKE NYC LOGO).

CONSUMER TELEVISION
:20 AND UNDER: SINGLE

573

ART DIRECTORS:
Ray Brennan
Stephen McKenzie

WRITERS:
Steve Meredith
Jason Gormly

AGENCY PRODUCER:
Nick Peers

PRODUCTION COMPANY:
Loose Moose

DIRECTOR:
Ken Lidster

CLIENT:
Van den Bergh Foods/
Peperami

AGENCY:
Ammirati Puris Lintas/
London

574

ART DIRECTOR:
Eric McClellan

WRITER:
Shalom Auslander

AGENCY PRODUCERS:
Andrew Chinich
Roxanne Karsch

PRODUCTION COMPANY:
Palomar Pictures

DIRECTOR:
Ben Stiller

CLIENT:
America Online

AGENCY:
TBWA Chiat/Day, New York

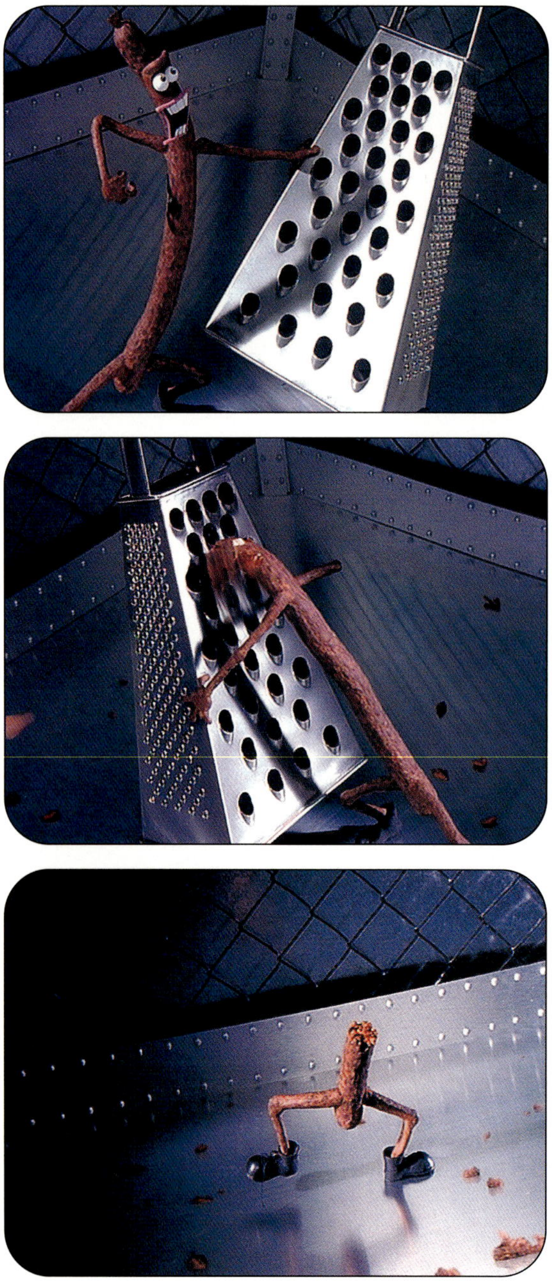

573

(SFX: SLICING, GRATING SOUNDS)

ANNCR: Peperami Mini. It's a little bit of an animal.

574

(SFX: TYPING)

ANNCR: Any ladies out there?

(SFX: TYPING)

ANNCR: Yes—ladies escaping the gender biases of the physical world.

(SFX: TYPING)

ANNCR: You sound really cute.

AMERICA ONLINE ANNCR: American Online—welcome!

SUPER: AMERICA ONLINE.

SUPER: FOR A FREE TRIAL CALL 1-800-4-ONLINE.

CONSUMER TELEVISION
VARYING LENGTHS
CAMPAIGN

575

ART DIRECTOR:
Martin Galton
WRITER:
Tim Delaney
AGENCY PRODUCER:
Matthew Jones
PRODUCTION COMPANY:
Delaney & Hart
DIRECTORS:
Andrew Douglas
Stuart Douglas
CLIENT:
Adidas
AGENCY:
Leagas Delaney/London

576

ART DIRECTOR:
Tom Notman
WRITER:
Alistair Wood
ILLUSTRATOR:
Mark Thomas
AGENCY PRODUCER:
Charles Crisp
PRODUCTION COMPANY:
Hibbert Ralph Animation
DIRECTOR:
Jerry Hibbert
CLIENT:
Whitbread Beer Company
AGENCY:
Lowe Howard-Spink/
London

575

MUHAMMAD ALI'S BROTHER: Muhammad Ali is my brother. When we was kids . . .

BROTHER (ANNCR): He used to get me to throw rocks at him so he could practice duckin' an' weavin'. He had natural ability, but he was short on muscles.

BROTHER: So he trained hard . . . and got real strong. So strong in fact he went on to be the greatest heavyweight of all time.

SUPER: MUHAMMAD ALI TRAINING SHOE, 1960.

SUPER: THE ADIDAS TRAINING SHOE, 1995.

MUHAMMAD ALI: I'm 22-years-old: I must be the greatest.

SUPER: ADIDAS.

576

SUPER: MR. FLOWERS' GUIDE TO WALKING STICKS.

(SFX: OUTDOOR SOUNDS)

MR. FLOWERS: Yes. A good stick is the gentleman's scepter, Derek. With it he may probe suspicious hollows in trees and reed banks.

(SFX: BICYCLE SOUNDS)

MR. FLOWERS: Wait a minute—that man's been fishing without a license. This is where a good stick earns its keep. Wait . . . gently bently . . . and now!

(SFX: BICYCLE WHEEL SPINNING)

POLICEMAN: There'll be a reward for this . . . two pints of Flowers Original.

SUPER: MR. FLOWERS CLAIMS HIS REWARD.

DEREK: How did you know he didn't have a license?

MR. FLOWERS: Derek, my father hasn't had a fishing license for 40 years.

SUPER: DAMNED FINE ALE.

CONSUMER TELEVISION
UNDER $50,000 BUDGET

577
ART DIRECTOR:
Bart Cleveland
WRITER:
Brian Sack
PRODUCTION COMPANY:
The Dxters
DIRECTOR:
Bobby Sheehan
CLIENT:
WNNX-FM
AGENCY:
Cleveland Clark/Atlanta

578
ART DIRECTORS:
Greg Wells
Carl Warner
WRITER:
David Parson
AGENCY PRODUCER:
Stan Hart
PRODUCTION COMPANY:
Teleworks
DIRECTOR:
Carl Warner
CLIENT:
American Airlines
AGENCY:
DDB Needham Worldwide
Dallas Group

579
ART DIRECTOR:
Jennifer Fleming-Balser
WRITER:
Rich Tlapek
AGENCY PRODUCER:
Tom Gilmore
PRODUCTION COMPANY:
Hank Kingsley
Productions
DIRECTORS:
Auggie Alcala
Rich Tlapek
Jennifer Fleming-Balser
CLIENT:
Live Oak Theatre
AGENCY:
GSD&M Advertising/
Austin

580
ART DIRECTOR:
Jim Baldwin
WRITER:
Ron Henderson
AGENCY PRODUCER:
Brent Holt
PRODUCTION COMPANY:
Post Op
CLIENT:
Motel 6
AGENCY:
The Richards Group/Dallas

577

(MUSIC: NINE INCH NAILS SONG THROUGHOUT)

GRANDMOTHER (READING FROM LYRICS OF RED HOT CHILI PEPPERS): What I got you got to give it to your mama.

MECHANIC (READING FROM LYRICS OF STONE TEMPLE PILOTS): Flies in the vaseline.

BIKER (READING FROM LYRICS OF NIRVANA): Throw down your umbilical noose so I can climb right back.

GRANDMOTHER: What I got you got to give it to your papa.

SWIMMER (READING FROM LYRICS OF WHITE ZOMBIE): I am the astro creep.

POOLSIDE COOK (READING FROM LYRICS OF PRIMUS): Winona's got herself a big brown beaver.

GRANDFATHER (READING FROM LYRICS OF JANE'S ADDICTION): And she don't want to pay for it.

SWIMMER: I am the crawling dead.

COWBOY (READS FROM BECK): I'm a loser, baby, so why don't you kill me?

TENNIS MOM 1 (READING FROM LYRICS OF R.E.M.): Oh no, I've said too much.

SUPER: PARENTS NOT INCLUDED.

SUPER: 99X.

TENNIS MOM 2: (READS FROM R.E.M.): I haven't said enough.

578

MAN: London, Heathrow. JFK, New York. That's what American Airlines do six times every day. You know. Fly planes, not hit sticks on maps. That'd be stupid.

SUPER: AMERICAN AIRLINES. SIX DAILY RETURN FLIGHTS BETWEEN HEATHROW AND NEW YORK'S JFK.

579

MAN: Hi, honey.

WOMAN: How was work?

MAN: Great. Say, did you remember to call Live Oak Theatre about our tickets?

WOMAN: I thought you said you were going to call.

MAN: As busy as our schedules are, I guess we both forgot! I'll call now. Where's that number?

WOMAN: Here it is: 472-5143. That's 472-5143.

MAN: Hello, is this the Live Oak Theatre? I'd like to order my season tickets.

(MUSIC: CHEESY)

ANNCR: We promise that none of the actors, directors, set designers, lighting people or writers responsible for this commercial are involved in any way, shape or form in any Live Oak Theatre production.

(MUSIC: STOPS)

MAN: I got the tickets!

KID: Guess what, dad, I got an "A" on my test today!

MAN: That's great, Tiger! I guess those phonics tapes we got him really helped.

ANNCR: Live Oak Theatre. Never a crappy production.

SUPER: FOR "ALL IN THE TIMING" OR SEASON TICKETS, CALL 472-5143.

580

(MUSIC: MOTEL 6 THEME)

TOM: Hi, Tom Bodett here for Motel 6 with a little memory device to help you remember our new 800 number. Okay, look deep into that spirally thing. All right, now you're gettin' sleepy . . . real sleepy. And since you're sleepy, you're gonna be needin' a place to sleep. So here's the number to call:

SUPER: 1-800-4-MOTEL-6.

TOM: 1-800-4-MOTEL-6. That's 1-800-4-MOTEL-6 . . . for a cleeeeean, comfortable roooom.

Well, I'm Tom Bodett for Motel 6 and we'll leave the light on for you. In case you're still kinda dizzy.

SUPER: MOTEL 6.

CONSUMER TELEVISION
UNDER $50,000 BUDGET

581

ART DIRECTORS:
Mark Arnold
John Roberts
WRITER:
Charlie Hopper
AGENCY PRODUCER:
Greg Malone
PRODUCTION COMPANY:
Technisonic Studios
DIRECTOR:
Lloyd Wolfe
CLIENT:
St. Louis Vipers
AGENCY:
TBWA Chiat/Day, St. Louis

INTERNATIONAL FOREIGN
LANGUAGE COMMERCIAL:
TELEVISION

582

ART DIRECTOR:
Elvio Sanchez
WRITER:
Juan Mariano Mancebo
AGENCY PRODUCER:
Marta Lugris
PRODUCTION COMPANY:
Studio Solanes
DIRECTOR:
Leo Solanes
CLIENT:
Ancora Publicaciones
AGENCY:
BDDP Mancebo Kaye/
Madrid

583

ART DIRECTOR:
Heinz Schwegler
WRITER:
Iwan Weidmann
PRODUCTION COMPANY:
PPM Filmproduktions AG
DIRECTOR:
Ron Eichhorn
CLIENT:
Telekurs AG
AGENCY:
Dubach Werbeagentur AG/
Wallisellen, Switzerland

581

ROLLER HOCKEY PLAYER: (LONG, GUTTERAL SCREAM).

(SFX: SCREAM REVERBERATING THROUGH EMPTY ARENA)

(SFX: STICK SLAMMING AND BREAKING)

(SFX: HELMET SMASHING)

(SFX: PADS CRASHING TO FLOOR)

(SFX: SCREAM REVERBERATING IN VACANT HALLWAYS, THEN DYING OUT)

SUPER: IF THEY DON'T WIN.

SUPER: THEY DON'T GET PAID.

SUPER: ST. LOUIS VIPERS.

582

ANNCR: The contents of the new magazine *Tendencias* are so interesting that you will not be able to do without a single one of its pages. Not even in the most critical situation.

583

(SFX: PATIENT BEING REMOVED FROM AMBULANCE)

ANNCR: With direct debits, your health insurance payments are always made on time. LSV. Intelligent payments. A Swiss bank service.

Years ago it was said that the pen would be the downfall of the pencil. More recently, nay-sayers have preached that the computer would cause its demise. Not only has the pencil persevered, it may in fact be turning the tables. At last count there were 1,748 web sites dedicated to pencils.

Interactive Finalists

584
ART DIRECTOR:
David Hunter
WRITER:
Mark Friedman
DIGITAL ARTISTS/DESIGNERS:
Russell Brown
Bruce Charonnat
WEB MASTERS:
Jocelyn Bergen
Andy Shore
CLIENT:
Adobe
AGENCY:
Foote Cone & Belding/
San Francisco

585
ART DIRECTOR:
Todd Bartz
WRITER:
Tim Pegors
PHOTOGRAPHER:
Jim Gallop
DIGITAL ARTISTS:
Todd Bartz
Patrick Maun
AGENCY PRODUCER:
Margaret Bossen
CLIENT:
BMW of North America
AGENCY:
Fallon McElligott/
Minneapolis

584 http://www.adobe.com

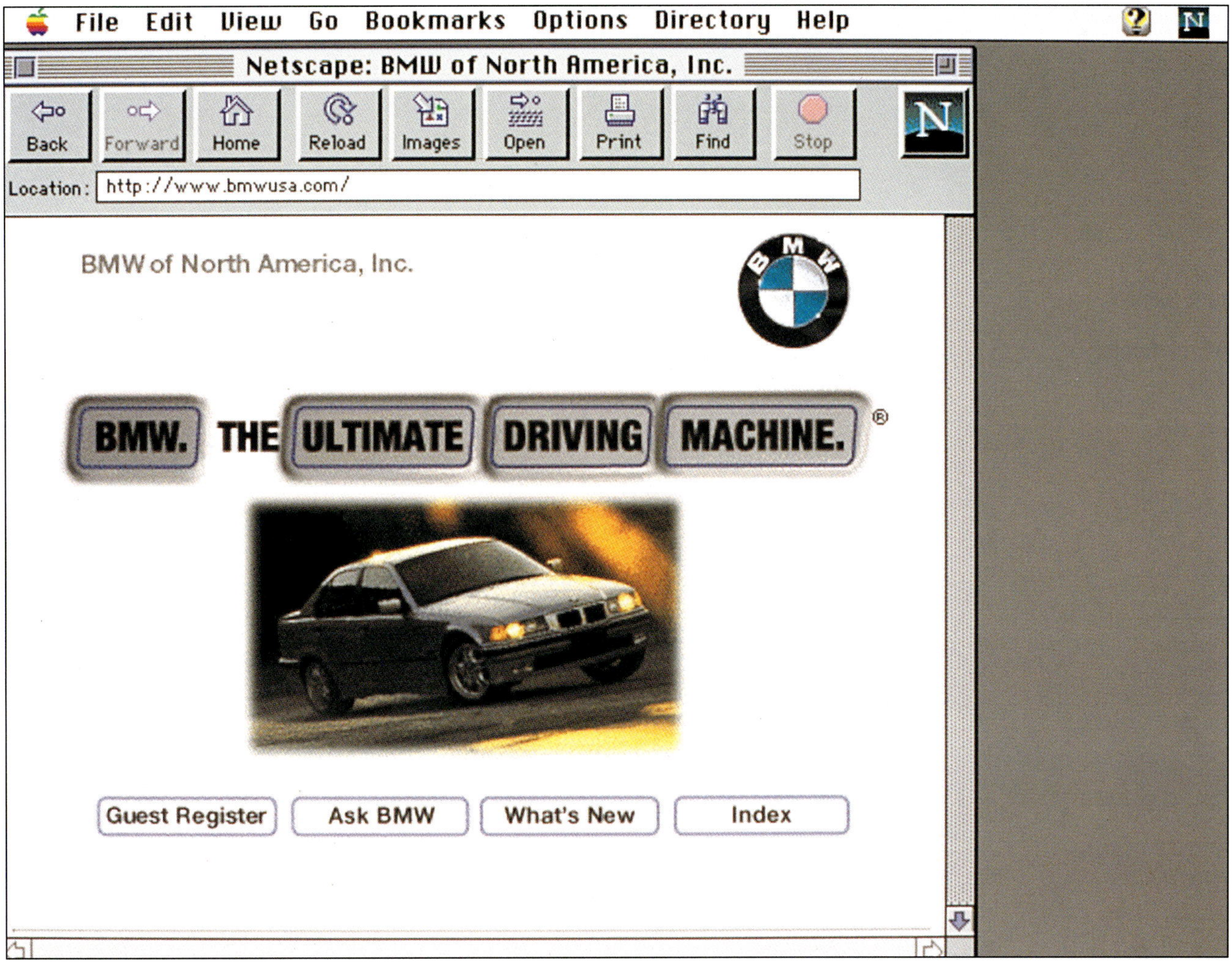

 http://www.bmwusa.com

INTERACTIVE: WEB SITE

586
ART DIRECTORS:
Alan Colvin
Eden Fahlen
WRITER:
Tim Pegors
DIGITAL ARTIST:
Patrick Maun
AGENCY PRODUCER:
Margaret Bossen
CLIENT:
Fallon McElligott
AGENCY:
Fallon McElligott/
Minneapolis

587
ART DIRECTOR:
Dana Wallace
WRITER:
Damian Fraticelli
AGENCY PRODUCER:
Sorel Husbands
PRODUCTION COMPANY:
Cybersight/Portland
CLIENT:
Carillon Importers/
Stolichnaya Brands
AGENCY:
Margeotes Fertitta &
Partners/New York

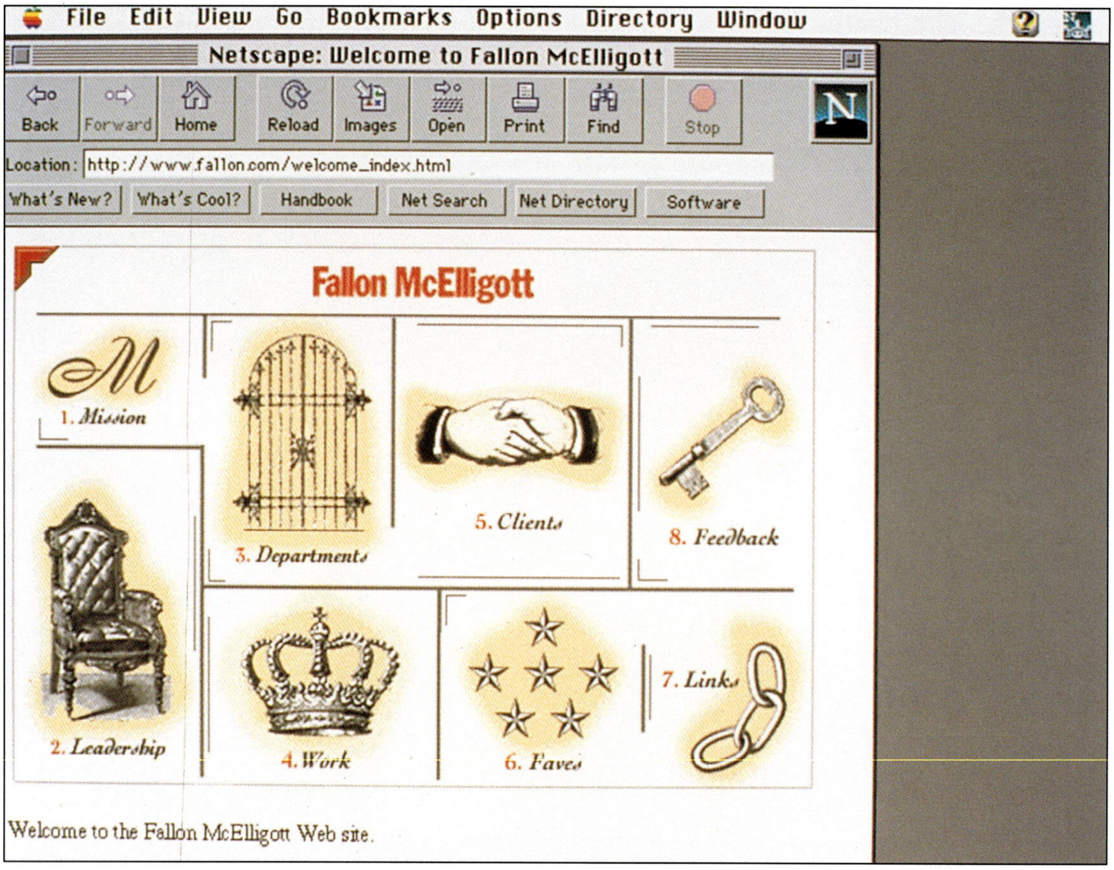

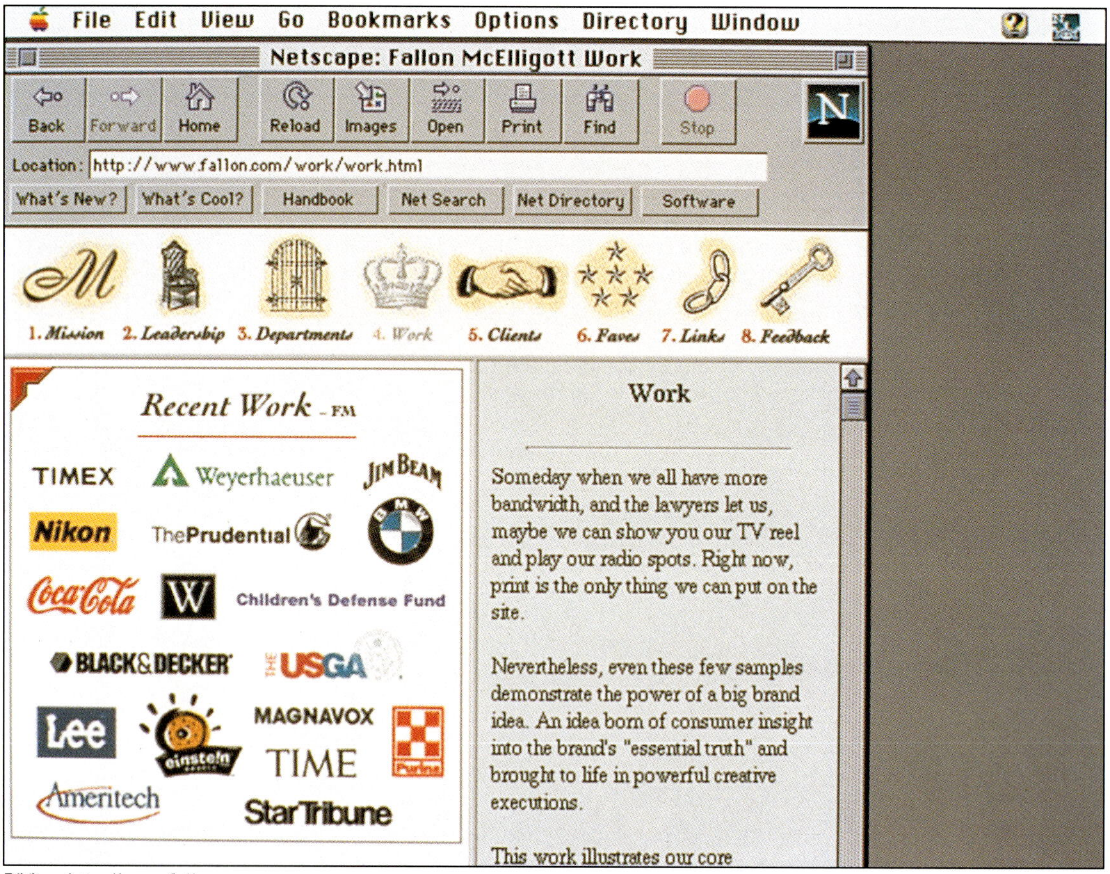

586 http://www.fallon.com

Netscape: Stoli Central
What's New?
What's Cool?
Handbook
Net Search
Net Directory
Newsgroups
THIS SITE IS INTENDED FOR AUDIENCES OF LEGAL DRINKING AGE ONLY
STOLI CENTRAL™
FREEDOM OF ADVENTURE
FREEDOM OF EXPRESSION
FREEDOM OF VODKA
SPIRITS OF THE WORLD
STOLI NOTE
Behold Stolichnaya(R)'s web site with a twist --- believed to be the only stop on the internet where you can be a creator and a critic, be in Moscow and Mexico, as well as become bemused, befuddled and benevolent all in a single visit. That's because at STOLI CENTRAL freedom reigns supreme.
So if you've yet to do so, add the site to your personal hotlist, because you won't want to miss any of our latest additions.
http://www.stoli.com/cgi-bin/imagemap/maps/new/stoli-central.map?

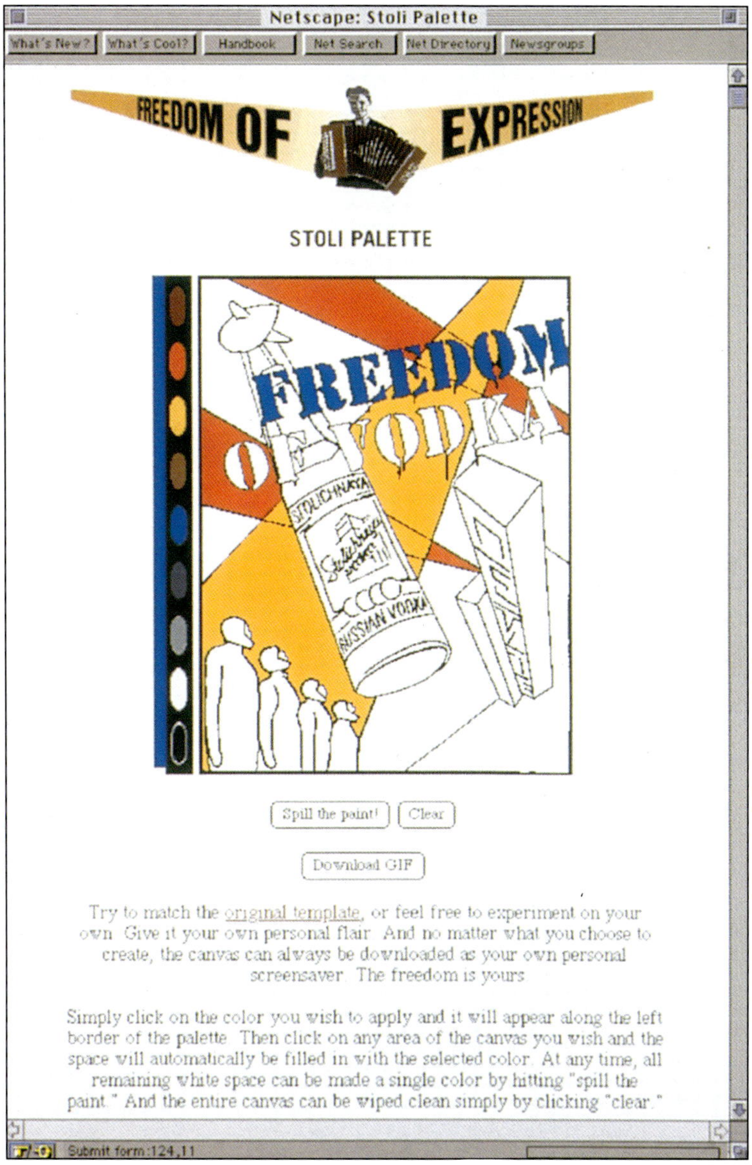
Netscape: Stoli Palette
What's New?
What's Cool?
Handbook
Net Search
Net Directory
Newsgroups
FREEDOM OF EXPRESSION
STOLI PALETTE
FREEDOM OF VODKA
STOLICHNAYA
RUSSIAN VODKA
Spill the paint!
Clear
Download GIF
Try to match the original template, or feel free to experiment on your own. Give it your own personal flair. And no matter what you choose to create, the canvas can always be downloaded as your own personal screensaver. The freedom is yours.
Simply click on the color you wish to apply and it will appear along the left border of the palette. Then click on any area of the canvas you wish and the space will automatically be filled in with the selected color. At any time, all remaining white space can be made a single color by hitting "spill the paint." And the entire canvas can be wiped clean simply by clicking "clear."
Submit form:124,11

587 http://www.stoli.com

INTERACTIVE: WEB SITE

588
ART DIRECTOR:
Dave Parrish
WRITER:
Amy Derksen
PHOTOGRAPHER:
Dean Hawthorne
DIGITAL ARTIST:
Holly Dickens
DESIGNER:
Michael Giarratano
AGENCY PRODUCER:
Evan Davies
PROP PRODUCTION:
Minniefax
CLIENT:
The Coca-Cola Company
AGENCY:
The Martin Agency/
Richmond

589
ART DIRECTORS:
Brook Boley
Todd Miller
WRITER:
Avery Carroll
DIGITAL ARTIST:
Brook Boley
CLIENT:
Rubin Postaer &
Associates
AGENCY:
Rubin Postaer &
Associates/Santa Monica

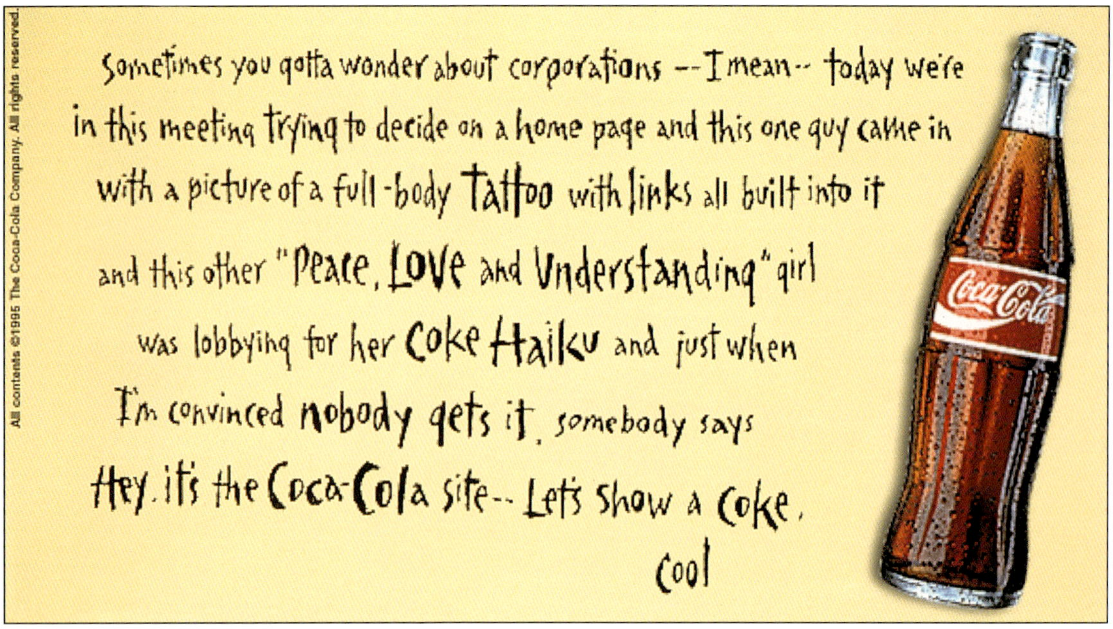

588 http://www.cocacola.com

Netscape: RPA-O-Matic
Back
Forward
Home
Reload
Images
Open
Print
Find
Stop
cation: http://www.rpa.com/
hat's New?
What's Cool?
Handbook
Net Search
Net Directory
Software
RPA-O-MATIC
HEY! Howyadoin'?
RUBIN POSTAER AND ASSOCIATES IS A PUSH OF THE BUTTON AWAY!
BUT THIS JUST IN! ER, MAKE THAT THESE JUST IN.
OUR NEWEST CLIENTS ARE ARCO AM/PM AND U S WEST INTERACTIVE SERVICES.

Back
Forward
Home
Reload
Images
Open
Print
Find
Stop
cation: http://www.rpa.com/Clients/index.html
hat's New?
What's Cool?
Handbook
Net Search
Net Directory
Software
CLIENT-O-RAMA
GO ON, CHECK OUT OUR FABULOUS CLIENTS
HONDA
USWEST
Discover
Disney
CALIFORNIA PIZZA KITCHEN
PHILIPS
Kubota
DO NOT PUSH THIS BUTTON

590

ART DIRECTORS:
Walt Morton
Nat Whitten
Marcello Guidoli

WRITERS:
Nat Whitten
Walt Morton

PRODUCTION COMPANY:
WWS Interactive

CLIENT:
Weiss Whitten Stagliano

AGENCY:
Weiss Whitten Stagliano/
New York

You've arrived at WWSWorld, a digital downtown of the not-too-distant future. Created by Weiss, Whitten, Stagliano, WWSWorld is here to fulfill all your virtual interests, whether they be mental, physical, or spiritual. Need a map to guide you? Click on the globe below. Or, if you'd rather dive right in, enter the Funhouse through the door above.

WWSWorld is best visited via Netscape. Please download your copy for Macintosh or Windows immediately. WWSWorld will not be liable for any brain injury incurred by visitors that fail to heed our health and safety injunctions.

 http://www.wwsworld.com

INSTRUCTIONS
1. FASTEN MACHINE FIRMLY.
2. KEEP MACHINE CLEAN AND OILED.
3. HOLD PENCIL STRAIGHT AND GRASP IT CLOSE TO MACHINE.
4 WHEN CUTTERS ARE DULL AND BEGIN TO BREAK LEADS INSERT NEW CUTTERS.
C. HOWARD HUNT PEN CO.
CAMDEN, N. J.
MADE IN U. S. A.

It has been reported that Ernest Hemingway got into the mood to write by sharpening pencils. He began each day with seven finely honed #2's. And he considered it a good day's work if he managed to dull all seven. For other writers this number was merely a warmup. John Steinbeck went through sixty pencils a day. The road to the Nobel Prize is paved with pencil stubs.

College Finalists

COLLEGE COMPETITION
ASSIGNMENT:
THE INTERNET

591
ART DIRECTORS:
Lisa Brink
Faria Raji
WRITERS:
Lisa Brink
Faria Raji
COLLEGE:
Art Center College of
Design/Pasadena

592
ART DIRECTOR:
Scott Vitrone
PHOTOGRAPHER:
Buddy Holly
WRITER:
Aaron Griffiths
COLLEGE:
Creative Circus/Atlanta

593
ART DIRECTOR:
Debby Yennaco
WRITER:
Colleen O'Hare
COLLEGE:
Creative Circus/Atlanta

594
ART DIRECTOR:
Don Shelford
WRITER:
Susan LaScala
COLLEGE:
Creative Circus/Atlanta

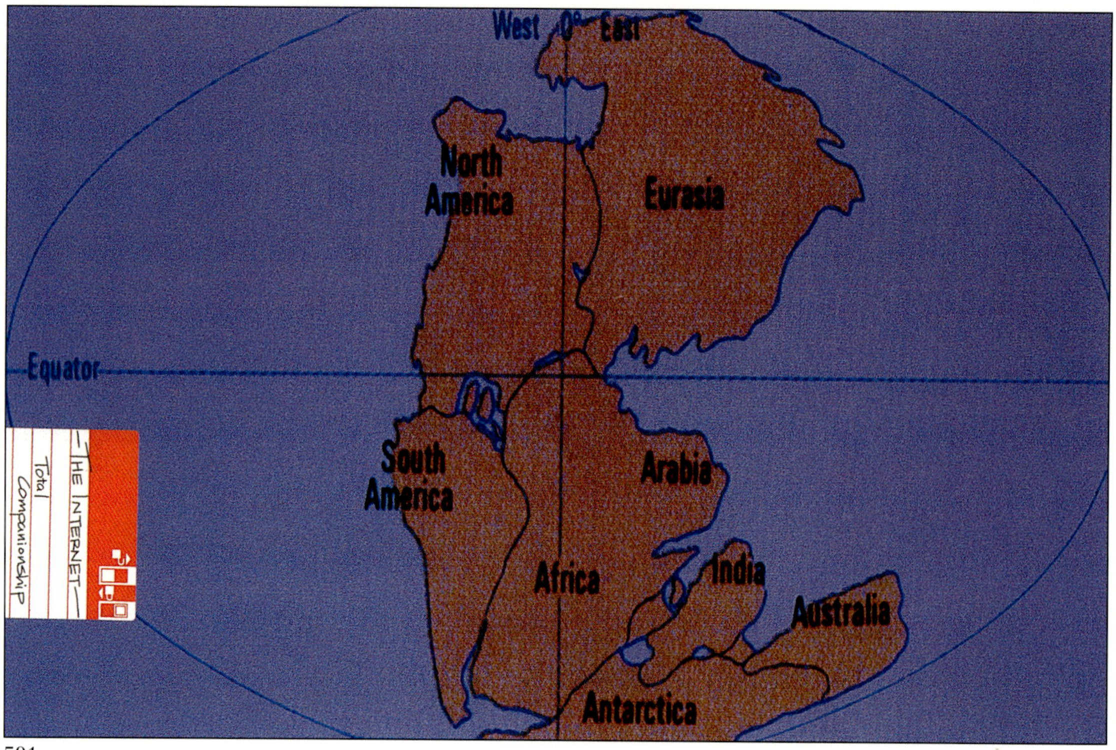

591

592

EVEN IF YOU FOUND SOME INGENIOUS WAY OF SCRAPING IT UP, YOU COULD ONLY REACH ONE PERSON.
ON THE INTERNET, IT'S THOUSANDS OF PEOPLE AT ONCE.
THE INTERNET.
1.800.898.9000

593

What if you never tried your favorite food? You can't learn anything from someone who agrees with you. Penicillin was discovered by accident. If you always go the same way, you'll never know what else is around. The Internet. There are no dead ends.
For more information call 1-800-4444-NET

594

COLLEGE COMPETITION
ASSIGNMENT:
THE INTERNET

595
ART DIRECTORS:
T.K. Long
John F. Gregory
WRITERS:
T.K. Long
John F. Gregory
COLLEGE:
Creative Circus/Atlanta

596
ART DIRECTOR:
Buz Davis
WRITER:
David Weist
COLLEGE:
Creative Circus/Atlanta

597
ART DIRECTOR:
Marcus Slaven
WRITER:
Marcus Slaven
COLLEGE:
East Texas State
University/Commerce

598
ART DIRECTOR:
Todd Sturgell
WRITER:
Todd Sturgell
COLLEGE:
East Texas State
University/Commerce

595

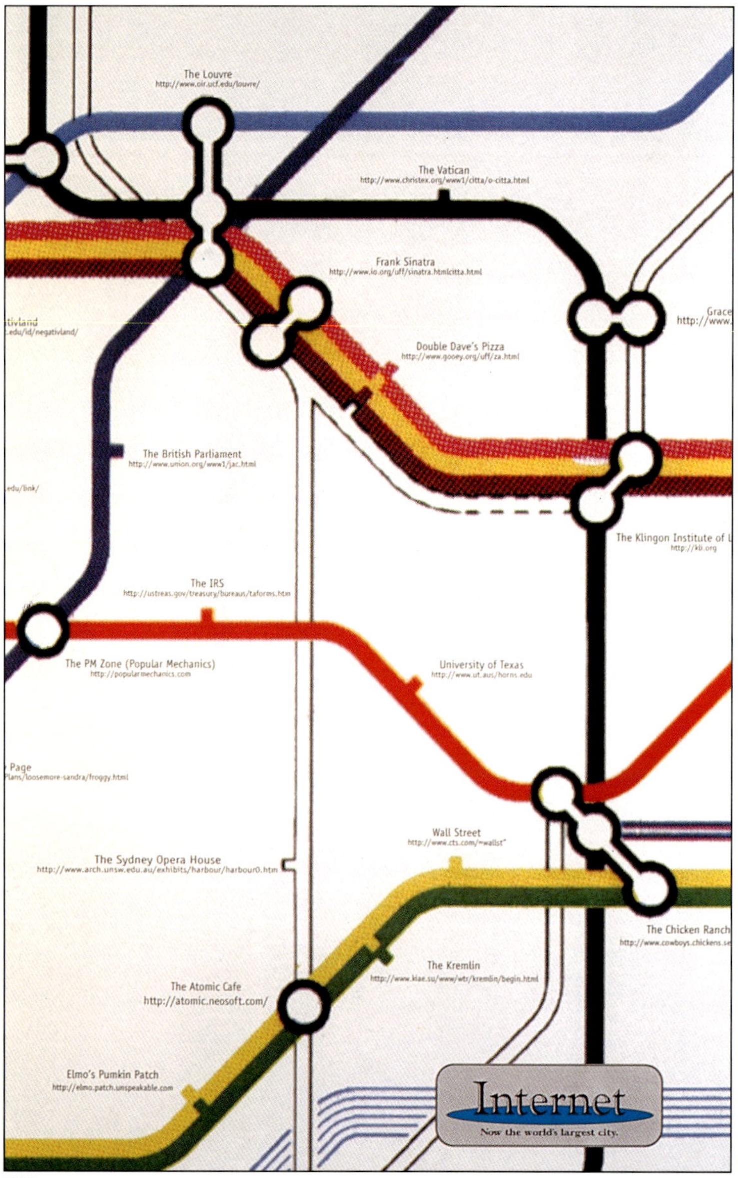

596

THE COOLEST PART IS
YOU'RE ON A COMPUTER,
WHICH MAKES PEOPLE
THINK YOU'RE WORKING.
Fool your boss. Fool your coworkers. They'll think you're on the Internet accessing your E-Mail, checking the latest stock reports, getting business updates, upgrading software, downloading data and all sorts of really neat things that successful executives do. But you're really on the Hollywood Movieline Site getting the latest scoop on Terantino's acting career. Is the Internet great, or what? Think of it as a powerful way to conquer the business world. Or a darn good way to kill about 8 hours.
THE INTERNET
CHANGING THE WAY WE, UM, WORK.

597

MELONS
SQUASH
ED'S
PRODUCE
www.veggies.com
The latest stock reports. Ski conditions in Aspen. The best time to plant asparagus.
The Internet
There's room for everyone.

598

COLLEGE COMPETITION
ASSIGNMENT:
THE INTERNET

599
ART DIRECTOR:
Jeanine Michna
WRITER:
Ian Graham
COLLEGE:
Miami Ad School/Miami

600
ART DIRECTORS:
John Huggins
Tia Lustig
WRITER:
John Huggins
COLLEGE:
Miami Ad School/Miami

601
ART DIRECTOR:
Laura Metrano
WRITER:
Eddie Hahn
COLLEGE:
Miami Ad School/Miami

602
ART DIRECTOR:
Jayson Szott
WRITER:
Jayson Szott
COLLEGE:
Michigan State
University/East Lansing

599

600

WHAT YOU FIND MAY BE BETTER THAN WHAT YOU ARE LOOKING FOR.
MAP of DISCOVERY
EASTERN HEMISPHERE
NORTH PACIFIC OCEAN
SOUTH ATLANTIC OCEAN
SOUTHERN OCEAN
COLUMBUS
WHY IS IT THAT WHEN YOU'RE LOOKING FOR ONE THING YOU'RE INEVITABLY DISTRACTED BY ANOTHER. SETTING ASIDE WHAT YOU WERE ORIGINALLY AFTER TO EXPLORE THE POSSIBILITIES OF YOUR DISCOVERY.
DURING THE RENAISSANCE CHRISTOPHER COLUMBUS SAILED THE SEAS LOOKING FOR A SHORTER ROUTE TO THE SPICE LANDS. INSTEAD HE RAN IN TO TRIBES OF WILD, NAKED INDIANS WILLING TO SHARE THEIR WEALTH AND KNOWLEDGE. FEEDING HIS CURIOSITY.
ALONG WITH MANY OF HIS CONTEMPORARIES, COLUMBUS CHALLENGED POPULAR BELIEF AND MADE HISTORY.
ON THE INTERNET IT'S YOUR TURN TO EXPLORE, SHARE IDEAS AND GAIN KNOWLEDGE. DISCOVER YOUR WORLD. THE INTERNET HAS IT ALL, EVEN A FEW WILD, NAKED INDIANS.
INTERNET
The New Age Of Discovery

601

If a big fat idiot like Rush Limbaugh can find love on the internet think what might be waiting out there for you.
We put the world at your fingertips
The Internet

602

COLLEGE COMPETITION
ASSIGNMENT:
THE INTERNET

603
ART DIRECTOR:
Jayanta C. Jenkins
WRITER:
David Weist
COLLEGE:
Portfolio Center/Atlanta

604
ART DIRECTOR:
Todd Jay Brunner
WRITER:
Todd Jay Brunner
COLLEGE:
School of Visual Arts/
New York

605
ART DIRECTOR:
John Carson
WRITER:
John Carson
COLLEGE:
Southern Methodist
University/Dallas

606
ART DIRECTOR:
John Carson
WRITER:
John Carson
COLLEGE:
Southern Methodist
University/Dallas

603

604

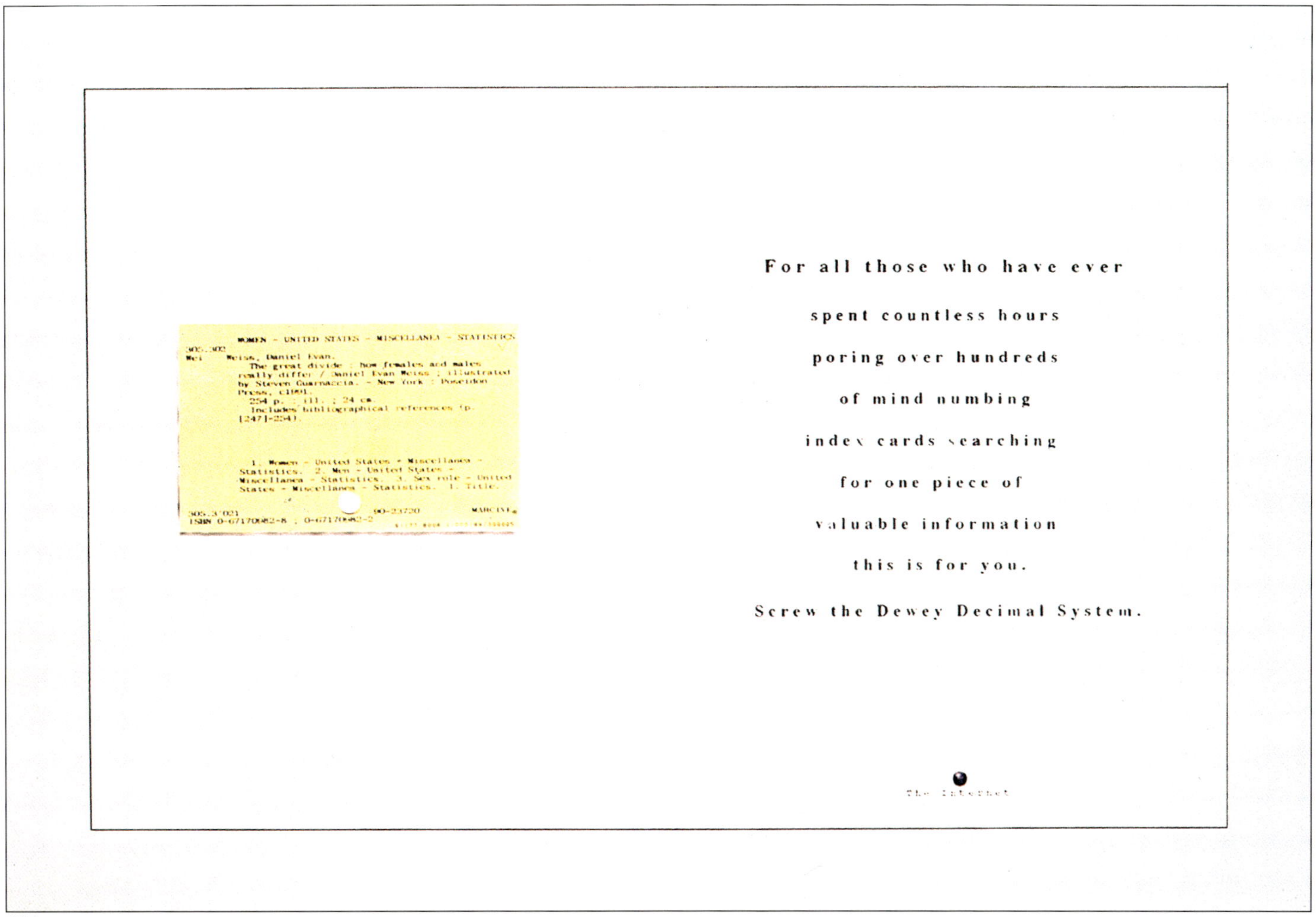
WOMEN - UNITED STATES - MISCELLANEA - STATISTICS
Weiss, Daniel Evan.
The great divide : how females and males really differ / Daniel Evan Weiss ; illustrated by Steven Guarnaccia. - New York : Poseidon Press,
254 p. : ill. ; 24 cm.
Includes bibliographical references (p. [247]-254).
1. Women - United States - Miscellanea - Statistics. 2. Men - United States - Miscellanea - Statistics. 3. Sex role - United States - Miscellanea - Statistics. I. Title.
ISBN 0-671700682-8 ; 0-671700682-2
For all those who have ever
spent countless hours
poring over hundreds
of mind numbing
index cards searching
for one piece of
valuable information
this is for you.
Screw the Dewey Decimal System.

605

When was the last time
you went to the library
in your underwear?

606

COLLEGE COMPETITION
ASSIGNMENT:
THE INTERNET

607
ART DIRECTORS:
Supriya Wagle
Maisie Scharold
WRITERS:
Supriya Wagle
Maisie Scharold
COLLEGE:
Southern Methodist
University/Dallas

608
ART DIRECTORS:
Carrie Jepsen
Bonnee Sharp
WRITERS:
Carrie Jepsen
Bonnee Sharp
COLLEGE:
Southern Methodist
University/Dallas

609
ART DIRECTOR:
Prisna Virasin
WRITER:
Mat McCaffree
COLLEGE:
Southern Methodist
University/Dallas

610
ART DIRECTOR:
Rossana Bardales
WRITER:
Tiffany Yeager
COLLEGE:
University of Texas at
Austin

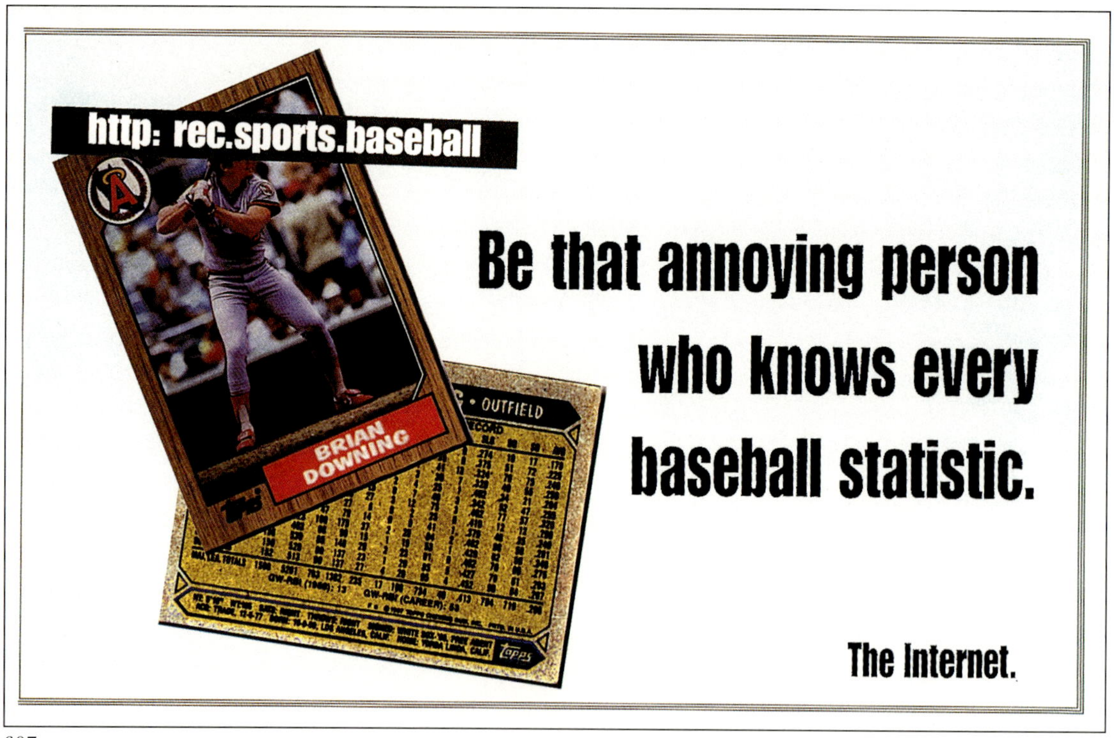

607

608

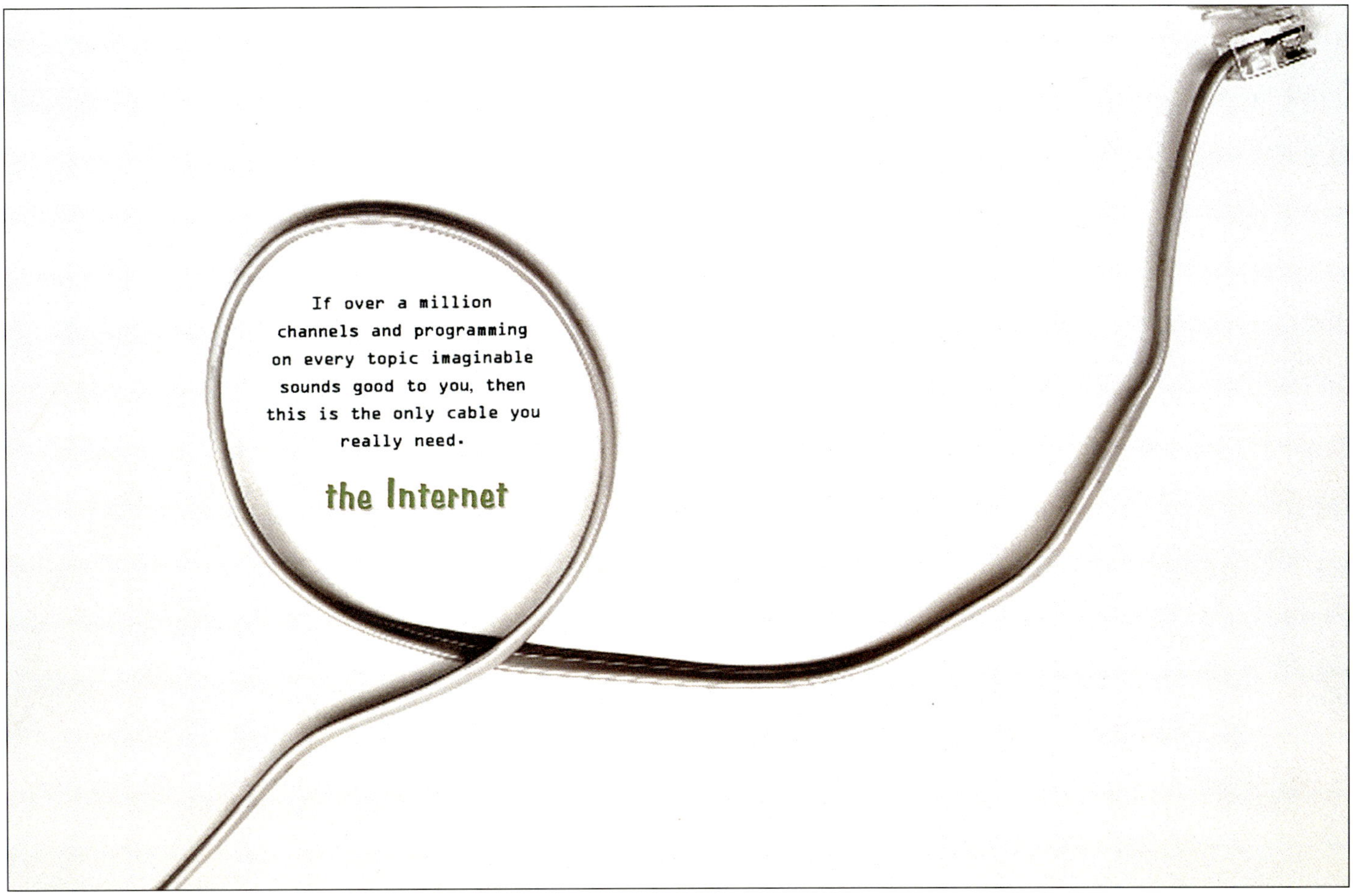
If over a million channels and programming on every topic imaginable sounds good to you, then this is the only cable you really need.
the Internet

609

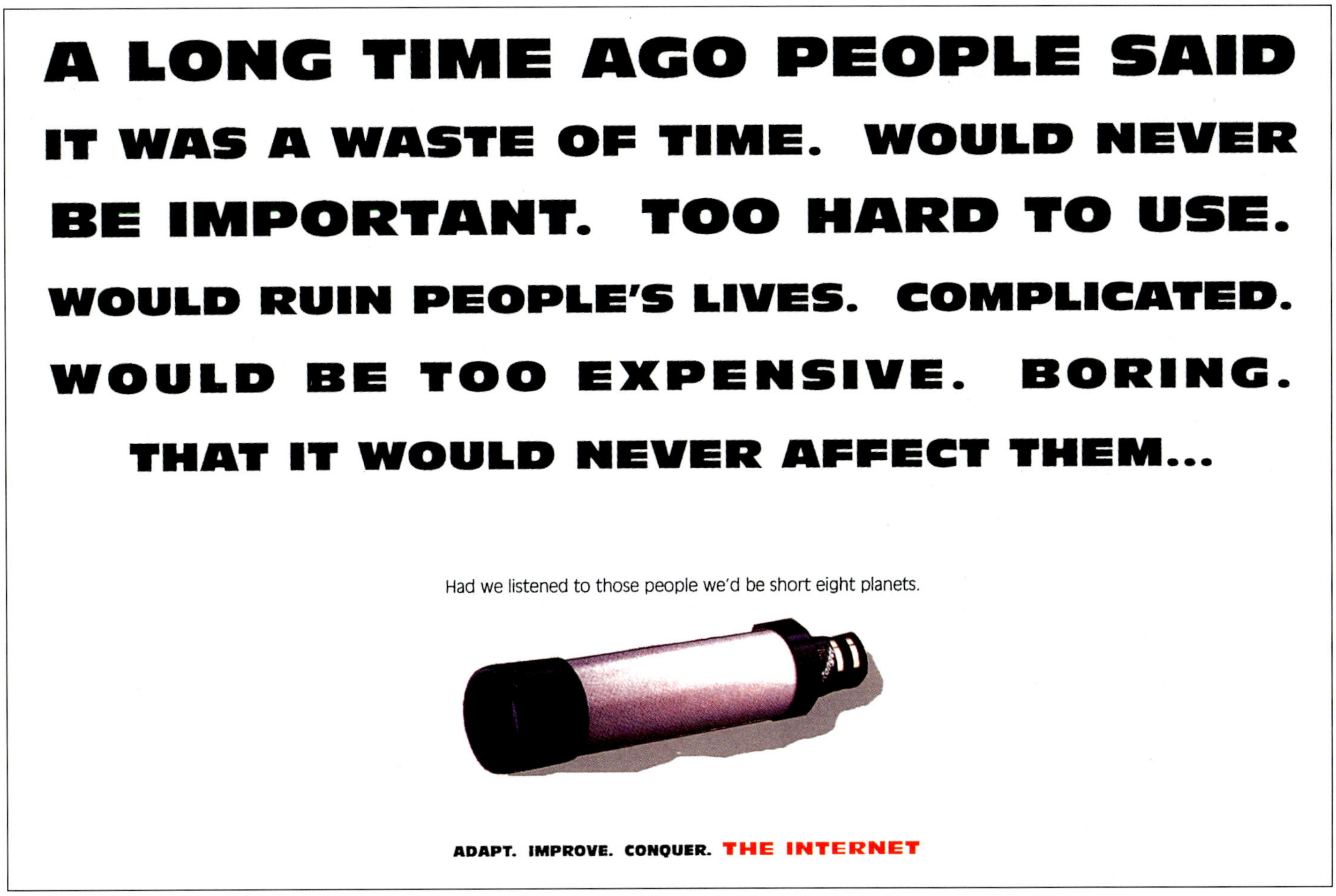
A LONG TIME AGO PEOPLE SAID IT WAS A WASTE OF TIME. WOULD NEVER BE IMPORTANT. TOO HARD TO USE. WOULD RUIN PEOPLE'S LIVES. COMPLICATED. WOULD BE TOO EXPENSIVE. BORING. THAT IT WOULD NEVER AFFECT THEM...
Had we listened to those people we'd be short eight planets.
ADAPT. IMPROVE. CONQUER. THE INTERNET

610

Considering all the different shapes, sizes and colors of pencils that have been produced in the last 2,000 years, it should come as no surprise that there are actually people who collect them. One such person in the Midwest has amassed over 25,000 of them. No, it's not Bob Barrie.

Index

AGENCIES

AGENCY PRODUCERS

ART DIRECTORS

CLIENTS

PRODUCTION COMPANIES

TYPOGRAPHERS

WRITERS